D1037360

Edvard Munch—Theme and Variation

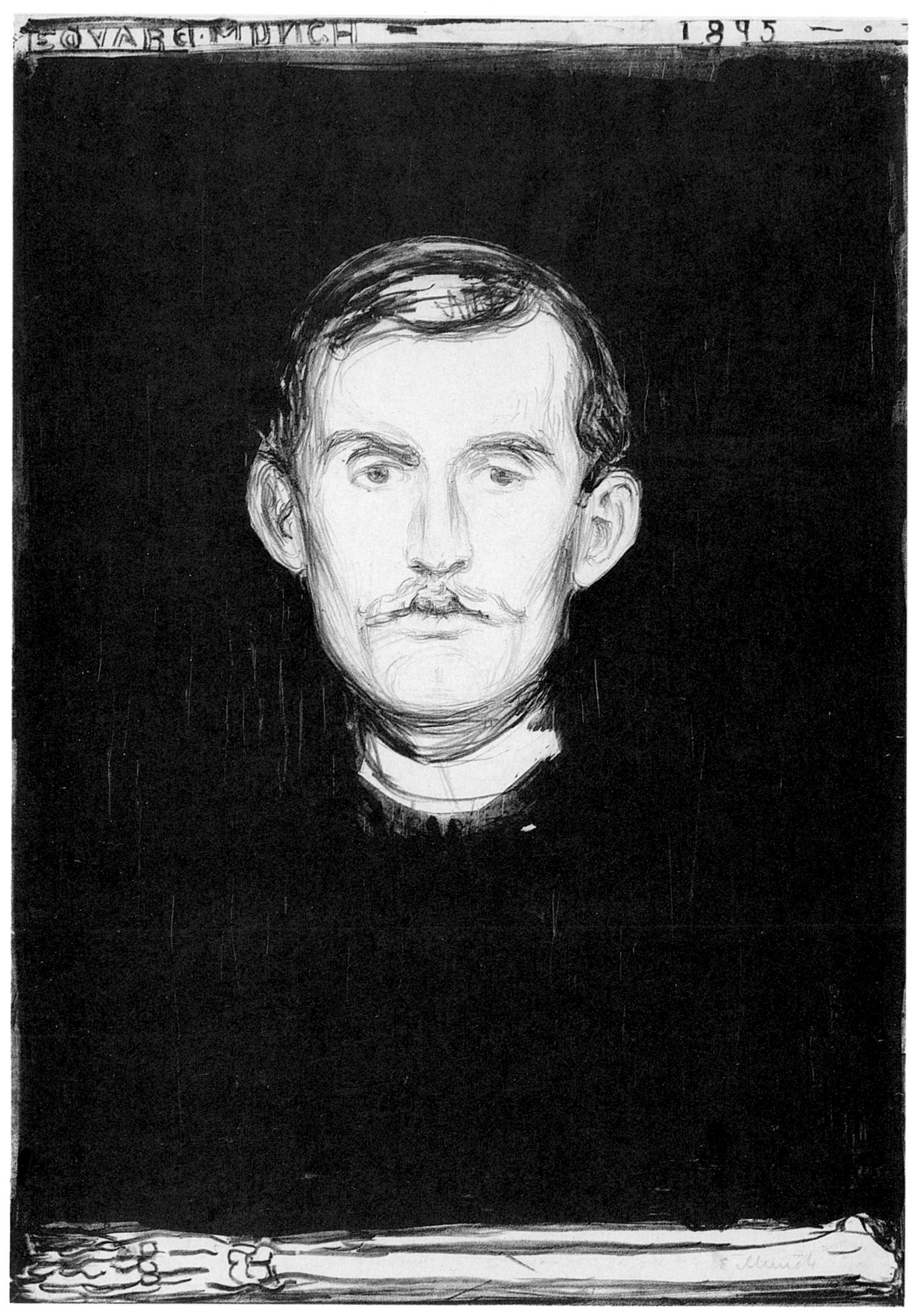
EDVARD MUNCH
1895

Edvard Munch

Theme and Variation

Edited by
Klaus Albrecht Schröder
Antonia Hoerschelmann

Contributions by
Christoph Asendorf
Dieter Buchhart
Antonia Hoerschelmann
Frank Høifødt
Marian Bisanz-Prakken
Iris Müller-Westermann
Gerd Woll

ALBERTINA

Hatje Cantz Publishers

Patronage

The exhibition is under the patronage of

H. M. King Harald V of Norway

and

the Federal President of the Republic of Austria Dr. Thomas Klestil

Lenders to the Exhibition

We would like to thank all private and public lenders.

Austria
Österreichische Galerie Belvedere, Vienna

Denmark
Galleri Faurschou, Copenhagen
Statens Museum for Kunst, Copenhagen

Finland
Ateneum, Taidemuseo, Helsinki

France
Musée d'Orsay, Paris

Germany
Stiftung Stadtmuseum Berlin
Museum Folkwang, Essen
Hamburger Kunsthalle
Sprengel Museum Hannover
Von der Heydt-Museum, Wuppertal

Liechtenstein
R. and H. Batliner, Vaduz

Norway
Rasmus Meyers Samlinger, Bergen Kunstmuseum, Bergen
Munch-museet, Kunstsamlingene, Oslo
Nasjonalgalleriet, Oslo

Sweden
Göteborgs Konstmuseum, Göteborg

Switzerland
E.W.K., Bern

Spain
Museo Fundacion Thyssen-Bornemizsa, Madrid

USA
Museum of Fine Arts, Boston
The Art Institute of Chicago
The Museum of Modern Art, New York
Catherine Woodard & Nelson Blitz Jr., New York
The Museum of Modern Art, New York
The Leon and Debra Black Collection, New York
National Gallery of Art, Washington, D.C.
Epstein Family Collection, Washington, D.C.

and all lenders who wish to remain anonymous.

Contents

Catalog

Acknowledgements

We would like to thank
for their help and support

Christoph Asendorf, Berlin
Hans Aurenhammer, Vienna
Friedrich Teja Bach, Vienna
Herbert Batliner, Vienna
Klaus Behrens, Mühlheim a.d.R.
Evelyn Benesch, Vienna
Torill Bjørdal, Bergen
Nelson Blitz, Jr., New York
Magne Bruteig, Oslo
Ingmarin Desaix, Göteborg
Wolfgang Drechsler, Vienna
Douglas W. Druick, Chicago
Earl A. Powell III, Washington, D.C.
Audun Eckhoff, Bergen
Arne Eggum, Oslo
Inger Engan, Oslo
Sarah M. Epstein, Washington, D.C.
Jens Faurschou, Copenhagen
Sabine Fehlemann, Wuppertal
Larry J. Feinberg, Chicago
Suzanne Folds MacCullagh, Chicago
Björn Fredlund, Göteborg
Gerbert Frodl, Vienna
Gary Garrels, New York
Hubertus Gassner, Essen
Meike Gerber, Hamburg
Arne Gjermundsen, Oslo
Magdalena Ufnalewska Godzimirska, Oslo
Gracia Pablo, Oslo
Aashild Grana, Oslo
Diana Griffin, Boston
Mette Havrevold, Oslo
Sidsel Helliesen, Oslo
Helga Hernes, Oslo
Anna Karina Hofbauer, Vienna
Frank Høifødt, Oslo
Lasse Jacobsen, Oslo
Anne Kaslegard, Oslo
Konstantin Klien, Vienna
Linda Klyve, Bergen
Kirsten Korff, Oslo
Eberhard W. Kornfeld, Bern
Annette Kulenkampff, Stuttgart
Diana Kunkel, New York
Gunnar B. Kvaran, Oslo
Serge Lemoine, Paris
Hilsen Karen E. Lerheim, Oslo
Marja Lilja, Helsinki
Mary Lister, Boston
Tomás Llorens, Madrid
Glenn Lowry, New York
Jan-Eric Lunström, Bergen
Mario-Andreas von Lüttichau, Essen
Mattias Malmberg, Oslo
Caroline Mathieu, Paris
Iris Müller-Westermann, Stockholm
Heribald Närger, Munich
Jane van Nimmen, Vienna
Hanne Storm Ofteland, Oslo
Eli Okkenhaug, Bergen
Silje Opdahl, Oslo
Knut Ormhaug, Bergen
Karin Osbahr, Stuttgart
Kim Pashko, Boston
Sue Welsh Reed, Boston
Petra Pettersen, Oslo
Angela Reimer, Berlin
Jennifer Roberts, New York
Andrew C. Robinson, Washington, D.C.
Malcolm Rogers, Boston
Cora Rosevear, New York
Gabriele Sabolewski, Stuttgart
Helmiriitta Sariola, Helsinki
Uwe M. Schneede, Hamburg
Siegfried Schöffauer, Vienna
George T. M. Shackelford, Boston
Alan Shestack, Washington, D.C.
Gunnar Sørensen, Oslo
Vivi Spicer-Turnball, Washington, D.C.
Andreas Stolzenburg, Hamburg
Tore Tanum, Vienna
Anniken Thue, Oslo
Jan Thurmann-Moe, Oslo
Biliana Topalova-Casadiego, Oslo
Martin Treml, Berlin
Margit und Rolf Weinberg, Zurich
Franz Wingelmaier, Vienna
Wolfgang Wittrock, Berlin
Gerd Woll, Oslo
James Wood, Chicago

Edvard Munch—Theme and Variation

Klaus Albrecht Schröder

No artist has ever achieved as radical a break with the visible world as Edvard Munch. And no artist before him created such powerful images from his own traumatic experience. *The Scream*, surely Munch's most famous work, still retains the inexorable quality of an obsession today. Born of absolute subjectivity, personal experiences crystallizes in the forms and colors of this painting into an icon of Modernism to which we all can relate—an image of fear, panic, and horror.

A genderless figure staggers into the foreground in front of a bridge that is drawn into the depths of the scene. Pressing its long, thin hands to its skull-like head, the figure cries out against a blood-red evening sky streaked with veins of sulphur-yellow. *The Scream* has become a symbol of the alienation of the human being from the real world that is unrivalled in the history of art. Like Paul Gauguin and Vincent van Gogh, its creator became a leading exponent of a modern art that culled its imagery from absolute subjectivity. To an even greater degree than can be said of his predecessors, personal biography and iconography appear to be inseparably interwoven in the art of Edvard Munch.

However, recent years have witnessed an increasing caution with respect to premature assumptions about the relationship between Munch's life and his work, and rightly so. Edvard Munch was certainly not immune to the progressive art of his time. Nor was that art resistant to his innovations. On the contrary, Munch gave more than he received, even to the expressionists. The most recent Munch exhibitions have explored the stylistic coordinates of his art. Yet they have also shown once again how difficult it is to define Munch's style in precise critical terms. And this difficulty has more to do with the impact of the artist himself than with his work. Celebrated as a symbolist after the publication of the first Munch monograph in 1894, he was prominently represented at all of the major exhibitions of expressionist art only a few years later. Shortly after taking part in the pioneering fauvist presentation at the *Salon des Indépendants* in 1906, he exhibited with the Brücke group in Dresden in 1908. Four years later, in 1912, he was given his own hall of honor along with Van Gogh and Cézanne at the legendary *Sonderbundausstellung* in Cologne.

In the 1880s, Munch abandoned impressionism, which had been imported to Norway not long before, as quickly as he had the naturalism of his older countrymen and patrons Christian Krohg and Fritz Thaulow, and largely without outside influence. Even his stays in Paris do not explain the radical newness of his first recognized trio of symbolist works: *The Sick Child*, *Puberty*, and *The Day After*. One need not read the expressions of outrage in the first reviews to gain an impression of how unprecedented and alien these paintings were. These works, some of which have survived only as later versions, reveal the profound influence of Munch's subjective experience. "I do not paint what I see but what I have seen." This statement also defines his aesthetic program: The filter of memory, the traces and scars of the mental process of coming to grips with experiences and emotions are the foundation both of his iconography and of his world of forms and colors. The anecdotal is totally eliminated from his works. They are genre pictures in title only.

Only in a formal, aesthetic sense was Munch's encounter with the Parisian revolt of the avant-garde against naturalism and its culmination in impressionism a catalyst for his rejection of external, visible processes in favor of the tremors of the soul. Yet Munch's position between symbolism—a badge of modernism before the turn of the century—and the expressionist approach to motifs illuminates nothing more than his renunciation of the *sensus literalis*. Neither his friendship with Mallarmé nor his admiration for Arnold Böcklin and Max Klinger prompted him to a more literal treatment of his subjects. Munch's pictures are never illustrative; they do not "mean something;" they carry no underlying symbolic meaning that could be expressed in words. Edvard Munch's pictures are emphatic existential expressions of archetypal life situations.

Munch's central position in the history of modern art is defined by his involvement in a wide range of anti-impressionist movements of the avant-garde and his contributions to equally heterogeneous and expressionist, symbolist, and art nouveau currents. But the essential principles of formal design that characterize both his paintings and graphic works were all shaped in France.

Munch observed the using of tree trunks, fence posts, window beams, and similar elements to subdivide the pictorial space in the work of Puvis de Chavannes, Seurat, and Emile Bernard.

He learned about the emancipation of color, deviation from object color and the resulting colorist exaggeration of objects, human figures, or atmospheric moods from Van Gogh and Gauguin.

The practice of separating fields of color with dark boundary lines, the resulting flattening of pictorial space, and the simplification of motifs call to mind the hallmark of the Pont-Aven School: the *Cloisonné*.

The rigid, iconic frontality of his protagonists—from *Puberty* to *The Scream*—is obvious evidence of Munch's admiration for Seurat's oeuvre.

Japonism taught Munch a new approach to the composition of the edges of his pictures, and the general tendency toward decorative simplification of forms was modeled on the Japanese woodcut.

Equipped with this new post-impressionist grammar, Munch developed a vocabulary of his own: symbolic figures of existential states cast in visual form. The exhibition at the Albertina presents all of the important symbols of Munch's art in multiple versions and variations, all of the symbolic figures of angst and love, separation and jealousy, panic and melancholy, estrangement from the self and estrangement from the world. Our Munch exhibition features many of the most familiar and the most disturbing visual images in the history of art, including Munch's best-known symbolic figures:

The human figure, usually female, facing the front. Her iconic austerity and rigidity inevitably confronts the viewer with his own personal feelings.

The figurative shadow. Its reification in *Puberty*, *Starry Night*, and *Moonlight* translates the Romantic doppelganger motif into modern visual language, making the shadow the uncanny companion of the self.

The column of moonlight. The reflection of the moon on the water's surface solidifies into a phallic-erotic figure. The column of moonlight is the luminous reverse image of the figurative shadow. For both are objectified light—in the one case its nocturnal presence, in the other as a place which no light can illuminate: the dark side of the soul.

The curvilinear liquefaction of the landscape as a vibrant image of personal moods. These gently curving seaside landscapes are in a sense the basso continuo of the *Frieze of Life*. They form the thematic link that joins the individual pictures.

The acceleration of perspective: a formal principle which Paul Cézanne employed as an anti-naturalistic impulse heralding the demise of the mathematically constructed central perspective. The rapidly vanishing perspective exposes the human figures to a powerful external pull and an overpowering inner compulsion: a symbolic figure of the rapid dissolution of the individual in the whole—the primal fear of society at the dawn of the modern era.

Foreground figures cut off abruptly by the edge of the picture. The Impressionists used this device to heighten pictorial reality. Munch took such a radical approach to these figures cut off by the edge of his pictures—legacies of Japanese woodcut art and early snapshot photography—that nothing is left to suggest the randomness of the facial field. The hardness of the cut strips the figures of any spatial repoussé function.

Thus although each of these symbolic figures of modernism corresponds to principles of formal design whose origin we rightly seek in the nineteenth-century French capital, Munch's new pictorial symbols are not mere expressions of these principles. This was not the least of the reasons why Munch found Paris less receptive to his themes and subjects than the artistically more backward capital of the German Reich. The bohemian community of Berlin, particularly the literary circle Zum Schwarzen Ferkel, exhibited a much greater sensitivity to the existential dilemmas of Munch's themes than the l'art-pour-l'art aesthetes of Paris. August Strindberg and Stanislaw Przybyszewski sensed the expressionist impulse in Munch's art even before expressionism was born. Munch's concept of death as metamorphosis was familiar to everyone in the avant-garde circles of Berlin. His idea of the antagonism of the sexes fell on fertile ground there. The visual and literary tradition of the three ages of woman had survived in Berlin since the age of northern German romanticism.

The artistic difference between the illustrative naturalism of Böcklin, Thoma, and Klinger, who enjoyed such success in Germany, and Munch's expressive symbolism could not have been greater, however. Yet what Munch shares with Max Klinger, in particular, is the conception of individual works as parts of a whole cycle. Serial works were especially prevalent in German graphic art of the 1880s and are likely to have helped inspire the Norwegian artist's concept for the *Frieze of Life*.

But only the medium of the exhibition offered Munch an opportunity to conceive of his images as a coherent sequence of emotions that achieve fateful dominance over life. Only in exhibitions does the symbolic character of Munch's cyclical production become evident.

It is only in the juxtaposition of the different techniques, of paintings and prints, that the interplay of individual images achieve its full orchestral effect, with all of its overtones and undertones. For Munch himself, the interaction of painting and graphic art was of essential importance. At the exhibitions in which he was able to influence the arrangement of his works, the bands of paintings hung high on the wall were accompanied by chains of prints hung below them at eye level.

Although Munch's motivation for his first prints was primarily commercial, as they were cheaper to make and easier to sell than paintings, he realized during his stay in Paris in 1896, if not sooner, that the media of color lithography, etching, and woodcut harbored an expressive potential of its own that was equal to that of painting. Paris was the Mecca of avant-garde graphic art during the 1890s. Henri de Toulouse-Lautrec and the Nabis associated with Edouard Vuillard revolutionized color lithography; Gauguin and Vallotton revived the artist's woodcut, which had deteriorated over the course of the nineteenth century into a masterfully employed but superficial medium of illustration in daily and weekly newspapers. Under the influence of French graphic art, Edvard Munch discovered the potential for pictorial concentration, for consolidation, and for expression-heightening simplification inherent in graphic art. Thus Munch joins the likes of Dürer, Rembrandt, and Francisco Goya, as an artist whose graphic oeuvre is regarded as at least equal in quality to his paintings.

The exhibition at the Albertina not only presents the essential stations of the *Frieze of Life* in a cyclical context once again, it also features the seaside landscapes and portraits, groups of works that were of great importance to Munch.

Yet the primary goal our Munch exhibition is to demonstrate the interdependence of his prints and paintings. We want to emphasize the process of cross-fertilization that took place as Munch alternated between different media in work on a given theme. Never before have the most significant works from this immense body of graphic art—encompassing more than 750 subjects and 30,000 prints—been gathered together in such concentration and quality. It is no coincidence that many of these prints are one-of-a-kind works—either because Munch reworked them after printing or because he actually made only one print on a specific kind of paper for experimental purposes. Munch discovered in the cosmos of graphic art the material qualities of paper and the wooden printing block as new, additional dimensions. Just as he incorporated the largely untreated canvas into his paintings, Munch also relied on the aesthetic effects that could be achieved by allowing the paper or the wood grain to play their parts as well. The end of the nineteenth century witnessed the final elimination of the genre boundaries between still life, portrait, and history painting that had so long been upheld by the academies. In much the same way, Munch did away with the hierarchy of techniques—painting, drawing, and printmaking. And the painted version no longer necessarily preceded, in a chronological sense, the print version as an *inventio princeps*. Some themes were articulated first as woodcuts or etchings before Munch varied them in paintings. Others were formulated only in prints, while yet others never found their way from canvas to paper.

Munch experimented with the blurring of boundaries between media, selecting black-and-white lithographs as starting points for various watercolor version, for example, or deliberately printed with thick oil paint to create effects similar to those of painting with such heavy, pasty pigments. Another aspect of this blurring of the boundaries between painting and printmaking is the phenomenon of the print without borders or margins. And by incorporating the wood grain, Munch found a graphic equivalent of his interest in the material qualities of the image-bearing medium, which is evident in so many of his paintings. The medium—canvas here, paper there—gives up its neutrality in both cases. It becomes a visual image in its own right. No longer was the woodcut merely a technique used for the reproduction of popular paintings.

For such artists as Nolde, Heckel, Kirchner, and Pechstein, in particular, the lithograph and the woodcut became media of expressive art *sui generis* for a quarter of a century.

The exhibition *Edvard Munch—Theme and Variation* has programmatic significance for the new Albertina. The integration of different techniques—70 paintings and 135 watercolors, drawings, gouaches, pastels, and prints—in a comprehensive survey presentation illuminates the principle of variation as a crucial driving force in Munch's art.

Perhaps more so than any other museum, the Albertina is ideally suited to the task of offering insights into what is supposedly such a familiar artist's oeuvre from the perspective of the drawings and prints. Yet this cannot be accomplished by placing the works on paper under quarantine in the interest of preserving the history of the collection and thus cutting them off from dialogue with the other media for which they served as preparation or to which they respond as variations. For Edvard Munch, variation meant much more than repetition and modification in the interest of variety alone. Variation, in the sense it is used in music, is the central creative principle in Munch's art.

We could not have achieved our ambitious goal of realizing such a comprehensive Edvard Munch exhibition without the assistance of numerous colleagues and lenders.

More than forty European and American lenders have provided major works from their collections for our exhibition. I wish to express my sincerest gratitude to them all.

Special thanks are due to the large Munch collections in Norway, without whose support we could never have realized this ambitious exhibition concept. I wish in particular to thank Arne Eggum, former director of the Munch-museet, his successor Gunnar Sørensen, and the members of their staff, Gerd Woll, Magne Bruteig, Petra Pettersen, as well as the team of conservators who carefully restored many works from Munch's estate for our exhibition. Without their efforts, these works could not have been loaned at all. The Nasjonalgalleriet in Oslo generously acceded to all of the Albertina's loan requests. I am very grateful to its director Anniken Thue and Sidsel Helliesen for their support. The Rasmus Meyers Samlinger of the Kunstmuseum Bergen also provided generous support for our project from the very start, for which I wish to thank Audun Eckhoff, the museum's director, and his predecessor Gunnar B. Kvaran. Many important paintings and unique prints are still held in significant private collections. I am profoundly grateful to all of these collectors for their willingness to support our exhibition.

I wish to thank exhibition curator Antonia Hoerschelmann, Dieter Buchhart, and the authors of the catalog for their important contributions.

We also owe a debt of gratitude to the Norwegian Embassy in Vienna under the direction of Ambassador Helga Hernes and her successor Arne Walther.

Last, but certainly not least, I wish to express special thanks to the main sponsor of this exhibition: the UNIQA Insurance Company. UNIQA's Director General Konstantin Klien accompanied this project with great interest and goodwill from the beginning. Without the professional know-how provided by this competent insurance partner, not to mention its essential financial assistance, it would have been impossible to realize an exhibition of this kind.

"... a Shedding of Skin ..."

Antonia Hoerschelmann

> Repetition is the definitive term for what the Greeks referred to as 'recollection.' Just as they taught that all knowledge is recollection, contemporary philosophy holds that all life is repetition. ... Repetition and recollection represent the same kind of movement but in opposite directions. For what is recollected is what was, and is repeated in reverse, whereas actual repetition recollects forward.[1]

Sören Kierkegaard expressed these thoughts in 1843. He is credited with being the first to have spoken of repetition as the crucial category of time in the modern era[2]—a theme on which Sigmund Freud and Friedrich Nietzsche also wrote significant and influential essays that have impacted on the ongoing discussion on art as well. Kierkegaard discusses his—simple—experiments on the consequences of repetition:

> During the time when I was devoting longer periods of thought, at least occasionally, to the problem of whether repetition is possible and what meaning it has, whether something gains or loses through repetition, the following thought occurred to me: You can travel to Berlin. You've been there before. And then you can learn whether a repetition is possible and what it means.[3]

Munch may well have been familiar with the writings of the Danish philosopher, who died in 1855. And he would have been able to read them in the original. At any rate, it is astonishing to realize that two Scandinavians agree in recognizing repetition as a crucial principle.

Repetitions have diverse facets. There are reproductions, copies, and variations; there are structures of organization in the form of series and cycles; and there is also the possibility of cyclical or irregular recurrence. Questions regarding the concepts of original and reproduction, uniqueness, diversity and multiplicity were the focus of particular interest in the 19th century, and the advent of photography and eventually of film made them themes of central concern. Walter Benjamin responded to these issues in "The Work of Art in the Age of Mechanical Reproduction," an essay first published in the 1930s which is still viewed as an inspiring analysis today. Thus one of the most important aspects of the art of Edvard Munch—the repetition of his own themes, subjects, and motifs in paintings and graphic works throughout his productive life—is firmly embedded in the cultural and social discourse of his time.

Despite its importance for an understanding of Munch, it was quite some time before scholars turned their attention to this principle. It was first examined more closely within the context of the exhibition *Edvard Munch. Symbols and Images* presented by the National Gallery of Art in Washington in 1978, primarily with reference to Munch's *Frieze of Life*. The exhibition *Edvard Munch. Love. Angst. Death* presented in Bielefeld in 1980 dealt in considerable detail with themes and variations. That exhibition focused solely on works on paper relating to subjects from Munch's *Frieze of Life* and covered—only—works from the period around the turn of the century. In his catalog foreword, Ulrich Weisner emphasized the network structure—as opposed to a linear chain structure—of Munch's oeuvre and went on to say that,

> Neither Munch's variable approach nor the sequential character of his oeuvre diminish the value of each individual piece. Indeed, every single print exhibits a significant degree of individuality, that is, uniqueness and unmistakable clarity. Each is capable of standing on its own and is also, in a certain sense, an end point rather than a temporary interim or transitional state preparatory to a final pictorial solution.

Arne Eggum has made a significant contribution to the study of Munch's working principle of multiple variation with his publications. He has devoted himself largely to compiling, publishing and interpreting the meaning and content of new artistic and autobiographical materials. During his many years of service as Director of the Munch-museet, he has supported a wide range of research projects, one of the fruits of which is an entirely new situation in Munch scholarship today. Nearly every specific subject has been studied in extensive projects and dissertations. The constantly changing focuses of different scholarly approaches ultimately tell us a great deal about the recent history of art scholarship, in which we recognize a progressive shift of emphasis, from stylistic and formal to sociological aspects, from psychological to literary approaches to Munch's art. The sustained, worldwide interest in the artist, which Japanese art historians have consistently demonstrated for many years with stimulating new insights, has produced an almost overwhelming abundance of publications devoted not only to Munch's significance to 20th-century art but also to the role he plays for artists today, based upon the impact of his influence in specific countries and on international movements.

Our exhibition and the accompanying catalog reflect the results of this research and add new insights to them. The starting point was the decision to present a selection of subjects from the *Frieze of Life* in deliberate juxtaposition with a group of works created outside the context of the series, including nudes, landscapes, portraits and self-portraits. It soon becomes evident that Munch's working method was the same, regardless of theme. This networking of thematic content and principles of form and composition is the essential foundation of his experimental, innovative, pioneering method (in its technical sense as well). Subjects, motifs, and motif groups as well as modes of representation used in the depiction of human figures and landscapes, remained available for use at different points in time. With this tightly interwoven body of art, Edvard Munch articulates one of the crucial turning points on the road to modernism. He remains within the framework of representational motifs. His worlds of imagery are filled with existential emotions and acutely sensitive atmospheres that can blend together in complete synthesis only with the aid of all our senses.

The individual variations are both experimental results and autonomous solutions, regardless of the techniques used, and they are expressions of Munch's ceaseless striving for the essence—in both meaning and composition—the heart of the work of visual art. Emanuel Goldstein discussed this aspect in a letter to Munch written in December 1891:

> You write that you cannot stop asking yourself 'Why?' with every picture. I think that is as senseless as asking yourself every morning 'Why get up? Why live when I'm going to die anyway?' After all, you paint because you cannot do otherwise. And every picture is really nothing other than a shedding of skin, like a day that has passed. . . . I think that if you work on it every day, your own true essence will emerge in all its originality in the end. And it will not be bound by a specific form of expression or any particular style of art.[4]

1 Quoted and translated from Udo Hock, *Das Unbewusste Denken. Wiederholung und Todestrieb*, Franfurt am Main 2000, p. 37.

2 Cf. *ibid.*

3 *Ibid.*

4 Quoted and translated from Reinhold Heller, *Edvard Munch. Leben und Werk*, Munich and New York 1993, p. 56.

Crossover
Munch and Modernism

Antonia Hoerschelmann

In the process of selecting subjects from art history for his silkscreen prints, in which he adapted his sources in different formats and color variations, Andy Warhol found in Edvard Munch an artist whose oeuvre exhibited very similar characteristics.

Warhol combined two lithographs from 1895, *Madonna* and *Self-Portrait (with Skeleton Arm)* (fig. 1). These two works, both from Munch's symbolist phase during the 1890s, relate in different ways to the theme of the transient nature of life and deal in thematic terms with the circle of life, the cycle of becoming and passing away.

Along with *The Scream*, *Madonna* is one of Munch's most popular images. This one subject and its many variations reveal essential aspects of Munch's working method. The first of five very similar surviving painted versions of *Madonna*, all of which were completed within a period of no more than three years, was shown for the first time in 1893. The painting triggered both immediate and sustained outrage and enthusiasm among the public. On the one hand, *Madonna* evokes a sense of serenity reminiscent of the "grandeur" of classical antiquity—and it is surely no coincidence that the position of the arms calls to mind the *Barberini Fawn*, a work dating from the late 3rd century B. C. (fig. 2), which Munch had seen when he visited Munich in 1893. Yet *Madonna* also personifies the epitome of lasciviousness and sinfulness in this particular pose. In the early years of the century, only a select few were permitted to view the picture, and then only in the back rooms of (German) galleries and exhibiting institutions.[1] Nevertheless—or perhaps for that very reason—it soon became a pseudo-sacred cult image. *Madonna* was elevated to the status of a secular goddess, a precursor of Warhol's *Marilyn* or *Jacky O.*, and a symbol for a broad range of contemporary ideas about the enigma of life and death, the mystery of human origin. These divergent aspects are reflected in the different titles: *Madonna*, *Conception*, *Loving Woman*, *Monna*, and *Annunziata*. Munch used multiple titles for other subjects as well, as he sought to evoke associative and inventive responses in different viewers.[2] In addition to the *Madonna* paintings, he also did a number of studies, large, intrinsically coherent drawings (cat. no. 20), and—beginning in 1895—lithographs with differing frames of view, some of them hand-colored. The Munch-museet alone is said to possess 116 examples of primarily autonomous variations—not repetitions.[3]

One of the two main versions conforms closely to the painted *Madonna* (cat. no. 22). In another, as in the source adapted by

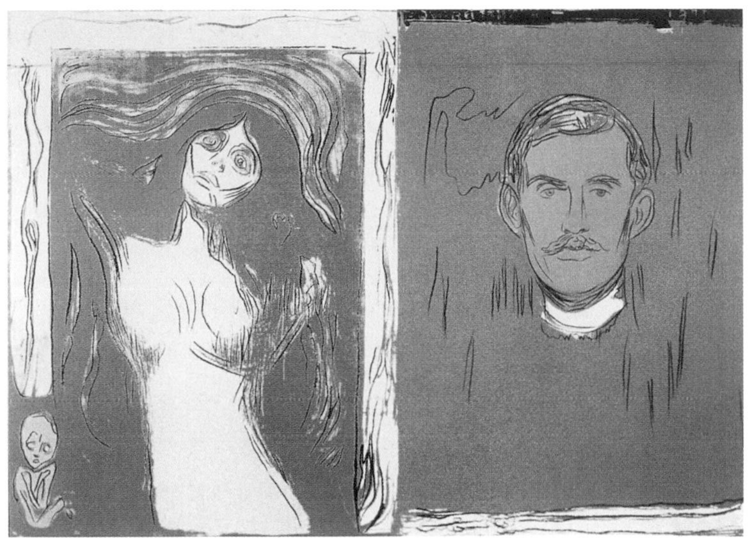

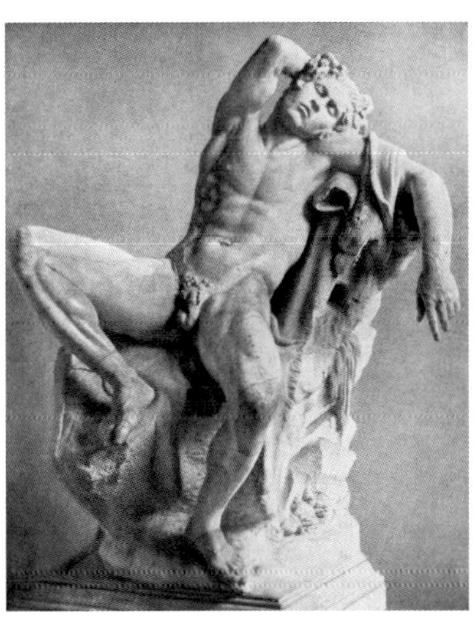

1 Andy Warhol, *Self-Portrait with Skeleton Arm and Madonna (after Edvard Munch)*, 1984, silkscreen (acrylics) on canvas, 129.6 x 180.4 cm, José Mugrabi Collection

2 *Sleeping Satyr (Barberini Fawn)*, end of 3rd century B. C., Glyptothek, Munich (left forearm and part of the rock are additions)

Warhol, she is surrounded by a frame comprising an embryo and spermatozoa. The origin of this element may be traceable to the original, no longer surviving frame of a (first?) painted version (cat. no. 23).[4] Formally speaking, this framing alters the proportions of the entire scene and focuses attention on the cycle of birth and death.

As is typical of many of Munch's graphic works, evidence of different print states is visible on the lithograph stone for *Madonna*, in the traces of multiple revisions, such as scrape marks and small changes in the form of modulating lines, and in the use of additional printing plates. These help differentiate between individual states and print editions and serve as points of reference for dating purposes. Aside from changes in the images on the printing plates, further variations involved the use of different coloring, paper with differing structures and colors, and the selection of different frames of view.

Madonna also provides an excellent example of Munch's practice of pulling individual compositional elements from specific works for use and further development in others. Thus he introduced the frame from *Madonna* in slightly altered form in the drypoint etching *Death and the Maiden* (cat. no. 44) of 1894 and another variation of the device in the lithograph *August Strindberg* of 1896 (cat. no. 190).[5]

Munch regularly drew material from previous works and used elements of earlier compositions, often at extended intervals. One example of this practice is the lithograph *Self-Portrait with Cigar* of 1908–09 (fig. 3), in which he paraphrased the *Madonna* image, possibly in response to a caricature (fig. 4)[6] printed in the *Vikinger* on October 12, 1895 following his major exhibition at Blomqvist's gallery in Kristiania. Other large-format lithographs of *Madonna* were done as long afterward as 1920 as rearticulations of the theme which reflect changes in his style over the course of the years.

Warhol's decision to combine and indeed complement *Madonna* with *Self-Portrait (with Skeleton Arm)* is understandable from both a formal and a thematic point of view. The skeleton arm completes the frame of the Madonna, just as birth also bears the seed of death within itself. Apart from the aspect of mortality, the skeleton arm also alludes to the exposure of the inner structure of objects and living beings with the aid of recently discovered roentgen technology but can also be interpreted as a reflection of esoteric ideas.[7]

One eye in the self-portrait is fixed on the viewer, while Munch gazes either downward or inside himself with the other. The "presence of absence" that spawned a wide range of different interpretations—and titles—in the case of *Madonna* is also evident here. This work is also open to a variety of interpretations, an attribute that is particularly characteristic of the works created during Munch's highly symbolic creative phase of the 1890s, with its strong literary orientation. In keeping with his own working principle, Warhol also varied the color combinations in his homage to Munch, in a sense adding new variations to the many that already existed.

Uwe Schneede emphasizes another analogy to Warhol in relating certain aspects of Munch's methodological approach to Warhol's "Factory Concept." Schneede cites an account by the artist Paul Herrmann (cat. no. 183), who was present the day the lithograph of *The Sick Child* was printed in Paris.

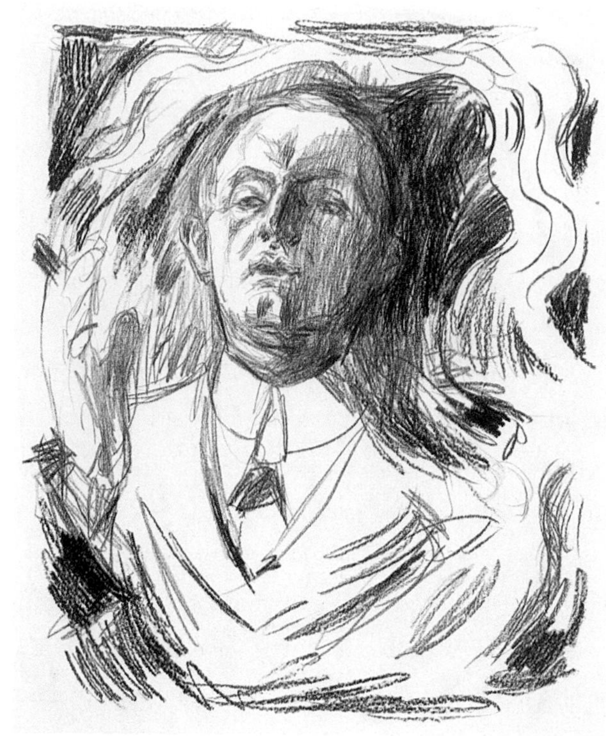

3 Edvard Munch, *Self-Portrait with Cigar*, 1908–09, lithograph on paper, 56.6 x 45.5 cm, Albertina, Vienna

I wanted to print at Clot's and was told it could not be done. Mr. Munch had an appointment. The lithograph stones with the large head were already laid out in a neat row for printing. Munch comes, stands in front of the row, closes his eyes tightly and begins to direct blindly in the air with his finger: 'Print ... gray, green, blue, brown.' Opens his eyes, says to me, 'Come, let's have a drink ...' And so the printer printed until Munch returned and blindly issued new commands: 'Yellow, pink, red ...' And so it went several more times ...[8]

This anecdote reflects a modern aspect, as it shows that Munch was not concerned with the physical presence of the artist as author during the production of his works but instead believed that the element of chance and other people can be involved on an equal basis in the process of realizing the fundamental idea proposed by the artist. Munch shifted back and forth between the interplay of built-in randomness and precise instructions and between the pure, perfect printing skill of another's hand and personal intervention on the part of the artist.

Experimentation, as expressed in his unique approach to graphic printing techniques, which included such practices as cutting wood blocks apart with a saw and using unorthodox combinations of woodcuts and lithographs, enabled Munch to explore new ways of articulating content, motifs, forms, and above all colors, and it resulted in the production of an extensive body of works in widely diverse variations. In addition to the mostly unnumbered editions, he also made a large number of prints in single copies. In the case of *The Lonely Ones*, *Two Women on the Shore*, and *Melancholy*, for example, the compositions themselves were altered only slightly, while the addition of printed or painted color to specific elements on the individual sheets produced variations in each print, as in the column of moonlight in *Two Women on the Shore*. Munch also achieved widely varying color nuances and as well as different interpretations of content and mood through the use of shading. In accordance with Munch's wishes with respect to the two groups of works mentioned above, several print sequences were to remain together, which suggests the possibility that he may have considered producing the works in series.[9]

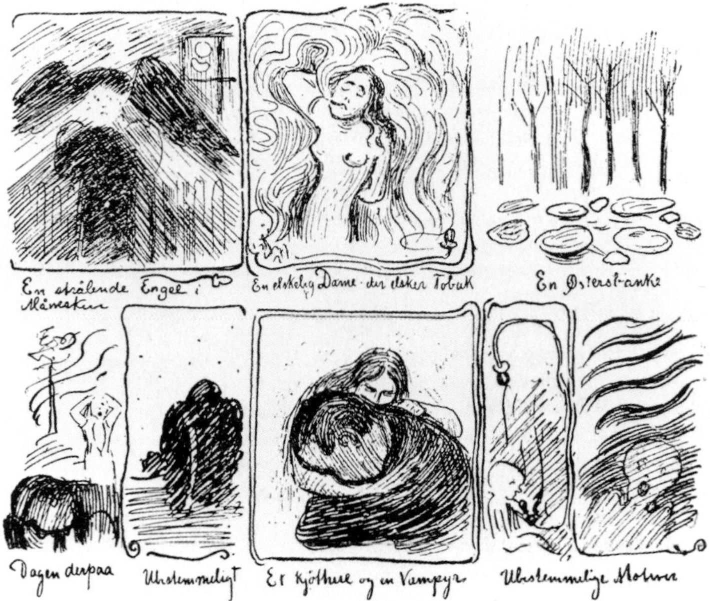

4 "An endearing lady who loves tobacco," caricature of the exhibition at the Blomqvist gallery in *Vikingen*, 1895

Claude Monet exhibited a series of fifteen paintings of haystacks at the Galerie Durand-Ruel in Paris in May 1891. Munch may have seen this exhibition, which history records as a last farewell to the aura of the individual work of art, as he did not leave the French capital until the end of May. Christoph Heinrich writes in this context that

Monet did not invent the series in art. Many artists did groups of works during the latter half of the 19th century in which they sought to achieve diversity in increasingly small variations within a range of deliberately established constants. In the process, they went far beyond what had previously been understood as repetition, replication, and variation on a theme: Thus Courbet, for example, presented no less than thirteen *Paysages de Mer* at an exhibition in 1867, and Degas showed a group of formally similar pastels of women at their toilets at the last impressionist exhibition in 1886. The lone wolf Cézanne began his painting of Mont Sainte-Victoire, and Vincent van Gogh planned to welcome his friend Gauguin in Arles with a group of twelve sunflower paintings. At the 1889 World's Fair, every Parisian had an opportunity to admire Hiroshige's *One Hundred Views of the Capital City of Edo*, and Sisley, Monet's comrade-in-arms, exhibited a group of works depicting the same motif in different atmospheric moods.[10]

Art history offers many examples of the repetition of subjects, and the practice is often and traditionally explained as a response to demand in the art market. What was new in Monet's case was the development, through reduction to very few central motifs, of a concept for repetitions that formed a series. With this accomplishment, he set new and essential accents for modern art and thus also represents a mirror of his time, which was characterized by interest in photography and the prevailing philosophy of positivism—which relies on precise scientific observation rather than metaphysical and theological structures of thought. Although each work is a finished and autonomous work of art in its own right, a group of variations of a single subject generates a very specific dynamic and statement. The work of art is at once a whole and part of a whole, and the basic structural principle of the series is repetition. Although this definition can be applied to Munch's graphic works and their serial aspects, it does not apply to his painting, since Munch was ordinarily motivated to do variations by the wishes of his clients or by his own, artistically inspired, desire to surround himself with multiple versions of his subjects. Munch expressed his own feelings on the matter: "You see, there are painters who collect the paintings of others. I know one who has a whole gallery full of French impressionists. He needs them for his work. I understand that very well. I need my own paintings for the same reason. I have to have them around me if I want to keep on working."[11]

If the structural principle of the series is repetition, then the series clearly differs from the cycle, in which all the parts relate to a coherent narrative. If one accepts Heinrich's contention that a cycle must be based first on one pattern, then on another, and later yet another, then it is evident that this concept does not apply to Munch, even though he occasionally grouped paintings together under the term "cycle" in his presentations. Munch used such terms as "cycle," "series," "variation," and "copy" quite arbitrarily and applied them randomly. But there is no narrative in his art that has a definite beginning or end, and no single theme occupies a necessarily fixed position within a given progression. The aspect of temporal narrative sequence in this sense is not present in his art. This is particularly evident in the *Frieze of Life*, in which the individual subjects were grouped freely and arranged in new constellations for every presentation.

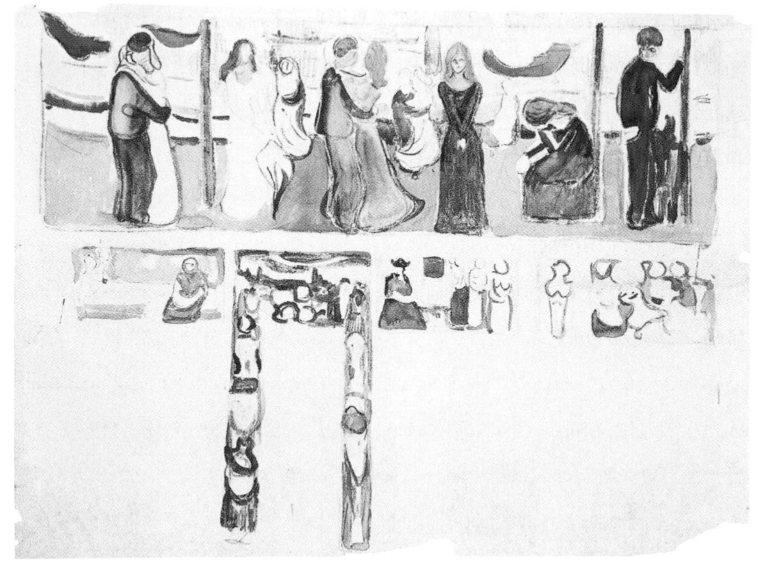

Theme and variation relate much more closely to the concept of series, as possibilities for change are also explored here on the basis of a visual idea. But variation has less to do with repetition, as it follows a different structural principle: first this one, and from it a second emerges, and from that a third, and so on. This accords with Munch's statement, cited above, that he always felt the need to use one of his paintings as a point of departure for the next.

In the *Frieze of Life*, Munch grouped what he regarded as the essential contents of his art as stations—and thus variations—of life (fig. 5). The complex presents the circle of life, growth and decline, and the unalterable mortality, vulnerability, love, and vileness of human beings. Munch's *Frieze of Life* developed slowly from his pictures and central themes over a period of years, as the painter had begun grouping individual paintings, drawings, and prints together under the thematic headings of motifs of love and angst even in the early 1890s.

In 1902, Munch exhibited twenty-two paintings under the collective title *Presentation of a Number of Images of Life* at a show to which he was invited by the Berlin Secession. Here, he included the aspect of death for the first time. Exhibited on the left wall was the

5 Edvard Munch, decorative design for *Frieze of Life*.
Entrance wall with *Angst* motifs, 1902–07, gouache, watercolor and charcoal on paper, 78 x 98 cm, Munch-museet, Oslo

Seeds of Love group, comprising six paintings, among them *Starry Night* (cat. no. 38), *Red and White* (cat. no. 30), *Eye in Eye* (cat. no. 33), *The Kiss*, and *Madonna*. The six paintings in the group *Love in Bloom and Decline* were presented on the front wall: *Ashes*, *Vampire*, *The Dance of Life* (fig. 4, p. 57), *Jealousy* (fig. 1, p. 69), *The Woman (Sphinx)* (cat. no. 27), and *Melancholy*. The *Existential Angst* group comprised five paintings positioned centrally on the right wall: *Angst* (cat. no. 116), *Evening on Karl Johans Gate* (cat. no. 114), *Red Virginia Creeper* (cat. no. 155), *Golgatha* (fig. 6, p. 60), and *The Scream* (cat. no. 118). Hung on the back wall were five paintings devoted to the theme of death: *By the Deathbed* (cat. no. 132), *Death in the Sickroom*, *Odor of a Corpse*, *Metabolism* (fig. 1, p. 53), and *Dead Mother with Child*.[12]

Munch replaced specific paintings both before and after the Berlin exhibition, showing different versions of certain subjects done in different years and creative periods, and thus it is virtually impossible to reconstruct the contents of some presentations exactly. Photos from his studio which document various groupings from different work phases tell us a great deal about Munch's approach to the *Frieze of Life* (figs. 6 and 7)

Munch's idea for the *Frieze of Life* emerged from his work with his own paintings, and he remained flexible and open with respect to questions of grouping and sequence from the outset, never establishing a fixed program. The pictures serve a dual function. Although they are autonomous works of art—in keeping with their specific origins—each also represents a thematic aspect of the *Frieze of Life*. Thus it comes as no surprise that the individual works differ in format and size.

Munch made the following remarks with regard to the presentation of his *Frieze* in Berlin:

> The Frieze was exhibited as a frieze at the Berlin Secession in 1902—all around on the walls of the large entrance hall—but rather high, as the pictures lost some of their intimacy if hung too high. The paintings were set in white frames—according to my drawing—by virtue of their similarities and their differences—different in color and size but related to one another by certain colors—and lines—the vertical lines of the trees and walls—the more horizontal lines of the floor—the ground—the roofs and tree-tops—in the lines of the sea—waves of cradle songs. There were sad, grayish-green shades in the colors of the death room—there were screams of fire—in blood-red skies and sound in red, strong, clear—yellows and greens. There was a symphonic effect.[13]

According to Werner Hofmann, "the four walls of the hall looked like an open winged altar and drew the scanning, combining, and selecting gaze of the viewer into their midst."[14]

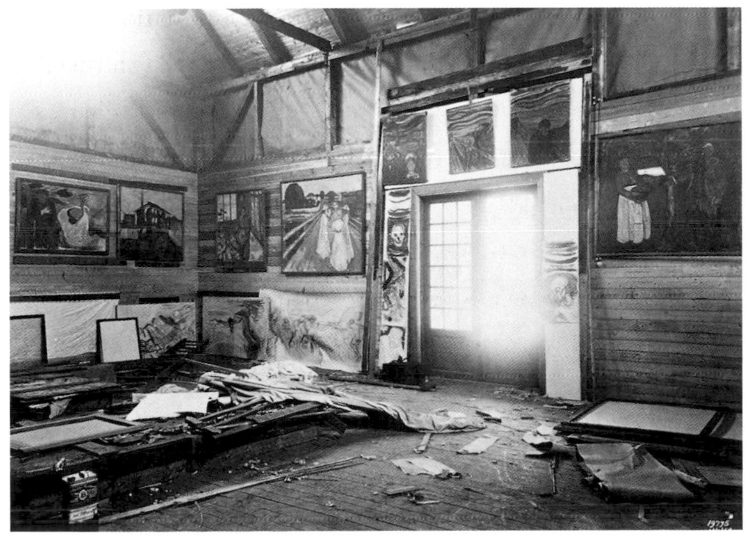

6 Studio in Ekely, c. 1927, photo: Anders Wilse

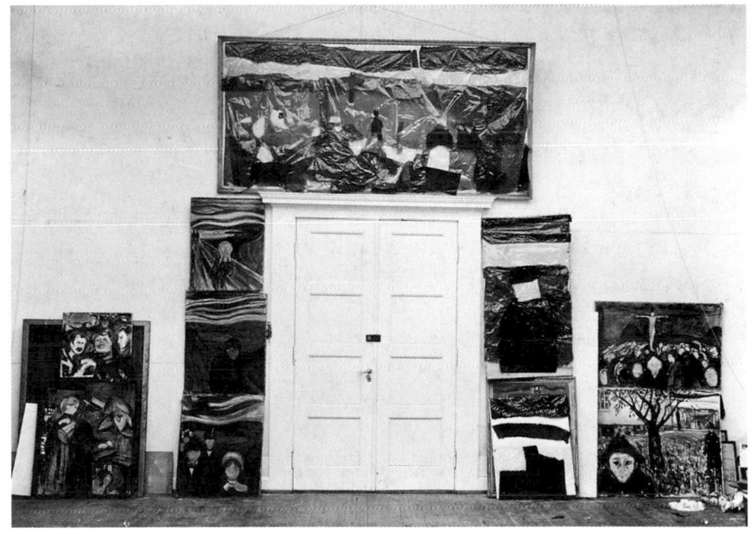

7 Wall in the winter studio in Ekely, c. 1933, photo: Ragnvald Væring

Clearly evident here is Munch's idea of constructing in a large spatial context, and we also recognize his often expressed desire to have his works presented in rooms devoted entirely to him, as he felt that they could be effective only in such settings.[15] This expansively staged exhibition event also helps us understand another of his wishes, namely to exhibit his paintings at the Vienna Secession, as he indicated shortly thereafter in a letter to Franz Servæs. The artists of the Vienna Secession had awakened interest throughout Europe with their exhibitions and staged presentations devoted to the idea of the total work of art. Yet, unlike Munch, they began with a single key idea, to which everything was subordinate in both formal and thematic terms. Munch's thoughts of Vienna may have inspired him to a modified form of staged presentation at an exhibition at the Beyer & Sohn art dealership in Leipzig the following year. In this case, we are blessed by the rare good fortune of having access to an extensive photographic documentation of that exhibition (fig. 8). These photographs show that Munch was obviously intent upon gathering all of his major works from the 1890s together in a frieze. In order to create a homogeneous impression, the paintings were hung in horizontal rows just below the ceiling line and—in the manner of a passe-partout frame for prints—fitted into a broad, continuous, light-colored construction. The graphic works were hung beneath them in a one- or two-row arrangement. The graphic works are variations of the four major themes of the *Frieze of Life*, but do not respond to the paintings hanging above them and are not presented in groups. This presentation also documents the change in Munch's attitude towards graphic art. At first, he used prints primarily for economic purposes and as an effective way of disseminating the subjects of his paintings. But the more he explored the technical possibilities of graphic art, the more autonomous the prints became. They were not only equally important but in turn also exerted an influence on the design and composition of the paintings. Consequently, in later years, the transparent, glazing color harmonies of the kind found, for example, in the woodcut variations of *Two Women on the Shore* provided inspiration for the markedly lighter color schemes of his late paintings devoted to this subject.

Just as Munch exhibited increasingly little preference for individual variations of a given theme, he also gradually eliminated the hierarchies among artistic techniques. This networking process expanded to encompass painting, drawing, graphic printing techniques, and, beginning in 1902, photography as well. From the 1920s on, watercolors document the unique possibilities offered by the expanded repertoire of technical resources, which Munch exploited above all to achieve subtle, transparent color qualities (cat. nos. 179–181).

An examination of the secular theme of *Girls on the Pier* provides another example of the multi-faceted interplay of creative phases and different techniques. Variant versions of the painting, in addition to those in the Munch-museet, are especially numerous and distributed all over the world. The boat dock is depicted from different points of view in the various versions, shifting the dynamics of the composition in each case. Different persons and groups of figures appear, depicted at different ages and looking in different directions, producing changes of mood and relationship to the viewer. Munch did numerous variations of this theme in various media after 1901: etchings (1903), woodcuts (1905), and lithographs (1912–13). In 1918, he created a particularly atmospheric, evocative variation of the theme using a combination of a wood

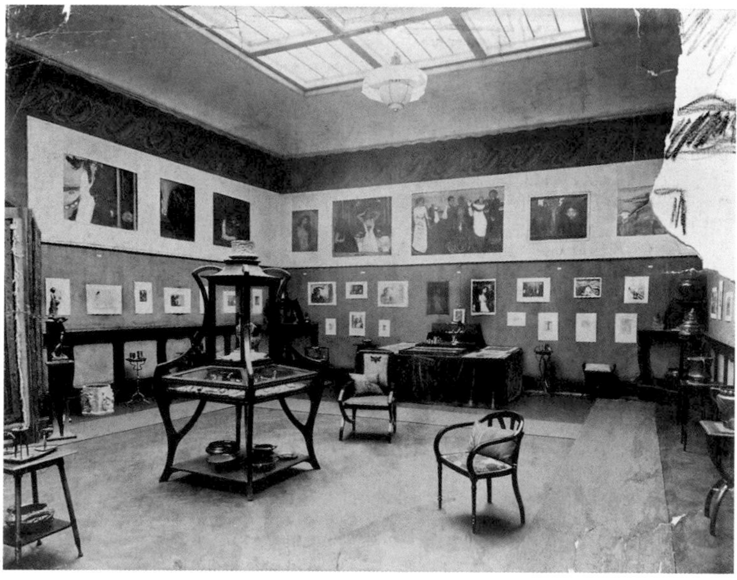

8 Munch exhibition at P. H. Beyer & Sohn, Leipzig 1903

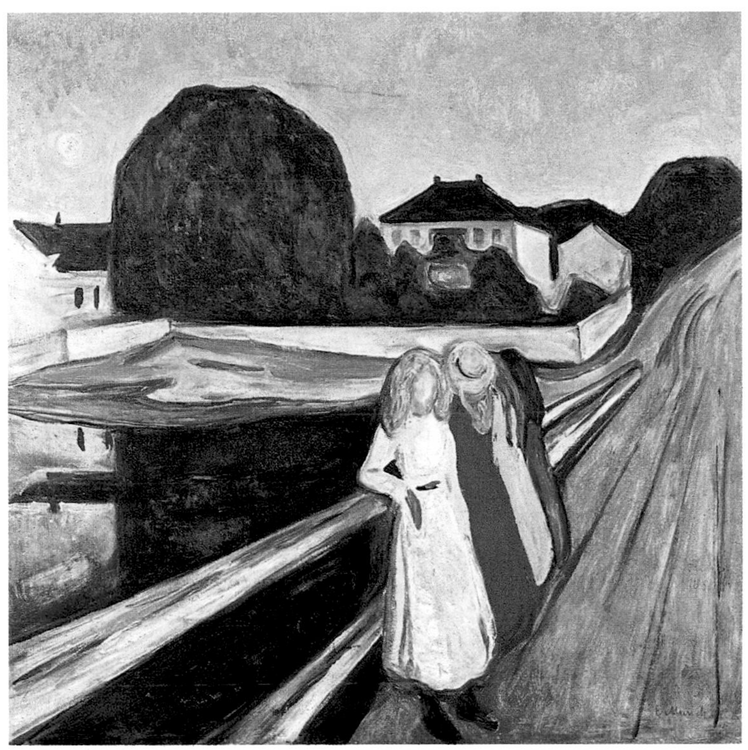

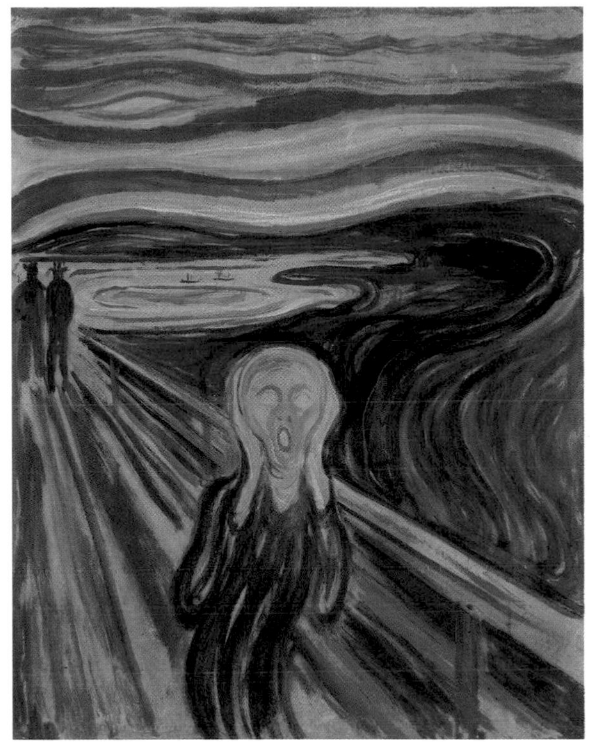

block and two lithograph plates. He also isolated individual elements of the composition and transformed them into autonomous subjects, rendering the harbor wall, the house, and the tree in the background as independent pictorial fields (cat. nos. 164, 165).

The practice of isolating and varying landscape motifs from the background of a composition reflects Munch's specific interest in capturing the mood of a landscape. He used color qualities such as warm and cold shades in diverse ways to shape the expressive content of the pictures. Titles refer to times of day, and the unique phenomenon of the midnight sun accentuates and guides the rendering of color and light. The sun and the moon produce areas of light and shadow over the course of the day. The seasons also change, calling attention to yet another aspect of variation in Munch's landscapes. Here as well, the qualities of the cold and warm colors dominate the mood and the expressive character of the individual scenes, which may thus be interpreted as images of the soul.

Hilly landscapes, and above all the Norwegian fjord coastline, dominate the landscape images and settings in Munch's theater of life. Munch noted the presence of this continuum in his paintings as early as 1902 in Berlin in his remarks on the *Frieze of Life*, quoted above. These coastal landscapes appear empty or populated in splendid atmospheric images. Their rocks offer places to sit for such figures as Jappe Nilssen (cat. no. 86) and the woman in *Melancholy* (cat. no. 91). The *Young Woman on the Beach* (cat. no. 93) gazes out at the sea, as do *The Lonely Ones* (cat. no. 98). The scene in *Separation* (cat. no. 40) is set at the seashore, that of *The Woman (Sphinx)* (cat. no. 27) at the edge of a lake. Here, as in Munch's earlier composition entitled *The Voice* (cat. no. 1), we also see the forest, in which the strict compositional rhythm of the tree-trunks clashes with the curving horizontal or diagonal lines of the shore. The detail of the variously interpreted column of moonlight also moves as a mystifying theatrical element from *The Voice* to *Summer Night on the Shore* (cat. no. 144), and is in 1914 an important formal and thematic element in *Kiss on the Beach* (cat. no. 48) and the painting *Two Women on the Shore* of 1935 (cat. no. 110).

9 Edvard Munch, *Girls on the Pier*, 1905,
oil on canvas, 126 x 126 cm, Wallraf-Richartz-Museum, Cologne

10 Edvard Munch, *The Scream*, 1893, oil, tempera and
charcoal on cardboard, 84 x 67 cm, Munch-museet, Oslo

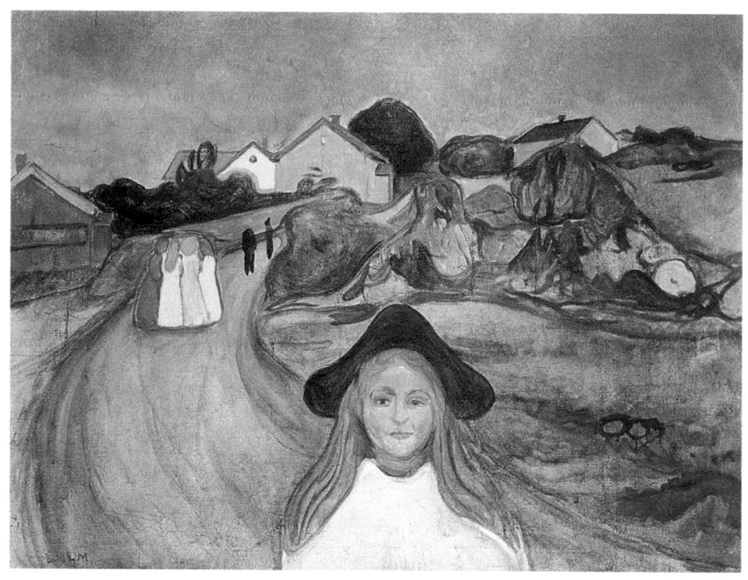

Strips of shoreline, sections of roads, and bridge structures serve as platforms for a wide variety of events. While the motif is entirely profane in *Girls on the Pier* (fig. 9), the bridge becomes a dramatic, dynamic element of composition in *Angst* and *The Scream* (fig. 10) There, it no longer evokes a sense of stability and spatial depth but threatens in its form as a steeply rising diagonal to destroy or reverse all spatial relationships.

In *Evening on Karl Johans Gate* (cat. no. 111), the street in the center narrows with frightening speed towards the vanishing point on the horizon, a device of composition that also appears beginning in 1907–08 in such works as *The Murderer* (cat. no. 157) and *Bricklayer and Mechanic* (cat. no. 159). As in *The Murderer on the Lane* (cat. no. 158) or *Country Road* (fig. 11), widely differing figures and groups of adults and children move along this road at many different distances from the viewer.

Moreover, the subjects of *The Kiss* (cat. no. 43), *The Sick Child* (cat. no. 122), and *Vampire* (cat. no. 65) escape from their interior settings to become "spaceless" and "timeless" compositions, in which the couples in the scenes are concentrated increasingly in the fusion of their two figures.

On the basis of his explosive early works, in which he developed the essential formal and thematic characteristics of his oeuvre within the period of a very few years, Munch wandered onward, symbolically speaking, along a progressively expanding spiral, adding new themes and artistic ideas in each new phase. Conditioned by new experiences gained along the way, his return to these themes did not produce pure repetitions, as the works done in Warnemünde and later in Ekely clearly show. Instead, his revisiting of the past served as a means of combining the results of previous experiments with current interests and experience gained in the interim, renewing them in such a way that they then provided new points of departure for the future: a working method characterized by simultaneity and timelessness at once.

Munch generally approached the factor of time in his own unique way. He liked to wait until the moment of sale to date his pictures, and then chose the date on which the idea had come to him as the decisive date of origin—a procedure that makes it difficult in many cases to determine the dates of origin of individual works today.[16] According to Munch, the period of step-by-step approach to the realization of a given idea—and thus a process of creation of the individual work which could last for years and was subject to periodic interruptions—was subordinate to the intellectual process involved in its conception. One visitor wrote the following account after a meeting with Munch in his open-air studio (fig. 12):

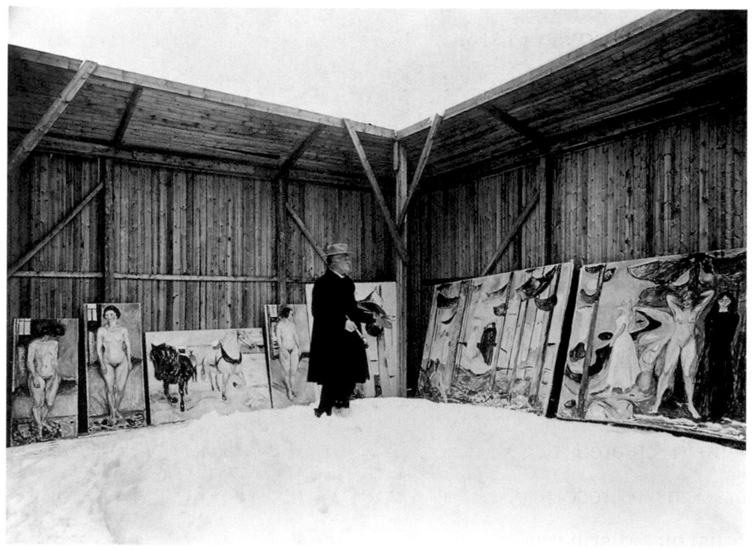

11 Edvard Munch, *Country Road (Street in Åsgårdstrand)*, 1902, oil on canvas, 88.5 x 114 cm, Öffentliche Kunstsammlung Basel

12 Edvard Munch painting in his open-air studio, Ekely, ca. 1925

Finished and unfinished canvases were leaning against the walls, multiple variations of his favorite subjects. I was horrified at the way he treated them, kicking them with his feet and generally showing no concern at all about any damage they might incur. He explained that the important thing was not the finished work or preserving it as such, but instead only that something assumed perfect artistic form at some point, even if it took several different tries to accomplish that. Then, he said, it would become a part of the fabric of the world, which could never be conceived without it again.[17]

In Munch's case, "several different tries" means numerous variations, all of which were equally important to him. A different decision could be made and thus a different solution found at any given time and depending upon his disposition. This touches upon a fundamental question of human existence that remains as current as ever today: To what extent do one's own decisions influence the course of actions and events, the nature of solutions and resolutions. *Lola Runs*, a feature film released in 1998, presents three variations of a basic situation which illustrate the diversity of possible decisions that could emerge from it and the resulting patterns of interconnected, interacting events. The characters in the stories of Milan Kundera repeatedly express despair in face of the recognition that in real life—in painful contrast to art and fantasy—one never has the chance to return to a fork in the path and take the other way. And unlike the protagonist in the continuous loop of time in which the plot of *Groundhog Day* (1992) unfolds, he avoided inconsequential repetitions by virtue of his ability to add new elements and variations continually as he proceeded up the ascending spiral of his life.

Munch's *Dance of Life* is not only the title of a painting that forms part of the *Frieze of Life* and now exists in a number of variations (fig. 13 and fig. 4, p. 57), it also integrates in the course of permanent questioning through experiments and serial trials the various combinations of tonal progressions, tempi, dynamics, and keys Munch created using a wide spectrum of different tonal colorations to record different worlds of mood and feeling and to construct distinctive sound architectures. Movement and speed are erratic in Munch's *Dance of Life*, *The Voice* is heard in different shades of sound, resonating in soft, variable timbres and freezing still in the presence of the *The Scream* that cuts through everything. Musical associations were a popular topic of discussion in visual art around the turn of the century and in the early years of the 20th century. Visual compositions by Kupka and Kandinsky come readily to mind in this context. Conversely, musicians also turned their attention to aspects of visual art. In 1874, Modest Mussorgsky composed the piano suite *Pictures at an Exhibition* in honor of his friend, the painter and architect Viktor Hartmann, who had died the preceding year. Again and again, the piece repeats the musical theme of the promenade in a series of variations corresponding to the subjects of the individual paintings. The images are varied in different motifs, moods, keys, volumes, tempi, and timbres. The suite was not printed until several years after Mussorgsky's death in 1886 and was almost never heard in concert halls. It was not rediscovered until the next century and became popular only after Maurice Ravel wrote an orchestral arrangement for Sergej Kussewitzky in 1922. Today, *Pictures at an Exhibition* is available in many other versions, not the least noteworthy of which is the one adapted for an entirely new audience by Emerson, Lake and Palmer in the 1960s, just as Andy Warhol did with his variations on themes by Munch.

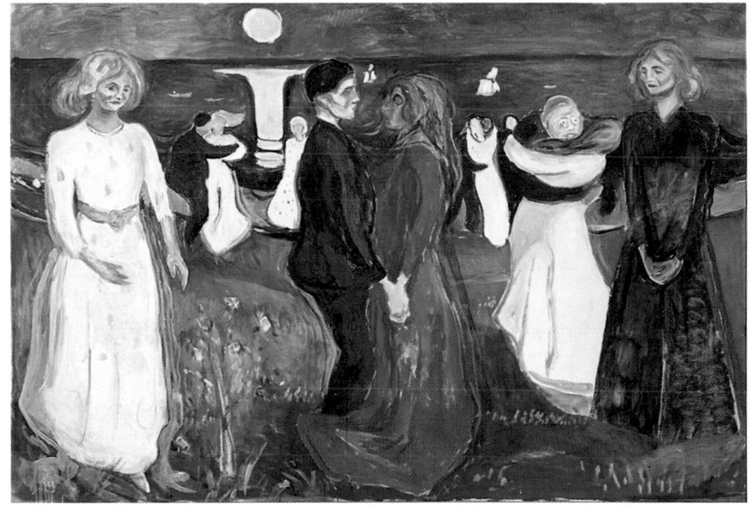

13 Edvard Munch, *The Dance of Life*, 1925–29, oil on canvas, 143 x 208 cm, Munch-museet, Oslo

1 Schiefler made the following entry in his diary on Dec. 28, 1903 with regard to Munch's visit to his exhibition at the Kunsthalle Hamburg: "He understands our reluctance to exhibit the *Madonna*. He thinks that something like that could indeed by dangerous for young girls. *The Kiss* as well." Edvard Munch/Gustav Schiefler, *Briefwechsel*, vol. 1: 1902–1914, Hamburg 1987, p. 71.

2 For the quotation see the chapter *Madonna*, p. 137.

3 Cornelia Gerner, *Die »Madonna« in Edvard Munchs Werk. Frauenbilder und Frauenbild im ausgehenden 19. Jahrhundert*, Morsbach 1993 p. 28.

4 *Ibid.*, pp. 15f.

5 On the variations of the image of the woman as Madonna see the chapter *Madonna*, pp. 137–147.

6 Three female characters in works by Henrik Ibsen appear relevant to the cigarette-smoking *Madonna* shown in the caricature and to refer to the image of the *femme fatale* and the emancipated woman. See Gerner 1993 (see note 3), pp. 169ff. Munch depicted himself smoking a cigarette in an early self-portrait in 1895; cf. fig. 8, p. 102.

7 See the text by Christoph Asendorf, pp. 83–90.

8 Quoted and translated from Uwe M. Schneede, *Edvard Munch, Das kranke Kind*, Hamburger Kunsthalle 2002, p. 28.

9 Norma S. Steinberg, "Munch in Color," in *Harvard University Art Museum Bulletin*, 1995, spring, p. 36.

10 Christoph Heinrich, "Une série d'effects différents. Monets *Getreideschober* als Hülle für das Licht, die Zeit, das Universum—und 'die märchenhafte Kraft und Pracht der Malerei,'" in *Monets Vermächtnis. Serie—Ordnung und Obsession*, Uwe Schneede (ed.), exh. cat., Hamburger Kunsthalle, Ostfildern-Ruit 2001, p. 13.

11 Quoted and translated from Matthias Arnold, *Edvard Munch*, Hamburg 2000, p. 134.

12 Reference is made here to examples shown in this publication. For exact information on the grouping of the paintings shown in Berlin see Jan Kneher, *Edvard Munch in seinen Ausstellungen zwischen 1892 und 1912. Eine Dokumentation der Ausstellungen und Studie zur Rezeptionsgeschichte von Munchs Kunst*, Worms 1994, pp. 151f.

13 Quoted and translated from *ibid.*, p. 152.

14 Werner Hofmann, *Die Moderne im Rückspiegel. Hauptwege der Kunstgeschichte*, Munich 1998, p. 222.

15 See, for example, "Edvard Munch and the Early Secessionist Woodcut in Vienna," pp. 91–96 and "Munch and Austria," pp. 97–109.

16 See also Rolf E. Stenersen, *Edvard Munch—Close-Up of a Genius*, Oslo 1994, p. 94.

17 Quoted and translated from Arnold 2000 (see note 11), p. 135.

Disappearance: Experiments with Material and Motif

Dieter Buchhart

The Artist's Act of Will

Adopting an unconventional painting technique, Edvard Munch distanced himself from the Scandinavian tradition of naturalism in the mid-1880s. In the following years, conservative critics referred to his works as unfinished, sketchy, "roughly executed,"[1] and "random experiments with color."[2] Working in a very direct manner, he applied paint in multiple layers, sometimes with a palette knife, made gaps in the painted surface by scraping away certain areas of color, scratching the skin of the paint, and creating works with palpable color volume. The traces of his work remain visible in the tactile structure of the body of color as evidence of the often time-consuming painting process and the material quality of the paint. Munch's *Self-Portrait* of 1886[3] (fig. 1) is marked by numerous scratches. The head is turned to the side in a three-quarter profile. The eyes continue the turning movement, watching attentively from their corners. Executed with more liquid paint, the hair flows in a smooth transition into the grayish, blueish-green background. The layers of paint in the face were applied with a palette knife and then partially scraped away again, leaving bare patches of canvas. In some places, Munch scratched and cut with a sharp object so vigorously that these wounds expose the canvas sizing, thus incorporating the color of the sizing into the overall color scheme of the painting. He inflicted severe injuries to the color skin of his *Self-portrait*, as an illusionistic representative of himself, as if he were tearing away lumps of flesh with his blows. The explanation for why Munch mistreated the painting in such an aggressive manner is less likely to be found in a biographical-psychological interpretation[4] than in Munch's unorthodox approach to technique and material. Around 1886, Munch explored the experimental potential of the body of color as a three-dimensional membrane in numerous applications of new paint to paintings and studies in which he often linked the original subject with the layers of color and motifs he applied over them and through his highly varied application of scratch and scrape marks. In his *Self-Portrait*, he made pointed incisions in the painted surface. In the first version of *The Sick Child*, he cut deep, mostly horizontal lines into the nearly dry paint using a pointed object, possibly a palette knife or the stem of a brush, thus exposing underlying layers of paint. In his portrait of *Dagny Bohr Konow* (fig. 2), he scraped broad vertical and horizontal strips of paint away with a palette knife applied with great pressure, destroying significant portions of the portrait image. Not only is the canvas sizing integrated into the overall color scheme, as in *Self-Portrait*, the canvas itself exerts a defining influence on the total structure of the work by virtue of its material quality, emphasizing its own materiality and presence as an indexical gesture. In this way, Munch probed the potential of the medium of painting, making the traces of the production process visible and palpable even in the final version of his painting. During his years in Paris between 1889 and 1892,

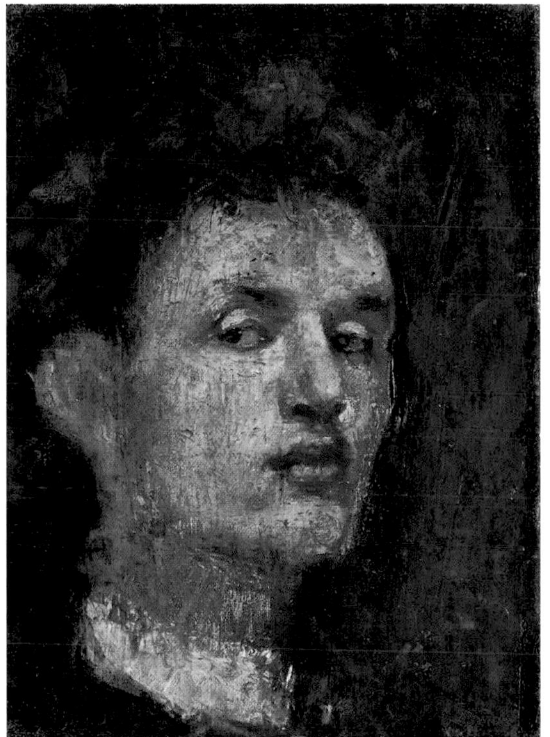

1 Edvard Munch, *Self-Portrait*, 1886,
oil on canvas, 33 x 24.5 cm, Nasjonalgalleriet, Oslo

Munch's interest shifted progressively from the impasto body of color to a more sparing use of paint influenced by the impressionists. It was probably not until after his arrival in Berlin in the fall of 1892 that he took up these experiments again, focusing on the inherent material properties of the image-bearing medium and the possibilities for variation offered by sizing and color combinations. A letter from the Swedish painter Richard Bergh to Edvard Munch in Berlin dated June 15, 1893 supports the assumption that Munch's experimentation with sizing and binders may have been a by-product of his acquaintance with the physician Carl Ludwig Schleich: "So now I would ask if you could send me the samples of tempera paints as Doctor Schleich kindly promised—provided he has not forgotten. I would very much like to try them out."[5] Schleich frequented the bohemian circle of Zum Schwarzen Ferkel and provided Strindberg, and presumably Munch, with his knowledge about recipes for paints and binders.[6] Strindberg himself experimented extensively in the media of painting and photography during this period. In his paintings, he vigorously pursued the autonomization of visual resources on the basis of his ideas regarding the subjective nature of what is seen. "One should paint his inner self and not draw sticks and stones, which are actually meaningless in themselves and can assume form only because they have passed through the smelting furnaces of the perceiving, feeling subject. That is why one did not study outdoors but instead painted at home, from memory and with imagination."[7] The dry, pasty layers of paint of the mid-1880s now gave way to partially unpainted, partially self-sized or unsized patches of canvas, and a glazing technique relying on heavily diluted paints and in some cases the use of casein as a binder.

Strindberg's principle of chance in creative art and Munch's "kill-or-cure treatment": the disappearance of matter through the workings of nature

Munch painted the portrait of *Stanislaw Przybyszewski (with Skeleton Arm)* (cat. no. 186) in Berlin in 1893–94. The head of the Polish author Przybyszewski, a leading figure in the Zum Schwarzen Ferkel group, appears in very dry, dull colors in the upper half of the painting executed on thinly sized canvas.[8] Visible in the lower section of the painting are a bone, on the left, and the vague form of a hand, on the right, which are separated from the molded, protruding face by a reddish horizontal line. The water and rust spots still recognizable today were imparted to the canvas perhaps prior to the painting process, in which Munch framed the face in blue, sketched in the collar and hem and crossed through the reddish dividing line with a few blue brushstrokes resembling hatched lines as an apparent corrective measure. Finally, he made both the blue strokes and the reddish horizontal line paler by applying a glaze of white paint below the face, while leaving the bone uncovered. In his autobiographical novel *Inferno*, published in 1897, Strindberg describes the portrait in a diary entry for June 18, 1896:

> In the studio of the Danish artist [Munch], we looked at a portrait of Popoffsky [Przybyszewski] painted two years ago. It shows only the head, separated from the body by a cloud, and beneath the cloud crossed bones like those one sees on gravestones. The severed head sends a shudder down our spines, and the dream I had on May 14 suddenly appeared again like a ghost in my mind's eye.[9]

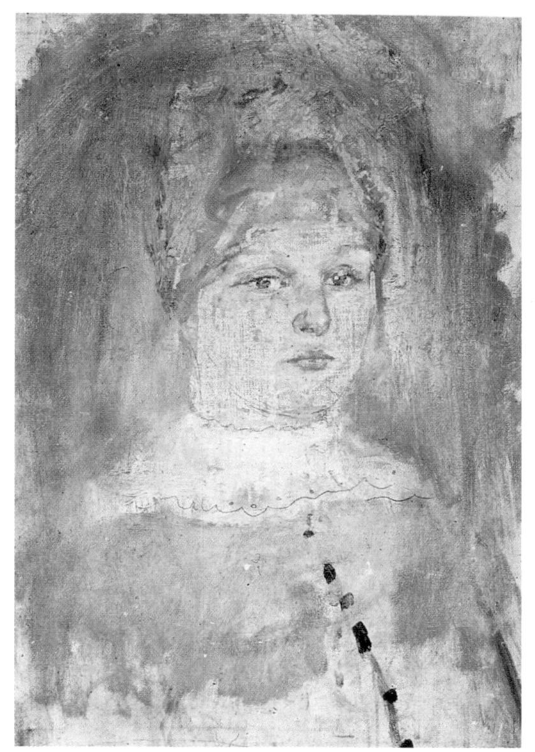

2 Edvard Munch, *Dagny Bohr Konow*, 1886, oil on canvas, 49.7 x 35 cm, private collection

These notes not only support a dating circa 1894, they also provide an early reference to the presence of large water spots, for since Munch painted no cloudlike structures, what Strindberg describes as a "cloud"[10] is presumably one of the cloud-shaped spots created by the action of water on the canvas. The likelihood that Munch caused this "water damage" deliberately by exposing the painting to wind and weather, as he did with many of his works, is confirmed by accounts and statements by several contemporaries, by photographs, by the paintings themselves, and by Munch's relations with Strindberg.

What is the significance of this process, referred to in the literature as a "kill-or-cure treatment," in Munch's art?[11] Was it carelessness and a lack of interest in preserving his works that lay behind his habit of exposing them to sunshine, rain, snow, and the cold, or was it a deliberate expression of artistic intent? Hermann Schlittgen mentions the chaos of Munch's working environment, which the artist himself documented in a number of photographs in 1902. He mentions tripping over "a fresh painting leaning in some place where it could not possibly have stood."[12] Other accounts go even further, citing incidents in which Munch actually encouraged visitors to damage his works: "'Go ahead and trample all over them,' he said, 'it will only make them better.'"[13] For "a good painting can take a lot of punishment. Only bad paintings must be whole and have expensive, heavy frames."[14] But the artist not only permitted these "injuries" to his works, he actually made them an integral part of his working method: "Just wait until it has survived a few showers, until it has suffered a few nail scratches and other things and has been sent around the world poorly packed. ... Yes, and it will become good as time goes by! It has to acquire a few faults before it becomes really good."[15] Yet he was also attentive to complaints by his customers, among them that of Gustav Schiefler, Director of the Hamburg Regional Court, who called his attention to the "quite severely damaged condition" of a painting sent through the mail, and probably poorly packed, in a letter dated February 9, 1913. Munch responded, saying, "I think the damage to the painting makes little difference—but it is unpleasant—and by the way, all of my paintings are a bit perforated (?)—it is a necessary part of being a genuine 'Munch'—I'll find another painting for you."[16] Munch's answer is ambiguous, for although he views such damage as characteristic of his paintings, he expresses regret for it and even offers to send a replacement. This may be understood as a concession on Munch's part to his financial dependence on his clientele, and it also indicates his awareness of the fact that such treatment of works of art was not tolerated at that time. Yet he continued to expose his paintings to natural weathering nonetheless, thus weakening the impact of the painter's act of will by figuring the random component of natural deterioration into the painting process. Munch expressed thoughts on the relationship of art to nature in notes written in 1903–04: "I do not paint from nature—I draw from its kingdom."[17] When the artist's estate was inspected and appraised following his death on January 23, 1944, "substantial parts of his collection were in miserable condition," according to Munch's contemporary Jan Thurmann-Moe,[18] as "many of the canvases were partially rotted, full of holes, tears, and gaps. Layers of paint and sizing in many of the canvases had more or less been peeled and washed away, and

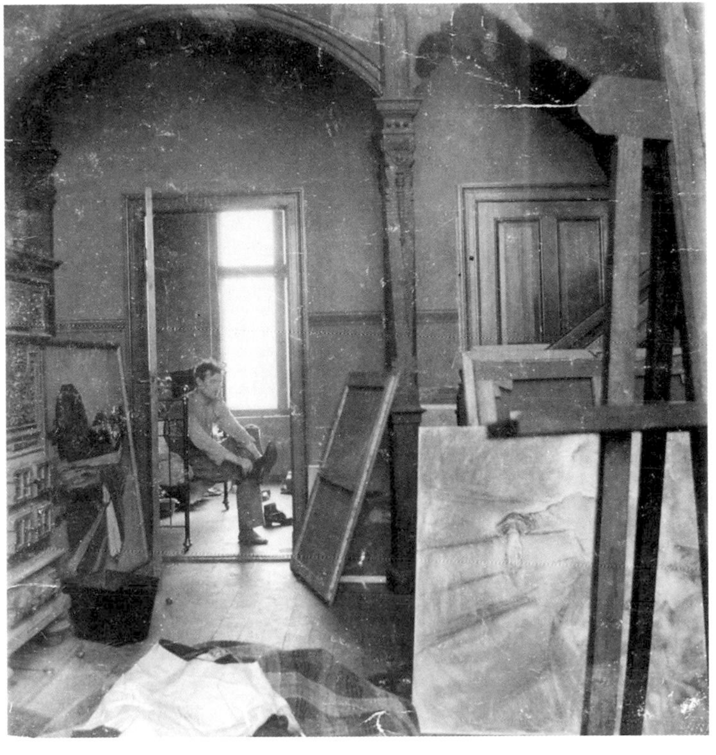

3 Edvard Munch in his studio apartment on 82, Lützowstrasse, Berlin, 1902, photo: Edvard Munch, Munch-museet, Oslo

a number of pictures exhibited large dark water, mold, and mildew spots. Nearly half of the pictures were covered with bird excrement."[19] Munch exposed his paintings to an accelerated aging process, which destroyed some of them, and introduced the factor of chance, which is not subject to human will or consciousness. While his experiments with scraping and scratching were clearly acts of will, the natural, largely uncontrollable weathering process now became a part of his art—entirely in the spirit of Strindberg, who concluded his 1894 essay on "New Forms of Art! Or Chance in Artistic Creation" with the following appeal: "The art of the future (which will disappear, like everything else): Imitate nature in an approximate way; imitate in particular nature's way of creating!"[20] Munch wanted not only to "imitate [nature's] way of creating," but actually to let it create. This is what Strindberg implies in his reminder that "everything" passes. There is no proof that Munch was familiar with the text of the essay, but we do know that he was in close contact with Strindberg from 1892 to 1896. It was precisely during those years that Strindberg sought in numerous experiments to establish a link between nature (or the study of nature) and art, and this clearly suggests that Munch was familiar with the dramatist's views. Further evidence is found in Munch's notes from 1907–08, in which he states in the spirit of Strindberg that "Art is the human urge for crystallization. Nature is the great eternal kingdom from which art draws sustenance."[21]

Yet Strindberg mixes several different levels in his discussion of a "theory of automatic art" and a "mixture of the unconscious [random events] and the conscious [acts of will]."[22] He speaks on the one hand of a creative process liberated to the extent possible from the influence of the conscious mind, "when [the] hand keeps moving the palette knife at random"[23] or when "in a fit of pique ... I brought my hand down on the poor wretch's head [the clay figure of a praying boy] and "transformed" him through "metamorphosis" into a "weeping nine-year-old boy."[24] One the other hand, he sees a piece of charcoal pulled from an oven as a "masterpiece of primitive sculpture"[25] and his experimental photograms of crystallizations (fig. 4) as works of art, and thus he recognizes nature's creative artistic potential. Munch, however, made no automatic art but instead employed a deliberate process of painting, scratching, and scraping to create visual representations of themes which he then exposed to natural weathering, thus exploiting nature's "way of creating" for his own creative purposes. Munch allowed nature to rework his paintings, relinquishing his tools of influence and control. The effects of his "kill-or-cure treatment" depend upon the material properties of the image-bearing medium but not on the subject. The type of sizing, the adhesive strength of the binder, or the tightness of the weave in the canvas determine the outcome. The subject is eliminated in two ways—in that the artist retreats as an active agent and exposes the subjectivized object depicted—the subject of the painting—and along with it his own unique style to alteration and possibly to total destruction.

The parallels between Strindberg's ideas regarding the role of chance in artistic creation and Munch's experimental investigation into nature's way of creating clearly support the presumption that Munch began integrating the element of chance and the influence of nature in the form of an accelerated aging process with his "kill-or-cure treatment" approach while in Berlin. The portrait

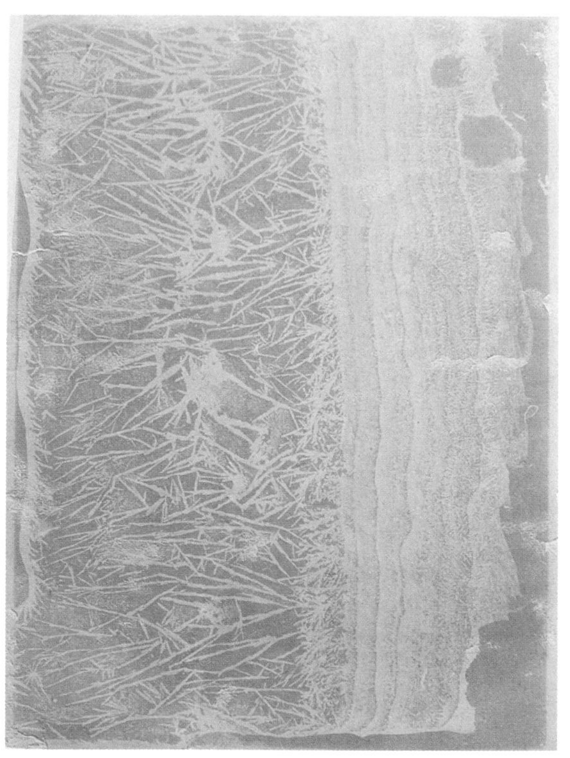

4 August Strindberg, photogram of a crystallization, 1892–96, 9 x 12 cm, Kungliga Biblioteket Stockholm

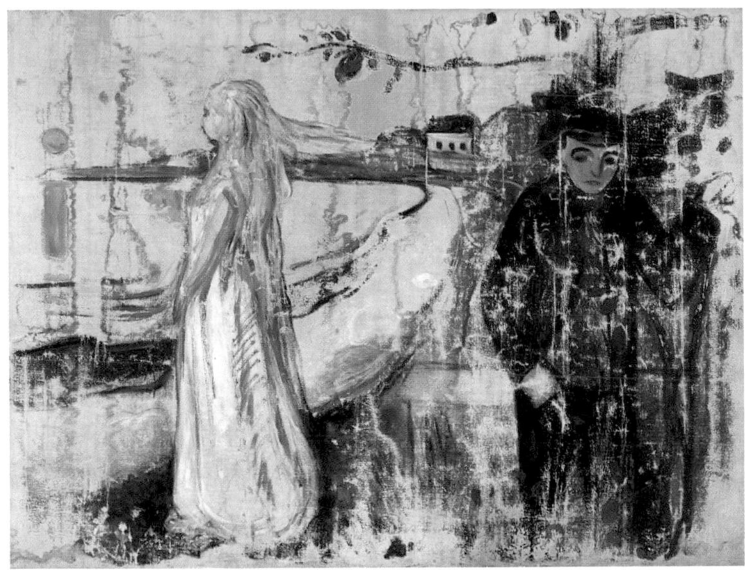

of *Stanislaw Przybyszewski (with Skeleton Arm)* (cat. no. 186) is one of a group of paintings from the mid-1890s that Munch placed outdoors during this period and which consequently also exhibit water spots and such severe damage as peeling layers of paint and patches of washed-out color (fig. 5).[26]

At this point, Munch attributed new significance to the canvas substrate of the painting in three different ways. First of all, he usually applied paint sparingly, sometimes as a thin glaze, thus allowing the color and structure of the canvas to remain visible beneath the transparent layer of paint. Secondly, he left substantial areas of his canvas blank, emphasizing its material character and making it a part of the total structure of the work so that the substrate lost its neutral status and assumed a pictorial quality in its own right. Thirdly, paint was peeled away or washed out by the influences of weather. The elimination of some areas left the surface of the canvas exposed. The remaining areas of illusionistic imagery are declared as applied layers, whereby Munch's abandonment of the painted layer as the medium of a seemingly immaterial surface, the subject, becomes obvious. The discoloration of the canvas by spots of water and mold identifies the image-bearing medium as an autonomous pictorial resource, which assumes an image-making function in terms of both color and structure. As evidence of the creative forces of nature, the disappearance of layers of paint and the emergence of the canvas substrate mark out a horizon of time that encompasses the entire process of creating the work and renders the temporal character of the natural aging process visible.

Munch consistently refused to inhibit the aging process by applying varnish, as these changes gave his paintings "the patina, the tone he wanted and planned for," as Jappe Nilssen pointed out in his vitriolic attack on the conservator at the Nasjonalgalleriet, who had varnished three of Munch's paintings, in his article entitled "Devastation" in the daily newspaper *Dagens Nytt*.[27] The artist himself made no official statement on this issue but is said to have confided in Sternersen that "I didn't recognize my own painting.—One of my very best pictures! And he [Jens Thiis, Director of the Nasjonalgalleriet] allowed Harald Brun [conservator at the Nasjonalgalleriet] to paint on it!" This statement suggests that Munch did not regard varnish as a final protective coating but as a layer of material in its own right, as a second skin that can only be a part of the artist's creative process. The fact that his working method did not include varnishing is evidenced not only by his "kill-or-cure treatment" but also by the fact that not a single one of the 1,100 paintings found in his studio after his death had been varnished.

Unfortunately, many of his paintings were coated with varnish afterwards. The resulting change in the refraction factor intensified the color depth and leveled the surface. Much of the bird excrement found on several hundred paintings was removed; brittle canvases and paintings with large gaps and tears were strengthened with backing canvases. As a result, one has only a vague sense of the actual effects of Munch's "kill-or-cure treatment" in many cases today. The water spots such as those in *Stanislaw Przybyszewski (with Skeleton Arm)* and *Death and the Maiden* (cat. no. 44) fade appreciably even without the intervention of conservators, as the natural process of creation initiated by Munch continues even today.

5 Edvard Munch, *Separation*, 1893, oil on canvas, 115 x 150 cm, Munch-museet, Oslo

Wood grain—the presence of the base material

In the fall of 1894, Munch began working on etchings and lithographs, the first of which were mirror images of subjects he had depicted in paintings. Following the dissolution of the bohemian Zum Schwarzen Ferkel group, which included such personalities as Strindberg and the Przybyszewskis, who had exerted significant influence on his development as an artist, he left Berlin in late February 1896 for Paris, where he turned his attention to graphic art and produced his first multichrome color lithographs, among them *The Sick Child* (cat. no. 123–130). In the fall, he began a period of intensive work with the medium of the woodcut, creating his first five prints in rapid order: *Man's Head in Woman's Hair*, *Moonlight* I, *Melancholy* I, *The Voice* (*Summer Night*) and *Angst*. The first prints were highly experimental. Munch focused on the printing process and combinations of different materials while exploring the potential inherent in printing paints and wood as a base material.

Moonlight I became the focal point of these early experiments. The motif is derived from the nearly square painting entitled *Moonlight* of 1893 (fig. 8), which shows a woman standing in the moonlight in front of a house surrounded by a white fence. Munch dispensed with the fence in the woodcut and reduced the composition in the horizontal format to a mirror image of the woman's head and shoulders, her shadow, a section of a tree, the wooden boards of the house and the window, in which the moon is reflected. Several variations hand-printed by the artist himself are characterized by thick, pasty layers of color, in some cases oil paint.[28] Unlike the earlier two-color prints in black and blue produced using the front and reverse sides of a wood block (cat. no. 11), these prints were executed with a third color plate, which Munch presumably cut into three parts with a fretsaw[29] before putting the differently colored sections back together. He often used this characteristic method for his woodcuts. Printed with thick oil paint, the variations (cat. no. 13) represent a link between painting and graphic art by virtue of the color material he used. Difficult to transfer to paper, the oily paint produced spotty, lumpy prints in the high-pressure printing process. The colors black, dark green, and yellowish-brown and the yellowish-brown paper, the fine structure of which give the prints a consistent underlying matrix, blend with one another. The color and material structure of the paper remain visibly present over the entire surface of the print, an effect that is not restricted to the areas corresponding to the cuts and gouges in the printing plate. By printing to the edges of the irregularly cut sheets, Munch not only saved paper,[30] but also treated the marginless print like a painting. The painterly character of these early experiments is emphasized by the fact that a version printed with a thick application of paint (cat. no. 14)[31] can be identified as a print only after "thorough examination."[32] Like a canvas, the paper structure appears as a substrate in places, but does not correspond to hollows in the woodcut. Munch must have applied his impasto paint like a painter to the third plate and then transferred it to the previously printed front and reverse sides of the printing block and then onto the paper. The print has irregular edges and fills the entire paper sheet. The outlines are blurred through the process of applying the paint. Red shines through the thick layers of black, blue, green, and reddish brown in the lower left, and white, the reflection of the moon, is visible beneath the opaque light blue of the window. The marginless print and the iridescent effect of the impasto paint also position this print between painting and graphic art. As in the painting *Moonlight*, body, hair, and hat disappear in this atmospherically charged version by virtue of the blending of the different areas of color. Yet the face does not stand out as a pale form but instead echoes the hues of the wooden boards in its subdued coloration.

In contrast to the painted variations, in which paper structure and color composition dominate the visual effect, Munch incorporated the natural structure of the grain in the wood block in his early two-color prints of *Moonlight* I (cat. no. 11). Munch always used lengths of wood cut parallel to the grain, selecting printing blocks of varying thicknesses ranging from pieces cut from large panels used in furniture manufacture to wooden boards prepared for use as painting substrates.[33] The vertical grain pattern in *Moonlight* I emphasizes the verticality of the figure, the wooden boards, and the window frame and cuts through the printed areas of the finished image. In a monochrome black version of the front side of the printing block (cat. no. 12)[34] the grain lies over the face, the window, and the surrounding black area like a veil, and the contourless body disappears entirely.

The sparing use of paint and the usually unsanded, unpolished surfaces of the printing blocks favor the transfer of the grain pattern and saw marks to the print and evoke an impression of transparency. Since Munch did not eliminate surface irregularities and accepted indentations and deformations in the printing block, his prints exhibit areas of differing color strength, whereby areas with thinner coverings of paint render the grain with particular clarity. This produces subtle effects, such as the delicate shimmer (of moonlight) at the level of the woman's face. The marked pattern of the wood grain obscures the paper structure and shifts the significance of the substrate in favor of the overall color scheme.

Munch's inclination to incorporate the structure of the wood into his early prints is only partially attributable to the influence of Paul Gauguin, Paul Herrmann, or Alfred Jarry.[35] Although Gauguin's *Noa Noa* prints from 1893–94 (fig. 6) exhibit a transparency achieved through the sparing use of paint, Gauguin worked with blocks of wood cut against the grain, thus greatly reducing the importance of the grain pattern. With the exception of Paul Herrmann, whose color woodcuts combined with lithographs reveal delicate wood patterns,[36] there is no evidence that Munch's contemporaries employed similar working methods. Munch's interest in the natural properties of wood is more likely an outgrowth of his Berlin experiments on the material qualities of pictorial resources. In his works from the Berlin period, both chance and the negation of the neutral character of the substrate play important roles, although the direct reference to the material gives way in the printing process to an impression in the sense of a trace.

Just as Munch introduced the factor of chance into his works in Berlin, thus interpreting and elaborating upon Strindberg's appeal to "imitate nature's way of creating" for his own purposes by exposing paintings to weathering, we also recognize other parallels to Strindberg in Paris in 1896. At the time, Strindberg was intensely concerned with overcoming the boundaries between scientific experimentation and the artistic process through a "form of associative aesthetics."[37] When he wrote, for example, "that trees are directly related to the sun by virtue of the concentric circles [annual growth rings] in their trunks," he was establishing relations and external affinities in forms and manifestations.[38] During his years in Berlin, Munch had become quite familiar with the unconstrained use of natural forms such as the annual growth rings which form the grain in lengths of wood, of new scientific insights such as the X-rays discovered by Conrad Wilhelm Röntgen in 1895, and even of aspects of the occult, as his depiction of spermatozoa and fetuses in his painting *Death and the Maiden* of 1893 (cat. no. 44) clearly shows. The significance of Strindberg's influence upon Munch's studies in science and his grasp of scientific principles cannot be overstated, and it is reasonable to assume that Munch continued to pursue these interests in Paris, where Strindberg introduced him to intellectual circles. Munch represented nature's way of creating in visual form by transferring the pattern of wood grain to his prints. The presence of the base material is more than the reproduction of a natural structure; it is also an expression of its yearly growth and thus of the factor of time, which is visualized

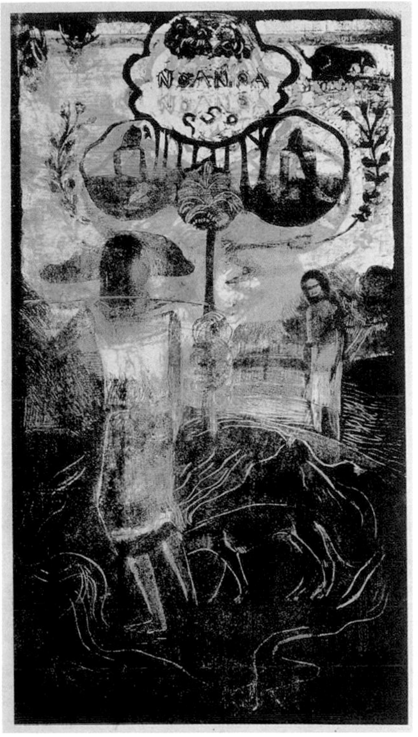

6 Paul Gauguin, *Noa Noa Fragrant*, 1893–94,
color woodcut, 35.8 x 20.4 cm,
Musée National des Arts d'Afrique et d'Océanie, Paris

in the random detail. It is a trace of nature and the material quality of the wood that Munch printed in and onto the paper as an image-bearing substrate as a way of linking his creative process with that of nature itself.

An impressive illustration of the manner in which Munch intensified the presence of the wood grain over the course of the following years is found in *The Kiss*, a work Munch revisited in a number of woodcut variations, the last of which was completed shortly before his death. Highlighted by the artist's sparing use of paint, the wood grain pattern plays an important role even in the first two woodcuts, *The Kiss* I (cat. no. 49) and *The Kiss* II of 1897 (cat. no. 50). A year later, Munch used a fretsaw to shape the silhouette of the kissing couple from the wooden block for *The Kiss* III (fig. 7). One recognizes immediately that the body of the woman is formed from an area of concentric, ellipsoid lines of grain—that is, the cuts in the wood are organically adapted to the natural growth pattern. In the early two-color prints of 1898, Munch printed the silhouette in black in a kind of experimental run onto the gray print of a rectangular wood block visibly marked by growth rings and knotholes in three different positions by turning the silhouette 90 degrees for each printing. This produced two types of variation in horizontal formats with vertical grain patterns. The first—type A—is characterized by nearly wedge-shaped growth rings which penetrate from the upper right and narrow to a point (cat. no. 51). The second—type B—is turned 180 degrees and exhibits the same remarkable grain pattern rising from the lower left (cat. no. 52). Type C (fig. 7) is a vertical format, and thus the grain pattern penetrates the silhouette horizontally. These grain patterns overlap in all variations and dominate the pictorial effect. While the background pattern in the horizontal formats enhances the vertical orientation of the couple, that of the vertical format creates a radical disturbance of the vertical effect. The image of the couple is laid over the wood background like a projection. Arne Eggum compares the results of such woodcuts with the results of an X-ray exposure of the motif through a wooden panel[39] and emphasizes its projection character. Whether Munch was actually influenced by the discovery of X-rays, as Eggum suggests in his simplistic comparison, is a matter of speculation. Yet it is highly likely that he was acquainted with the subject matter, since Strindberg was involved in the study of X-rays[40] and this new scientific discovery was rapidly gaining popularity, among other things at carnivals and fairs, where performers used X-rays to reveal the contents of handbags and purses. The gray-black color scale and the transparency of the prints are reminiscent of black-and-white negatives and roentgenograms or shadow images. The transparent motif of the kissing couple is declared as the material wood in its own right and threatens to disappear amongst the annual growth rings and knotholes. Munch's technique of printing to the edge of his paper makes the paper itself an illusionistic substitute for a wood block, a material print. Munch does not emphasize the "non-material quality of the woodcut," as Eggum contends,[41] but indeed its very opposite, the material character of the original wood material.

More than thirty years later, Munch used this characteristic spruce block once again for the slightly horizontal, monochrome reddish-brown print *Starry Night* (cat. no. 150), thus turning the background plate into a primary printing plate (fig. 8). The prominent wedge-

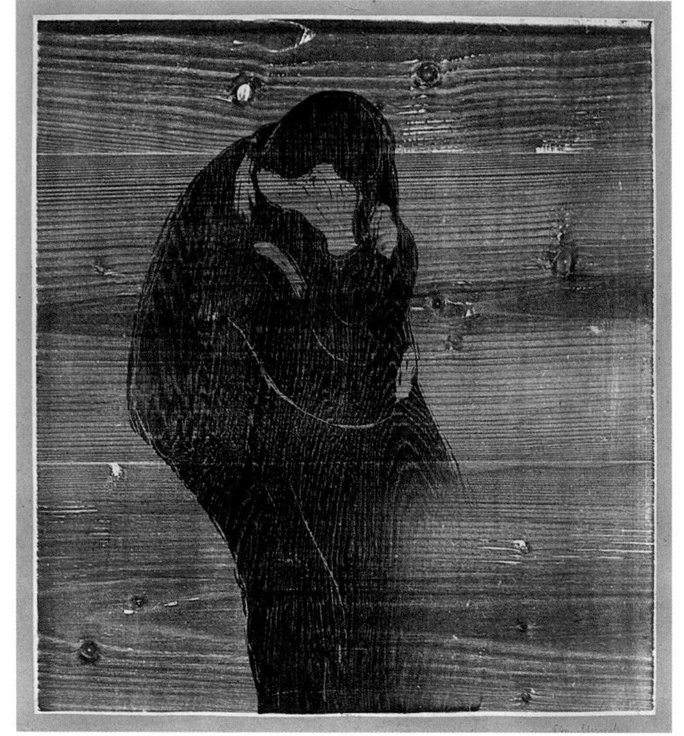

7 Edvard Munch, *The Kiss* III, 1898,
color woodcut on paper, 45.8 x 40.3 cm, private collection

shaped grain pattern is clearly recognizable—now in a vertical configuration—in the upper left-hand portion of the print. The knotholes serve as pictorial elements—the stars in the nocturnal sky. The dimensions of the print block preserved at the Munch-museet show that this block is the same one used for *The Kiss*. A fracture line at the bottom provides evidence that a sizable portion was broken off—presumably deliberately by Munch himself—thus altering the format. The grain of the wood overlaps the lines, some of which are very finely drawn, and the motif of this sole surviving print disappears into the structure of the wood. The reddish-brown color is a further reference to the original wood material, although the printing block was selected with regard for the motif and relies on the natural markings. By using the same printing block employed for one of his most important prints a second time, Munch incorporated his own life cycle alongside the natural temporal character of the annual growth rings into the work.

In contrast to the agitated, prominent wood grain pattern of the background plate for the early prints of *The Kiss* III, the parallel grain pattern in the fourth woodcut version of 1902 corresponds to the configuration of the grain of the silhouette of the kissing couple. Almost all of the nearly square, two-color prints in black and gray are printed on gray paper without margins (cat. no. 53) and have a decorative quality. The pattern drawn by nature is concentrated and evokes an almost ornamental effect, like that of a fabric pattern. In a later dark-blue print (cat. no. 54), which shows only the slightly reworked silhouette of the couple, Munch intensified the presence of the wood in the print by adding traces of brown in the troughs of the grain as a reference to the color of the original material.

Shortly before his death, Munch took up the theme of the kiss one last time in the monochrome woodcut *Kiss in the Field* (cat. no. 56). Using a few fine lines, he cut the figures of a kissing couple into the background of a mountainous landscape. The pair literally melts into the prominent grain pattern of the wood block in the brown print.[42] Here, the motif disappears and gives way to the material character of a wood block, which is reflected in both the color and structure of the print. Munch reveals the aesthetic potential of nature's way of creating in a temporal context, which he expresses in the form of the record of time contained in the annual growth rings.

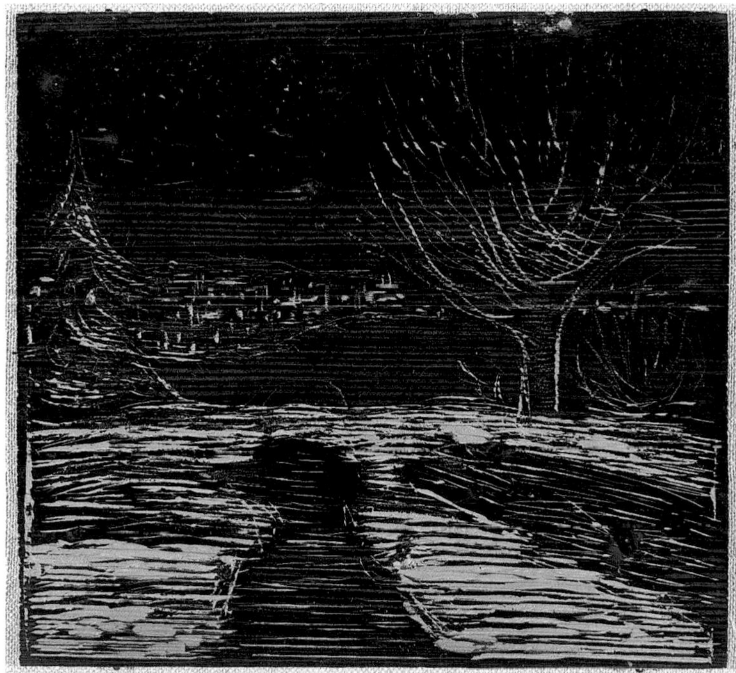

8 Block of the woodcut *Starry Night*, 1930 (cat. no. 150), 37 x 40 cm, Munch-museet, Oslo

Transparency in revised prints

Munch's lack of concern for the boundaries between different artistic techniques becomes evident not only in his early painterly variations of *Moonlight* I but also in the numerous revisions of prints he executed using drawing pencils, chalk, ink, watercolor and opaque paints ranging from gouache to oils. We recognize three different working methods in these revised versions: correction, glazing and opaque coloring, and the addition of new motifs. In several prints, including *Moonlight* I,[43] Munch corrected printing faults and covered over presumably unwanted blank areas. This type of retouching seems surprising, since Munch not only accepted misprints and faults as natural products of his unorthodox working method but actually regarded them as essential programmatic features, as the "kill-or-cure treatment" to which he subjected his paintings would indicate. Thus, one is inevitably compelled to ask whether he actually made these corrections—or at least some of them—himself. The question can no longer be answered with certainty today.

It is an established fact, however, that Munch colored numerous prints, including etchings, lithographs, and woodcuts, during the years beginning in 1895. Most, though by no means all, of the works in question were monochrome black prints. Gerd Woll assumes that these additions of color were made in preparation for color printing and points out that "it looks as in other cases as though he simply enjoyed painting over the monochrome print."[44] This casts doubt upon their significance as autonomous variations. According to Woll, Munch transferred only very few of these variations to color prints,[45] although this actually tells us very little about the importance of these works, since Munch repeated specific themes in many variations throughout his life. It is more likely that these numerous one-of-a-kind pieces are products of his ceaseless striving to explore the experimental potential of the processes of artistic production and that of theme and motif, without regard for historical genre boundaries.

Munch executed a number of hand-colored versions of his two lithographs, both completed in 1896, devoted to the theme of jealousy and concerned with his triangular relationship with Stanislaw Przybyszewski und Dagny Juel. The painting completed the preceding year shows Przybyszewski *en face* in the foreground (fig. 1, p. 69); Munch and Juel are positioned in the middle ground as Adam and Eve standing at the Tree of Knowledge. Whereas *Jealousy* II (cat. no. 72) is largely a mirror-image version of the painting, although the woman no longer reaches for the apple and the reddish-orange wall near the left-hand edge of the print is missing, Munch moved closer to the motif in *Jealousy* I (cat. no. 73) and placed the couple closer together. In a version of *Jealousy* I colored with transparent watercolors (cat. no. 74), he accentuated Przybyszewski's pupils, the dots on the woman's open dress, the apples, and the male figure on the right in intense red, thus establishing a connecting thread of color and content. Using thick orange paint, he set the woman's hair in complementary contrast to the blue of the sky. He intervened even more vigorously in a variation of *Jealousy* II (cat. no. 71) by shifting the right-hand edge of the lithograph to the extent that the male figure in the middle ground is intersected by the edge of the print and the view of the horizon line disappears. The man is dressed in a top hat and tailcoat; the woman wears a yellow hat with prominent hatbands tied at her throat and, in contrast to the lithograph, a voluminous, open red dress, the billowed sleeves of which join with the blue contours of the background to conceal the last section of the horizon. Munch cut off the "flower of pain" that appears in front of the section of the wall on the left in the painting but is missing in *Jealousy* I with the strip of meadow and added it, intersected at the lower right-hand corner, with rounded, reddish-orange forms. Przybyszewski's face is rendered paler by the addition of grayish-greenish paint with a strong glazing effect. Munch followed the model of the lithograph in his variation of *Jealousy* I, accentuating certain details. But in *Jealousy* II he altered the composition by fragmenting the print, attacking the image-bearing surface, and destroying the coherent whole of the print. The woman is now positioned between the two men, whose figures are intersected by the edges of the picture. In the absence of a horizon line, her avenue of escape towards the rear is blocked. The artist undertakes a social re-evaluation through his transformation of the clothing,

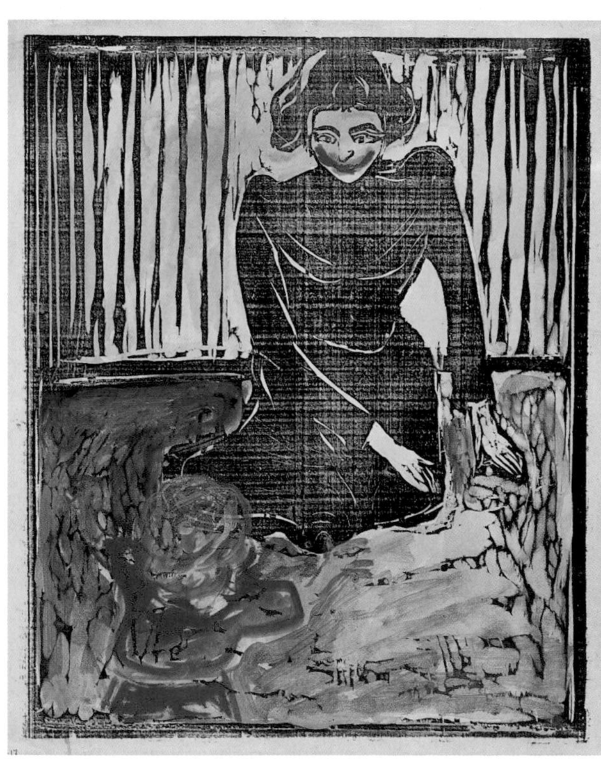

9 Edvard Munch, *Woman Sitting on the Floor*, 1899, hand-colored woodcut on paper, 52 x 42 cm, Munch-museet, Oslo

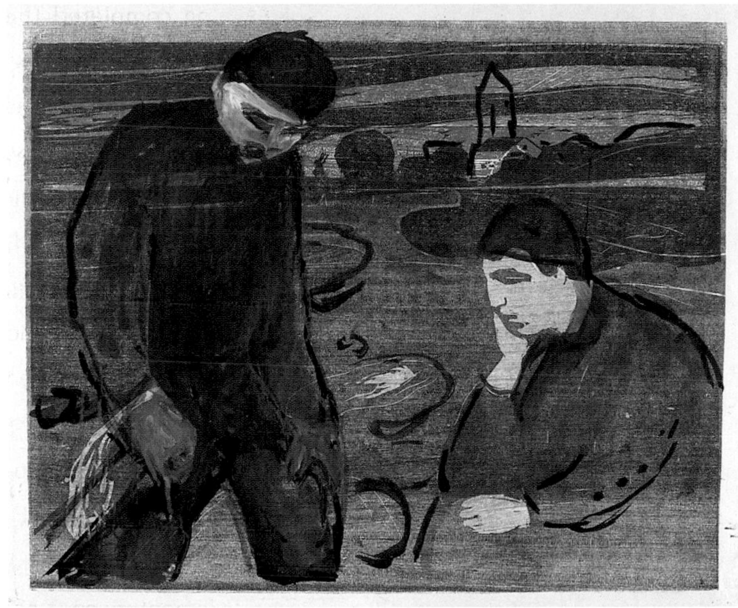

which changes from plain to festive, whereby the now grotesque nakedness of the woman opens the way for an interpretation of the group of figures as a concubine and her patron. The opaque, in some places relief-like paint imbues the couple with a marked painterly quality in contrast to the graphically smooth, delicately washed face of Przybyszewski.

The interplay of graphic and painterly elements is intensified in a variation of the woodcut *Towards the Forest* I of 1897 (cat. no. 57). This version bears the signature "E Munch 97" in the lower right-hand corner and on the grayish cardboard in which the marginless print is encased. The inscription "not for sale" appears on the reverse. The print shows a couple walking towards a forest, their arms around each other. The man is dressed in a suit, while the woman, who is usually described in the literature as nude,[46] wears a transparent dress, the outline of which is most clearly evident along the hem. The total transparency of her dress reveals her nakedness and alternates between exposure and potential concealment at the same time. As in a roentgenogram, the outer covering, which is intended to serve as protection against the male's gaze upon the naked skin beneath it, is transparent. The "birthday suit" establishes a substantive link between this work and the image of male desire in *The Hands* (cat. no. 24–26) and *Inside the Man's Brain* (fig. 5, p. 87). In 1915, Munch reworked the wood blocks, experimenting in multiple variations of *Towards the Forest* II (fig. 1, p. 188, cat. no. 61) with the full spectrum of possibilities ranging from transparency to total concealment from view by printing dresses of varying transparency over the main plate of the first version using a second plate.

Most of the print variations of *Towards the Forest* I (cat. no. 58–60) are characterized by the clear visibility of the horizontal grain pattern. The couple, and especially the man, who is described only by an outline, seems on the verge of disappearing into the structure of the wood, which counteracts the vertical orientation of the trees and the couple itself. The vertical aspect is echoed by the frame-like molding affixed to the left and right edges of the wood block and its vertical grain pattern. Because these strips of molding are both neutral with respect to the subject and related to it as part of the print, they represent, as a pre-existing pictorial structure, a situation in which the observer appears to gaze at the couple. In the heavily revised version of 1897 (cat. no. 57), the strips of molding, each separated by a small gap, retain their dual character. The contrast between the man's suit and the woman's apparent nudity is heightened by the transparency of the dress and the highlighting of the man's legs with opaque paint. The gouache, applied very thickly in some places, serves to restructure the composition. A section of meadow is suggested in green in the lower part of the print. It appears as a transparent film overlay over the trees, which are represented by only a few lines. A red line forms both the edge of a seemingly impenetrable forest, in which the tree-tops are emphasized by broad contour lines and dark interior markings, and the line of a bank, above which a body of water suggested in blue gouache appears, bounded below the midline by a blue horizon line. The fact that Munch also gave *Towards the Forest* I the alternative title *The Lake*[47] confirms that he was experimenting here with the visual notion of a couple at the water's edge, as in the motif of *The Lonely Ones (Two Human Beings)*, a work he first executed as a painting (which has not survived) in 1891–92 and then repeated in a woodcut in 1899 (cat. nos. 98–103). The transparency of the added layers of paint contributes to an overlapping of the forest

10 Edvard Munch, *Melancholy* III, 1902,
hand-colored woodcut on paper, 38.5 x 49.5 cm,
Munch-museet, Oslo

and lake images in the sense of a calculated duality of painting and graphic art. Parts of the woodcut print disappear beneath the impasto paint, and the material quality of the wood characteristic of most of the other variations is lost.

The degree to which underlying elements remain visible varies from nearly total concealment to sketchy additions that set color accents or introduce new motifs. Both of these effects are found in variations of the color lithograph *The Sick Child* of 1896,[48] which features the figure of a girl with shoulder-length hair against a portion of an oversized pillow. The horizontal frame of view corresponds to that of the second version of the painting *The Sick Child* of 1896 (cat. no. 122), although Munch simplified the composition substantially and eliminated the bowing female figure, whose head obscures part of the pillow. According to an account attributed to Paul Herrmann, the printing process did not involve a carefully considered selection of colors: "Munch comes, stands in front of the row, closes his eyes tightly and begins to direct blindly in the air with his finger: 'Print ... gray, green, blue, brown.' ... And the printer printed until Munch returned and blindly issued new commands: 'Yellow, pink, red ...' And so it went several more times ... "[49] The diverse color schemes of the surviving prints[50] and the different papers, some of them colored, on which they are printed serve to confirm this account. The printing process is declared an experimental series and the element of chance is calculated as a part of the process of creating the work and its aesthetic effect. Munch pursued these experiments further in his hand-coloring work (cat. no. 124, 127): "I have continued to work constantly on my graphic pieces and experimented with various prints—I often use prints as a resource for drawing and hand-coloring."[51]

In two versions, Munch added a bowed woman's head with knotted hair—as in the painting—in the lower right-hand corner. The first variation is a print made with three stones in red, yellow, and grayish-blue in which he confronts the delicate lithograph-chalk drawing with the profiled woman's head (cat. no. 129) in gouache applied in broad, partially black brushstrokes. In contrast to the painting, the woman is shown facing the girl, but the two do not communicate visibly, as her head is bowed. Her eye recedes into a large, black socket resembling that of a skull, and the mouth disappears within the broad contour line. Her flesh is rendered in vertical strokes set against the direction of the chalk lines in dark pink. The rough, black brushstrokes of her hollow cheek reinforces the association with a skull. The head is neckless and framed in darkness, apparently separated from the body, so that the woman is not physically fixed in place. In the second variation (cat. no. 130), a print made with five stones in black, two red hues, blue, and yellow, Munch reduced the woman's head to a few black, glazing lines applied over the lithograph in three-quarter profile turned away from the girl. This sketchy application of color describes transience as a state between presence and absence. Although the woman's head is present as a motif, its physical transparency, which exposes the background, suggests that it is about to disappear. The addition of the woman's head initially establishes a closer iconographic link between the lithography and the painted version, although its transparency represents a different form of presence. In this work, Munch combines two visual and temporal levels by laying the woman's head as a kind of memory image like a transparent film over the primary motif of the sick girl. Yet this addition is less a kind of "mourning commentary"[52] than a means of emphasizing transience as a symbolic reference to the passage from life to death,[53] from being to non-being.

Transparency and Dissolution

Munch's stay at the seaside resort of Warnemünde in 1907–08 was a period of intensive experimentation in painting and photography, and it produced marked stylistic changes in his painting, in particular. Henceforth, his paintings would be characterized by vivid coloration and direct application of paint. *The Drowned Boy* of 1908 (cat. no. 160) is a powerful summation of his experiments with color, in which, among other things, he took up the thread of his work with the body of color during the 1880s. His unorthodox approach to the application of paint ranged from the use of highly diluted, watery paint to the direct application of thick paint from the tube to the canvas.

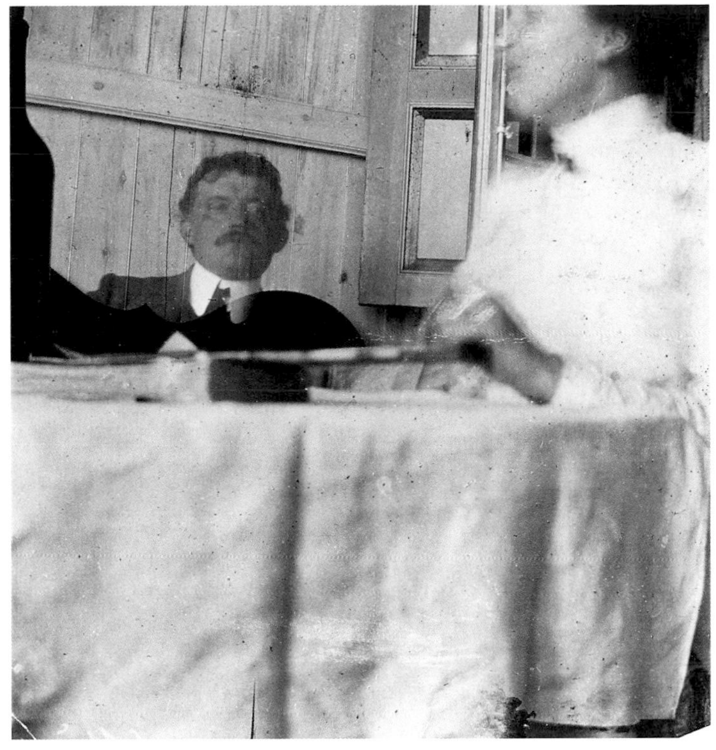

11 Edvard Munch and his housekeeper, Warnemünde, 1907, photo: Edvard Munch, Munch-museet, Oslo

The horizontal-format painting exhibited in Stockholm under the title *Mechanic and Peasant* in 1913[54] is dominated by two male figures viewed from the rear, one dressed in dark, the other in light clothing—mechanic and peasant—in the middle of the scene. In the foreground, Munch added a horse's head facing the viewer on the left and a sketchy figure of what is presumably a dog on the right. The scene to which the title refers takes place in the background in front of a suggested harbor, where a man holds the dead boy in his arms and strides past a group of women. The setting for this complex scene is the beach promenade outside Munch's rented fisherman's house in Warnemünde. It is no coincidence that the transparency of the animals and the dissolution of the light-colored male figure call to mind Munch's experimental "photographs of fate"[55] from the years 1902 to 1908, in which such effects as double-exposure, uncontrolled light, transparency, ghostly blurring resulting from the movements of the models, and outright aggressive close-ups were used. The horse's head is laid like a transparent film, resembling a double-exposure, over the lines of the beach promenade, which vanish towards the horizon.

A comparison of this work with the photographic self-portrait entitled *Munch and his Housekeeper*, which was taken in Warnemünde in 1907 (fig. 11), reveals a similar presence of the background, wooden boards and the back of a bench, which show through his body. His housekeeper is seated on the right. The lack of transparency in her figure indicates that she remained sitting at the same spot during both exposures. In contrast to the sharp focus of his own image, hers shows some motion blurring, which may have occurred when she possibly covered the lens with an object she was holding in her hand during one of the exposures.[56] Munch's free space is reduced to a bare minimum by the tablecloth that covers the entire surface of the image above a point just below the midline, by the wine bottle cut off by the left-hand margin, the fragmented image of the housekeeper and the window shutter on the right, and a wooden beam that ascends at an angle above his head. The figure of the artist escapes this claustrophobic closeness, which is heightened by the long object in the housekeeper's hand, by virtue of his transparency. Yet like a raised index finger, the object points in a warning gesture towards the wine bottle in an unmistakable reference to Munch's severe alcoholism as the cause of his fragile psychological condition. The artist employs the stylistic tool of double-exposure to unite two images—the room with and without his presence—capturing at the same time the interval of time between the two events. He creates an image in a state between absence and presence representing the disappearance or the appearance of the protagonist—Munch himself—in the photograph. Yet his notes from the period, in which he expresses several times his belief that he will soon die, suggest that he was concerned with the phenomenon of disappearance in the sense of a localized material loss. The implied shift of location, transformation, destruction, or death is the result of disappearance from the pictorial format as the viewer's sphere of visual perception.

In his oil painting entitled *The Drowned Boy*, Munch applied the transparency achieved through double-exposure to the representation of the animals in the foreground and the key scene in the background, linking the two events together, much as he did in the photograph. This transparency achieved with the techniques

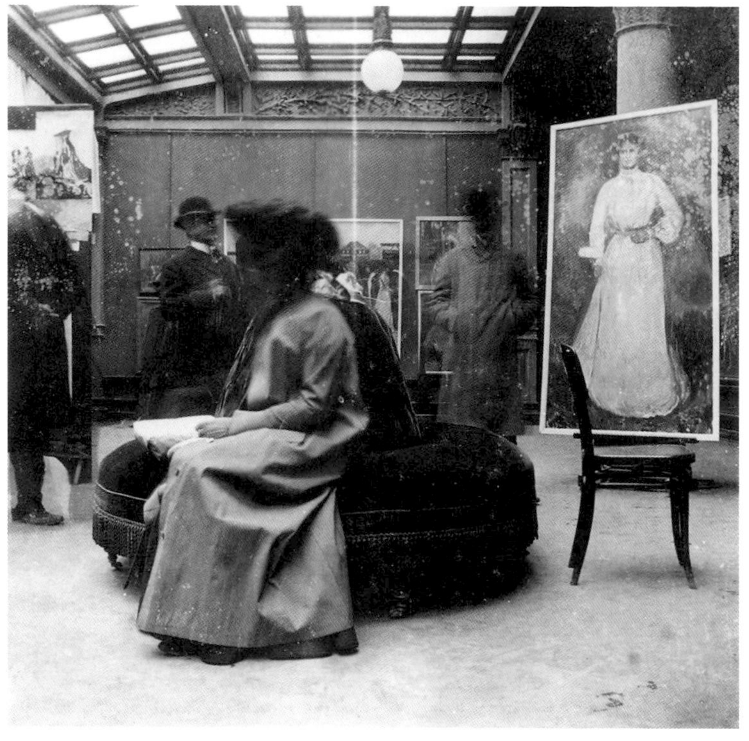

of painting may signify both a trace of the past—a kind of mental image of an event—and physical movement out of the picture, or disappearance. As a record of movement, however, this overlaying of two events calls attention to the interval of time between the beginning and the end of the movement in contrast to the motion blurring evident in the figure in the whitish clothing seen from the rear, which corresponds to the photographic image of motion recorded by a camera during an extended exposure period. The displaced outlines of the right leg suggest both dissolution and the man's forward walking movement. Munch obviously related the representation of the time continuum of a movement to the motion blurring of a photograph and translated it into an organic, whitish-yellowish color surface modeled with white paint applied directly from the tube. This recording of a continuous motion stands in opposition to the transparency of the animals and the background scene as a simultaneously displayed trace of the past.

Through this application of photographic effects, Munch forged a link between two other artistic media, painting and photography. His painting *The Drowned Boy* stands at the point at which these media and the resulting artistic possibilities intersect, which Munch continued to investigate until the end of his life.

In *The Murderer* of 1910 (cat. no. 157) and *The Murderer on the Lane* of 1919 (cat. no. 158), Munch symbolically linked the subject of murder with that of escape in the transparent image of the murderer. In *The Murderer*, the three-quarter figure in dark purple and cobalt-blue strides towards the viewer. His movement is suggested by the forward position of the right leg and the transient quality of the depicted figure. Marked by a broad, red line, the path leading into the depth is bounded on both sides by rock formations reminiscent of Kragerø and at the level of the "murderer's" forehead by the background landscape. The transparent green face of the murderer is elaborated with broad, yellowish-white brushstrokes. Without a mouth or nose, it remains anonymous, like a mask. The advancing figure, the disfigured fingers of the clenched hands, which stand out clearly against the light background, and the purple and reddish color to the figure's right heighten the dramatic tension. Perhaps the deed has already been committed and the murderer is already fleeing the scene, as some authors contend,[57] or is approaching his victim to carry out the inevitable act of murder. It is a question that cannot be answered. In either case, the figure's transparency expresses both physical and psychological movement as a transient state of constant tension between past and future, event and expectation.

In *The Murderer on the Lane* (cat. no. 158), the deed is already done. The murder victim lies as a glazing bluish-purple shadow on the lane, and the sketchily drawn head of the murderer appears on the verge of disappearing from the viewer's sight. As in *The Drowned Boy*, Munch added the scene last to the composition. The landscape drawing entitled *Avenue* (fig. 13) done the same year is an indication that the artist originally planned to do a straight landscape and that he probably added this scene to the canvas once it was completed, as a kind of second exposure of a frame of film. The dematerialized character of the transient image corresponds to a recollection of the event even in the act of fleeing the scene of the crime and can, if one considers the aspect of the avenue as a

12 Edvard Munch exhibition at Blomqvist
in Kristiania, 1902,
photo: Edvard Munch, Munch-museet, Oslo

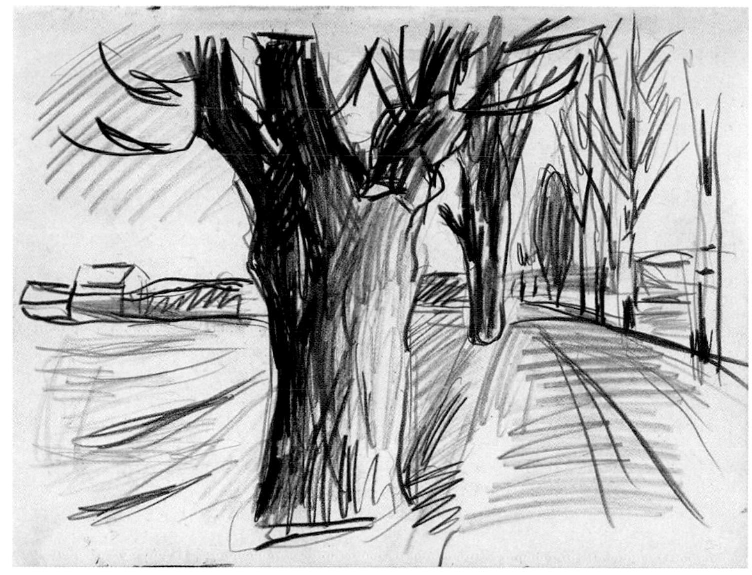

symbol of death,[58] be interpreted as an expression of growth and decline, of life and death.

More than twenty years later, Munch summarized his experiments with transparency and dissolution as symbols of death in the gouache entitled *Self-Portrait at Quarter past Two in the Morning* (cat. no. 203). Munch is shown seated and about to stand up from a chair—the very same chair in which his sister Sophie died nearly seven decades before. His emaciated, bald head resembles a skull, and his suit hangs loosely on his haggard frame, which is painted in transparent color on a prepared background. A blanket draped over his thighs, vaguely suggested in broad brushstrokes, is slipping to the floor. Rendered in spaced, primarily vertical brushstrokes, the room in the background appears, like Munch's own body, to be in a process of dissolution, a dominant impression to which the irregular pattern of glazing and opaque areas of paint applied directly from the tube contributes substantially. The brushwork, which appears quite spontaneous in places, calls to mind Strindberg's appeal for a creative process liberated from the artist's consciousness, "in which the hand moves at random with the palette knife [or with brush and tube, in Munch's case]."[59] Even the shadow splits away from the body and develops a life of its own as a dark, translucent spot. The transparency of the body is reminiscent of Munch's experiments with double-exposure in the photographs he categorized as *Photographs of Fate* 1902–08.[60] In the sequence of images in the process of dissolution, transparency is used to describe the simultaneity of absence and presence as an expression of his intimation of impending death. Over his face, which is reduced to a few light brushstrokes, Munch applied vigorous yellowish-green strokes that extend to the back of the chair. Thus by obliterating his image with brushstrokes, presumably shortly before his death, Munch clearly announced the end of his lifelong struggle to come to grips with the phenomenon of disappearance, a struggle he had pursued intensely since he began damaging the painted surface of his face in his *Self-portrait* of 1886. The elimination of the subject is iconographic; its disappearance beneath a transparent layer of color is in keeping with the thoughts about death he articulated even before reaching the age of thirty: "And it is very strange, to disappear entirely—that you must—that the hour must come when you can say to yourself—now you have ten minutes more, five minutes more, and then it will happen—and then you will feel yourself gradually being transformed into nothing."[61]

13 Edvard Munch, *Avenue*, 1919, chalk drawing on paper, 21.3 x 27.9 cm, Munch-museet, Oslo

1 Andreas Aubert, in *Morgenbladet*, Nov. 9, 1886, n. p.

2 N. N., "Kunst und Wissenschaft. Edvard Munch," in *Deutscher Reichs-Anzeiger und Königlich Preußischer Staats-Anzeiger*, no. 269, Nov. 12, 1982, n. p.

3 Although the self-portrait is signed but not dated, the dating of its origin to 1886 has not been questioned since 1927 and is regarded as certain by Müller-Westermann. Cf. Iris Müller-Westermann, *Edvard Munch. Die Selbstbildnisse*, Ph. D. dissertation, Oslo 1997, p. 26, note 24.

4 Iris Müller-Westermann describes "skin as a mirror of self-discovery" and interprets injured facial and paint skin as a "metaphor for the traces left behind by life." *Ibid*., pp. 13ff and 22.

5 Letter from R. Bergh to Munch dated "Gottland, Visby, June 15, 93," archives, Munch-museet. Quoted and translated from Jan Thurmann-Moe, *Edvard Munchs "Hestekur." Eksperimenter med teknikk og materialer*, exh. cat., Munch-museet Oslo, Oslo 1995, p. 30.

6 Cf. Göran Söderström, *Strindberg och bildkonsten*, Uddevalla 1972.

7 August Strindberg, *Die Entwicklung einer Seele*, Munich 1919, p. 5.

8 Thurmann-Moe 1995 (see note. 5), p. 25.

9 The English translation is based on a literal translation of the Swedish original by the author: August Strindberg, "Inferno," in *August Strindbergs Samlade Verk. Inferno*, vol. 37, Stockholm 1994 [original edition Stockholm 1897], p. 117.

10 The Swedish word "töcken" can also be translated as "fog" or "mist."

11 The Norwegian term "Hestekur," horse treatment, translated here as "kill-or-cure treatment," is attributed to Munch himself, but is not found in any of his surviving notes. Munch's neighbor in Ekely, the draftsman, graphic artist, and painter Chrix Dahl wrote: "And so I listened with a certain feeling of trepidation as Munch praised the benefits of this kill-or-cure treatment, which seemed more like an effective method of destroying the paintings." Chrix Dahl, "Mesteren på Ekely," in *Edvard Munch. Mennesket og kunstneren, Kunst og Kultur*, Oslo 1946, pp. 145–156. According to Munch's friend and biographer, the banker and writer Rolf Stenersen, the artist coined the term "horse treatment" himself. Rolf E. Stenersen, *Edvard Munch—Close-Up of a Genius*, Oslo 1994 [original edition: Stockholm 1944], p. 79.

12 The painter Hermann Schlittgen describes Munch's chaotic living and working environment as witnessed during a visit in Berlin during the 1890s. Hermann Schlittgen, *Erinnerungen*, Hamburg 1947, p. 175.

13 Grünewald, quoted and translated from Josef Paul Hodin, *Edvard Munch*, Stockholm 1948, p. 96.

14 Munch, quoted and translated from Stenersen 1994 (see note 11), p. 84.

15 Munch/Gierløff, quoted and translated from Ragna Stang, *Edvard Munch. Der Mensch und der Künstler*, Königsstein 1979, p. 230.

16 The undated letter of response to Schiefler's letter of February 9, 1913 was presumably written several days or weeks later. Edvard Munch and Gustav Schiefler, *Briefwechsel* 1902–1914, vol. 1, Hamburg 1987, p. 453, No. 600.

17 Literally translated by the author from *Edvard Munch, Livsfrisens tilblivelse*, Oslo n.d. [1928?], p. 1 (retranslated into English).

18 Having worked since 1950 as a student on the conservation project devoted to Munch's artistic estate, consisting of more than 1,100 paintings, which had been acquired by the city of Oslo following the artist's death, Jan Thurmann-Moe was placed in charge of restoration work in 1954 and, as Director of the Restoration Department at the Munch-museet until 1996, guided the course of restoration work on Munch's surviving oeuvre, some of which was in very poor condition.

19 Jan Thurmann-Moe, "Roßkur und Firnis bei Edvard Munch," in Heinz Althöfer, *Das 19. Jahrhundert und die Restaurierung*, Munich 1987, p. 112.

20 The essay was first published in French under the title "Du hasard dans la production artistique" in *Revue des Revues*, Nov. 1894. Quoted from Thomas Fechner-Smarsly (ed.), *August Strindberg: Verwirrte Sinneseindrücke. Schriften zu Malerei, Fotografie und Naturwissenschaften*, Dresden 1998, p. 38.

21 Translated from Poul Erik Tøjner, *Munch med egne ord*, Oslo and Copenhagen 2000, p. 131, N 57.

22 Fechner-Smarsly (ed.) 1998 (see note 20), pp. 34 and 31.

23 *Ibid*., pp. 31 and 34.

24 *Ibid*., p. 34.

25 Strindberg, "Inferno" (see note 9), p. 71.

26 These include, among others, *Death and the Maiden*, 1893 (cat. no. 44), *Separation*, 1893, oil on sized canvas (MM M 884), *Sitting Nude and Grotesque Mask*, 1893, casein tempera/oil on sized canvas (MM M 91), *Two Women in a Seaside Landscape*, 1893, casein tempera/oil on sized canvas (MM M 732), *Old and Young Woman in the Landscape*, 1895, casein tempera/oil on canvas sized by the artist (MM M 860), and *Brothel with Hats*, 1894–97, casein tempera on unsized canvas (MM M 149).

27 As a close friend of Munch's who, as far as is known today, made no official statement, Jappe Nilssen commented the term "Hærverk," as meaning "destruction" or, translated as a legal term, "destruction of property," with respect to the varnishing of the paintings. Jappe Nilssen, "Hærverk," in *Dagens Nytt*, June 14, 1909, n. p. Christian Krohg attempted to calm the debate he had triggered, yet noted that painters "must now fear that their pictures will suddenly have their turn as well and be stripped of the beautiful patina they have spent so much time acquiring over the years." Christian Krohg, "Fernis," in *Dagens Nytt*, June 17, 1909, n. p.
Three years later, Munch wrote to Nilssen on the occasion of his participating in the exhibition of the Kölner Sonderbund: "There is hardly a varnished painting here—Never has a warning appeared with such perfect timing as your article about the varnishing of my paintings—People here regard it as vandalism." Munch/Nilssen, spring 1912, in Hermann Uhde-Bernays, *Künstlerbriefe über Kunst. Bekenntnisse von Malern, Architekten und Bildhauern aus fünf Jahrhunderten. Von Alberti bis Kandinsky*, Dresden 1956 [first printing 1926], p. 933.

28 Gerd Woll groups these variations under "state II," although prints MM G 570–4,–15,–16 were printed with oil paint. Gerd Woll, *Edvard Munch. The Complete Graphic Works*, London 2001, p. 115.

29 Due to the blurred color margins, it is no longer possible to determine whether the wood block used in these versions had already been cut apart. Woll 2001 (see note 28), p. 115. Like Woll, Akira Kurosaki regards these variations as trial prints but assumes that the process was a test preparatory to Munch's subsequent division of the wood block into three color sections. Akira Kurosaki, "Moonshine: A Study of the Paper Used for Edvard Munch's Color Woodcut," in *Journal of Kyoto Seika University*, 4, Jan. 20, 1993, p. 125 and Table 4.

30 In these variations with thick applications of paint, Munch used paper similar to packing or commercial paper. Cf. Kurosaki 1993 (see note 29), p. 121. Thus the most frequently cited cost argument is open to question.

31 This version is inscribed by the artist: "E Munch/ Mondschein mit Hand gedruckt."

32 Gerd Woll, "Grafikeren," in *Munch og Frankrike*, exh. cat., Musée d'Orsay Paris, Munch-museet, Oslo, Paris 1991, p. 264.

33 Woll writes, "The wood blocks remaining after his death include almost every possible type of wood such as thick, heavy pieces made from several boards in spruce or pine, thin plywood, blocks in various types of hardwood, and in later years a number of mahogany panels from Le Franc, primed with a grayish paint." Woll 2001 (see note 28), p. 13.

34 Kurosaki regards this print as a trial print for the front face of the printing block. Cf. Kurosaki 1993 (see note 29), p. 123. Woll classifies the print as unfinished, along with the eight of the thirty-four other prints in the collection of the Munch-museet. Woll 2001 (see note 28), p. 113. However, the fact that Munch saved a significant number of "unfinished" prints which he did not process further suggests that he regarded them as finished. Such an argument also derives support from the fact that fragmentation played an important role in many of his works and that Munch prints all four of the other woodcuts of 1896 in a single color, primarily black.

35 Woll 1991 (see note 32), p. 273; Richard S. Field, in Jacquelynn Baas and Richard S. Field, *The Artistic Revival of the Woodcut in France 1850–1900*, exh. cat., The University of Michigan Museum of Art, Yale University Art Gallery, The Baltimore Museum of Art, Ann Arbor 1984, p. 128f.

36 Woll and Field cite *Undine* (1896), Woll 1991 (see note 32); Baas and Field 1984 (see note 35). The woodcut published in *Pan* in 1897 is one of at least three other prints in which Herrmann, who worked under the pseudonym Henri Héran, printed the wood color blocks over a lithograph and which he first published in 1896 in the French journal *Le Centaure*, which was not widely circulated. It is not unlikely that Munch was familiar with Herrmann's prints, since the two spent time together in Paris in 1896, as evidenced, among other things, by Herrmann's eyewitness account of the printing of the lithograph *The Sick Child* I at the Clot printing shop. However, the wood grain played a subordinate role in these prints and is only vaguely discernable. Unlike Munch, Herrmann was interested in achieving an organic structure, which he laid like a curtain over the motif, through the use of bridges joining worked areas.

37 Fechner-Smarsly (ed.) 1998 (see note 20), p. 283.

38 August Strindberg, *The Sunflower* (*Helianthus annuus*), first published in the occult journal *L'Initiation* in 1896. Quoted and translated from Fechner-Smarsly (ed.) 1998 (see note 20), p. 108.

39 Arne Eggum, *Munch og fotografi*, Oslo 1987, p. 63.

40 Strindberg wrote his scholarly essay "Über die Lichtwirkung bei der Fotografie. Betrachtungen aus Anlass der X-Strahlen" [On the effect of light in photography. Reflections in connection with X-rays] about this time. The essay was first published in 1897 in volume 4 of *Tryckt och utryckt*.

41 Eggum 1987 (see note 39), p. 63.

42 According to Woll, the wood grain is prominently visible in several of the brown to reddish-brown prints. Woll 2001 (see note 28), p. 435.

43 *Ibid.*, p. 115.

44 Gerd Woll, "Prints from 1896," in *Edvard Munch. Grafikk fra 1896/Prints from 1896*, exh. cat., Munch-museet, Oslo 1996, p. 22.

45 Although Woll contends that Munch transferred a few of these variations to color prints, he does not cite examples. *Ibid.*, p. 12.

46 Schiefler called attention to the woman's nudity as early as 1907. Gustav Schiefler, *Verzeichnis des graphischen Werks Edvard Munchs bis 1906*, Berlin 1907, p. 86. Eggum's argumentation regarding the "relation of opposition" between the genders is also based upon the tension between the clothed man and the "naked" woman. Arne Eggum, "Zum Walde," in Ulrich Weisner (ed.), *Munch. Liebe. Angst. Tod*, exh. cat., Kunsthalle Bielefeld, Bielefeld 1980, p. 151. Eggum later revised this assessment, cf. Arne Eggum, *Edvard Munch. The Frieze of Life from Painting to Graphic Art*, Oslo 2000, p. 147.

47 Woll 2001 (see note 28), p. 129.

48 Woll distinguishes in this context between two versions, of which *The Sick Child* II is presumably a reworked version of the color stone used for the first version. *Ibid.*, pp. 98ff, No. 72 and 73.

49 Quoted and translated from Erich Büttner, "Der leibhaftige Munch," in Jens Thiis, *Edvard Munch*, Berlin 1934, p. 92.

50 Although Woll 1991 cites "nearly one hundred" prints, she lists only a total of forty-eight prints in the catalog of graphic works. Woll 1991 (see note 32), p. 267; Woll 2001 (see note 28), pp. 99f.

51 Munch-museet, MM T 2705. Quoted and translated from Woll 2001 (see note 28), p. 24.

52 Uwe M. Schneede, *Im Blickfeld: Edvard Munch. Das Kranke Kind*, exhib. cat., Hamburger Kunsthalle, Hamburg 2002, p. 30.

53 Cf. Søren Kierkegaard, *Die Krankheit zum Tode*, Stuttgart 1997 [first edition 1849].

54 Eggum 1987 (see note 39), p. 134.

55 Munch presumably referred to his experimental photographs from this period as "Skjæbnefotografier," which can be translated from Old Norwegian as "photographs of fate." Munch-museet T 2731.

56 Arne Eggum explains in detail which of the photographs are preserved in the archives of the Munch-museet and attempts to determine to the extent possible what types of camera Munch used. He argues that the camera used for these photographs could open its shutter but that the exposure had to be interrupted manually by covering the lens. Eggum 1987 (see note 39), p. 97.

57 Cf. Arne Eggum, "James Ensor and Edvard Munch. Mask and Reality," in *James Ensor. Edvard Munch, Emil Nolde*, exh. cat., Norman Mackenzie Art Gallery, University of Regina, Saskatchewan (Canada) 1980, p. 29; Matthias Arnold, *Edvard Munch*, Reinbek 1986, p. 123; Simon Maurer, "Der Mörder, 1910," in Guido Magnaguagno (ed.), *Edvard Munch*, exh. cat., Museum Folkwang Essen, Kunsthaus Zürich, Bern 1987, cat. no. 86.

58 Munch himself made use of this symbol in the drawing *Death Raking Leaves*, 1891–92, Munch-museet MM T 290.

59 Fechner-Smarsly (ed.) 1998 (see note 20), p. 31.

60 In manuscript MM T 2731. Eggum 1987 (see note 39), p. 123.

61 Manuscript, Munch-museet T 2761, c. 1889, p. 21.

Paper in Prints by Edvard Munch

Gerd Woll

Paper is a very important part of a drawing or graphic work—not merely as the underlying material for the image, but also as an important aesthetic factor. Large parts of the picture often remain untreated so that the paper plays an independent role. Most evident, of course, is the tone or color of the paper, but the surface too is important for the way in which ink is absorbed or light reflected. Similarly, the size of the sheet, the margins and the paper's edges can be important for the overall appearance of an artwork on paper and how it is experienced.

These, however, are qualities that are seldom experienced by the public, as artworks on paper almost without exception are covered by glass or placed in glass showcases when exhibited. In addition, the sheet is frequently mounted in a passe-partout so that margins and paper edges are hidden. When it comes to older works, the sheet often has been cut to fit into a passe-partout, a frame or an album. This makes knowledge of paper into pure *Feinschmeckerei*—an exciting exercise for the connoisseur—but the importance of paper for the artwork in a larger context is thereby easily overlooked or underestimated.

Munch's graphic works, and his use of paper in this connection, stretches over a period of fifty years, from 1894 to 1944, and comprises most types of standard paper available during this period. Everything leads us to believe that Munch was aware of the characteristics and qualities of the various paper types, and that he made his considered choices, although as far as we know he never searched for the quite special paper. Rather, it was as if he knew how to utilize the possibilities in the types of paper usually obtainable. The governing terms in his first years as a graphic artist were primarily decided by the price, later mostly by availability. In most cases, availability meant the types of paper the printers had in stock—we have no instances to support Munch's ever having procured paper on his own before he installed his own presses in Norway after 1911.

In all, Munch created more than 750 subjects as prints; these are divided into the three most usual methods: intaglio, lithography and woodcut. Totally he can have printed close to 30,000 impressions. From the very beginning it was his policy to retain the plates and lithographic stones for his prints, in order to make new prints from them as needed. In other words, he did not follow the more recent custom of destroying the plates after printing a fixed number. As a rule, Munch printed rather few impressions at a time, and it is therefore only exceptionally that one can speak of editions in connection with Munch's graphic art.

This led to the printing of his most popular themes at various times and by different printers. In some cases, there can be an interval of twenty years between the first and the last impression from the same plate or lithographic stone. We have examples where the same lithograph has been printed in Paris, Berlin and Oslo.[1] Sometimes Munch worked on the plates before such new impressions were made, but by no means always. This was done because of wear or damage to the plates and stones that he wished to repair, or because he wanted to try out other possibilities. In any case, it was unavoidable that usually there is a clear difference in the quality of the earliest and latest impressions.

Although Munch printed many trial proofs and the more experimental prints on his own, he usually entrusted this work to professional printers. He used the best printers in Berlin, Paris, Copenhagen and Oslo, and the printers had their definite opinions and ideas about how the printing was to be carried out in order to achieve the best results. It is probable that Munch learned most of what he needed to know about prints in the printing offices, either in collaboration with the printers, or by studying the work of other artists whom he met there. In any case, we have no information about his learning the secrets of intaglio printing or lithography anywhere else. When it comes to woodcuts, he appears to be largely self-taught, and it was not always easy to get professional printers to tackle his woodblocks. Usually, the woodblocks he used for his colored woodcuts were cut up into many pieces, colored individually, then put together again like a jigsaw puzzle before being printed.

The choice of paper and printing ink was an important part of the printers' profession, and usually they had their specialties and preferences. This does not mean that artists did not have their opinions about this, but normally choice of paper and ink was made in the printing houses. A systematic examination of the types of paper used in Munch's graphic works will probably help to throw light on the various impressions as to when they were printed and the print shop responsible for the printing.

Unfortunately, we know little about the cooperation between Munch and the printers, and today there are few sources able to supply information about the special characteristics of the individual print shops. Only sporadically do we have extant correspondence that allows short glimpses into facets of this important process unfortunately underestimated by the history of art. Our most important source is and will remain the prints themselves, but it is a laborious and time-consuming task to examine such large numbers of prints as is the case here. To this are added the difficulties in describing or documenting paper types, an absolute necessity when it is not possible to make a direct comparison. Although the greater part, 17,000 impressions, are to be found in the Munch-museet in Oslo, a great many of Munch's earliest prints were sold. Today Munch's graphic art is spread over large parts of the world and is found in great numbers in museums and private collections.[2]

Unfortunately, graphic works by other artists from the same period are not described in such a way that, from information given in catalogs or museum registrations, one can agree to whether the types of paper used are the same as those, for example, one finds in Munch's prints. At exhibitions, it is seldom possible to identify the paper in a graphic work by examining it oneself. In order to establish anything about the paper, not only must one have access to the impression when not under glass, one should also have the opportunity to hold it up against the light or place it on a light box, and preferably also feel it with the fingers. There are extremely few museums that allow outsiders to make this type of examination—and in any case it is very time-consuming work that, unquestionably, is done by the professional staff of the museum concerned. However, it is important that standards be developed for description and documentation so that information can be exchanged.[3]

Munch made his first intaglio prints in the late fall of 1894. Apparently, he began rather carefully with drypoint, but he must have learned the etching technique very quickly—both line etching and the possibilities that lie in etching the plane. We have extremely few examples to show that Munch used traditional aquatint, but he used open bite extensively. He worked industriously with intaglio prints as the winter of 1895 progressed and he must have thrown himself into lithography at an early stage. Munch was living in Berlin at the time and had his intaglio prints printed at well-known printers such as Sabo or Angerer, while Liebmann or Lassally printed the lithographs.

Our most important source of information concerning the printers Munch used in this early period is Gustav Schiefler who published the first volume of his catalog of Edvard Munch's graphic work in 1907.[4] Schiefler was in close direct contact with Munch and discussed with him many problems concerning cataloging. When it comes to the early intaglio prints Schiefler, in many cases, gives both Sabo and Angerer as the printers, without indicating differences that can tie them to one or the other. Notwithstanding, Schiefler describes early prints from both Sabo and Angerer as carried out in black on white paper. This stands in contrast to later prints carried out by Felsing which were usually printed in brownish black ink on yellowish paper.

Intaglio prints require paper that is soft and strong enough to withstand being pressed down into the incisions in the metal plates and receptive enough so the ink in the incisions fastens to the paper. Usually, Munch's intaglio prints are printed on rather heavy paper and among both early and late impressions we find many on markedly white paper. A number of these come, in all likelihood, from Sabo or Angerer, but some of the early impressions can be traced to Norges Geografiske Oppmåling (NGO) (the Geographical Survey of Norway). There, Munch had a contact in the map-printing department, so that he was able to print trial proofs when home in Norway. In those days, many maps were still made as engravings and the paper for these was chosen with great care for clearness and precision of detail and lines. We have some impressions showing that Munch has printed his intaglio prints on the back of maps of various districts in Norway or sea areas along the coast. The printing ink used on the white paper is pure black—sometimes thinned to a grayish tone. These prints from the NGO are, in fact, not so very different from the early prints identified with Sabo or Angerer.

In these impressions, there was maximum contrast between the black line and the white surface, and in most cases, this functioned well. However, in many of Munch's more evocative subjects—for example, *The Voice* (*Summer Night*) (cat. no. 2), *Tête-à-tête* (Sch. 12, Woll 9) or *The Lonely Ones* (*Two Human Beings*) (fig. 1, p. 223) it was perhaps desirable with a more toned down quality. The use of open bite and drypoint, as in *The Voice* (*Summer Night*) (cat. no. 2), made it possible to deepen the tone in the entire picture, but the use of paper with a somewhat deeper tone could have the same effect.

In June 1895, Meier-Graefe published a portfolio with eight of Munch's intaglio prints.[5] Angerer printed them for the ordinary edition on English intaglio printing paper, a relatively heavy paper with a matte surface and a somewhat gray tone. At the same time, however, ten impressions of each motif were printed on thick Japan paper for a special de luxe edition. These, moreover, were printed from copperplates that were not steel-faced and they were numbered and signed by the artist. The ordinary edition, on the other hand, was printed on steel-faced plates and was unsigned.

Handmade Japan paper was expensive and certainly not something Munch could afford in his first years as a graphic artist when he had to carry the printing costs himself. It is possible that economic reasons were a contributory factor in Munch's beginning with graphics in the first place. At the end of 1894, he had reached the age of 31 and had already carried out many of his most important themes as paintings. After the so-called scandal exhibition in Berlin in 1892, his name became known outside Scandinavia as well, but he sold next to nothing. For many years, his most important source of income came from exhibition entrance fees. In such a situation, it was perhaps not so strange that he also wished to try his hand at print versions of special subjects, in the hope that these would be easier to sell than the paintings. At the same time, it was important for him to spread his artistic message to as many as possible, and for that purpose prints were more advantageous than paintings. Economically however, the result was disheartening—even though he sold some prints, this was not sufficient to cover the extra expenses involved in equipment and printing. The so-called Meier-Graefe portfolio, for which the publisher had such high regards, proved difficult to sell.

Another more elaborate paper used by Munch in many early intaglio prints—most probably both in those printed in Berlin and in Paris—was a deckle-edge paper in a gray-brownish shade from Arches. The sheets have a watermark making them easy to identify (fig. 1). This paper has some of the qualities otherwise found in handmade paper, and a faint texture corresponding to chain lines and laid-lines has been introduced. The sheets have deckle edges similar to handmade paper. This paper type—"mouldmade paper"—is also produced by machine, but in a way that is closer to the traditional craftsman-like product than paper made in the faster paper machines.

The choice of paper can have a further function, in addition to the aesthetic and technical—it can have a social function. When the first ten impressions of the Meier-Graefe portfolio were printed on expensive Japan paper from plates that were not steel-faced, then numbered and signed by the artist, while the ordinary edition is neither signed nor printed on special paper—the object is not chiefly aesthetic. There is, indeed, a certain difference in quality in this case, but in fact, it is rather marginal. However, the result of doing this was a product to be aimed at various collectors—the exclusive to those who could afford it, and a more reasonable version to those who were most interested in the subject matter itself and the artistic message.

Such devices were quite usual at the time, and for an artist wishing to work his way into a market already overfilled with protagonists, it was wise to tread lightly. Meier-Graefe composed a lengthy introduction to Munch's art that was issued with the

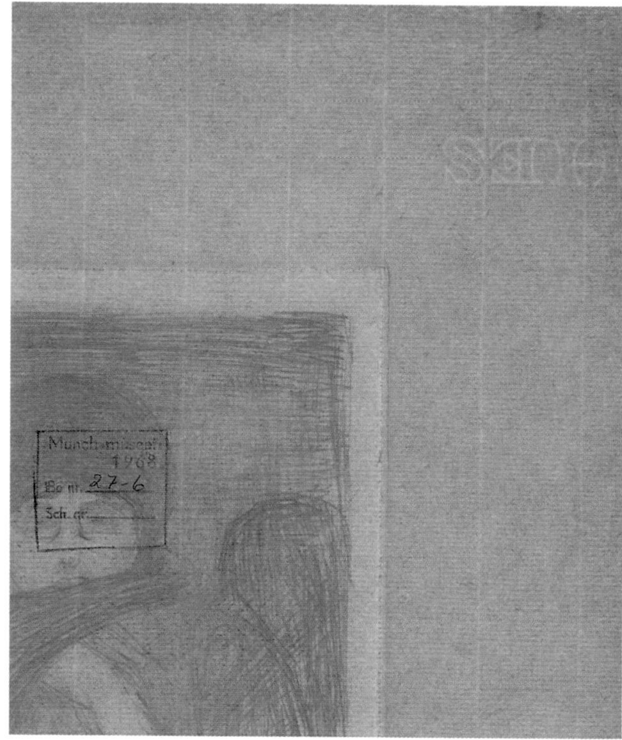

prints. Clearly, he was quite aware that Munch's subject matter in itself was controversial enough, and wished therefore to launch the print versions as less offensive, for a decidedly conservative Berlin public, than his paintings that only a few years before had led to scandal and the closing of his first solo exhibition there. Therefore, it was perhaps not so strange that he wanted the most conventional form possible for the intaglio prints he put out. Possibly, it was also he who, for the same reason, chose a grayish ink on light grayish-brown paper—instead of a more pronounced black-and-white contrast that otherwise was the most usual in the early intaglio prints as they were printed by Angerer and others.

Arches paper that we find in many of the early impressions—perhaps particularly in the ones he sold—has the same effect. With its laid lines and deckled edges, the paper has an air of old-fashioned handmade paper. Although these impressions were not particularly emphasized in comparison to other impressions of the same print, they lend the prints a certain conventional exclusiveness. We find Arches paper in prints that in all probability have been carried out in Berlin—by Angerer or Sabo—just as we do in prints originating in Paris. This French paper was well established and in use all over Europe.

Most of the early lithographs from Liebmann are printed on heavy paper with quite a smooth surface giving a precise representation of all details in the drawing. In most cases, he has used white paper, but there are also some dramatic examples of strongly colored paper. The other printer in Berlin used by Munch for his early lithographs was Lassally. There, Munch became acquainted with the grayish-white China paper used in so many of his lithographs and woodcuts. Whether it was due to economic or aesthetic reasons remains unsaid, but typical for the editions on China paper is that the sheet is cut in such a way that it is barely larger than the image itself. In prints such as *Madonna* (cat. nos. 22, 23), *Vampire* (cat. nos. 68–70,), *Self-Portrait* (with Skeleton Arm) (cat. no. 200) and some others, the margins are so narrow that Munch has had to sign the prints on the picture surface itself. In many cases, Munch has aided the modest size by mounting the prints on large sheets of heavy paper or cardboard in a darker grayish or gray-brown tone. Probably, he did this already in 1895 with the prints from Berlin, but it was in the course of the succeeding years that he developed this into quite a specialty.

China paper with its even gray-white surface was highly recommended for the printing of lithographs. Printers all over the western world used it. The production method was known in large parts of Asia and is recognizable by the way the pulp was spread out on a smooth wall or something similar. On the verso of the sheet, one can usually see the marks of the brushes used for this purpose. On the face of the paper, the surface is even and smooth as silk, and with its distinctive tone, because of the special fibers used in production, this was a beautiful paper suited to many uses. Thus, it is not surprising that Munch used it for many of his lithographs and woodcuts.

Another typical material from the early days in Berlin is a grayish cardboard, which in most cases has now become a clear green color. We find, for example, *Vampire*, *Madonna* and *Self-Portrait* on this paper. Munch, however, was not satisfied with only gray or blue-gray paper, he could also make a splash with far stronger col-

1 Edvard Munch, verso of *Woman with a Shawl*, 1895, intaglio print on Arches paper, 44.5 x 30.8 cm, Munch-museet, Oslo. Photographed on a screen to make the paper structure and the watermark visible.

ors. Some impressions of *The Scream* are printed on a bright purple paper, while *The Hands* (fig. 3) is found on bright red. In these cases, the paper color collaborates directly with the black printing ink and contributes appreciably to the strong effect in these impressions.

A problem with such colored paper, however, is that the color is seldom light-resistant. When exposed to light, the paper will fade easily and lose its original intensity, which of course influences the entire expression. This also applies in cases where the effect is less dramatic, for example in the many impressions in which the original grayish or blue-gray tone in the paper has turned to a far warmer green tone. However, we have become so accustomed to seeing these impressions on "green" paper that we have come to consider them as quite correct. On the rare occasion when one finds an impression in which the original paper color is preserved, one is struck by the fresher and clearer effect of such a print.

There are, however, other ways of bringing color into a graphic work than printing it on colored paper. In Paris, where he lived in 1896–97, Munch also learned several ways of making color prints: intaglio prints, lithographs and finally woodcuts which he first began to create during the time he spent there. Multi-colored prints, in which the sheet of paper is pulled through the press several times, made special demands on the paper used. Not least was the capability to absorb several layers of color. In Paris Munch made a series of exceedingly delicate colored intaglio prints, carried out as scraped aquatint on pre-prepared zinc plates. The colors were laid on the plate *à la poupée*, in such a way that the already inked plate was run only once through the press.

Most of these prints were carried out on Arches paper and probably printed by Porcabœuf.

For colored lithographs, on the other hand, one stone for each color was normally needed. These were printed one after the other as the underlying color dried. Munch had a number of his color lithographs printed by the well-known lithographer August Clot—one of the leading printers of color lithographs.

The most thoroughly carried out color lithograph is *The Sick Child* (cat. nos. 123–130), but Munch also made some others in several colors. He used China paper in many of these prints, as he also had done with a number of lithographs printed in Berlin in previous years. Munch's lithographs continued to be printed on sheets of paper only barely larger than the image itself, and in many cases mounted on large sheets of heavy, grayish or gray-brown cardboard. This method, in a way, is related to *chine collé*, in which a

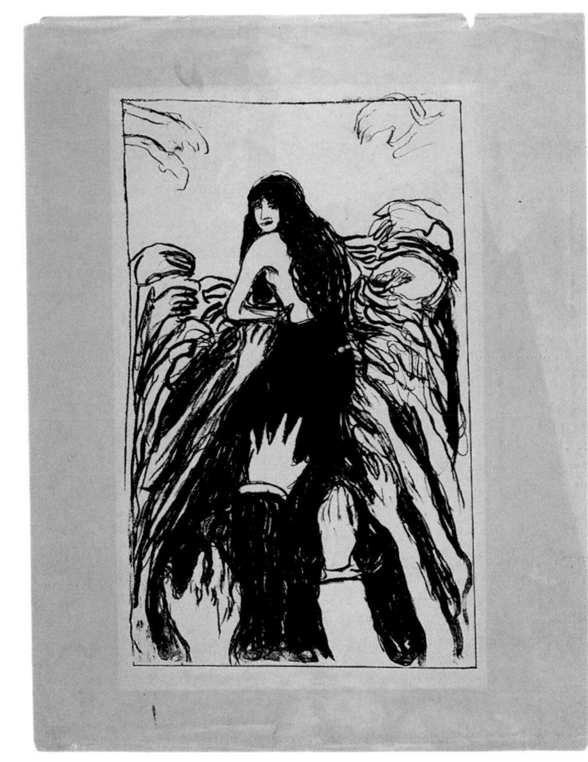

3 Edvard Munch, *The Hands*, 1895,
lithograph on bright red paper, 62 x 46.7 cm,
Munch-museet, Oslo

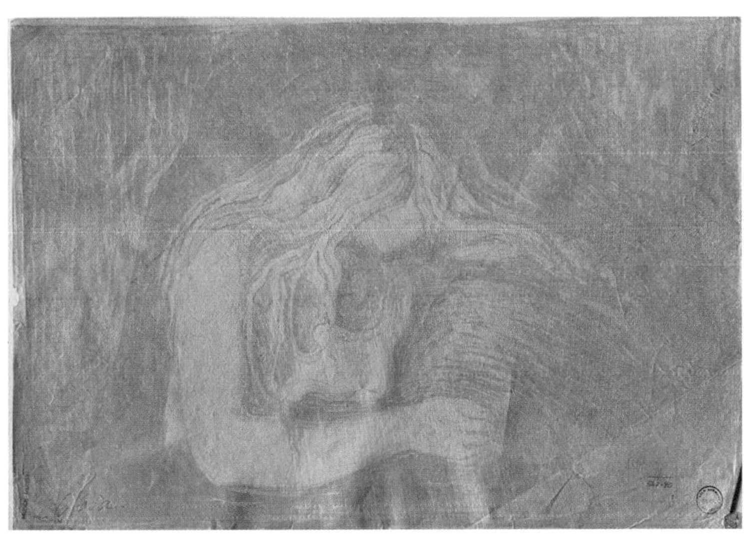

2 Edvard Munch, verso of *Vampire*, 1895,
lithograph on China paper, 38.9 x 55.6 cm,
Munch-museet, Oslo. Photographed with a sidelight
to make the brushstrokes in the paper visible.

sheet of very thin paper, usually China paper of the thinnest sort, is laid on top of a heavier sheet of paper. When these are run through the press, the thin paper is firmly glued to the heavier sheet. Munch has used *chine collé* in both intaglio prints and lithographs.

In mounting the thin grayish-white China paper on cardboard in a darker color, however, he achieved more than merely making the sheet larger and stronger. He also introduced a new color in interplay with the white paper and printing ink. This effect is unusually successful in well-known prints such as *The Scream*, in several impressions of the woodcut *The Kiss* (cat. nos. 51, 52) and in a magnificent hand-colored woodcut of *Angst* (fig. 4).

Munch, however, has also printed lithographs and woodcuts straight onto large sheets of grayish cardboard. In one specific case, he did this because he thought that these prints could be used as the cover for a portfolio of prints he planned to publish. He fastened two such sheets together along one long side—with the woodcut *Man's Head in Woman's Hair* (fig. 5) printed on one side. The prints he presented as belonging to such a portfolio—which he called *The Mirror*—are printed on China paper mounted on the same sort of large cardboard sheets. It is still uncertain whether Munch himself considered this only as a "model" for a series of such portfolios he wished to print, or whether he actually meant that they were to be a selection of such impressions collected in the portfolio cover. In any case, he must have sold the impressions originally presented this way, because they were privately owned for many years, until, at the end of the 1970s, they were donated to the Harvard University Museums by the then owner.[6] For a number of years, Munch tried to realize this project that was a sort of frieze of life in graphic works, but he never succeeded in finding someone willing to publish it. He had no possibility of paying the cost of printing the number of prints in question, and nothing ever came of it.

From 1897 until 1901, Munch spent long periods home in Norway and did a lot of experimenting with both woodcuts and lithographs. He did the printing himself and was responsible for many distinctive impressions. He had bought and installed a small press that he could use for trial proofs, and he even prepared a number of lithographic stones himself. Many of the prints from this period carry obvious signs of experimentation, with uneven coloring and printed on coarse brownish paper that looks more like wrapping-paper than anything else (fig. 6). Frequently, the sheet of paper is torn crookedly and the print rather haphazardly placed on the sheet. Nevertheless, there is an unusual presence in these prints and they completely lack the superficial perfection of the professional print. Of the prints shown in the exhibition, *Rouge & Noir* (cat. no. 41) is an example of this.

Towards the end of 1901, Munch decided to try Berlin once again, and, gathering all he had of money and artworks, he rented a fine, large atelier there. On this occasion, he had all his copperplates at the Geographical Survey of Norway sent to the printer Angerer, but already in early 1902, they must have been transferred to Felsing.[7] As late as fall 1902, both Felsing and Lassally in Berlin refused to deliver any prints to Munch until they were paid for the work done. Albert Kollmann, Munch's faithful helper at this time, had to mediate and pay the money for him so that it was possible for Munch to have prints on hand in order to sell them. After these difficul-

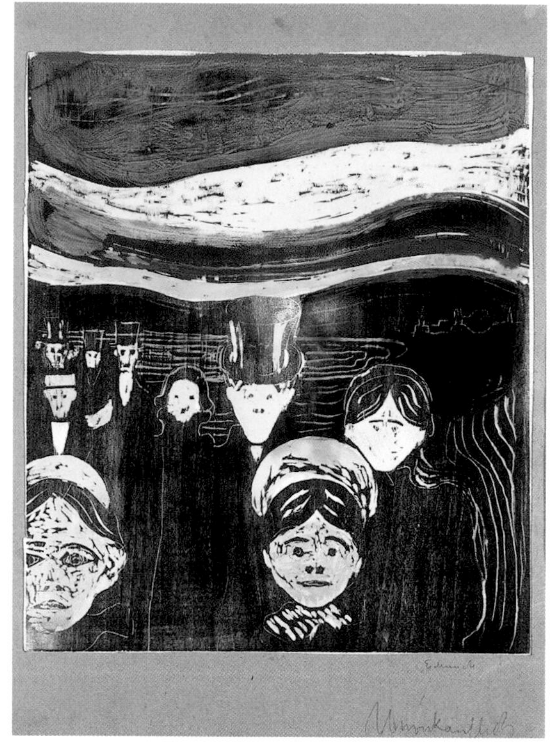

4 Edvard Munch, *Angst*, 1896, hand-colored woodcut on paper on gray cardboard, 45.3 x 37.8 cm, cardboard: 56.9 x 42.5 cm, Munch-museet, Oslo

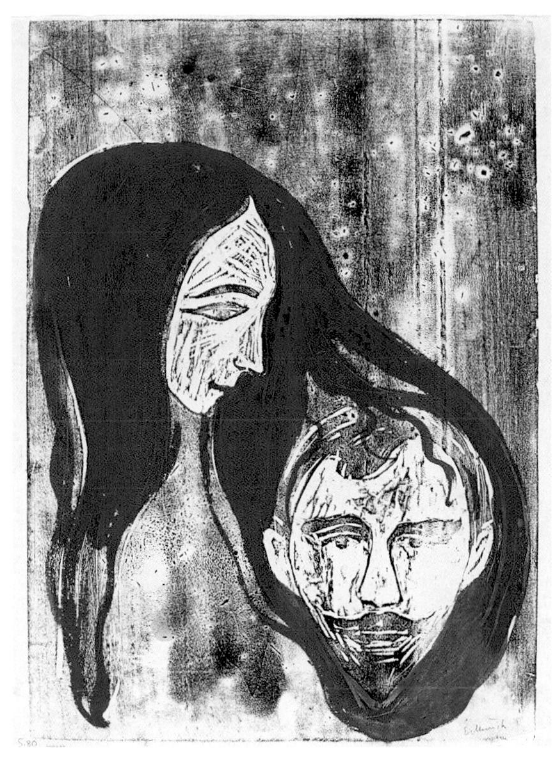

ties, however, things developed swiftly and in a positive direction for Munch as a printmaker. Dr. Linde in Lübeck bought practically all his available intaglio prints and lithographs, adding them to his collection of modern art. Gustav Schiefler, who saw the prints while visiting Linde, was so delighted by them that shortly afterwards he began a complete cataloging of Munch's graphic works. In a short time the demand for prints increased considerably and in 1904 Bruno Cassirer signed a three-year contract for all sales of Munch's graphic works in Germany.

In many ways the choice of Felsing for the printing of the intaglio works in 1902 is rather surprising. Presumably, it must be seen in the light of Munch's intense wish to make an artistic breakthrough—also as a printmaker. Felsing was highly esteemed and used by many prominent artists in Germany. The printing firm was a family concern that had existed for several generations and had its own special profile.[8] Wilhelm Felsing who ran the printing house from 1892 to 1940 had his own distinct ideas about printing ink as well as paper. He preferred a warm, brownish-black tone, printed on paper also with a tone tending towards the yellowish.

We know very little about whether or not Munch himself liked the typical Felsing style, but, among his supporters in Germany, both Schiefler and Kollmann had expressed criticism several times and maintained that impressions printed in black on white paper were better than the typical Felsing prints. The judgement of posterity has been the same—Felsing prints are usually regarded as less interesting than other impressions from the same plate. However, in all fairness, prints from Felsing also vary greatly in quality and expression. Nor is it true that all the prints are on a heavy yellowish-white intaglio printing paper. In fact, rather many are printed on a warm, yellowish white van Gelder paper with a faint texture, and a number are printed on heavy Japan paper. The brown tone of the ink varies accordingly from a rather deep, warm black to dark yellowish brown.

However, compared to both early prints and later impressions, with Munch generally responsible for the printing, Felsing's prints, in most cases, have something dully professional and almost commercial about them. The majority are printed in the decade 1902–1912, a period in which Munch sold a huge amount of graphic art and printed in large quantities.

The same applies to lithographs from the same period and to some degree even to the woodcuts. Just as Felsing became his

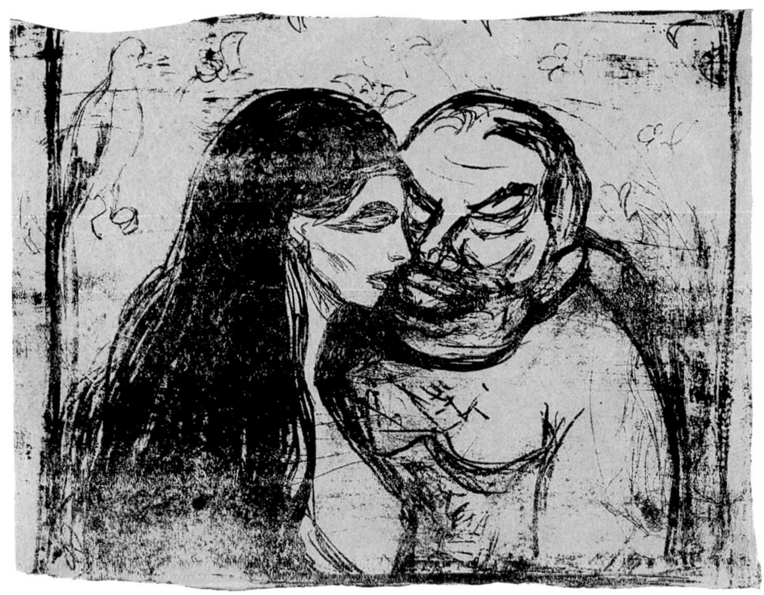

5 Edvard Munch, *Man's Head in Woman's Hair*, 1896, color woodcut on gray cardboard, 71.9 x 62.5 cm, Munch-museet, Oslo

6 Edvard Munch, *Burlesque Couple* I, 1898, lithograph on coarse brownish paper, 29.5 x 38 cm, Munch-museet, Oslo

permanent printer of intaglio prints, Lassally took over the printing of practically all lithographs and woodcuts. With an improved economy Munch was able to use more expensive paper, and woodcuts on handmade Japan paper with clearly visible chain lines, wide margins and deckled edges mainly stem from the period between 1906 and the outbreak of the First World War.

For colored woodcuts, this strong, soft and absorbent paper was exceptionally well suited. The color was usually thinned out so that it had a certain transparency—such as was usual in Japanese woodcuts. There is, however, nothing to suggest that Munch used water-based ink as did the Japanese, but he obtained a corresponding appearance by thinning the oil-based ink.

A characteristic feature in many of Munch's woodcuts is the way in which he allows the wood itself to play an active role in the picture—so that the knots and growth rings create an intricate and attractive background for the image. This is perhaps most pronounced in the many versions of *The Kiss*, but it is also true of many others. In one of his last woodcuts, *Kiss in the Field* of 1943 (cat. no. 56), the subject is barely suggested with careful sketch marks, while the restless pattern of the wood is what characterizes the print. There has been much speculation as to how Munch has so clearly revealed the structure in the wood—whether he has worked on the woodblocks in a particular way with sandpaper or done something else in order to bring forth these lines—although nothing certain can be said about this.

In addition to thin Japan paper he also printed numerous lithographs and woodcuts on thin, transparent machine-made European paper—which we commonly call tissue paper—of various qualities. In some cases, he has utilized the paper's transparency by mounting the sheet with the reverse side out, so that the color takes on a more diffuse quality. An impression of *Seated Nude* of 1897 (Sch. 99, Woll 111) on thin Japan paper is painted in watercolor and mounted in this way. In 1908–09, Munch spent several months in Dr. Jacobson's private clinic in Copenhagen, but he was far from inactive during this period. Among other things, he drew the *Alpha and Omega Series* that came out as a portfolio of lithographs printed at Dansk Reproduktionsanstalt in Copenhagen. As with his first portfolio of prints, this one, too, was printed on paper of various qualities. The ordinary edition was printed on thick white vellum, while a smaller number was printed on Japan paper pasted to sheets of the same paper as in the ordinary edition and, in addition, a small number were printed on thick gray paper.[9]

When he left Dr. Jacobson in the spring of 1909, Munch decided to find a place in Norway where, in peace and quiet, he could work on large projects such as, for example, the competition for the decoration of the new University Assembly Hall in Oslo. First, he rented a large house in Kragerø, and then in 1911 he bought a house in Hvitsten and shortly after rented a large property outside Moss. In 1916 he bought the property at Ekely on the outskirts of Oslo and moved most of his possessions and his work there. Although the work with the Assembly Hall decorations took up most of his time in the period 1909–16, he managed to install his own print-workshop. Before 1913, he had bought presses for printing intaglio prints and lithographs, ordered paper and printing-ink from Germany and created prints with renewed energy.[10] Early on, possibly already in 1910, he was in contact with lithographer Nielsen (later Kildeborg) who, for a number of years, came to his various working places and assisted him with printing of lithographs and woodcuts.

Although Munch created his own possibilities for printing lithographs and woodcuts at home in Norway, most of his older plates and stones remained with the printers in Berlin. Therefore, until the breakout of the First World War, Felsing and Lassally continued to print the majority of his graphic works. Although his finances no longer made it necessary to limit the number of impressions he printed, it appears that Munch continued to print only a small number at a time from each plate or stone. Orders to Lassally usually consisted of three to six impressions from each—but usually from all the plates and stones he had in his keeping.[11]

The result was that Munch now had close to a complete collection on the same type of paper—and with approximately the same ink-color. It seems that he deliberately aimed at just such a common characteristic when sending his graphic art to exhibitions. It was the case, for example, with the prints he sent to *The Armory Show* in USA in 1913. All his prints shown there that have been identified are printed on thin Japan paper. Another large order to Lassally in 1913 resulted in a quantity of lithographs and woodcuts on large sheets of heavy, porous white paper. This paper seems highly light-resistant and the Munch-museet impressions, that have never been exhibited, look almost as if they came off the press yesterday. Here, however, the size of the sheets presents a perceptible problem, in that they are as large as 600 x 800 mm. Even relatively small images such as, for example, the woodcuts *The Heart* (fig. 7) and *Encounter in Space* (fig. 8) are printed in these large formats, which can make them less usable in an exhibition context than earlier impressions on smaller sheets.

Munch, however, could also print on less conventional paper, for example coated paper on which a number of his lithographic caricatures of 1903 are printed. This smooth paper, totally without surface texture, resulted in an extremely precise print of all details, and may have been used when Munch wished to transfer a lithograph to a new stone. From existing correspondence we know that lithographer Hagen in Oslo wanted to grind down the stones on which the caricatures were drawn, and that Munch urged his relative and faithful helper Ludvig Ravensberg to visit the printer and make sure that impressions were made on suitable transfer paper before any grinding-down took place.[12]

The printer Clot in Paris introduced Munch to transfer lithography, and it was there he became familiar with Clot's special paper for executing the original drawing. It was made from Clot's own recipe and contained an artificial grainy substance to prevent the surface of the finished lithograph from appearing too smooth and dead. Much later on in life, Munch declared that he disliked this paper, and preferred ordinary paper for such drawings.[13] In order to obtain a lively effect in the surface, he could even place a portfolio with canvas cover underneath. This has been done in *Attraction* II (cat. no. 37) and in *Separation* II (cat. no. 39). In a number of cases even a wooden board has been used, so that the structure in this material would show in the drawing—and consequently also in the lithograph.

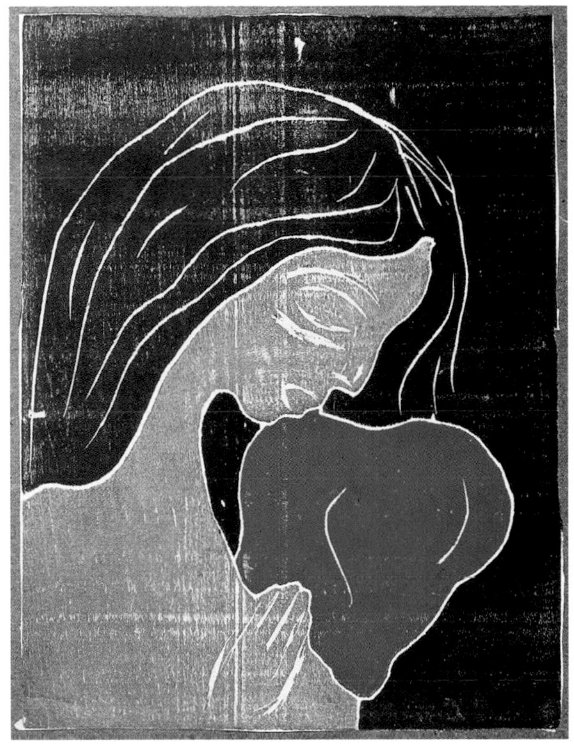

At the outbreak of war in the fall of 1914, Munch, as mentioned, had established a satisfactory situation in Norway for work with graphic art, and there was a great demand for his prints. However, as most of his earlier plates and lithographic stones remained with the printers in Berlin, Munch, with good reason, was worried about what could happen to them. He arranged, therefore, in the fall of 1914, to have all the copperplates and woodblocks, as well as some lithographic stones, sent home. Of the remaining lithographic stones, he had impressions on transfer paper sent to him, so that he could transfer them to new stones in Norway. The reunion with the old plates led to the reworking of some of them into completely new versions, while others were printed with many curious experiments in coloring and printing. In some of the later woodcuts that he printed at home in Norway, he experimented with floating transitions between the color fields, and allowed the color layers to bleed into one another in an unusually soft manner. These color woodcuts, printed around 1917, are mainly on soft, heavy white paper, probably manufactured in Norway. During the war, it was impossible to obtain Japan paper or

7 Edvard Munch, *The Heart*, 1898–99, color woodcut on paper, 25 x 18, 4 cm, Munch-museet, Oslo

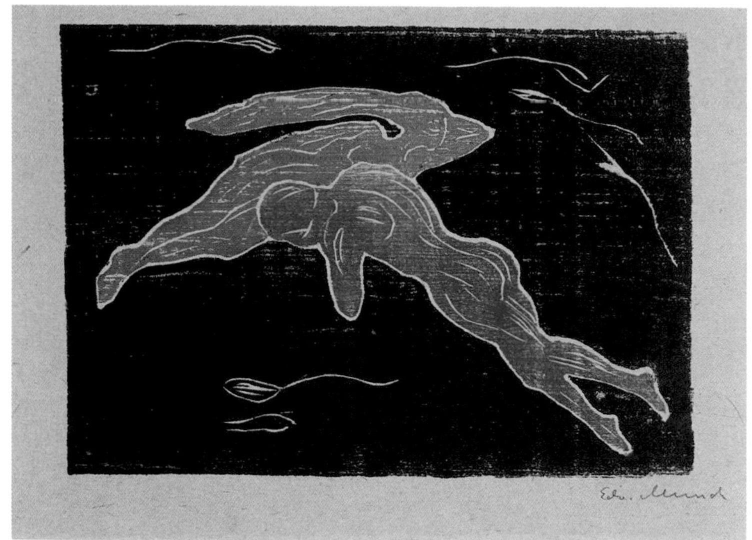

other types of paper that had to be imported. However, a number of Munch's prints from the war years are printed on a rather special Japan paper with narrow chain lines. We have a number of lithographs on the same paper, dated 1913 by the artist, and it seems therefore likely that this is paper procured by Munch in good time before the outbreak of war.[14]

Munch continued to make prints up until the end, and made many curious experiments with woodblocks and copperplates. From 1917, we have some quite special monoprints of the etching *Houses in Kragerø* (cat. no. 147), in which he appears to have inked the plate with oil paint. These are printed on heavy, white paper that makes a good background for the strong colors. Largely, he ceased working with intaglio prints around 1916–17, and lithographs, with a few exceptions, he made only as transfer lithographs. With woodcuts, however, he continued to explore the many possibilities that lay in the treatment of the woodblocks, and this he did just as extensively as the inking and printing itself.

Munch was never afraid to stretch the borders of the possible, and this included his relationship to the material on which he printed his graphic works. He could use unusual types of paper, such as thick paper with a strong canvas texture, for example, and on one occasion he even printed a woodblock straight onto a canvas so that the woodcut could serve as the outline for a painting![15] In these cases, the texture in the paper and the canvas was so pronounced that it was pressed into the woodblocks, and can be sensed as a faint texture in all later impressions printed from the same block.

Munch used several printers in Oslo, and accounts coming from them relate that he was most exacting in his choice and treatment of paper. Of his later prints, however, few are printed on the more exclusive types of paper. Everything indicates that he chose the best machine-made paper that the Norwegian printers had on hand, and was satisfied with that. In his later years, Munch was just as careless in his treatment of the artworks on paper as of the paintings. Photographs from his studios and contemporary descriptions of Ekely bear witness to chaotic conditions; prints and drawings lay strewn about in heaps and piles, unprotected from dust and light. In all, at his death, he bequeathed close to 18,000 graphic works to the municipality of Oslo. This must have been an impossible amount for him to look after. That they are in such good condition as they are, despite everything, shows that he must have been very much aware of quality in his choice of paper.

8 Edvard Munch, *Encounter in Space*, 1898–99,
color woodcut on paper, 18 x 25 cm, Munch-museet, Oslo

1 Probably 10 of Munch's lithographic stones were sent from Paris to Berlin in 1904, where they were printed by Lassally. After the outbreak of the First World War, eight of them were, in any case, sent home to Norway in the course of the autumn 1914, and most of them were later printed in Oslo by lithographer Nielsen.

2 A comprehensive survey of museums owning graphic works by Edvard Munch is found in appendix VI of Gerd Woll, *Edvard Munch. The Complete Graphic Works*. London et al. 2001.

3 A useful tool for descriptions of paper types is *The Print Council of America Paper Sample Book. A practical Guide to the Description of Paper*, with introductory text by Elizabeth Lunning and Roy Perkinson, The Print Council of America 1996. Also to be recommended is a symposium with accompanying report from Toronto, in May 1999: *Looking at Paper. Evidence & Interpretation*. A classic in the field of paper history is still Dard Hunter, *Papermaking. The History and Technique of an Ancient Craft*, 1st edition 1947, 2nd edition 1947 and new edition 1974. In recent years, much useful information has been available on the internet, where IPH—International Association of Paper Historians in particular has been active. On their homepage http://www.assiph.com one finds links to water mark archive, literature and conferences.

4 Gustav Schiefler, *Verzeichnis des graphischen Werks Edvard Munchs bis 1906*, Berlin 1907. The second volume was published 20 years later: *Edvard Munch. Das graphische Werk 1906–1926*, Berlin 1928. (Both reproduced in facsimile in Oslo 1974).
The correspondence between Munch and Schiefler has been published in two volumes: Edvard Munch and Gustav Schiefler, *Briefwechsel Band 1 1902–1914*, Hamburg 1987, and *Briefwechsel Band 2 1915–1935/1943*, Hamburg 1990.

5 The eight intaglios are: *The Girl at the Window* (Sch. 5, Woll 5), *The Sick Child* (Sch. 7, Woll 7), *Kristiania Bohemians I* (Sch. 10, Woll 15), *Tête-à-tête* (Sch. 12, Woll 9), *Moonlight. Night in St. Cloud* (Sch. 13, Woll 17), *The Lonely Ones (Two Human Beings)* (Sch. 20, Woll 13), *Dr. Asch* (Sch. 27, Woll 25), *The Day After* (Sch. 15, Woll 10).

6 This series was first shown to the public in 1978 in connection with a large exhibition of Munch's works in the National Gallery, Washington DC. The series was specially treated in an article in the exhibition catalog, cf. Bente Torjusen, "The Mirror," *Edvard Munch. Symbols & Images*, Washington 1978. The theme was further developed and illustrated in color in Bente Torjusen, *Words & Images of Edvard Munch*, Vermont 1986.

7 In an undated letter to his sister, Inger Munch, written just before Christmas 1901, Edvard Munch writes: "If you are in town will you do me a favor and go up to the Geographical Survey of Norway where my intaglio copperplates are stored— You must ask them to send them to me in the fastest possible manner, as express goods to the following address: Angerer, Kunstanstalt Druckerei für Kupferstich, Wasserthorstrasse 50, Berlin. [...] The forwarding charges, packing and so on will be paid here by Angerer..." (Original letter in Munch-museet, N 1103). On October 31, 1902, Albert Kollmann wrote to Munch telling him that he had fetched the collection of intaglio prints, in all 39 prints, from Felsing and had shown them to anyone who wished to see them. Dr. Linde in Lubeck was interested and would like to buy them, but first Kollmann had to pay Felsing M 221.68 for the job, after that he sold all 39 intaglio prints to Dr. Linde. According to the same letter, at this time Felsing had more than 93 intaglio prints by Munch. (Original letter in Munch-museet).

8 For a supplementary story about the printing house just before Munch began to use it, see Willibald Francke, *100 Jahre im Dienste der Kunst. Erinnerungs gabe der Firma O. Felsing aus Anlass des hundertjährigen Bestehens der Kupferdruckerei*, Berlin 1897. A more recent history is found in *Die Felsings aus Darmstadt*, exh. cat., Kunsthalle, Darmstadt 1987.

9 According to information on the title page, there were 50 impressions in the initial printing of the portfolio, with 20 impressions on Japan paper, 5 on gray cardboard and 25 on white cardboard. Later, considerably more were printed on heavy white paper (white cardboard); later in a catalog, Munch states that 60 portfolios are printed on heavy white paper.

10 In a letter to Gustav Schiefler of August 7, 1912 Munch writes: "I am setting up a lithograph press—and expect to be doing etchings—and lithographs—very soon," Munch and Schiefler 1987 (see note 4), no. 587, the original privately owned), and in a letter of September 18, 1912: "You should have seen me during the fast few days—very busy printing with my new lithograph press—It is going very well—and I've done various new wood[cuts] and litho[graphs]," Munch and Schiefler 1987 (see note 4), no. 590, the original privately owned). In a letter from Schiefler dated November 2, 1912 he has looked into prices and suppliers of presses for the printing of intaglio prints, Munch and Schiefler 1987 (see note 4), no. 595.

11 From October 26, 1911 there is an invoice from Lassally for "3 prints each of 35 monochrome sheets at 3 M" and "3 prints each of 21 multicolored works at 5 M" (original in Munch-museet), and from April 19, 1913 a similar invoice for 3 consignments to Munch: "on April 1, 6 prints each of 27 monochrome lithographs, 6 each of 5 multicolored ditto," "on April 9, 6 prints each of 15 multicolor woodcuts and 6 each of 1 monochrome," "on April 17, 6 prints each of 20 monochrome woodcuts." (original in Munch-museet).

12 In an undated letter to Ludvig Ravensberg, the envelope postmarked 12.11.1904, Munch writes: "There are some stones at Lithographer Hagen's (*Bohemians' Heroic Deeds*) and he wants to grind them down—I ask you to look into this and have them transferred to suitable paper and then again transferred to stones at Lithographer Petersen and Waitz—Petersen and Waitz will look after this." (original in the Munch-museet).

13 In a retrospective note Munch wrote: "I used an excellent paper at Clot's, the first-rate printer in Paris—which he prepared himself, with albumen—I find the grainy appallingly dull—and found that paper prepared in another way usually became hard when transferred—I then hit upon the idea, despite all printers' and overprinters' protests, of using, in some cases, ordinary paper—preferably newspaper—I found that for certain purposes it was useful. Everywhere it was at hand—it gave a livelier pattern and softer print.—For things that did not demand that the smallest grain be included—it was good." Undated note from 1922 (original in Munch-museet, N 290).

14 A letter from the company R. Wagner, Japan-Papiere Direkt-Import und Lager, Berlin, dated December 20. 1912, reveals that Munch had had a number of samples sent to him—with accompanying price list—on Japan paper that was particularly suitable for printing. Unfortunately, only the letter has been preserved, and we do not know what Munch eventually ordered in the line of Japan paper.

15 An impression of the woodcut *Engineer Frølich* (Woll 725) from 1931 is printed directly on painting canvas (MM G 683–1). The woodblock previously owned by the lithographer Nielsen, was acquired by Munch-museet in 1968 and according to information from the printer, this woodcut was carried out as study material for Munch's painted portrait of Engineer Frølich.

Edvard Munch—Style and Theme around 1900

Frank Høifødt

The years around 1900 were a crucial period in the life and art of Edvard Munch. It was then that he developed a more strongly colored and decorative style, and finished the thematic *Frieze*, exhibited in Berlin in 1902 as *Eine Reihe von Lebensbildern* [A Series of Paintings of Life]. During these years, his decidedly problematic love affair with Mathilde (Tulla) Larsen was to play a role that is difficult to disregard.[1]

Towards the turn of the century, Munch was absorbed in the correlation in his own world of symbols. He returned to earlier subjects and pictorial forms, trying them out in new variations. Neither theme nor iconography, however, is "private" in an exclusive sense. When crystallizing themes from his own life, he did so within the characteristic horizons of the period, *fin-de-siècle*, in a close relationship with artistic and literary patterns.

In the second half of the 1890s, Munch had worked mostly with prints, at the expense of paintings. Many of the print subjects from around 1900 are difficult to date exactly, even though the high level of precision in Gerd Woll's catalog of graphic works presents completely new possibilities of seeing relationships.[2]

In his prints, Munch was also preoccupied with thematic correlations. The title *Love*, which he had already used in a series of paintings in 1893, he used also in 1897 for a portfolio of prints, or group of subjects.[3] Later the same year he announced the impending publication of a series of portfolios entitled *The Mirror*.[4] The new title, in all probability, relates to the enlargement of the theme framework with, among other things, more metaphysical subjects, such as *In the Land of Crystals*, *Funeral March*, *Metabolism* and *The Urn*.[5]

"Are you continuing with your lithographic portfolio?" asks William Molard in a letter to Munch in the spring of 1898.[6] In the summer, Munch meets Tulla Larsen.

Monumentality

Traditional keywords for Munch's style at the turn of the century are monumentality and color art. Pictures such as *Metabolism*, *Red Virginia Creeper*, *Melancholy* (*Laura*), *Fertility* and *The Dance of Life* are all painted in a somewhat large format, and are considered to be a rounding-off of the original *Frieze of Life*, the main theme in Munch's art. Munch was in Italy in 1899. In Munch literature, from Jens Thiis to Arne Eggum, a "monumental-decorative tendency" is seen against a background of impressions from the visit there. Uncertain and mistaken dating has made it difficult to follow a logical development from picture to picture—when, for example, the decorative and monumental *Mother and Child* is dated 1897, the dynamic *Fertility* with its strong colors 1898, and the somber *Metabolism* 1899.[7]

Metabolism (fig. 1) is associated with German romantic symbolism, of the type practiced by Hans von Marrées and Ludwig von Hoffmann. Among Munch's *Frieze* pictures, it relates to *The Woman* (*Sphinx*) of 1894. *The Dance of Life* is French decorative color art, an expression of the new times. Between these two works, *Metabolism* and *The Dance of Life*, there is a stylistic quantum leap.

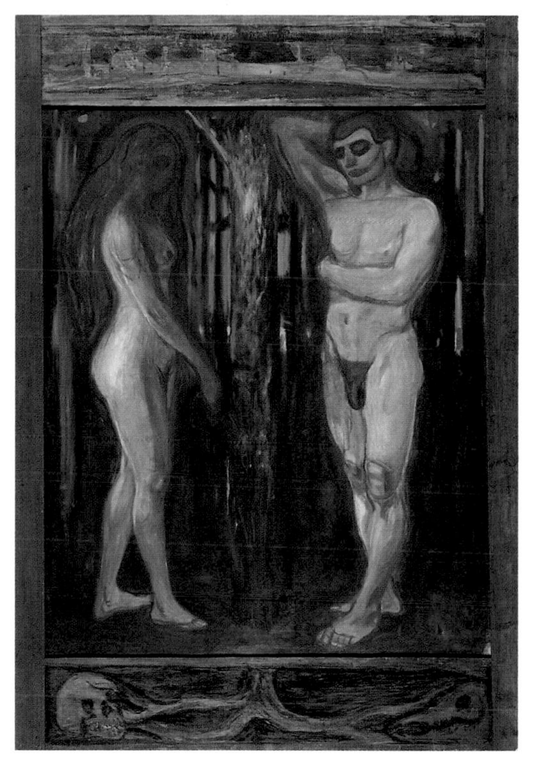

1 Edvard Munch, *Metabolism*, 1898–1900/before 1915, oil on canvas, 172 x 143 cm, Munch-museet, Oslo

Metabolism

Love as a theme framework also had become too narrow for the series of paintings. Subjects concerning death had gained new topical interest, and during the fall of 1898, Munch was in the process of painting *Metabolism*.[8] The size in itself is an indication of the picture's importance. The same female model, in an almost identical pose, appears in *Nude Study* (cat. no. 172), presumably painted at the same time. *Metabolism* is provided with a striking frame of iconographic significance. Thus, it is linked to the main subject in the *Love* series, *Madonna*, which was emphasized by means of "a symbolic frame showing sperm and embryo."[9] Roots and skulls—the subject on the lower part of the wide, carved frame—are a direct reference to metabolism, the eternal earth-bound cycle. The subject matter on the top of the frame, an urban silhouette, suggests "a further sacred context."[10] This can be perceived as analogous to the lithographic subject *In the Land of Crystals*, also entitled *In the Beyond*. Thus, *Metabolism* stands as a synthesis of old and new themes. The title *Metabolism* was first used in 1914. In 1900, the picture was called *Adam and Eva*, in 1902 *Life and Death*.[11] Ingrid Langaard has suggested that the picture was intended to play a cardinal role, "meant as a sort of finish to the frieze."[12] Much suggests that this is so.

Metabolism is Munch's most explicit allusion to the Fall of Man myth. One of the models may have been Jan van Eyck's *Ghent Altarpiece*.[13] In fact, the Fall of Man myth runs all through Munch's art. There are distinct references to it in *Frieze* subjects such as *Eye in Eye* of 1894 (cat. no. 33), *Ashes* of 1895 and *Jealousy* of 1895 (fig. 1, p. 69). "The tree of knowledge for good or ill" is the symptomatic title Munch later gave to a binder filled with key subjects and matching texts—the closest he came to a realization of *The Mirror*. In connection with the *Frieze of Life* exhibition in Kristiania in 1918, Munch wrote that *Metabolism* is "... as necessary for the whole frieze as the buckle is for the belt." In the literature, little attention has been paid to that striking statement. It is *The Dance of Life* that has received special status as the actual rounding off and synthesis of the *Frieze*.[14] However, when both pictures were shown for the first time at Arno Wollfram's in Dresden in 1900, evidently *The Dance of Life* was for sale and not *Metabolism* (*Adam and Eve*).[15] Munch could not part with the "belt buckle" of the *Frieze*! His high opinion of *Metabolism* in 1918 appears to be equally valid in 1900.

To Italy, Spring 1899

The monumental *Metabolism* was painted before the journey to Italy. What specific stimuli can Munch have received in Italy? Julius Meier-Graefe has been used as cicerone in the terrain in question. This leading German art critic was Munch's good friend from Berlin days. He moved to Paris in 1895, where he persuaded Siegfried Bing to establish an Art Nouveau style salon, and the gallery L'Art Nouveau opened that same fall. Bing was a keen promoter of the art of the Nabis. Munch was invited to exhibit, and he moved to Paris early in 1896. In collaboration with Hugo Bruckmann, Meier-Graefe founded the magazine *Dekorative Kunst* in 1897, modeled on the English publication *Studio*.[16]

In the beginning of the new year 1899, the National Gallery of Norway bought the pictures *Spring* (1889) and *Inger* (1892) for NOK 3.500. "For Munch this was a great deal of money and he decided to travel to Italy," writes Munch's biographer Jens Thiis in 1933 about this ever-recurring *topos* in Munch literature.[17] The correspondence between Edvard Munch and Tulla Larsen, however, reveals that Paris and not Italy was the destination when Munch departed from Norway early that spring. Munch's health was poor, the weather was bad, so they did as his companion suggested, and continued on to Italy in hopes of warmer weather. In Florence Munch became worse and he asked Tulla Larsen to go on ahead of him back to Paris. Munch was "stranded" in Florence for almost two months. In a letter to him from Grez, not far from Paris, Tulla Larsen writes: "... that there is no end to your feeling so ill—and when I think that I alone am to blame—I got you down there—and this is the result!"[18]—Before returning to Paris from Florence, Munch spent a few days in Rome.

"So, willingly I gave up the whole object of this trip" he writes to Tulla Larsen. The purpose was, among other things "the printing of my large lithographic work—that I ... have striven for four years to do."[19] When Munch traveled south in the spring of 1899, the plan had been to complete *The Mirror* in Paris.[20]

On the way home from Italy, Munch allegedly looked up Meier-Graefe in Paris and expressed "... his enthusiasm for Raphael's inspiring *stanze* ..."[21] This is evident from an article in *Dekorative Kunst*, most of which was written by Meier-Graefe.

Munch in *Dekorative Kunst* 1899

In the autumn, 1899, *Dekorative Kunst* contained two modest paragraphs about Edvard Munch. The style does not carry the serious engagement we usually find in Meier-Graefe, and it seems more impersonal, more like an informal chat.

"MUNCH has just returned from a journey to Rome and Florence ..." writes the author.[22] "The juxtaposition of MUNCH and RAPHAEL is, indeed, one of the strangest imaginable." It should be noted, however, that it has not been said that these are Munch's words; rather, the names of the two artists are used as a stylistic device. Earlier in the text we read for example: "There can hardly be a greater contrast than LAUTREC and MUNCH." Who could have made such an assertion? In 1904, Meier-Graefe writes that Toulouse-Lautrec has been of greater importance for Munch than anyone else.[23]

It seems that the author uses "RAPHAEL" as a synonym (or rather: *metonym*) for "Rome and Florence" and the general impressions for which the artist is said to have expressed his enthusiasm. Despite this "strange" constellation—Munch and "Italian Renaissance," one might perhaps say "... he seemed thrilled by his impressions; *not by the paintings but rather the architecture*... [my italics]." These impressions "...have given him the urge to create large-scale decorative art, which he now intends to carry out in Norway." There is nothing to say that Munch has expressed enthusiasm for Raphael, let alone "his inspiring *stanze*."

Meier-Graefe did not sign his contribution in *Dekorative Kunst* with his own name, but used the Greek letter gamma as his signature.[24] At the end of the small, rather insignificant article "E. Munch" of fall 1899, this sign does not appear. It would seem that Meier-Graefe did not write the article.[25] Moreover, he withdrew from the editorial staff that fall, and established his own fashionable Art Nouveau gallery, La Maison Moderne, in rue de la Paix.[26]

"I look forward to starting to work, one becomes tired of travelling by train—but it has indeed been useful for me to see all the splendid pictures," Munch writes home from Florence.[27] Among other things, he bought a portfolio of Botticelli reproductions.[28] He is reported to have said that he had this artist in mind when, a couple of months later, he painted *The Dance of Life* (fig. 4).[29] There was great interest in Botticelli among artists at the time, but where *The Dance of Life* is concerned, other influences are far more striking and conclusive.

Munch did not realize the plans for his graphic works in Paris in spring 1899. Evidently, sickness made work impossible for several months. He was still sick when he arrived in Paris on his way home. He insisted that Tulla Larsen should remain in Grez. "I am on my feet but am very weak," he writes in a letter to her on May 25.—"I wonder whether I am still able to paint.—I have surely forgotten how."[30] On June 5, he sailed from Le Havre for Kristiania.[31]

Summer 1899

Munch arrived in Kristiania at the end of the first week in June. It is probable that he painted *Studenterlunden* (fig. 2) immediately after his homecoming. The picture portrays a luxuriant park, known as Studenterlunden in Kristiania, with a brownish-yellowy gravel walk winding its way between chestnut trees and lilac bushes, and a tall poplar-like formation in the background. In the foreground on the right a couple sit on a bench locked in an embrace. Two amorous couples sit beneath the chestnut tree, and further along the path, yet another couple is indicated with cursory brushstrokes. "In *Studenterlunden*, the park's deep green mass flows together into an expanse of beautifully undulating contours in which the bright figures of girls glow like beautifully set precious jewels," wrote a Czech writer in 1905.[32]

Studenterlunden shows signs of stylistic ambivalence and experimentation. The chestnut tree and the distant gravel walk are realistically depicted, with heavy volumes and pictorial space. On the

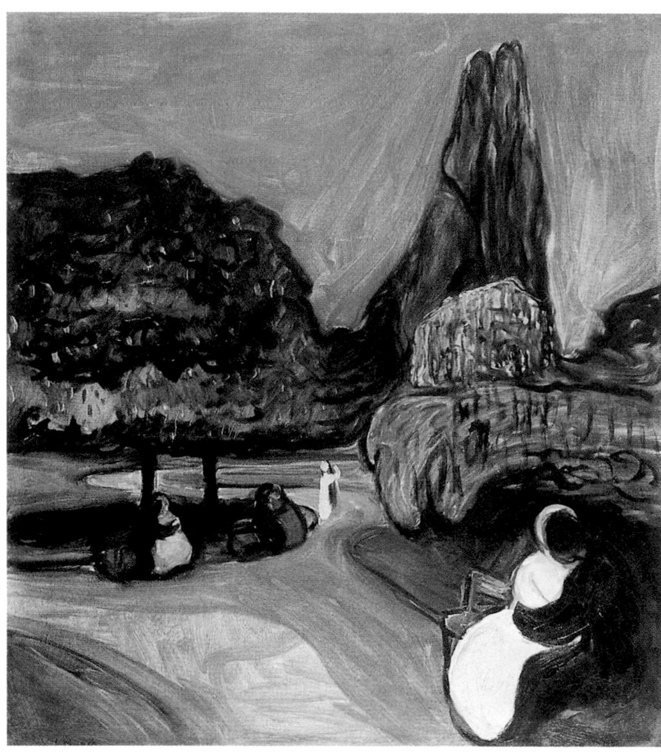

other hand, the figures and the flowering bushes on the right are greatly simplified and held to the picture plane. The couple in the foreground is severely stylized; undulating lines delimit a black and a white patch with no modeling whatsoever. Stylistically, the couple is almost identical with the background figures in *The Dance of Life* (1899).[33]

As a motif, *Studenterlunden* is well known. Munch returned to it again in 1904 when he painted a series of pictures for his patron Max Linde in Lübeck, *Lovers in the Park* of 1904 (cat. no. 47). Here the painterly expression is quite different. Our picture has scarcely been depicted or treated in Munch literature, apart from an exhibition in Basel in 1985.[34] The picture was sold in Prague already in 1905, in connection with the last of the original four exhibitions of the *Frieze* (Berlin, Leipzig, Kristiania, Prague). It has been dated 1902.[35] However, Munch mentions the picture in a letter from Berlin to Andreas Aubert, dated February 7, 1902.[36] A summer picture from Kristiania is hardly likely to have been painted in Berlin in the New Year 1902, and in 1994, the dating was changed to 1901.[37] The picture, however, was also mentioned in connection with Munch's exhibition in the Diorama premises in December 1900.[38] New *terminus antequem*: summer 1900.

The late summer of 1900 saw a dramatic and painful break between Munch and Tulla Larsen in Switzerland. It was not until September that Munch returned to Norway. He went straight away to Holmenkollen Turisthotel, and from there for a prolonged stay at Hammers Pension at Ljan. Thus, a dating to summer 1900 is unlikely. It follows that summer 1899 is the most plausible dating. Flowering lilacs and chestnut trees point to the beginning of June—when we dare to draw that sort of matter-of-fact information from such a symbolic rendering.[39] It fits well with the time of Munch's return from Paris. Tulla Larsen arrived in town barely fourteen days later. Munch had already moved on to Åsgårdstrand.[40]

A relatively contemporary critic described *Studenterlunden* as "... a truly misanthropic spring impression and nature *seen with eyes that hate it*."[41] The subject was perceived in a similar way when it was shown in Zurich in 1922: "Munch fears, hates, desires woman. Love is for him a dark, sensuous urge—it is thus he presents it in the park scene *Summer Night* ... These couples, always a pale and a dark mass intertwined, are no longer human beings, they are like mating beetles driven by natural desire."[42]

Dance on the Shore

When one becomes aware of the close kinship between *Studenterlunden* and *The Dance of Life* (fig. 4), a third motif, dated to about 1900–1902, fits naturally into this stylistic context, namely *Dance on the Shore* (fig. 3). This image is less realistic, in both form and content. A mystical natural experience has taken on the character of a hallucination. Figures of women dancing on the shore, framed by dark tree trunks, are the picture's main elements. A path leading down to the shore continues into the sea—"Death's Dwelling."[43] As so often with Munch, here the symbolic function of the sea is connected with eroticism and perdition. By the side of the path lies a large cat, the symbol of both the female sex and calamity. Like an archaic pillar guarding a gruesome secret, it portends Eros and doom.[44]

2 Edvard Munch, *Studenterlunden*, 1900–02 (1899), oil on canvas, 101 x 91 cm, private collection

On the open shore, two young girls dance with abandon. They have not yet crossed the boundary of eroticism, but they are dancing dangerously close to the water's edge. The small inlet resembles an open jaw that can swallow them. The wildness of the dance intimates that there are forces within them that drive them towards the abyss. The girl dressed in yellow seems to have the strongest affinity with the sea. In accordance with an established typology, her hair is red and conforms with the ominous reflections of the sun on the water, rocking and throbbing like large drops of blood.

The women in black dance alone. The color indicates that they have left the battlefield of love behind them. The figures are as if locked in between the dark tree trunks. Have they shaken the hand of death, dedicating themselves to the generations of family that have gone before, to nature's merciless cycle?

Dance on the Shore shows the somewhat similar alternation between a spatial and a flat mode of presentation that we saw in *Studenterlunden*. In the cell-like, ornamental, flat painting, one also sees close ties with the Pont-Aven painters and the Nabis.[45] The small "jewels" in yellow, white and red we also recognize from *Studenterlunden*. The detail with the two young girls who dance together we find, in a forerunner to *The Dance of Life*, a monochrome ink drawing.[46] The typology and color symbolism of *Woman (Sphinx)* (1894 [cat. no. 27; fig. 2, p. 70] and later variations) lurks in the background of both *Studenterlunden* and *Dance on the Shore*. In *The Dance of Life* Munch has kept more explicitly and consistently to the *paradigmatic* image of the *Frieze*. The genesis of *The Dance of Life* also contains a new literary inspiration. In 1898, Munch's good friend, the Danish writer Helge Rode, had brought out a new play, *Dansen gaar* (*Dancing*). In the second act, during a garden party, the following dialog takes place between the two main characters:

Claire: "I thought we were alone among all the others, when we were dancing."

Aage: "Yes, how true, Claire. For us, they were only colors. (Smiles) Dancing, well—People do the same thing, yet it is so different. For some, dancing is something primitive; for others something wild and gay. For us I think it was something serious, although we were happy. I think it was the Dance of Life."[47]

In the large painting both women, one dressed in a pale color, the other in a dark color, have Tulla Larsen's facial features. A biographical level is introduced. Based on Munch's own writings, it is possible to interpret the subject as a thematic presentation of the

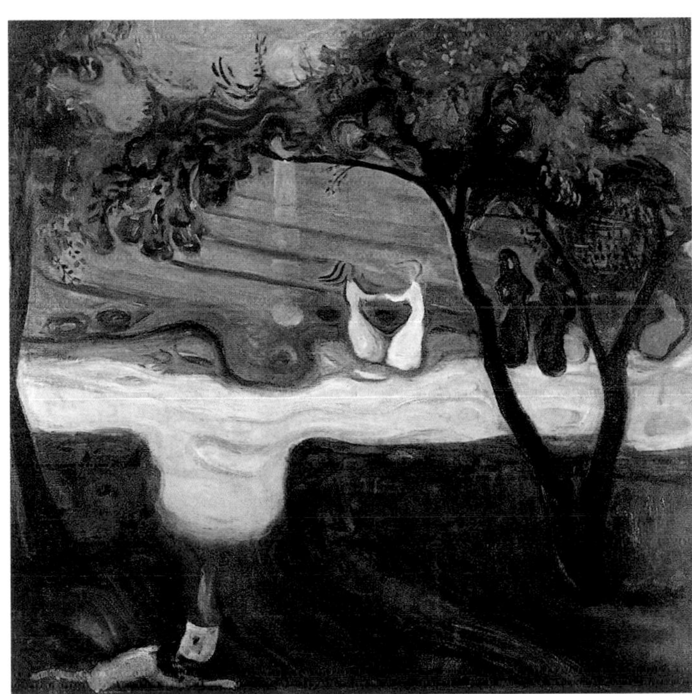

3 Edvard Munch, *Dance on the Shore*, 1900–02 (1899), oil on canvas, 96 x 99 cm, Narodnie Galerie, Prague

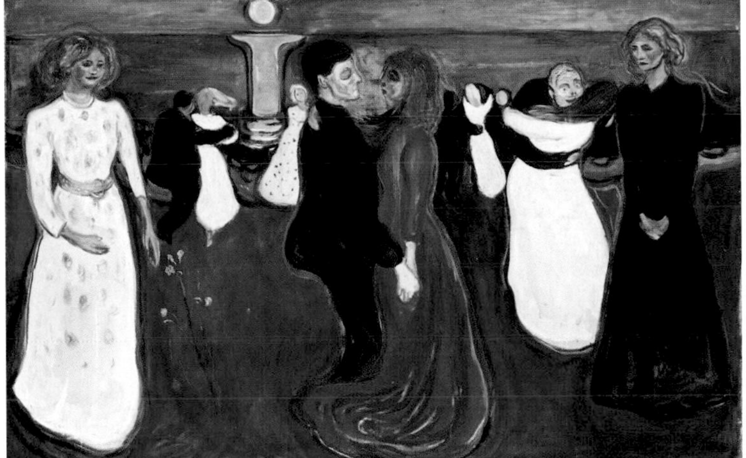

4 Edvard Munch, *The Dance of Life*, 1899–1900 (1899), oil on canvas, 125 x 191 cm, Nasjonalgalleriet, Oslo

break that had to come between Munch and Tulla Larsen with Munch's choice of Art and rejection of Love. The couple in the center then becomes a symbolic presentation of the artist who dances with his "First Love", the inspiration for the *Frieze*.[48] Naturally, the immediate layers of content are of a more ordinary character.

The Dance of Life presents a more consistent development of the stylistic tendencies we have seen in *Studenterlunden*. Here, there is no vacillation between different methods of presentation. The entire motif consists of bright color patches, clearly delimited, with no modeling or spatial recess. All three pictures are clearly French in style, with *The Dance of Life* a daring and personal monumental realization of decorative flat painting. Renaissance art may have played a minor role in both *Metabolism* and *The Dance of Life*, but after the Italian journey—perhaps one should rather say, the Paris journey—it is chiefly the influence of contemporary French painting that has gained renewed impact.[49]

Mother and Daughter

We have now ascribed definite style characteristics to the summer of 1899, although one must not presume that these apply to all his work. There is a fourth subject that begs to be included, namely *Mother and Daughter* (fig. 5) in Norway's National Gallery. The picture, however, is dated 1897. This was a year in which Munch painted little; for, as has been said, he was mainly taken up with printmaking. No known paintings of 1897 relate stylistically to *Mother and Daughter*. Nor do the prints from that year have anything to do with the picture's splendid "monumental-decorative" style. When, on the other hand, it comes to woodcuts from 1899, one finds definite stylistic parallels, with *The Lonely Ones* (*Two Human Beings*) (cat. nos. 98–103) as an illustrative example.

The cautious dating "prob. 1897" was used in Munch's exhibition at the National Gallery in 1927. Later this dating was ascribed to a letter written by Munch to his Aunt Karen, dated Berlin March 19, 1898. In it he mentions a picture probably to be shown at *The Free Exhibition* in Copenhagen that spring: "You and Inger from last summer."[50] In a comment to *The Family Letters*, Johan Langaard

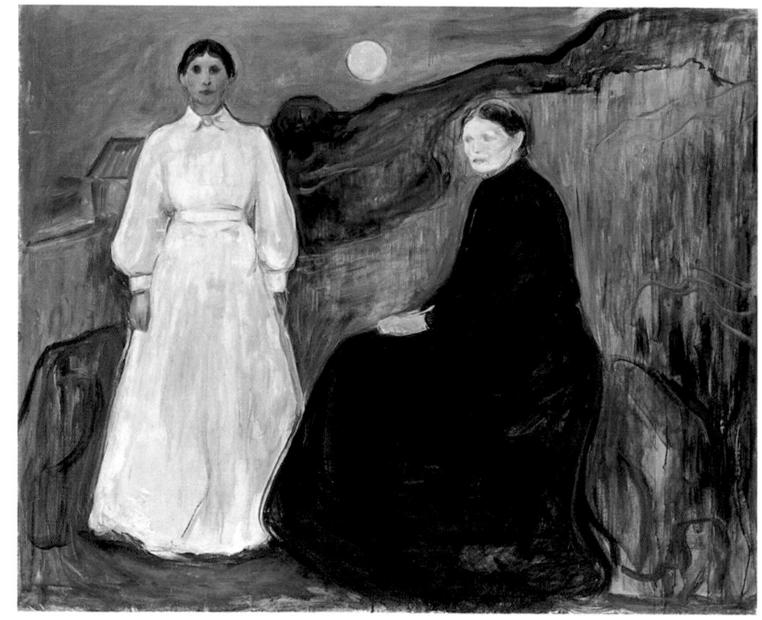

writes that this "possibly refers to 'Mother and Daughter' in the National Gallery."[51]

Tone Skedsmo has concluded that *Mother and Daughter* is identical with Copenhagen catalog no. 126, *Summer Night*.[52] According to the catalog, this picture belongs to art collector and art patron Olaf Schou. The given measurements, however, indicate that this is a somewhat larger picture. It may apply to *The Lonely Ones* (c. 1891), also entitled *Summer Night*. This picture belonged to Olaf Schou and was destroyed in a fire on board a ship in December 1901.[53] It could be that Aunt Karen and Inger are hidden behind no. 127 in the exhibition, a picture with the title *Double Portrait*. This image, however, is much smaller than *Mother and Daughter*. The foundation for Johan Langaard's careful supposition is, consequently, rather weak, and a stylistic appraisal must carry more weight. The striking similarity to *The Dance of Life*, right down to details, points to the summer of 1899 as a dating. In addition, from the exchange of letters with Tulla Larsen we find that Aunt Karen and Inger visited Munch in Åsgårdstrand in June.[54]

Mother and Daughter is the least literary subject in this group. In no way do I suggest that it is without symbolic intentions and levels, but *Studenterlunden* and *Dance on the Shore* to a greater degree repre-

5 Edvard Munch, *Mother and Daughter*, 1897 (1899), oil on canvas, 135 x 163 cm, Nasjonalgalleriet, Oslo

sent a decorative mosaic of hieroglyphs. *The Dance of Life*, for its part, is the consummate symbolist *The Woman* (*Sphinx*) in a modern vitalized version.

Winter 1899–1900

The traditional dating of *Red and White* (cat. no. 30) to 1894 is without professional foundation. Stylistically the painting is much closer to *The Dance of Life* than to *The Woman* (*Sphinx*) of 1894 (cat. no. 27). The colors have a greater degree of "rawness" than we find in *Ashes* (1895), and the brushstrokes are freer and more summary. Large, intense color planes resound freely—as in *The Dance of Life*. In my consideration of the motif, I have reached the conclusion that it was painted in the late summer or fall 1899.[55] In relation to other pictures from that same summer, *Red and White* shows a certain expressive disharmony.

The most striking aspect, in relation to the concept *The Woman* (*Sphinx*), is the absence of the third woman. It can look as if she has been there, but has been over-painted. In addition, the absence of the woman in black is strikingly accentuated. Between two parallel tree trunks, one sees a formless element, perhaps a stone? In his study of the painting, Gösta Svenæus' associates these elements with a gravestone and a coffin or grave. It then becomes reasonable to associate the "flowing" red area between the stone and the figure in red with blood!

Red and White stands as an experimental variation on the theme *The Woman* (*Sphinx*). And, it is not simply an amputation or removal that has taken place. "The woman in white," a positive, poetic and dynamic figure, appears here as a tragic figure, unmoving as a pillar of salt, her visible arm hanging loosely at her side. Her neck is hidden by the dress. The fair hair is thin. The visible eye appears as a downward slanting line, giving the face a tragic and resigned expression. To crown it all, a heavy branch hangs immediately in front of her face.

In the etching *The Woman* II of 1895 (cat. no. 32) the figure in the pale dress is a young woman with a firm figure, her hands held behind her back, her head turned towards the sea in intense, dreamy longing. If, with a keen eye, one studies the corresponding woman's figure in the lithograph of 1899 (cat. no. 31), the contrast is striking. Here, the woman in the pale dress is depicted flat and plain, a rather stupid cardboard figure, silent and slightly sinister. Can it be accidental that in exactly 1899 we find these two examples in which "the pale-clad one" is perverted in a negative direction?

"In comes the smiling fair-haired woman, who wishes to pluck Love's flower—but it will not be plucked—," Munch writes in connection with *The Dance of Life*.[56] The reference is to Tulla Larsen. One wonders whether the special presentation of "the pale-clad one"—as tragic or "stupid"—relates on one level to Munch's changed feelings for Tulla Larsen after the summer of 1899. It is not the same as saying that this is the picture's "actual" content. A stimulus from life shows itself in a new variation on Munch's old theme—in the everlasting interplay between life and art.

Fall and Winter 1899–1900

The strong coloring in *Red and White* is pursued further in the expressive *Red Virginia Creeper* (cat. no. 155) that I suggest is painted in late 1899.[57] The composition has a more open structure than earlier pictures, it seems loose and uncertain: "... brushstrokes now move almost at random, no longer following a structured pattern."[58] It may be a dangerous parallel to draw, but I am not the first to suggest a connection between visible stylistic characteristics on one hand and Munch's steadily more problematic life situation on the other. It does not mean that the style is a spontaneous reaction to the biography. The style is chiefly a result of the artist's deliberate search for an adequate expression.

Red Virginia Creeper is almost obtrusive in its symbolism. The picture's structure brings to mind *Jealousy* (1895). In *Jealousy*, however, the "picture within the picture" reveals the thoughts of the figure in the foreground. In *Red Virginia Creeper* the house stands as a threatening and mysterious symbol without given meaning.[59] It is reasonable to interpret the house psychologically, as the symbol of the individual and the first person. Munch's friend, the poet Sigbjørn Obstfelder, offers a "link" to a well-known theme complex: "The woman is like a garland. She is in everything; she is like a dangerous ivy. She winds herself around all men and houses."[60] The relationship with Tulla Larsen steadily became more traumatic. Munch spent the months around the turn of the century 1899–1900 at Kornhaug Sanatorium in Gausdal. Here he drew several variations of *The Empty Cross*. The subject shows the artist's role in a world where everything is doubtful. A personal level is striking. This applies equally to the painting *Golgatha* (fig. 6)—also called *The Last Hour*. Here the formal tendencies seen in *Red Virginia Creeper* have received a more deliberate and consistent application. To all appearances, the painting has been created in a spontaneous and crazed state of mind; the expression is strongly emotional. Most of the canvas is covered with thinned-out paint, creating a translucent effect, and with pronounced brushstrokes. The artist has allowed some parts to remain with an aggressive, unfinished sketch-like character with the ground visible, while selected elements have been given thicker layers of paint in strong colors. Not since *The Scream* of 1893 (cat. no. 118) has Munch been so expressionistic. It is reasonable to regard the crucified figure as representing the Artist, both personally and in general. Some of the other figures invite identification. The Kristiania Bohemians, for example, begin to play their unpleasant roles on Munch's stage.

In the spring of 1900, Munch traveled to Germany where Tulla Larsen had been waiting for him for close to five months. He exhibited at Hugo Wolfframm's gallery in Dresden. Travelling constantly, in the (repeatedly interrupted) company of Tulla Larsen, the following months see the culmination—and for the time being, the end—of the traumatic relationship. For Munch, there was little peace or concentration to paint anything of importance before his return to Norway in September, leaving a broken-hearted Tulla Larsen in Switzerland.

Fall 1900

The curious picture known as *Parisian Boulevard* (fig. 7) has caused puzzlement among researchers, and seldom has been commented upon. It is in poor condition and probably has not been exhibited during the artist's lifetime. It differs from Munch's other works, making it difficult to place chronologically, stylistically and thematically. Again, it is a case of the impact of French decorative symbolism, here in a particularly severe and intricate form. As a formal element, the broken, vertical border in the right half of the picture, in the form of a sinuous green line, has no direct parallel in Munch's work, and appears almost as a token of Art Nouveau. The formal relationship with the art of the Nabis is clearly seen if one compares it to *The Chestnut Trees* by Edouard Vuillard, a design made for stained glass paintings that were ordered by Siegfried Bing in 1894.[61]

In the right-hand part of Munch's picture sits a woman clad in black, on the far left a small figure wanders along the boulevard. The little manikin is painted with elementary brushstrokes in a cursory manner, like a calligraphic character. The picture is usually dated 1896–97.[62] After a study of other motifs, of Munch's private iconography, biography and "private mythology," I have concluded that the picture dates from the fall of 1900.[63] In theme and to a degree formally, it is akin to the etching *The Girl and the Heart* of 1896. In content it also relates *Studenterlunden*—in both pictures flowering chestnut trees form the frame around springtime's eroticism. *Parisian Boulevard* is in many ways atypical, and placed as it is in the chronology, it may be considered a regressive experiment in a period of searching and uncertainty. It is here the voice of Julius Meier-Graefe breaks in.

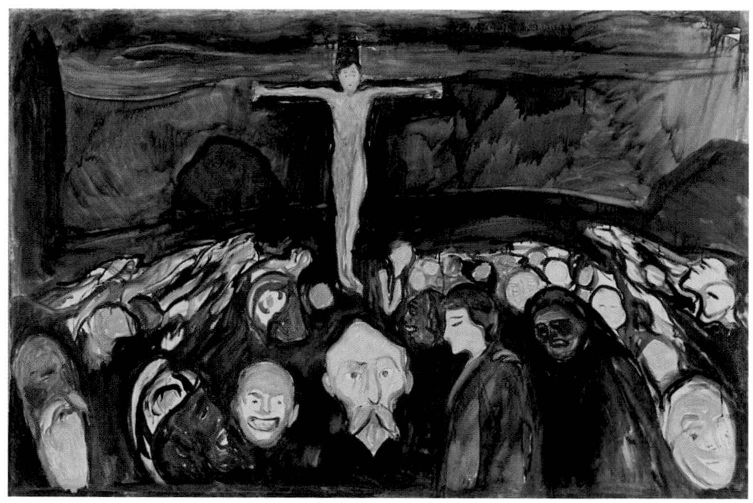

6 Edvard Munch, *Golgatha*, 1900,
oil on canvas, 80 x 120 cm, Munch-museet, Oslo

In 1895, Meier-Graefe had published a portfolio of eight Munch etchings, on his own initiative and at his own expense. During the fall of 1897, he began to prepare a large portfolio of prints entitled *Germinal*, with contributions from a number of leading *"peintres et graveurs."* He wished to include Munch, and asks him—with steadily growing urgency—to provide something he can use. The last in this series of requests is a postcard from spring 1899. Meier-Graefe begs Munch to send him immediately a graphic plate, long since paid for.[64] The card, however, is addressed to Norway and dated May 15—precisely the time at which Munch arrives in Paris from Italy. As already indicated, it is uncertain whether these two met at all in Paris that spring. In any case, Meier-Graefe did not receive a plate or a print that he could use.

In October, Munch receives a rather cool letter: "I regret that because of your negligence I have not received a lithograph from you, and now it is too late."[65] Meier-Graefe wishes compensation for his loss and asks for a drawing with specified measurements that he can publish. And, if this is not convenient, "please return my money."

If Meier-Graefe is disappointed, it is hardly less humiliating for Munch. After that bitter message, there is a hiatus in (extant) letters from Meier-Graefe. The next is dated November 1901. "Dear friend," writes Meier-Graefe, "I am glad to hear from you again and that you are feeling better," signed "your old Meier-Gr."[66] Could it be that Meier-Graefe's evaluation of Munch's art, which we will now examine more closely, comes at a time when there is a certain coolness in the friendly relations between them?

Meier-Graefe on Munch in *Die Insel* 1900

Otto Julius Bierbaum founded the Art Nouveau magazine *Die Insel* in 1899. The first three quarterly issues in the initial year (1900) contained Meier-Graefe's "Beiträge zu einer modernen Ästhetik" [Contributions to a Modern Aesthetics], the forerunner to his large *Entwicklungsgeschichte der modernen Kunst* [History of the Development of Modern Art] published in 1904.[67] In the third quarterly issue, the author presents a number of contemporary artists and gives an appraisal of their relationship to tradition and to modern endeavors. Munch is given modest space, half a page of twenty-four in all. Moreover, he receives rough treatment; Meier-Graefe points to the anarchistic in van Gogh's art, and continues:

> One finds a similar hostility with Munch, the equally sincere anarchist. However, what appears to the bourgeois to be barbarism in van Gogh, is truly so with Munch. The latter stands on a lower cultural level as an artist, his works are largely thoughts; he goes further than van Gogh in one respect; his paintings are nothing but denial, and in another respect van Gogh's level is totally alien to him, since several of his pictures refuse a purely aesthetic consideration. To us van Gogh is the more convincing; in that he does not make use of the subjectively psychological, but is a mere painter, a temperament, which in this art alone could express itself and seek expression. One should not conceal the impossibility, and undesirability, of an environment where typical paintings by Munch would be appropriate, and this circumstance from the outset reduces his significance to the utmost abstract.[68]

The article has a subtitle and a recurring theme: "The Influence of Millet." Contemporary artists are measured against the master from Barbizon. Modern art is indebted to the great masters, and, at the same time, it sheds new light on them. In his art, Constantin Meunier, for example, reveals a rarely acknowledged connec-

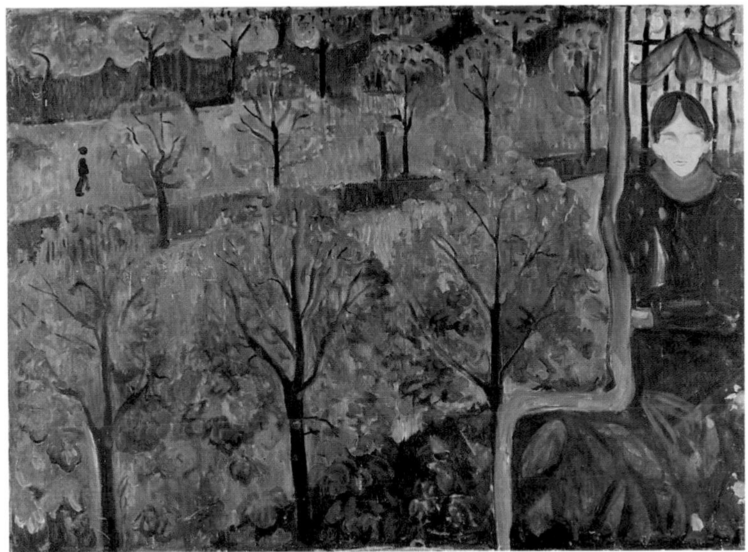

7 Edvard Munch, *Parisian Boulevard*, 1896–98 (1900), oil on canvas, 97 x 130 cm, Munch-museet, Oslo

tion between Michelangelo and Rembrandt, in that he endows his figures with dignity, as does Millet.

Fertility

"Not since Millet has peasantry been endowed with comparable attributes of dignity," writes Thomas A. Messer about Munch's painting *Fertility* (fig. 8).[69] "Am I reminded of Millet or some other Master, in any case it does not matter, it is so delightful," writes "Constance" in *Verdens Gang* in December 1900.[70]

In *Fertility* a man and a woman are placed on either side of a fruit tree, in an open and luxuriant landscape. The man is sitting, while the woman stands, holding a basket filled with red berries. The subject of the painting is usually mentioned in the same breath as *Metabolism* in the literature covering Munch's art from the turn of the century. Thematically the relationship is evident, but stylistically the distance is great. Metabolism is somber symbolism, with subdued colors and a traditional modeling of the forms. *Fertility* is an exuberant outdoor scene, carried out in fresh colors and dynamic lines. Compared to *Metabolism* it appears realistic and down to earth. When *Fertility* is dated 1898 and *Metabolism* 1899, the style development becomes incomprehensible.[71]

Commentators have been almost unanimous in perceiving *Fertility* as "a pastoral idyll"—"a song of praise to the exuberance of life and all life-giving forces," as Ingrid Langaard expresses it.[72] In the fall of 1900, Meier-Graefe dismisses Munch's art as "... nothing but negation."[73] In describing *Fertility*, Roy Boe writes: "The painting is a paean to a state of well-being, harmony and love..."[74] Why does Munch suddenly paint a "pastoral idyll" with reference to Millet, if it is not in answer to Meier-Graefe's article? Quite simply, it gives Munch's picture a *terminus postquem*. *Fertility* was Max Linde's first acquisition. He gave the picture the title *Earth's Blessing*, in the very spirit of Millet.[75] The simple greatness we see in Millet's figures "... belongs to the farmer, who knows hard work, yet has faith in its fruits," as Meier-Graefe writes.[76] Differing descriptions of Munch's picture may lead one's thoughts to Millet's *L'Angelus de soir* (1857–59), but Munch has not necessarily had a particular picture in mind. For example, in *Potato Planters* of 1861–62 (fig. 9) there are several striking parallels to *Fertility*. The flat landscape in Munch's picture falls into place as a "Barbizon landscape." The placement and proportions of the country couple are close to those of the *Potato Planters*. The similarity also extends to the couple's rustic clothes—the men's hats seem to be of the same type.

According to Meier-Graefe it is van Gogh who gathers the threads together; in him is concentrated modern painting's endeavors, while at the same time he is "elementary like Millet."[77]

Van Gogh *identifies* with his pictures, he does not speculate, and his concrete importance lies quite literally in his colors and lines.[78] "In him the strongest coloring is combined with the strongest linear expression; he crowns impressionism from Manet and its master Cézanne, and at the same time intensifies Millet."[79]

Once, while in the clinic in Copenhagen, Munch was asked who had written most knowledgeably about him; he answered without hesitation: "Julius Meier-Graefe."[80] It must have been bitter—but perhaps thought provoking and a relief?— to read his friend's critical evaluation of his art in the fall 1900. In *Fertility* Munch—in competition with van Gogh, but in his own way—has attempted an "intensification" of Millet.

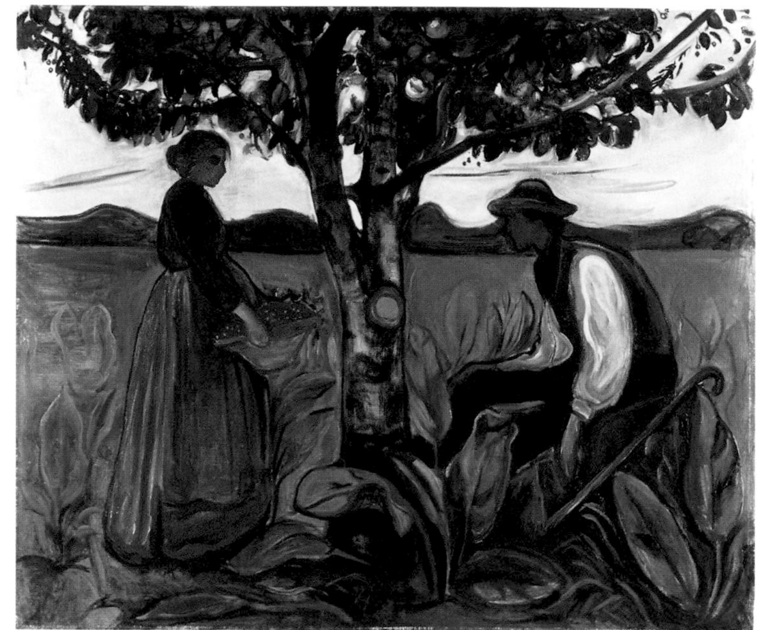

8 Edvard Munch, *Fertility*, 1898 (1900), oil on canvas, 120 x 140 cm, private collection

As a subject, *Fertility* is perhaps no less programmatic than *Metabolism*, but it expresses a different, a more extroverted attitude, it shows a new type of decorative endeavor—an endeavor that may be said to culminate in the Aula (the University Assembly Hall in Oslo) pictures, Munch's life-loving, decorative and monumental wall embellishment.

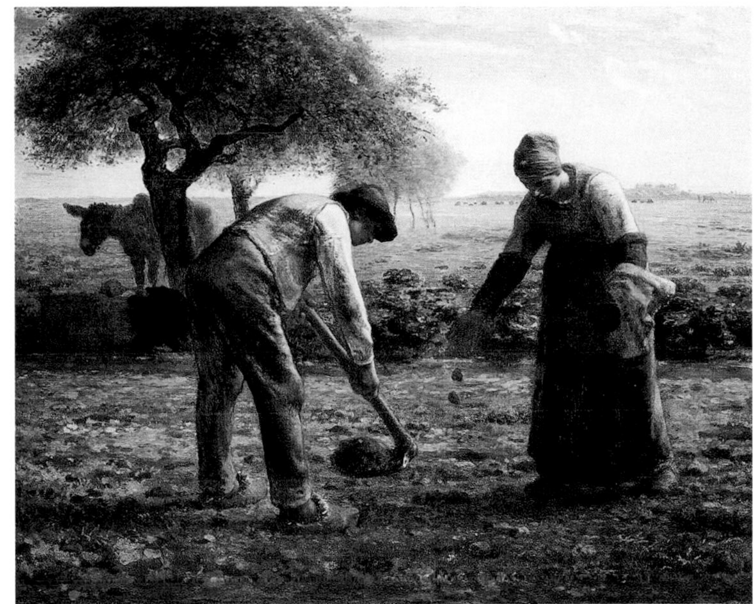

1 This period has been illuminated in Frank Høifødt, *Kvinnen, kunsten, korset. Edvard Munch anno* 1900, unpublished dissertation, University of Oslo 1995. Some relevant factors are presented by Reinhold Heller, "Malattia, arte e castità. Edvard Munch alla fine del XIX secolo," in *Edvard Munch*, exh. cat., Museo d'Arte Moderna Città di Lugano, Lugano 1998.
2 Gerd Woll, *Edvard Munch. The Complete Graphic Works*, London et al. 2001.
3 Mentioned in the draft of a letter from Munch to Meier-Graefe, dated Åsgårdstrand June 26, 1897.
4 The catalog for Munch's exhibition in the Diorama premises, Kristiania, September/October 1897, ms. in Munch-museet. See Bente Torjussen, "The Mirror," in *Symbols and Images*, Washington, 1978.
5 *Ibid.*, p. 192.
6 Letter from William Molard to Munch, dated Paris, March 7, 1898, ms. in the Munch-museet.
7 See, for example, *Edvard Munch*, exh. cat., Folkwang Museum, Essen 1987, cat. nos. 47 and 48.
8 Munch meets Tulla Larsen in August, and I have suggested that Munch has used her as a model. Naturally, the work could well have stretched into the new year, but he is soon plagued by sickness. In February/March he is hospitalized, followed by a fortnight's convalescence at his family's at Nordstrand. See thorough argumentation for the dating in Frank Høifødt, "Metabolism—the 'belt buckle' of the *Frieze*," *Kunst og Kultur*, no. 3, Oslo 2001.
9 Jens Thiis, *Edvard Munch og hans samtid*, Oslo 1933, p. 218. It concerns an exhibition at Blomqvist in 1895.
10 Gøsta Svenæus, *Stoffveksling—Im männlichen Gehirn*, Lund 1973, p. 195.
11 The title *Metabolism* evidently was used for the first time in 1914. See Høifødt 2001 (see note 8), p. 135.
12 Ingrid Langaard, *Edvard Munch. Modningsår*, Oslo 1960, p. 408.
13 Svenæus 1973 (see note 10), p. 195.
14 "*The Dance of Life* may be seen as the centerpiece in the great thematic cycle that comprises the human condition," writes Thomas A. Messer, a formulation that is frequently paraphrased, *Edvard Munch*, New York 1973, p. 144.
15 See Jan Kneher, *Edvard Munch in seinen Ausstellungen zwischen* 1892 *und* 1912, Worms 1994, p. 188 and note 10, p. 601.
16 Kenworth Moffett, *Meier-Graefe as art critic*, Munich 1973, p. 28.
17 Jens Thiis, *Edvard Munch*, Oslo 1933, p. 266.
18 Letter from Tulla Larsen (in Grez) to Munch, dated "Sunday afternoon" (May 7?), tl-B13.
19 Undated draft for a letter from Munch to Tulla Larsen, written in Florence, em-B9 and em-B8.
20 See Torjussen 1978 (see note 5), p. 193. She has mistakenly dated the quotation from the letter 1900–1901.
21 Arne Eggum, "Edvard Munch. A biographical Background," in *Edvard Munch. The Frieze of Life*, exh. cat., The National Gallery, London 1992, p. 21.
22 "E. Munch," *Dekorative Kunst, Illustrierte Zeitschrift für angewandt Kunst*, vol. 4, 1899, the article about Munch is on p. 133.
23 "Lautrec also belongs in this context, to which Munch owes a great deal; indeed, he may have had a more beneficial influence on the Norwegian than all the others." Julius Meier-Graefe, *Entwicklungsgeschichte der modernen Kunst. Vergleichende Betrachtun der bildenden Künste, als Beitrag zu einer neuen Aesthetik*, vol. I, Stuttgart 1904, p. 394.
24 Moffett 1973 (see note 16), p. 29, with note 95.
25 As a result, "E. Munch is not included in the résumé of Meier-Graefe's contributions in *Dekorative Kunst*," Moffett 1973 (see note 16), p. 186.

9 Jean François Millet, *The Potato Planters*, 1861–62, oil on canvas, 82.5 x 101.3 cm, Museum of Fine Arts, Boston, gift of Quincy A. Shaw through Quincy A. Shaw, Jr., and Marion Shaw Haughton

26 *Ibid.*, p. 38.
27 Undated letter (May 1899) from Munch to Aunt Karen, no. 194, *Edvard Munch's brev. Familien*, Oslo 1949.
28 This is shown in a letter from Tulla Larsen to Munch, dated "Friday 11." (11 August, 1899), TL-C22, ms. in Munch-museet.
29 See Gösta Svenæus, *Das Universum der Melancholi*, Lund 1968, p. 121.
30 Draft of a letter from Munch to Tulla Larsen, dated Paris May 25, 1899, em-B8, ms. in Munch-museet.
31 See letter from Tulla Larsen to Munch, dated Paris Monday morning (June 5), tl-B27, ms. in Munch-museet.
32 Milos Marten (pseudonym for M. Sebesta). His book about Munch was published in 87 numbered copies by an avant-garde publishing house. See *Edvard Munch og den tsjekkiske kunst*, exh. cat., Munch-museet, Oslo 1971, p. 14 and p. 50.
33 *Livets Dans* is dated in two places, with both 1899 and 1900. Everything, however, leads us to believe that the picture was considered finished in 1899. It was exhibited in Dresden in May 1900, and when Munch refers to it as "the large picture I painted that summer" (T2759, p. 7), it is without doubt 1899 he means. For a more extensive commentary see Høifødt 1995 (see note 1), p. 127.
34 Commented upon by Christian Geelhaar, "Gemälde," in *Edvard Munch. Sein Werk in Schweizer Sammlungen*, exh. cat., Kunstmuseum, Basel 1985. Three years before, the picture was commented upon by Arne Eggum, but without illustration, *Der Linde-Fries. Edvard Munch und sein erster deutscher Mäzen, Dr. Max Linde*, Lübeck 1982, p. 6 and p. 40. See also Frank Høifødt, "Livets dans," *Kunst og Kultur*, no. 3, 1990, p. 170.
35 Eggum 1982 (see note 34), p. 40 and p. 6.
36 "The Students' Grove which you remember, with the lovers an early summer night," letter from Munch to Andreas Aubert, dated Berlin, February 7, 1902.
37 Iris Müller-Westermann in *Munch und Deutschland*, exh. cat., Kunsthalle, Hamburg 1994, p. 269, note 1, with reference to Arne Eggum and the letter to Andreas Aubert (see note 36).
38 "Constance," "Hos Munch," *Verdens Gang*, December 11, 1900, "It is a park on a moonlit night. The chestnut blossoms shine against a black-blue sky and all the benches are filled with couples kissing."
39 To a surprising degree Munch was faithful to—or tied to—the visual basis for a subject. This also applies to the next subject to be treated, the intensely symbolic *Dance on the Shore*.
40 See letter from Tulla Larsen to Munch dated "Josefinegade Wednesday, 4 p.m." (June 21), TL-C1. Support for biographical details such as this are to be found in the already mentioned correspondence between Munch and Tulla Larsen.
41 William Ritter, "Un peintre norvégien, M. Edvard Munch," *Études d'Art étranger*, Paris 1906. Quoted from *Edvard Munch og den tsjekkiske kunst*, exh. cat., Munch-museet 1971, p. 50.
42 Georg Schmidt, "Edvard Munch II," *National-Zeitung*, no. 490, October 18, 1922. Quotation from exh. cat. Basel 1985, p. 26.
43 Shortly after the turn of the century, Munch writes about his *Leitmotif* from Åsgårdstrand, "The shorelines became life's eternally changing lines—the sea became death's dwelling." T 2704, p. 29, ms. in Munch-museet.
44 For a detailed analysis and interpretation of the subject see Høifødt 1995, (see note 1), p. 110. There I enlarge upon the special role of the woman in red.
45 Jürgen Schutze gives a thorough formal analysis of *Dance on the Shore* in *Edvard Munch*, exh. cat., Folkwang Museum Essen and Kunsthaus Zurich 1987, commentary on cat. no. 58.
46 *The Dance of Life* I, T 2392 (1898–99).
47 Helge Rode, *Dansen gaar* (*Dancing*), Copenhagen 1898, Act II, pp. 70, 71. The quotation corresponds well with the already mentioned preliminary work for the painting, T 2392.
48 Known as "fru Heiberg" in Munch's notes.—This "identification" of the participants in *The Dance of Life* was published for the first time by Iris Müller-Westermann, in *Edvard Munchs Selbstbildnisse. Widersprüche als Herausforderung*, Vienna 1989, p. 519.
49 Gösta Svenæus points to Adam and Eve in van Eycks' Ghent altarpiece as the possible model for Munch's figures Svenæus 1973 (see note 10), Lund 1973, p. 195. According to the same author, Munch said that he had Botticelli in mind when he painted *The Dance of Life*, Svenæus 1968, p. 121.
50 Inger Munch (ed.), *Edvard Munchs brev. Familien*, Oslo 1949, no. 191.
51 *Ibid.*, p. 300.
52 Tone Skedsmo, *Olaf Schous gaver til Nasjonalgalleriet*, Oslo 1987, p. 113.
53 Olaf Schou handed over the entire sum of the insurance for the picture, NOK 1,600, to Munch, as payment for *The Girls on the Pier*, the Åsgårdstrand subject from the summer of 1901, that Munch had promised Schou.
54 Letter from Tulla Larsen to Munch, dated "Josefinegade Wednesday 4 p.m." (June 21), TL-C1.—"The setting" in *Mother and Daughter* is probably just south of Munch's house, which he bought in 1898.
55 Possibly worked on the following year. See Frank Høifødt, "Edvard Munchs 'Rødt og hvitt'—1894 or 1900?," *Kunst og Kultur*, no. 2, 1998.
56 T 2759, p. 2 (1905–06?), ms. in the Munch-museet.
57 Langaard and Revold have dated the picture 1900, Gösta Svenæus 1900–1901, Reinhold Heller autumn/winter 1898 and Arne Eggum 1898–1900. My argument for dating the picture to autumn 1899 is found in Høifødt 1995 (see note 1), p. 141.
58 Reinhold Heller, *Edvard Munch. His Life and Work*, London 1984, p. 170.
59 For a detailed interpretation see Høifødt 1995 (see note 1), p. 134.
60 Quotation from a short novel, Sigbjørn Obstfelder, *Korset*, Kristiania 1896. Ivy is another word for Virginia creeper. One of Munch's own drawings, *Hageskulptur*, illustrates the connection: In the foreground a man who suffers in a woman's embrace, on the right a naked tree that is smothered by a luxuriant bush, and in the background an elegant house, its façade covered by Red Virginia creeper.
61 Claire Frèches-Thory and Ursula Perrucchi-Petri (eds.), *Die Nabis. Propheten der Moderne*, Munich 1993, p. 396.
62 Arne Eggum, *Edvard Munch. Malerier, skisser og studier*, Oslo 1983, p. 145. The most thorough analysis of the subject matter has been made by Rudolph Rapetti, "1896–1898: Pariser-boulevard," in *Munch og Frankrike*, exh. cat., Munch-museet, Oslo 1992, p. 170.
63 Høifødt 1995 (see note 1), p. 177.
64 Letter from Meier-Graefe to Munch, dated Paris, May 15, 1899, ms. in Munch-museet. See also Woll 2001 (see note 2), p. 14.
65 Postcard from Meier-Graefe to Munch, dated Paris October 15, 1899, ms. in Munch-museet.
66 Letter from Meier-Graefe to Munch, dated Paris November 26, 1901, ms. in Munch-museet.
67 See Ron Manheim, "Julius Meier-Graefe," in Heinrich Dilly (ed.), *Altmeister moderner Kunstgeschichte*, Berlin 1990, p. 98 and note 5 p. 113.
68 Julius Meier-Graefe, "Beiträge zu einer modernen Aesthetik. Der Einfluss Millets," *Die Insel*, nos. 3–4, 1st year, 1900, p. 215.
69 Thomas A. Messer, *Edvard Munch*, New York 1973, p. 155.
70 "Constance", "Hos Munch," *Verdens Gang*, 11 Dec., 1900.

71 For example Arne Eggum 1983, p. 154 and p. 157. Reinhold Heller is alone in his early dating of *Metabolism* to 1894–95, *Edvard Munch. Leben und Werk*, Munich 1993, p. 90. *Fertility* is dated 1898, p. 101. In the new large catalog of graphic works, the painting *Fertility* and the woodcut version of the subject are both dated 1900, with reference to my doctoral thesis. Woll 2001 (see note 2), p. 167.

72 Langaard 1960 (see note 12), p. 396. "If one looks more closely, one finds that it is difficult to describe the scene as a pastoral idyll" according to Svenæus 1973 (see note 10), p. 238. I concur with this divergent viewpoint, but in this article focus to a greater degree on the subject's "face value"—a general, spontaneous level.

73 Meier-Graefe associates van Gogh with Nietzsche, the great yes-man. Munch, too, develops a renewed interest in Nietzsche around the turn of the century, mainly the more dynamic and vitalistic sides of the many-sided philosopher.

74 Roy Boe, *Edvard Munch. His Life and Work from* 1880 *to* 1920, dissertation, New York University 1971, p. 255.

75 See Eggum 1982 (see note 34), p.6.

76 Meier-Graefe 1900 (see note 68), p. 208.

77 *Ibid.*, p. 208.

78 *Ibid.*, p. 216.

79 *Ibid.*, p. 207.

80 A conversation with the Danish writer Anders W. Holm, recorded by H. P. Rohde, "Edvard Munch på Klinikk I København," *Kunst og Kultur*, 1963, p. 266.

"The Age of Carmen"—Gender Relationships in the Art of Edvard Munch, 1890–1920[1]

Iris Müller-Westermann

As early as 1885, at the age of twenty-one, Munch expressed his fascination with the female gender in a letter: "Women are beautiful creatures, by the way. I think I shall paint only women from now on."[2] The relationship between men and women is indeed a central theme and a continuous thread in Munch's art.

Munch first presented scenes of erotic encounter in its various phases at *Unter den Linden* 19, an exhibition of his paintings presented in Berlin in December 1893. His *Study for a Series on "Love"* comprised six paintings, namely *The Voice*,[3] *The Kiss*, *Vampire*,[4] *Madonna*,[5] *Melancholy*[6] and *The Scream*.[7]

These paintings alone cover a broad spectrum. At first, man and woman attract one another and are joined together; the woman then leaves the man, and consequences of their separation are manifested as jealousy in *Melancholy* and despair in *The Scream*, which complete the series.

First Awakening of Feeling

A man and a woman stand facing each other, mute and motionless, in a landscape immersed in mystical green light in the painting *Eye in Eye* of 1894 (cat. no. 33). They gaze into each other's eyes, exploring the mystery of their mutual attraction. The huge, cavernous eyes seek insight into the inner world of the other. While strands of the woman's red hair reach out towards the man and bind the couple together, the tree that rises vertically between them serves as a separating element that divides the picture into the man's half, on the right, and the woman's on the left. The woman is integrated into the coloration of the landscape with the reddish house and the reddish-brown tree, but the man appears as a foreign body. If the house is interpreted as a metaphor for familiarity with the world of emotions—with nature in its broadest sense—then that world belongs to the woman, and the man is a stranger in it. His pale face already bears the signs of future agony, for which Munch's symbol is the "blood flower" or "flower of pain" that rises into the air behind him. In this painting shown in the section entitled *Seeds of Love* as part of the comprehensive presentation of the *Frieze of Life* at the Berlin Secession in 1902, Munch illustrates how thin the dividing line between attraction and angst is in sexual relationships—for the man in this case. He also describes this ambivalence in various autobiographical notes: "I stood before the mystery of woman—I gazed into an unknown world—My curiosity was awakened—What did it mean—that look I did not know—That look came from a terribly strange—and marvelous world—what did that world consist of –"[8]

In terms of iconography, the positioning of the two people on each side of the tree alludes to Adam and Eve and the theme of The Fall of Man.[9] Munch also dealt with the attraction motif in four graphic variations. In the lithograph *Attraction* II of 1896–97 (cat. no. 37), he placed the couple in the foreground of the landscape at Åsgårdstrand, which runs with its curving shoreline like a melody through the *Frieze of Life*. The tree in the painting *Eye in Eye* is replaced by a column of light produced by the full moon shining on the water. With its phallic form, the column of the moon emphasizes the erotic character of the encounter. But the shape of the column of light with the moon above it and the horizontal reflection on the horizon also call to mind the figure of the crucified Christ as Munch rendered it explicitly in the painting entitled *Golgatha* (fig. 6, p. 60) in 1900. The full moon and its reflection on the water becomes a metaphor that heralds both the promise of fulfillment and martyrdom.

From Devotion to Loss of Control

In *The Kiss*, man and woman blend together visually to form a unity. In the painted versions (cat. nos. 43, 46), Munch contrasts the intimate interior setting of the couple's kiss with the hustle-and-bustle outside the window, but in the woodcut variations, he focuses entirely on the couple (cat. nos. 49–54). The pair stands out as a monumental form against the background, and their faces merge into a single shape. Only the four hands indicate that they are two people locked in intimate embrace. In one of the woodcut versions (cat. no. 50), Munch cut lines around the couple's silhouette, creating the impression of an aura and thus heightening the sense of the unity of man and woman in the moment of mutual devotion. This fusion also appears to dissolve the identities of the man and the woman. Yet here as well, the composition suggests in the precarious balance in the form of the couple that this condition is not permanent.[10]

Munch had the painting now known as *Vampire*—entitled *Love and Pain* at the time—reproduced on the cover of the catalog as an emblem for his exhibition of the *Frieze of Life* in Berlin in 1893. Apparently, he felt that the motif expressed essential aspects of man's relationship to woman. The title *Vampire*—which appeared for the first time at Munch's exhibition in Stockholm in 1894—probably goes back to Munch's friend Stanislaw Przybyszewski:

> A broken man, and the face of a biting vampire on his neck... There is something terribly calm and passionless in this picture; an immeasurable, fatal quality of resignation. The man there rolls and rolls in abysmal depths, without will, powerless, and he is happy to be able to roll on with as little will as a stone. Yet he cannot rid himself of the vampire, cannot rid himself of the pain either, and the woman will always sit there, biting forever with a thousand adders' tongues, with a thousand poison fangs.[11]

Neither the title *Vampire* nor Przybyszewski's description does justice to the complexity of the painting. There is something menacing in the way the woman's red hair entwines the man like the arms of an octopus, as if to consume him. Yet the woman is tenderly affectionate and protects the man at the same time. This ambivalence in the woman's image is heightened by the shadow, which joins the couple at the formal level, emphasizing its unity and intimacy, but also looms behind them as a dark threat.

Munch's depiction of a red-headed woman in the painting is interesting in itself. In the literature and visual art of the nineteenth century, the woman with red hair embodies the image of the dangerous female who causes suffering, the vamp who destroys men.[12] Yet instead of employing that image as a simple stereotype of femininity, Munch also attributes qualities of warmth and compassion to the woman. This enables him to expose the more subtle aspects of devotion in sexual relationships.

The women in Munch's paintings assume the active role, while the men are passively submissive. Whether the woman kisses the man on the neck or bites and destroys him is beyond his control. The man's yearning for affection, intimacy, and fusion reaches its limit in his fear of losing control, a loss he experiences himself in his submitting to the woman's attraction. Thus in the erotic encounter, she appears to be the stronger of the two, to have power over the man. Precursors of the *Vampire* motif clearly show that Munch was there emphasizing only one of many aspects of the relationship between the genders at the time.[13] Munch himself never took the one-sided view of the motif described and interpreted by Przybyszewski. In the painted version of *Vampire*, Munch succeeded for the first time in expressing the duality of man's relationship to woman—longing to abandon oneself to love, on the one hand, and fear of losing control, on the other. He described these conflicting emotions in a diary entry: "And he laid his head on her breast—he felt the blood pulsing through her veins—he listened to the beat of her heart—He buried his face in her lap and felt two burning lips on his neck—a shiver shook his body—an icy feeling of ecstatic desire—and he pressed her to his body convulsively."[14] In his treatment of the relationship between devotion and vulnerability, longing and fear, Munch probes new dimensions in the visual representation of relations between men and women. He describes emotional reactions rather than external actions.

Women in the Bohemian Community

During this period, which witnessed the first stirrings of a women's movement in Europe, gender relations were a focus of considerable discussion. It was also one of the most important topics of discussion among the bohemians in Kristiania, with whom Munch was involved in the 1880s. Hans Jæger, the leading figure in this bohemian circle, had questioned the foundations of prevailing social norms, Christian doctrine, morals, and the dominant concepts of law, by pointing out the relationship between prostitution and the prevailing double standard of bourgeois morality, which demanded that women retain chastity before marriage but tolerated brothels for men at the same time. Jæger advocated free love between men and women and the liberation of sexuality from the bonds of matrimony.

While freedom for the individual and liberation from social constraints occupied the foreground of a debate regarding gender relations in Kristiania, the discussion within the bohemian circle Zum Schwarzen Ferkel in Berlin revolved around the life-determining power of the sexual drive and sexuality as a universally destructive force. In 1893, Munch's friend, the Polish writer Stanislaw Przybyszewski, opened his novel *Totenmesse* [Mass for the Dead] with the lines "In the beginning was sex. Nothing else—everything subsumed within it. ... Sex is the basic substance of life, the stuff of development, the innermost essence of individuality. Sex is the eternally creating, the rebuilding-destroying force."[15]

Munch's pictures relate to the experiences of men with women seeking to redefine their roles. The painter Oda Krohg was one of the few women in the bohemian community in Kristiania. She was attractive, self-assured, emancipated, and hopelessly disgraced within the bourgeois society from which she came due to her "scandalous lifestyle." In the watercolor drawing *Kristiania Bohemians* II of 1895 (cat. no. 195), Munch depicts Oda Krohg in a red dress standing confidently at the end of a table around which all of her lovers are gathered. Gunnar Heiberg, Jappe Nilssen, Hans Jæger, and the cuckolded latest husband Christian Krohg, are there, but her former husband is present as well. The bowl of fruit in front of her lap underscores her erotic aura.

It was the music student Dagny Juel who turned the heads of all the men of the Zum Schwarzen Ferkel circle. Introduced to the group by Munch in the spring of 1893, she succeeded almost immediately in sowing such confusion among the men that jealous intrigues developed, eventually leading to the dissolution of the

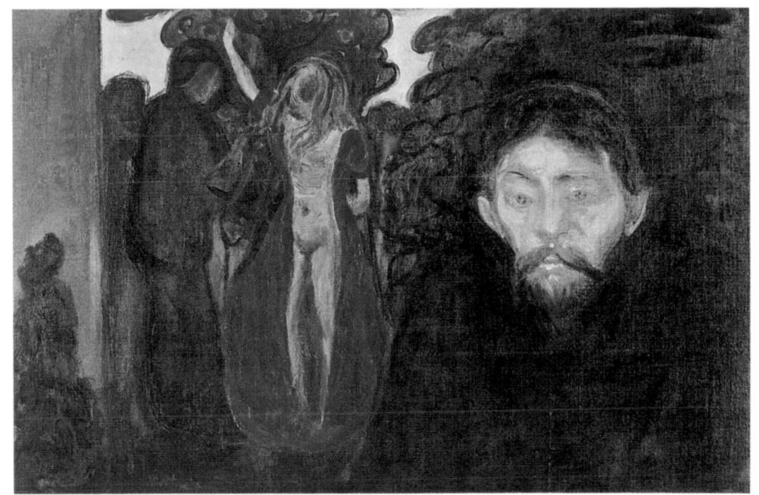

group (fig. 1). Munch painted the portrait of *Dagny Juel* in 1893 (cat. no. 185), shortly after she joined Zum Schwarzen Ferkel circle and before she married his friend Stanislaw Przybyszewski in September.

Intent upon liberating themselves from the old rules of behavior, Oda Krohg and Dagny Juel were prototypes of the modern woman. They and others of similar persuasion helped expose as a lie the popular notion that women have no sex drive. Although they received intellectual support from their male fellow bohemians, Munch's pictures clearly reveal the changes that affected men's roles when women emancipated themselves and chose their own lovers.

Stereotypes of Femininity

We regularly encounter three types of women in Munch's art: the sensual woman, who presents herself red-haired and nude to the viewer in the painting *The Woman (Sphinx)* (fig. 2); the innocent woman dressed in white and shown gazing longingly at the sea in the same painting; and the third, the grieving woman dressed in black. "Woman, in all her diversity, is a mystery to a man," Munch wrote, "Woman, saint—whore and unhappy devotee in one."[16]

Munch explained *The Woman (Sphinx)* to Henrik Ibsen during an exhibition: "They are the woman who dreams—the sensual woman—and the woman as a nun."[17] He painted over the woman dressed in black in the painting entitled *Red and White* (cat. no. 30),

1 Edvard Munch, *Jealousy*, 1895,
oil on canvas, 67 x 100 cm,
Rasmus Meyers Samlinger, Bergen Kunstmuseum

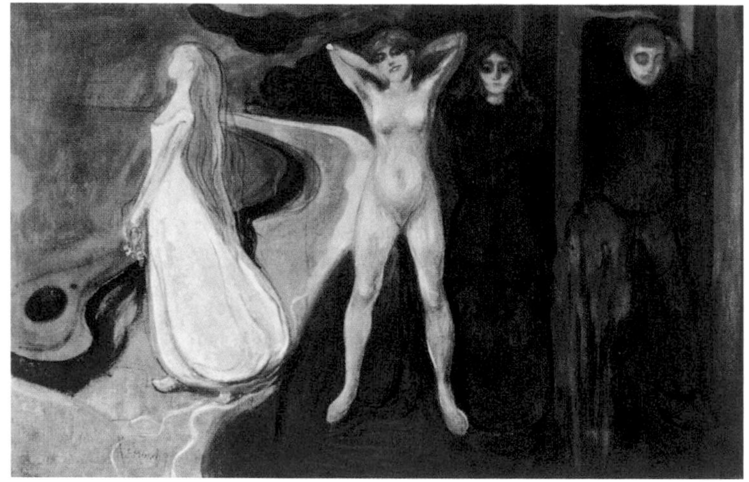

leaving the sensual woman in the red dress to lure the man and the woman in white facing the sea.

Women were commonly classified into two groups—virgins and whores, good women and bad—in the waning years of the nineteenth century. The symbolists used a wide range of female figures belonging to one or the other of these categories in their pictures—Venus, Salome, Delilah, Judith, Mary, and Eve, to name only a few examples. The categorization of women as innocent or sinful enabled men to retain control over "woman as a mystery" in every conceivable situation and to classify a given woman accordingly with respect to his own desires and purposes.

Although Munch employed these stereotypes of femininity as well, we encounter men in his pictures who no longer have and can no longer gain control over these women. Not only does the woman leave the man in such paintings as *Separation* (cat. no. 40), it is the blonde, innocent woman dressed in white who parts from the man, leaving him behind, slumped and clutching at his heart with a hand outlined in blood-red, his only support the tree on his left. The strands of her long, blonde hair, which, like invisible threads, wind themselves around the neck of the abandoned male, are his only remaining connection to her; and as a symbol of his broken heart, the "flower of pain" rises from the ground in front of him like a crimson bush.

Woman's hair is a recurring motif in Munch's art, a symbol of female strength and power and a symbol of the invisible vital link between man and woman.

None of the obsolete stereotypes is valid in the world of Munch's art. He developed an image of the man plagued by insecurity in the erotic encounter with a woman. His treatment of the diverse psychological consequences of the relationship between the genders introduced a new theme to visual art.

Metabolism: Man and Woman in the Cycle of Life

In *Jealousy*, for example, the sensual, alluring, and thus also dangerous woman appears as a descendant of Eve, yet she also has a counterpart in *Madonna*, the image of the expecting mother. *Madonna*, or *Loving Woman* (cat. no. 19), as it was also entitled, presents a woman at the moment of conception. Munch provides the following description in *Kunskabens træ på godt og ondt*:

The interlude in which the whole world comes to a stop
Your face contains all the earthly beauty there is
Your lips crimson like the coming fruit
Slide apart in pain
The smile of a corpse
At this moment life extends its hand to death
The chain is forged that binds the thousand dead generations to the thousand yet to come.[18]

In the lithograph version of *Madonna* (cat. no. 23), the concept of the cycle of life is symbolized by the small fetus and the spermatozoa along the edges of the print. In the fulfillment of her natural function of reproducing life, the woman does not appear menacing but saintly. Thus *Madonna* represents a "beatification of the sex act,"[19] since it becomes part of a larger context through the conception of new life. No longer merely a vehicle of pure sexual pleasure, it serves a useful purpose. By ensuring the survival of the species over generations, woman is linked with both immortality and death. This makes her a symbol of all of the uncontrollable forces of life in the eyes of men.

2 Edvard Munch, *The Woman (Sphinx)*, 1894,
oil on canvas, 164 x 250 cm,
Rasmus Meyers Samlinger, Bergen Kunstmuseum

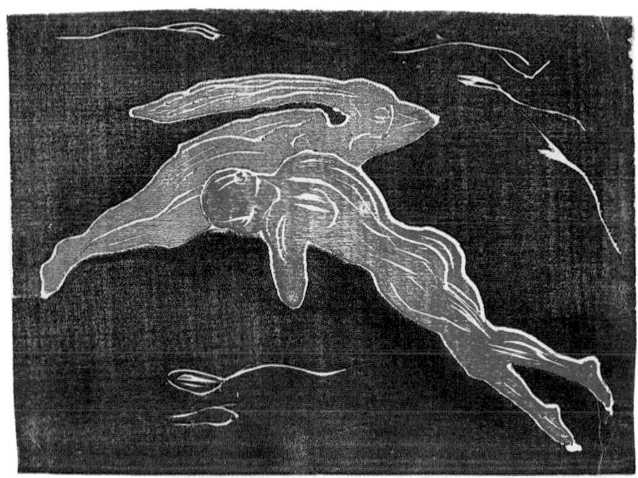

In *Metabolism* (fig. 1, p. 53), a painting that is to the *Frieze of Life* "as the buckle is to the belt," Munch places the fate of the individual, as in *The Voice, The Kiss, Melancholy,* and *Jealousy,* within a broader context. As the tree draws its nourishment from the skulls decomposing in the earth, the present Adam and the present Eve have grown forth from the dead of the preceding generation. Entering the image of the golden silhouette of the new Jerusalem at the upper edge of the painting, Munch introduces the vision of a state of heavenly bliss that follows the agonies of life on earth, combining past, present, and future in this painting. He compares human destiny with the movements of the stars (fig. 3): "Like a star that ascends from the darkness—and encounters another star—and shines brightly for a moment before disappearing into the darkness—so do man and woman meet—rising together, shining forth in flames of love—only to disappear in different directions ..."[20] And despite all the uncertainty about the meaning and purpose of human existence, the interrelationships of life-determining forces are made accessible to the human being only through the individual experiences that comprise the theme of the *Frieze of Life*.

Yet there is no harmony between the genders in Munch's world of images. Men remain immobilized, caught between longing for intimacy and fear of closeness. That the painter was well aware of his own historical position is clearly suggested by a diary entry made in 1929:

I have lived in an age of transition

in the midst of the emancipation of women

Then it was the woman who seduced and lured and betrayed the man—

The age of Carmen—

In the age of transition, man became the weaker sex.[21]

The Inferno Crisis, 1902–08

On the Operating Table

The period from 1902 to 1908 witnessed Munch's long-awaited breakthrough as an artist in Germany, but those same years were also marked by increasingly severe mental crisis, which culminated in complete physical collapse in October 1908. Munch continued to struggle with the traumatic end of his complicated love affair with Tulla Larsen, which lasted from 1898 to 1902, until 1908. He mercilessly expressed his hate and his powerlessness in paintings, notes, and letters.

The relationship with the wine merchant's daughter from Kristiania came to a dramatic end in the fall of 1902 in a dispute at Munch's house in Åsgårdstrand. The conflict was the product of the lovers' different expectations with regard to their future life together. Tulla Larsen wanted to marry. Munch did not, preferring to maintain his independence as an artist. As Tulla Larsen had threatened to commit suicide, the decision to end the relation-

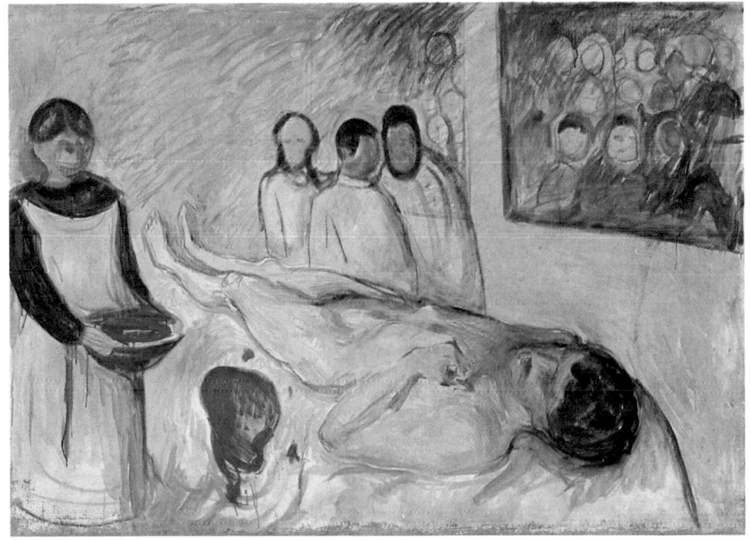

3 Edvard Munch, *Encounter in Space*, 1898–99, color woodcut on paper, 19.9 x 25.2 cm, Munch-museet, Oslo

4 Edvard Munch, *On the Operating Table*, 1902–03, oil on canvas, 109 x 149 cm, Munch-museet, Oslo

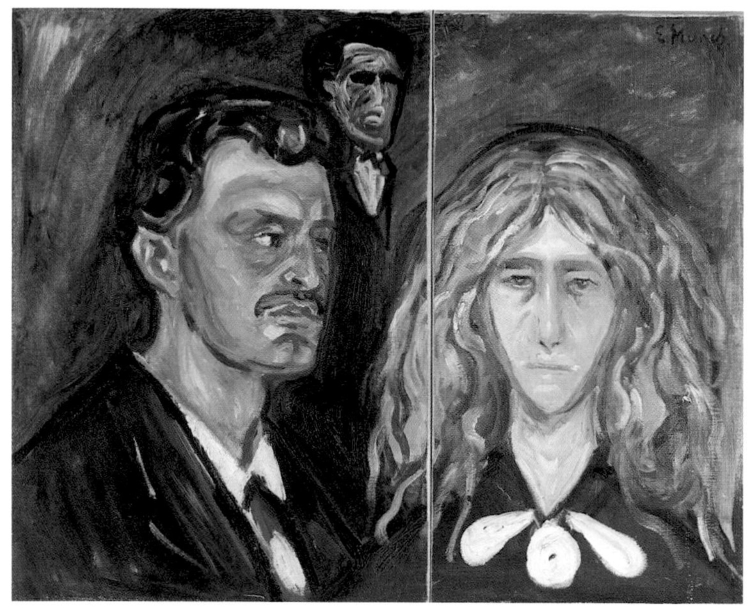

ship was a difficult one for Munch, who had been raised in a religious family. The best solution would have been for her to leave him.[22] Munch appears to have seen no way of resolving the dilemma. During this last encounter, he shot himself with a revolver in the left hand—"in a state of distress," as he later described it. The bullet remained lodged in his middle finger and had to be removed at a hospital. Cut off at the last knuckle, the finger remained as a reminder throughout his life of his desperate attempt to escape from a seemingly hopeless situation.

Munch dealt directly with the subject of the gunshot wound in *On the Operating Table* (fig. 4), a painting in which he employed the historical motif of the *Theatrum anatomicum*.[23] The nude body of the artist lies stretched out on a bed on a diagonal across the pictorial surface. His left hand lies clenched into a fist above his heart. A huge "red blood spot" on the sheet in the extreme foreground calls attention to the wound.[24] The nurse on the left faces the viewer, holding a bowl of blood, while the three physicians on the other side of the bed appear to be discussing, rather than treating, their patient. Curious students observe the scene from behind a pane of glass.

On the Operating Table is not an objective depiction of the surgical procedure. There is no need for a patient to undress entirely to have a bullet removed from his finger. Indeed, the sense of drama evoked by the scene stands in stark contrast to the actual severity of the injury.

In this painting, Munch condensed the experience into an image of his personal and artistic situation as he perceived it at the time.[25] In the spring of 1902, he had exhibited the *Frieze of Life*, his most important work from the 1890s, in its full breadth in a presentation comprising twenty-two paintings. He had also met Albert Kollmann, the Lübeck ophthalmologist Dr. Max Linde, and Gustav Schiefler, Director of the Regional Court—all patrons who committed themselves tireless to promoting Munch's art through purchases and commissions. All in all, the year 1902 appeared to herald the artistic breakthrough Munch had worked so hard to achieve for so many years.[26] But the shooting incident at the end of his summer stay in Norway completely destroyed his already precarious emotional and psychological balance. What made matters even worse was the negative response to Blomqvist's extensive exhibition of his most recent works in Kristiania, which clashed painfully with the positive reception of his art in Germany.[27]

The exposure of the nude, unprotected, wounded artist to the curious gazes of a crowd of spectators while those responsible for caring for him neglect their duty became for Munch a metaphor for the ridicule and rejection to which his art—itself an extreme form of self-revelation—was subjected in Norway.

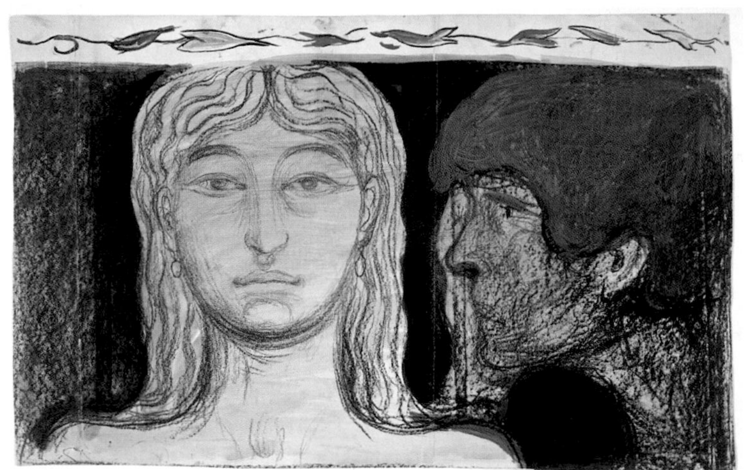

5 Edvard Munch, *Self-Portrait with Tulla Larsen*, c. 1905, oil on canvas, 64 x 45.5 cm, Munch-museet, Oslo

6 Edvard Munch, *The Woman (Sphinx)*, 1896, hand-colored lithograph on paper, 47, 2 x 35.5 cm, Munch-museet, Oslo

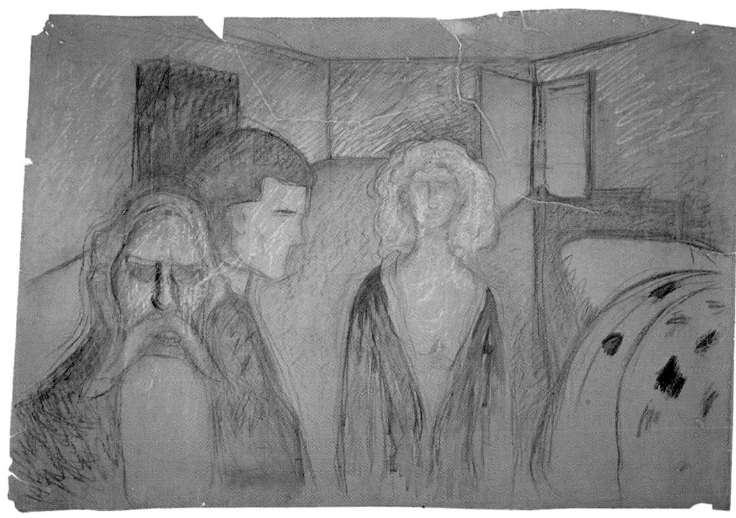

Moreover, he felt personally betrayed by those among his friends who sided with Tulla Larsen following the shooting incident. She herself married his young fellow-artist Arne Kavli only shortly afterward. In Munch's disturbed state of mind, he fantasized that the whole episode had been planned by these "supposed friends" as a way of destroying him. In the manner of a public accusation, Munch exhibited the painting *On the Operating Table* at Blomqvist's gallery in his home city of Kristiania in September 1903.[28]

The Man and the Artist as the Victim of Demoniacal Femininity

Another very interesting attempt to come to grips with his experience with Tulla Larsen is found in a self-portrait with her of 1905 (fig. 5). While his head appears as a straight portrait, the figure of Tulla Larsen, with her greenish-white, stony face and her flaming red hair, has the look of a caricature. Like the male figure that seems to grow from Munch's shoulder as a kind of alter ego, she appears as a creation of the artist's imagination.[29] Peter Krieger characterizes this fantastical apparition as "a demon of destruction."[30] The contrasting gradations of orange and green intensify the fundamental undertone of disharmony, while the green background evokes a ghostly atmosphere and exposes the figures, rather than binding them into a context.

In portraits of couples since the Renaissance, the man is often shown gazing out of the picture, while the woman faces the man, the focus of her attention.[31] Here, however, it is clearly evident that these traditional role assignments have lost their meaning for Munch.

In this double portrait, Munch employed a visual formula he had developed ten years before in the lithograph entitled *The Woman (Sphinx)* as a means of expressing the enigma of woman (fig. 6). In that work, the man depicted in profile stares at the woman, who faces the viewer, in the hope of discovering her secret.

The woman in *Self-Portrait with Tulla Larsen* (fig. 5), however, is no longer mysterious and puzzling but downright dangerous. She appears to be the cause of a kind of schizophrenic split in Munch's personality, as represented by the ghostly, green shadow-being next to him, which apparently emerges from his own body.[32]

Self-Portrait with Tulla Larsen may be interpreted as an attempt to come to grips with her at the personal level through the medium of the painting. Yet the victim-perpetrator relationship is not as clear-cut here as Munch's written notes would suggest. Tulla's frozen, masklike facial features show that she has lost all vitality and is thus in her own way a victim of the situation described, in

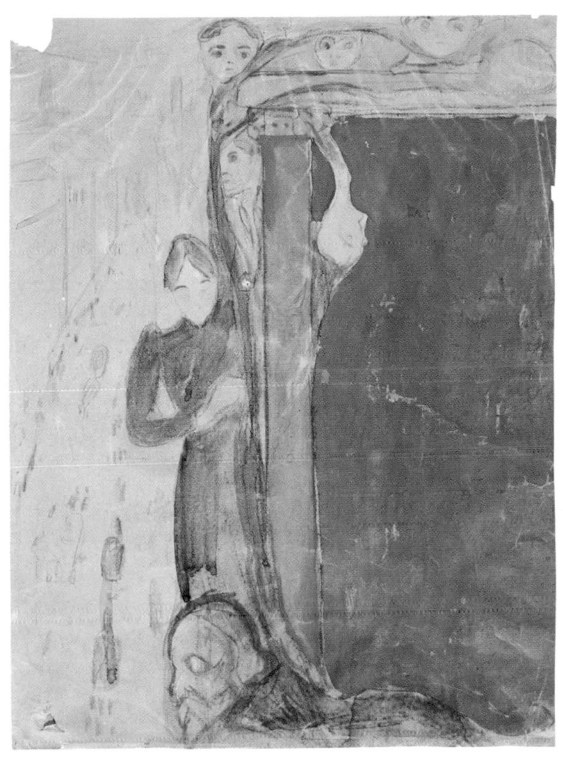

7 Edvard Munch, A *Woman and Two Men in an Interior*, c. 1905, charcoal, pastel, watercolor on paper, 108 x 151 cm, Munch-museet, Oslo

8 Edvard Munch, *Family Tree*, 1894–95, charcoal, watercolor on paper, 63.1 x 47.2 cm, Munch-museet, Oslo

which she does not appear actively involved—in contrast to Munch, who evokes the impression of a strong-willed, vigorous man with strength enough to defeat this "demon Tulla Larsen."

After completing *Self-Portrait with Tulla Larsen*, Munch cut the painting apart, separating Tulla's portrait from his own. This appears to have been a symbolic act of liberation, a ritual re-enactment of his separation from Tulla Larsen with which he severed all ties irrevocably.[33]

There is a drawing at the Munch-museet that traces its source to the double portrait with Tulla Larsen (fig. 7). Here, however, Munch focused on a different, highly revealing aspect. A woman resembling Tulla Larsen and an older, bearded man—a stylized image of Munch's father (fig. 8),[34]—are shown standing in a room face to face. The two figures appear as antipodes, unconnected by contact of any kind. Each dominates one-half of the picture: Tulla Larsen on the right near the bed with its covers pulled down; the father on the left next to the cupboard. Munch's body, with his head rendered in profile, emerges from the figure of the father and turns towards Tulla Larsen, whose breast is bared. The large format of this drawing (108 x 151 cm) suggests that Munch may have toyed with the idea of doing a painted version of the motif.

In this picture, Tulla Larsen personifies the bohemian community and its ideals of free love, while the father represents family origins and traditional values, for which the cupboard as a place to store valuables serves as a metaphor. Although father and son turn their heads in different directions, Munch is unable to entirely abandon the values his father represents and remains fused with his figure even as he turns his attention to the new—Tulla Larsen and free love. He himself commented upon the pain he caused his father during the 1880s through his contacts with the Kristiania bohemians: "How he suffered because of me—nightly—and my lifestyle—because I could not share his faith."[35]

Munch also described the difference between his and Tulla Larsen's philosophies of life: "You have the gospel of a life of enjoyment—I that of pain."[36] Yet it is clear that there was no convenient either/or solution for the artist; indeed, conflict and ambivalence were the status quo for a restless soul in times of transition.

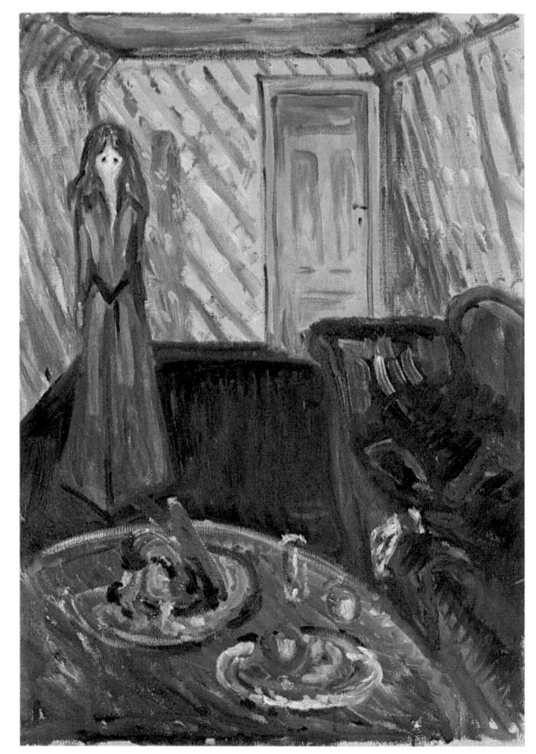

9 Edvard Munch, *The Murderess*, 1907,
oil on canvas, 88 x 62 cm, Munch-museet, Oslo

Peak of the Inferno Crisis and Collapse

The Green Room

In 1907, Munch did a series of paintings in Warnemünde devoted to the battle of the sexes. He called it *The Green Room*. In part, he employed motifs from the *Frieze of Life* in these works, although all of the scenes are set in a small room with green wallpaper and a low ceiling. His brushwork here is rapid, spontaneous, and aggressive, and he often applied paint directly from the tube.[37]

In *Jealousy* I (cat. no. 77), we see a man with a green face sitting at a table in the extreme foreground. His stony gaze is directed forward. A woman is seen kissing another man in the background. Is this the scene the protagonist sees in his mind's eye, the cause of his jealousy?

In *The Murderess* (fig. 9), a woman stands rigidly, as if rooted in the floor, facing the viewer in the room. She has a cold-blooded, remorseless look. All we see of the victim is the body stretched out on the sofa on the right and a limply hanging, bleeding hand. His head is cut off by the edge of the painting.

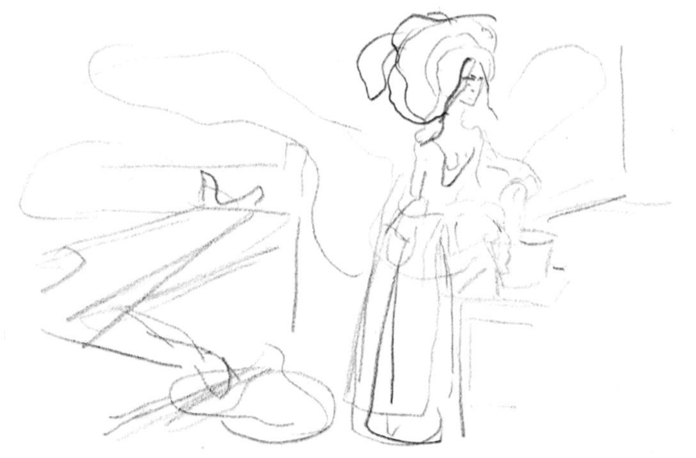

Munch dealt with the motif of the murder of a man by a woman in several different versions in 1906–07, works he entitled *Murder, Still Life (The Murderess)*, and *The Death of Marat*. In addition to the paintings, he also devoted a lithograph and a number of drawings to the same theme.

By that time, Munch had already begun work on stage-sets and scene designs for performances of Ibsen's *Ghosts* and *Hedda Gabler* at Max Reinhardt's Kammerspiele in Berlin. The similarity between Hedda Gabler and Tulla Larsen and the woman in *The Death of Marat* series is not coincidental. In the figure of Hedda Gabler, who causes Ejlert Lövborg to shoot himself to death, Munch saw a direct parallel to Tulla Larsen, who had caused him—Munch—to shoot himself in the finger.

Munch had also seen a performance of Hebbel's *Judith* at the Hamburger Schauspielhaus the year before and written the following note: "Judith by Hebbel—He is killed by the woman—interesting—Ibsen learned from him." [38]

In one of the many literary fragments Munch wrote on the subject of the shooting incident, he described the moments immediately following the shot: "I heard nothing I lay on the bed half anaesthetized I bled—the air smelled of gunpowder—She went about the room and washed the blood from the floor—I was overcome with anger—You monster—You abominable creature—are letting me bleed to death go and fetch the doctor at least."[39]

A chalk drawing (fig. 10) shows Tulla rinsing out the rag she had used to wipe the blood from the floor instead of—by Munch's account—attending to the injured man and calling a doctor.[40] The scene shows her with her head raised and a visionary expression on her face, as two shadows alight on her shoulders like wings, giving her the appearance of an angel of death. Cut off by the edge of the picture, the missing head of the man and a huge pool of blood beneath his outstretched hand convey an unmistakable message—that the injured man is already dead.

In the spring of 1907, Munch began work on a large-format version of this theme, which he entitled *Marat's Death* or *The Death of Marat* (fig. 11).[41] Although he used models for the figures,[42] it is impossible to overlook their resemblance to Tulla Larsen and himself. The basis for composition of the painting was derived from *On the Operating Table* and *Still Life (The Murderess)*, but here, he depicts both the man and the woman nude.[43] In this way, he strips the figures of all protective covering and exposes them mercilessly to the viewer's gaze. The staging in this picture, which confronts us frontally with Tulla Larsen, makes the viewer the judge of the depicted crime. Whereas the clenched fist in the self-portrait *On the Operating Table* signifies the will to live, there is no such sign in this work. The man has spread his arms and calls to mind the image of Christ after his removal from the cross.

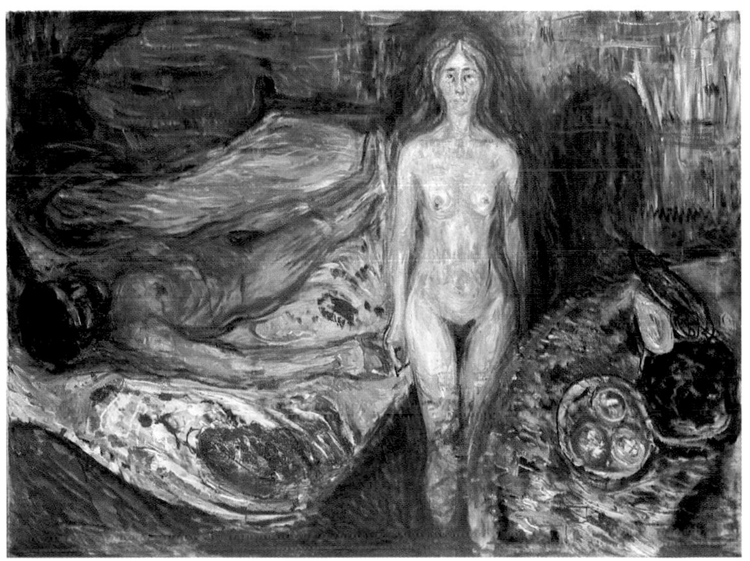

10 Edvard Munch, Study for *The Death of Marat*, c. 1906, pencil on paper, 13.8 x 22.4 cm, Munch-museet, Oslo

11 Edvard Munch, *The Death of Marat*, 1907, oil on canvas, 150 x 200 cm, Munch-museet, Oslo

While Munch strictly avoided any physical contact between the man and the woman in the earlier versions, he now joins his right arm and his body with her right arm to form a triangle. Although the touch of their hands almost suggests a hint of tenderness, the triangle—the space the man and the woman create through their encounter—is filled with blood as a metaphor of destruction. Munch confronts the yearning for intimacy between man and woman with its own futility. The large spot of blood on the sheet is evidence enough that intimacy leads only to destruction and suffering.

By covering the pictorial space with a fabric of long, horizontal brushstrokes and dabs of red paint, the artist creates a spatial mood that evokes the sense of an atmosphere of tension, in which the tension is visually present in the air. However, the characterization of victim and perpetrator is much less one-sided here. Despite her upright posture and unrelenting rigidity, she is imbued with a certain quality of vulnerability by the large shadow behind her and the coloration, while the colors used to depict the man also make him look more vital and alive than she.

Munch's title, *The Death of Marat*, calls to mind the murder of the French revolutionary Jean Paul Marat by Charlotte Corday in 1793. But Munch was not interested in either the political background or the details of the crime. Under the pretense of seeking to expose a plot against him, Corday, the counter-revolutionary, obtained an audience with Marat. Plagued by a skin disorder, Marat received her lying in his bathtub, where she stabbed him to death. Probably the best-known memorial to the fallen revolutionary is Jacques Louis David's painting *The Murdered Marat*.[44] Apparently, Munch regarded the fact that a woman had destroyed a man's life as the essential parallel in the story. Although his choice of the Marat motif was prompted by his own personal experience, Munch transcends the personal sphere in this work.[45]

In October 1908, Munch suffered a total nervous breakdown. After spending a number of months at the mental hospital run by Professor Jacobson in Copenhagen, he moved back to Norway in 1909, where he lived a healthy life in retreat and abstinence from drugs.

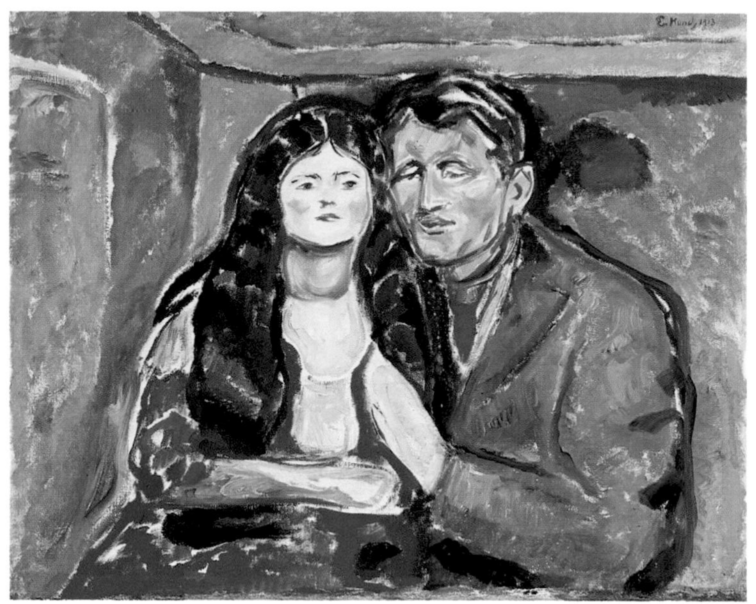

12 Edvard Munch, *The Seducer* I, 1913, oil on canvas, 80 x 99 cm, Munch-museet, Oslo

Renewed Interest in the Opposite Sex

The Seducer and *Beneath Red Apples. Man and Woman in the Garden*

In 1910, Munch purchased *Nedre Ramme*, an idyllic estate to the east of the Kristiania Fjord, north of Hvitsten. It was not long before seventeen-year-old Ingeborg Kaurin from the town of Moss became his model.[46] With her youthful freshness, her spontaneity, and her ample female attributes, she introduced an entirely new type of woman to his art. She was neither the dangerous woman who destroys men nor the embodiment of innocence. The Ingeborg Kaurin in his paintings is a genuine living being made of flesh and blood.

During the periods in which she posed as his model, Ingeborg also worked as his housekeeper. Munch depicted her washing herself in the garden and painted her both as a reclining and a weeping nude. He also painted a new version of *Madonna* using her as a model—a worldly Madonna, a real human being. She also inspired the artist to do two self-portraits.

In the double portrait entitled *The Seducer* I (fig. 12), Munch and his model are shown sitting next to one another. The artist is pressed so closely to the girl with the soft facial features that their heads touch. His left hand is placed gently on her breast, both of their arms form an interlocking horizontal configuration and fuse the couple into a unit around which the low, boxlike stage setting encloses them like a protective cave. Unlike the low-ceilinged rooms in *The Green Room* series of 1907, this space no longer seems threatening. Munch's painting technique and coloration also show a new freshness and spontaneity, to which Munch may have been inspired by the works of the expressionists shown at the *Sonderbund-Ausstellung* in Cologne in 1912.[47]

In this frontal presentation, in which the viewer and the mirror become one, Munch once again offers his relationship to woman as an issue for discussion. A harmonious relationship between man and woman is obviously only an expression of longing in this case. Though Munch and his model are close to one another, a sense of distance predominates. She gazes dreamily outward, while he listens to his inner self.

The painting was presented under the title *The Seducer* at its very first showing at Gurlitt's gallery in Berlin in February 1914.[48] But one is prompted to ask who actually seduces whom in this scene. The artist depicts himself as rather more sensitive and hesitant, qualities one does not immediately associate with a seducer. Is the title perhaps ironic? Or is life itself the seductress the fifty-year-old artist now encounters anew in the form of a young woman?

Numerous sketches, drawings, and graphic works related to *Seducer* bear witness to the intensity with which Munch, inspired by his encounter with Ingeborg Kaurin, took up the theme of erotic love once again. They also give an impression of the breadth of the spectrum within which Munch visualized his different scenes of encounter between man and woman.

The other self-portrait with Ingeborg Kaurin is entitled *Beneath Red Apples*,[49] a painting also known as *Man and Woman in the Garden* I and *Adam and Eve* (fig. 13). The Adam-and-Eve motif can be traced back in Munch's art to the early 1890s. *Eye in Eye* of 1893 (cat. no. 33) and *Jealousy* of 1895 (fig. 1) both have origins in those years. Towards the end of the 1890s, the Adam-and-Eve motif in the large-format painting *Metabolism* (fig. 1, p. 53) became a central linking element in the *Frieze of Life*. Such paintings as *Earth's Blessing* (*Fertility*) of 1898 (fig. 8, S. 62) and *Adam and Eve* of 1908 are also contemporary renditions of this Christian motif.[50]

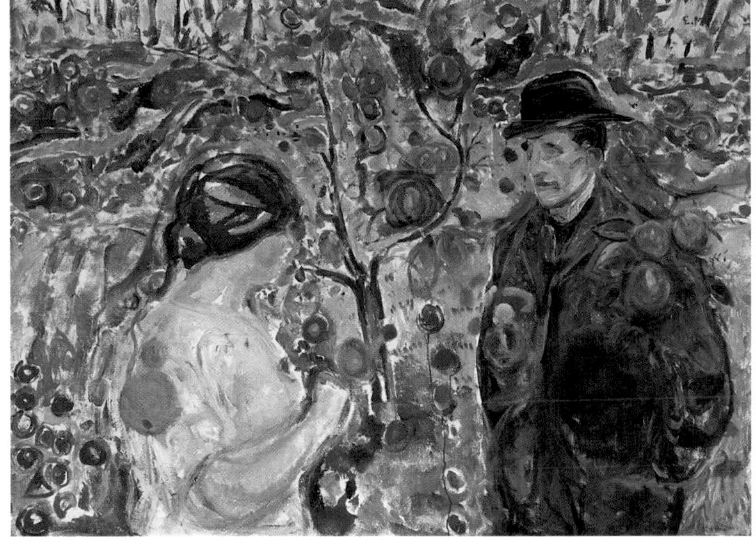

In the vividly colorful double portrait of 1913–14, Ingeborg Kaurin and Munch stand facing each other in the artist's garden, which is covered with ripe apples. The apple tree between the two both joins and separates them. Ingeborg, in her light-colored dress, with bare arms and a face that looks like one of those plump, shiny apples, merges and becomes one with her natural surroundings. Munch stands opposite this personification of fertility as an elderly gentleman in a coat and hat. Rather than extending his hands to touch her, he keeps them hidden in his pockets. Although he looks at the young women in fascination, he makes no effort to approach her, remaining instead an admirer from a distance. Amidst the fertile splendor of nature, Munch is an observer and not a participant. A huge, round spot on the left side of his chest alludes perhaps to old wounds and to the price he has paid for his encounters with the opposite sex.

This is the first work in which Munch introduced the aspect of aging in his depictions of relationships between men and women. Here, we see a man fifty years of age in the presence of a woman thirty years younger. In the *Seducer*, Munch seeks to come closer to the young woman; in *Man and Woman in the Garden* I, the distance between them is too great.

13 Edvard Munch, *Beneath Red Apples* (*Man and Woman in the Garden* I), 1913–15, 109 x 133 cm, oil on canvas, Munch-museet, Oslo

Man and Woman—An Old Theme in a New Light

Artist and Model

Munch once again approached the theme of gender relationships in a series of paintings entitled *Artist and Model* in the late second and early third decades of the twentieth century.[51] Although the subject is an art-historical topos in which the artist reflects upon his relationship to the model within the context of their work—which is not to say that sexual tensions did not come to the surface[52]—what Munch examines here is not the painter-model relationship. These works are concerned with the relationship between a man and a woman in various constellations, and the scene of these encounters is the artist's bedroom in Ekely.[53]

Annie Fjeldbu,[54] who served as Munch's model from 1919 to 1923, is his female counterpart in these works. In *Artist and Model* I (fig. 14), Munch depicts himself and his model facing the viewer. Props in the picture include the unmade bed with the hanging blanket on the right and a round table with a yellowish-blue glazed vase on the left. Although the artist stands behind the model in this painting, his body forms the central pictorial axis, making him appear as the dominant figure in the scene.

The scene is viewed from a slightly elevated vantage point, which diminishes the sense of intimacy and introduces an element of scientific objectivity. In this pictorial configuration, what the artist and model see in the mirror is identical with what the viewer sees in the painting.[55] Instead of the erotic mood one might expect of a scene in which the model appears in the artist's bedroom in a nightdress, Munch confronts the intimacy of the setting with the distance that separates the two people.

This distance is achieved through several different types of contrast. Unlike the model, who stands there with loosened hair in a nightdress and dressing gown, the artist is dressed in a dark suit with a white shirt and tie. The girl's face is shadowed, while the artist's appears to be illuminated—except for a narrow strip of shadow in the middle of his face.[56] Her wide-open, cavernous eyes suggest fright, but the artist stands stiffly erect, his arms hanging weakly at his sides, his facial expression revealing practically no emotion at all.

The colorful carpet and the spontaneous, uninhibited painting style, combined with the vivid shades that dominate the overall color scheme, create an impression of liveliness and vitality that stands in strong contrast to the still, lifeless-looking figures.

The frontal presentation of the woman, the bed on the right, and the open space towards the rear are anticipated in the drawing *A Woman and Two Men in an Interior* (c. 1905) cited above (fig. 7). In that work, Munch dealt with both his relationships to Tulla Larsen and to his father in terms of the conflict between Christian morals and bohemian ideas about free love. In the painting, the two male figures are merged into one—that of the artist. The positions of the figures relative to one another are also different than in the drawing.

In *Artist and Model* II, the man-and-woman constellation has changed (fig. 15). The two are no longer positioned one directly behind the other. The man has assumed a dynamic frontal pose, hands in his pockets, his legs spread apart, farther towards the background. He exudes a sense of power, strong will, and aggressiveness. The woman in the extreme foreground, turned in three-quarter profile towards the viewer, has lowered her gaze in a gesture of humility and submission. Although she is bowed to the right, into the scene and towards the man, no communication

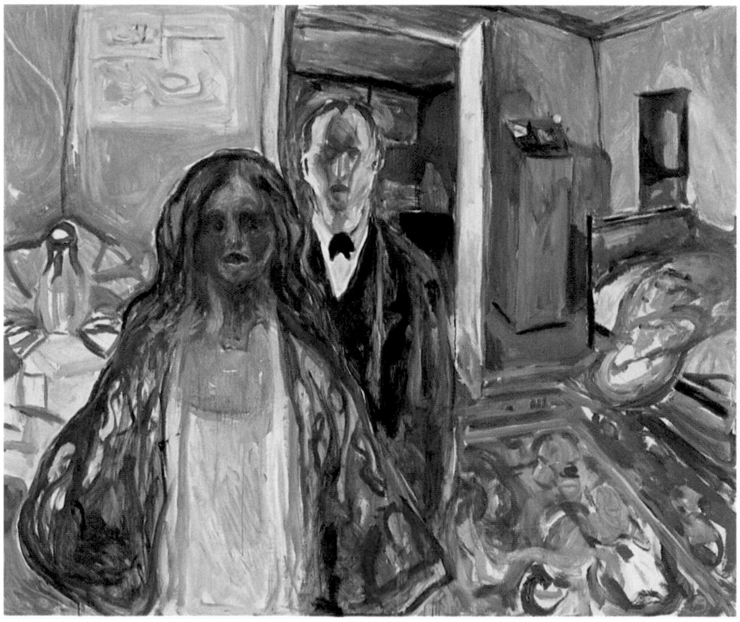

14 Edvard Munch, *Artist and Model* I, 1919, oil on canvas, 134 x 152 cm, Munch-museet, Oslo

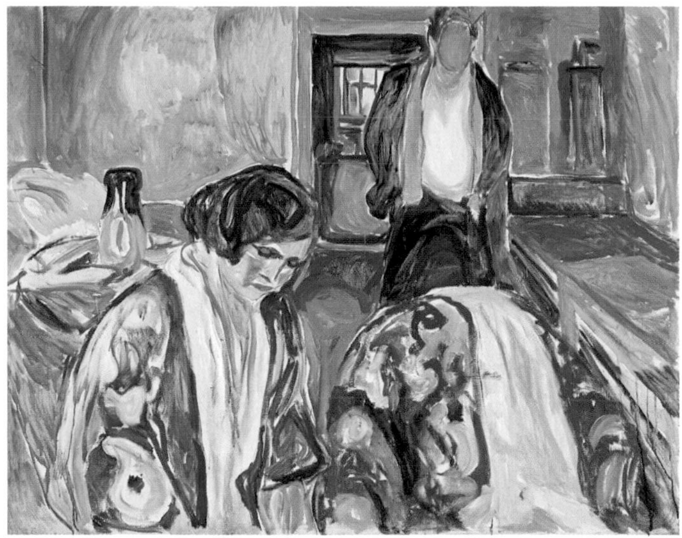

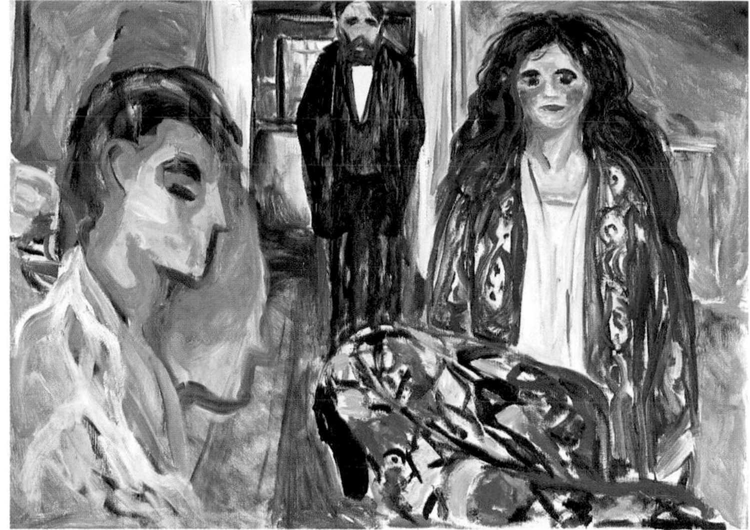

takes place. Her face clearly exhibits the features of Annie Fjeldbu, while the man has no face at all.[57] The unbridgeable gap between man and woman is emphasized by the composition, in which the right-hand half of the picture is allotted to the man, the side on the left to the woman, the partition formed by the vertical line that runs through the door frame over her left shoulder towards the floor. The chair with the colored blanket heightens the sense of the spatial barrier separating the man and the woman. Munch invented metaphors of alienation that rule out all hope of change in the relationship with the opposite sex.

The painting entitled *The Artist and his Model (Jealousy Motif)* (fig. 16), represents a kind of final installment in the *Artist and Model* series.[58] The model faces the viewer and occupies the right-hand half of the picture, while a young man is turned towards the woman, his face shown in profile. Between the two, an older, bearded man stands in the doorway behind them. The blanket that hangs over the chair in *Artist and Model* II is draped in front on the model here and resembles more a many-veined leaf than a blanket. In terms of composition, it forms a barrier for the viewer and the two men in the picture, separating them from the woman. Structural similarities to the drawing of 1905 (fig. 7) are evident. In the painting, however, both male figures represent the artist. He turns as a young man towards the woman but appears as an older man together with the viewer as an observer of the scene—as in *Artist and Model* II. The blurring in the figure of the young man may indicate that it represents the artist at some point in the past. This lack of sharpness might then be understood as a state of being out of focus with time, while the figure of the older man is sharp, since it designates the present.[59]

The distance between himself and women Munch felt as a young man has not changed with age. Now, however, his real lovers have been replaced by models. By playing roles with them, he confronts his hopes and desires with reality.

A drawing in a sketchbook from the 1890s contains an interesting variation of the *Ashes* motif (fig. 17).[60] The disappointed, weakened man who sits slumped on the left, while the woman—strengthened by their sexual intimacy—vigorously stretches her limbs,[61] is joined by the female mask from the self-portrait of 1893, a symbol of sexuality that dominates the scene.[62]

A study relating to *Artist and Model* II and III is directly traceable to the 1895 drawing of the *Ashes* motif, although the roles of the man and the woman are reversed here (fig. 18). The woman now sits in the foreground, bowed and grieving, whereas the man stands strong and upright in the background.

The message could be read like this: While the woman draws new energy from her closeness to the man, closeness to the woman

15 Edvard Munch, *Artist and Model* II, 1920–21, oil on canvas, 119 x 150 cm, Munch-museet, Oslo

16 Edvard Munch, *The Artist and his Model (Jealousy Motif)*, 1920–21, oil on canvas, 85 x 115 cm, Munch-museet, Oslo

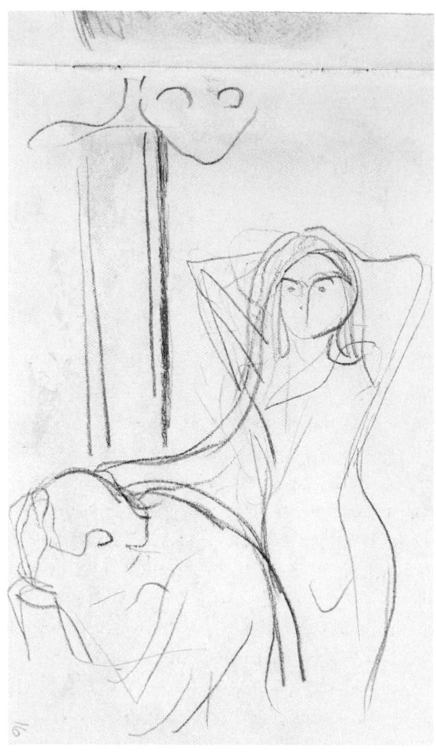

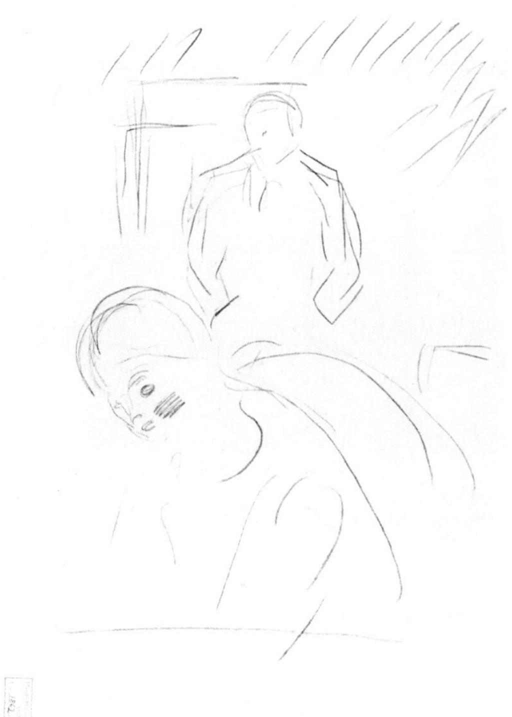

brings the man to the edge of the abyss and robs him of his power. The man draws strength from distance from the woman, whereas the woman suffers in a state of separation from the man.

And thus man's longing for woman and woman's for man remain an unachievable utopia in the world of Munch's art. The freshness and spontaneity of his later painting, which was entirely absent in his earlier images of relationships between the genders, prompts one to assume that Munch—as a consequence of his own experience—shifted from the role of the participant to that of the observer.

17 Edvard Munch, *Ashes Motif with Mask*, c. 1895, pencil on paper, 18.4 x 11.8 cm, Munch-museet, Oslo

18 Edvard Munch, Study for *The Artist and his Model*, c. 1920, pencil on paper, 50.7 x 35.4 cm, Munch-museet, Oslo

1 This essay is a revised and expanded version of "Im männlichen Gehirn," published in *Munch und Deutschland*, exh. cat., Kunsthalle der Hypo Kulturstiftung, Munich, Hamburger Kunsthalle, Hamburg, Nationalgalerie, Berlin, Ostfildern-Ruit 1994, pp. 30–38. In that article, I examined the gender relationships in Munch's art of the 1890s. In "The Age of Carmen," the study extends into the early 1920s.

2 Munch in a letter, 1885.

3 Exhibited under the title *Summer Night's Dream*. This version is now in the collection of the Museum of Fine Arts, Boston.

4 Exhibited under the title *Love and Pain*. The version shown at the time is now part of the collection of the Göteborgs Konstmuseum.

5 Exhibited under the title *The Face of Madonna*.

6 Exhibited under the title *Jealousy*.

7 Exhibited under the title *Despair*.

8 Munch's writings, Munch-museet, Oslo, reg. no. T 2704.

9 Arne Eggum cites later overpaintings in the areas of the woman's hair and the tree. Judging from old exhibition photos, this work must have been done after 1906. The underlying mood of the painting was originally more coherent and somber.

10 With regard to the various versions of this motif see also Arne Eggum, *Lifsfrisen fra Maleri til grafikk*, Oslo 1990, pp. 157–171.

11 Stanislaw Przybyszewski, *Das Werk des Edvard Munch*, Berlin 1894, p. 20.

12 Cf. Cornelia Gerner, *"Die Madonna" in Edvard Munchs Werk. Frauenbilder und Frauenbild im ausgehenden 19. Jahrhundert*, Morsbach 1993, pp. 139ff.

13 Cf. Müller-Westermann 1994 (see note 1), p. 34.

14 Munch's writings, Munch-museet, Oslo, reg. no. T 2771, p. 9.

15 Stanislaw Przybyszewski, *Totenmesse*, 1893, quoted and translated from Stanislaw Przybyszewski, *Studienausgabe*, Michael M. Schardt (ed.), Paderborn 1990, vol. 1, p.10.

16 Munch's writings, Munch-museet, Oslo, reg. no. N 30.

17 Edvard Munch, *Livsfrisens tilblivelse*, n.d., p. 14 (translated into English from the author's translation from the Norwegian)

18 Munch's writings, Munch-museet, Oslo, reg. no. T 2547, copy p. 9.

19 Holger Koefoed, *Eros i norsk kunst, 1880–1980-årene*, Oslo 1986, p. 52.

20 Munch's writings, Munch-museet, Oslo, reg. no. T 2782-C, p. 29.

21 Munch's writings, Munch-museet, Oslo, reg. no. T 2744, 27.2.1929; translated into English from the author's translation from the Norwegian.

22 Munch discussed the manner in which he tried to persuade Tulla Larsen to end their relationship in his notes, among other sources: Munch's writings, Munch-museet, *Den gale dikters dagbok*, p. 1, and Munch's writings, Munch-museet T 2734. The latter is dated *c.* 1929.

23 Two paintings by Rembrandt on the subject of anatomy instruction are worthy of note in this context. In the first, a work dated 1632 and now in the collection of the Mauritshuis in The Hague, the corpse is surrounded by students and the anatomist is positioned diagonally in the picture, just as it is in Munch's painting. In the other painting (1656, Rijksmuseum in Amsterdam), a student is shown standing on the left—analogous to the nurse holding the bowl of blood in Munch's picture—holding the removed dome of a skull like a bowl.

24 Stephanie von der Wense speaks of the "skull-shaped spot of blood." Cf. Stephanie von der Wense, *Der Künstler und sein Modell. Mann und Frau im Spätwerk Munchs*, unpublished M.A. thesis, University of Hamburg, 1986, p. 28. The form can also be seen as a heart-shaped spot, which would open a view to a new thematic dimension in the interpretation of the self-portrait based on the visual parallels to *Self-portrait with Lyre* and *The Girl and the Heart*.

25 Cf. Pål Hougen, "Kunstneren som stedfortreder," in *Höjdpunkter i norsk konst. Årsbok för Svenska statens konstsamlingar*, Stockholm 1968, pp. 123–140, p. 124.

26 On Munch and his patrons in Germany during the period 1902–12 see Stefan Pucks, "'Und die Deutschen begannen, mich kräftig zu unterstützen.' Edvard Munchs Förderer in Deutschland 1902–1912," in *Munch und Deutschland* (see note 1), pp. 91–99.

27 Under the headline "Vi gjør Streik!" [We shall go on strike!] a certain R wrote in the Oct. 2, 1902 issue of *Aftenposten*, "This is not art. This is paint-smearing. This is disgusting." Two days later, O. D. A., writing in the same newspaper, argued that Munch's paintings were dangerous for young, unformed minds.

28 *Edvard Munchs Udstilling*, Blomqvist, Kristiania, (from Sept. 16, 1903), as cat. no. 10 *Paa Operationsbordet*. The painting was reviewed in *Aftenposten*, Sept. 16, 1903. Eggum dates the painting to 1902–03. Cf. Arne Eggum, *Munch og fotografi*, Oslo 1987, p. 139. In that article, he expresses the opinion that the painting was done at Linde's home in Lübeck. While working on commissions, Munch stayed with Linde in the late fall of 1902 and again in the spring of 1903. Eggum bases his dating on a photograph, Munch-museet B 2146 (F) showing the painting in an unfinished state. According to Eggum, the photo was taken at the home of the Lübeck ophthalmologist. I have doubts that the photograph was actually taken at Linde's house. Linde lived with his family in an elegant Empire-style mansion. The photo shows the unfinished painting leaning against a door. Recognizable are a plank floor and a washing pail on the left. The molding on the three-part door is typical of those found in apartment buildings in the 1890s. Thus the photograph suggests instead that Munch took the picture at his own apartment in Berlin sometime between late 1902 and the early summer of 1903. As no photographs of the exhibition in September 1903 are available, it is not out of the question that the photo was taken after the exhibition and that Munch did not finish the painting, i.e. in the form in which it now appears today, until later. Contrary to Eggum, we regard it as unlikely that the painting was done in 1902—that is, several weeks after the shooting episode—1903 seems more likely.

29 Art history offers numerous examples of the depiction of the thoughts of a thinker behind his head. These include scenes of visions and dreams in medieval and Renaissance art. Such motifs were secularized in the late nineteenth and early twentieth centuries, e. g. in Heinrich Füssli's *Nightmare*, Francisco Goya's *The Sleep of Reason Gives Birth to Monsters*, and Jean Auguste Dominique Ingres's *Ossian's Dream*. See also Reinhold Heller, "The Riddle of Edvard Munch's Sphinx," paper presented at the 10th AICA Conference, Munch-museet, Oslo, Aug. 29, 1969, p. 4.

30 Peter Krieger, "Selbstbildnisse," in *Edvard Munch. Der Lebensfries für Max Reinhardts Kammerspiele*, exh. cat., Nationalgalerie Berlin, 1978, pp. 86–95, p. 87.

31 See also Iris Müller-Westermann, *Frau und Mann als Paar im Bild. Darstellung zwischen Realität und Utopie*, (*Hintergründe und Materialien*), Hamburg 1986, pp. 12–15.

32 In other paintings from the same period, Tulla Larsen is depicted as *Salome*, MM G/r 715; *Salome* II, 1905, MM G/r 107-20; or simply as a destructive female force, as in *Cruelty*, 1905, MM G/r 109-19; all now at the Munch-museet, Oslo.

33 The two parts were not put back together until after Munch's death. But they were mounted on two separate stretchers, so that the cut line is still visible.

34 See also Munch's rudimentary image of his father in the drawings *The Family Tree*, T 391, and *The Family Tree*, T 387A, and in the painting *By the Deathbed* (*Fever*) of 1895 (cat. no. 132).

35 Munch's writings, Munch-museet T 2770, St. Cloud, Feb. 4, 1890.

36 From the draft of a letter by Edvard Munch to Tulla Larsen, dated June 1899—March 1900, Munch-museet, Oslo, EM / C55.

37 *The Green Room* series includes, among other works, *To the Sweet Girl*, M 551; *Jealousy*, M 573; *The Murderess*, M 588; *Desire*, M 552; *Hate*, M 625; all at the Munch-museet, Oslo.

38 Munch's writings, Munch-museet, *Tilbakeblikk* 1902–08, p. 9a.

39 Munch's writings, Munch-museet, T 2568 p. 19.

40 In light of the Thuringian landscapes contained in this sketchbook, which both precede and follow this sketch, we date drawing T 132, 19 to c. 1906.

41 Gustav Schiefler reports in a diary entry for March 9–12, 1907 of a visit at Munch's room at the Hotel Hippodrom am Knie: "He was painting a large picture in which the towering figure of a nude woman, shown as a full figure from the front, stands. Behind her is the corpse of a naked, murdered man. He calls it the Death of Marat." Edvard Munch / Gustav Schiefler, *Briefwechsel*, Hamburg 1987, vol. 1, p. 232.

42 "A couple named Grävenitz served as his models," *ibid.*, p. 232.

43 Arne Eggum cites Max Liebermann's *Samson and Delilah* as another possible source of inspiration for *The Death of Marat*. The painting was shown at the Berlin Secession in 1902, where it created quite a sensation. Munch undoubtedly saw Liebermann's painting, since he showed his *Frieze of Life* there at the same time.

44 The painting is now in the collection of the Musées Royaux des Beaux-Arts, Brussels.

45 Munch took up the Marat theme again many years later. In *Marat and Charlotte Corday. In the Bathtub*, c. 1930 (Munch-museet, Oslo, M 311) he depicted the nude man in the bathtub and the woman, turned facing the viewer, is seen holding a weapon concealed beneath a bouquet of flowers held in front of her breast. Like the figure in *The Death of Marat* I, she is accompanied by a dark shadow. Munch's treatment of the subject is evidence of a detachment from the original event. None of the sense of hate or aggression evoked by the earlier versions is noticeable here. In this work, Munch was concerned with reconstructing a historical event. He experimented with the motif in several variations characterized by a new approach to coloration and more relaxed brushwork.

46 Ingeborg Kaurin (1894–1972), also known as "Mosse-piken" (the girl from Moss). She was Munch's model from 1911 until she married the Norwegian painter Søren Onsager in early 1915.

47 The 1912 *Sonderbund-Austellung* in Cologne was devoted to the goal of presenting a survey of expressionism as the most recent current in painting, a movement joined by the most progressive artists in all of the countries of Europe. Expressionism was understood to include all of the movements and tendencies whose advocates had turned away from naturalism and impressionism and strove for simplicity and intensification of forms of expression, for a new rhythms and coloration, and for decorative or monumental artistic design. Cf. Richard Reiche in the foreword to the exhibition catalog, Cologne, p. 3. In addition to Van Gogh, Cézanne, and Gauguin, Munch was also honored at the *Sonderbund-Ausstellung* as a pioneer of expressionist art. He was the only living artist given an entire room of his own, where he exhibited thirty-two works from all of his creative periods. This exhibition represented Munch's final breakthrough. Munch traveled via Copenhagen and Paris to Cologne to appear at the show and wrote to his friend Jappe Nilssen the day before the opening ceremony: "I have been given a very large room, 10 x 15 m. It is the largest room at the exhibition. Van Gogh, Gauguin, and Cézanne will make up the main exhibit. 3 rooms with Van Gogh! 86 extremely interesting paintings. ... Gathered together here is the wildest painting being done in Europe—I am a pure classic and pale in comparison—the Cologne Cathedral is shaken to its foundations." Letter from Edvard Munch to Jappe Nilssen, dated Cologne, spring 1912. (The *Sonderbund-Ausstellung* opened on May 25, which means that the letter was presumably written on May 24.) Printed in Erna Holmboe Bang, *Edvard Munch og Jappe Nilssen. Efterlatte brev og kritikker*, Oslo 1946, pp. 55f. On the relationship between the Brücke group and Edvard Munch, see Marit Werenskiold, "Die Brücke und Edvard Munch," *Zeitschrift des deutschen Vereins für Kunstwissenschaft*, vol. 28, no. 1/4, 1974, pp. 140–152; Arne Eggum discusses the influence of the Brücke artists on Munch following the 1912 "Sonderbund-Austellung" in Part II of his essay "Die Brücke und Edvard Munch." Arne Eggum, "Munch's Self-Portraits," in *Symbols & Images*, exh. cat., National Gallery of Art, Washington 1978, pp.11–33.

48 *Edvard Munch*, exh. cat., Kunstsalon Fritz Gurlitt, Berlin 1914, cat. no. 78, *The Seducer*.

49 The painting is listed in the 1919 catalog of Blomqvist's in Oslo as cat. no. 22 under the title *Under de røde Æbler* (*Beneath Red Apples*).

50 Munch painted other versions of this theme in *Adam and Eve* (M 592) and *Adam und Eve* (M 741), dated 1928, both at the Munch-museet, Oslo.

51 The title originated with Arne Eggum. Eggum also refers to the series as *The Bedroom—Artist and Model*. Cf. Arne Eggum, "Sovrummet," in *Edvard Munch*, exh. cat., Liljevalchs konsthall & Kulturhuset, Stockholm 1977, pp. 104–108.

52 Cf. Picasso's work on this theme, for example.

53 There is no evidence that Munch exhibited the *Artist and Model* series during his lifetime.

54 Annie Fjeldbu (1897–1969), whose real name was Anna Hansen, worked full-time as a model and later as a dancer. She first served as Munch's model in the late fall of 1918, at the earliest, and continued to model for him until she married a Swedish nobleman and moved to Sweden in 1923. Twenty letters from Munch to his model have survived, the content of which also includes suggestions for modeling dates. The first of these is dated Feb. 19, 1919. Annie Fjeldbu was also the model for such works as *Nude at a Wicker Chair*, M 499, the four times of day, *Morning*, M 382, *Noon*, M 759, *Evening*, M 380 and *Night*, M 384; all at the Munch-museet, Oslo. The artist also used her as his model again in his revised versions of *Nude Weeping* of 1907 and 1913.

55 See also Arne Eggum, *Edvard Munch und seine Modelle*, Stuttgart 1993, p. 88.

56 Stephanie von Wense has interpreted the cross on the forehead as a sign of martyrdom. Cf. Wense 1986 (see note 24), p. 76.

57 Stephanie von der Wense has called attention to overpainting on the man's face. Cf. *ibid.*, p. 79.

58 We assume that it was executed in 1920–21, along with *Artist and Modell* II and III. See also Eggum 1977 (see note 51), p. 113.

59 On sharpness and blurring tools of expression, see also Rolf Stenersen, *Nærbilde av et geni*, Oslo 1945, p. 64. On Munch's experiments with photography and its artistic potential see. Eggum 1987 (see note 28).

60 Page 10 of sketchbook T 131 contains a drawing dated 1895 by the artist. This clearly supports the dating of the drawing under discussion here to c. 1895.

61 Cf. the painting entitled *Ashes*, 1894, Nasjonalgalleriet, Oslo.

62 Cf. *Self-Portrait under a Mask of a Woman*, c. 1893, M 229, Munch-museet, Oslo.

Power, Instinct, Will—Munch's Energetic World Theater in the Context of the Fin de Siècle

Christoph Asendorf

I.

The first attempt to assess Munch's position within the context of the artistic possibilities of his time was undertaken in 1894 in a publication devoted to the artist, edited by Stanislaw Przybyszewski (fig. 1) and published by S. Fischer. Przybyszewski's own contributions were complemented with articles by Franz Servaes, Willy Pastor, and Julius Meier-Graefe, and thus the book presented the thoughts of four authors, each of whom was associated in his own way with the theory, practice, and propaganda of the artistic revolution that took place around 1900. In his preface, Przybyszewski emphasizes the aspect that contributed most to the disruptive influence Munch exerted from the very outset—the fact that his art broke away from ruling doctrine of naturalism to venture forth into new, uncharted terrain and into the "abysmal depths" of the "most subtle and delicate stirrings of the soul."[1] His exploration of the realm of the subconscious exposed layers of personality which the prevailing cultural consciousness of the time would have preferred to leave concealed. Indeed, referring specifically to the *Love* series, Przybyszewski sees Munch's paintings and prints as "images of the human soul in the moment at which all reason grows silent and all imaginative activity has ceased."[2]

Without actually using the term, Przybyszewski firmly positions Munch's oeuvre within the system of reference of symbolism, the most powerful and influential movement within the anti-naturalist revolt at the *fin de siècle*. As in the case of Mallarmé and Maeterlinck, Przybyszewski contends, his art no longer recognizes external processes; the only reality is the uncontrollable "come-and-go" of emotional-spiritual movements.[3] Franz Servaes argues along similar lines, although from a different background. His frame of reference is Gauguin's symbolist painting from the period following his break with impressionism. On his quest for a new language for his art, Gauguin had also discovered a new realm of life. He replaced the weary intellectualism of European civilization with the freshness and primitive originality of Polynesia. And Servaes sees a similar departure in Munch's case as well—albeit with one significant difference: "He carries his own Tahiti within himself, and so he proceeds with the unerring sense of a sleepwalker through our confusing cultural life, never straying from his path, in full command of his utterly cultureless Parsifalian nature."[4]

Willy Pastor cites another important symbolist artist in his attempt to describe the distinctive qualities of Munch's art. Comparing Arnold Böcklin's *Storm* (fig. 2) with Munch's painting of the same title (cat. no. 10), he discovered that, while the latter "does not yet dispense with clarifying symbolism,"[5] the weight of the work shifts towards the effects of the fundamental forces themselves and thus, one might say, amounts to symbolism at a higher level of abstraction.

Only Meier-Graefe appears uninterested in such classifications. His article reads at first like a literary text devoted over many

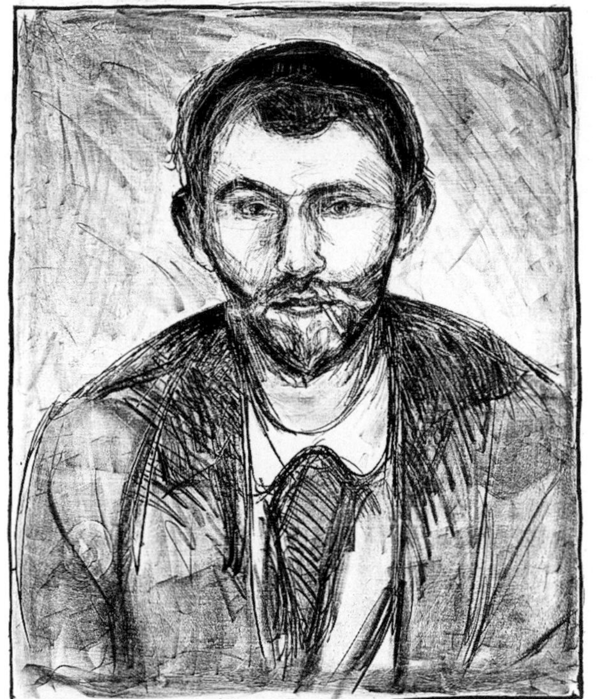

1 Edvard Munch, *Stanislaw Przybyszewski*, 1895, lithograph on paper, 54.5 x 45.8 cm, Munch-museet, Oslo

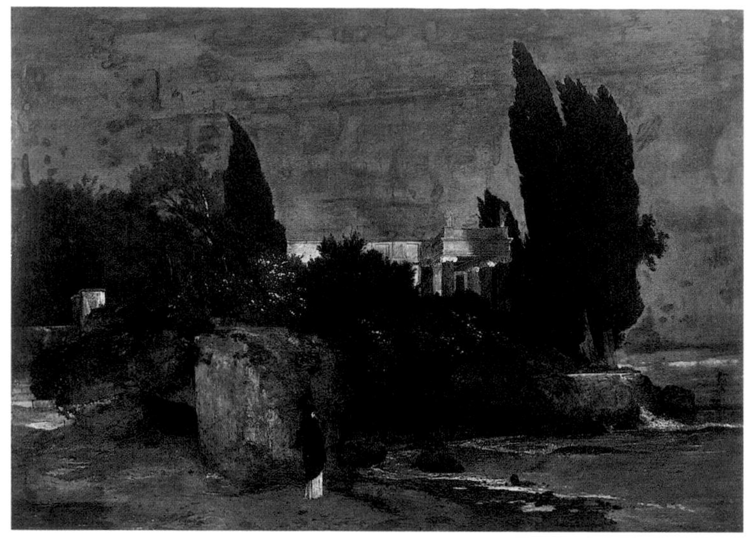

pages to a description of the internal development of a girl into a young woman. Only then does he note casually in a footnote that he has just "narrated" three works of Munch's, including *Puberty* (cat. no. 16). Yet this narrative leads to the heart of Munch's works, which the author describes as "grandiose images of fundamental psychological states."[6] Meier-Graefe pursues two lines of argumentation: While he distinguishes Munch's radical art from the accommodating style of a Ludwig von Hofmann, an artist he otherwise quite admires,[7] he writes consistently as a social critic who rejects the saturated complacency of the *Gründerzeit*.

Przybyszewski's Munch book is not the product of casual cooperation but a document of the personal and intellectual relationship between the individuals involved. The hub of communication was the Zum Schwarzen Ferkel in Berlin, a tavern which Strindberg (and later its owners as well) so named in reference to the Bessarabian wine bag that served as its sign. It was a gathering place for artists of various nationalities in the early 1890s. Frequent visitors included Strindberg as well as Munch, Dehmel, and Przybyszewski.[8] The scandal surrounding the Munch exhibition of 1892, which prompted the founding of the Berlin Secession, established the Ferkel group as pioneers of modern art and literature. The journal *Pan*, published by Meier-Graefe beginning in 1895, was born of this context.

That Munch was celebrated here as a symbolist artist is proof of his modernity. Symbolism was a favored form of expression among innovators in the field of art during the late 1880s and early 1890s. Przybyszewski was influenced by the French symbolists. Where Servaes emphasizes Munch's modernity[9] and his interest in the unexplored and the imponderable, he, like many symbolists, recalls Baudelaire's theory of modernism. In Berlin, Strindberg met Hermann Bahr, who shortly before had proclaimed the "end of naturalism" in Vienna and appealed to artists "to seek out the mysterious instead of pursuing the obvious and to express precisely that in which we feel and understand differently than in reality." He was concerned with a "mystique of the nerves."[10] Thus the Berlin Ferkel group was in step with the most recent developments in the mood of European art, and it had in Munch an outstanding artist as its shining example. The symbolist interpretation developed in this context dominated the critical reception of his oeuvre; it was not revised by expressionist theorists until a good ten years later.

II.

That Munch preferred to present his major works of the 1890s, with the exception of his portraits, in cyclical form—that is, in a coherent thematic context—is a well-known fact, although this is made apparent to museum visitors only on occasion in partial reconstructions at exhibitions today. He exhibited a first frieze, entitled *Love*, composed of six paintings in 1893, and several expanded versions with variations appeared in the course of the next ten years. Outstanding among these is the extensive version of 1902, his *Frieze of Life*, shown in Berlin. In response to a suggestion by Max Liebermann, Munch hung what his mentor Albert Kollmann referred to as "an entire cycle of symbolist paintings" in the Secession's exhibition building.[11] He devoted two of the walls in the room reserved for him to the thematic complex of love, the third to existential fear, and the fourth to death. Because the pictures were of different formats and had not been composed for presentation within a single context, Munch had to find a means of establishing unity among them. This he accomplished with the aid

2 Arnold Böcklin, *Villa by the Sea* (1st version), 1864,
oil on canvas, 125.2 x 174.7 cm,
Bayerische Staatsgemäldesammlungen, Schack-Galerie, Munich

of a broad strip of fabric along which the paintings were arranged. The title chosen for the cycle as a whole was less than succinct, and thus the *Presentation of a Number of Images of Life* was given a much more striking title at the Oslo exhibition two years later: *Frieze. Motifs from Modern Spiritual Life.*

The expressive power of *The Scream* (cat. no. 118) could hardly be more intense: the genderless individual beneath a bloody sky, shown as if sliding from the diagonal formed by the bridge, its terrified gaze fixed upon a scene of horror the viewer cannot see. Although this image of almost absolute alienation from the reality of the world sets a certain tone, the painting actually stands alone. In contrast, the works devoted to the problems of gender relationships form an unmistakable thematic focus within the *Frieze of Life*. Even the painting entitled *The Kiss* (cat. no. 46), which appears at first to show only a couple united in intimacy in an interior setting, places the pair in a disturbing state of suspension. If we examine the painting from left to right, our gaze wanders from a small detail of the outside world in daylight to the shapeless darkness of the right-hand half of the picture, into which the outlines of the woman appear to flow. The painting *Vampire* (cat. nos. 65, 66) evokes an entire sinister mythology—the man is a victim, drawn as if unconscious into the sphere of the woman with the flowing red hair. *Jealousy* (cat. no. 71) separates the couple; the woman is associated with the world (and the biblical apple tree), while the pale man's head apparently submerged in its dark surroundings gazes in desperation from the picture. A similar head—probably Przbyszewski's here as well[12]—appears in *Red Virginia Creeper* (cat. no. 155); covered with blood-red foliage, the house seems alive, while the man has the look of an outcast, unsheltered as in the painting *Eye in Eye* (cat. no. 33), where he is encircled by the woman's hair but separated from her by a tree. Other paintings in the *Frieze of Life* appear embedded in an energetic world theater, in the constant flow of forces, the natural rhythm of nature. Remarkably often (in *Melancholy*, *The Voice*, *The Woman [Sphinx]*, and *Red and White*, for example) a seashore is the stage upon which the human drama unfolds. This is true of *The Dance of Life* (fig. 4, p. 57), perhaps the most ambitious work in the *Frieze*. A group of dancers circles around a central pair of figures, which remains motionless in the middle of the scene as if spellbound, illuminated by a moon whose light intersects with the horizon. Two passive, flanking figures, a girl and an old woman robed in white and black, frame the scene on either side of the central figure of the woman in the red dress, whose size corresponds to their own; they represent the flow of time to which all are subject. Though he treats it symbolically here, Munch dealt in a more direct way with this motif of constant transformation, of growth and decline, and of the painful processes of incessant attraction and repulsion, elsewhere, namely in the title of his painting *Metabolism* (fig. 1, p. 53). With reference to the other painting, he described this work as being as necessary "as the buckle for the belt."[13]—and thus the prosaic concept of physiological metabolism becomes a symbol of the complex pictorial world of the *Frieze* as a whole.

III

But on what theoretical ideas is based the energetic view of the world visualized in these paintings? There is, of course, no solid theoretical foundation underlying Munch's art. What we have,

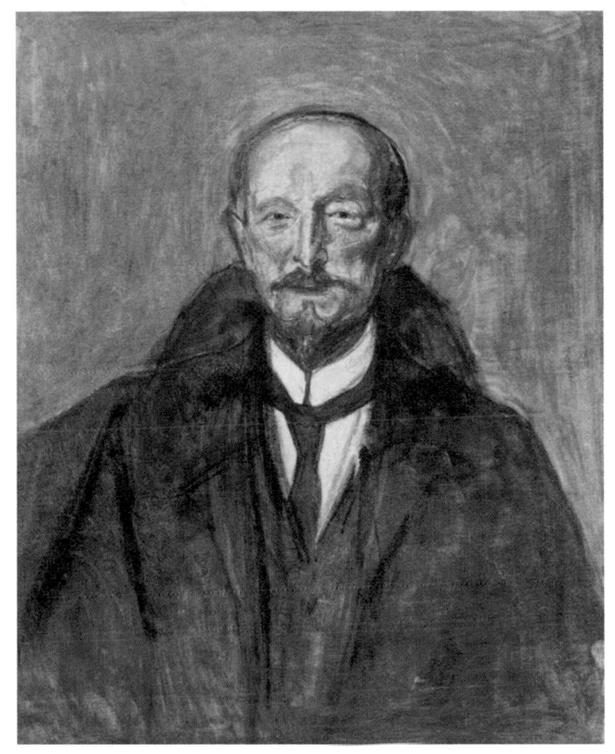

3 Edvard Munch, *Albert Kollmann*, 1901–02,
oil on canvas, 81.5 x 66.5 cm, Kunsthaus Zürich

however, are isolated indicators, readings, and expressions of interest in his environment which provide at least some clues to the attitudes that may have influenced his art. We encounter quite a unique theory of energy in the writings of his long-standing patron Kollmann, for example, who was a fervent advocate of Reichenbach's "od" theory. The "od" is a natural force, "a so-called dynamide,"[14] the existence of which was first postulated in the *Odisch-magnetische Briefe* [Odic-magnetic letters] of Baron Reichenbach in 1852. It is a force "similar to electricity, magnetism, and heat [which] actually stands in the midst of these three natural forces" but differs from them by virtue of its specific behavior. The "od" is an omnipresent, permeating force; it adheres to persons and flows out from them; it exhibits polar behavior like magnetism and affects the eye and the emotions. But its influence touches only the sensitive. Sensitive people, according to Reichenbach, are restless because they are constantly surrounding by "odic" emissions and thus "are always seeking change in their situations, their activities, etc." Thus their daily lives engender nervous agitation.

We encounter currents and rays in Munch's art of the 1890s in a variety of forms—as extended flows of lines, for example, or as a diaphanous veil around the figure's head that appears almost to be blowing into the picture in his 1901 portrait of Kollmann himself (fig. 3). An echo of Reichenbach's theories may be audible here. The entire Ferkel group was interested in Kollmann himself, whom Theodor Däubler once referred to as a "phenomenon of materialization,"[15] and in ideas about energy in general. One visitor wrote of Dagny Juel that her hair crackled when touched.[16] Strindberg depicted himself as electrically charged in *Inferno*. Przybyszewski spoke of a divided self consisting of a civilized and an explosive component, "in whose brain the receptive and motor leads formed a single circuit, not yet interrupted by resistance between the stations."[17] Thus theirs was a club of people highly charged with energy and without stable subject unity, who explored new combinations in life and art. It was also Przybyszewski who told Strindberg about forces affecting him from a distance, among them the "od" rays with which he had formerly been unfamiliar,[18] indicating that the tortures inflicted upon Strindberg by the sorcerer Popoffsky in *Inferno* were a residual reflex of these tales.

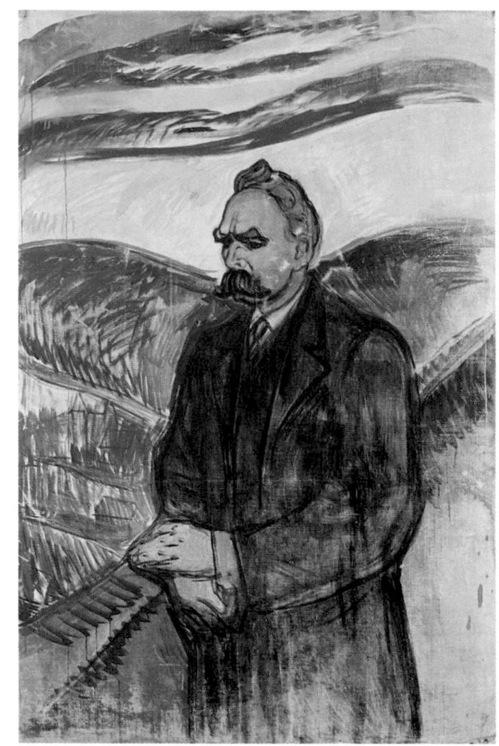

4 Edvard Munch, *Friedrich Nietzsche*, 1906, oil on canvas, 200 x 130 cm, Munch-museet, Oslo

Reichenbach's energy theory had a variously meandering effect on the Ferkel group. Yet some of the questions under discussion here could also be approached from the perspective of Freud's theory of drives. Freud also explored the modern psyche. His dynamic concept of drives encompasses both physical forces and spiritual forms of energy; the human being is subject to a constant "pressure" from both sides. The psychoanalyst's famous statement that "Drives are mythical beings, magnificent in their indeterminacy" reads like a caption for Munch's *Frieze of Life*.[19] On the whole, however, these links tend to be coincidental.

More immediately graspable is an entirely different influence. Munch, like many of his contemporaries, was not only a devotee of Nietzsche (fig. 4) but also of Schopenhauer and his theory of will. The impact of Schopenhauer's theory of *fin-de-siècle* consciousness as a whole was significant. Even the French symbolists had cited Schopenhauer. Particularly striking evidence of the breadth of the philosopher's reception is found in *Buddenbrooks*. Thomas Mann passes review of the chapter on death from *The World as Will and Idea*: "Who, what, how could I be if I were not I, if this, my personal manifestation, did not enclose me and separate my consciousness from that of all those who are not I! Organism! Blind, irrational, regrettable eruption of relentless will!"[20] Reality is but illusion, the individual but a temporary and often painful objectification of spaceless, timeless will. If we consider Munch's *Metabolismus* in the context of his readings of Schopenhauer, the paintings assume a meaning that transcends the crude biologism of its title.

Whatever the guiding principles of the theories of the influences of energy discussed amongst the members of the Ferkel group may be, and whatever images of the world they inform, if we examine them against the whole background of the *fin de siècle*, they become interpretable as representations of a general discourse on the characteristics of the present under the aspect of modernity. And all of these can be related to a basic model of energy. Bergson's central theory of the current of life, the *élan vital*, is based on a higher concept of reality as a process of becoming. Georg Simmel observes that, under the influence of the money economy, everything of substance dissolves into relationships and thus into open-ended processes; accelerated circulation in the big cities goes hand and hand, he argues, with an "intensification of neural life."[21] In his *Sociology*, he frames the corresponding form of socialization in a philosophical image, the metaphor of a "fluctuating, continuously developing process."[22] Even in the arts—in the sculpture of Rodin, for example—he points out, one observes a "dissolution of solid contents into the liquid element of the soul."[23] He regards this general fluidity as characteristic of modern society and the aspect that distinguishes it from all preceding societies.

IV.

Munch himself developed a number of techniques for visualizing flows of energy. These can be tentatively and very roughly classified under three different approaches, each of which he varied in a number of ways: the use of lines of force, the depiction of auras, and the division of the pictorial surface, of figure and background, into strips. In such paintings as *Melancholy* (cat. nos. 85, 86) and *Red and White* (cat. no. 30), flowing lines of force move through the sky or indicate the motion of the sea. This visual language, which serves a rather more illustrative purpose in these works, is charged with drama and transformed into a medium for existential expression in paintings such as *The Scream* (cat. no. 118) and *Angst* (cat. no. 116). The sky and the landscape are set in motion, melt away, cause the human figures to freeze, or threaten to pull them into the maelstrom. Yet it is not these spaces in which havoc is wreaked by expanding lines of force that tear people from their customary daily lives, as would a natural disaster. Indeed, Munch's human figures are already torn from their lives; his landscapes are landscapes of the soul, interior spaces of motion dissolving in all coordinates.

Although it is not immediately evident in terms of theme or intensity, these works bear a certain relationship to Art Nouveau by virtue of their formal aspects—a style of art for which Henry van de Velde sought to articulate a theory of lines charged with energy. He begins with several general presumptions: Lines are transposed gestures, expressions of vitality. And thus they are inscribed as expressions of emotional states on previously blank surfaces—psychic powers guide the hand; natural forces leave traces like a falling rock on these surfaces upon which it impacts or the wind in the arabesque linear patterns of moving water. Such lines "are born of the observation of an interplay of forces, and they demonstrate in the least of their subordinate components the current of non-intermittent power and energy."[24]

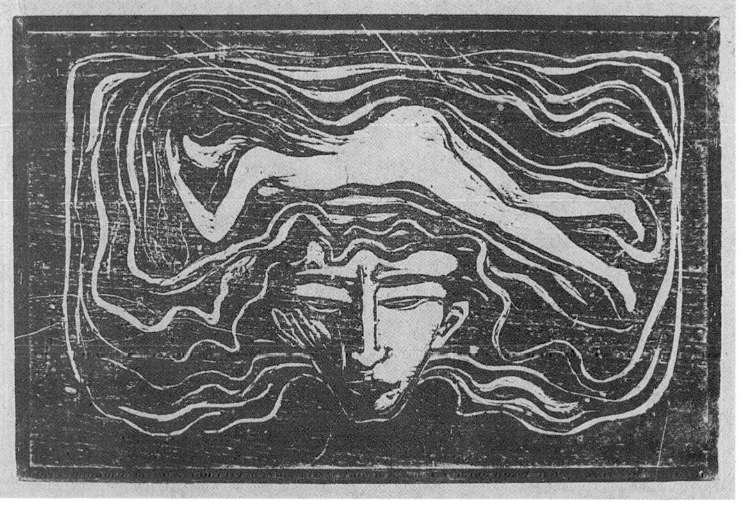

5 Edvard Munch, *Inside the Man's Brain*, 1897,
woodcut on paper, 37.3 x 56.9 cm, Munch-museet, Oslo

Yet Munch is not a commercial artist who, like Van de Velde, aims to symbolize the flow of energy in a column; he is an artist of expression. In one large group of his works, lines of force serve the purpose of illustrating his view of the fundamental antagonism underlying gender relationships. Hair represents the flowing lines of the soul—erotic communication appears in the image of the couples who are interwoven or intertwined by it. These processes are illustrated paradigmatically in the pair of lithographs entitled *Attraction* II (cat. no. 37) and *Separation* II (cat. no. 39), both of 1896. Even farther removed from the sphere of representation is the woodcut *Inside the Man's Brain* (fig. 5)—a head above which, as an externalized version of an inner image, a woman's head is positioned and connected to it in a compositional sense by an ornament consisting of hair and lines of force. Only once did Munch express an ironic view of this whole complex of ideas (while inverting it at the same time), when he wrote the following words on a casual sanatorium sketch in 1908–09 (fig. 6): "Professor Jacobson electrifying the famous painter Munch and applying positive male and negative female forces to his weakened brain."[25]

In contrast, depicting halos instead of lines of force requires the use of painterly rather than linear means. Halos originate in Christian iconography, in which an entire ensemble of different types of halo was developed to signify divine powers. However, it appears that a generation intent upon severing the bonds of naturalism and positivism discovered new opportunities for expression in this context. If we divest the halo of its original context, it can become a sign of a more general kind of spiritual halo or energy radiation. Kandinsky, for instance, was inspired by the freely floating halos illustrated in theosophical books in his efforts to develop a concept of non-representational painting.[26] Munch was not concerned with such things. Yet his oeuvre offers numerous examples of how halos can be used to allude to states of the mind and soul. These range from the shadow behind the figure of a young girl (*Puberty*) (cat. no. 16) to the erotic corona of his *Madonna* of 1893–94 (cat. no. 19) to the device he employed in the portrait of Dagny Juel Przybyszewska (cat. no. 185), who floats almost bodiless in pictorial space against a unreal-looking vibrating bluish background—an impalpable manifestation in a field of energy.

Munch pursued a different approach with his strip paintings. They are the product of an experimental phase which coincided with the period of mental crisis in 1907–08. Here, he wanted to make a new start: "I felt the need to break up the line and the planar surface. ... And so I started a series of paintings with very broad, often meter-long lines or vertical, horizontal, and diagonal brush-

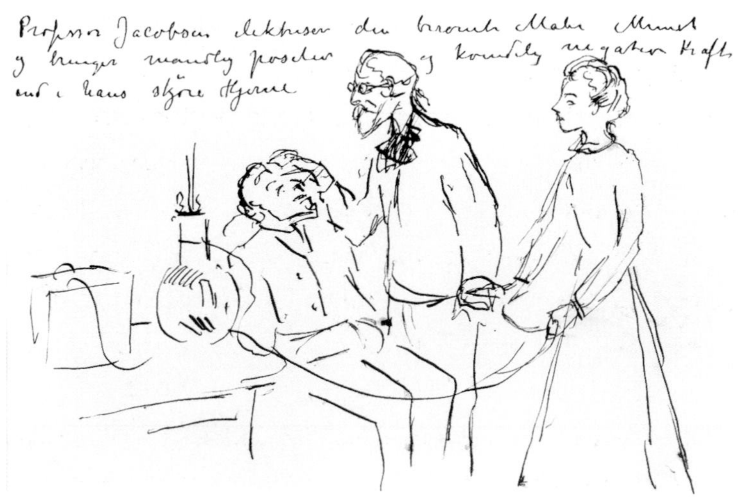

6 Edvard Munch, "Professor Jacobson electrifying the famous painter Munch and applying positive male and negative female forces to his weakened brain," 1908, pen and wash on paper, 13.7 x 21.2 cm, Munch-museet, Oslo

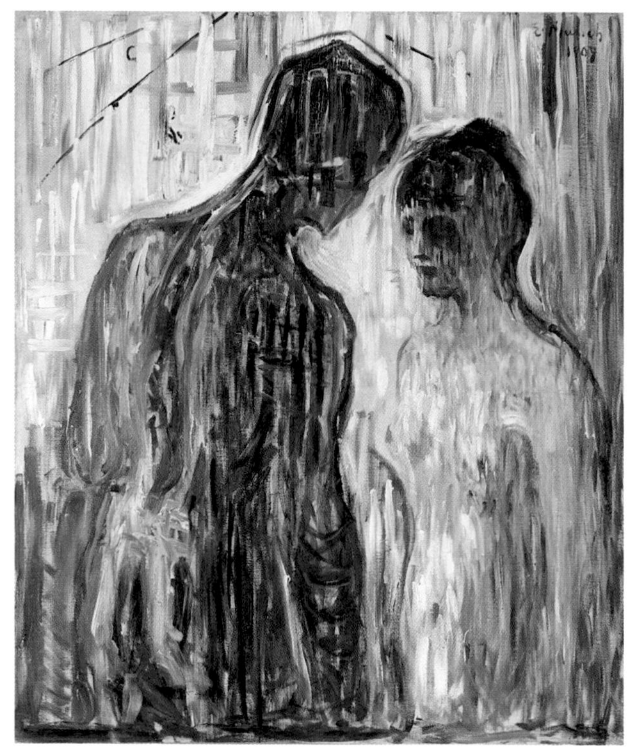

7 Edvard Munch, *Cupid and Psyche*, 1907, oil on canvas, 119 x 99 cm, Munch-museet, Oslo

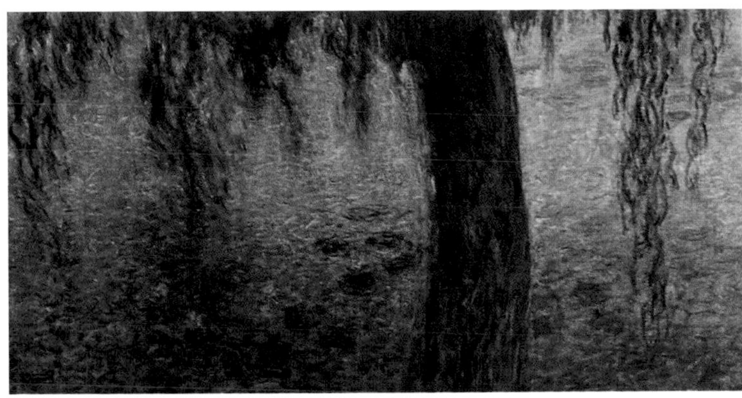

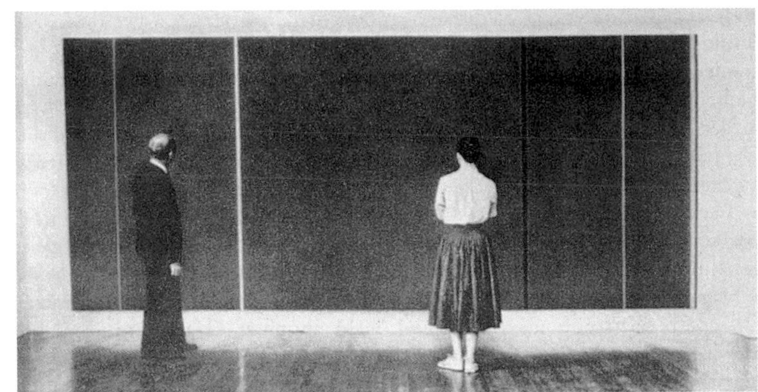

strokes. This relaxed the structure of the two-dimensional surface."[27] One of the most important works created during this period is *Cupid and Psyche* (fig. 7). The two figures stand facing each other, nude, bowed towards one another and observing each other cautiously. They are clearly distinguished by light and color; yet the overall impression is blurred by the vertical strips that run through the entire painting, as if the energies flowing through the space and the bodies were passing along these strips.

We recognize the effect of a space left open above and below in one of Munch's earlier works. In his *Voice* of 1893 (cat. no. 3), the naturalistic "strips" of the largely rootless and topless trees—a technique used to dissolve the boundaries of pictorial space that can also be found in Claude Monet's *Nymphéas* (fig. 8) or, much later and in abstract form, in Barnett Newman's *zips* (fig. 9). And there is something else which contributes to the unique effect of *Cupid and Psyche*: The strips in this painting blur the boundaries between the figures and the background, obscuring the outlines of the figures, each of which appears to melt into its surroundings. In this way, Munch achieves a strange state of suspension between figuration and dissolution, an effect that had also occupied the attention of other *fin-de-siécle* artists, including the Nabis painters and Gustav Klimt, in whose portrait of Adele Bloch-Bauer "garment and home interior melt together into a single, ornamental continuum."[28]

Works by artists of this generation exhibit a well-developed sensitivity to the relationship between figure and background, which now become potentially capable of exchanging roles; the clarity of spatial relationships and stable boundaries in generally are questioned. Munch's strip paintings, however (*Cupid and Psyche*, *Comfort* and *The Death of Marat*, in particular, and, in a more general sense, the series entitled *The Green Room*[29]) belong primarily in their own pictorial cosmos. All of the techniques with which he experimented until 1910 were employed in an effort to achieve direct representation of something that is almost impossible to represent—Munch's strips, halos, and lines of force are all means used to visualize, in particular, the dynamics of an intrapsychic play of forces in a world drama charged with energy.

V.

Munch's visual language began to grow calmer in 1910, although the change did not involve a diminution of quality, as it did in the late work of many expressionist artists. An important cycle of paintings was done for the auditorium of the university in Oslo, a group of works Munch himself related to his earlier oeuvre: "The *Frieze of Life* represents the concerns and the joys of individual people, viewed from close up; in contrast, the paintings for the university show the great, eternal forces."[30] The central work is the painting *The Sun* of 1909–11 (fig. 10), a radiant circle of light above a broad landscape, in which his theme of energy is synthesized, so to speak.

On the occasion of a major Munch exhibition in 1985, Joseph Beuys characterized Munch's oeuvre as part of a constellation that

8 Claude Monet, *Nymphéas*, 1920–26 (detail), oil on canvas, 200 x 425 cm, Musée de l'Orangerie, Paris

9 Barnett Newman, *Vir heroicus sublimis*, 1950–51, oil on canvas, 242.2 x 513.6 cm, The Museum of Modern Art, New York, donation by Mr. and Mrs. Ben Heller

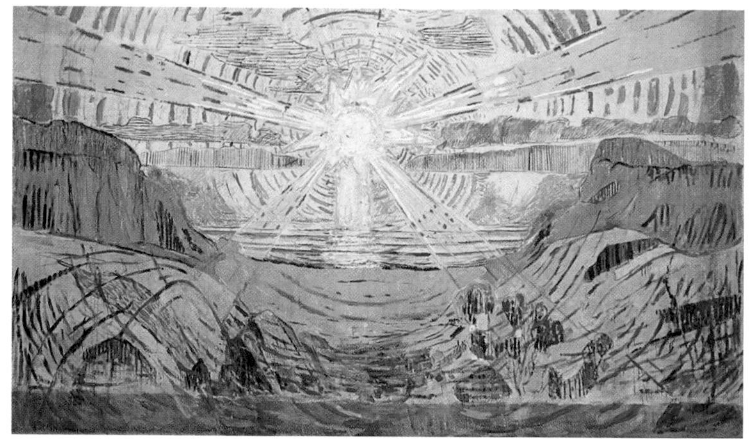

also comprised the art of Vincent van Gogh and Giovanni Segantini,[31] and the consistent leitmotif of energy was surely one aspect that prompted his assessment. One senses such a link between Van Gogh's *Starry Night* of 1889 and Munch's *The Sun*, for example. The workings of cosmic forces are also a theme in Segantini's great Alp triptych of 1896–99, in which the central painting, *Being*, shows a radiant sky above the unshakeable solidity of the Engadine alpine landscape. The peasants appear integrated within the natural cycle of life beneath the canopy of a heaven that appears to protect their earth-bound life while opening it at the same time to the abundant light of cosmic vastness.

For Beuys, the energy theme stood for something else as well. Aside from all their specific differences, he saw Munch, Van Gogh, and Segantini as embodying a "fundamental striving" for a "new spirituality." He did not mean this in a specifically religious sense, however, but was concerned instead with a position of independence and self-reliance, a state of being torn from all traditions that enabled these artist to venture forth into new realms. These new realms offer the opportunity to recreate a link with forces of a spiritual nature that have been lost in everyday life—and that is what interested Beuys in his own work. He apparently regarded the three artists as kindred spirits—and indeed, some of the tendrils of Segantini's pantheism and Munch's idea of the permanent metabolism of nature lead to his own theories of energy and heat. At the close of the twentieth century, Beuys reflects the situation at the preceding *fin de siècle* and sees the old questions as still unresolved in the present.

1 Stanislaw Przybyszewski (ed.), *Das Werk des Edvard Munch. Vier Beiträge*, Berlin 1894, pp. 3f.
2 *Ibid.*, pp. 16f.
3 *Ibid.*, pp. 28ff.
4 *Ibid.*, p. 37.
5 *Ibid.*, p. 71.
6 *Ibid.*, pp. 77ff, here p. 90.
7 *Ibid.*, pp. 92f.
8 See Angelika Gundlach (ed.), *Der andere Strindberg*, Frankfurt 1981, pp. 109ff.
9 Przybyszweski 1894 (see note 1), pp. 55f.
10 Hermann Bahr, "Die Überwindung des Naturalismus" (1891), and again in Ulrich Karthaus (ed.), *Impressionismus, Symbolismus und Jugendstil*, Stuttgart 1977, pp. 122, 124.
11 Cf. the thorough discussion of the history and background of the *Frieze of Life* by Uwe M. Schneede, "Munchs *Lebensfries*, zentrales Projekt der Moderne," in *Munch und Deutschland*, exh. cat., Hamburger Kunsthalle 1994, pp. 20ff, here p. 23.
12 See Thomas M. Messer, *Edvard Munch*, Cologne 1989, p. 90.
13 Ragna Stang, *Edvard Munch*, Königstein/Taunus 1979, p. 123.
14 On the following see Ludwig Büchner, "Die Röntgenschen Strahlen und die Reichenbachsche Od-Lehre," in *Gartenlaube*, 1896, p. 141ff.
15 Werner Helwig, *Capri. Magische Insel*, Frankfurt 1979, p. 13; on Kollmann in general, pp. 11–18.
16 Gundlach 1981 (see note 8), p. 127.
17 Stanislaw Przybyszewski, *Erinnerungen an das literarische Berlin*, (1926), Munich 1965, p. 46.
18 *Ibid.*, p. 195.
19 Translated from Sigmund Freud, "Neue Folge der Vorlesungen zur Einführung in die Psychoanalyse," in Sigmund Freud, *Gesammelte Werke*, Frankfurt 1999, vol. 15, p. 101.
20 Translated from Thomas Mann, *Buddenbrooks*, Frankfurt 1974, p. 657.
21 Georg Simmel, "Die Großstädte und das Geistesleben" (1903), in *Brücke und Tür*, Stuttgart 1957, p. 228.
22 Georg Simmel, *Soziologie*, Leipzig 1908, pp. 587f.
23 Georg Simmel, "Die Kunst Rodins und das Bewegungsmotiv in der Plastik," in *Nord und Süd*, no. 129, vol. 33, 1909, pp. 189ff.
24 Henry van de Velde, "Die Linie" (1902), in Hans Curjel (ed.), *Zum neuen Stil*, Munich 1955, pp. 192f.
25 Quoted and translated from Messer 1989 (see note 12), p. 108.
26 See Sixten Ringbom, "Kandinsky und das Okkulte," in *Kandinsky und München*, exh. cat., Städtische Galerie im Lenbachhaus München, Munich 1982, pp. 87ff.
27 Stang 1979 (see note 13), p. 202.
28 Carl E. Schorske, *Wien. Geist und Gesellschaft im Fin de siècle*, Frankfurt 1982, p. 258.
29 On this cycle see *Munch und Deutschland* (see note 11), pp. 216ff.
30 Stang 1979 (see note 13), p. 235.
31 *Edvard Munch*, exh. cat., Kunstmuseum Basel, Basel 1985, pp. 139f; cf. Günter Metken, "Von Montesquieu bis Beuys," in *Segantini*, exh. cat., Kunsthaus Zürich, Zurich 1990, pp. 32ff, esp. 42ff.

10 Edvard Munch, *The Sun*, 1911,
oil on canvas, 450 x 780 cm, Munch-museet, Oslo

Edvard Munch and the Early Secessionist Woodcut in Vienna—a Comparative Assessment

Marian Bisanz-Prakken

On the occasion of the present comprehensive exhibition of the art of Edvard Munch in Vienna, it seems appropriate to explore possible points of contact between the Norwegian artist and the early Secessionist avant-garde around 1900 with respect to a medium in which outstanding and innovative accomplishments can be attributed to both—that of the woodcut, which enjoyed a period of extraordinary bloom in the early years of the Secession from 1901–02 until the departure of the Klimt group (1905). Edvard Munch exhibited paintings and etchings at three Secession exhibitions during that very same period.[1]

Munch was not featured as a woodcut artist at these shows, however, although he had already made quite a name for himself in this context, especially in Germany. And he had not even been invited to the large-scale *Fifth Exhibition* (1899), a show devoted entirely to contemporary international graphic art. It should be noted, however, that this exhibition was organized by Josef Engelhart, President of the Secession at the time and an advocate of the "naturalist" position, as was clearly reflected in the largely traditional selection of exhibiting artists.[2]

At the twelfth, "Nordic" exhibition (1901–02), where Munch made his Vienna debut with his paintings *Beach* and *Angst* (cat. no. 116), Chairman Alfred Roller and his colleagues focused on painting. The works of Scandinavian, Russian, and Finnish artists presented at this show along with paintings by Ferdinand Hodler and Jan Toorop were highly significant in light of the upcoming *Beethoven Exhibition*, for which preparations had already begun.[3] This ambitious cooperative project, which was to highlight a contemporary form of "temple art" in the spirit of interaction among all the arts, featured both examples from the distant past and achievements of contemporary monumental art.

It was at this epoch-making exhibition, in which artists experimented demonstratively in a mood of euphoria with "simple" materials, unorthodox combinations of materials, and wholly new techniques, that the modern Viennese woodcut was born.[4] A series of square woodcuts by a total of twelve artists—including Carl Moll, Koloman Moser, Friedrich König, Maximilian Kurzweil, and Ferdinand Andri—were printed in the fittingly square exhibition catalog. Even the experimental approach to the technique of woodcutting—which was new to them at that time—pursued by the artists involved in the Beethoven project inevitably calls to mind Munch's intense and primary concern with the processing of the wood surface. The art critic Karl Kuzmany, who observed the artists of Vienna in their "experimental laboratory for modern woodcutting art," as he described the workshop located in the basement of the Secession building—remarked that

> Only a few had worked with graphic media before; as experienced and, to a certain degree, mature painters, they were dilettantes at woodcutting. It was quite enjoyable, for a change, to take advantage of the full potential inherent in the material and to present one's ideas in the lively, decorative areas and lines that emerged from their impassioned working of wood surface to the public in multiple reproductions. Yet they went to extremes in blithely evading the conventional visual image and reducing both outlines and aspects of color to primitive forms.[5]

At first glance, some of the woodcuts printed in the catalog suggest associations with Munch. Symbolized in a simplified formal vocabulary which emphasizes contrast—the color orange appears with a uniform surface quality in some of the black-and-white prints—are such themes as threatened existence, fear, and loneliness. Yet a closer examination of these works, which were presented in similar fashion but differed significantly from one another, reveals that only two or three actually relate at all closely to Munch.

Thus, for example, the woodcut by Friedrich König with the image of a nude figure resembling a witch shown floating above a seaside

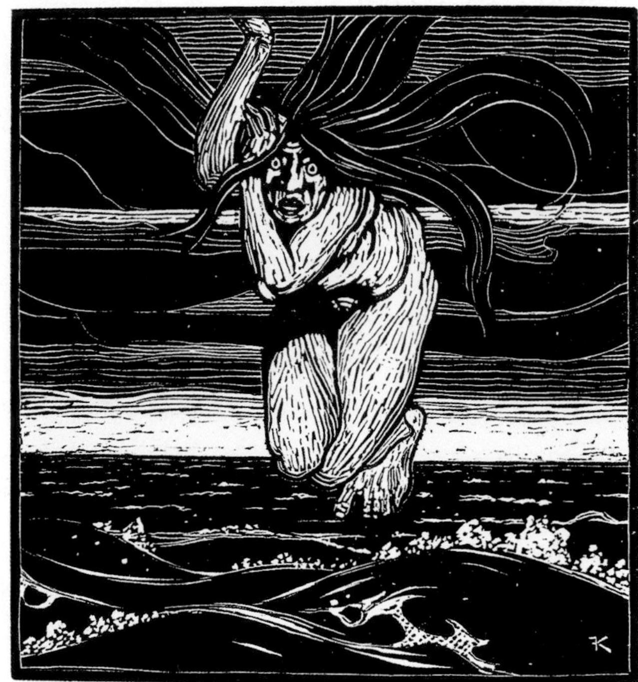

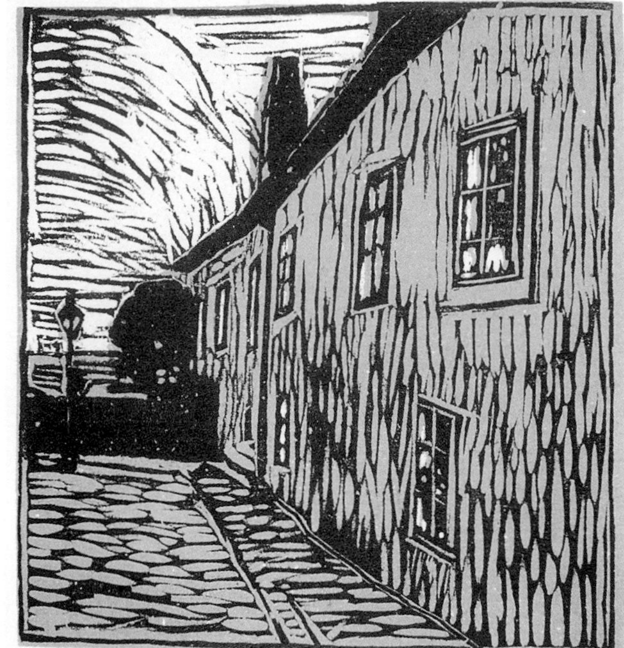

landscape is in certain ways reminiscent of Munch's painting *Angst*, which had been shown previously at the *Twelfth Secession Exhibition*—in the emphatic frontal view, the wide-open eyes with their sharply accented pupils, and the pulsating lines of the waves and sky (fig. 1).[6] Yet the caricature quality of the fantasy figure—though typical of König—has nothing in common with Munch's painting.

There are readily apparent technical similarities between Carl Moll's woodcut *Beethoven House on Eroikagasse* (fig. 2) and Munch's woodcuts, particularly in the density and dynamics of the broad, rough-cut lines used to depict the structures of the wall, the pavement, and the sky in parallel rhythms (with respect to technical execution, see, for example, Munch's woodcut *The Old Fisherman*, 1897).[7] Especially noteworthy here are the strong depth effect and the colliding directional systems projected over the flat surface, a principle of composition that Munch employed in his painting *The Scream* and the corresponding lithographic versions. Whether Munch's work actually served as a source remains a matter of conjecture. In any event, the general decorative character of Moll's woodcut is without parallel in Munch's art.

The most artistically mature work reproduced in the catalog is Koloman Moser's woodcut depicting a monumental figure in a primarily abstract, storm-lashed setting (fig. 3).[8] At first glance, the irregular structures of the white dots, spots, and lines call Munch to mind; yet the intricacy of these patterns bears a closer resemblance to those found in the works of the Karlsruhe painter and graphic artist Wilhelm Laage, a contemporary influenced by Munch, whose woodcuts were featured in a special issue of the journal *Ver Sacrum* in 1901.[9] This is another example of the selective perception of developments in international art by Viennese artists. Munch was ignored by *Ver Sacrum*, both as a painter and a graphic artist, whereas considerable attention was devoted to one of his successors.

Both ideologically and practically speaking, we recognize significant differences between the woodcuts produced for the *Beethoven Exhibition* and those of Edvard Munch. In the latter case, we see an individual artist working on the basis of his own subjective experience, devoting himself over a period of many years to profound themes of life and, using different techniques—including wood-

1 Friedrich König, *Untitled*, 1902,
woodcut for the *Beethoven Exhibition*, 15 x 14.1 cm,
Albertina, Vienna

2 Carl Moll, *Beethoven House on Eroikagasse*, 1902,
woodcut for the *Beethoven Exhibition*, 14 x 13.1 cm,
Albertina, Vienna

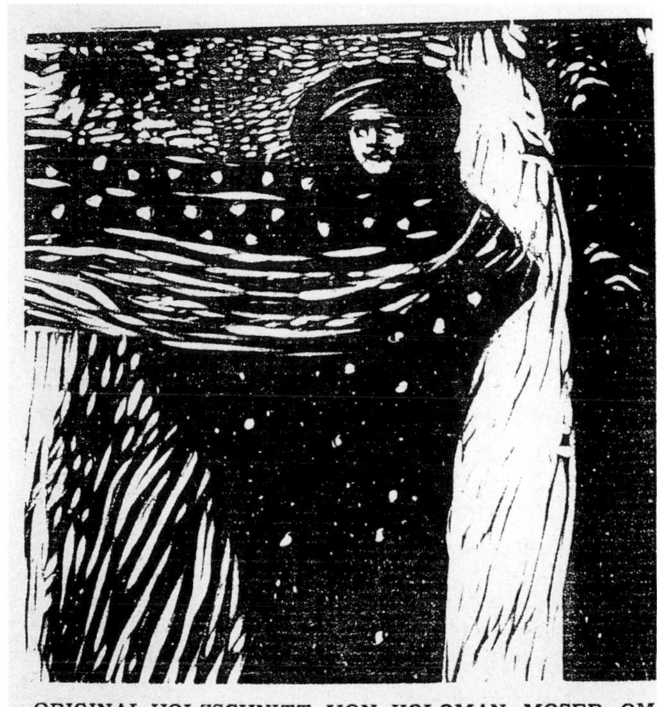

cut—creating an extended series of new variations. In the former, we observe a group of artists which discovers the woodcut in a mood of euphoria associated with a short-term cooperative, experimental project. Their woodcuts were not the products of personal or inner stirrings, as were Munch's, but were created in response to a thematic program. The artists involved in the project joined in focusing their attention on a single idea embodied in Max Klinger's Beethoven figure, the keynote image of the exhibition. In terms of format and subject matter, the woodcuts reproduced in the catalog relate—in some cases directly—to the square decorative plaques that were hung in a rhythmic arrangement on the walls of the side rooms beneath the frieze-style paintings (Klimt's *Beethoven Frieze* extended over three walls in the left side room). These decorative plaques served as thematic or atmospheric accompaniments to the more important paintings, which in turn—in the spirit of the complex iconography of the Beethoven sculpture—dealt in allegorical form with the dialectics of longing and fulfillment, suffering and redemption, struggle and survival. Accordingly, the themes of decorative plaques and the woodcuts are worlds apart, the former showing paradisiacal, pastoral, bucolic scenes, the latter concerned with such fundamentally pessimistic themes as fear, loneliness, mortality. Thus artists' attempts to come to grips with these existential themes were carried out within the context of the strict hierarchy of the total work of art.

Yet the rugged, primitive quality of the prints, a natural consequence of the often forceful working of the wood surface, appears to anticipate expressionism in some cases. It should be emphasized in this context, however, that the origins of this modern impulse, in itself a surprising development for Vienna, are to be found in the enthusiastic experimentation in handicraft techniques by the artists' group and in the maxims—cited in the catalog—that called for the use of "simple" principles of design and "honest" materials. According to the catalog, these principles represented a reaction to the "illusion" and the "lie" of Viennese "Ringstrasse art." Another factor involved in this creative impulse was the desire to achieve the "antithesis of the excessively refined painting technique of the impressionists," as Karl Kuzmany expressed it. This remark by the critic refers to a debate that polarized the entire German-speaking region at the time.[10]

The programmatic ambition of this philosophy of originality, which underlay the Secession's collective quest for a new kind of "temple art," had nothing in common with Edvard Munch's artistic goals. His experiments in the art of the woodcut and the formal reductions he achieved in the process were devoted to the symbolic representation of subjective, spiritual phenomena and states of mind. His repetitive printing of the woodcuts in differing color nuances must be understood in this context. Thus the "primitive quality" of his prints—which even included the incorporation of the natural wood grain and the grooves cut with a saw—assumes a character that is entirely different from that of the works created by the Viennese artists for the *Beethoven Exhibition*. Munch's woodcuts are the product of a constant interplay between manual and intellectual-spiritual activity. In contrast, the woodcuts exhibited at the *Beethoven Exhibition* must be classified—despite their often expressive character—as primarily decorative examples of two-dimensional art (*Flächenkunst*), which appear by virtue of their square

3 Koloman Moser, *Untitled*, 1902,
woodcut for the *Beethoven Exhibition*, 14 x 13.5 cm,
Albertina, Vienna

format as integral components of a total work of art. The black, planar woodcuts of William Nicholson or Félix Vallotton—both of whom were exhibited at the Secession—were more likely to have served as sources of inspiration for the Viennese woodcuts than the spiritual creations of Edvard Munch, which are characterized by subtle, often transparent color effects. The reception of Japanese woodcut art provides a point of encounter between Munch and the Viennese artists, in particular with respect to the reduction of flat forms and the two-dimensional rendering of spatial relationships. These sources of stimulus must be regarded in light of the general enthusiasm for Japanese art that had spread throughout Europe, however.

The catalytic effect of the *Beethoven Exhibition* soon became evident at all levels of artistic endeavor, including the art of the woodcut. Many woodcuts were created specifically for publication in *Ver Sacrum*, whose final year of publication (1903) was devoted primarily to this medium. Some of the contributions printed in the journal are works by students from the classes of Felician von Myrbach and Koloman Moser, both of whom taught at the Kunstgewerbeschule [Academy of Crafts]. Perhaps the most outstanding figures among the artists who continued to work with this technique during the years of change following the *Beethoven Exhibition* were Koloman Moser, Carl Moll, Maximilian Kurzweil, and Ferdinand Andri.

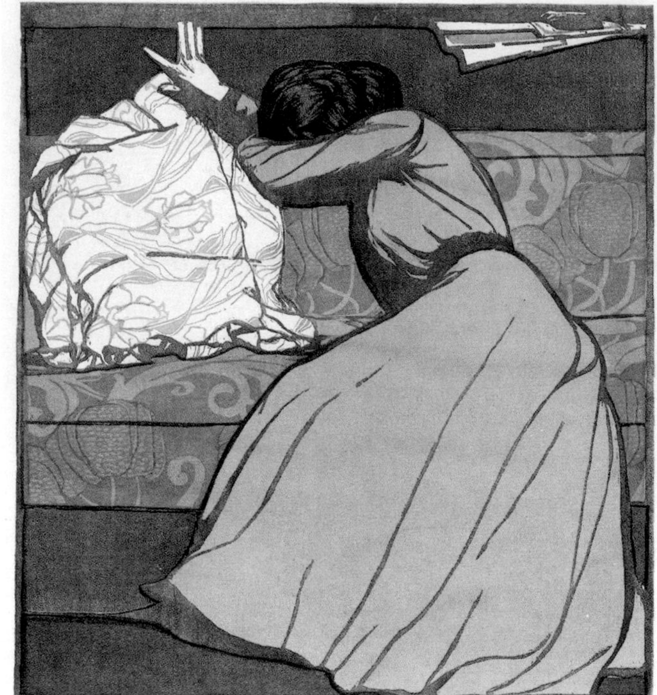

Their woodcuts produced around 1903 are undisputedly the finest examples of early Secessionist printmaking. In these works, the rugged character of the first experimental prints gives way to a cultivated technique based on effects of tension on the flat surface; and they were also printed in different colors. At the same time, the artists abandoned the ideologically German, symbol-laden allegories of the *Beethoven Exhibition*, which remained an isolated phenomenon in turn-of-the century Vienna. The Secession artists now turned their attention to less weighty themes—landscapes, city scenes, and interiors. These woodcuts, which exhibit an unmistakable Viennese identity, are even farther removed from Munch than their immediate predecessors shown at the *Beethoven Exhibition*. The differences can be illustrated by comparing several pairs of works devoted to similar motifs.

In his color woodcut *Mystical Shore* of 1899 (cat. no. 143), Munch achieved a highly symbolic abstraction of the seacoast motif. In this work, the reflection of the moon in the midst of the parallel lines of the waves, which are printed in bluish-green and follow the grain of the wood, creates an emphatic, mystical accent. The

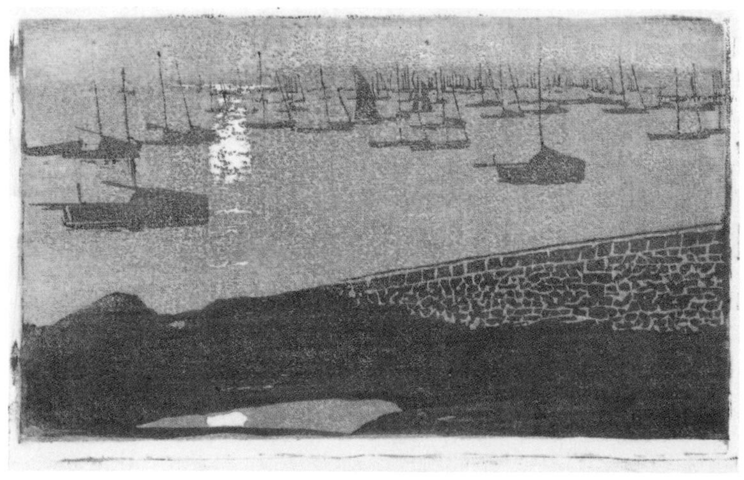

4 Maximilian Kurzweil, *Sunset over the Harbor*, 1903, color woodcut, 13.8 x 19.5 cm, Albertina, Vienna

5 Maximilian Kurzweil, *Cushion*, 1903, color woodcut, 55.5 x 45.2 cm, Albertina, Vienna

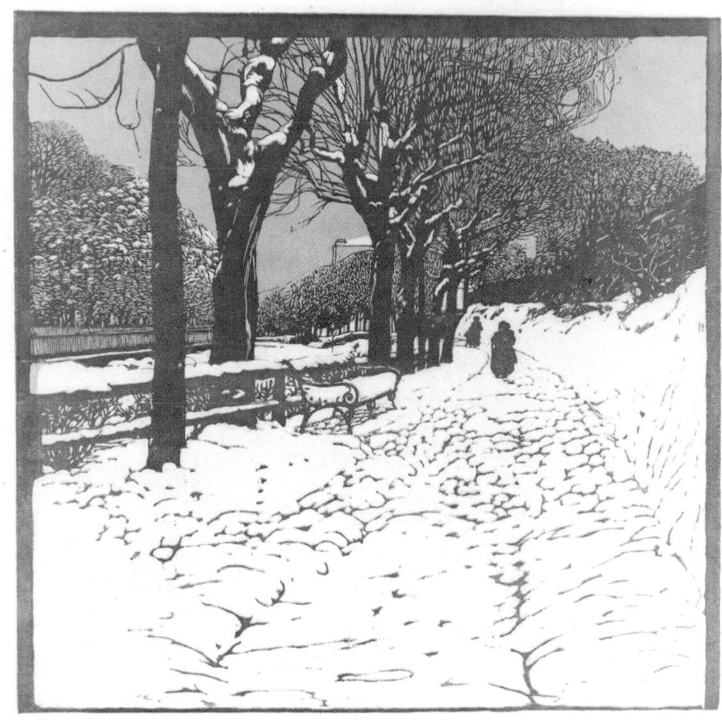

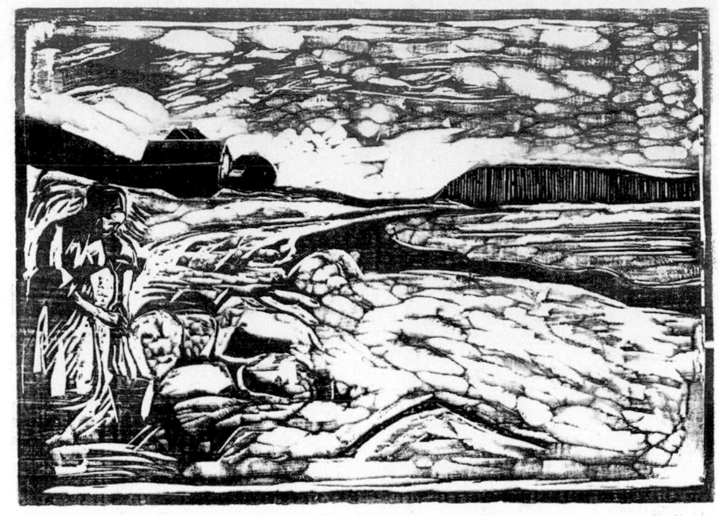

version of the woodcut by Maximilian Kurzweil entitled *Sunset over the Harbor* of 1903 shown here (fig. 4), which is one of several produced in different colors, depicts an evening scene—as does Munch's woodcut as well; yet this print is entirely lacking in "spiritual dimension."[11] In this work, the flat areas of base colors—subdued blue and light purple—enter into a subtle dialog with the gray of the silhouette-like shapes of boats grouped along the horizon and the decoratively structured shoreline in the foreground. The white reflection of the moon was not cut into the wood itself but achieved by leaving out color at this point. In this work, inspired in part by Japanese art and in part by the Pont-Aven School, the printed areas of color, which take on a suggestive effect by virtue of tiny irregularities, create a sense of mood. Kurzweil's composition derives its vitality—in a manner quite typical of the Viennese art of the period—from the tension-filled balance between large and small areas of color and the deliberate intersection of forms and lines.

The woodcuts *Winter Scene on the Hohe Warte* by Carl Moll (fig. 6) and *Washing Clothes on the Shore* by Edvard Munch (fig. 7) were both done in 1903; the red version of Munch's woodcut shown here was presumably first printed in 1918.[12] These two works, each of which presents a specific local motif, represent two fundamentally different worlds. Moll's monumental, square composition—the hallmark of Viennese two-dimensional art (*Flächenkunst*)—is characterized by harmonious proportions and balanced, subtly matches color constellations. The subdued winter mood is evoked in congenial fashion by the three print colors—white, light gray and dark gray. On display here is the solemn assumption of the subject into the total work of art—which still had an imperial quality at that time—and into the holy "world of the artist," which was governed by higher laws. In Munch's print, however, we recognize the reaction of the sense of self, which appears directly transposed into the vigorous dynamics of the landscape structures. In his beach landscape, Munch systematically incorporated the smooth color transitions caused by the exposed grain of the wood, heightening the expressive power of the areas of cliff and sky. In contrast, Moll's winter scene is dominated by uniform color effects. In some of his woodcuts, however—such as *Church of St. Michael* and the series of watercolor prints entitled *Beethoven Houses*—Moll also experimented with flowing color transitions. Yet this procedure still serves the function of filling areas of surface, and it forms a decorative contrast to the uniformly black lines and forms of the print.

6 Carl Moll, *Winter Scene on the Hohe Warte*, 1903,
color woodcut, 52.7 x 43.2 cm, Albertina, Vienna

7 Edvard Munch, *Washing Clothes on the Shore*, 1903/1918,
color woodcut on paper, 48.5 x 62 cm, Albertina, Vienna

Of all Viennese artists, Maximilian Kurzweil was most interested in the overlapping of different color areas in his prints. This is particularly evident in his color woodcut entitled *Cushion* of 1903, another outstanding example of turn-of-the-century Viennese print art (fig. 5).[13] The position and gestures of the sitting figure, which is integrated into the harmonious pattern of lines and the overall tectonic structure of its surroundings, appear remarkably controlled. Whereas the expressive urge is subordinate in this work to the dominant emphasis on the elements of space and two-dimensionality, the priorities are precisely reversed in Munch's woodcut. Where he is concerned with the relationship between figure and surroundings—as in the woodcuts *Moonlight* and *Melancholy*, both of 1896 (cat. nos. 11–15, 87, 88), for example—the forms and colors of architectural and landscape elements respond to the moods or emotional states of the depicted persons.

On the whole, the question posed at the outset as to whether there were points of contact between Munch's woodcuts and those of Viennese artists around 1900 must be answered in the negative. The respective positions and artistic objectives are simply too different. We are undoubtedly confronted here with an aspect of the North-South dialectic that was manifest at all levels of culture. A letter of March 7, 1904, in which Carl Moll expresses lavish praise for his Norwegian colleague on the occasion of the extensive presentation of his pictures at the *Nineteenth Secession Exhibition*, sheds revealing light on the lack of attention given Munch's woodcuts by the artists of the Vienna Secession:[14] Although Moll himself had reached the peak of his woodcut production at that time, he does not devote a single word to the subject in his letter to one of the greatest exponents of the modern European woodcut.

1 *12th Exhibition*, 1901–02, cat. nos. 66, 67 (paintings); *15th Exhibition*, 1902, cat. nos. 32, 50, 65 (etchings); *19th A-Exhibition*, 1904, cat. nos. 32–51 (paintings).
2 Marian Bisanz-Prakken, *Heiliger Frühling—Gustav Klimt und die Anfänge der Secession*, exh. cat., Graphische Sammlung Albertina, Vienna 1998, p. 22.
3 *Ibid.*, pp. 26, 166, 169.
4 For a discussion of the early Secessionist woodcut in Vienna, see "Die frühe Secession und der Holzschnitt," in *Heiliger Frühling* (see note 2), pp. 144–155.
5 Karl Kuzmany, "Jüngere österreichische Graphiker, II, Holzschnitt," in *Die Graphischen Künste*, 31, 1908, p. 70.
6 Catalog for the *14th Exhibition* (*Beethoven*), Secession, Vienna, 1902, p. 54.
7 *Ibid.*, p. 38. Edvard Munch's *The Old Fisherman*, Woll 116.
8 *Ibid.*, p. 32.
9 *Ver Sacrum*, 4, 1901, pp. 256–274; 5, 1902, pp. 140, 150.
10 Kuzmany 1908 (see note 5), p. 74.
11 Woodcut in grayish-blue, light purple, and gray, 13.8 x 19.5 cm, Albertina, Vienna, inv. no. 1997.
12 Woodcut in dark gray, light gray, and white on Japan paper, 556 x 453 mm, Albertina, Vienna, inv. no. NF 9691. Edvard Munch's *Washing Clothes on the Shore*, woodcut in red and black, 48.5 x 62 cm, Albertina, Vienna, inv. no. 1924–440; Woll no. 246.
13 Woodcut in grayish-blue, light blue, brown, green, and yellow on Japan paper, 55.5 x 45.2 cm, Albertina, Vienna, inv. no. NF 9691/1.
14 Letter from Carl Moll to Edvard Munch, dated Vienna, July 3, 1904, Munch-museet, Oslo; cited from *Sehnsucht nach Glück. Wiens Aufbruch in die Moderne: Klimt, Kokoschka, Schiele*, Sabine Schulze (ed.), exh. cat., Schirn Kunsthalle Frankfurt, Ostfildern-Ruit 1995, p. 226. The other letters from Carl Moll to Edvard Munch in the archives of the Munch-museet in Oslo also make no mention of the woodcuts of either artist. (Thanks to Inger Engan, librarian at the Munch-Museet, for her kind assistance.)

Munch and Austria—Traces of Encounter

Antonia Hoerschelmann

Vincent van Gogh, Edvard Munch, and Diego Velázquez are the painters with whom Maria Lassnig surrounds herself in her painting entitled *Traditionskette* of 1983 (fig. 1). As Wolfgang Drechsler points out,

> What she shares with these pioneers of modern art and what creates the contextual bond with the seventeenth-century Spanish artist Diego Velázquez, who is also cited in the painting, goes beyond the formal aspects of painting; it is also the substantive component which justifies this appeal to tradition. Yet Maria Lassnig's art hardly ever involves autobiographical narrative. She does not show what she does but rather what she feels.[1]

Since the early 1980s, Maria Lassnig has been reflecting upon pictorial themes and formal solutions from her early work. In contrast to Edvard Munch, her rediscoveries lead to variations and developments in her art which are also capable of accommodating entirely new contents. Thus, for example, she has transformed the animal, which always plays an important role in her art, from the artist's alter ego to a partner and point of reference and eventually to a representative of endangered nature.

Lassnig's retrospective view of her own work and her own development also involves recollection of her artistic origins, of her "forefathers" and mentors. Munch and Van Gogh are placed as honorable busts on a pedestal, Velázquez as a "painters' painter" in the pose of his own self-portrait. Lassnig herself kneels between them and the viewer in the foreground. What the painters depicted here have in common is the consistent transformation of complex reality through the workings of internal and external perception. In the course of their search for seismographic traces, all artistic activity—every brushstroke, every spot of paint, and every line—becomes subordinate to the goal of grasping in the visual image the essence of the object in its totality and thus of transposing it from the sphere of individual experience to the level of universal validity, regardless of whether the point of departure for the subject is a real object, such as a portrait, an idea, a feeling, or a sensation. According to Maria Lassnig, the intensity and precision of the artist's work requires that one "has seen and felt the world; in other words, that one must 'know' something specific in order to choose and paint it, and not simply wade in the fog and mud of randomness."[2]

Edvard Munch explained his approach to the object and content of his pictures in the often cited statement, "I do not paint what I see but what I have seen."[3] Temporal distance transforms the objects of experience into memory images which, isolated from the space-time continuum and controlled by moods, feelings, and sensation, take shape on the canvas.

> I do not believe in art that has not developed necessarily from the heart's urge to reveal itself. We want to create more than a mere photograph of nature, and we are not content to paint only pretty pictures to be hung on

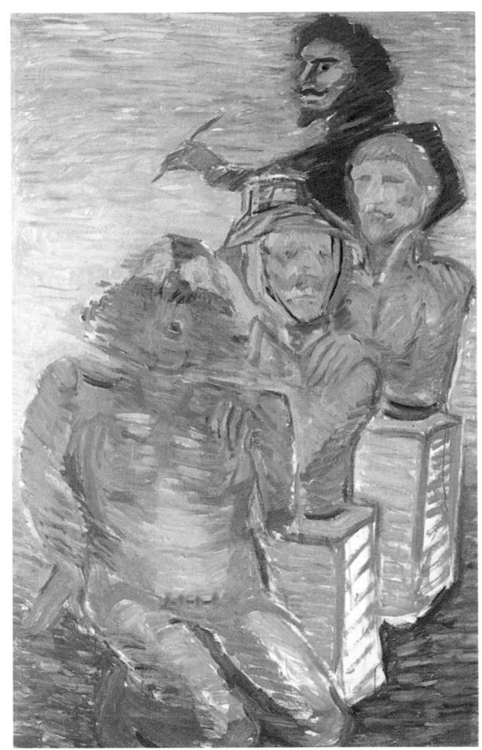

1 Maria Lassnig, *Traditionskette*, 1983, oil on canvas, 204 x 130 cm, private collection

the living room wall. We want to attempt, if we cannot achieve it ourselves, at least to establish the foundation for an art that can be a gift to humanity, an art that we have created from our own heart's blood, an art that touches and takes hold of people.[4]

Munch achieved that goal in his images of fear and despair and of love and yearning. He captured a "sense of the world" that remains relevant even in our time, and in the intensity with which he expressed his message, he himself remains both a challenge and a guiding standard.

Edvard Munch first exhibited in Vienna at the *12th Exhibition of the Vienna Secession* in 1901. A touring exhibition organized by the Kunsthandlung Lichtenberg in 1893 had been cancelled due to financial losses.[5] The theme of the Secession exhibition was Scandinavian and Russian painting, complemented by works by Ferdinand Hodler, Cuno Amiet, Jan Toorop, and others. The exhibiting artists were carefully selected in keeping with the by-laws of the Vienna Secession—the goal was to educate the public. According to the catalog, Munch was represented by two paintings. Mentioned in addition to *Angst* of 1894 (cat. no. 116) is the title *Beach*, a painting that can no longer be identified today.[6]

In his review of the exhibition, the Vienna critic Ludwig Hevesi devoted extensive and lavish praise to Ferdinand Hodler and surveyed the Russian section with favor. With respect to Munch, he had only this to say:

One sees a crowd of people that appears to be moving towards the viewer. Ten faces are discernable, all pale, with eyes full of horror, distorted by fear, caricatured. A Carrièresque manner of blurring a scene. But the artist also renders their fear visible in a symbolic way, making an ornament of fear. The water in the background, the fiery sky—everything comes together in swirling waves. The fear that grips these brains is transmitted to their surroundings and dissolves them in colorful lines of emotion that intertwine in uncanny patterns and confusing tangles. Carrière with Toorop.[7]

Munch exhibited in Vienna again the following year, showing a group of twenty etchings at the 15th exhibition of the Secession.[8]

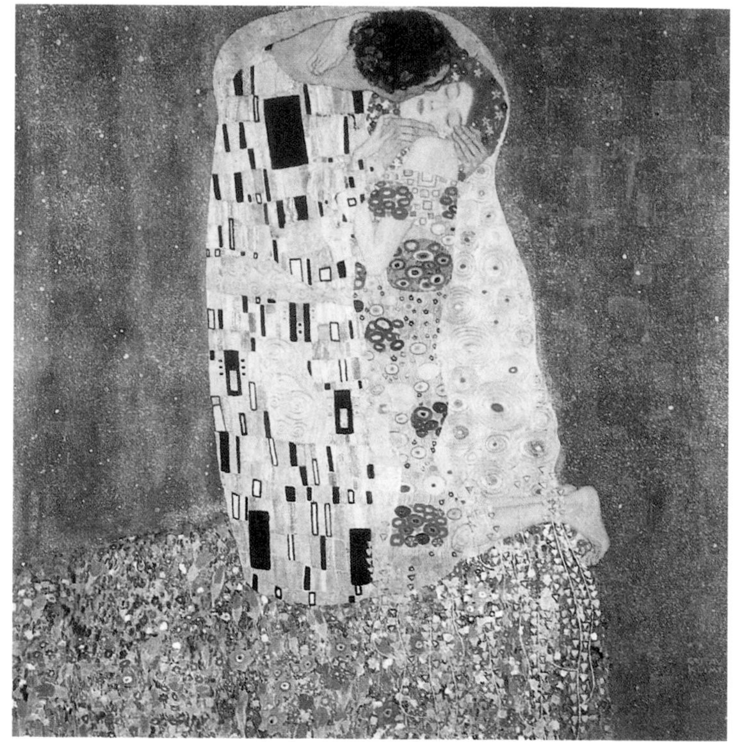

2 Gustav Klimt, *The Kiss*, 1907–08,
oil, plated with silver and gold on canvas, 180 x 180 cm,
Österreichische Galerie Belvedere, Vienna

His woodcuts would surely have been more interesting to the artists of the Vienna Secession, since they were working with the technique themselves a lot at the time, as the illustrations in the journal *Ver Sacrum* so strikingly document.[9] Munch's woodcuts (cat. nos. 51–54) most certainly inspired Gustav Klimt (fig. 2) or at least provided him moral support in his work. Both artists chose the harmonious square pictorial format for their images of the *Kiss* to achieve symmetrical compositions of monumental character. In both the painting and the woodcut, a common outline encloses the two bodies, joining them in a closed formal block and incorporating them into the flat surface. Each of the isolated groups of figures is interwoven with its surroundings, with nature—in the woodcut through the integration of the actual grain of the wood in the block and in the painting through the use of corresponding formal elements and color accents. In this way, not only do the figures melt together into a unified form but this form itself also forges a strong substantive bond with nature.[10]

Again in 1904 works by Munch were shown at the 19th Secession exhibition in Vienna. Featuring twenty paintings, this was the first presentation of his art on a larger scale.[11] Considerable effort was made to recruit Munch for this exhibition. As early as 1903, Felician von Myrbach, President of the Secession, wrote to the artist: "This exhibition is to have an élite character and will comprise only a small number of selected paintings and sculptures by artists to whom we have extended personal invitations."[12] Carl Moll wrote to Munch as well, explaining that "[the Secession] plans to reserve a separate room for your works."[13] Munch expressed thanks in his response and indicated that he agreed with the proposed approach: "My works lose much of their effect when shown together with others."[14] Munch had considered exhibiting in Vienna several years earlier. After the first comprehensive presentation of the *Frieze of Life* in Berlin in 1902, he was evidently so impressed with the unity of the works in the cycle that he wrote early in the year to his friend Franz Servaes,[15] saying, "I would very much like to exhibit this frieze in Vienna, for I regard it as my most important work. The artists of Vienna are the only ones who can help me show the frieze in a fitting architectural setting."[16] Munch was apparently familiar with the exceptional exhibitions of the Vienna Secession, presentations such as the *Beethoven Exhibition* of 1902 that had the quality of total works of art.

Given the admiration expressed in the Secession's invitation and Munch's favorable impression of the Secession's exhibition activities, which he had expressed some time before, the presentation realized in Vienna was astonishing. Munch's works—although shown like those of the other artists in a separate room—were grouped around the central exhibit devoted to Ferdinand Hodler, the star of the show. The works were selected by the hanging commission[17] on the basis of criteria described in the foreword to the catalog: "The character of the exhibition is determined by an orientation towards the monumental, towards simplicity and the development of style in form and color." Accordingly, the commission focused on paintings by Munch that tended to emphasize the decorative and the monumental, works in which sweeping line structures appeared as defining elements of composition,[18] much like those found in turn-of-the-century stylized art.[19] Only about one-third of the works shown belonged to the *Frieze of Life*, and thus, like the preceding Vienna exhibitions, the presentation failed for the most part to represent the essential focus of Munch's artistic concerns at the time.[20] The selection reflected Hevesi's assessment, cited above, that *Angst* assumed the quality of an ornamental painting in such a context. The works sold after the exhibition in Vienna corroborate this observation.[21] Even Richard Muther, who had still been skeptical with respect to Munch in 1901,[22] emphasized the monumental, decorative aspects of the Norwegian artist's work in his review of the exhibition. He saw Munch's most admirable qualities in his use of color and used such terms as "color mass," "expression" and "rhythm" to emphasize expressionist characteristics.

The image of a Nordic summer night is almost too overpowering for the small room …; it would even dominate the main room—so massive and coherent are the chords of color that flow from this work. And what rhythm there is in these small landscapes! How well he succeeds in imbuing even these small works with a monumental effect through the clear distribution of color masses and by relating all details to the defining fundamental

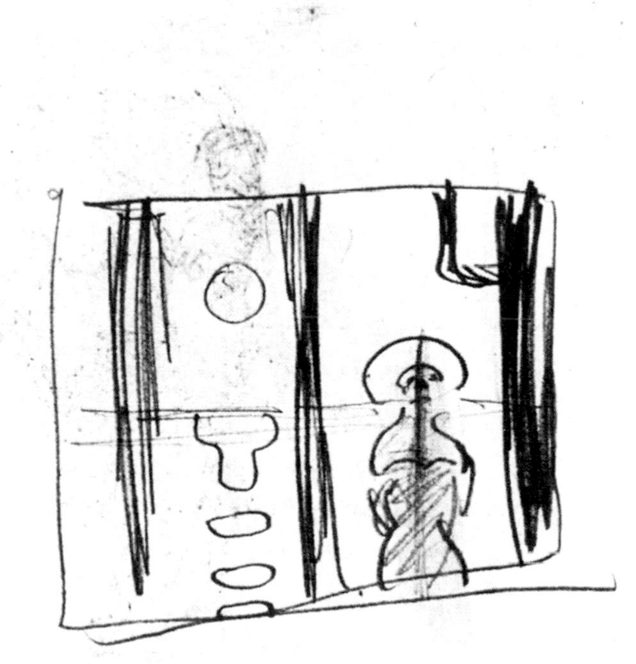

3 Alfred Kubin, *Study after Munch*, c. 1903, pencil on paper, sketch book 8, Oberösterreichische Landesgalerie, Linz

form! One has the sense in Munch's case ... of a ... genius who achieves expression in the simplest and least constrained manner possible.[23]

Munch did not travel to Vienna for any of these exhibitions. It is likely that he was personally acquainted with only one Austrian artist. Alfred Kubin mentions having met Munch at the Galerie Paul Cassirer in Berlin in 1903: "I also got to know Munch personally. I was his and his bride Tulla Larsen's guest on several occasions. Munch was a difficult man to get close to, an introvert who opened up only after a considerable amount of drink, but I was very touched by his reserve."[24]

The small drawing in one of Kubin's sketchbooks, a rendition of *The Voice* (*Summer Night*) (fig. 3), of which Munch produced many different variations, was probably done about this time. Although the encounter did not lead to a close friendship between the two artists, they are known to have been in touch with each other more than thirty years later: "I heard from Edvard Munch, who remembers me fondly from 1903 and wishes to have one of my works."[25]

Munch and Kubin also shared Nietzsche's heroic idea of the great, lonely, creative human being far removed from social contacts. Both artists tended to stylize themselves in keeping with this image to the point of manipulation in their writings, letters, public appearances, and correspondence. Munch pointed out, for example, that his name meant "monk" and thus symbolized and gave direction to his life. He cultivated his loneliness, and Kubin, the "Magician of Zwickledt," described his house as a monk's cell. There are several remarkable parallels in the lives of the two artists—the early death of their mothers and the resulting changes in family circumstances, their "absent" fathers, and other deaths within their immediate families, events that shaped their childhood and adolescent years.

The first signs of expressionism began to appear in Viennese art in 1904. Muther suggested as much in the review cited above, and elements of expressionism are evident in the painting of Richard Gerstl. "A comparison of Richard Gerstl with the Secession reveals that the Secession was more a standard-bearer for traditional values, more a swan-song of the nineteenth century than a prelude to the twentieth,"[26] wrote Werner Hofmann in 1965, adding that "the intellectual situation in Vienna at the dawn of our century rested on a foundation of severe tensions."[27] Polar oppositions, not in personal sense but with respect to matters of principle, were embodied by such pairs of figures as Richard Strauss and Arnold Schönberg or Gustav Klimt and Richard Gerstl. According to Hofmann, Klimt stood for the position of the artist at the turn of the century, whereas Gerstl represented the turn towards expressionism in Austria, although his oeuvre remained largely hidden from the public eye until 1931.

Two exhibitions presented by the Vienna Secession played a decisive role in Gerstl's development as an artist. An extensive exhibition of impressionist art in 1903 provided Gerstl an opportunity to study original works and prompted numerous artistic experiments. The 1904 exhibition of the works of Edvard Munch mentioned above offered him new perspectives on aspects of pictorial

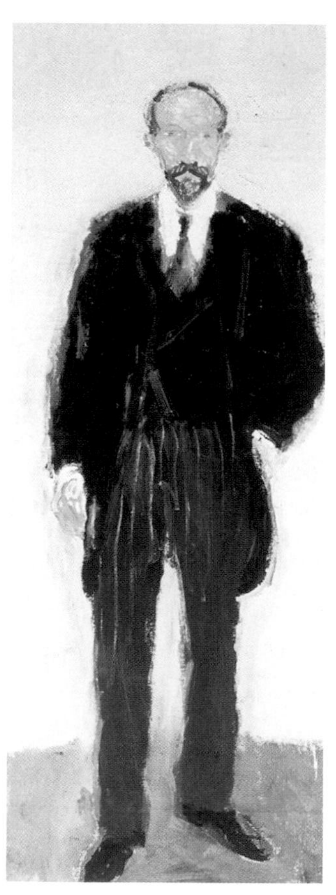

4 Richard Gerstl, *Portrait of Ernst Dietz*, before summer 1907, tempera and oil on canvas, 184.5 x 73 cm, Österreichische Galerie Belvedere, Vienna

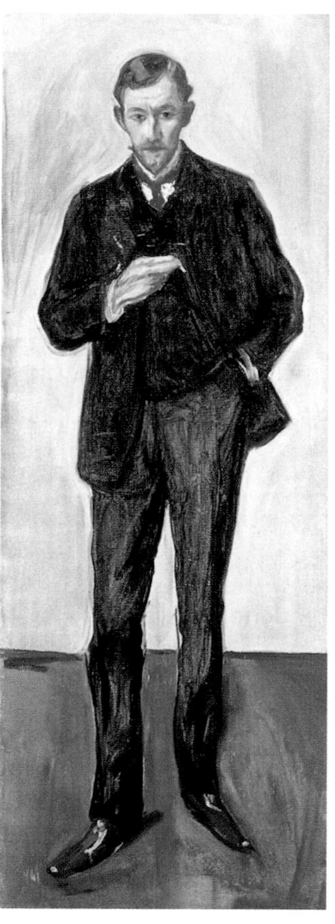

5 Edvard Munch, *Portrait of a Frenchman*, 1901, oil on canvas, 185 x 70 cm, Nasjonalgalleriet, Oslo

design, particularly in the field of portraiture. This is revealed by a now historic comparison[28] between Gerstl's *Portrait of Ernst Dietz* of 1907 (fig. 4) and Munch's painting *Angst*, with respect to the schematic rendering of the head, and *Portrait of a Frenchman* of 1901 (fig. 5), with respect to composition.

Two traditions of different ages are apparent in this sketchy painting style: that of the impressionists—in the dissolution of contours and the loosely organized interior drawing of the clothing—and that of the symbolist painting of Edvard Munch. *Angst* of 1894 [cat. no. 116], his most important work, was not only exhibited at the Secession but was also available, like many of his other works, in the form of reproductions in art journals and books. The barely suggested, pin-point eyes, the unmodelled surface of the face, and the short, dark strokes of paint in the outline and the beard are direct descendents of Munch's faces.[29]

In the art of Arnold Schönberg, who took painting lessons from Gerstl, Munch's masks of fear mutate into transparent grimaces and faces which emerge as visions from ethereal color spaces and appear as bodiless shadows on the narrow dividing line between the visible and invisible worlds on the canvas (fig. 6).
In *Self-Portrait on a Blue Background* of 1905 (fig. 7), Gerstl obviously referred in his selection of color contrasts to works done by Munch during the 1890s, such as the portrait of *Dagny Juel Przybyszewska* of 1893 (cat. no. 185) or the *Self-Portrait with Cigarette* of 1895 (fig. 8). Both artists depict themselves surrounded by an indefinable, dark-blue color space. In Munch's works, the head and the hand — the artist's most important working tool, shown in the middle of the painting—emerge clearly and unmistakably as light-colored areas, while the body blends in its three-quarter presentation into the indefinite blue surrounding space. Gerstl, however, presents himself frontally to the viewer, with a brightly illuminated, naked upper body which, as a central column of light, also illuminates the surrounding space and forms the pictorial axis. While the two artists are alike in their loneliness and isolation, they differ in terms of their chosen role images. Gerstl depicts himself as a saint with a halo of light in the tradition of images of Christ, the saints, hermits, and martyrs, whereas Munch retreats into darkness. This becomes even more obvious in *Self-Portrait in Hell* (fig. 10, cat. no. 202), in which Munch positions the glowing inferno of the flickering light of hell at the point at which the light of the fire and the dark shadow meet. Gerstl takes his interpretation a step further in *Self-Portrait as a Nude in Full Figure* of 1908 (fig. 9), a work in which he depicts himself fully nude for the first time. Here, the artist cites the iconography of Dürer's pen-and-ink self-portrait of 1503–04[30] in the end. Munch also focused on the subject of the nude male in photography including self-portraits while working in Åsgårdstrand in 1904 and again on the beach at Warnemünde in 1907. In their self-portraits, both artists dealt with the quest for self-identity and a fitting new approach to the expression of their life and role as artists, and each articulated a contemporary position of reorientation.

Whereas the role of the artist as victim and social outsider—as expressed in the art of Van Gogh and Gauguin—was a dominant theme in artists' self-portraits in the nineteenth century, this image appears to have faded in the

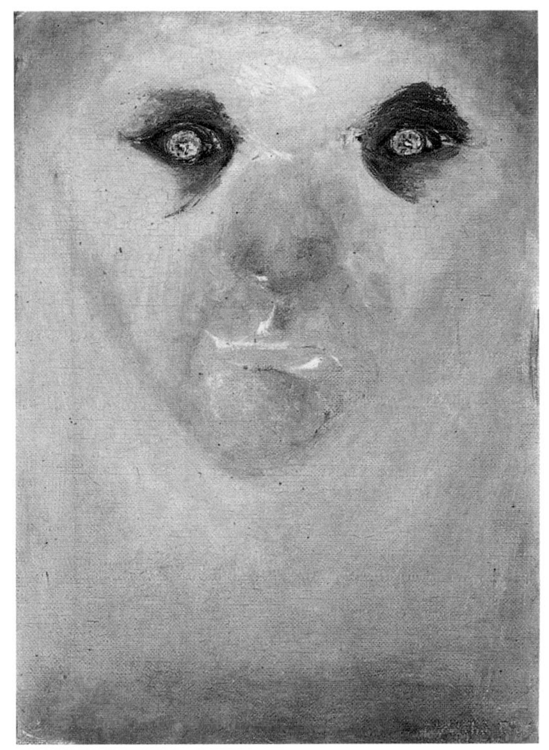

6 Arnold Schönberg, *Staring Gaze*, 1910,
oil on canvas, 28 x 18.8 cm,
Lawrence and Roland Schönberg and
Nuria Schönberg Nono collection

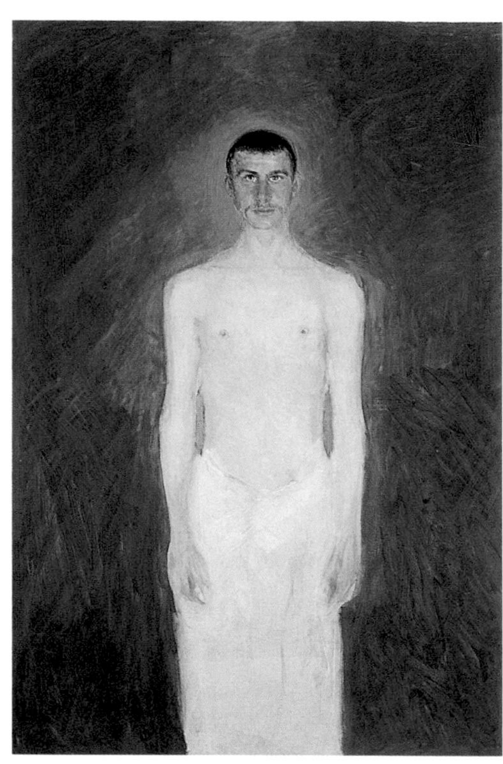

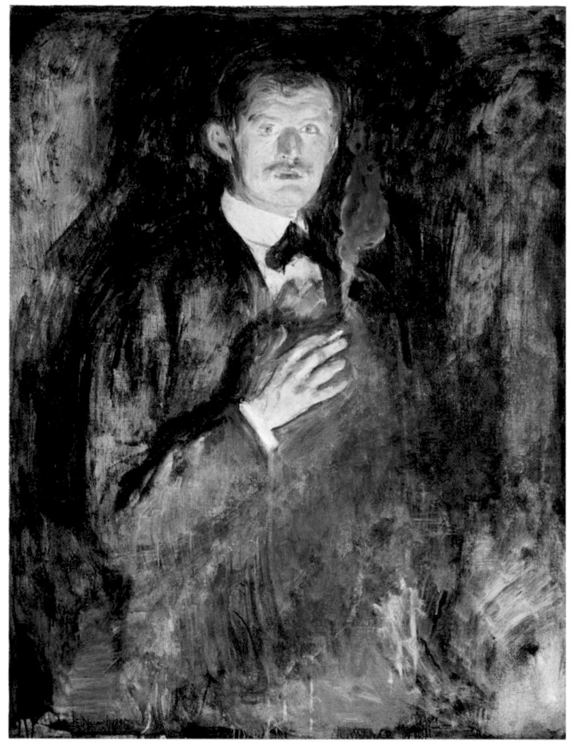

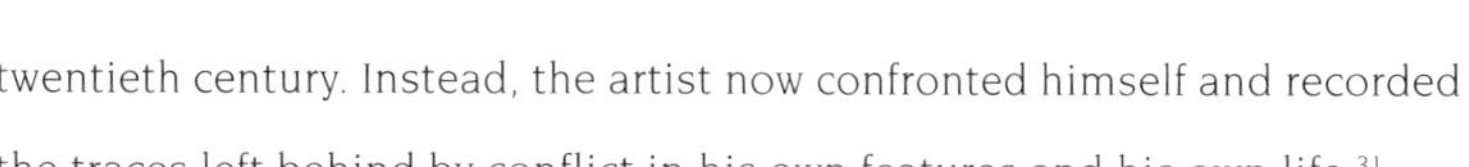

twentieth century. Instead, the artist now confronted himself and recorded the traces left behind by conflict in his own features and his own life.[31]

As a "hopelessly lost self"—to cite Hermann Bahr—the visual artist sought to visualize the invisible aspects of human individuality—his own and that of others—in the intellectual climate of the turn of the century, not writing of life but painting it, as Munch's fatherly friend Hans Jæger had expressed it. Munch himself expressed thoughts on the subject: "My pictures are diaries;"[32] and "You know my pictures, and you know I have experienced all that myself."[33]

Works by Munch were not shown again in Vienna until 1909, at the *Internationale Kunstschau*,[34] which featured four of thirteen painted sketches done in 1906 for Ibsen's play *Ghosts*, which was performed at the Berliner Kammerspiele under the direction of Max Reinhardt. At this exhibition, he encountered a new generation of artists represented by the young Egon Schiele and Oskar Kokoschka. Both had attracted considerable attention the preceding year at the *Wiener Kunstschau*, for which their work had been chosen by Gustav Klimt. By the time Munch next appeared in Vienna—in early 1912 at the group exhibition *Norwegische Künstler im Künstlerbund Hagen*—the two artists had become so well-known and firmly established that it was possible to present them along with Munch. A. F. Seligman remarked that Munch represented the lesser evil as compared to the Austrians, Schiele in particular, writing that "I note with pleasure the absence of gross indecencies at this exhibition."[35] His comment refers to the difficult situation facing expressionist artists in Vienna and the partial lack of currency in Viennese art criticism. In general, criticism of Munch was quite positive, and critics praised the "color synthesist, who is striving to achieve increasingly grand monumental effects."[36] Munch was represented with eleven paintings, thirty-one prints, and the folio *Alpha and Omega*. Important paintings such as *Melancholy (Laura)* (cat. no. 92), *Self-Portrait with Bottle of Wine* (cat. no. 201), or prints such as *August Strindberg* (cat. no. 190), *The Kiss* (cat. no. 45), and *Madonna* (cat. no. 22 or 23) were shown.[37]

Works by the Norwegian were exhibited alongside those of Austrian artists at the extensive international *Sonderbund-Ausstellung* in Cologne in the summer of 1912. We read in the foreword to the

7 Richard Gerstl, *Self-Portrait on a Blue Background*, c. 1904, oil on canvas, 159.5 x 109 cm, Leopold Museum – Privatstiftung, Vienna

8 Edvard Munch, *Self-Portrait with Cigarette*, 1895, oil on canvas, 110.5 x 85.5 cm, Nasjonalgalleriet, Oslo

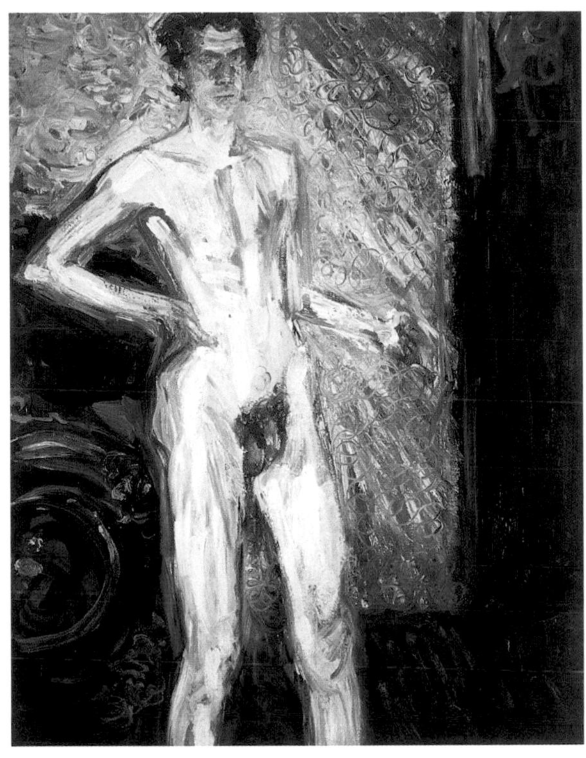

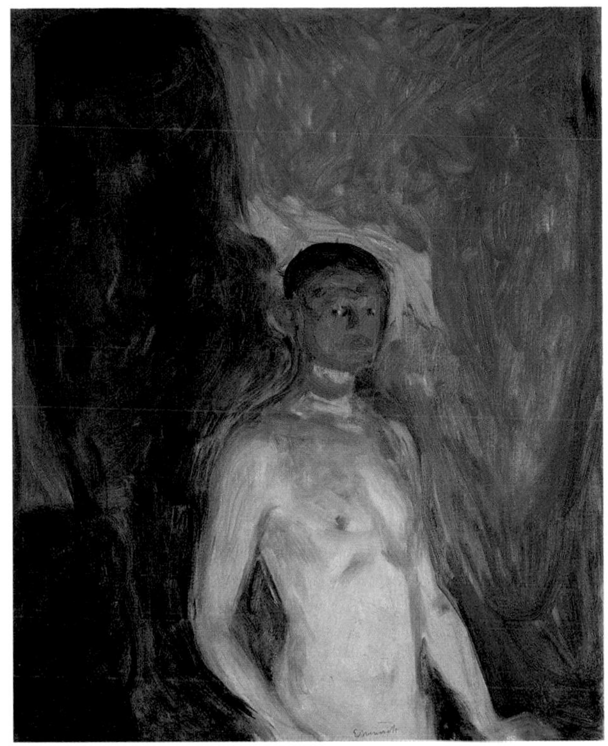

catalog: "While this international exhibition of works of living artist seeks to show a cross-section of the expressionist movement, a retrospective section is devoted to the historical roots from which this controversial contemporary painting style has emerged: the art of Vincent van Gogh, Paul Cézanne, Paul Gauguin."[38] However, the exhibition made no distinction between fauvism, expressionism, or cubism but instead equated expressionism with innovative contemporary expressive art. Also featured in other special exhibits were the neo-impressionists Henry Edmond Cross and Paul Signac as well as Pablo Picasso: "And thus we hope to close the chain of relationships that links modern painting with the art of the last classic painters."[39]

Edvard Munch was celebrated with thirty-two paintings from all of his creative periods as the leading protagonist of expressionism and thus achieved his final breakthrough to success. Reflecting the geography of the Habsburg Empire, artists from Prague, Krakow, and Vienna were represented in the Austrian sections, among them Albert Paris Gütersloh with two, Egon Schiele with three, and Oskar Kokoschka with six paintings.[40]

Beginning in 1910, these three artists worked in a climate influenced by *Der Sturm* and *Die Aktion*, journals published in Berlin which had a significant impact on the expressionist movement, and the Berlin art dealers, editors, and publishers Herwarth Walden and Paul Cassirer.[41] In contrast to Vienna, Berlin was relatively receptive to the expressionist movement at the time. "For us, Berlin was disreputable, spoiled, cosmopolitan, anonymous, gigantic, full of future potential, literary, political, and painterly (as the city for painters),"[42] wrote the now nearly forgotten author Hans Flesch-Brunningen, providing a vivid description of what made Berlin so attractive for Austrian artists in the years beginning in 1910.[43]

The influence of the art of Edvard Munch on Oskar Kokoschka grew appreciably between 1909 and 1912, particularly with respect to portraiture. Writing on Munch in 1954, Werner Hofmann discussed the "narrative portrait"[44] as a visual medium which goes beyond pure depiction of the portrait subject, as can be seen in the painting *Paul Herrmann and Paul Contard* (cat. no 183) shown in Vienna. New characteristics of this approach to portraiture are the reduc-

9 Richard Gerstl, *Self-Portrait as Nude in Full Figure*, 1908, oil on canvas, 140.5 x 110.5 cm, Prof. Dr. Rudolf Leopold, Vienna

10 Edvard Munch, *Self-Portrait in Hell*, 1903, oil on canvas, 82 x 66 cm, Munch-museet, Oslo

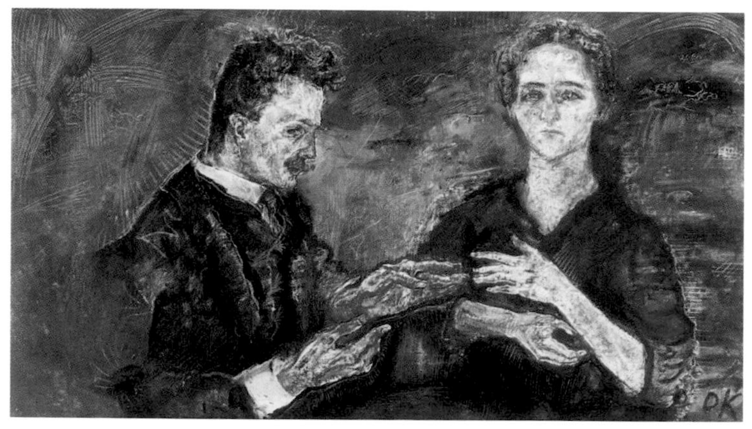

tion of surrounding space and greater proximity to the subject. In his double portrait of the art historians Hans and Erica Tietze (fig. 11) done in 1909, Kokoschka took Munch's approach a step further by heightening pictorial emphasis on the relationship between the married couple, which set the dominant thematic tone in the work.[45] Typical features of his painting technique in this early phase are thinly applied iridescent colors and agitated brushstrokes which render the full essence of the personalities of the subjects and thus go far beyond the traditional boundaries of portraiture. Through color and dynamics, the figures mark out their surroundings as their personal fields of energy, their aura. Thus, and by virtue of Kokoschka's treatment of the painting surface by scratching, a technique with which Munch had also experimented in his early paintings, we recognize certain affinities between the two artists, for "as is also true of Munch, Kokoschka's effect is that of extreme reality,"[46] as Anton Faistauer pointed out as early as 1923.

Kokoschka remained an admirer of Munch throughout his lifetime, citing him as a key witness in support of his argumentation in favor of figuration versus abstraction. In his emphatically philosophical 1953 essay entitled "Der Expressionismus Edvard Munchs," he stated in his preface that "The art of Edvard Munch belongs to the future, of course, when this generation 'lost' in two World Wars, which is reflected today in a fashionable 'non-figurative' art, will have been forgotten."[47]

"There is an oil painting by Schiele," wrote Franz Theodor Csokor on the occasion of the painter's death, "that was done in 1918, *Crouching Couple*, a tragedy with a background of stone. ... It brings to mind a master with whom Schiele otherwise has nothing in common, either formally or psychologically, namely Edvard Munch."[48] Csokor emphasized the importance of the Norwegian artist, in whose paintings he saw the tragic themes epitomized—themes which also occupy a significant position in the art of Egon Schiele, however.

Hans Bisanz identifies points of common ground shared by Munch and Schiele particularly in their portraits, which represent a core concern of expressionist art,[49] although Van Gogh, Hodler, and Klimt had greater impact on Schiele's development as an artist. In both his portrait of *Poldi Lodzinsky* of 1908 (fig. 12) and the portrait of *Eduard Kosmack* of 1910 (fig. 13), Schiele quite obviously drew inspiration from the composition of Munch's *Puberty* (cat. no. 16),

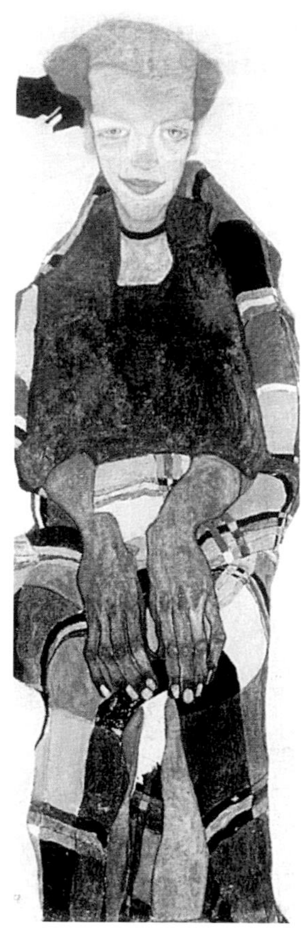

11 Oskar Kokoschka, *Hans Tietze and Erica Tietze-Conrat*, 1909,
oil on canvas, 76.5 x 136.2 cm,
Museum of Modern Art, New York, Abby Aldrich Rockefeller Foundation

12 Egon Schiele, *Poldi Lodzinsky*, 1910,
oil on canvas, 109.3 x 36.5 cm,
Private collection Ferdinand Eckhardt, Winnipeg

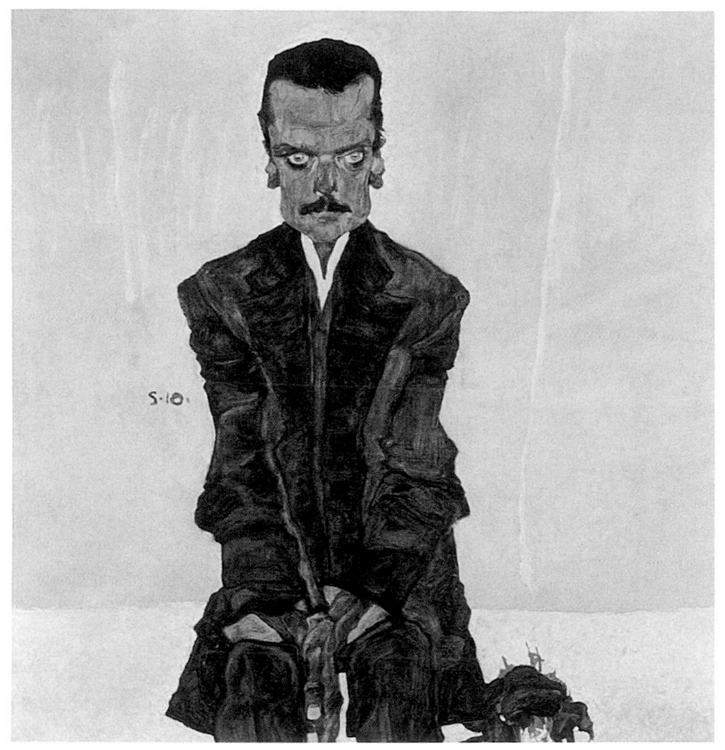

paraphrasing the striking posture which serves as the medium for articulation of the essential substantive qualities of his portraits. Schiele's death in 1918 coincided with Austria's defeat in the First World War. The small nation that remained was compelled to develop new social, cultural, and socio-economic structures. The art scene was also shaken to its foundations and confronted with massive problems.[50] Only a few enjoyed success during those years. Otto Kallir-Nirenstein proved to be one of the most important pioneers of artistic and cultural life in Vienna with his Neue Galerie on Günangergasse in the heart of Vienna, established in 1923. As early as 1924, he organized in his sixth gallery exhibition the first presentation in Vienna devoted solely to the art of Edvard Munch, featuring more than 100 works from all phases of Munch's creative life.[51] The show was accompanied by a catalog containing an introduction by Curt Glaser, author of the comprehensive monograph on Munch published in 1917. With reference primarily to the artist's more recent work, Glaser wrote that "One must become acquainted with and learn to love this second Munch like the first in order to grasp the whole Munch, who is both the one and the other, as it is not the changing moods of progressing age but rather the fundamental artistic philosophy and the enduring form in which it is embodied that defines the essential foundation of the creative personality."[52] The response of the press to the extensive exhibition, the artist himself, and the gallery's accomplishment in having brought the exhibition to Vienna, was largely positive. Yet some critics took the opportunity to recall past omissions with regard to Munch and international modern art. We read in an article printed in the *Wiener Tagblatt*:

This poor audience has been thoroughly bored for decades at the conservative exhibitions; and it is bored as well at exhibitions that show new things, finding itself unable to grasp the new because no one offers any guidance and because it has been raised over decades, sadly enough by the press as well, in the spirit of 'knowing better' and 'nothing to it anyway' that is so typical of the philistine. And the result, particularly among the broader public, is the attitude that the audience is called upon to 'judge' the artist, to 'accept' or to 'reject' him instead of approaching every work of art, even the most modest, with a certain degree of respect and striving to find a point of view from which to understand what the artist wanted to achieve. ... Here is an artist personality of outstanding stature, and if the Viennese pass him by without a thought, they will remain the same dunces they were twenty-five years ago, when the old Miethke spent so much time and money in vain to show Manet and Renoir, Gauguin and Cézanne in Vienna and make them at home there—a loss that can never be made good. ... I cannot allow myself to describe this oeuvre here; one must see it and be shaken.[53]

Press reviews raised a number of questions—about the importance of the artist, about his significance to painting and graphic art and as to which of these media profited most from Munch's contribution,[54] about his roots, and about the impulses he followed.[55] At age sixty, the artist was praised as "the greatest psychologist of portraiture since Rembrandt and El Greco."[56]
By the time this exhibition was presented, discussion regarding the "crisis of expressionism" had already progressed to an advanced stage. The Vienna art historian Hans Tietze, a herald and

13 Egon Schiele, *Eduard Kosmack*, 1910,
oil on canvas, 100 x 100 cm,
Österreichische Galerie Belvedere, Vienna

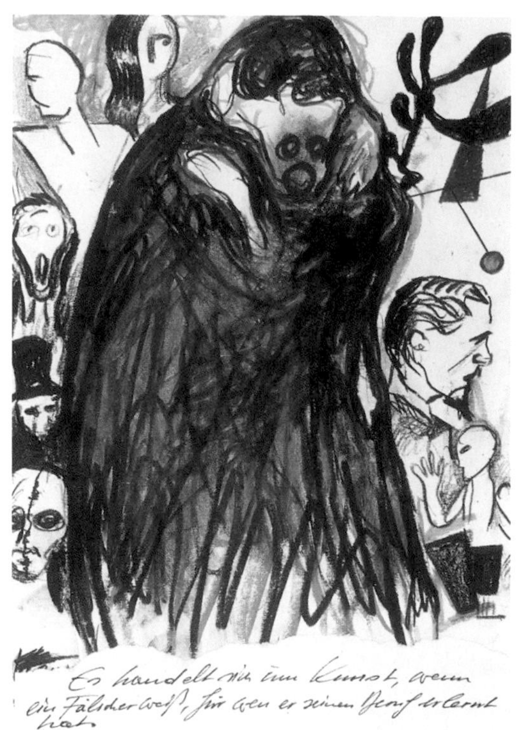

14 Günter Brus, *Es handelt sich um Kunst, wenn ein Fälscher weiss, für wen er seinen Beruf erlernt hat*,
color crayon and color chalk on paper, collection of the artist

advocate of contemporary art, called attention as early as 1921 to the "existential lie of expressionism," which, he said, had shattered and dissolved relationships and thus failed to fulfill its social mission.[57] Yet by this time, Munch had also long since passed beyond early expressionism and begun to devote his attention to new themes and contents, so that he was able to sustain his success in the 1920s and 1930s. One unmistakable sign of that success is the fact that, supported by Joseph Goebbels, he was awarded the silver Goethe medal for art and science by Reichspräsident Hindenburg as a "true German" in 1932. That did not prevent him from being banned along with his fellow expressionists as degenerate artists in 1938, however.[58]

Thus Munch's exhibitions in the years immediately following the Second World War—like those of all artists once declared degenerate—can also be seen as political statements in which he distanced himself from the recent past. Such exhibitions also served as a means of rehabilitating the artists in question. The first major, comprehensive exhibition of the art of Edvard Munch presented in Vienna took place at the Akademie der bildenden Künste in 1959. The organizers of this show scheduled during the Wiener Festwochen had high expectations, fueled in part by the success of the Vincent van Gogh exhibition the preceding year, which drew 140,000 visitors. In the exhibition catalog, author Fritz Novotny explained the reasoning behind the presentation of these two great painters in close succession and compared them as "two fundamental types, two fundamental manifestations of modern expressionism."[59] Kristian Sotriffer first explored the relationships of these two artists to Austrian art in 1963, focusing on correspondence relating to the exhibitions presented at the Vienna Secession around the turn of the century, in which the friendship between the Viennese artist Carl Moll and Edvard Munch is also documented.[60] This attitude of admiration is confirmed again forty years later by Maria Lassnig in her painting *Traditionskette*.

Cooperation with the then newly founded Munch-museet in Oslo led in 1966 to the first Munch exhibition at the Albertina in Vienna. In contrast to the very hesitant and circuitous approach to Munch's oeuvre at the turn of the century and during the ensuing fifty years, the Norwegian catalog authors emphasized the rela-

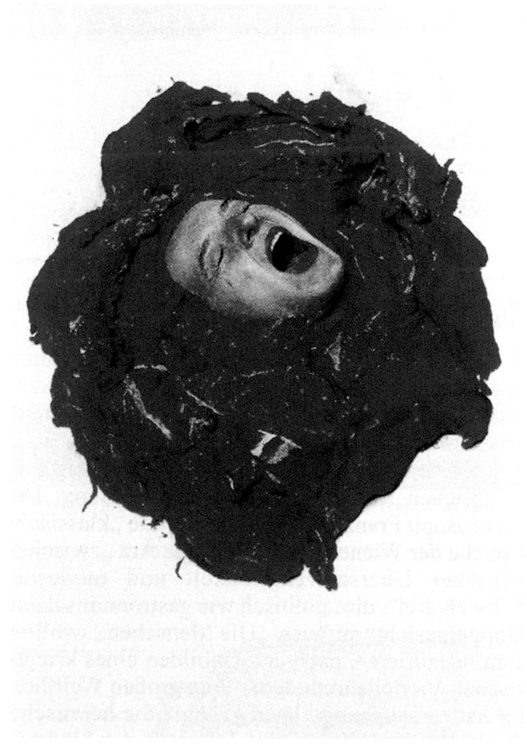

15 Julia Kissina, *Ohne Titel*, 1998,
from the installation: *Fleischästhetische Maschine*,
Cibachrome, 110 x 110 cm

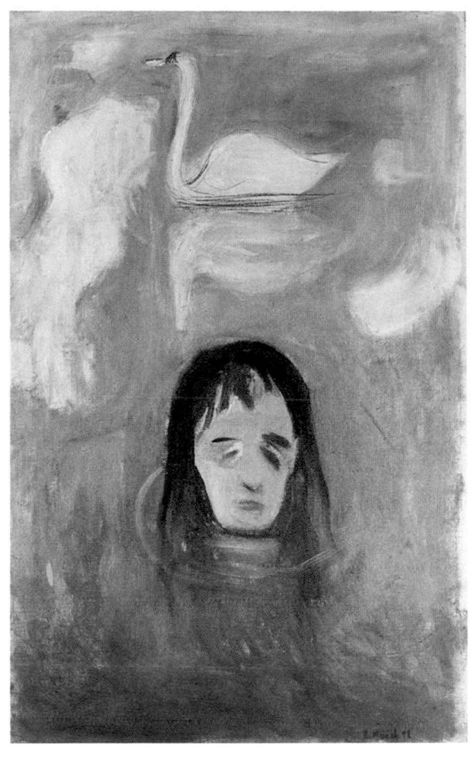

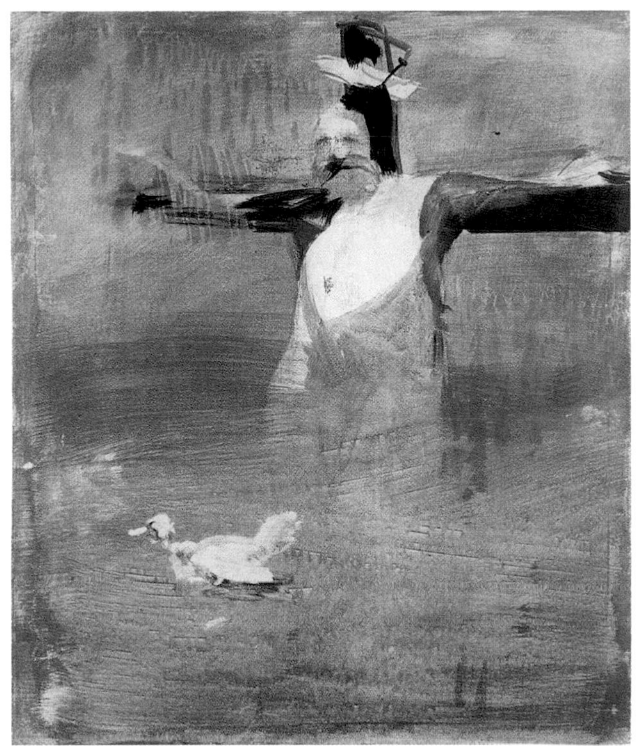

tively strong presence of Munch in Austrian public collections (four paintings are now on exhibit at the Österreichische Galerie Belvedere, and the Albertina holds a collection of 120 prints) and the interest of Austrian art historians in Munch.[61]

The real future significance of these two exhibitions lay in the fact that they gave a young generation of artists an opportunity to study the work of the Norwegian artist. One such artist was Günter Brus, who saw the exhibition at the Albertina as an art student at the age of twenty-four and was fascinated by Munch's works and their technical brilliance. Brus was able to examine the injuries to the human body Munch frequently inflicted by cutting and scratching the surfaces of his paintings as a young artist. He later pursued this theme in a much more direct manner through the immediate experience of wounds on his own body. Both artists used bodily injury as a means of expressing personal concerns. In more recent works, Brus again refers directly to works of Munch's which represent icons of existential feelings (fig. 14).

Munch's impact on post-1945 international art has been the focus of scholarly attention for a number of years. Some of the responses to the artist and his work are very direct and assume the form of citations—the spectrum ranges, to note two prominent examples, from the works of Günter Brus to the photographs of the artist Julia Kissina (fig. 15),[62] a native of Russia who now lives in Germany. At the same time, however, Munch's painting as such can pose a challenge to contemporary artists.[63] More than 100 years after Munch's symbol-laden and pathbreaking self-portrait *Vision* (fig. 16), Siegfried Anzinger painted the work entitled *Crucifixion and Baptism* (fig. 17). Using the possibilities offered by painting, his aim is to evoke striking, penetrating images—entirely in keeping with the tradition and spirit of Edvard Munch.

16 Edvard Munch, *Vision*, 1892, oil on canvas, 72 x 45 cm, Munch-museet, Oslo

17 Siegfried Anzinger, *Crucifixion and Baptism*, 2000, distemper on canvas, 130 x 110 cm, Stift Admont

1 Wolfgang Drechsler, "Aussen und Innen. Zur Malerei von Maria Lassnig," in Wolfgang Drechsler (ed.), *Maria Lassnig*, exh. cat., Museum Moderner Kunst, Vienna 1985, p. 9.

2 Maria Lassnig, *Die Feder ist die Schwester des Pinsels, Tagebücher* 1943–1997, Hans Ulrich Obrist (ed.), Cologne 2000, p. 87.

3 Quoted and translated from Matthias Arnold, *Edvard Munch*, 6th edition 2000, p. 7.

4 Arnold 2000 (see note 3), p. 8.

5 According to contractual agreements, the exhibition was to be presented in Breslau, Dresden, Munich and at the Künstlerhaus in Vienna. Cf. Jan Kneher, *Edvard Munch in seinen Ausstellungen zwischen* 1892 *und* 1912. *Eine Dokumentation der Ausstellungen und Studie zur Rezeptionsgeschichte von Munchs Kunst*, Worms 1994, p. 27.

6 Munch had exhibited with success at the Munich Secession just prior to this event. Thus the selection of only two works for this showing in no way reflects his true importance at the time.

7 Ludwig Hevesi, *Acht Jahre Secession*, Vienna 1906, reprint edited by Otto Breicha, Klagenfurt 1984, p. 356.

8 The twenty etchings were selected from a group of thirty-nine works brought from Lübeck to Vienna through the efforts of the Munch admirers, collectors, and "market strategists" Albert Kollmann and Dr. Max Linde, who were especially enamored of his etchings at the time, after a visit by Secession President Wilhelm Bernatzik to Linde in Lübeck. Seven works were sold in Vienna. See Kneher 1994 (see note 5), pp. 162–163; and *Edvard Munch / Gustav Schiefler. Briefwechsel*, vol. I, 1902–1914, edited by Arne Eggum in collaboration with Sibylle Baumbach, Sissel Biörnstad und Signe Böhn, Hamburg 1987, p. 41, Linde to Schiefler, dated January 25, 1902: "Indeed, Vienna has already kept seven of the most beautiful pieces."

9 See the catalog essay by Marian Bisanz-Prakken, pp. 91–96.

10 See Hans Bisanz, "Zur Bildidee *Der Kuss*—Gustav Klimt und Edvard Munch," in Tobias Natter and Gerbert Frodl (eds.), *Klimt und die Frauen*, exh. cat., Österreichische Galerie Belvedere Vienna, Cologne 2000, pp. 226ff.

11 See Iris Müller-Westermann, "Edvard Munch und Wien. Österreichs Begegnung mit dem Werk von Edvard Munch 1901–1918," in Sabine Schulze (ed.), *Sehnsucht nach Glück. Wiens Aufbruch in die Moderne: Klimt, Kokoschka, Schiele*, exh. cat., Schirn Kunsthalle Frankfurt, Ostfildern-Ruit 1995, pp. 224ff.

12 M May 28, 1903—Munch-Archiv, see Kneher 1994 (see note 5), pp. 189f.

13 M June 23, 1903—Munch-Archiv, see Kneher 1994 (see note 5).

14 Archives of the Vienna Secession, archive no. 28.3.2. Munch's friend and collector Rolf E. Stenersen recalls that Munch categorically rejected the idea of being presented along with other artists. Rolf E. Stenersen, *Edvard Munch—Close-Up of a Genius*, Oslo 1994, pp. 105f.

15 Member of the Zum Schwarzen Ferkel group in Berlin, originally from Vienna.

16 Quoted and translated from *Edvard Munch. Sommernacht am Oslofjord, um* 1900, *Kunst und Dokumentation* 12, Städtische Kunsthalle Mannheim, Mannheim 1988, p. 244.

17 Wilhelm List, Carl Moll, Koloman Moser, and Felician von Myrbach.

18 Despite reservations expressed by his friend and collector Max Linde, Munch accepted the selection made by the Secession. See Kneher 1994 (see note 5), p. 190.

19 Cf. Marian Bisanz-Prakken, "Khnopff, Toorop, Minne und die Wiener Moderne," Schulze 1995 (see note 11), pp. 172ff., Otto Benesch, "Hodler, Klimt und Munch als Monumentalmaler," in *Wallraf-Richartz Jahrbuch. Westdeutsches Jahrbuch für Kunstgeschichte*, vol. 24, Cologne 1962, pp. 333–358.

20 His paintings from the major project devoted to the *Frieze of Life* were the focus of many presentations during those years, the first of which took place in Berlin (1902), Leipzig (1903), Kristiania (now Oslo; 1904), and Prague (1905). The selection of subjects from the *Frieze of Life* shown in Vienna was supplemented by landscapes, portraits and a female nude.

21 Three paintings shown at the exhibition were sold: Carl Moll purchased *Winter Night* (*Winter Landscape in Moonlight*), now at the Kunsthaus Zürich. In a letter dated March 7, 1904, Moll had written to Munch near the end of the Vienna exhibition, stating that "your paintings [have] so touched my heart that it pains me to think that I may not be able to enjoy them again. ... I, myself, would dearly love to acquire one of your paintings." But he found the quoted price too high. Moll also complained in the same letter than he had been unable to find a buyer in Vienna and that the only work sold had gone to Breslau. Two days later, however, he wrote a joyful letter to Munch, informing him that a "friend and devoted art-lover is very enthused with your works" and had asked him to make an offer for two paintings. "The one is the evening scene at the seashore—with the rising moon ... the other painting my friend is interested in is *The Child and Death*. (letter from Moll to Munch dated March 9, 1904; both letters are now held in the archives of the Munch-museet. I wish to thank Inger Engan for this information.) The work *Summer Night on the Shore* (1902) mentioned in the letter is now at the Österreichische Galerie and comes from the collection of Alma Mahler. With regard to this work, Alma Mahler writes in her autobiography that "Gropius, who is an extraordinarily noble person, fervently wished to present me a gift after the birth of the child. He wrote to Karl Reininghaus, who occasionally sold one of the paintings in his large collection, asking him to sell him the *Midnight Sun* by Edvard Munch. That very same day, two servants appeared with the painting and a touching letter from Karl Reininghaus, who wrote that the picture had belonged to me for years, since I loved it so. He had lacked only the right occasion to send it to me. I had acquired it with a smile!—Now I could immerse myself for days in this oily, calm, yet so agitated sea. No painting has ever touched me as deeply as this one." Alma Mahler, *Mein Leben*, Frankfurt am Main 1997, pp. 82f. (I wish to thank Tobias Natter for this information.) Thus Carl Reininghaus was probably the art-lover mentioned by Moll in his letter. *Dead Mother with Child* (1899–1900) is now in Bremen. See Kneher 1994 (see note 5), p. 190.

22 "I stand helpless even in the face of Edvard Munch's *Angst*. A symbolist theme appears to have been put to rest here in genre-style." See Kneher 1994 (see note 5), pp. 145f.

23 Kneher 1994 (see note 5), p. 191. See Munch to Schiefler, dated February 11, 1904: "Richard Muther has just written an enthusiastic review of my exhibition in Vienna." Eggum 1987, vol. I (see note 8), p. 77.

24 Alfred Kubin, *Autobiographie* 1898–1904 (1911), included in the Sansara Folio.

25 Letter to L. Rosenberger, dated May 20, 1939, in *Wanderungen zu Alfred Kubin. Aus einem Briefwechsel*, Munich 1969, pp. 53ff. Kubin left an extensive collection of works of art by his contemporaries to the Albertina. Among these are three works by Edvard Munch, the woodcut *Moonlight* (inv. no. 1961/422), the lighograph *Tiger and Bear* (inv. no. 1961/424), and the etching *Dead Lovers* (inv. no. 1961/423). See Peter Assmann and Annegret Hoberg (eds.), *Alfred Kubin. Kunstbeziehungen*, exh. cat., Oberösterreichische Landesgalerie, Salzburg 1995.

26 Werner Hofmann, *Moderne Malerei in Österreich*, Vienna 1965, p. 94.

27 Hofmann 1965 (see note 26), p. 100.

28 Wolfgang Born first drew this comparison in 1931 in a text written in response to the—then very recent—discovery of Richard Gerstl by the art

dealer Otto Kallir-Nirenstein. It has since been affirmed by other authors. See also Hans Bisanz, *Edvard Munch und seine Bedeutung für den mitteleuropäischen Expressionismus*, Ph. D. dissertation, Vienna 1959, pp. 53f.

29 Klaus Albrecht Schröder, *Richard Gerstl*, exh. cat., Kunstforum der Bank Austria Wien, Kunsthaus Zürich, Zurich 1993, p. 90.

30 "Even before Schiele, Kokoschka, Oppenheimer and other Austrian painters began depicting themselves in various Christological and martyrological roles in 1910–11, Richard Gerstl made reference in form and motif to elements of the Christ image as a means of giving expression to his concept of self as an artist." Schröder 1993 (see note 29), p. 48.

31 Iris Müller-Westermann, *Edvard Munch. Die Selbstbildnisse*, Ph. D. dissertation Hamburg, Oslo, 1997, p. 6.

32 Quoted and translated from Arnold 2000 (see note 3), p. 8.

33 Arnold 2000 (see note 3), p. 8.

34 Bruno Cassirer promoted plans for a small exhibition of some ten drawings and possibly a small selection of prints in Vienna in 1906–07, but the show was probably not realized. See Kneher 1994 (see note 5), p. 242.

35 A. F. Seligmann in *Neue Freie Presse*, January 13, 1912.

36 "OP," in *Kunstchronik*, March 8, 1912; quoted and translated from Kneher 1994 (see note 5), pp. 318f.

37 Cf. Kneher 1994 (see note 5), pp. 316ff.

38 *Internationale Kunstausstellung des Sonderbundes westdeutscher Kunstfreunde und Künstler zu Cöln* 1912, exh. cat., Städtische Ausstellungshalle am Aachener Tor, Cologne 1912, pp. 4f.

39 Cologne 1912 (see note 38).

40 Egon Schiele: no. 369 *Lady in Black*, no. 370 *Mother and Child*, no. 371 *The Self-Seer*. Oskar Kokoschka: no. 358 *Annunciation*, no. 359 *Sposalizio*, no. 360 *Portrait (Actor)*, no. 361 *Still Life*—owned by Dr. Reichel, Vienna, no. 362 *Portrait of a Woman*, no. 363 *Dent du Midi*—private collection (fig. 37). Also represented were: Ernst Ascher, Vincenz Benes, Emil Fila, Bohumil Kubista, Willi Nowak and Antonin Prochazka, all from Prague; St. Herburg, R. von Felsz-Fynski, both from Krakow; Anton Faistauer and Anton Kolig, from Vienna, each with one picture. *Internationale Kunstausstellung des Sonderbundes* 1912 (see note 38), Austria, room 15, pp. 54f.

41 Aside from those mentioned, Felix Albrecht Harta and Max Oppenheimer also had contacts in Berlin.

42 Quoted and translated from Peter Sprengel and Gregor Streim, *Berliner und Wiener Moderne. Vermittlungen und Abgrenzungen in Literatur, Theater, Publizistik*, Vienna et al. 1998, pp. 569ff, quotation p. 575.

43 Kneher 1994 (see note 5), pp. 327ff.

44 Werner Hofmann, "Zu einem Bildmittel Edvard Munchs," in Werner Hofmann, *Bruchlinien. Aufsätze zur Kunst des 19. Jahrhunderts*, Munich 1979, pp. 111ff.

45 Cf. Bisanz 1959 (see note 28), p. 76.

46 Anton Faistauer, *Neue Malerei in Österreich. Betrachtungen eines Malers*, Zurich et al. 1923, p. 76

47 Oskar Kokoschka, *Der Expressionismus Edvard Munchs* (with three illustrations by Edvard Munch), Vienna et al. 1953, p. 5.

48 Quoted and translated from Christian M. Nebehay, *Egon Schiele 1890–1918. Leben Briefe Gedichte*, Salzburg and Vienna 1979, pp. 488f.

49 Hans Bisanz, "Edvard Munch und die Wiener Porträtmalerei um 1900—Zusammenfassung, Særtrykk av Årbok 1963. Edvard Munch 100 år. Oslo Kommunes Kunstsamlinger," special issue of *Jahrbuch* 1963, p. 143.

50 See Antonia Hoerschelmann, *Tendenzen der österreichischen Malerei zwischen 1918 und 1938 und ihre Relationen zur europäischen Kunst des 20. Jahrhunderts*, VWGÖ Vienna 1989.

51 The gallery opened in 1923 with an exhibition of the work of Egon Schiele; it showed Gustav Klimt in 1926 and first presented works by Richard Gerstl in 1931. It made its rooms available to a number of contemporary artists, including Oskar Kokoschka, Otto Rudolf Schatz, Alfred Kubin, Oskar Laske, Wilhelm Thöny, and Herbert Boeckl, but also presented work by nineteenth-century German and Austrian artists such as Ferdinand Waldmüller as well as Paul Signac and the French impressionists and Max Beckmann. See *Otto Kallir-Nirenstein. Ein Wegbereiter österreichischer Kunst*, exh. cat., Historisches Museum der Stadt Wien, Vienna 1986.

52 *Edvard Munch. Gemälde und Graphik*, VI. Exhibition, exh. cat., Neue Galerie, Wien I, Grünangergasse 1, Vienna 1927, pp. 5f. The catalog lists eleven paintings, twenty-two etchings, twenty-one woodcuts, and sixty-seven lithographs from all of the artist's creative periods.

53 *Wiener Tagblatt*, March 25, 1924, "Ausstellungen. Munch—Nolde. V.Tr;" On the Galerie Miethke in the years up to 1912, see G. Tobias Natter and Gerbert Frodl, *Carl Moll* (1861–1945), exh. cat., Österreichische Galerie Belvedere Wien, Salzburg and Vienna 1998, pp. 191ff.

54 *Volkszeitung*, March 14, 1924.

55 *Neue Freie Presse*, March. 14, 1924; *Arbeiter-Zeitung*, March 19, 1924.

56 *Das Wiener Journal*, April 5, 1924.

57 Hans Tietze, "Künstlerische und kunstliterarische Zeitfragen," in *Kunstchronik und Kunstmarkt*, July 22, 1921, no. 43, pp. 773ff.; Hans Tietze, *Lebendige Kunstwissenschaft. Zur Krise der Kunst und der Kunstgeschichte*, Vienna 1925.

58 See Jean Clair, *Die Verantwortung des Künstlers. Avantgarden zwischen Terror und Vernunft*, Cologne 1998, pp. 42f.

59 *Edvard Munch* 1863–1944, exh. cat., Wiener Festwochen, Kulturamt der Stadt Wien, Akademie der bildenden Künste, Vienna 1959.

60 Kristian Sotriffer, "Edward Munch und Österreich," first printed in *Die Presse*, December 7–8, 1963. Reprinted in *Edvard Munch. Aus dem Munchmuseet Oslo*, exh. cat., Villa Stuck Munich, Salzburger Landessammlungen Rupertinum Salzburg, Brücke-Museum Berlin, Munich 1987, pp. 45ff. The article is regarded as an important contemporary document on the state of research on Austrian art at the time, as it cites desiderata that have since been fulfilled, such as a study of the painter Richard Gerstl. See also the correspondence relating to this matter between Moll and Munch in the archives of the Vienna Secession and the Munch-museet in Oslo.

61 "The art historians of the Vienna School have made a significant contribution to research on the art of Edvard Munch. Worthy of particular note in this context are Otto Benesch, author of several seminal studies. Hans Tietze, Fritz Novotny, and Werner Hofmann have gained important insights in isolated studies, as has Hans Bisanz in his dissertation." Thor Brodtkorb, "Norwegischer Botschafter in Wien," in *Edvard Munch, Zeichnungen und Graphik aus dem Munch-Museum Oslo*, exh. cat., Graphische Sammlung Albertina, Vienna 1966, p. 5.

62 The analogy to Munch's *The Scream* may well have prompted the decision to place the photograph on the cover of the highly reputed art journal *Kunstforum international* in the June–July issue, no. 160.

63 The Oslo exhibition, *Echoes of the Scream*, presented in 2001, also shed light on Munch's current relevance to contemporary art. The following artists took part in the presentation: Asger Jorn, Joseph Beuys, Georg Baselitz, Per Kirkeby, Günther Förg, Jasper Johns, Marina Abramovic, Antonio Saura, Yannis Kounellis, and Francis Bacon.

Catalog

The Voice

Munch's first studies on the theme of *The Voice* are found in his literary notes and sketches from the winter of 1891–92. They presumably relate to Munch's first sexual encounters with Milly Thaulow, a married woman three years older than he, whom he refers to as "Mrs. Heiberg." Munch recorded his thoughts: "When we stand like this—and my eyes look into your big eyes—in the pale moonlight—you know, where—delicate hands spin invisible threads—that are bound around my heart—are pulled through my eyes—through your big, dark eyes—into and around your heart—Your eyes are so large, now, when we are so close—They are like two vast, dark skies."[1]

The two painted versions of 1893/94 show a woman in the foreground, left of center, with her hands concealed behind her. She faces the viewer in an attitude of expectation. The setting is presumably a place near Åsgårdstrand in 1950 on what was then Kristianiafjord, today's Oslofjord. The erotic undercurrent is created by the interplay of the vertical trunks of the spruces, the phallus-shaped reflection of the moon, and the woman's posture, which suggests something between presentation and expectation.

In what is regarded as the first painted version, the woman wears a hat, and her head is framed by two tree trunks (cat. no. 3). A couple in white appears on the sketchily drawn boat. The horizon is merely suggested by the reflection on the water. The only evidence that it is the moon, and not the sun, that is depicted here is found in a literary note written by Munch about Mrs. Heiberg: "How pale you are in the moonlight and how dark your eyes ..."[2]

Munch presented this version of the painting[3] under the title *Summer Night's Dream* at his solo exhibition *Unter den Linden* 19 in Berlin in 1893. The work represented his first approach to the principles of composition of his *Frieze of Life*, and he grouped it together with one version each of *The Kiss*, *Vampire* (*Love and Pain*),[4] *Madonna* (*The Face of Madonna*), *Melancholy* (*Jealousy*) and *The Scream* (*Despair*) under the title *Study for a Series on "The Love."* This version was later purchased by Helge Bäckström who helped arrange for an exhibition of Munch's work in Stockholm in 1894, at which one of the two painted versions of *The Voice* was shown under the title *In the Forest*.

In the second version (cat. no. 1), the artist has moved closer to the woman. Her hair now falls loosely, and she is intersected by the upper margin and held tightly between the upper and lower boundaries of the picture. The contours of her face are blurred in the twilight, and her eyes are widened, forming impenetrable caves of darkness. The unprimed canvas is visible at certain spots beneath the more thinly painted areas. The painting is first documented in a photograph taken at the solo exhibition at the Beyer & Sohn art dealership in Leipzig in 1903 (fig. 3, p. 158). A comparison with photos from the 1920s and 1930s, which show the present condition of the painting, suggests that the impasto layers were painted at a later date. It was probably during or following his period of experimentation with painting techniques in Warnemünde in 1907–08 that Munch added the orange boats and blue, white, and yellow to heighten the contrasts between the water, the beach, and the reflection, which he outlined with white paint squeezed from the tube. The woodcut entitled *The Voice* (*Summer Night*) of 1896 (cat. nos. 4, 5), a reverse image of the first version documented in 1903, also supports the assumption that the meaning of the motif has shifted.

In the woodcut, Munch covered the face and throat with dark, vertical bridge lines and joined the eyes and eyebrows to form dark sockets like those of a skull. In the four surviving prints of the woodcut now at the Munch-museet, he exploited the experimental potential of the print-making process, varying forms, colors, and formats. One of the two hand-colored versions is light, the other dark, representing day and night. In the monochrome version printed with a very sparing application of grayish-black exhibiting small splinters of wood (cat. no. 4), Munch used opaque and transparent paints to color the tree-trunks and the coastline in vivid ultramarine, the branches and forest floor in blue-green and yellowish green. He retouched the woman's silhouette with orange and red fading to pink, the lamp post with yellow. The strong glazing effect of the blue of the water's surface makes it appear bright as daylight, in contrast to the version colored with dark blue. The second—nighttime—version (cat. no. 5) was printed in

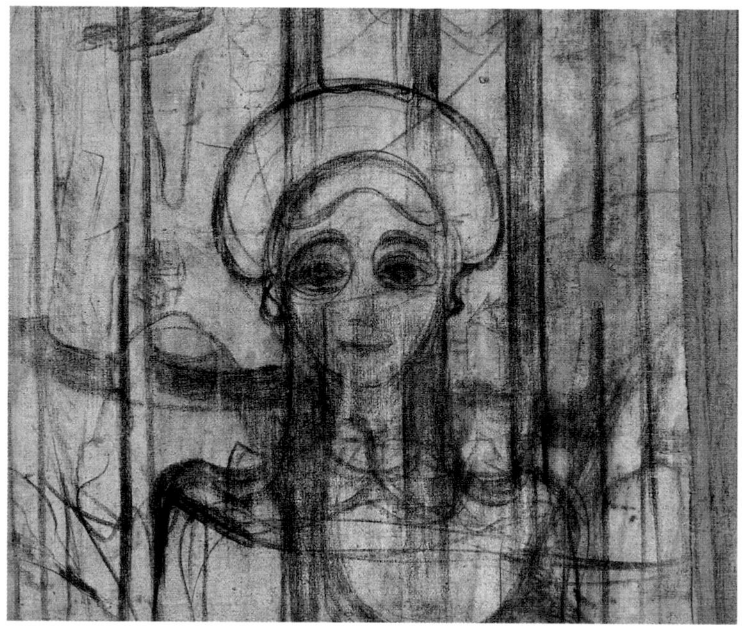

black, grayish-purple, and reddish-brown, using both wood blocks, one of which was sawed into two parts, with the addition of yellow to the reflection and blue to the water. Munch's experiment with nighttime and daytime versions shows that the light preserves the duality of moon and sun even in the paintings.

The frame of view in the etching *The Voice (Summer Night)* of 1894, which Munch also entitled *Woman in a Summer Night*, conforms very closely to that of the first painted version, although the woman with the hat has moved almost to the center of the scene between the column of moonlight, which has shifted towards the left, and the boat. The group of people in the background reappears in the later revisions of the second version of the painting, supplementing the couple relationship with a lovers' triangle.

In a version hand-colored with extensive areas of gray (cat. no. 2), Munch accentuated the column of moonlight with yellow, like that of the sun, and added spots of dark green among the branches. He retraced the contours of the sun or moon, the reflection, the brim of the hat, the arms and the tree-trunks in ink and added vertical hatching in the lower right-hand corner. After processing and etching most of the plate, he de-emphasized the boat and focused the action of the scene more fully on the woman.

Munch achieved his most radical solutions for this theme in drawings. The painting entitled *View from the Balcony in Åsgårdstrand* was discovered behind the wall of his studio in Åsgårdstrand in 1950. On the back of the painting is another large-format drawing (fig. 1), which Munch probably also planned to execute as a painting in 1893–94. In keeping with the description in his literary notes, the woman in the drawing has "big eyes." She wears a hat, like the one in the first version, and is presented as a bust figure in full frontal view. Her face and body are crossed by the tree-trunks in a pattern of bars. Thus the forest and the woman's image appear as an overlay similar to a photographic double-exposure.

In the charcoal drawing of 1893 (cat. no. 7), which also bears the title *The Voice (Summer Night)*, the eyes are defined and imbued with particular liveliness, while the nose, mouth, and chin are absent. The forehead is distinctly separated from the hat, the brim of which is highlighted like a halo, by fine lines. The body contours are formed by the sweeping curves of strands of hair, and a voluminous, meshlike structure below the throat accentuates the dress. The absence of a mouth, the organ through which the voice is articulated, appears to prevent communication. Yet Munch experimented with more than the motif. He colored the print and sprayed it with transparent gray and brown paint, covering the face and the area of foliage on the left with a structure of large spots.

Probably somewhat later, Munch juxtaposed this radical disruption of communication with the fragmentation of the head below the eyes in a drawing done in pencil and black chalk (cat. no. 6). The portion of the face below the mouth disappears entirely from the field of view defined by a hand-drawn frame. In a note written below the picture, Munch emphasizes the ambivalence inherent in this disappearance: "Your eyes are as big as half of the sky when you stand near me, and your hair has gold dust, and I cannot see your mouth—see only that you are smiling." DB

1 Munch-museet T 2782. Quoted and translated from Arne Eggum, "Sommernacht," in Ulrich Weisner (ed.), *Munch. Liebe. Angst. Tod*, exh. cat., Kunsthalle Bielefeld, Bielefeld 1980, p. 60.

2 *Ibid.*, p. 60.

3 Based on the description of *Summer Night's Dream* in *Morgenbladet*, Dec. 7, 1893, the version shown here can be identified as that from the Museum of Fine Arts in Boston.

4 Titles used at the *Unter den Linden* 19 exhibition which deviate from those commonly accepted today are given in parentheses.

1 *The Voice (Summer Night)*, 1893–94, drawing on canvas, verso of *View from the Balcony in Åsgårdstrand*, c. 1900, oil on canvas, 90 x 103 cm, Borre Kommune, Norway

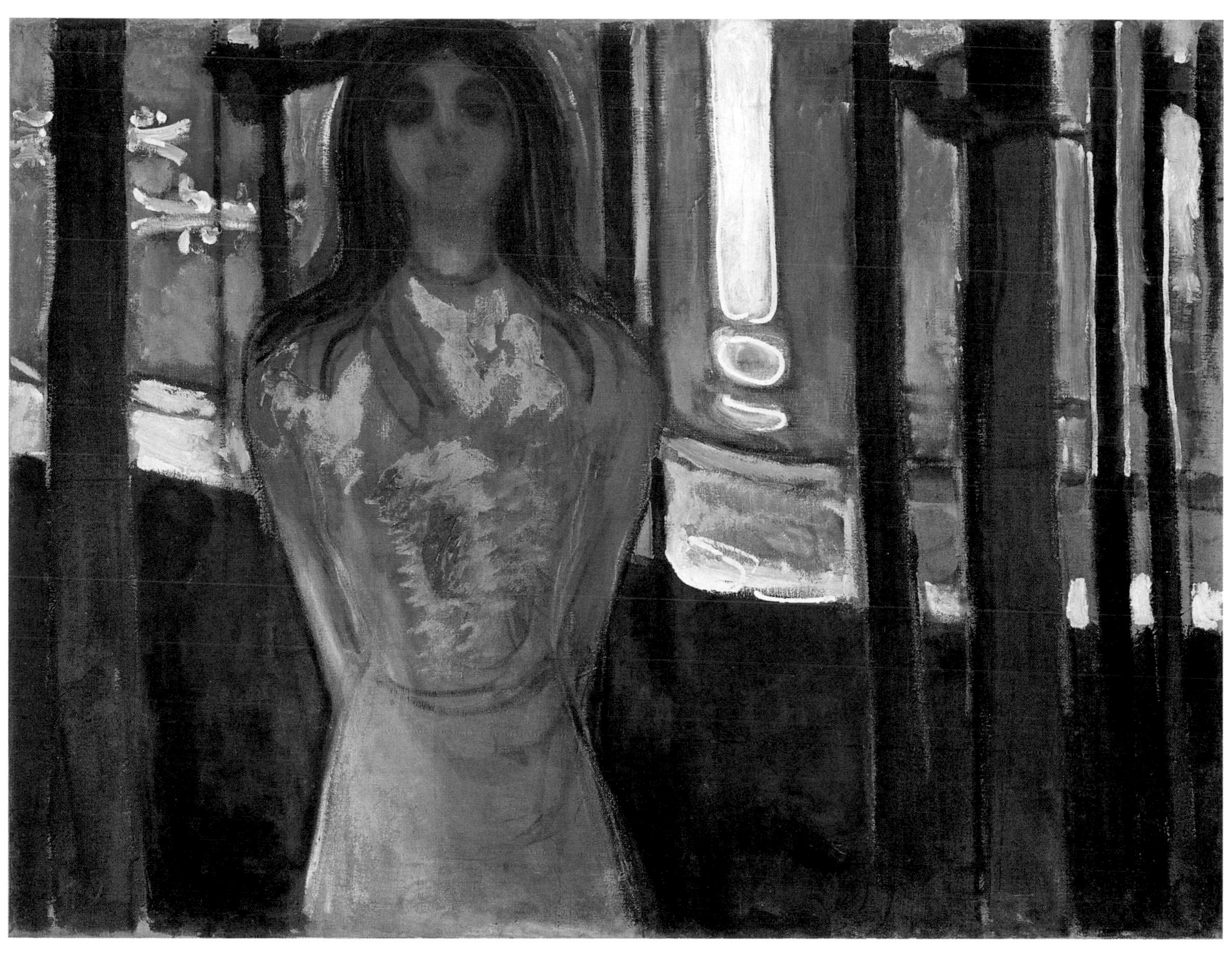

Cat. no. 1 *The Voice (Summer Night)*, 1893/after 1907
Oil on canvas, 90 x 119.5 cm, Munch-museet, Oslo

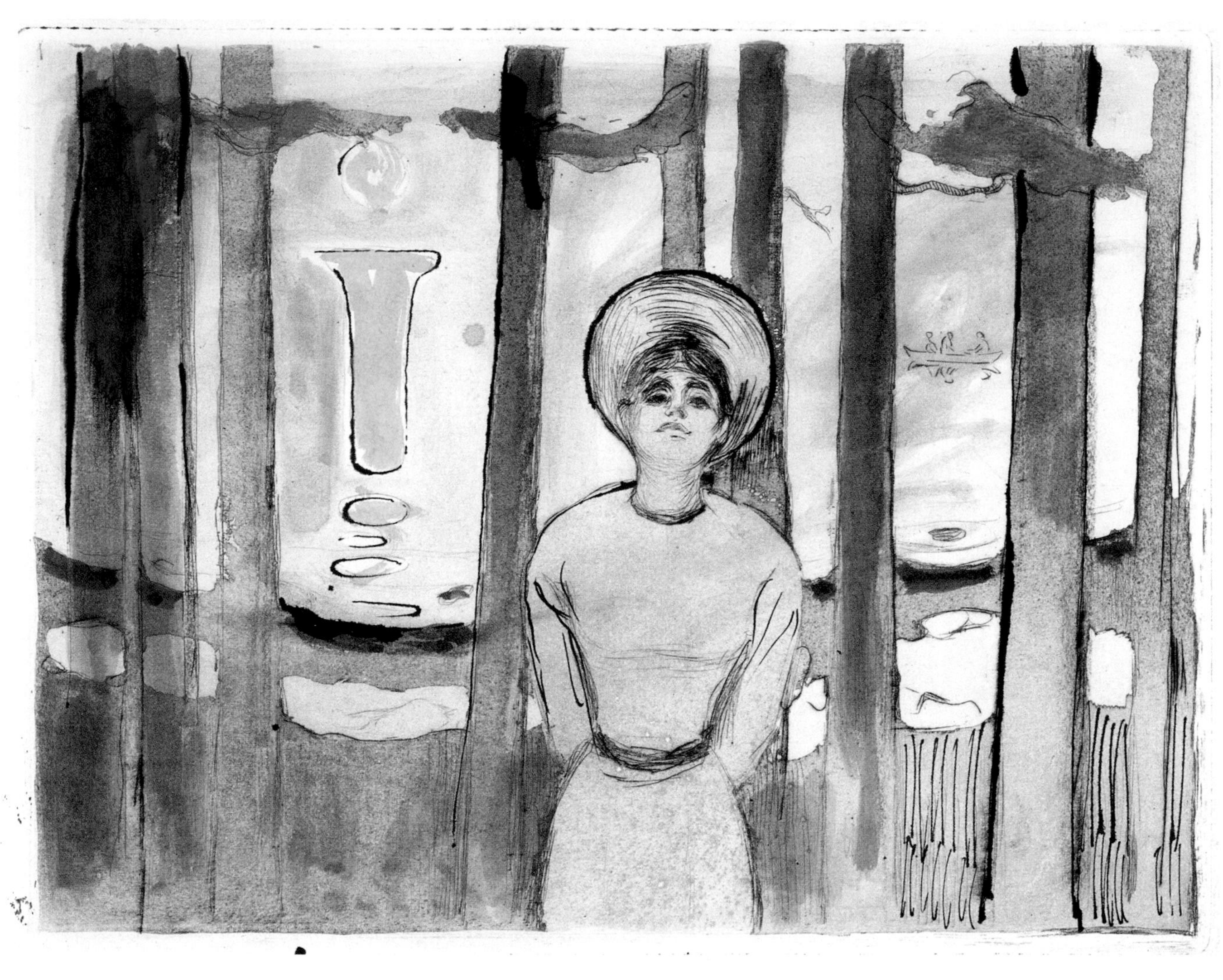

Cat. no. 2 *The Voice* (*Summer Night*), 1894
Hand-colored etching on paper, 23.7 x 31.4 cm
Munch-museet, Oslo

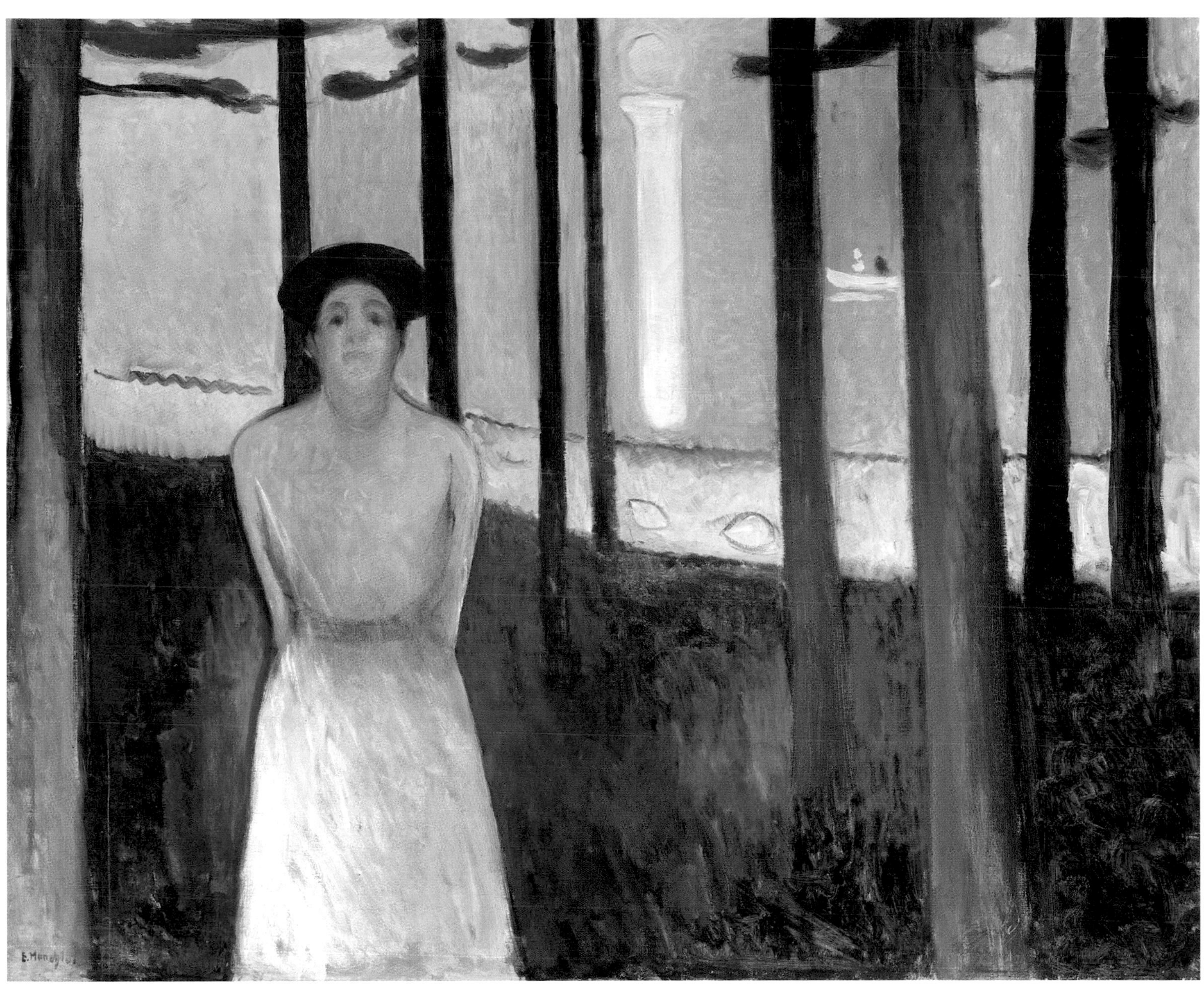

Cat. no. 3 *The Voice (Summer Night)*, 1893
Oil on canvas, 87.9 x 108 cm
Museum of Fine Arts, Boston; Ernest Wadsworth Longfellow Fund

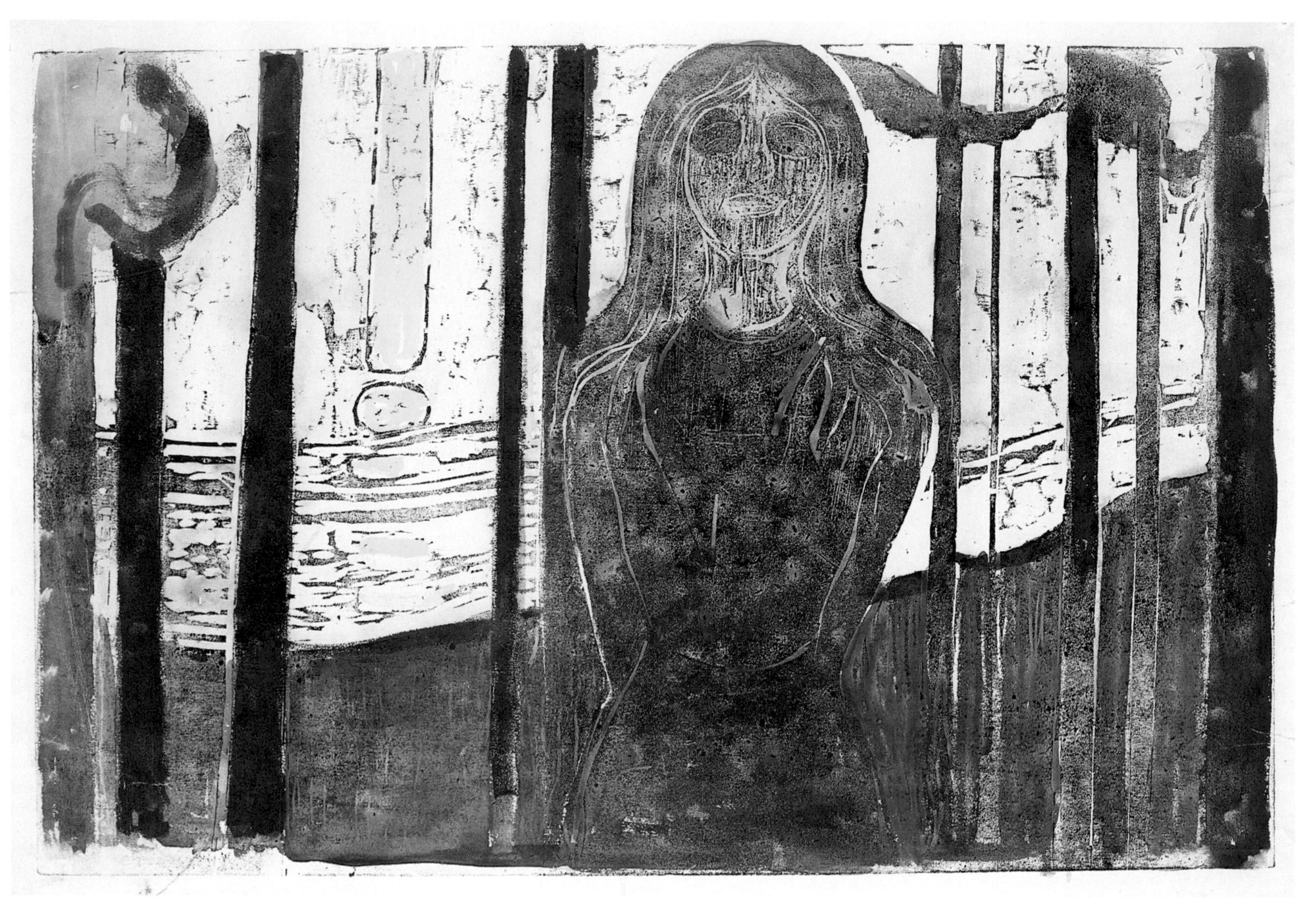

Cat. no. 4 *The Voice (Summer Night)*, 1896
Hand-colored woodcut on paper, 37.8 x 56.9 cm
Munch-museet, Oslo

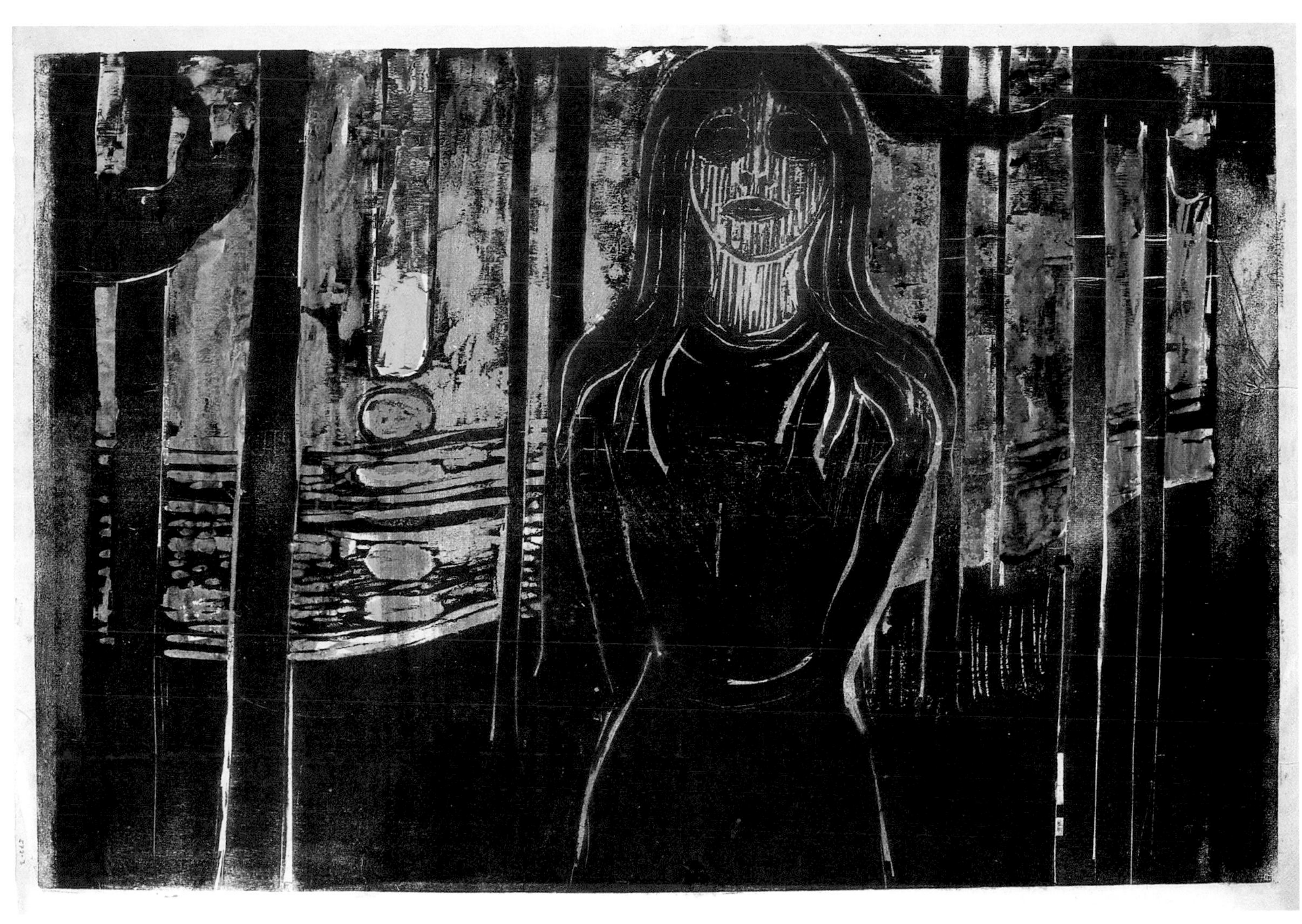

Cat. no. 5 *The Voice (Summer Night)*, 1896
Hand-colored color woodcut on paper, 37.6 x 57.7 cm
Munch-museet, Oslo

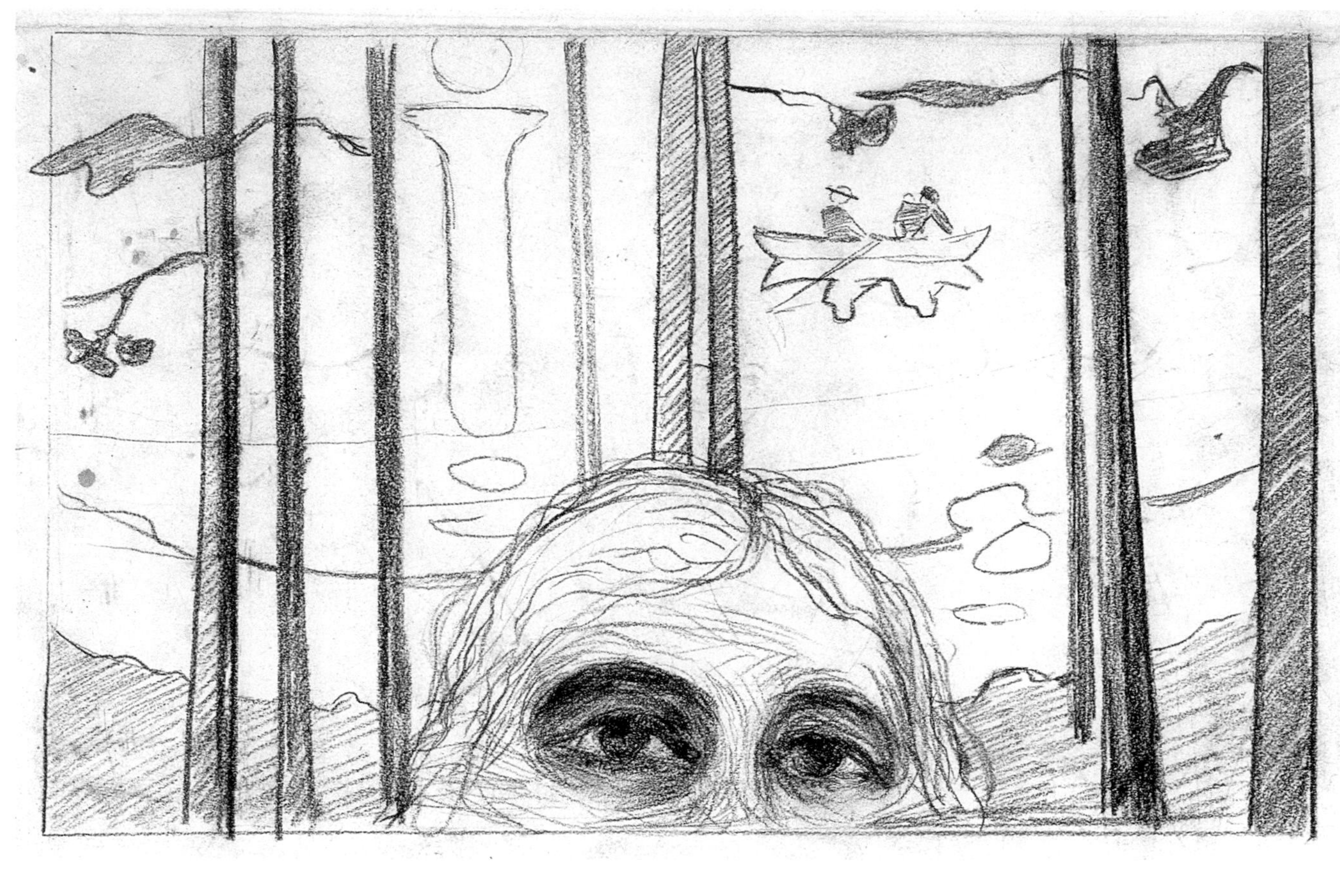

Cat. no. 6 *The Voice* (*Eyes*), 1893–96
Drawing on paper, 41.5 x 50 cm
Munch-museet, Oslo

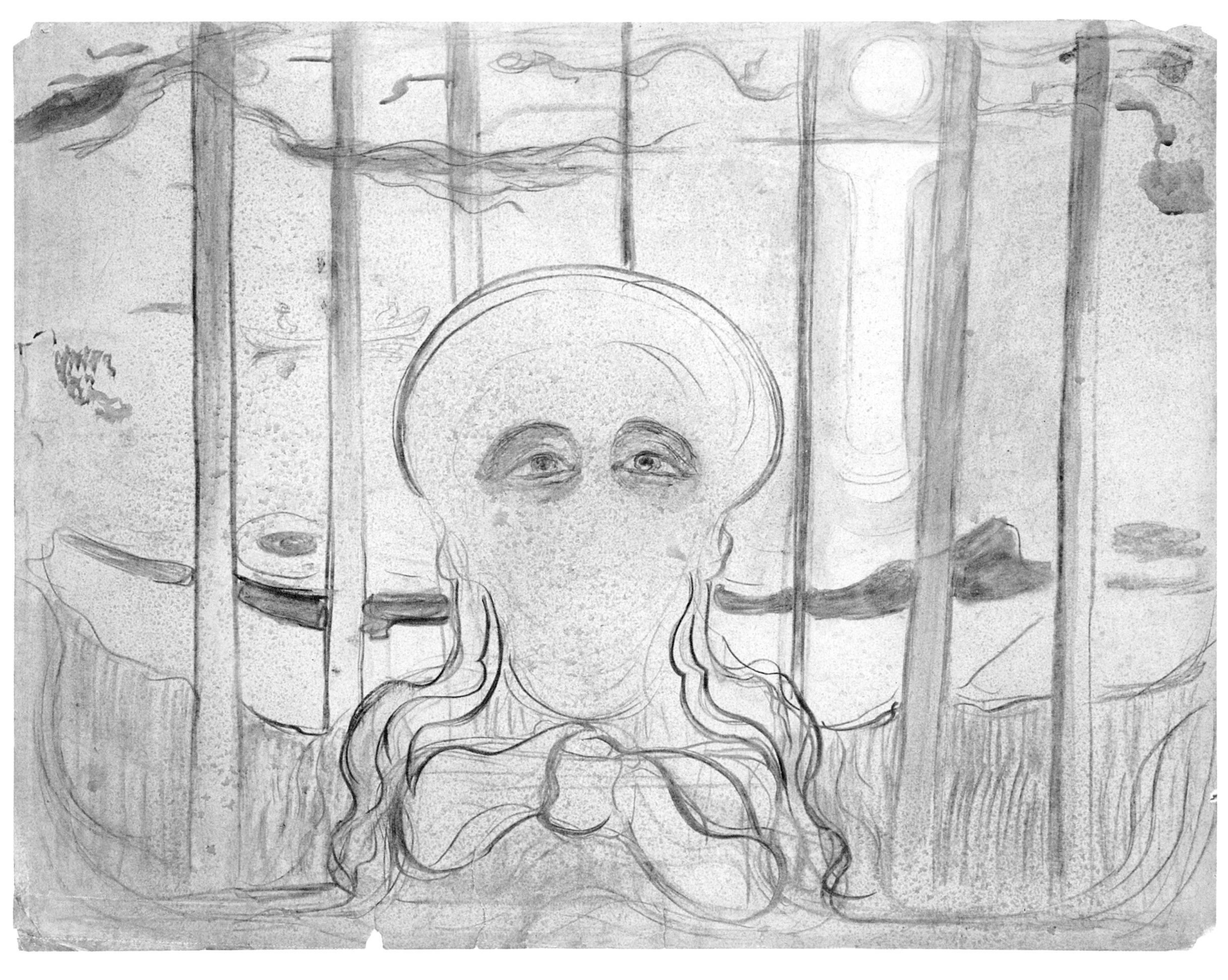

Cat. no. 7 *The Voice (Summer Night)*, 1893
Drawing and watercolor on paper, 50 x 64.7 cm
Munch-museet, Oslo

Moonlight

The nearly square painting entitled *Moonlight* (cat. no. 8) shows a woman standing in front of a white fence. Her hands are not visible—as they are in the preliminary studies done in 1891 and 1892—but disappear behind her body. In contrast to *The Voice*, the scene is illuminated by the moon from the front. The woman's face emerges in a blur from the darkness of the background and matches the coloration of the bright, white window frame and wooden slats of the fence. Her dress and hat appear to blend into a large, shadowlike area on the left, which echoes the forms of her body. A shadow, often interpreted as the umbra cast by the protagonist, although it does not conform to her outline, falls on the wall of the house behind her on the right and is bounded by an area of light color which extends as an oblique patch towards the fence. Space appears dissolved in the ambiguous interaction of individual pictorial elements. Uncertainty as to whether the shadow on the house wall has developed from that of the woman and assumed autonomous form in a figural transformation, or whether it signals the presence of a second person, contributes to the mysterious, unreal mood evoked by the picture.

In late 1893, Munch exhibited *Moonlight* at his *Unter den Linden* 19 exhibition in Berlin along with a number of symbolic works, including *The Storm*, a painting with a similarly indeterminable, uncanny atmosphere. The dark tones and glowing colors prompted Willy Pastor to associate the work with Arnold Böcklin's symbolic landscapes (fig. 2, p. 84) in his review of the exhibition in the *Frankfurter Zeitung* published in January 1894:

> The artist must use drastic means to bring to the light of understanding what stirs deep within him. The dragon of his alpine landscape, the dead horseman in the autumn painting, the furies of the storm, all of these are but makeshift solutions. ... I refer to Böcklin's Storm. One might compare this landscape to that of the same title by Eduard Munch. This work, which stands at the very heart of the creative method of these two artists, offers an excellent illustration of the progress Munch represents in the history of painting.[1]

Munch's fascination with Böcklin is evident in his account of a visit to the Kunsthalle in Hamburg in the fall of 1891: "Disgusting German art—languid women—battle scenes with towering steeds—and shiny cannonballs—you feel disgust, until you stop to look at a Böcklin painting—The Holy Flame."[2] Munch expressed his thoughts more precisely in a letter to Johan Rohde: "As horrid as the general state of art in Germany is—I must say one thing—it has the advantage down here that it has brought forth individual artists who stand so far above all others and so alone—e.g. Böcklin, of whom I almost think that he stands above all painters of our time—Max Klinger—Thoma ..."[3] Munch's enthusiasm suggests that he had studied the work of the German painter closely. The influence of Böcklin's view of the landscape on *Moonlight* and *The Storm* seems evident in their clear surface configuration, the isolation of central motifs, the glaring coloration, and the hard contrasts.

The Storm (cat. no. 10) is set in Åsgårdstrand and shows the Kiøsterud estate—a recurring motif in many of Munch's works—in the background and the Grand Hotel, which the artist frequented. The focus of the nocturnal scene is a woman in white, standing in front of the monumental hotel building with brightly illuminated windows. Like the figure in *The Scream* (cat. no. 118), she covers her ears with her hands. She stands apart from a group merged into a single form on the left. The people hold their hats or cover their ears with their hands as protection against the storm. Communication has ceased; the action has shifted, as in *The Scream*, to the inside, from the physical to the psychological realm. The attitude of the isolated protagonist's arms and her pear-shaped head recall the image of the screaming figure. But her anonymous face is devoid of detail. She feels the great outcry both physically, through nature—the storm—and mentally, through her isolation. The sketchy brushstrokes and the areas of partially thinned, running oil paint on the right create a sense of agitation in the picture. The signs of the storm's fury are concentrated in the people and the dramatically bowing tree in front of the hotel, which is thus drawn into the social context. The theatrical effect of the brightly illuminated windows is intensified by the areas where paint has been scratched away, injuring the painted surface. Munch transposed the dramatic tension of the scene to his working process.

While Munch dealt with the subject of *The Storm* only once again, in a small woodcut of 1908–09 in which the image is reversed (Sch. 341, Woll 371), he continued to work on the *Moonlight* theme during the years immediately following completion of his first version, always altering the frame of view. In the painting *House in the Moonlight* (cat. no. 9) the mood of uncertainty that prevails in *Moonlight* is resolved by the clarity of spatial relationships in the expanded frame of view. In front of the gate stands a woman dressed in a white skirt, whose torso, head, and hat disappear into the blue of the background. Behind her on the right is the house seen as a cut-off fragment in *Moonlight*. The organic, reddish-ochre form in the lower left-hand corner of *Moonlight* has its counterpart in the stone wall that now encircles the house. The focal point of the scene has shifted upward and to the right, thus increasing the distance between the woman and the corner of the house. The shadow of a man intrudes at an angle from below, signaling to the presence of a second person. The dynamic energy and organic character of the bushes and stones recalls the dramatic tension of *The Storm*, which is heightened in *House in the Moonlight* by the reddish borders around the shadows. As in *The Voice*, Munch may have been alluding here to his first erotic encounters with the married woman Milly Thaulow, symbolizing in his shadow and her disappearance in the background both the secrecy and threatening aspects of their love affair. The uncertainty as to whether the approaching shadow signifies danger or fulfillment clearly associates this painting with the mood of mystery in *The Storm* and *Moonlight*.

Munch continued his experiment with the frame of view in the color woodcut of 1896, in which the viewer is brought closer to the motif. The horizontal-format woodcut depicts the head and shoulders of a woman, her shadow, a tree, the house wall, and the window with reflections of the moon in a mirror-image of the earlier scene. Focusing on depiction, Munch dispenses with the uncertain interplay of pictorial elements. The shadow on the house wall conforms largely to the outline of the woman's body, but the dark shape next to the wall does not take up her profile. The dissolution of pictorial space compels Munch to strive for a planar, two-dimensional presentation in almost painterly prints with thickly applied paint, in some cases oils, and in the versions printed with thin applications of paint which incorporate the structure of the wood. Munch initially made two-color prints in black and blue using the front and reverse sides of a wood block (cat. no. 11). The grain pattern of the block is visible in these prints, whose sparsely colored areas represent reflections of the moon. For his experiments with oil paint (cat. no. 13) and impasto (cat. no. 14), he made a third color plate, which he presumably then cut into three sections. The intermingling areas of color dissolve the forms into entirely flat elements on the boundary between painting and graphic art. The strongest concentration on the pale reflection of the moonlight on the window and the face is achieved in the monochrome prints made with the front side of the main printing block. The shapeless body disappears into the black, which is broken up by the grain of the wood.

These highly experimental variations were followed by five-color prints made with the front and reverse sides of the main printing block and the three-part color plate, the different-colored sections of which Munch reassembled for the printing process. The wood structure is constantly present in the form of the imprint of the grain pattern in the prints (cat. no. 15). These variations focus on two-dimensionality.

Munch pursued his experiments with the frame of view using approximately square wood blocks in 1902, expanding the scene upward and adding a section of house wall and a tree. The resulting shift of proportions diminishes the concentration on the pictorial elements and the tension in the composition of the first woodcut version and thus transposes the motif into the non-directional square format of the first painted version. DB

1 Willy Pastor, quoted and translated from Jan Kneher, *Edvard Munch in seinen Ausstellungen zwischen* 1892 *und* 1912, Worms 1994, p. 37.

2 Sketch book T 128-22, Munch-museet.

3 Undated letter, presumably written in early 1893, published in Gran Henning, "To brev fra Edvard Munch til en dansk maler," in *Verdens Gang*, Aug. 26, 1950.

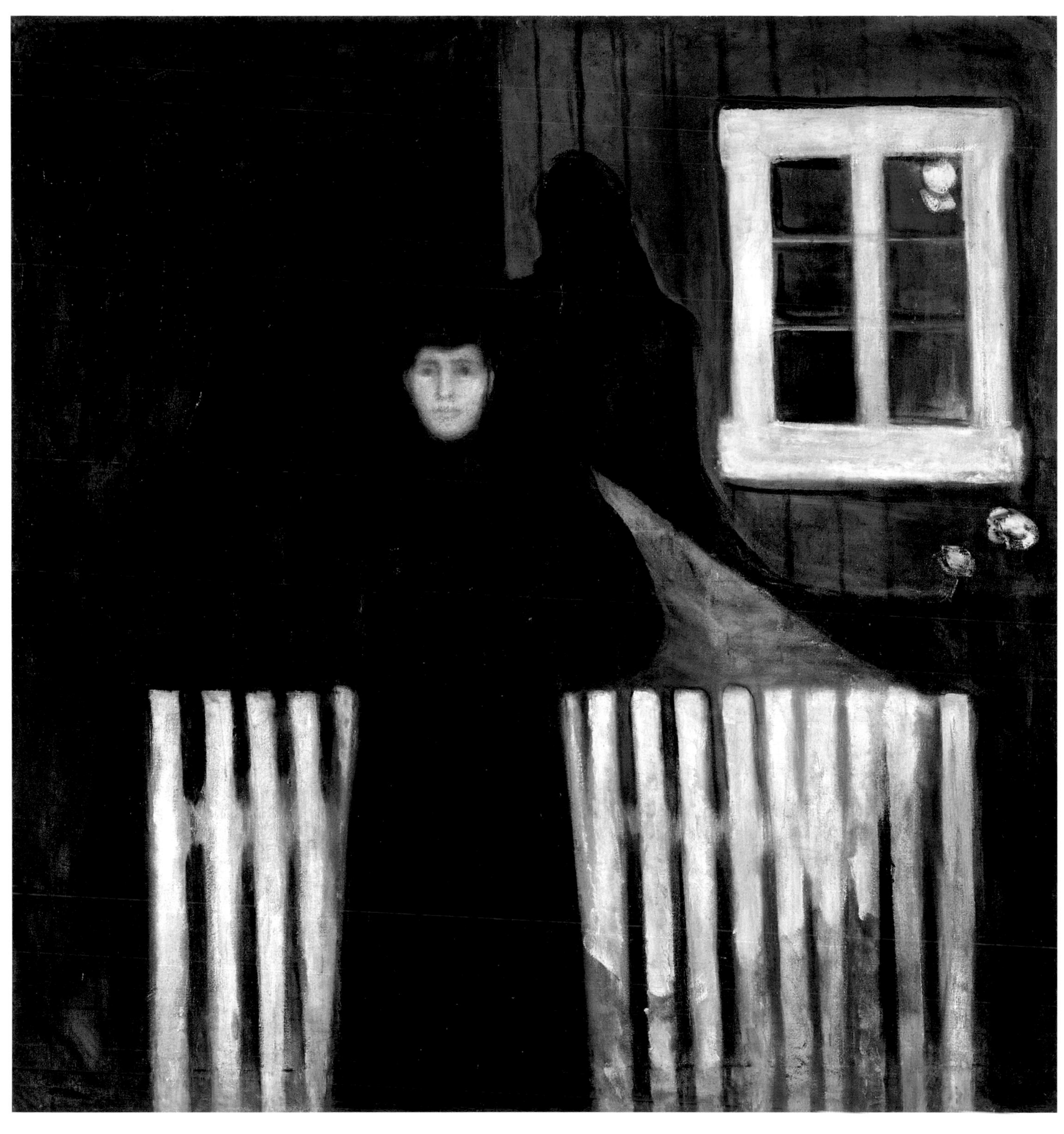

Cat. no. 8 *Moonlight*, 1893
Oil on canvas, 140,5 x 137 cm
Nasjonalgalleriet, Oslo

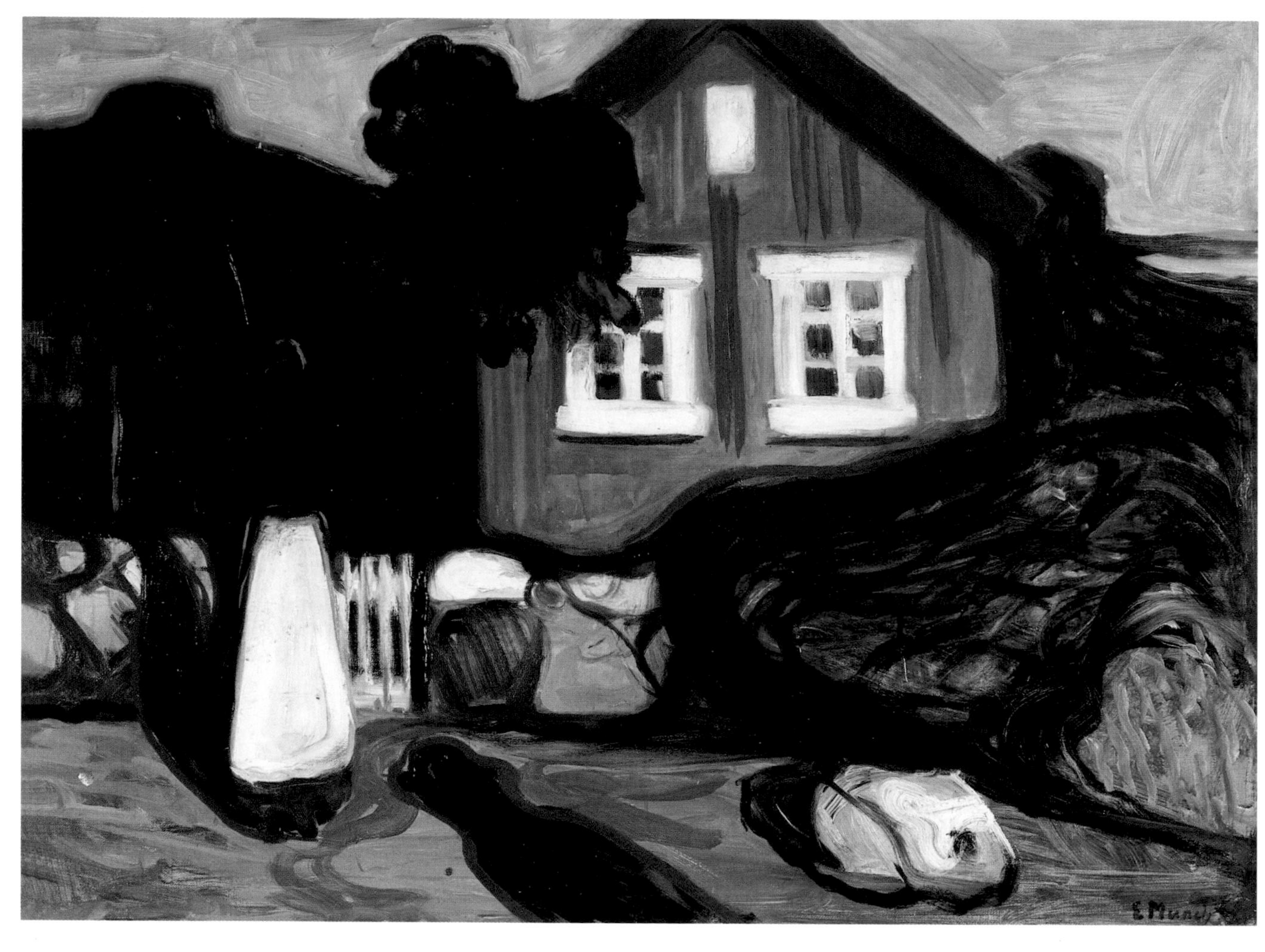

Cat. no. 9 *House in the Moonlight*, 1895
Oil on canvas, 81 x 100.5 cm
Rasmus Meyers Samlinger, Bergen Kunstmuseum

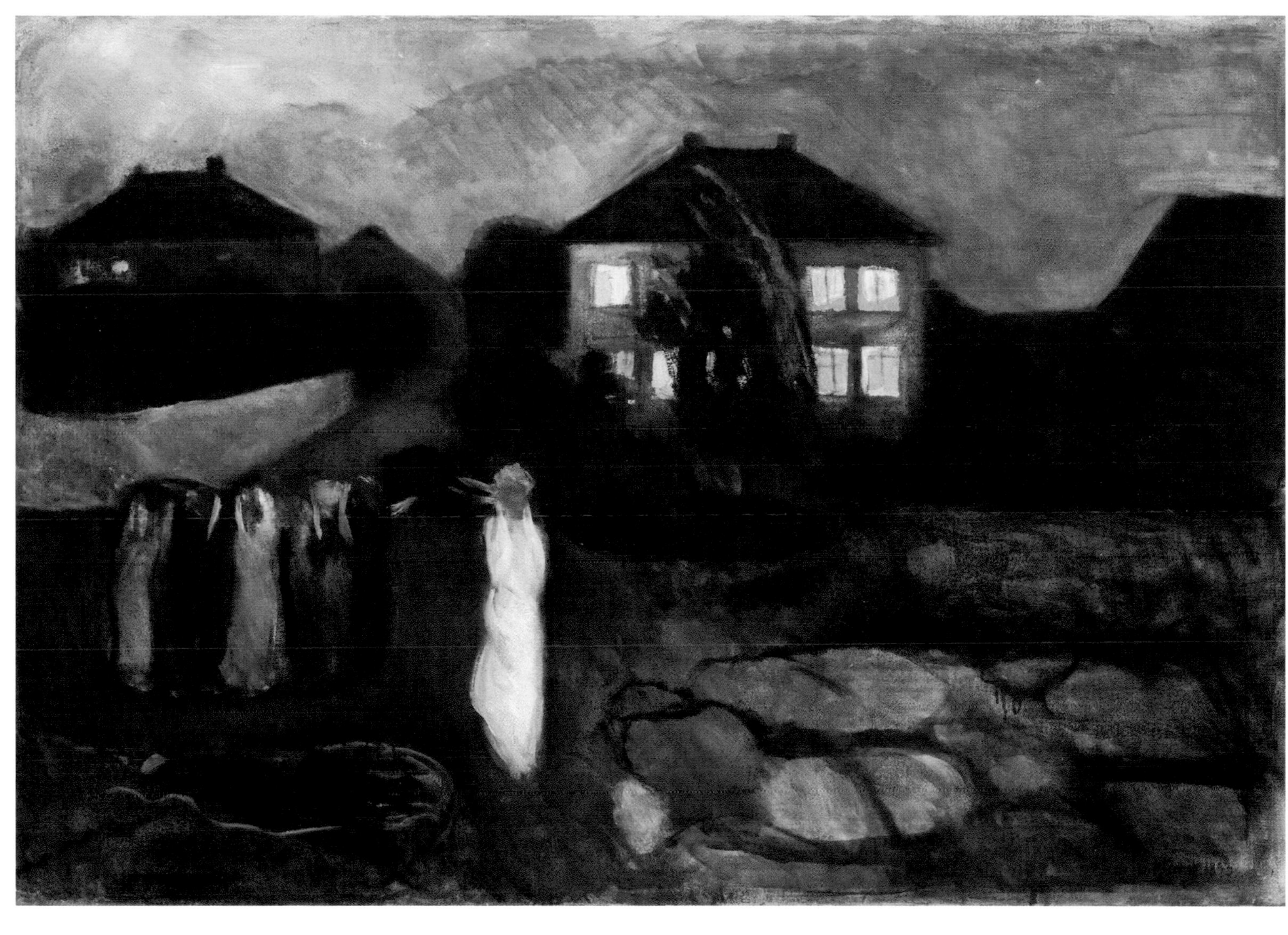

Cat. no. 10 *The Storm*, 1893
Oil on canvas, 91.8 x 130.8 cm
The Museum of Modern Art, New York, Gift of Mr. and Mrs. H. Irgens Larsen and acquired through the Lillie P. Bliss and Abby Aldrich Rockefeller Funds, 1974

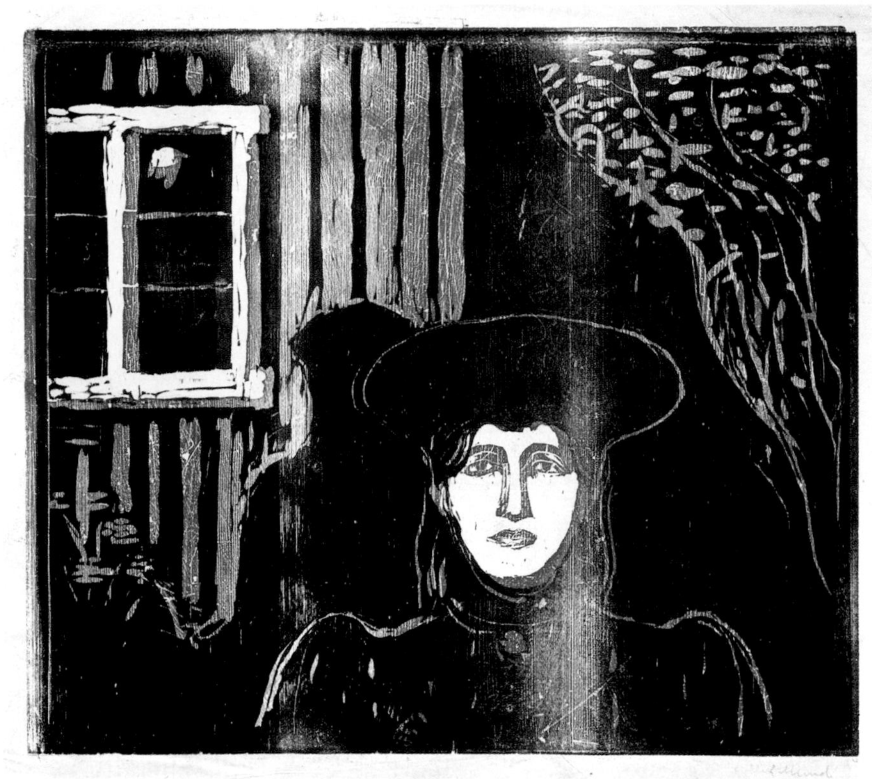

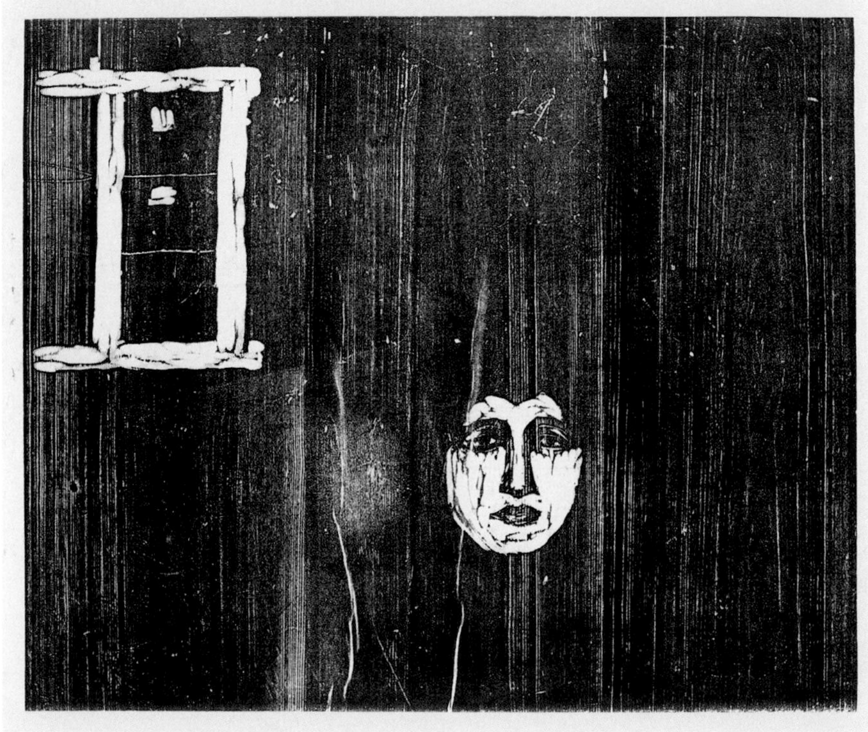

Cat. no. 11 *Moonlight* I, 1896
Color woodcut on paper, 41.5 x 47.1 cm
Munch-museet, Oslo

Cat. no. 12 *Moonlight* I, 1896
Woodcut on paper, 39 x 46.8 cm
Munch-museet, Oslo

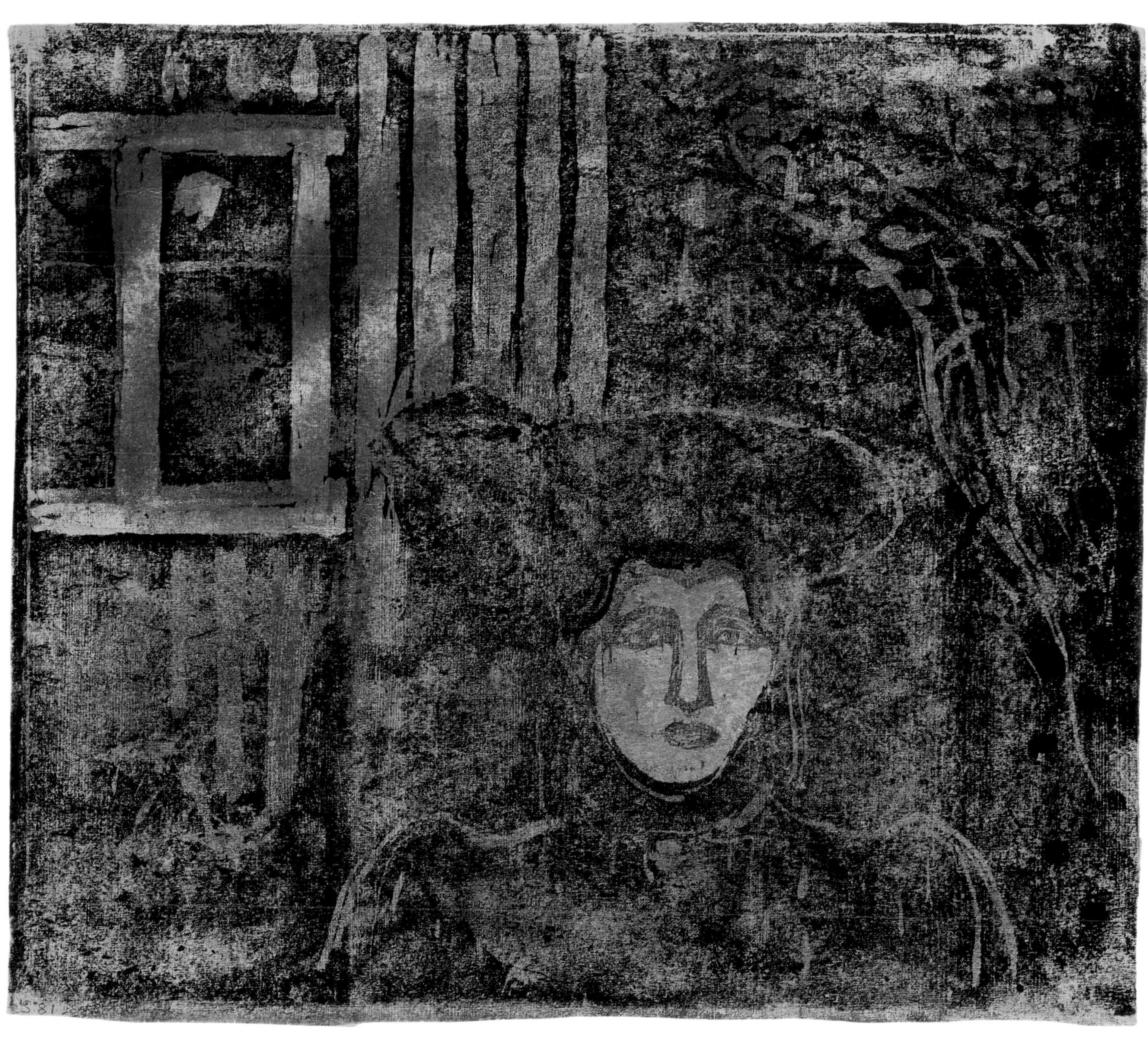

Cat. no. 13 *Moonlight* I, 1896
Color woodcut on paper, 41.2 x 47 cm
Munch-museet, Oslo

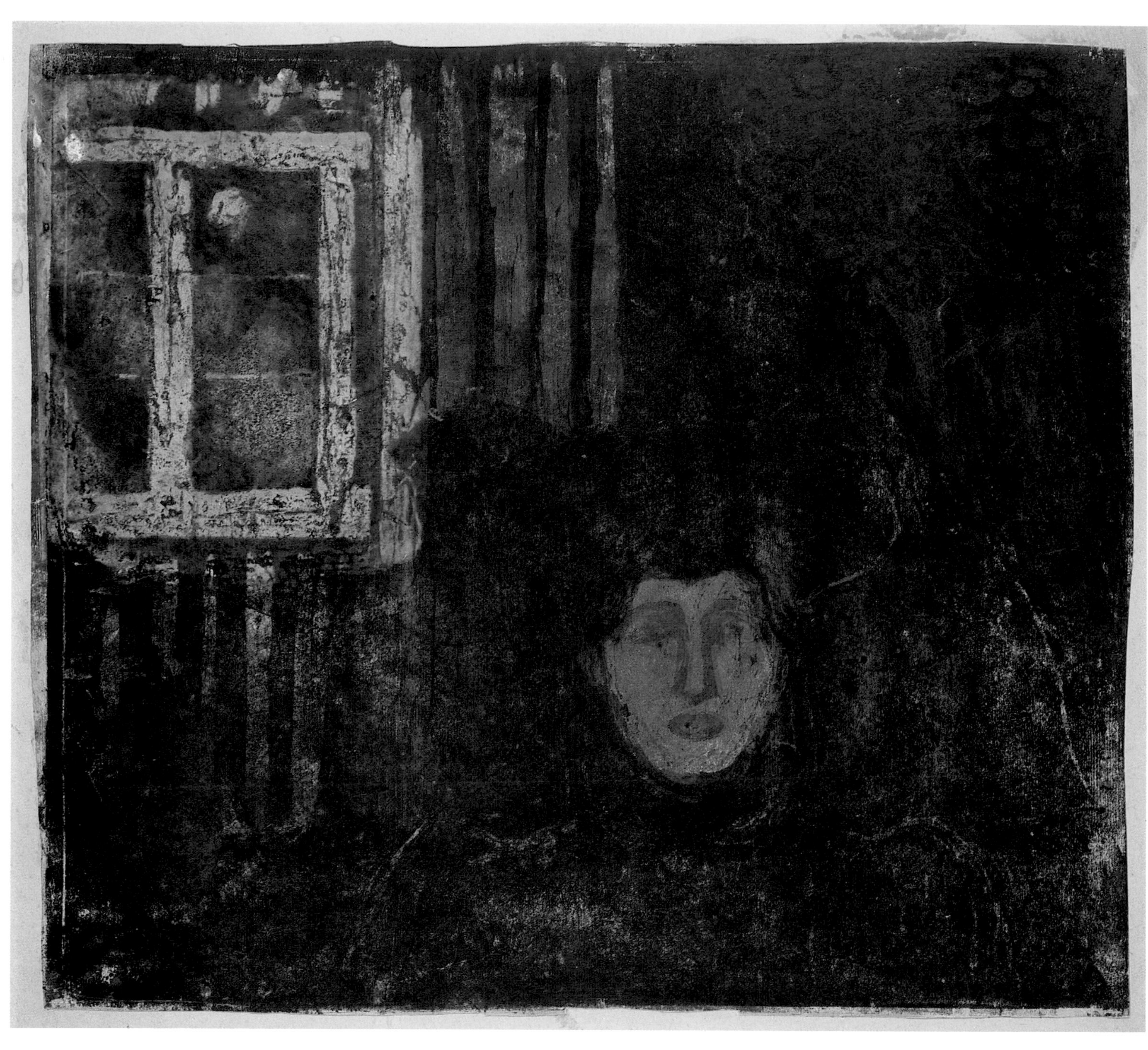

Cat. no. 14 *Moonlight* I, 1896
Color woodcut on paper, 41.7 x 47 cm
Munch-museet, Oslo

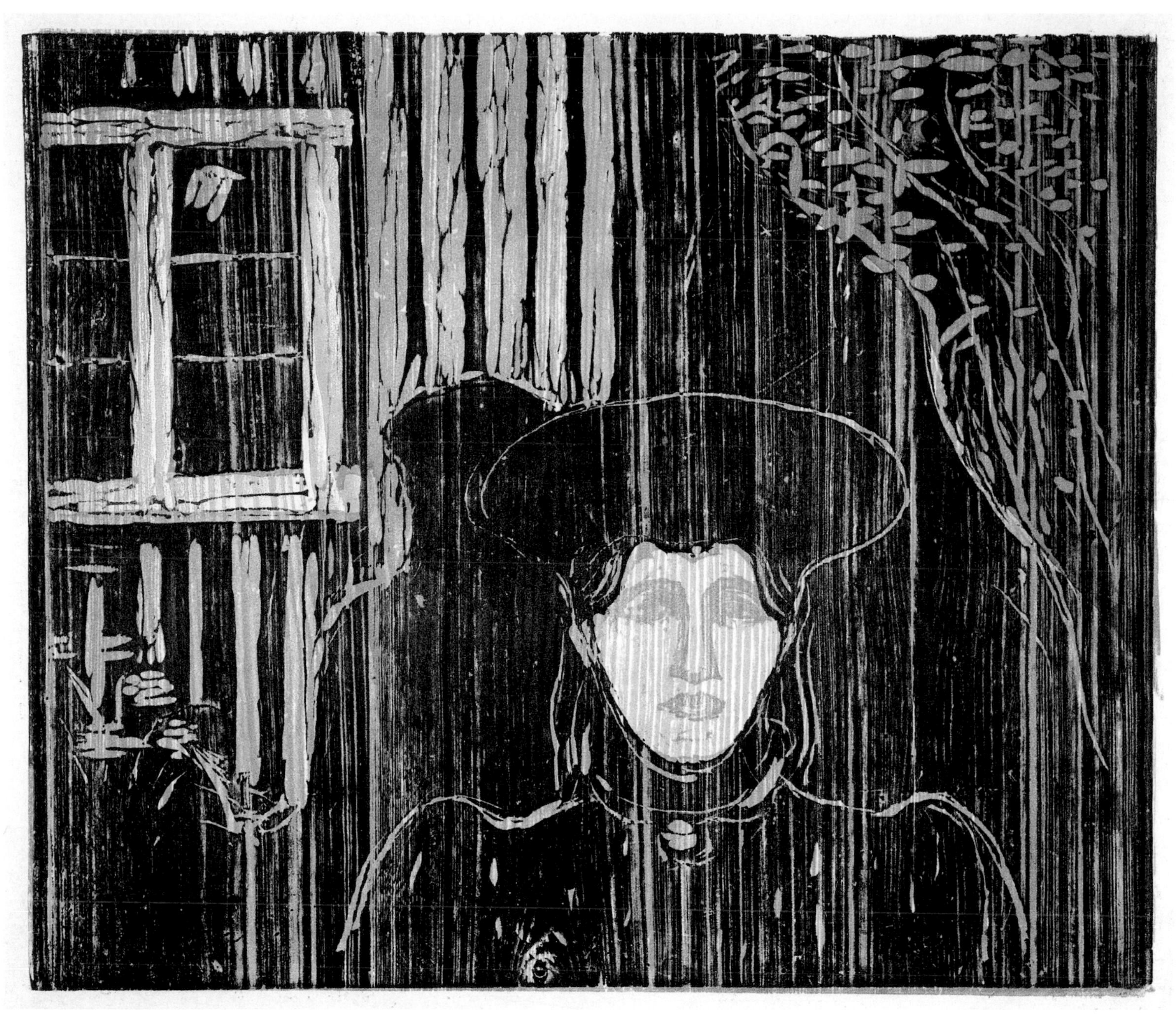

Cat. no. 15 *Moonlight* I, 1896
Color woodcut on paper, 41 x 46.7 cm
Albertina, Vienna

Puberty

In *Unterwegs*, part of his *Homo Sapiens* trilogy, Stanislaw Przybyszewski describes the adolescent awakening of a girl in puberty: "She sensed it; she did not understand it. ... She could not think, she only felt the wild shudder of desire that shook her body. She thrust both hands between her knees, bent forward, and pulled her legs towards her chest. And thus she sat cowering on the edge of her bed, listening in anxious pain to the unknown, the terrifying."[1]

Published in 1895, this substantially autobiographical novel, which recalls events of the year 1893, along with the other two parts of the trilogy, deals with the turbulent life of the author as a member of the Scandinavian-German bohemian circle associated with the Berlin wine tavern Zum Schwarzen Ferkel at a time when Munch was also a frequent visitor there. Munch finished a painting devoted to the theme of puberty in 1893 (fig. 1) and another in 1894 (cat. no. 16), both of which seem to fit Przybyszewski's description. In addition to a number of drawings, Munch presumably executed five paintings and three prints relating to puberty. The first Berlin version remained in his possession and is now at the Munch-museet. The 1894 version was purchased by Jens Thiis, Director of the Nasjonalgalleriet in Kristiania, in 1909 for only 10,000 kroner, a third of its market value at the time, along with four other major works by the artist. According to Munch, The "first lost version of 1886," as it is described in the catalog for the comprehensive retrospective at the Berlin Nationalgalerie in 1927,"[2] was destroyed in a fire.

A comparison of the two Berlin versions of the painting suggests that Munch was intent upon exploring the artistic potential of the subject at the level of meaning. In both versions, the same young girl is depicted with only a suggestion of budding breasts. She sits upright and rigid, with wide-open eyes, on the edge of her bed. Her legs are pressed tightly together, her feet defensively turned to one side. The bright lamplight casts an oversized shadow on the bare wall behind her.

In the 1893 version, which has survived in extremely fragile condition, Munch experimented with heavily thinned, running and sprayed paint. The viewer looks down at the girl from a somewhat elevated vantage point. Her hands are reddened, set off against her body by blue outlines, and emphasize the physical aspect of her situation, while her absent gaze suggests a state between daydream and pensive reflection. The pale blue bed sheet covers the edge of the bed and forms a largely unstructured area between the strict horizontal boundaries above and below. The clearly outlined, transparent shadow falls over the sheet and the wall and assumes a threatening existence of its own at the level of the girl's buttocks, where it appears to separate from the outline of her body. The viewer immediately notices that the outline connects the shadow to the rear corner of the bed with a straight line, forming an anthropomorphic shape that emerges from there. Here, we recall Przybyszewski's description: "She sensed it; she did not understand it. ... [and listened] in anxious pain to the unknown, the terrifying."[3]

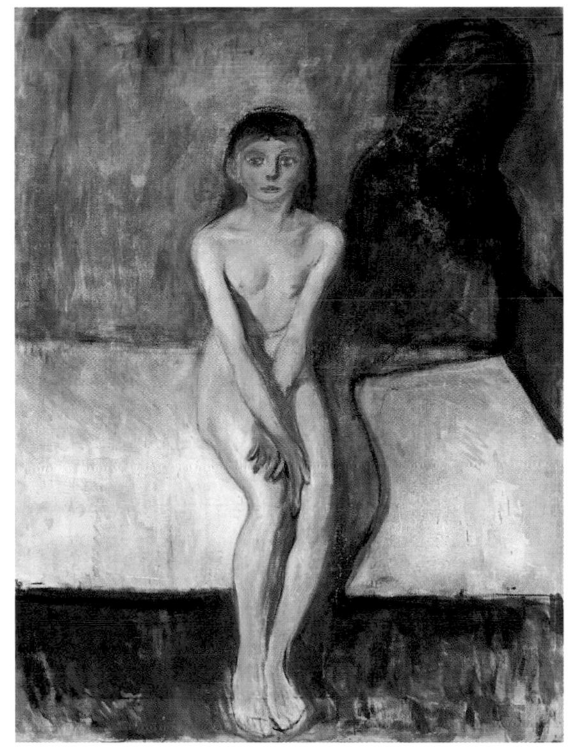

1 *Puberty*, 1893,
oil on canvas, 149 x 112 cm,
Munch-museet, Oslo

In the 1894 version from the Nasjonalgalleriet (cat. no. 16), this intimation gives way to certainty. The gaze of the girl, whose sitting position is unchanged, is now fixed on the viewer, who faces her almost at eye level. The painting style is more open and dynamic, though less experimental, and the colors are more vivid. The girl's hair falls more loosely, and her hands—no longer set apart from the body by color—are much more relaxed. The section of bed sheet left undefined in the other version is now clearly recognizable as a bed frame and sheet. The oblique line on the left, which is echoed in the double outline on the right-hand side, is emphasized with a broad, dark brushstroke and serves as a counterweight to the shadow, which is now consolidated into an organic form. The scene is imbued with greater energy by a very few changes and vigorous brushstrokes, and it expresses a will to act driven by the girl's sense of what is happening to her, a feeling of curiosity in the tension-filled relationship to the monumental shadow. Thus the painting identifies the two poles which define the phase of human development between childhood and youth, fear and curiosity, innocence and intimation. The variation from the Munch-museet emphasizes loneliness and fear, while the Nasjonalgalleriet painting focuses on desire and curiosity. The lithograph dated 1894 (Sch. 8, Woll 14)[4] is one of a group of Munch's early prints which depict, in mirror-images, themes (except for portraits) represented in paintings. As the lithograph is a literal rendition of the version from the Nasjonalgalleriet, the painting can also be dated to the year 1894.[5]

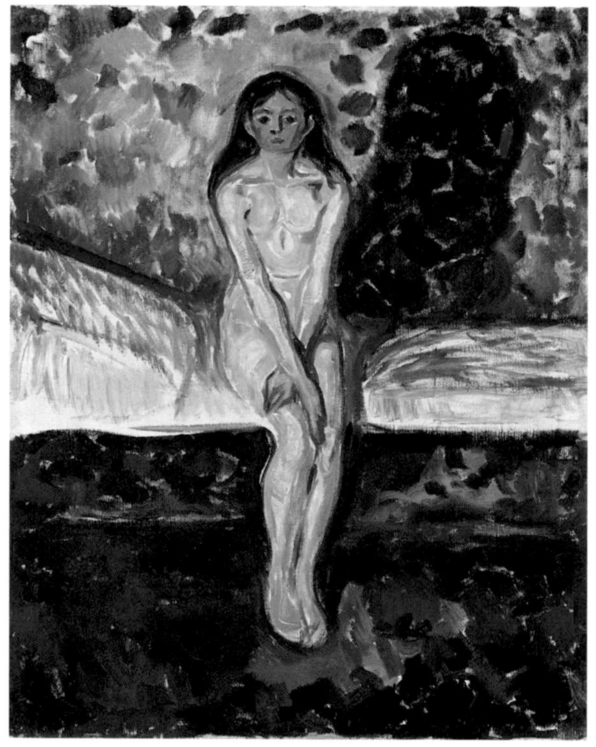

Munch took up the theme of puberty again in the 1910s in a work based on the version of 1894 (fig. 2). The patchy fragmentation of the foreground and background and its vivid coloration gives the picture a new and threateningly expressive quality. The figure, which occupies a smaller portion of the pictorial space, the enlarged shadow, and the dark, impenetrable eyes unite the elements of fear and curiosity. DB

1 Stanislaw Przybyszewski, *Unterwegs*, Berlin 1895. Quoted and translated from Przybyszewski, *Werke, Aufzeichnungen und ausgewählte Briefe*, vol. III, Paderborn 1993, p. 148.
2 *Edvard Munch*, exh. cat., Nationalgalerie Berlin, Berlin 1927, p. 18, cat. no. 40.
3 Cf. Przybyszewski (see note 1).
4 Gerd Woll, *Edvard Munch. The Complete Graphic Works*, London 2001, p. 54.
5 This dating is also supported by a studio report printed in *Morgenbladet*, May 1, 1894, which cites variously newly painted pictures, including *Puberty*.

2 *Puberty*, 1913–15,
oil on canvas, 97 x 77 cm,
Munch-museet, Oslo

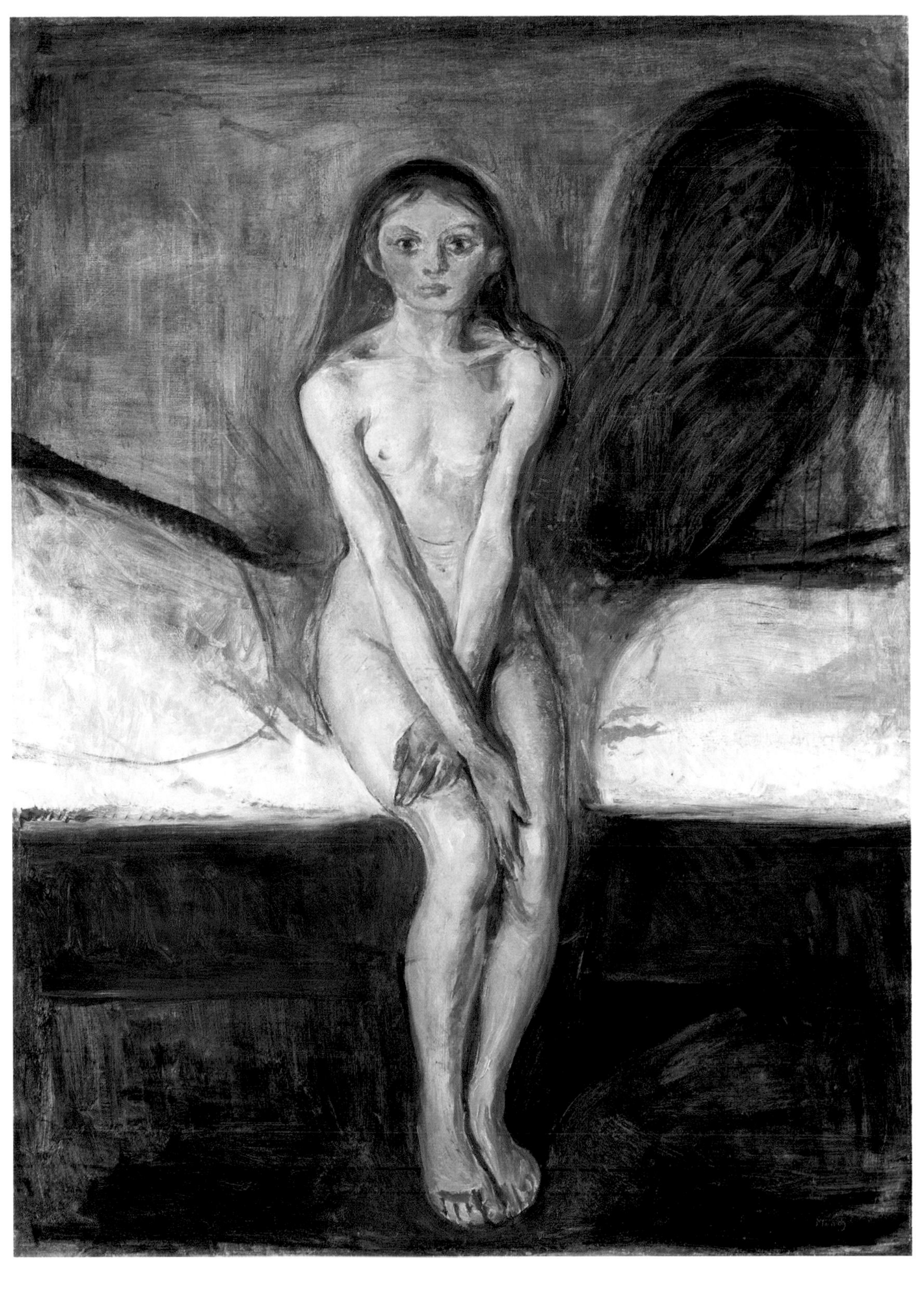

Cat. no. 16 *Puberty*, 1894–95 (1894)
Oil on canvas, 151.5 x 110 cm
Nasjonalgalleriet, Oslo

Madonna

Edvard Munch worked intensely on the theme of the *Madonna* during the mid-1890s, producing five paintings and a monochrome lithograph, to which he later added color plates. Numerous other drawings, prints, and paintings exhibit iconographic, thematic, or formal associations with the subject and may be classified within or related to the broad category of the *Madonna* group.

As is true of many of his titles, the designation *Madonna* was by no means Munch's original choice. He first showed a version entitled *The Face of Madonna* at his solo exhibition *Unter den Linden* 19 in Berlin in late 1893, as the catalog indicates. Two versions, both entitled *The Woman Who Loves*, were exhibited in Stockholm in 1894. It seems unlikely that Munch himself actually chose the titles used today. Indeed, the banker and writer Rolf Stenersen states in his highly personal biography that

> Munch often asked critics or art dealers to choose names for his pictures. It pleased him when they were given literary titles—*Two People*, *The Encounter*, *The Sea of Love*, *The Dance of Life*, *Consolation*, *Vampire*, *The Death of Marat*, *Ashes*, etc. Many of them have several names. In a cunning move, Director Jens Thiis brought the picture originally entitled *Loving Woman* and *The Conception* to the Nasjionalgalleriet and renamed it *Madonna*. Even if someone had suggested a title like *The Wave of Love*, Munch would have agreed.[1]

Thus there is little certainty about the early titles. They are indicative of Munch's complex approach to the subject, which makes it difficult to establish clear thematic classifications.

The scene depicted in all five painted versions is based upon the same compositional scheme. The paintings show the three-quarter figure of a nude woman with a finely drawn face. Her closed eyes are set in deep sockets, and her cheekbones are visible beneath the slightly sunken cheeks. The slightly upward view is underscored by the backward-leaning position of the head, which fully exposes the upper lip and forms the sides of the nose into a triangle. Although the woman's hips are still visible in the picture, the pudenda is absent—replaced in most of the paintings by undulating framing lines. The halo-shaped ring behind her head, her lips, and her nipples are associated and accentuated by luminous red.

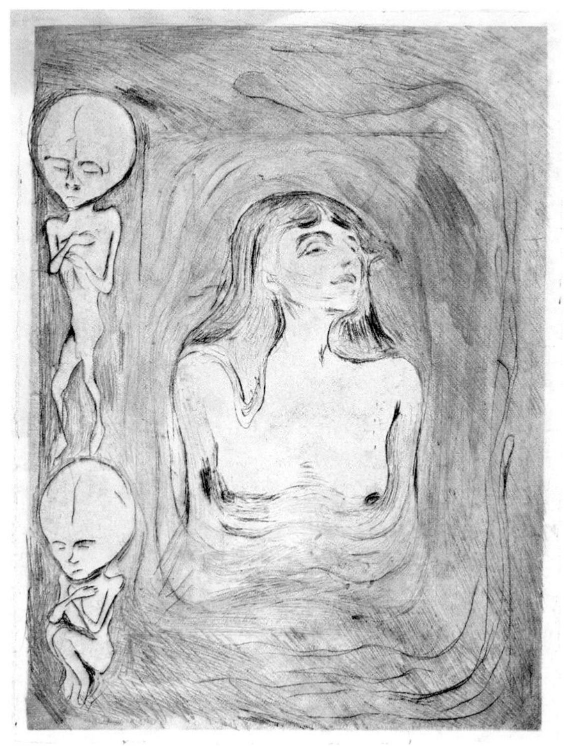

1 *Madonna*, 1894, hand-colored etching on paper, 36 x 26.5 cm, Munch-museet, Oslo

A comparison of the version from the Munch-museet (cat. no. 19) and the painting from the Blitz Collection (cat. no. 21) shows that Munch used the same pictorial structure but experimented with the use of color. The version from the Munch-museet dated to 1893–94 exhibits fine transitions without hard contrasts and derives its darker coloration from an underlying layer of green, among others. The hair and body outlines are emphasized in places by scratch marks, and substantial portions of the painting surfaces were sprayed with light-red paint. In contrast, the variation from the Blitz Collection is characterized by a very sparing use of paint. The contours of arms and legs, which are reinforced in part by dark brushstrokes, are left over from the preliminary drawing. The undulating framing was painted and sprayed onto the canvas in very pale blue and red tones, and the body is integrated into the background through the overlapping of the blue and red sprayed areas.

Evidence of Munch's experimentation with painting techniques is visible in all five surviving painted versions. Thurmann-Moe has shown that Munch used a mixture of turpentine and varnish as a thinner in a version now held in a private collection and that he sprayed the colorless liquid onto the completed painting.[2] Within a very short period of time—no more than three years—Munch completed five variations in a kind of experimental series. These works differ from one another primarily with respect to characteristics of the painted surface—modeled, laid on in thick, pasty layers, or applied sparingly—and Munch's varying use of spraying techniques and thinners. All of these differences establish paint as an autonomous pictorial resource. The character of these works as part of an experimental series supports the presumption that they were completed within a very short period. The artist may well have worked on several different variations at the same time.

In the lithograph (cat. no. 23), Munch added a frame of embryo and sperm motifs to the picture. In his biography published in 1933, Jens Thiis cites a similar frame in a painting: "*Madonna* or *Loving Woman* was painted in Berlin during the winter of 1893–94 and shown at the exhibition ... as a kind of triptych or in a symbolic frame consisting of spermatozoa and embryos, which appear again in the first version of the color lithograph; the tasteless frame was later eliminated."[3] Two newspaper caricatures printed on the occasion of Munch's exhibition at Blomqvist's gallery in fall 1895, where he showed three now unidentifiable painted versions under the title *A Woman Who Loves*, also refer to framelike elements. The caricature in the October 18, 1895 issue of *Tyrihans* shows a version with frame executed by Munch as a mirror image in the first stage of an etching (fig. 1). The caricature (fig. 2) is the only evidence of the existence of that work, however. On the basis of this evidence, it seems reasonable to assume the existence of another variation that differed significantly from the known versions but has not survived. Munch experimented with the frame in his lithograph prints, in some of which it is covered over (cat. no. 22).

Only four distinct formats have been identified among the more than 150 surviving prints. The multicolored prints made with a main lithograph stone and two color plates, which according to Schiefler (Sch. 33) were first printed in 1902, include a large number of variations which differ primarily with respect to the type of paper used, the choice of colors, and the frame of view.

The diversity is also reflected in the abundance of differing interpretations of the theme. Cornelia Gerner regards the "multiplicity of meaning and the complexity of the *Madonna* as the product of a range of different ideas," whereby the "typification" as a "hybrid type" united the "female art figures of the 19th century in a single 'person'" positioned between the *femme fragile* and the *femme fatale*.[4] This hybrid type develops not only from the frame motif but from the interplay of reclining and standing motifs, of stillness and movement, of exposure and concealment. Gerner calls attention in particular to the ambivalence between the erotic, ecstatic reclining motif and the standing motif, which positions the woman between dancer and mermaid. This is also true for the skeletal embryo and the spermatozoa as an allusion to conception and birth. Comparisons with works exhibiting formal and thematic similarities extend to nudes and portraits as well as symbolic pieces. A large-scale drawing of a nude in three-quarter figure (cat. no. 20) marked by numerous vertical water tracks combines the posture of the *Madonna* with arms bent upwards and downwards, which disappear behind the head and the body. The drawing reverses the representation in the painting and the lithograph, extending the turn of the body and emphasizing upward view. The ring is now clearly identifiable as a halo. It is possible that Munch experi-

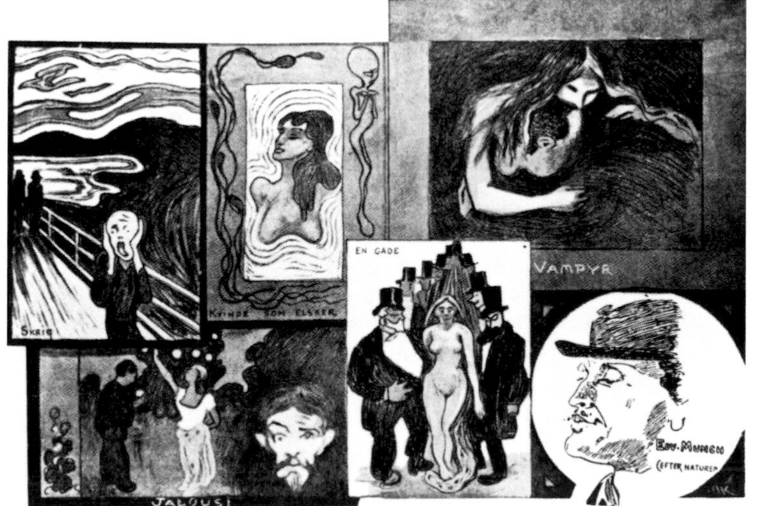

2 "From the Munch Exhibition," caricature in *Tyrihans*, no. 42, Oct. 18, 1895, Munch-museet, Oslo

mented here, as in the painted versions, with a liquid, which he allowed to run in vertical rivulets over the sheet and sprayed and/or splashed onto the paper. Other works, including the lithographs *Woman with Red Hair and Green Eyes (The Sin)* (cat. no. 18) and *The Brooch (Eva Mudocci)* (cat. no. 17) exhibit similar formal characteristics. *The Brooch* is a portrait of the violinist Eva Mudocci, whom Munch met in Paris in the spring of 1903 and with whom he developed a close friendship. The print is listed by Schiefler under the title *Madonna* (Sch. 212) and is thus associated with this group of works, although the only similarities found in the half-figure portrait are the head inclined to one side, the slightly upward view, and the figure's facial features. Evidence opposing this interpretation includes the open eyes and the body covered by the woman's hair and the robe to which the brooch is fastened.

In the painting *The Hands* (cat. no. 26), the aspect of male desire, visually represented by the hands, is involved in the interplay of concealment and exposure. Although the composition of this work differs from that of the *Madonna*, there are certain other similarities. In both works, the woman's hands disappear behind her body—although they are concealed behind her head in *The Hands*. One notes immediately that the pudenda is absent here as well, although the body is naked to a point below the hips. The nude body is surrounded by a dark, shadowy area; the sketchily suggested hands, some of which are severely disfigured, replace the undulating framework of lines. Although the ambivalence of sitting and reclining positions and of concealment and exposure is comparable to that in *Madonna*, this work is concerned with woman as an object of male desire. The ring-shaped element behind her head can be associated with both the halo-shaped form in *Madonna* and the woman's own hair. Yet the large number of hands and the claustrophobic closeness of the scene appear to emphasize a state of distress. The sparkling red of the woman's lips and her right nipple create a link with the two red hands below.

In the drawings (cat. no. 25) and the lithograph (cat. no. 24), the presentation of the nude body shifts to a rear view of a woman looking backwards over her left shoulder. Yet while a young, shy girl with closed eyes dressed in red pants is the object of male desire in the drawing, the smug smile of the woman in the lithograph calls to mind a different scene in an establishment in which the woman, as the attitude of her arms suggests, is about to let the last concealing garments fall from her body.[5] DB

1 Rolf Stenersen, *Edvard Munch*, Stockholm and Frankfurt am Main, 1950, p. 95.
2 Jan Thurmann-Moe, *Edvard Munchs "Hestekur." Eksperimenter med teknikk og materialer*, exh. cat., Munch-museet Oslo, Oslo 1995, p. 40.
3 Jens Thiis, *Edvard Munch og Hans Samtid*, Oslo 1933, p. 218.
4 In her dissertation presented in 1990, Cornelia Gerner offers a detailed discussion of the *Madonna* group and referes with considerable emphasis to the difficulties of interpretation. Cornelia Gerner, *Die "Madonna" in Edvard Munchs Werk*, Ph. D. dissertation, Morsbach 1993.
5 In one watercolored chalk drawing (c. 1893, Munch-museet, MM T 2292), the woman appears to be in the process of loosening her skirt.

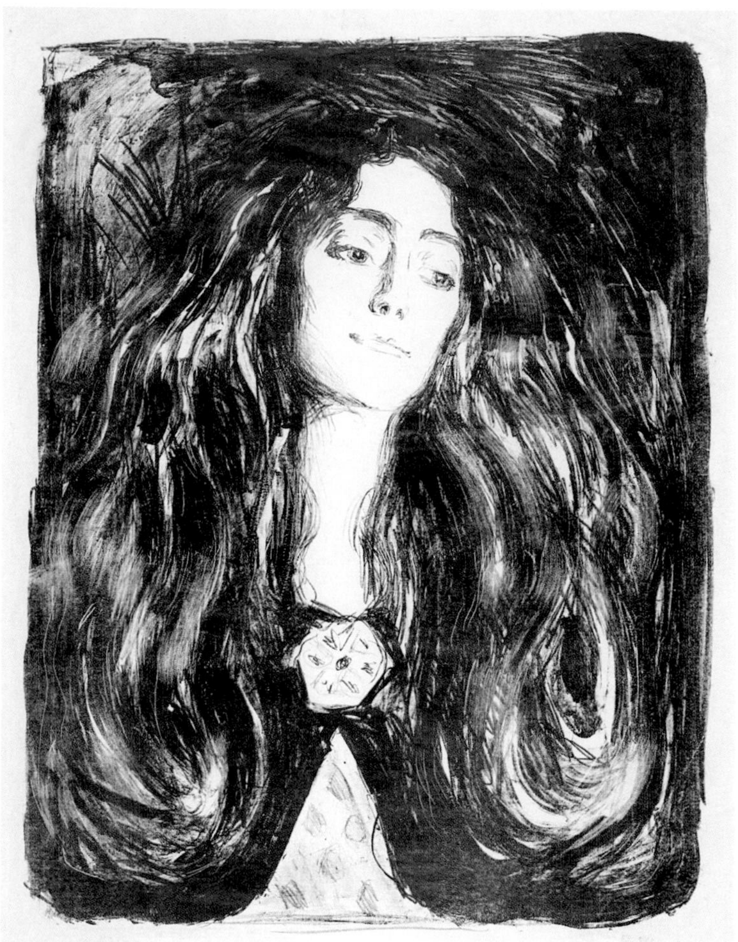

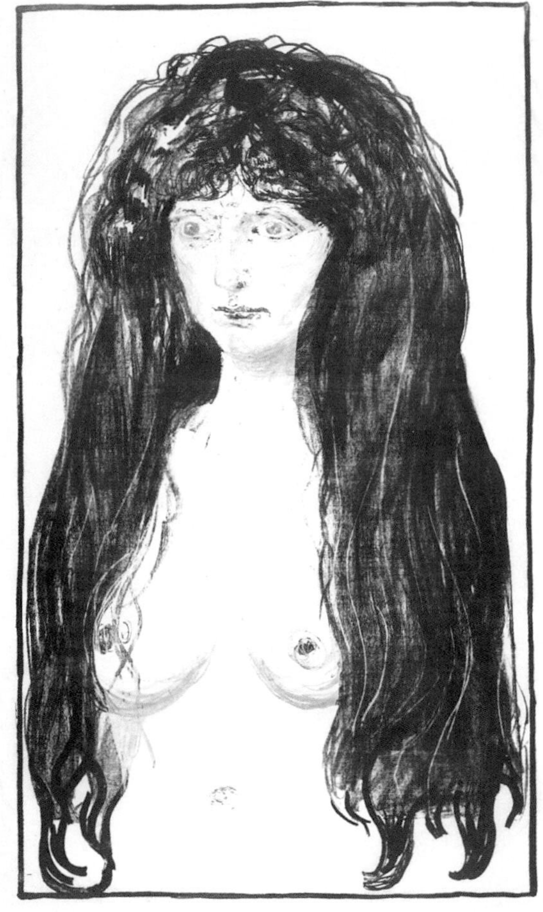

Cat. no. 17 *The Brooch* (*Eva Mudocci*), 1903
Lithograph on paper, 60 x 46 cm, Albertina, Vienna

Cat. no. 18 *Woman with Red Hair and Green Eyes* (*The Sin*), 1902
Color lithograph on paper, 69.7 x 40.2 cm, Albertina, Vienna

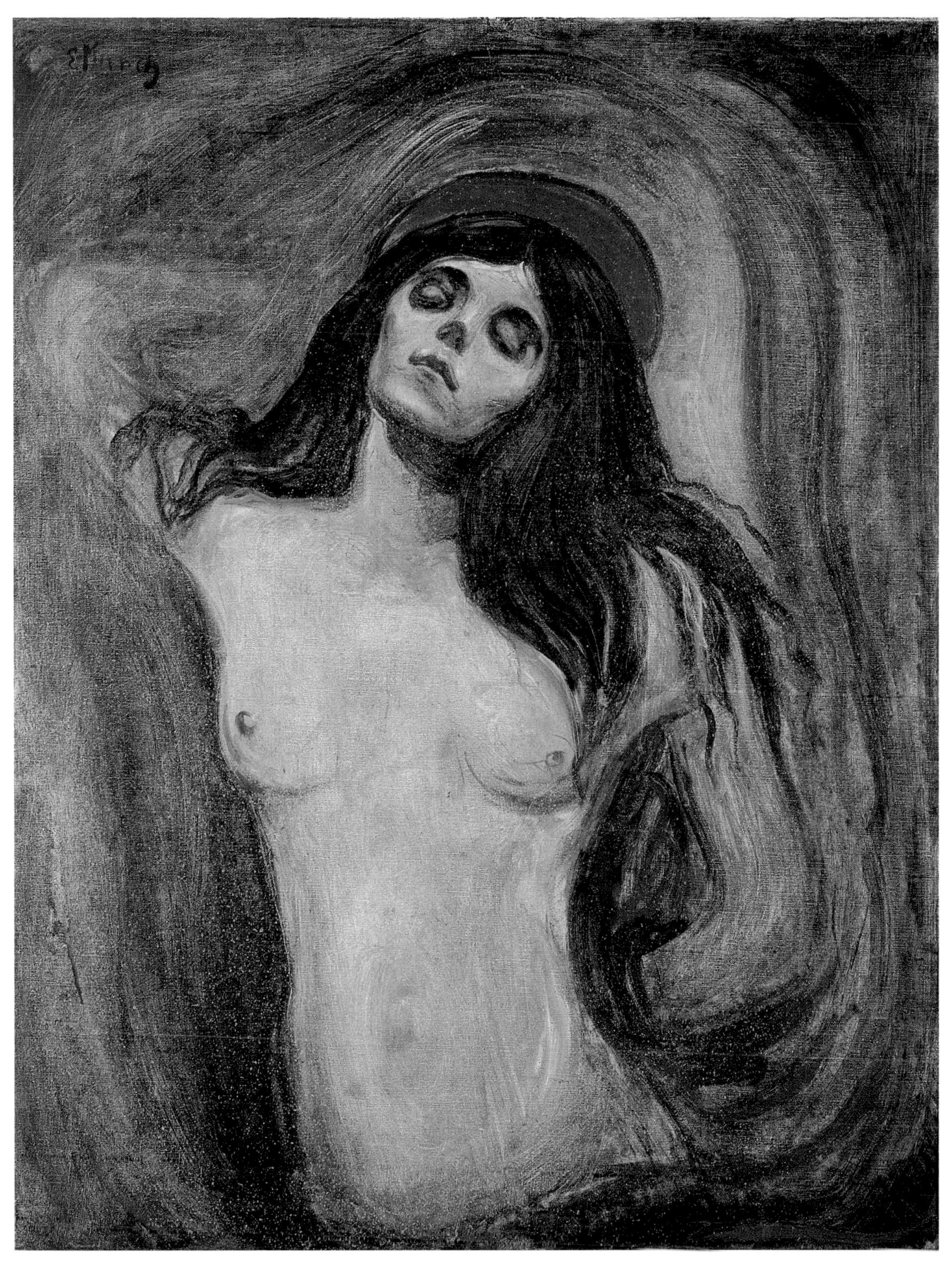

Cat. no. 19 *Madonna*, 1893–94
Oil on canvas, 90 x 68.5 cm, Munch-museet, Oslo

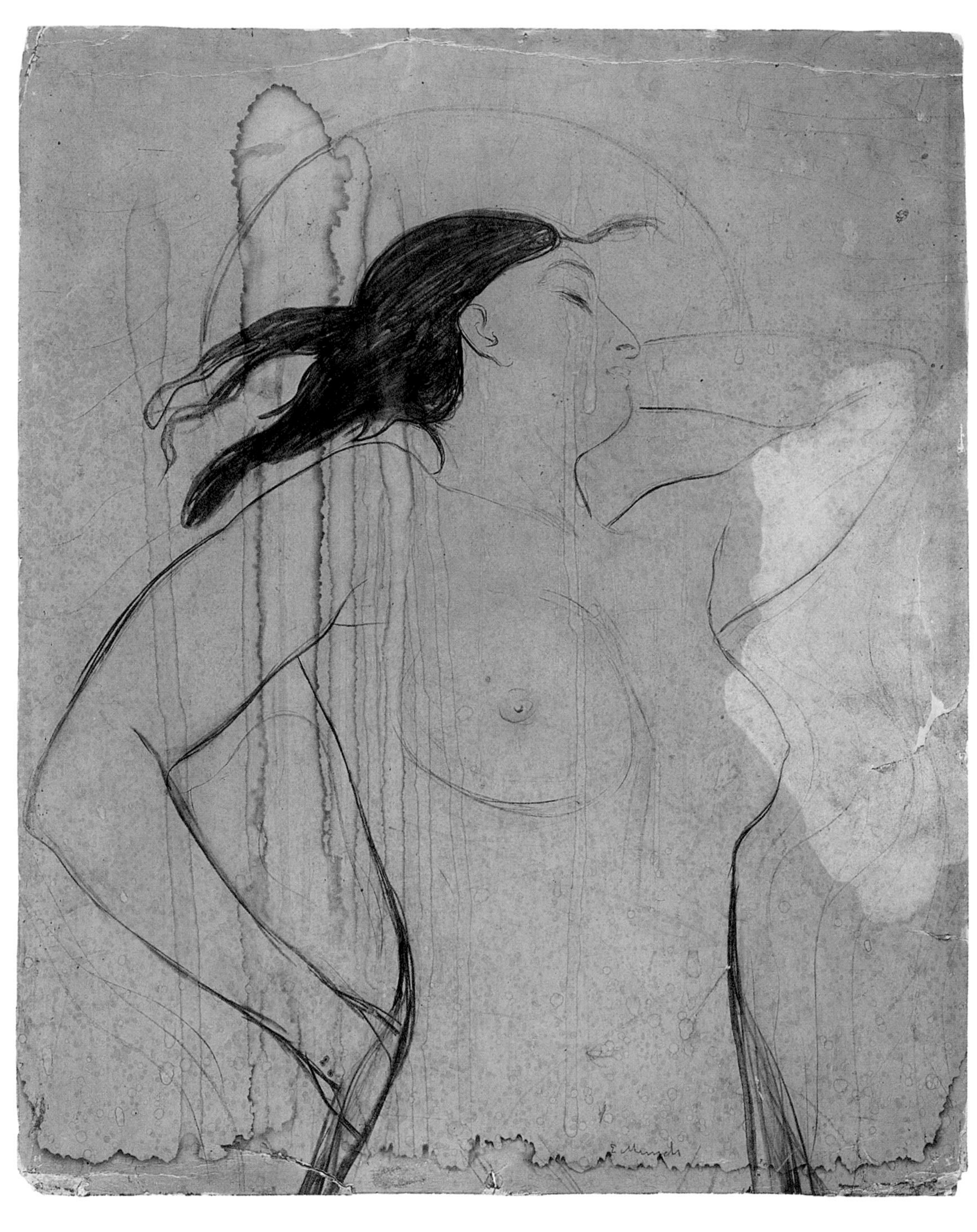

Cat. no. 20 *Female Nude*, 1893–94
Drawing on cardboard, 73.8 x 59.8 cm
Munch-museet, Oslo

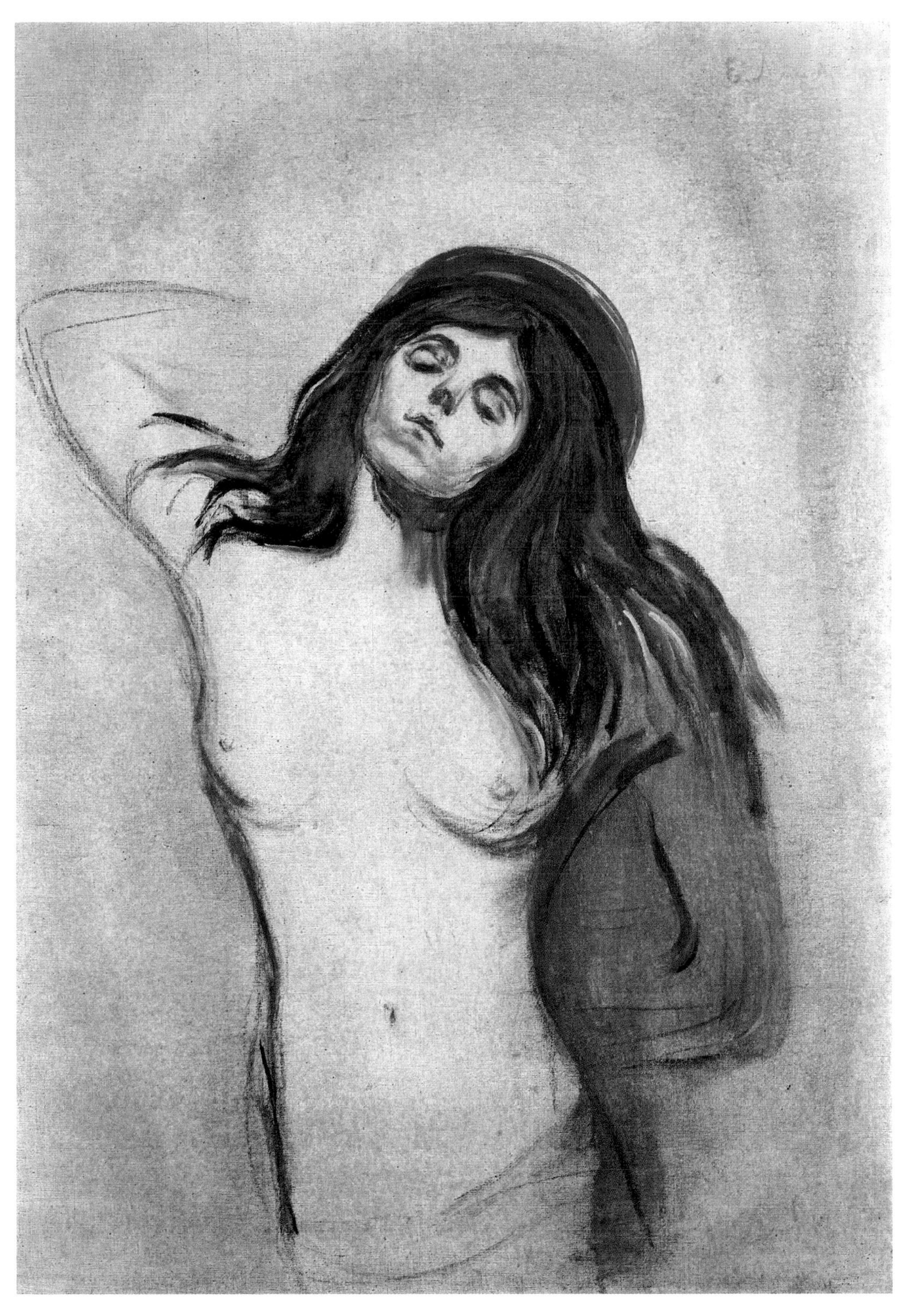

Cat. no. 21 *Madonna*, 1894–95
Oil on canvas, 97 x 75 cm
Collection of Catherine Woodard & Nelson Blitz, Jr.

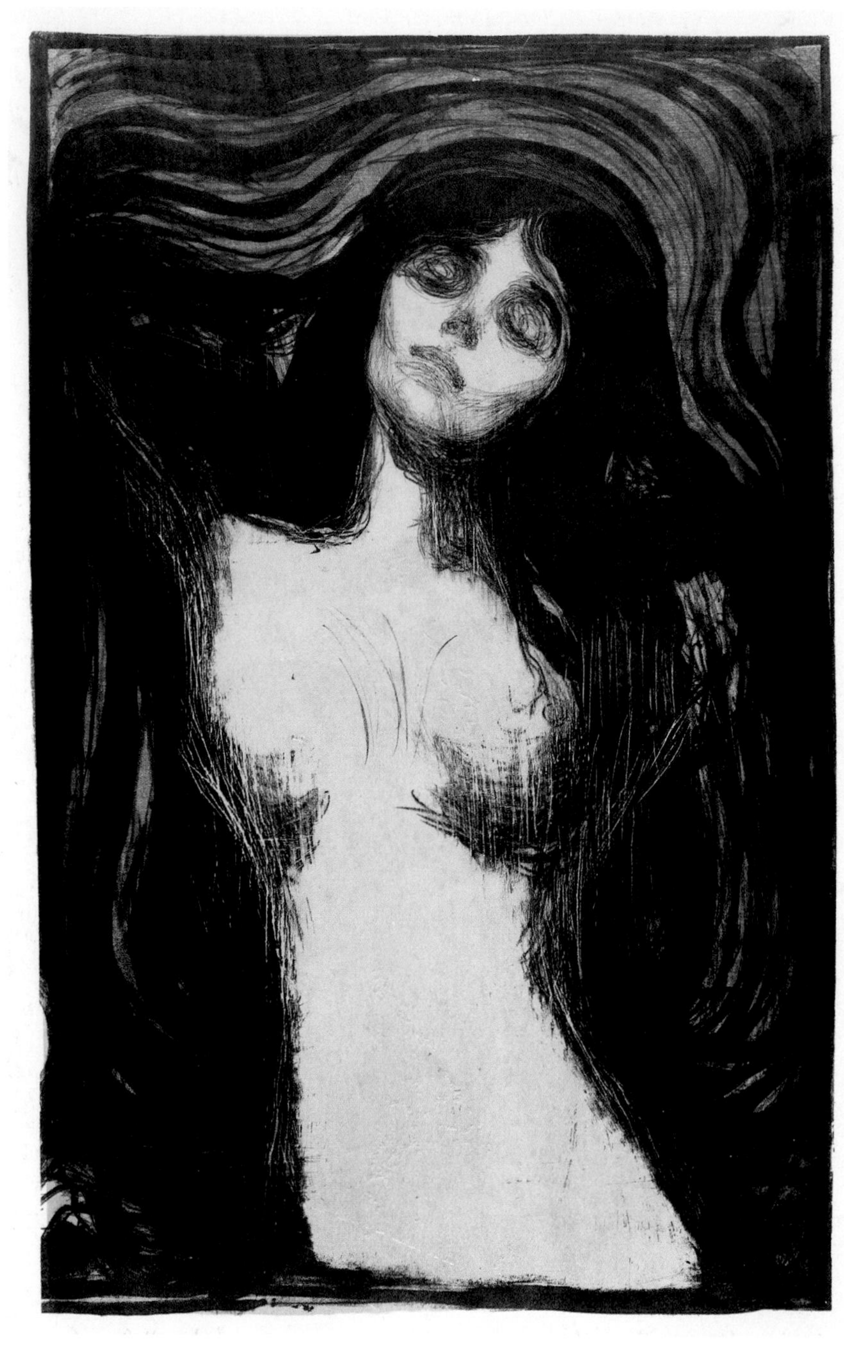

Cat. no. 22 *Madonna*, 1895/1902
Color lithograph on paper, 55.6 x 34.1 cm
Albertina, Vienna

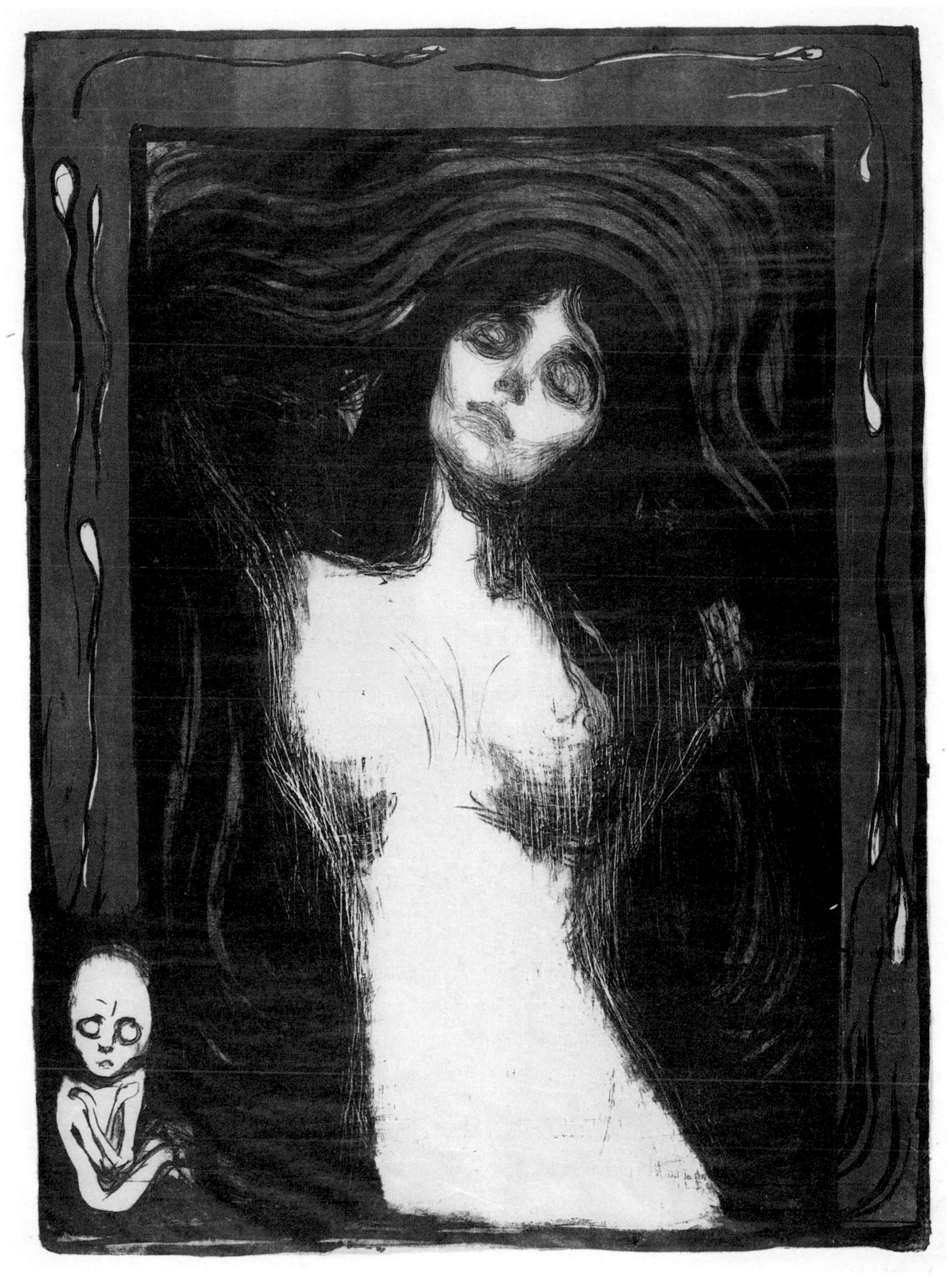

Cat. no. 23 *Madonna*, 1895/1902
Color lithograph on paper, 60.5 x 44.2 cm
Albertina, Vienna

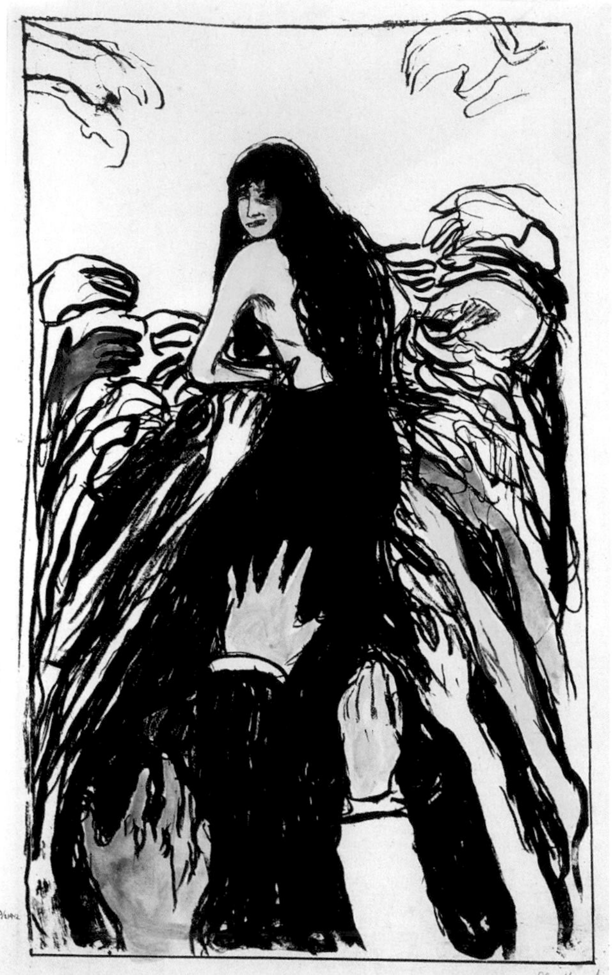

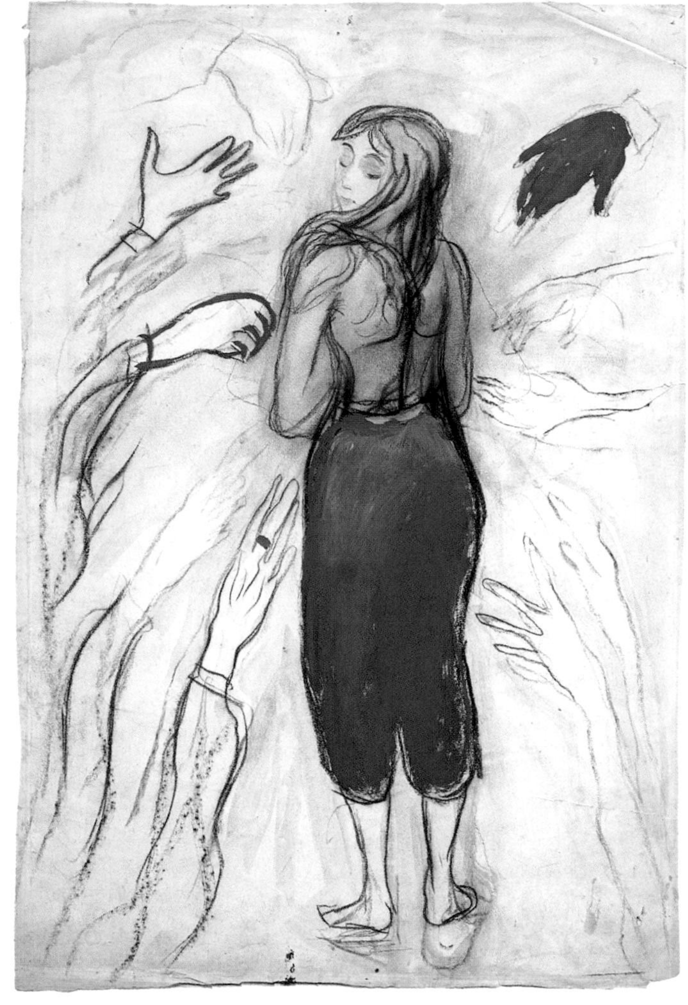

Cat. no. 24 *The Hands*, 1895
Hand-colored lithograph on paper, 48.4 x 29.1 cm
Epstein Family Collection

Cat. no. 25 *The Hands*, 1893–94
Drawing and gouache on paper, 67.2 x 45.2 cm
Munch-museet, Oslo

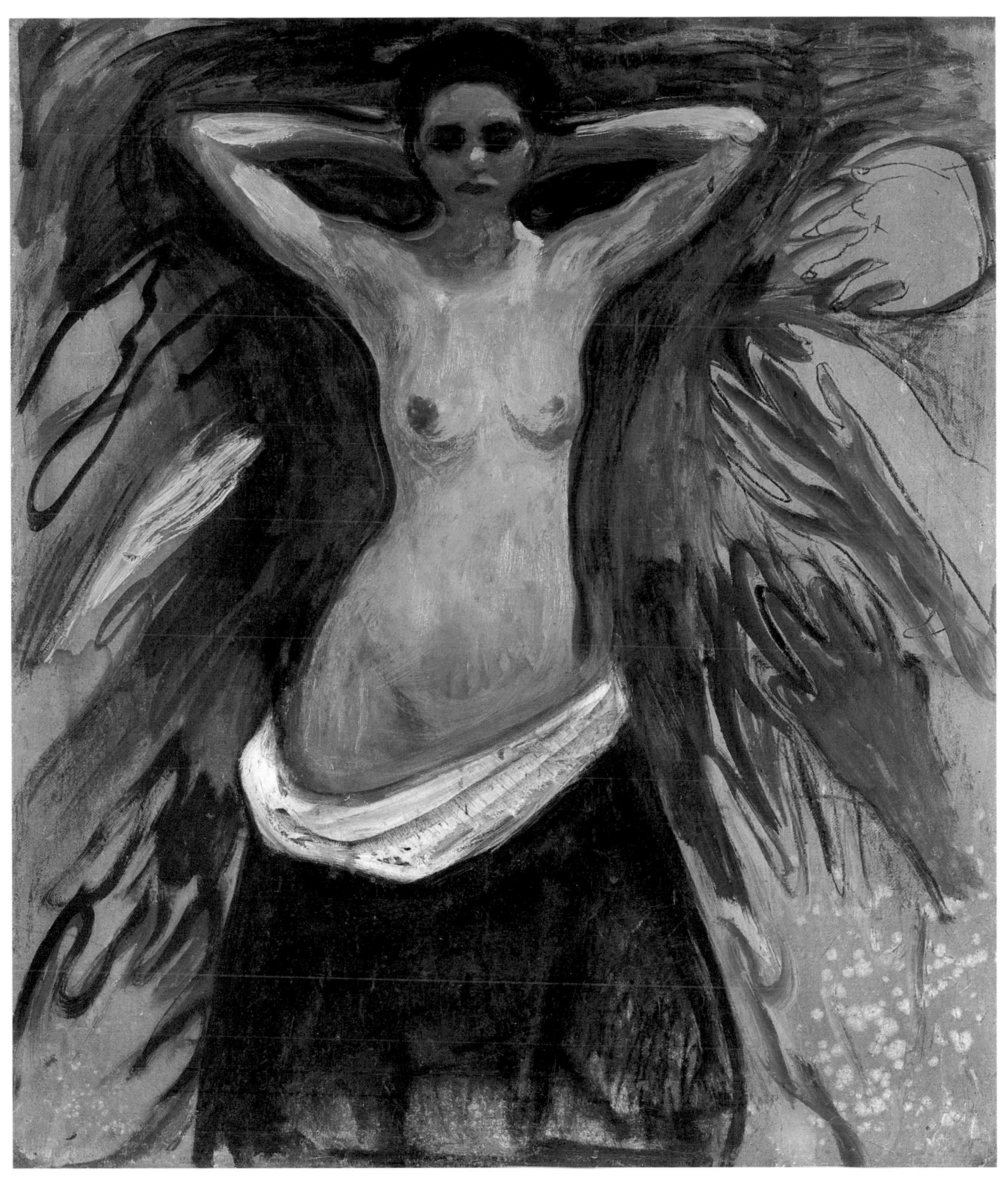

Cat. no. 26 *The Hands*, 1893
Oil and crayon on cardboard, 91 x 77 cm
Munch-museet, Oslo

The Woman

Munch produced variations of *The Woman* (*Sphinx*) over a period of three decades, from 1893–94 to 1925. Like *The Voice*, *Moonlight*, and *Eye in Eye*, it is a subject he developed early in his career. With roots in both classical mythology (the judgment of Paris) and Christian iconography (*Three Women at Christ's Grave*), the three-women motif was very familiar to nineteenth-century artists and is found in many different works. Wilhelm Leibl dealt with the theme in 1881, Jan Toorop in 1892 (Munch is said to have been familiar with the *Three Brides*), and Gustav Klimt in 1905. It also appeared in literary works, most notably in Chekov's drama *The Three Sisters*. One of Munch's personal acquaintances who used the three-women theme was Gunnar Heiberg, a member of the Kristiania bohemian community. A character in his play *The Balcony* utters the words "All the others are a single being—you are a thousand." Munch cited this sentence in his commentary on the painting in the catalog for the exhibition at which it was first shown.

Two painted versions (cat. no. 27 and fig. 2, p. 70) were completed around 1894 on the basis of sketches and were given several different titles at first: *Sphinx*, *The Woman*, *The Norns*, and *Drops of Blood*. The latter title refers to the image of the "flower of pain" or "blood flower," which Munch used numerous times as a symbol for the art "we have created with our heart's blood." Just as women bear children in pain and blood, so did Munch create his pictures. Here as well (cat. no. 27), the symbol sprouts from the ground and rises towards the heart of the depicted male figure. Munch also used it to symbolize the renunciation of happiness on earth—which he regarded as necessary—in favor of fulfillment in life as an artist. Munch was convinced that the only way to maintain the full creative power required for artistic work was by living an ascetic life. The presence of the male figure suggests that the three women are the products of his imagination and symbolize the different patterns of behavior in women's lives, and thus could be used to represent three phases of sexual development.

When Henrik Ibsen visited Edvard Munch's exhibition at the Blomqvist Gallery in 1895, Munch offered him the following explanation of the image of the three women: "She is the woman who dreams—the woman who enjoys life—and the woman as nun—who stands as a pale figure behind the trees." This suggests that Munch was less concerned with depicting the three phases of life and more interested in the three forms a woman's life could assume. The different roles associated with these three forms were the focus of heated discussion among men (and of their fantasies as well) around the turn of the century and were expressed by visual artists in diverse ways.[1]

In both painted versions, Munch positions the middle, nude woman very close to the one in dark clothing. The innocent woman, whose image calls to mind the figure in *Separation* (cat. no. 40), stands somewhat apart on the left, gazing at the sea. In keeping with Munch's characteristic color symbolism,[2] the figure dressed in white represents the innocence of youth, the red-haired woman a life of pleasure, and the dark-clothed figure a state of mourning. Their long, flowing hair is an important element of composition and iconography. It can separate (*Separation* of 1894 [cat. no. 40]) or join (*Lovers in the Waves* [Sch. 71, Woll 81]) or encircle and torment (*Man's Head in Woman's Hair* [fig. 5, p. 47]). In *Madonna* (cat. no. 19) and *Woman with Red Hair and Green Eyes* (cat. no. 18) hair is symbolic of the strong sensual appeal of the women depicted.

Two other works, *The Woman* (*Salome Paraphrase*) (cat. no. 28) and *Beach near Åsgårdstrand* (cat. no. 29), were completed about the same time as these paintings. They provide insight into a facet of Munch's working method and its complex structures and flexible combinations. In comparison, they have the appearance of two transparencies which, if laid one over the other, could produce another variation of the three-women theme. In the drawing of 1895 (cat. no. 28), Munch moves the three women closer together, emphasizing the central axis of the picture. The figure of the woman in mourning looks down at the head of a man in her arms. The man (Munch?) stands off to the side, his eyes closed. The hatched lines generate a complex light configuration consisting of light-dark contrasts, and the alternating fields of lines join the individual parts and blocks both on the flat surface and in abruptly emerging levels of space. In contrast, the seashore landscape

Beach near Åsgårdstrand (cat. no. 29) is dominated by the gentle line of the shore. This is an important element in Munch's world of images and one that he appears to have internalized. He renders a highly sophisticated interpretation of its light atmosphere, for example, in *Mystical Shore* and *Moonlight*. It links a number of subjects as a shared spatial setting in such works as *The Woman (Sphinx)*, *The Dance of Life* (fig. 4, p. 57), *The Voice* (cat. no. 1), *Separation* (cat. no. 40), and *Melancholy* (cat. nos. 85–92). This shared aspect creates the impression of a connecting band of waves, especially in the extensive presentations of the *Frieze of Life*.

In 1895, Munch began to focus on this subject in his graphic works, initially in etchings (cat. no. 32). He altered his previous versions somewhat, concentrating entirely on the group of three women and dispensing with the presence of the male figure. Here, the women are shown standing close together. The tree (of life) behind the nude figure, who stands facing the viewer with her legs spread widely, emphasizes the middle and provides a link to the innocent figure standing at the shoreline. She gazes towards the column of moonlight, an image interpreted as a phallic symbol which Munch incorporated throughout his life into many different scenes and also used as a meaningful element of variation in a number of hand-colored prints (cat. no. 105). In this work, she appears at eye level with the light-colored figure and is thus seen as representing awakening sexuality. The embodiment of provocative femininity that shines brightly in the light of the moon—and thus relates to *Madonna* as well—also has a connection with the moon, which is associated with birth and conception. The frontal presentation correlates to several full-figure portrait images and to *The Voice* (cat. no. 1) and *Moonlight* (cat. no. 8). The dark woman turns away, denying her femininity. In one version, the hands are empty, as in the drypoint etching; in another, they are shown holding the man's head, as in the drawing. Ultimately, all three relate in some way to the column of moonlight, which represents—in terms of content as well—a fourth pictorial figure in its own right.

In the hand-colored variation of 1895 (cat. no. 32), the three-colored masks on the upper strip echo the color symbolism of the three figures in the painting. In a lithograph done in 1899 (cat. no. 31), Munch dispenses entirely with color and its symbolic content. This work exhibits stronger light-dark contrasts and is a mirror image compared to the other presentations. The arc of the undulating strip of coastline now leads towards a higher horizon, causing the contour lines of the figures to blend more completely with the lines of the landscape. The dominant nude middle figure is positioned in an area of transition between light and dark, which is also symbolic. In the dark figure, Munch emphasizes the dark, sunken eyes; her body is nearly absorbed by the deep black; fine, white lines tracing her outline are all that distinguish her from her surroundings. The dominant eyes are also found in *Eye in Eye* (cat. no. 33) and in two versions of *The Voice*. In one drawing, *The Voice (Eyes)* of 1893–96 (cat. no. 6), only the eyes of this figure look over the horizon, fixing an ambiguous, because also inward gaze upon the viewer. The mouth is missing in another drawing (cat. no. 7).

Eggum presumes that Munch knew about the controversial experiments in hypnosis performed by the psychiatrist Charcot on young women as a means of exploring their personality structures. In his lectures, Charcot hypnotized women into three different states. In the first, cataleptic state, the women were rendered absolutely immobile and exhibited rigid, statuesque postures and blank, staring eyes. In the second state of lethargy they appeared relaxed and dreamy yet acutely sensitive. In the third state, somnambulence, they were subject entirely to their senses.

In *Red and White* of 1894 (cat. no. 30) dominates the intensity of the radiant colors and links this painting with compositions from around the turn of the century which exhibit especially vivid coloration, such as *Girls on the Pier* (cat. no. 163). Originally, this painting must have had a structure similar to that of the etching. The frontal position of the woman in red with her arms crossed behind her back calls to mind the female figures in *The Voice* (cat. no. 1) and *Moonlight* (cat. no. 8). The figure in white is believed to be traceable to the painting *The Lonely Ones* (which has since disappeared), a work in which this variation appeared for the first time. AH

1 Helmut Friedel (ed.), *Barbara Eschenburg, Der Kampf der Geschlechter. Der neue Mythos in der Kunst* 1850–1930, Munich 1985.

2 Iris Müller-Westermann relates this color symbolism very closely to Munch's self-portraits. Cf. Iris Müller-Westermann, *Edvard Munch. Die Selbstbildnisse*, Ph.D. dissertation Hamburg, Oslo, 1997.

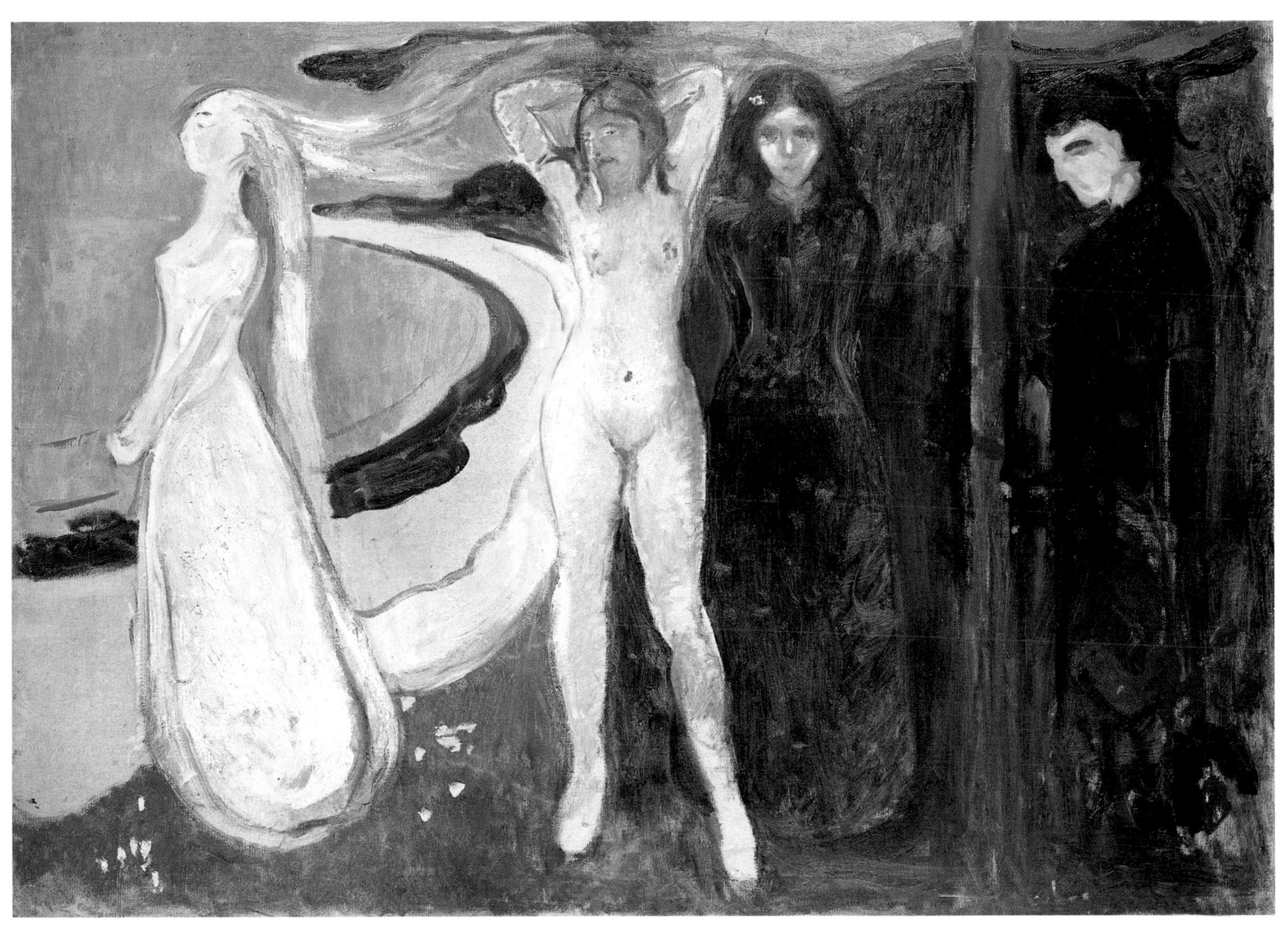

Cat. no. 27 *The Woman (Sphinx)*, 1893–94
Oil on canvas, 72 x 100 cm, Munch-museet, Oslo

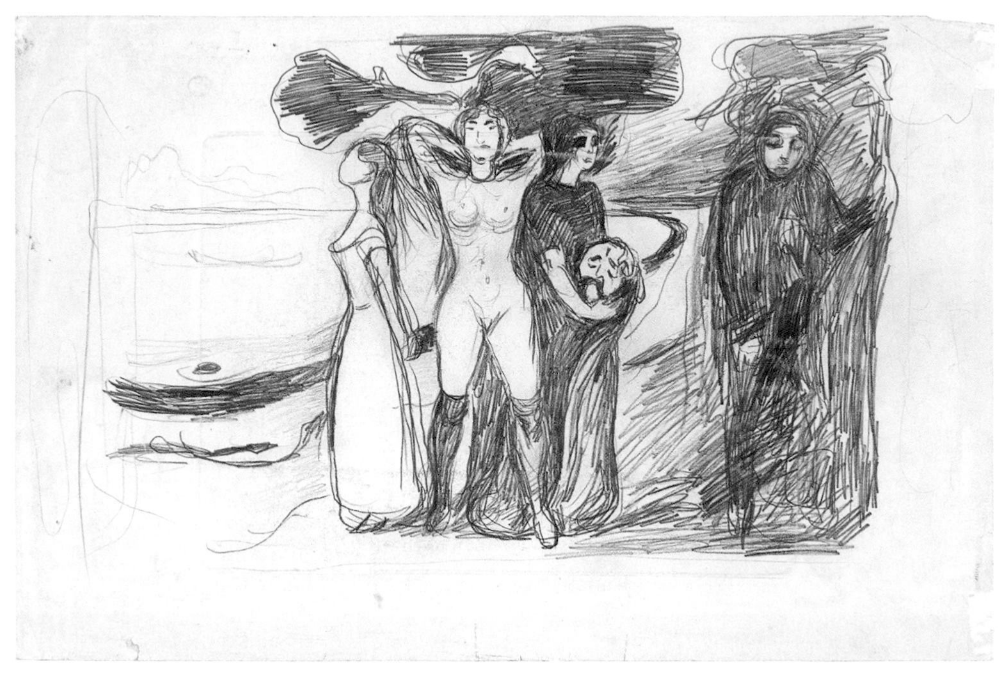

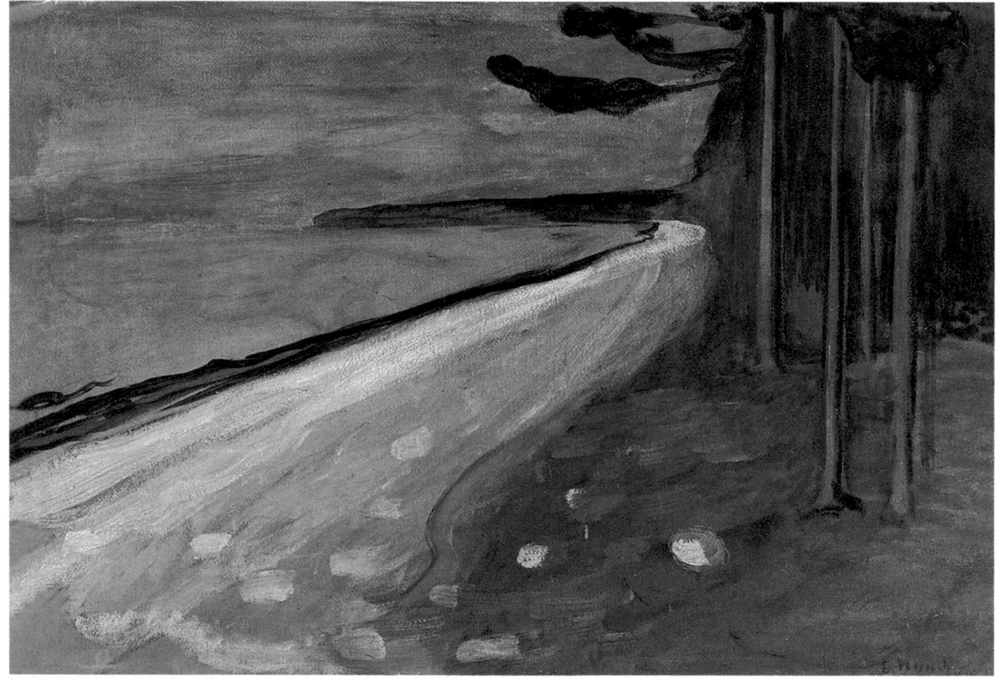

Cat. no. 28 *The Woman (Salome Paraphrase)*, 1895
Drawing on paper, 30.5 x 46 cm, Munch-museet, Oslo

Cat. no. 29 *Beach near Åsgårdstrand*, 1895–96
Oil on canvas, 57.5 x 83.5 cm
Collection of Catherine Woodard & Nelson Blitz, Jr.

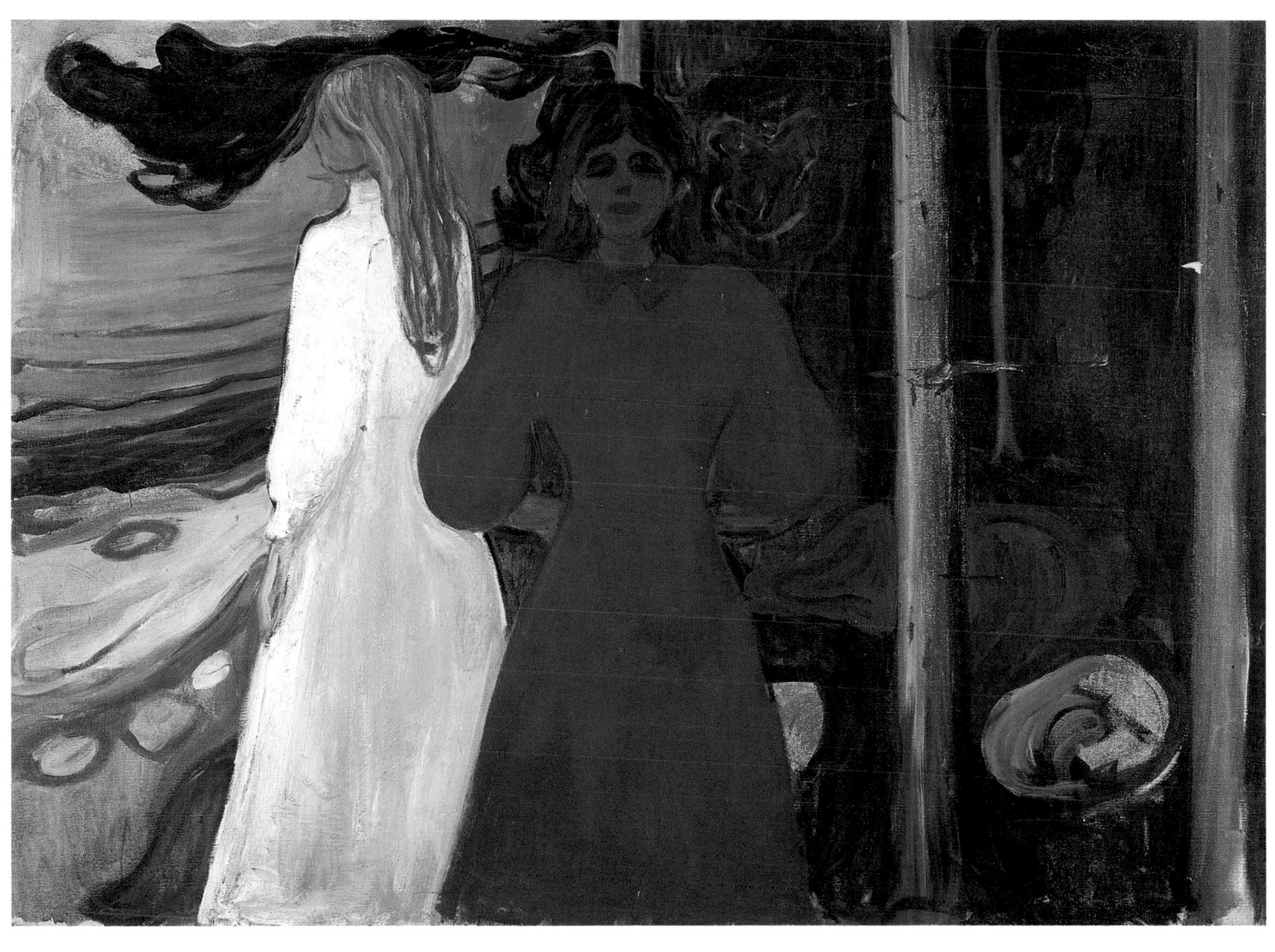

Cat. no. 30 *Red and White*, 1894 (1899)
Oil on canvas, 93.5 x 129.5 cm, Munch-museet, Oslo

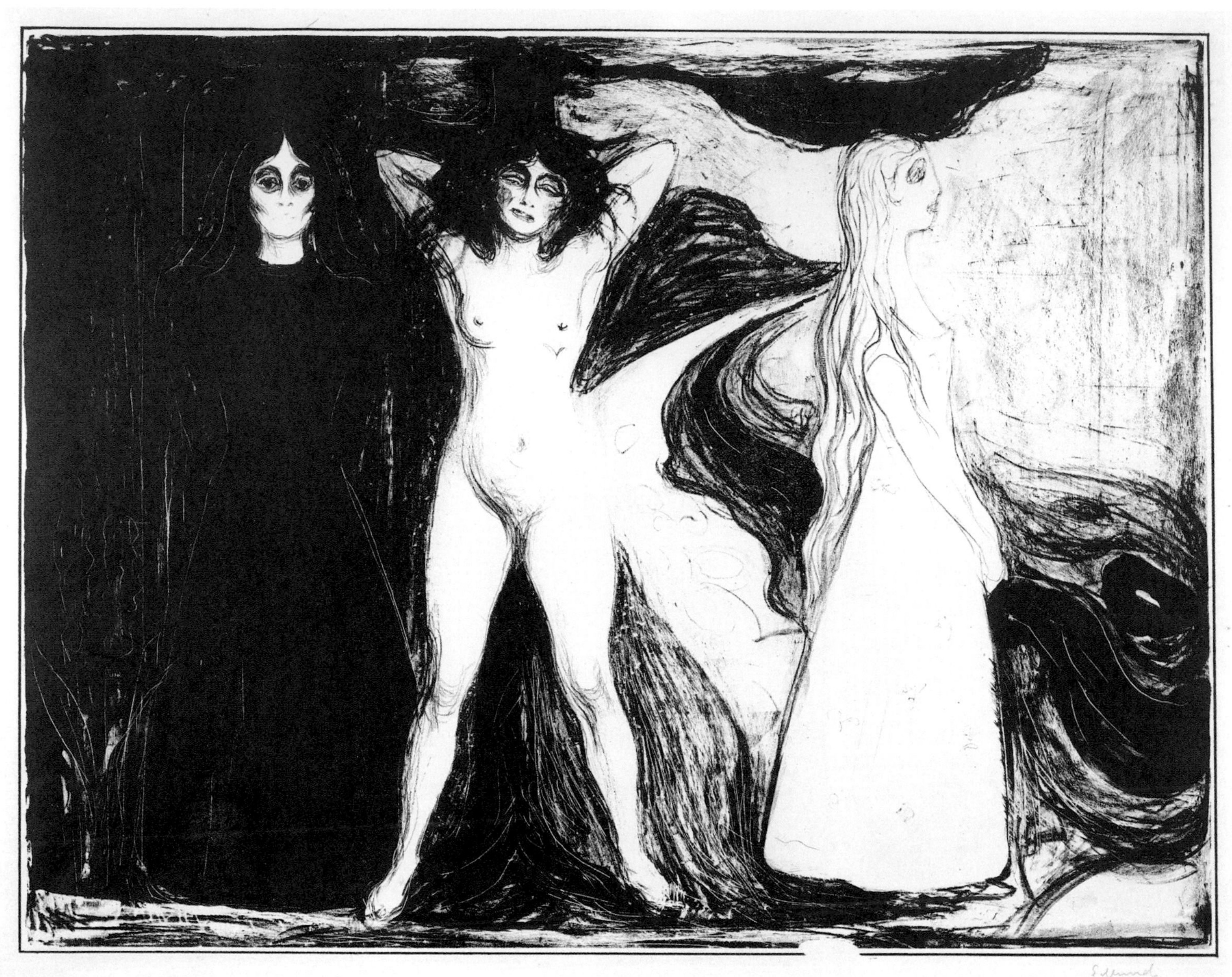

Cat. no. 31 *The Woman (Sphinx)*, 1899
Lithograph on paper, 46 x 59.6 cm
Albertina, Vienna

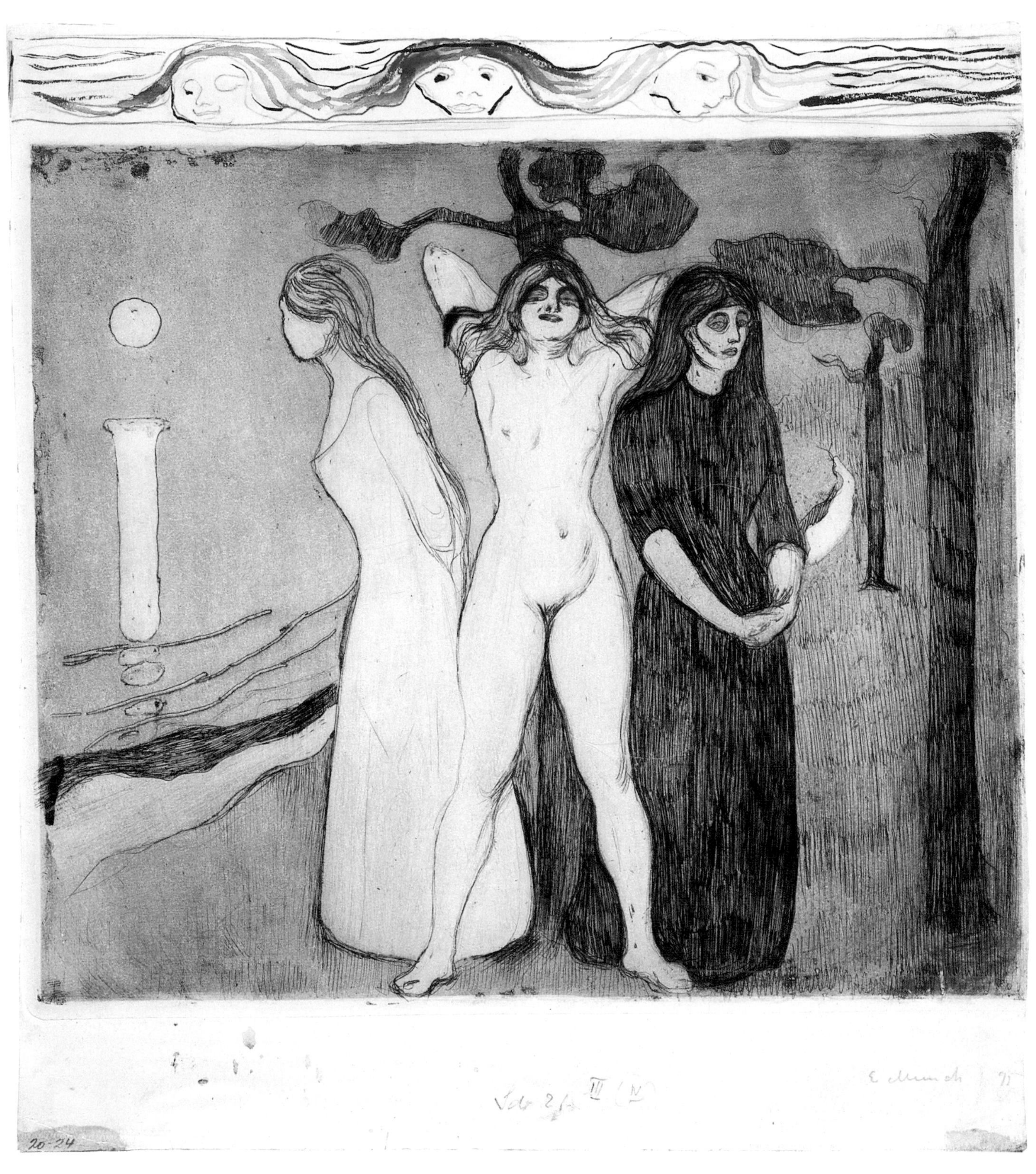

Cat. no. 32 *The Woman* II, 1895
Hand-colored aquatint and etching
on paper, 28.7 x 33.5 cm
Munch-museet, Oslo

Attraction

In *The Dance of Life* (fig. 4, p. 57), a man—Munch himself—dances at the seashore with a woman in a long, red dress—Milly Thaulow, his first mistress. Her right arm, as an extension of her hair, is around his shoulder, and she appears to pull his arm tensely towards her with her left. Her hands are outlined in red, as is the couple's entire silhouette, and her dress covers his feet like a wave. The force of attraction between the genders appears to originate with the woman, while the man stands rigidly, preserving a certain distance.

This view of the two heads presented in strict profile and the couple's specific physiognomy (fig. 1) are also found in *Attraction* II (*Two Heads*) of 1896 (cat. no. 37), a lithograph in horizontal format. Here, the figures of the man and woman are reduced to their heads and shoulders, and they nearly fill the format in the twilight scene set in the vicinity of Åsgårdstrand at Kristiania Fjord. They are separated from the sea by a row of tree-trunks and branches. The full moon and its reflection are thrust in a cross-shaped configuration—both as a phallic symbol and a sign of suffering—between the two. The woman's hair, shown encircling the man's head, embodies her powers of sexual attraction, which are underscored by the orientation of the branches. It is impossible to tell whether their eyes are open or closed, as they are hidden within diffuse, dark caverns. This ambivalence is apparent in all four graphic variations of *Attraction*, which move back and forth between seeing and not-seeing against noticeably changing backgrounds.

In the vertical-format etching dated by Schiefler to 1895 (cat. no. 35), the back of the Kiøsterud estate rises above the couple's heads, presenting a view of its characteristic grove of linden trees and the white fence beneath a starry sky. The man and woman have no mouths and are literally depicted as mute. Their heads remain separate from one another. The man's figure intersects the geometric form of the fence, and the woman's hair blends into the area of hatched lines surrounding her. In the version hand-colored with opaque paint, Munch highlighted the stars with dabs of pink and yellow and intensified their reflections in the water. The background motif corresponds in reverse to the two painted versions of *Starry Night* (cat. no. 38), works completed in the mid-1890s which show a view from the window of the adjacent Grand Hotel. Munch exhibited the presumably later variation in a horizontal format (cat. no. 38) under the title *Evening Star* at the *5th Secession Exhibition* in Berlin in 1902 as part of the *Frieze of Life* in the *Seeds of Love* group. In a literal sense, the bright evening star and its prominent swath of light can be understood as a seed of love in analogy to the column of moonlight as the planet of Venus, the Goddess of Love. In the etching, the heavenly body is positioned directly above the woman's head as a sign of the forces of sexual attraction that radiate from her. The painting's close connection with the theme of attraction is also emphasized in the ghostly red woman's head with its dark eye sockets and smiling mouth between the swath of starlight and the fence in the foreground, cut off by the edge of the picture. A shadow, possibly the couple's, appears in the other painted version, now in the collection of the J. Paul Getty Museum in Los Angeles. The energetic red lines beneath the dome-shaped group of trees are decipherable in the vertical-format lithograph *Attraction* I of 1896 (cat. no. 34) as the outlines of shrubbery. The pictorial structure is reversed again in the etching and matches the topography of *Starry Night*. The star-studded sky now forms a complete arc resembling the firmament, as it also ap-

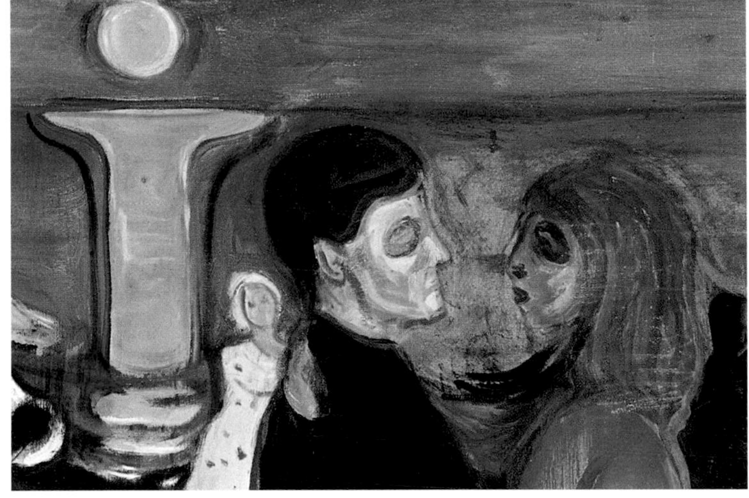

1 *The Dance of Life*, 1899–1900 (1899) (detail), oil on canvas, 125 x 191 cm, Nasjonalgalleriet, Oslo

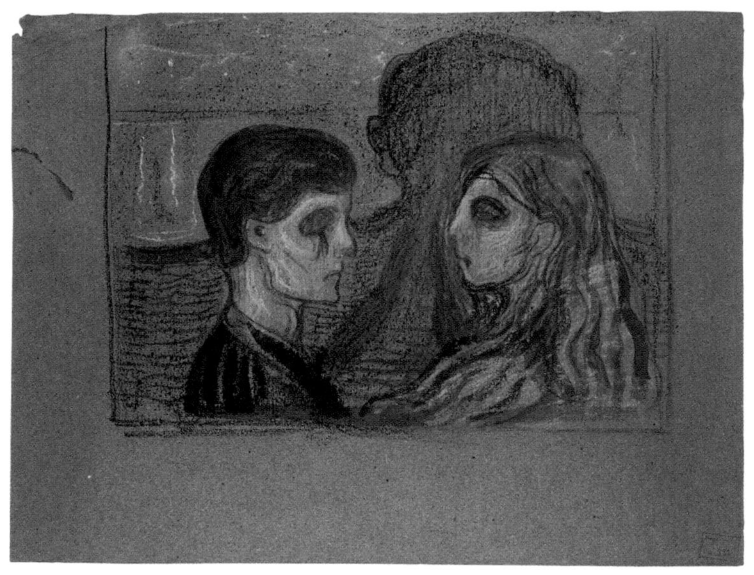

pears in a hand-colored version of the etching. The sense of togetherness of the foreground figures is mirrored in the two reflected bands on the water. As in the lithograph version, the woman's hair encircles the man's head as an expression of the attraction between the two. The title *Eye in Eye* noted by Munch himself on one print[1] suggests the presence of eye contact and communication between them, although communication between the mouthless heads with vacant eye sockets is limited to the bond created by the woman's hair. In contrast, the alternative title *Stars* shifts the level of interpersonal communication to the cosmic, symbolic sphere and calls attention to thematic affinities with *Starry Night*.

The expression of togetherness is most clearly developed in the horizontal-format etching entitled *Attraction* II of 1895 (cat. no. 36). The point of view is no longer elevated, as in the vertical-format prints and *Starry Night*, but is fixed instead at eye level. The crown of the woman's head now touches the horizon line, and the man's head intersects the fence and the group of trees. Ears, nose, mouth, and wide-open eyes make both verbal and non-verbal communication possible. The couple's togetherness is visually re-emphasized in the two long shadows, the two brightly shining stars, the swath of light and their presentation in profile. Although the alternative title *Man and Woman in the Moonlight* suggests that the light comes from the moon, Eggum contends on the basis of his reconstruction that the real source of light is the brightly illuminated window of the Grand Hotel.[2] This would also explain the shallow angle at which the light falls on the scene. Munch uses the shadow to move the man and the woman closer together. His use of hair as a symbol of the woman's power of attraction first appears in the lithographs of 1896, however. The print from the Museum of Modern Art was printed from a plate in bluish-green, brown, and yellow and, as the only surviving color print, represents Munch's earliest experiments in multi-color printing.

Munch altered the background again in two drawings.[3] In both of these works, the woman's head is positioned in front of the dome-shaped group of trees, which has become an autonomous, organic form. The group of trees also echoes the shape of the head and actually assumes head-shaped features in the pastel drawing (fig. 2). In the painting *Eye in Eye* (cat. no. 33), Munch replaced the background scenery of *Starry Night* with a meadow landscape with a clearly defined horizontal boundary in the upper third of the picture. Only the wavelike shadow encircling the couple recalls the shoreline in *Starry Night*. A small house appears as a kind of prop on the horizon line on the left above the woman. This house actually existed, as is documented by a realistic depiction in *Landscape with Red House* (fig. 4). The couple is shown standing in front of a

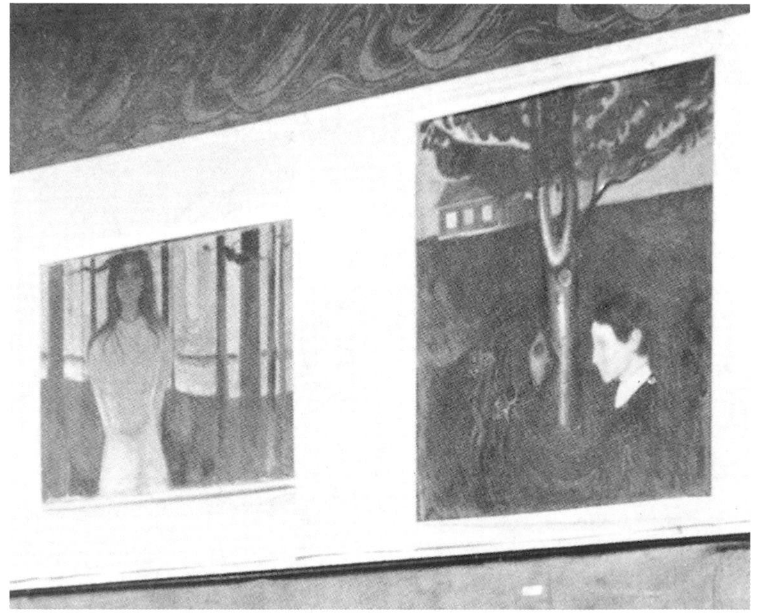

2 *Attraction*, c. 1895,
pastel on cardboard, 43 x 56.8 cm,
Munch-museet, Oslo

3 Exhibition of the *Frieze of Life* at P. H. Beyer & Sohn, Leipzig, 1903, (detail of installation photograph)

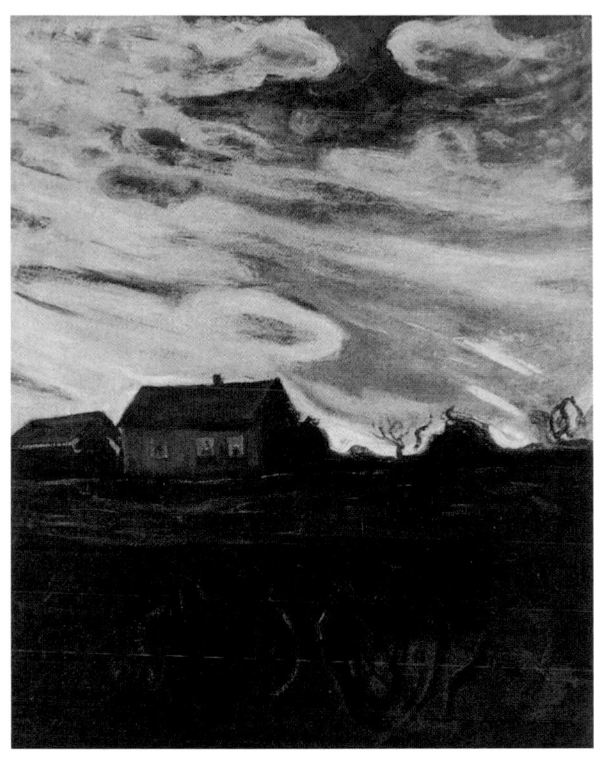

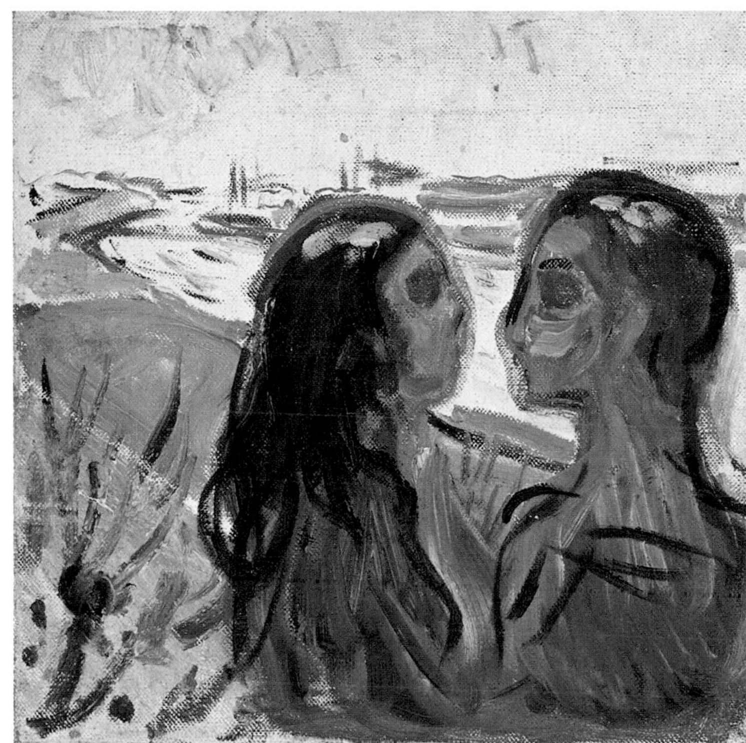

tree that divides the picture symmetrically in half and separates the genders. The image of a man and a woman beneath a tree links the theme of attraction in an iconographic sense with that of Adam and Eve beneath the Tree of Knowledge.

The painting is known to have been shown for the first time as *Eye in Eye* at the 5th exhibition of the Berlin Secession along with several other works, including *Evening Star*, in the *Seeds of Love* group as a part of the *Frieze of Life*. It may have been shown previously at a solo exhibition at the Diorama Center in Kristiania under the title *Green Air*, in reference to the dominant blues and greens.[4] As in *The Voice*, which was hung next to *Eye in Eye* at the solo exhibition at the Beyer & Sohn art dealers' in Leipzig in 1903 (fig. 3), Munch applied the impasto layers—in part directly from the tube—later. The more intense coloration and the unorthodox application of paint indicate that these additions were probably made during or following his painting experiments in Warnemünde beginning in 1907–08[5]. Munch added an eyebrow to the man in orange and opened his closed eyes with a dark-green dot but emphasized the dark cavern of the woman's eye, retaining the ambivalence between seeing and not-seeing. Stylistically speaking, the decorative surface orientation and Munch's monumentalization of the theme point to an origin in the latter half of the 1890s—later, that is, than the previously assumed dating of 1894. This is supported by the fact that Munch consistently coupled the theme of attraction with the background motif from *Starry Night* in his drawings and in etchings done in 1895. It was not until 1896 that he placed the couple in front of a column of moonlight in a wooded fjord landscape in a lithograph version (cat. no. 37). In *Eye in Eye*, he replaced the column of moonlight as an analogy to the evening star with a tree, the Tree of Life, thus anticipating pictures done shortly before the turn of the century, such as *Fertility* (fig. 8, p. 62). Munch's use of paint and the subdued blueish-green coloration achieved before a later revision are reminiscent of the original version of *Metabolism* (fig. 1, p. 53) and suggest an origin around 1896 to 1898.

Having returned to the view of two heads facing each other in profile around the turn of the century in *The Dance of Life* (fig. 1), Munch did another version devoted to the theme of attraction in Warnemünde in 1908. The background of this small, square painting is the harbor of Warnemünde, and the scene is depicted during the day rather than at night. The man and the woman now appear

4 *Landscape with Red House*, before 1905,
oil on wood, 80 x 66 cm, private collection

5 *Attraction (Landscape Motif)*, 1908,
oil on canvas, 34.7 x 34.5 cm, Munch-museet, Oslo

near the right-hand edge of the picture and are closer together. They have large eye cavities and no mouths. The two heads facing each other in profile appear again in a woodcut from the 1910s, this time in a jealousy scene in which a third face turned toward the viewer separates the pair (fig. 6). The foreground motif of attraction is interwoven here with the theme of jealousy in anticipation of the probable consequences of attraction. DB

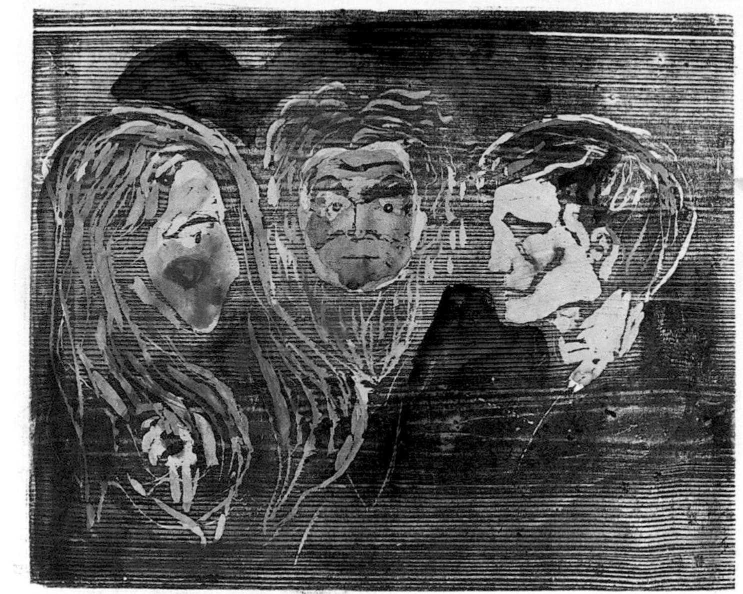

1 Gerd Woll, *Edvard Munch. The Complete Graphic Works*, London 2001, p. 101.
2 Arne Eggum, "Attraction," in Arne Eggum, *Edvard Munch. The Frieze of Life from Painting to Graphic Art*, Oslo 2000, pp. 76f.
3 Eggum regards these as "direct studies for the etching." Ibid., p. 80. This is not the case, however, as neither the format nor the composition corresponds.
4 *Green Air* was cited in the Sept. 18, 1897 issue of *Dagbladet* as an example of Munch's more recent paintings, which would refute a dating of 1894. Kneher shows that it was not *Eye in Eye*, as was previously assumed, that was shown under the title *Man and Woman* in Stockholm in 1894 and at Ugo Barroccio in 1895 but *Two People*, a painting later destroyed in a fire. Cf. Jan Kneher, *Edvard Munch in seinen Ausstellungen zwischen 1892 und 1912*, Worms 1994, pp. 57, 65 and 110.
5 The photograph, taken for an inventory of paintings by Munch offered by the art dealer Commeter in Hamburg in January 1907, shows clearly that *Eye in Eye*, listed under no. 35, has not yet been overpainted.

6 *Three Faces (Tragedy)*, 1913, hand-colored woodcut on paper, 36.5 x 44.2 cm, Munch-museet, Oslo

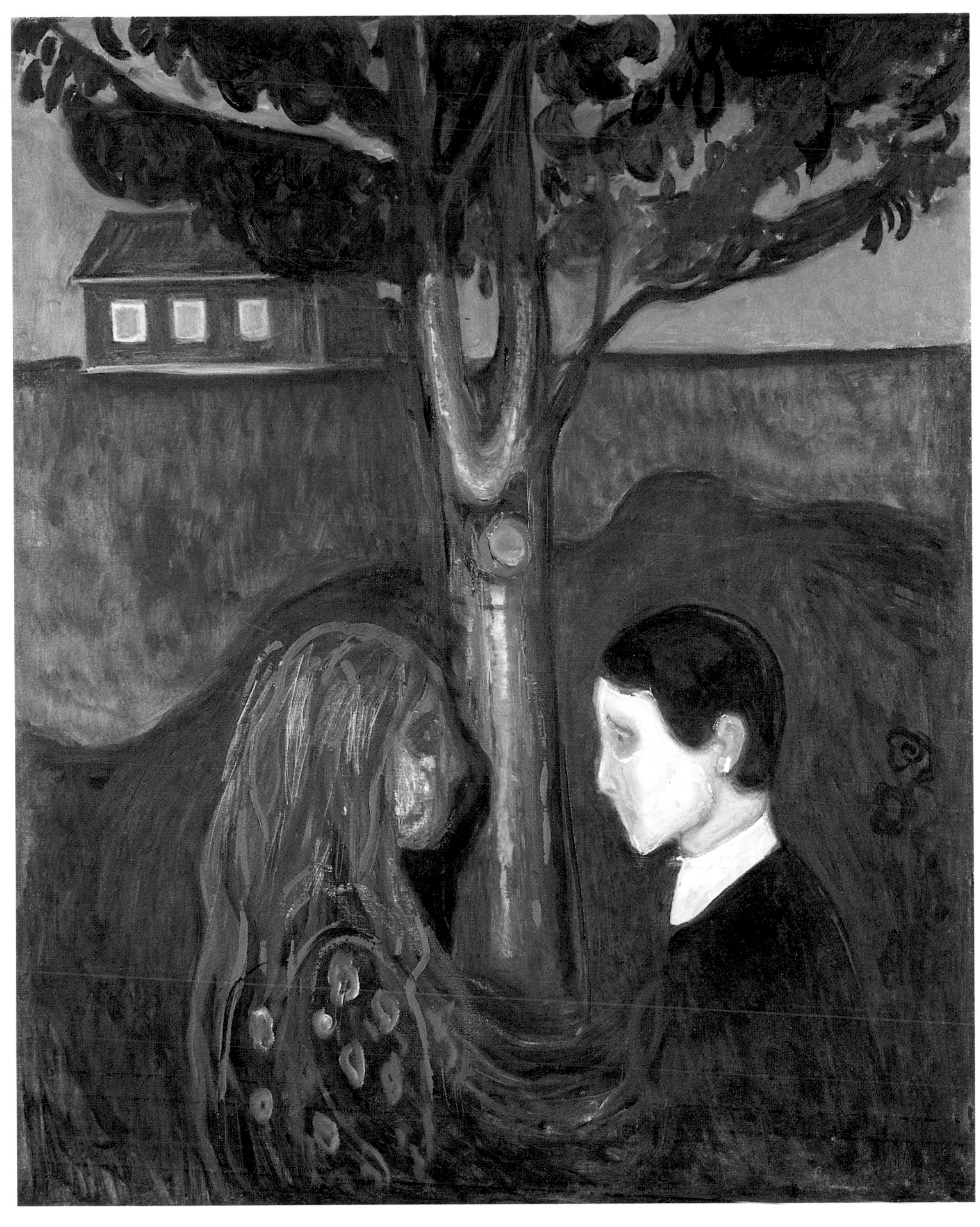

Cat. no. 33 *Eye in Eye*, 1894 (1896–98)/after 1907
Oil on canvas, 136 x 110 cm, Munch-museet, Oslo

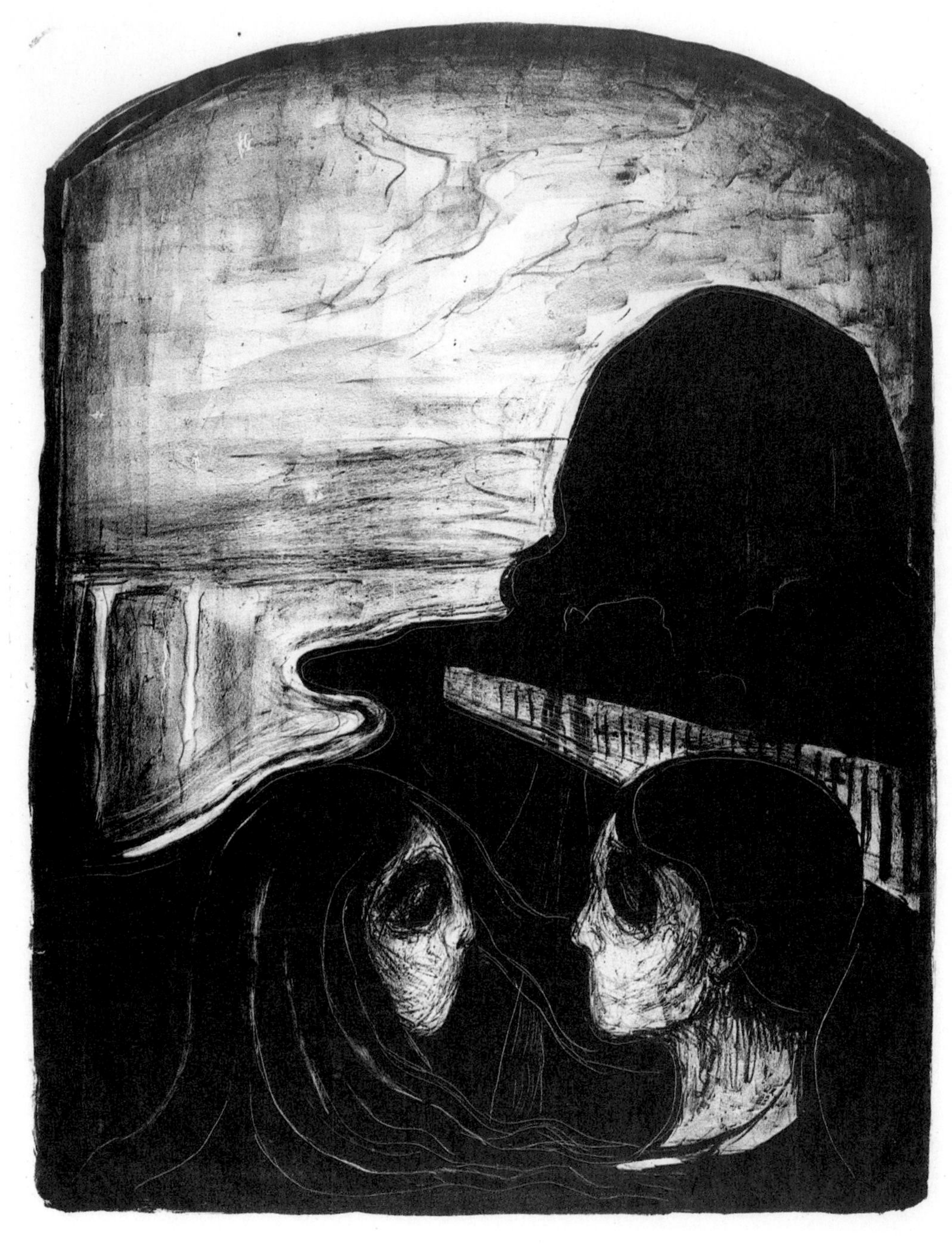

Cat. no. 34 *Attraction* I, 1896
Lithograph on paper, 59.3 x 43.2 cm
Albertina, Vienna

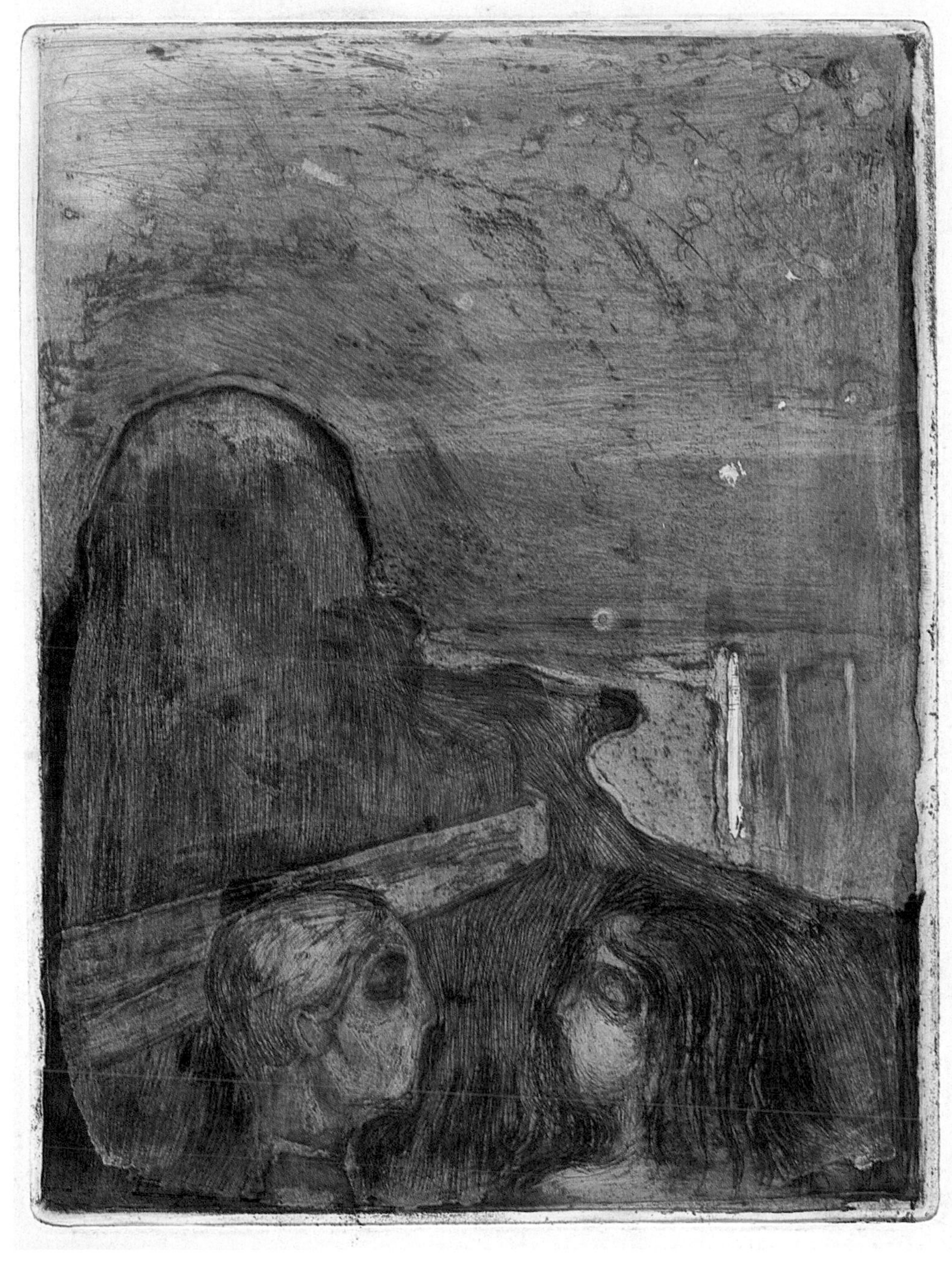

Cat. no. 35 *Attraction* I, 1895
Hand-colored etching on paper, 32 x 23.9 cm
Munch-museet, Oslo

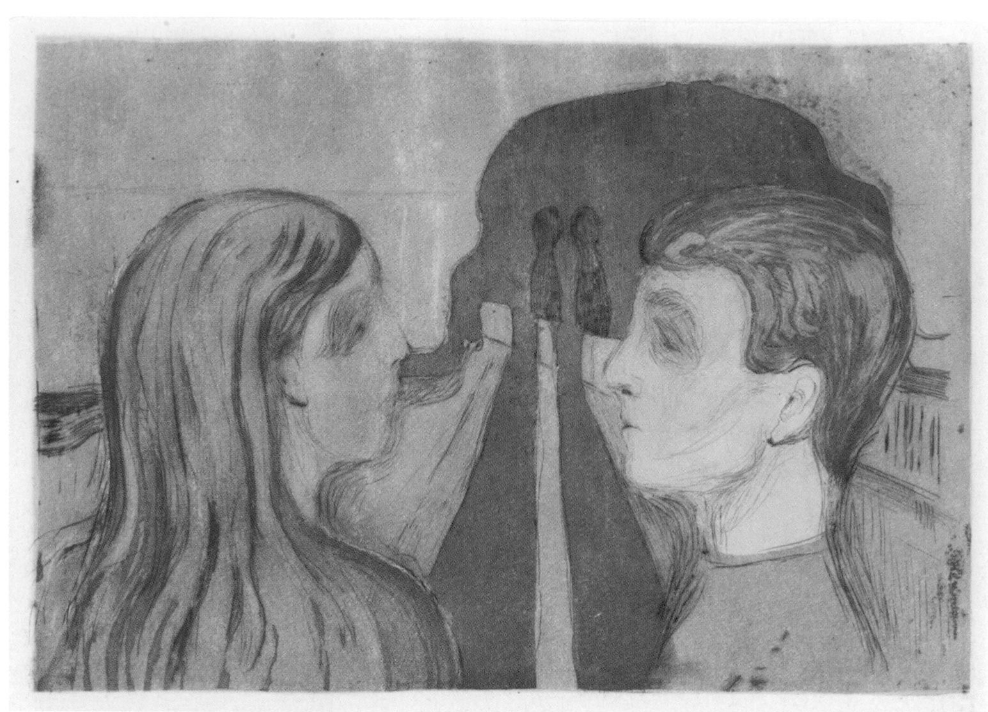

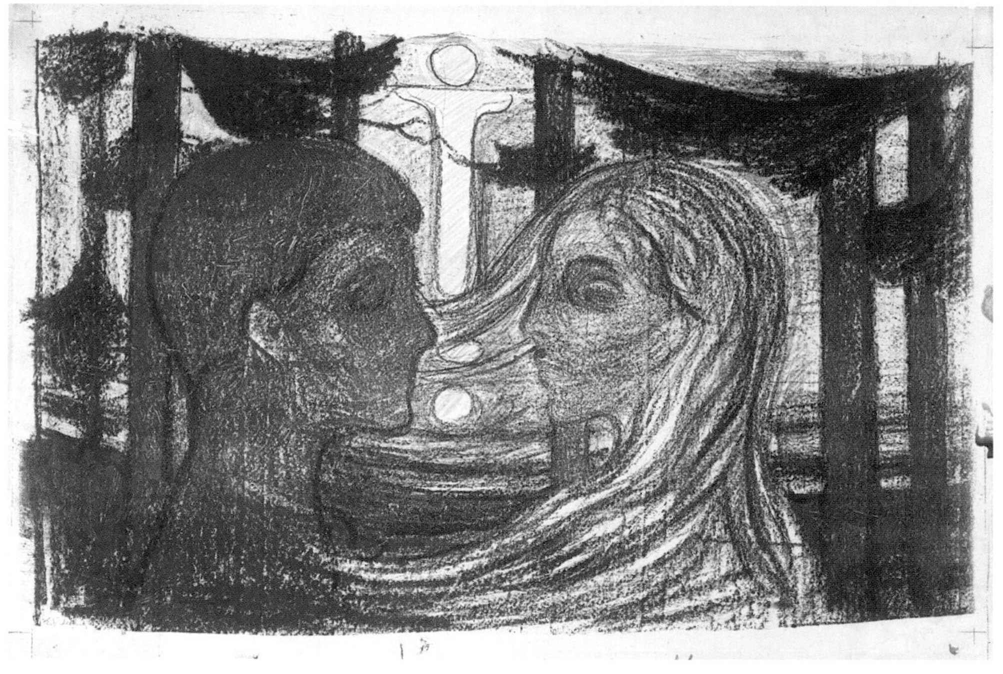

Cat. no. 36 *Attraction* II, 1895
Etching on paper, 26.7 x 33.1 cm
The Museum of Modern Art, New York.
Given anonymously, 1942

Cat. no. 37 *Attraction* II (*Two Heads*), 1896
Lithograph on paper, 41 x 63.5 cm
Munch-museet, Oslo

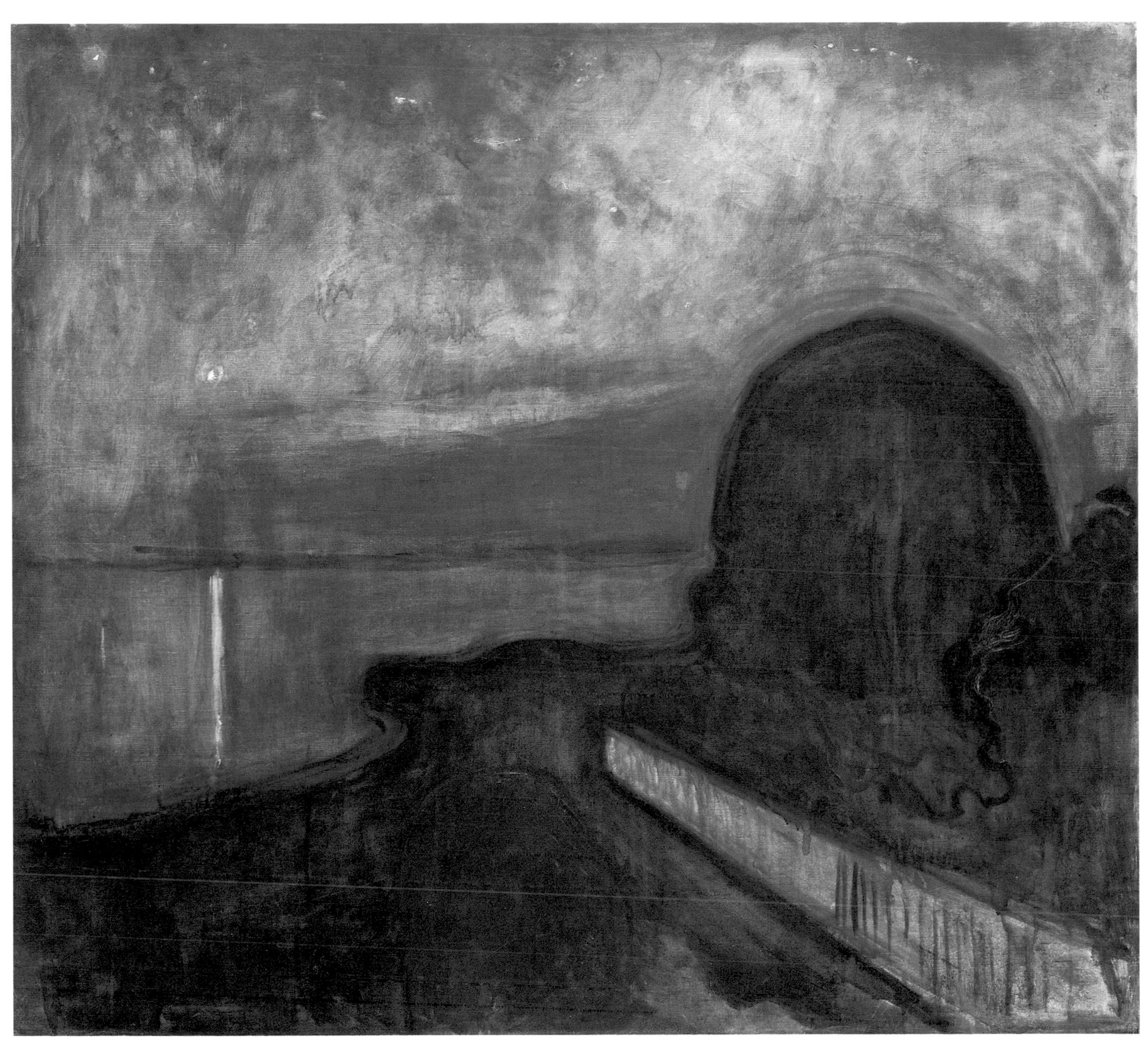

Cat. no. 38 *Starry Night*, 1895–97
Oil on canvas, 108.5 x 120.5 cm
Von der Heydt-Museum, Wuppertal

Separation

The point of departure is the attraction between a man and a woman, who merge into one in the kiss. In Munch's works, erotic encounters between two people and their affection for one another always contain the seed of failed love and eventual separation. With reference to the two brightly shining stars in *Attraction*, Munch remarked that "Like a star that ascends from the darkness—and encounters another star—and shines brightly for a moment before disappearing into the darkness—so do man and woman meet—rising together, shining forth in flames of love—only to disappear in different directions..."[1] Just as the star burns out, so is human love extinguished. Erotic attraction—symbolized in physical terms by the hair—originates with the woman, who leaves the man in *Separation*. His painful experience of separation is the subject of this work.

As an opposing pair, the lithographs *Separation* II (cat. no. 39) and *Attraction* II (cat. no. 37) symbolize separation as an inevitable consequence of attraction. The pictorial detail focuses on the heads and shoulders of the man and the woman, who first face one another and then, in *Separation*, turn their heads away from each other. The woman faces the opposite direction and gazes towards the open sea on the right-hand side, which is visible in *Attraction* as well. As a sign of warning, the full moon and its reflection has moved between the couple in the form of a cross as a phallic symbol and a sign of suffering—the two are now separated by the line of the seashore. The man's suffering is suggested by the fact that he has turned his light, finely drawn face towards the dark forest, while the woman, whose eyes are focused on the open sky and the vast sea, anticipates their separation as liberation. The ocean wind still appears to blow her hair towards the man, who has already turned away, as an expression of her seductive powers. We read in Munch's notes that

> ... she walked slowly towards the sea—farther and farther away—and then something very strange occurred—I felt as if there were invisible threads connecting us—I felt the invisible strands of her hair still winding around me—and thus as she disappeared completely beyond the sea—I still felt it, felt the pain where my heart was bleeding—because the threads could not be severed.[2]

Munch visualized the "invisible strands of her hair" as a bond encircling his bleeding heart in the second painted version of 1896 (cat. no. 40). The composition corresponds to that of *The Woman* (*Sphinx*), although the two central female figures are absent in the mirror-image rendition. The woman is depersonalized and depicted as a symbol of innocence in a white dress. Her blonde hair merges with the outline of her dress and blends into the coastline, forming a unified whole. But it also represents the threads of memory that encircle the man, prolonging his agony. The translucent colors culminate at the hem of the dress in spots and traces of running paint, which call to mind the blood flowing from the man's heart. The man remains behind and clutches his heart with his hand, which is outlined in red. The nearly leafless tree to his right serves as both a support and a frame. The "flower of pain" grows from the tree as a symbol of his broken heart.

The dramatic sense of suffering appears to have given way in the lithograph *Separation* II to melancholy and impending loneliness, as in the painted version of 1893, a mirror-image of the scene (fig. 5, p. 27). Munch presumably exposed this picture to the weather for quite some time, although some areas of paint were obviously more resistant to moisture than others and have remained in place as islands. After completing the "kill-or-cure treatment", Munch may have added layers of thick paint to the sun or the moon, the woman's hair, and the "flower of pain." To the extent still recognizable today, the application of paint suggests a combination of translucent, glazing and heavy impasto techniques. The brown color in the area of the man's head was actually applied using a spraying method. Munch used the house in the background again in *Eye in Eye*, thus establishing yet another link between the themes of attraction and separation. DB

1 Munch-museet T 2782-c.

2 Munch-museet T 2782-l.

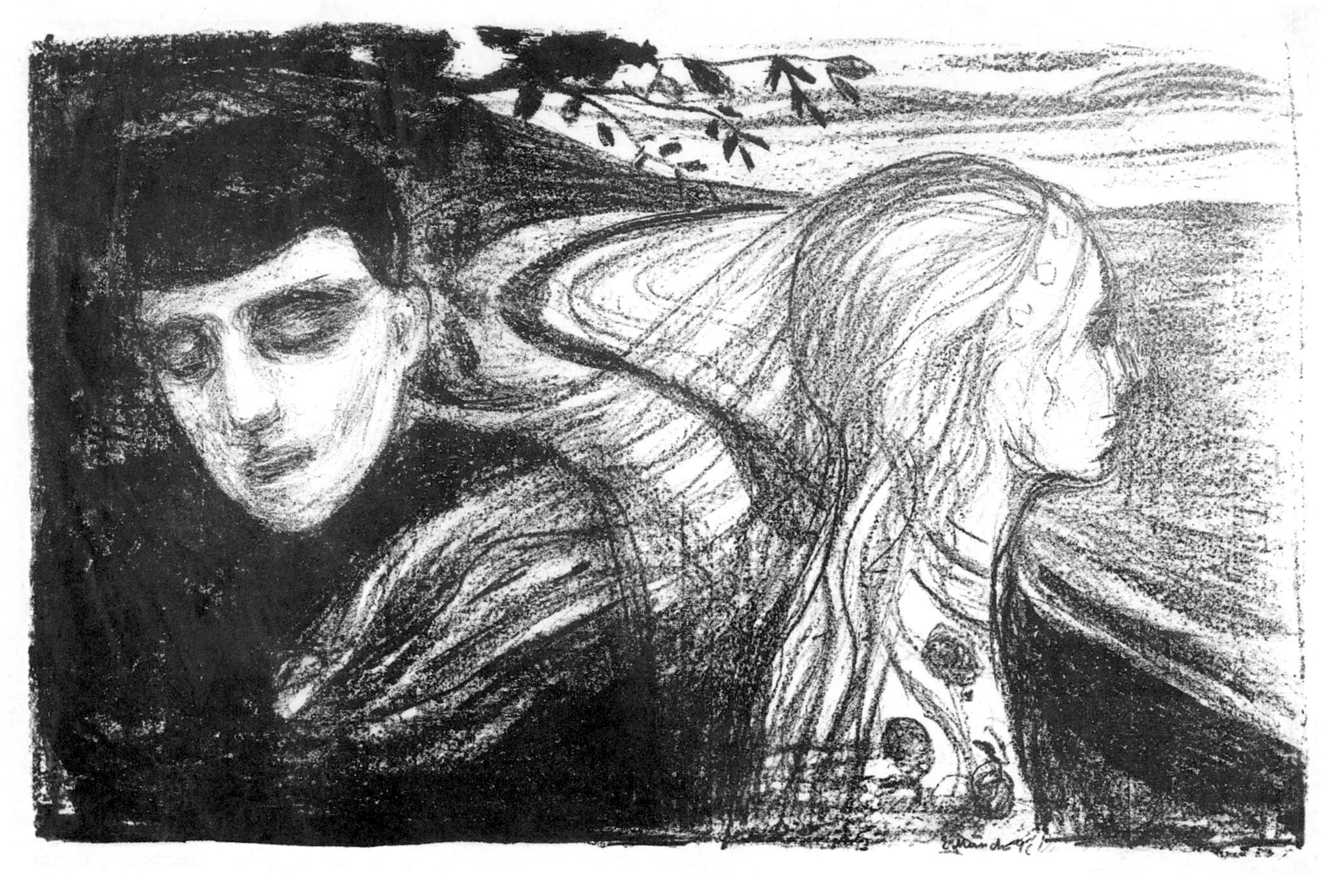

Cat. no. 39 *Separation* II, 1896
Lithograph on paper, 41 x 64 cm
Albertina, Vienna

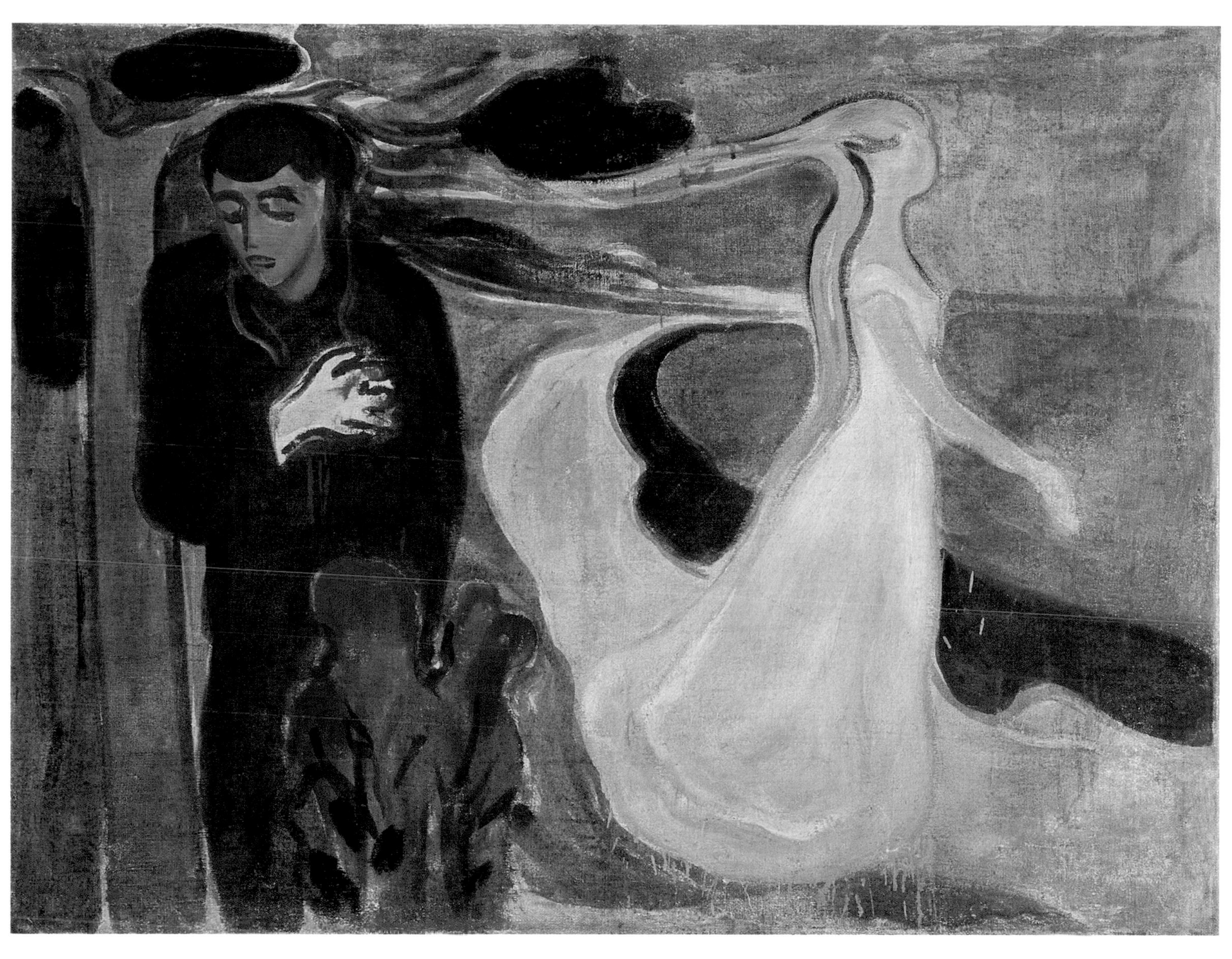

Cat. no. 40 *Separation*, 1896
Oil on canvas, 96.5 x 127 cm
Munch-museet, Oslo

The Kiss

"One sees two human figures whose faces are melted together. There is not a single recognizable feature ..., but the consuming passion of the kiss, the terrific force of sexual, painfully hungering longing, the loss of self-consciousness, the union of two naked individual personalities is so honestly felt..."[1] Thus wrote Stanislaw Przybyszewski in *Das Werk des Edvard Munch* (1894), the first monograph devoted to Munch, in his description of a painted version of *The Kiss* which can no longer be identified. Przybyszewski emphasizes the visual merger of man and woman at the moment in which they succumb to their passion. Their union is purchased at the price of their individuality and is only temporary in Munch's view, as the paintings *Separation*, *Jealousy*, *Melancholy*, and *Ashes* that follow *The Kiss* in his *Frieze of Life* clearly indicate. Thus the subject is always a fleeting image with an eternal character.

Munch remained concerned with this subject from the 1880s until shortly before his death, and we find variations on the theme in numerous sketches, studies, and drawings, in ten prints, and in more than a dozen paintings.[2]

With reference to a few noteworthy examples, the following discussion focuses on the development of the motif of the kissing couple and the artist's efforts to embed it within a changing pictorial structure determined not least of all by his choice of artistic media.

Munch's early work with the theme of *The Kiss* was largely inspired by personal experience. The oldest surviving drawing dates from the early 1880s and shows Munch's sister Laura, knitting, and a transparent image of a kissing couple in the background—presumably his father and his aunt Karen Bjølstad (fig. 1). The pair seems on the verge of disappearing in the diffuse light of the room, which is suggestive of domestic comfort. Munch may have been describing his father's relationship with his aunt, who had rejected the father's proposal of marriage in order to avoid becoming the children's stepmother.

In 1889, Munch wrote the word *Adjø* [farewell] on a drawing of a kissing couple (cat. no. 42) as an allusion to his separation from Milly Thaulow, a married woman with whom he had been involved a love affair for several years. The drawing shows a couple standing at the left near a studio window from which a gas streetlight can be seen. The couple is kissing, although the two figures are clearly separated from one another by the energetic pencil strokes and the outline of the man's face.

Munch began a period of intensive work on the theme of the kiss in the spring of 1892. He is believed to have finished three painted versions depicting the couple in an interior room near a window that year. Stylistically speaking, all three paintings reflect Munch's interest in impressionism, but each differs markedly from the others in terms of format and coloration. Munch arrived at the most dramatic pictorial solution in the horizontal-format version now in the collection of the Nasjonalgalleriet (cat. no. 43), which shows the couple framed by the window and shielded by a curtain from the gazes of others from outside. The window is the boundary between the public and private spheres, the outside world and the interior refuge, and it offers a view of the street at night. The couple is forced into the right-hand section of the picture and fragmented by the right and lower margins of the painting. Although the faces remain separated from one another, as in the drawing, the couple's shoulders and lower bodies melt together in the blue of the night.

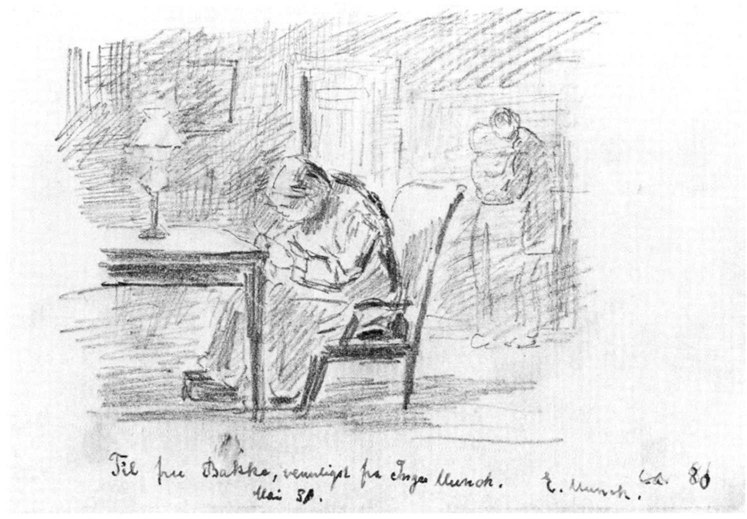

1 *Laura Munch and Kissing Couple*, beginning of the 1880s, pencil on paper, private collection

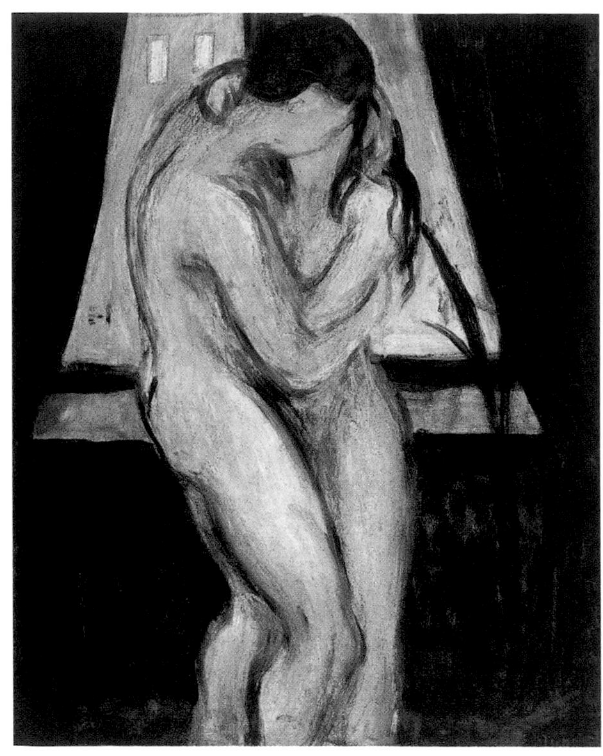

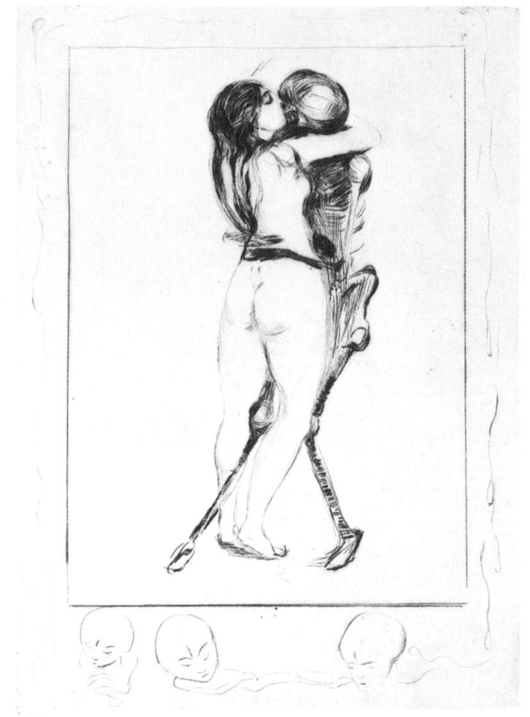

Under the influence of August Strindberg and the author Stanislaw Przybyszewski in Berlin, Munch elaborated on the theme in the painting entitled *Death and the Maiden* of 1893 (cat. no. 44), which he transposed as a mirror image into an etching (fig. 3)—a rendering of the Dance of Death—the following year. Here, a naked woman kisses a man reduced to a skeleton. The format-filling image is framed by threads of sperm and two huge embryos. In his symbolic interpretation of the traditional motif of the Dance of Death, Munch visualizes the union of the act of love with death in the cycle of life.

Munch used the nudity of the protagonists in *Death and the Maiden* again in several drawings and in the vertical-format etching *The Kiss* of 1895 (cat. no. 45). In the latter work, the couple occupies the center of the scene and stands in front of a window, the centerpost of which is positioned precisely in the middle of the picture and joins with the framing curtain to establish a strict visual symmetry. In contrast to the *The Kiss* of 1892, the pair does not hide from view in this version.

Munch turned his attention to the woodcut in the fall of 1896 and may well have already decided to transpose the etching into this medium by that time. This conclusion is supported by the fact that he painted the picture as an almost literal replica of the print in nearly identical dimensions on a wooden panel (fig. 2); the relatively small size and the choice of wood as an image-bearing medium are the key indicators here. Munch completed two woodcut variations and two paintings in 1897. In both media, the degree of abstraction of the couple—now clothed once again—reaches a first peak, as the bodies and faces are melted together. In the paintings, a curtain separates the lovers from the outside world, while only a small exposed section of window offers a view of the hustle and bustle in the street. In the somewhat larger painted version (cat. no. 46), the effect of backlighting is intensified by the strong coloration of the world outside the window, and the faces, hair, and bodies of the figures blend entirely together.

In the first woodcut version, *The Kiss* I (cat. no. 49), the window appears as a reference on the left-hand side of the scene, and the couple is merely suggested by a few outlines. Blended into a single, organic area, the faces exhibit traces of the woodcutting process. The thin coat of paint allows the pattern of the wood grain to appear in the print.

2 *The Kiss*, c. 1896–97,
oil on wood, 38.5 x 31 cm,
private collection

3 *Death and the Maiden*, 1894,
etching on paper, 30.1 x 22.8 cm,
Munch-museet, Oslo

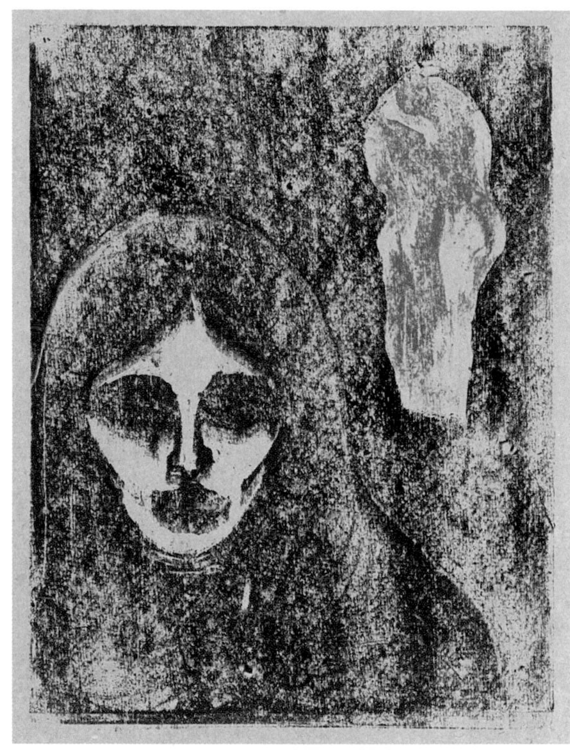

In *The Kiss* II (cat. no. 50), Munch eliminates the window and envelops the couple in a halo of undulating lines that roughly trace the outlines of their bodies. The same lines are already vaguely suggested in the painting (cat. no. 46). Present in the two earlier woodcut versions, the grain becomes a key element of pictorial design in *The Kiss* III (cat. no. 51). The couple, which has now melted into a single, depersonalized silhouette, was cut from the wood block with a fretsaw. The outlines of the arms are marked with fine incisions, while the hands and intermingling faces remain as open areas. The early prints of *The Kiss* III (cat. nos. 51, 52) exhibit the characteristic growth rings and knotholes of the background plate. Munch transferred the material features of the wood to the print. In *The Kiss* IV of 1902 (cat. no. 53), Munch opposed this agitated, prominently visible grain pattern with the vertical orientation of a mostly parallel grain configuration. Later on, he reworked the couple slightly and achieved the highest level of motif focus in prints that show only the silhouette (cat. no. 54). Now liberated from all spatial bonds, the kissing couple becomes an emblem of love. Yet this melting together in the moment of mutual devotion is tantamount to the loss of their personal identity and individuality.

Munch used the figure of the couple as a symbol of love in the small woodcut of 1898 entitled *Rouge & Noir* (cat. no. 41), in which he positioned it like a template in the upper right-hand corner. In contrast to the black of the dominant woman's head in the foreground, the kissing couple is printed in red, and the themes of the kiss and jealousy are joined in this depiction of the lovers' triangle, as in the painting *Jealousy* I of 1907 (cat. no. 77) and the lithograph *Jealousy* IV of 1930 (cat. no. 76). This is an indication of the increasing freedom with which Munch approached his subjects and their possible combinations.

Munch opposed the notion of the complete union of the genders with images of rift between them in *Studenterlunden* (fig. 2, p. 56) shortly before the turn of the century and in the painting *Lovers in the Park* (cat. no. 47) from the *Linde Frieze*. In these works, he used uniform contours to create forms of couples which are abstracted into organically united masses in the background but whose inner cohesion is negated by the color contrasts—the woman in white and the man in a dark color. Munch presents the two genders as opposing poles whose light-dark contrast, much as in *The Split of Faust* (cat. no. 154), signifies the division of the human soul into positive and negative, light and dark forces. In a later revision of *Summer Day* (fig. 4), another painting in the *Linde Frieze*, Munch added a couple in the foreground. The woman's head is turned slightly away from the man, and she appears to draw away from the union of the kiss, although the transparency of the couple against the background could also be read as a recollection of the past in the sense of a mental image of a bygone event.

In both paintings from the *Linde Frieze*, Munch shifts the kissing couple to an outdoor setting—a park in the one version and a

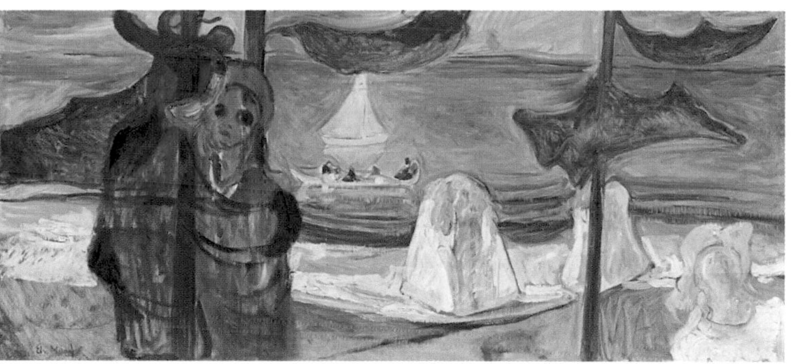

Cat. no. 41 *Rouge & Noir*, 1898
Color woodcut on paper, 25.2 x 19 cm
Munch-museet, Oslo

4 *Summer Day*, 1904–08,
oil on canvas, 90 x 195 cm,
private collection, Oslo

beach in the other. In *Kiss on the Beach* (cat. no. 48), the couple appears as a film image captured in a fleeting moment and laid over the landscape. The few tree trunks and the phallus-shaped reflection of the moon or the sun underscore the couple's vertical orientation and counteract the horizontal configuration of the landscape. Compared to those in *Lovers in the Park*, the color contrasts between the man and the woman are weaker, although the colors actually blend together only in the faces and hair.

Munch addressed the theme of the kiss one last time in 1943 in his monochrome woodcut entitled *Kiss in the Field* (cat. no. 56), a mirror-image version of his *Kiss in the Field* of 1905 (cat. no. 55) rendered in reduced form with very few fine lines. The kissing couple stands in front of the background of a mountainous landscape. Clearly distinct from its surroundings in the earlier version, it virtually disappears in the prominent wood grain visible in brown print in the final version. Here, the kissing couple literally becomes one with the nature of the wood.

DB

1 Stanislaw Przybyszewski (ed.), *Das Werk des Edvard Munch. Vier Beiträge von Stanislaw Przybyszewski, Dr. Franz Servaes, Willy Pastor, Julius Meier-Graefe*, Berlin 1894, p. 18.

2 The following list identifies most of the surviving painted versions, but is not to be regarded as exhaustive: *The Kiss*, 1892, oil on canvas, 71.5 x 64.5 cm, Munch-museet MM M622; *The Kiss*, 1892, oil on canvas, private collection; *The Kiss*, 1892, oil on canvas, 73 x 92 cm, Nasjonalgalleriet Oslo NG.M.02812; *Death and the Maiden*, 1893, oil on canvas, Munch-museet MM M 49; *The Kiss*, 1897, oil on canvas, 99 x 80.5 cm, Munch-museet MM M 59; *The Kiss*, c. 1897, oil on canvas, 87 x 80 cm, Munch-museet MM M 64; *The Kiss*, c. 1896–97, oil on wood, 38.5 x 31 cm, private collection; *Studenterlunden (Summer Night)*, 1901, oil on canvas, 101 x 91 cm, private collection, Switzerland; *Lovers in the Park (Linde Frieze)*, 1904, oil on canvas, 91 x 170.5 cm, Munch-museet MM M 695; *Summer Day (Linde Frieze)*, 1904/after 1907, oil on canvas, 90 x 195 cm, private collection, Oslo; *Couple on the Beach (Reinhardt Frieze)*, 1906–07, tempera on canvas, 90 x 155 cm, Staatliche Museen zu Berlin, Nationalgalerie; *Summer Day*, 1913–18, oil on canvas 105 x 220 cm, Munch-museet MM M 722; *Kiss on the Beach*, c. 1914, oil on canvas, 77 x 100 cm, Munch-museet MM M 41; *Kiss on the Beach*, 1921, oil on canvas, 89 x 101.5 cm, Sarah Campbell Blaffer Foundation, Houston, Texas 1968.1; *The Kiss*, c. 1920–22, oil on canvas, 203 x 152 cm, Munch-museet, MM M 363.

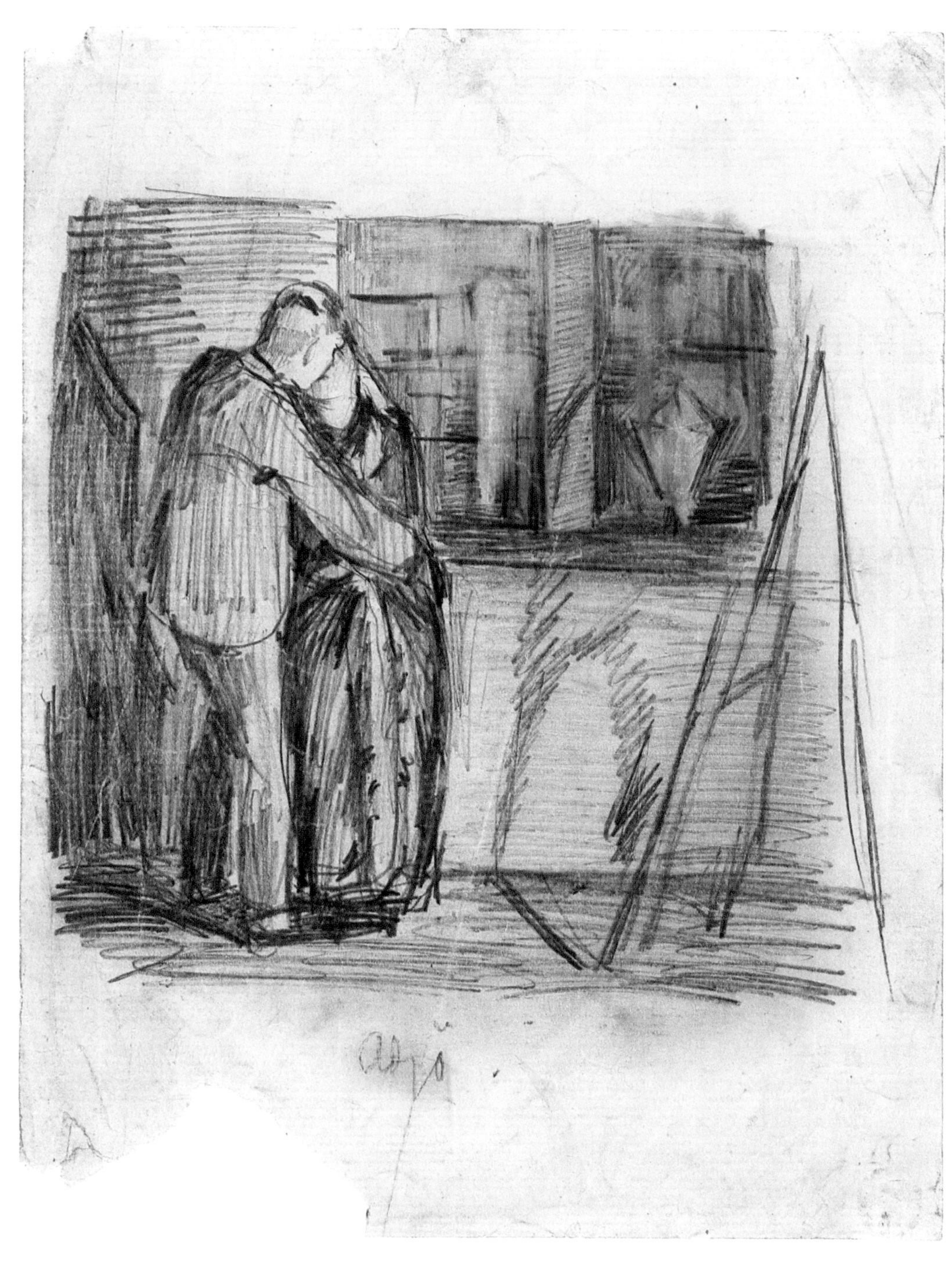

Cat. no. 42 *Adieu (Scene in the Studio)*, 1889
Drawing on paper, 27 x 20.5 cm, Munch-museet, Oslo

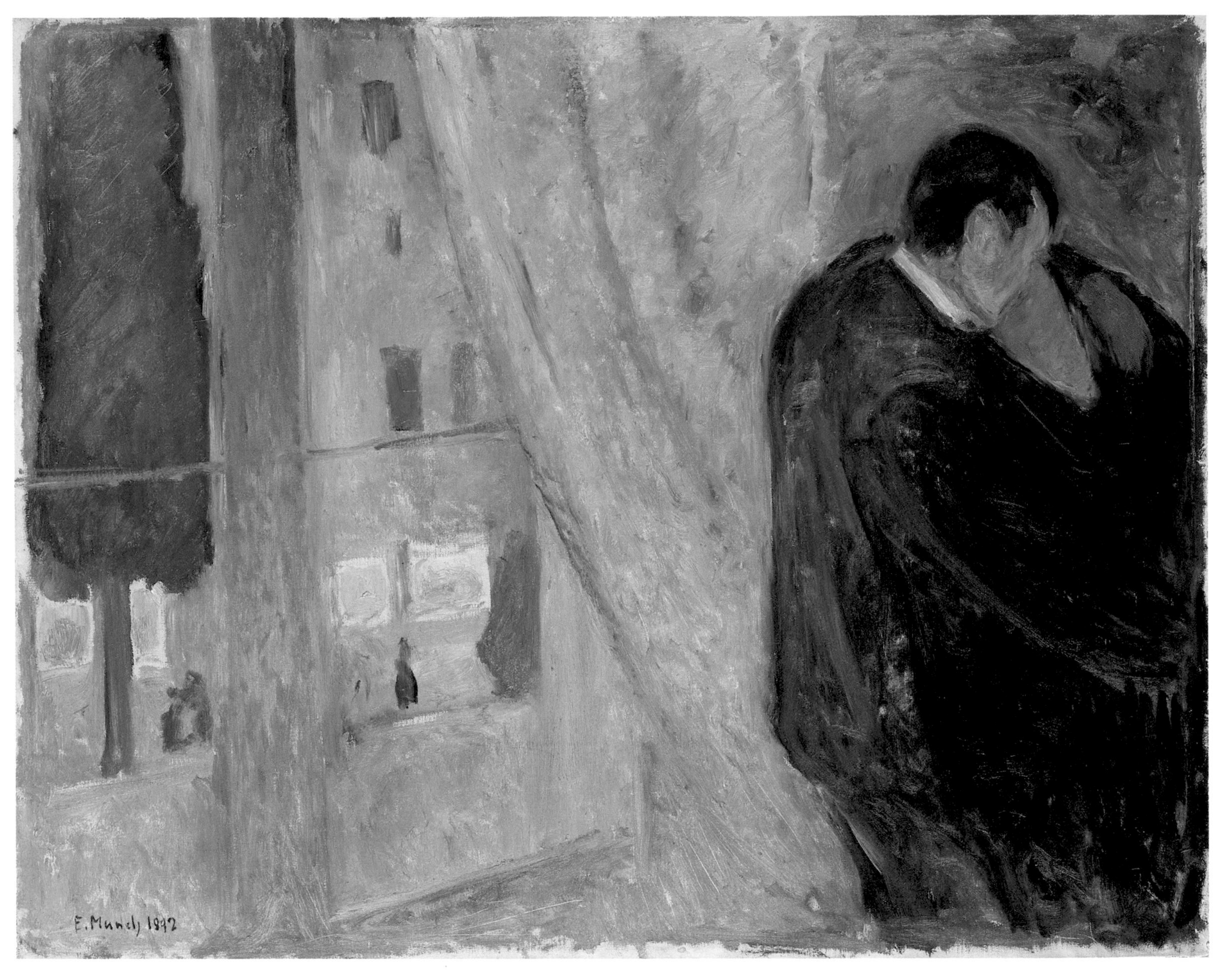

Cat. no. 43 *The Kiss*, 1892
Oil on canvas, 73 x 92 cm
Nasjonalgalleriet, Oslo

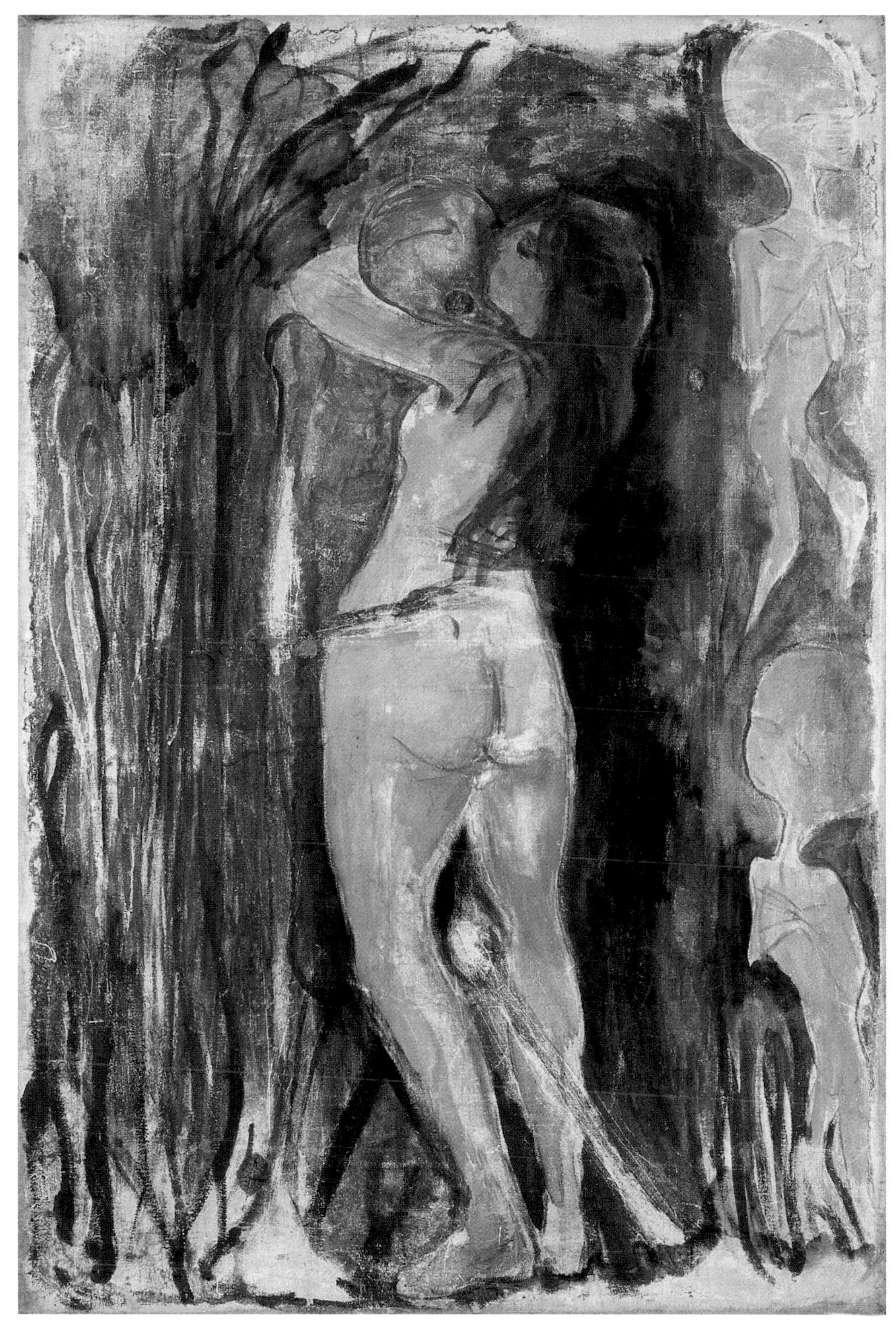

Cat. no. 44 *Death and the Maiden*, 1893
Oil on canvas, 128.5 x 86 cm
Munch-museet, Oslo

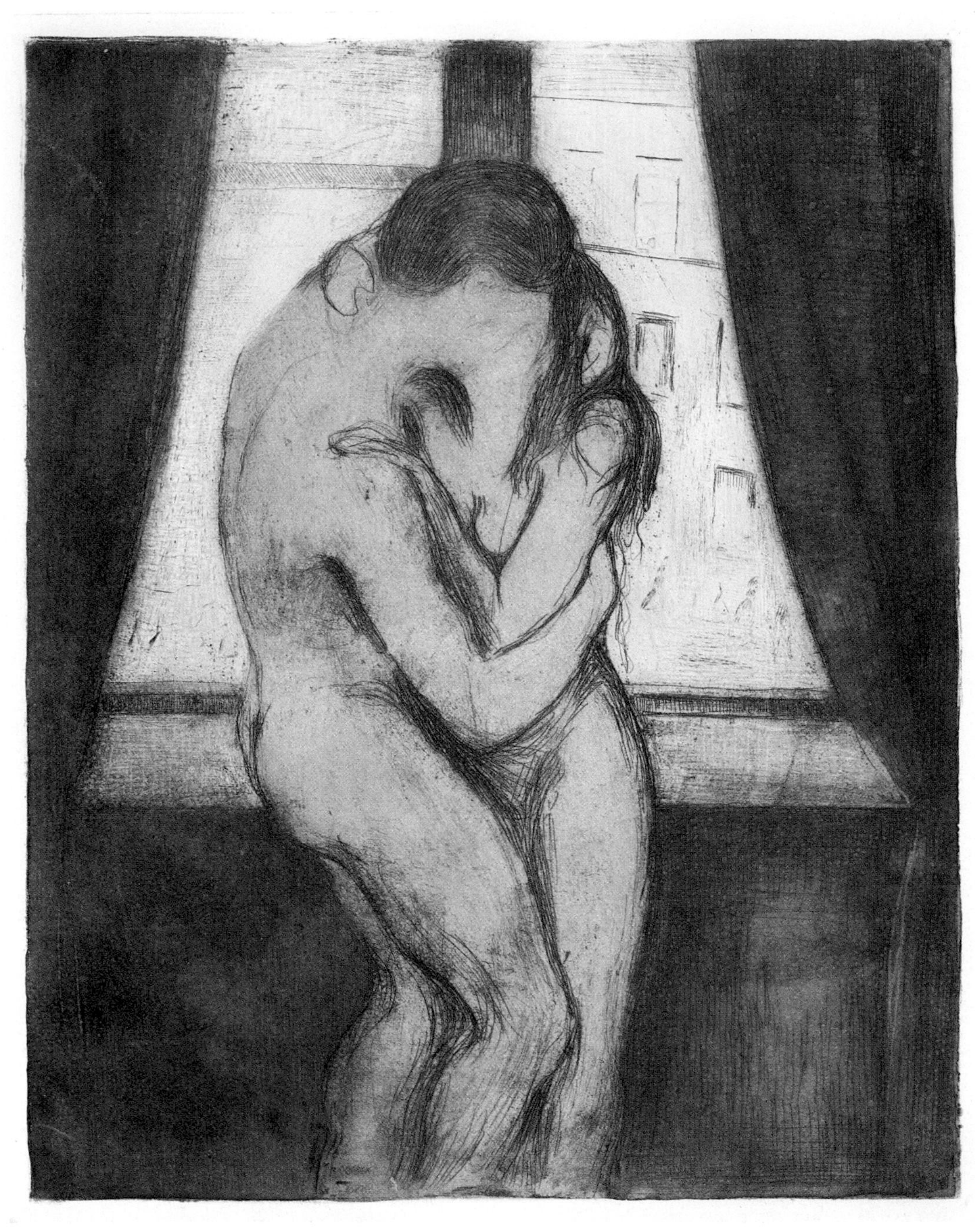

Cat. no. 45 *The Kiss*, 1895
Etching on paper, 32.7 x 26.3 cm
Albertina, Vienna

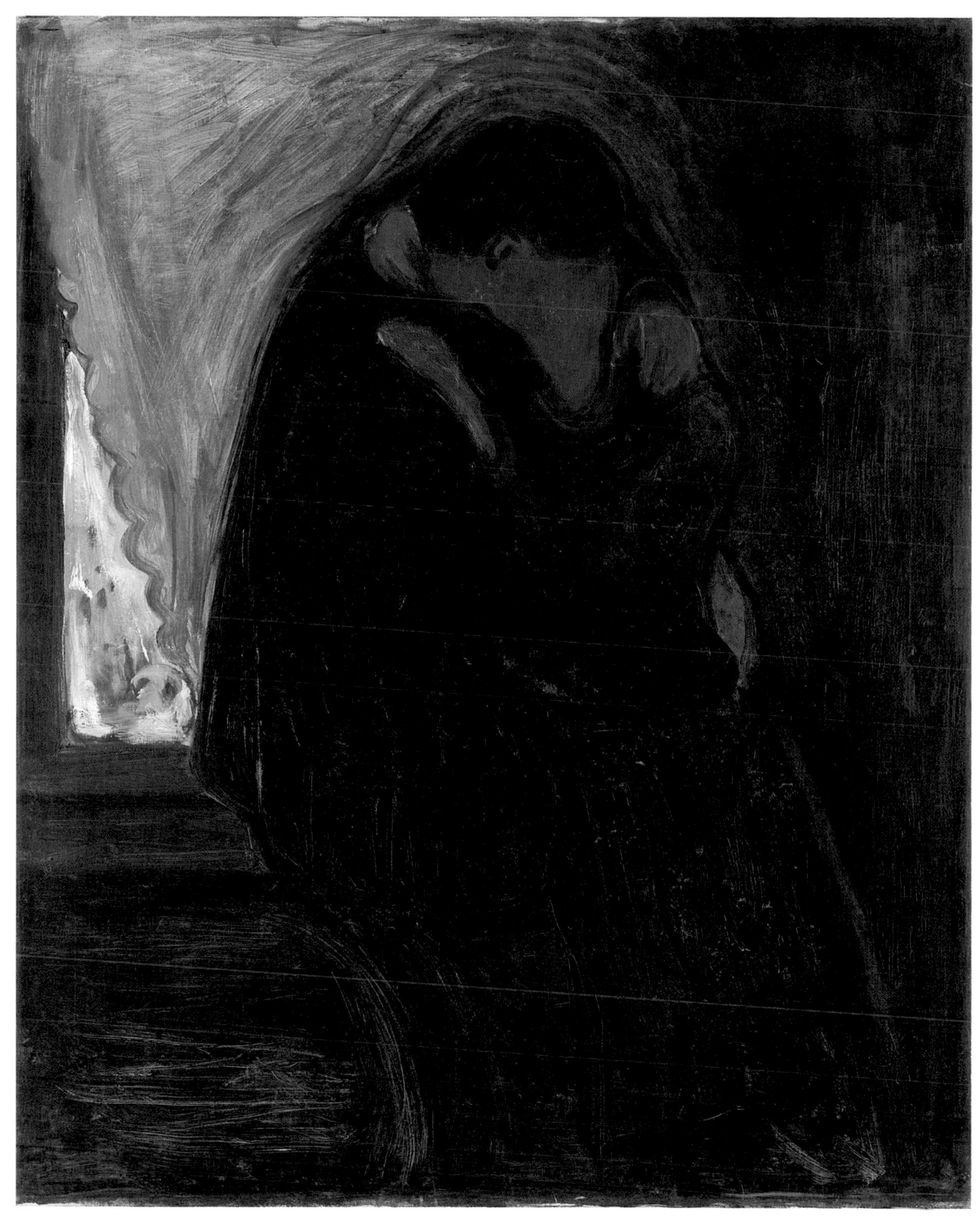

Cat. no. 46 *The Kiss*, 1897
Oil on canvas, 99 x 81 cm
Munch-museet, Oslo

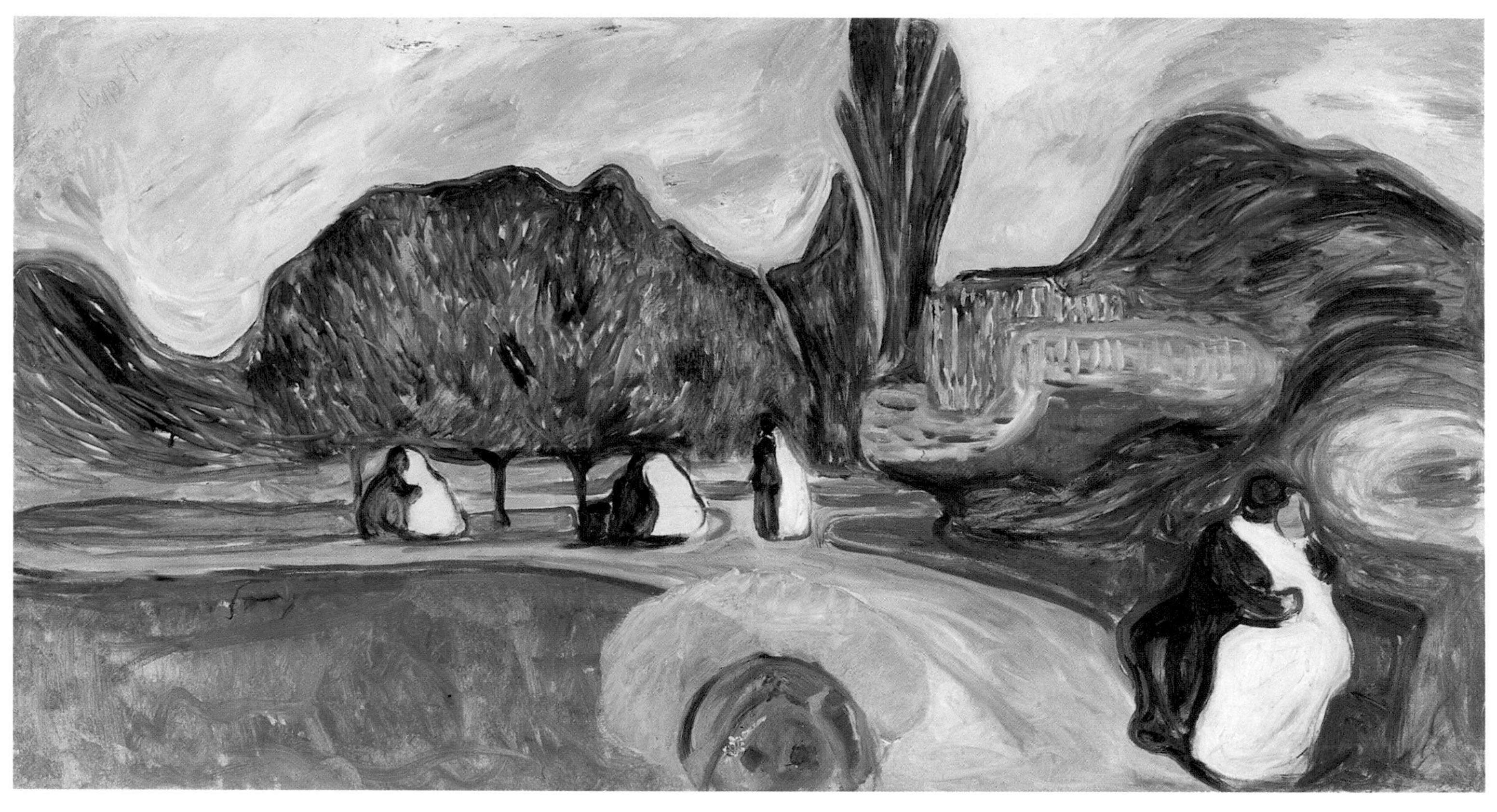

Cat. no. 47 *Lovers in the Park (Linde Frieze)*, 1904
Oil on canvas, 91 x 170.5 cm, Munch-museet, Oslo

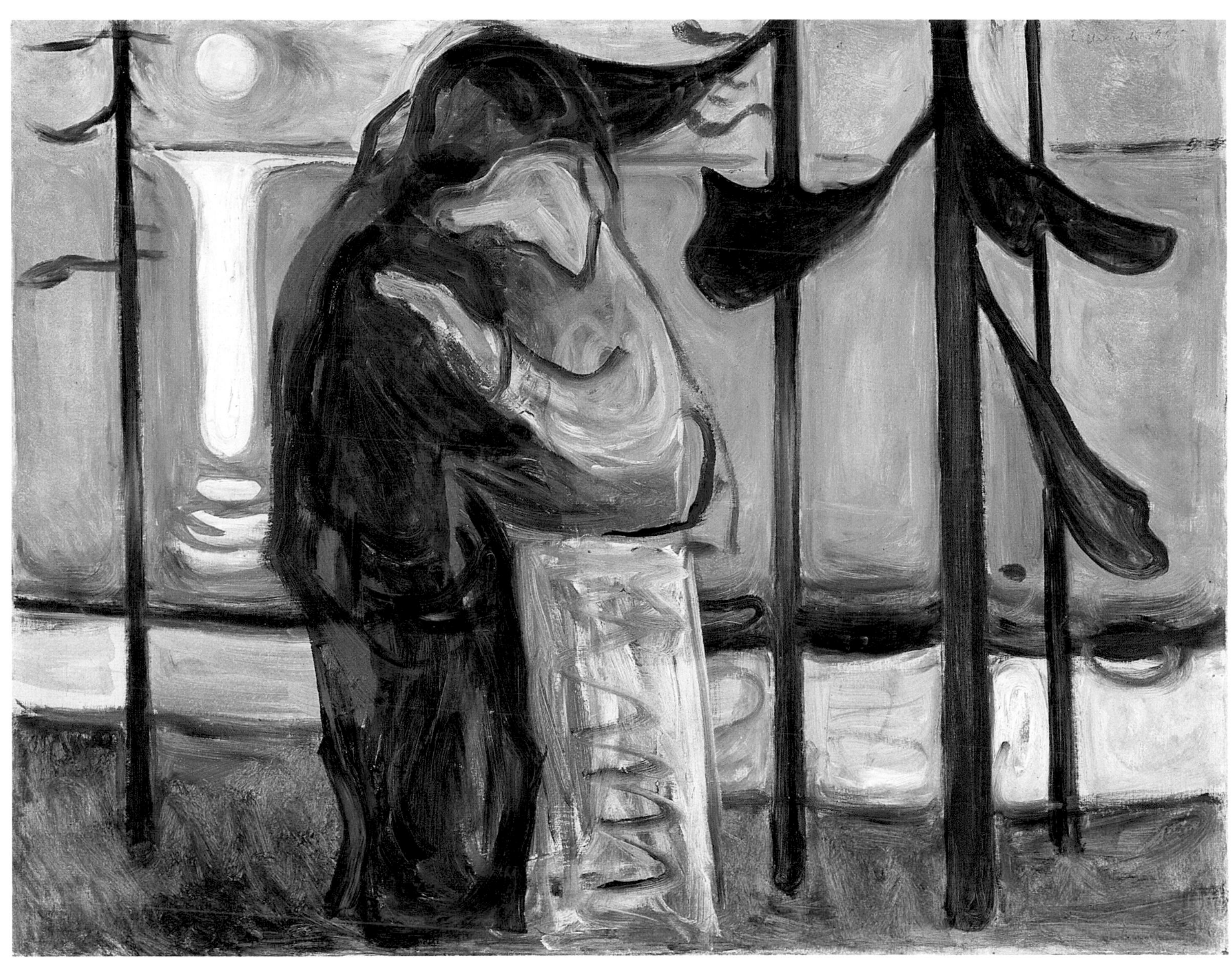

Cat. no. 48 *Kiss on the Beach*, c. 1914
Oil on canvas, 77 x 100 cm, Munch-museet, Oslo

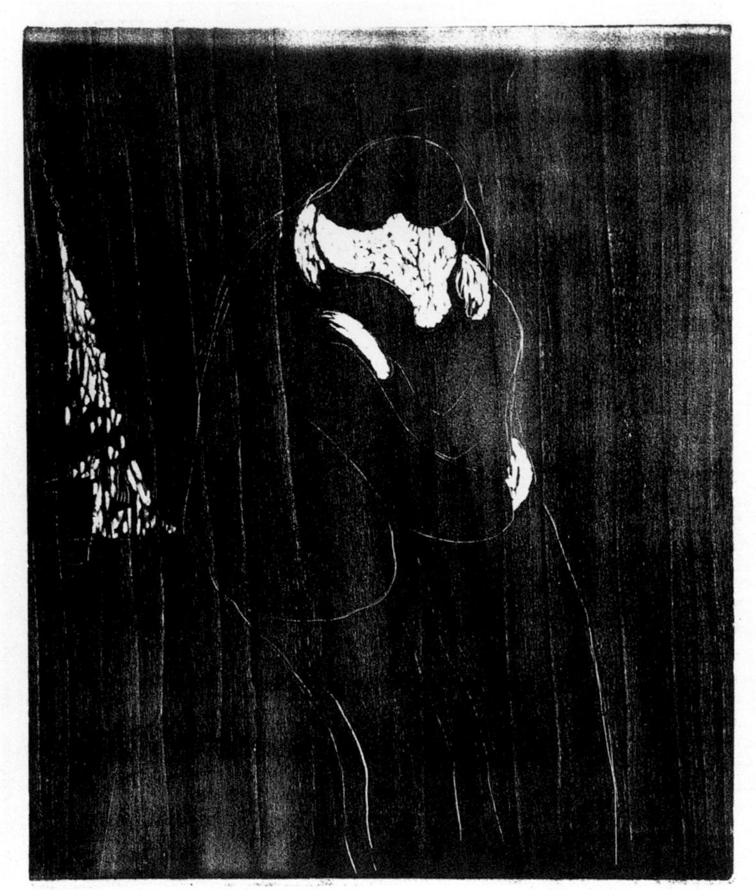

Cat. no. 49 *The Kiss* I, 1897
Woodcut on paper, 45.7 x 38 cm
Munch-museet, Oslo

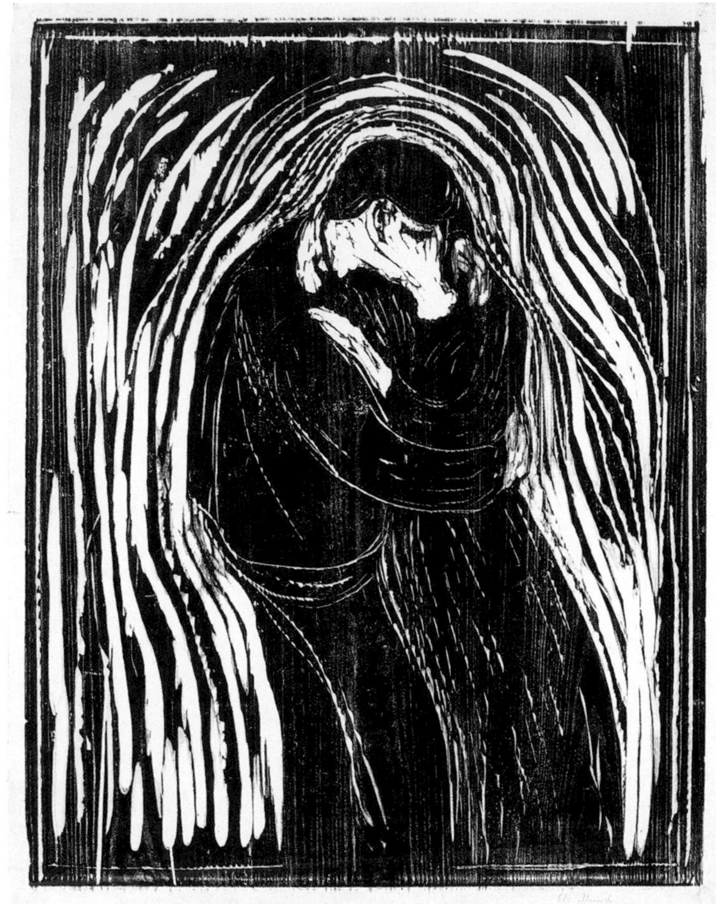

Cat. no. 50 *The Kiss* II, 1897
Color woodcut on cardboard, 58.8 x 46.1 cm
Munch-museet, Oslo

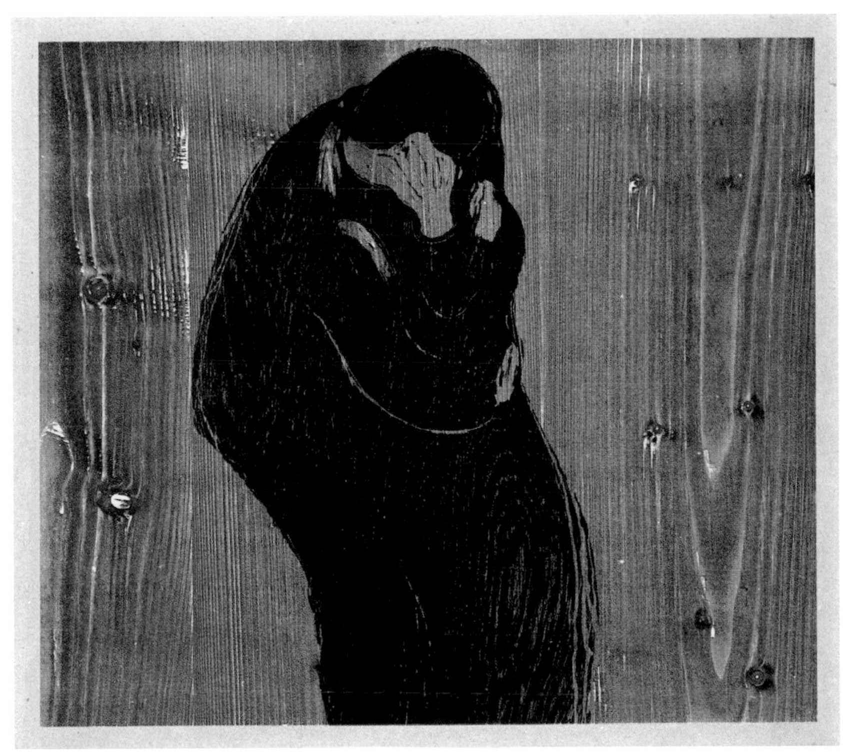

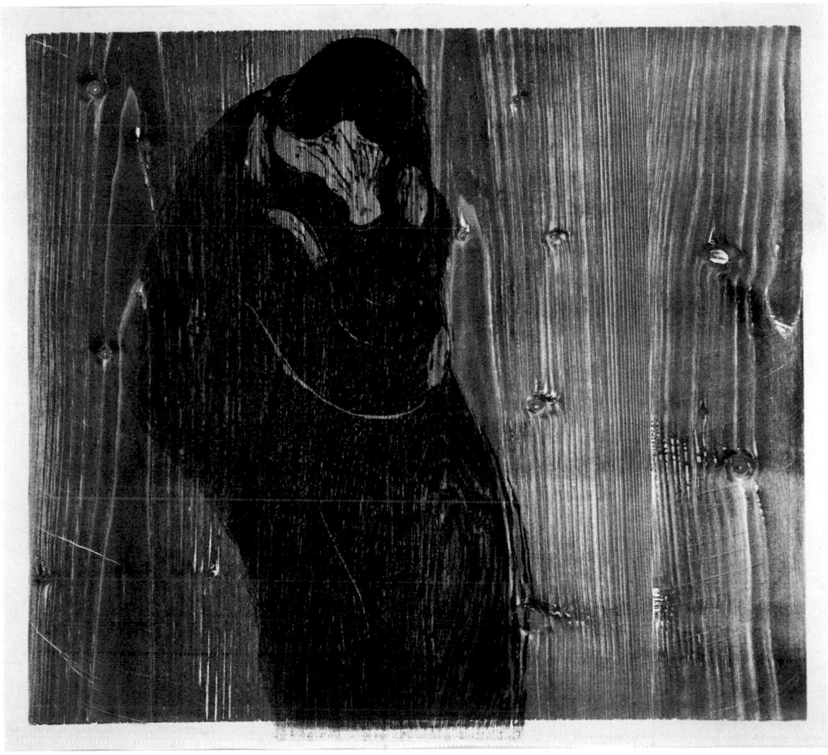

Cat. no. 51 *The Kiss* III, 1898
Color woodcut on paper, 40 x 45.6 cm
Munch-museet, Oslo

Cat. no. 52 *The Kiss* III, 1898
Color woodcut on paper, 40.6 x 46.3 cm
Epstein Family Collection

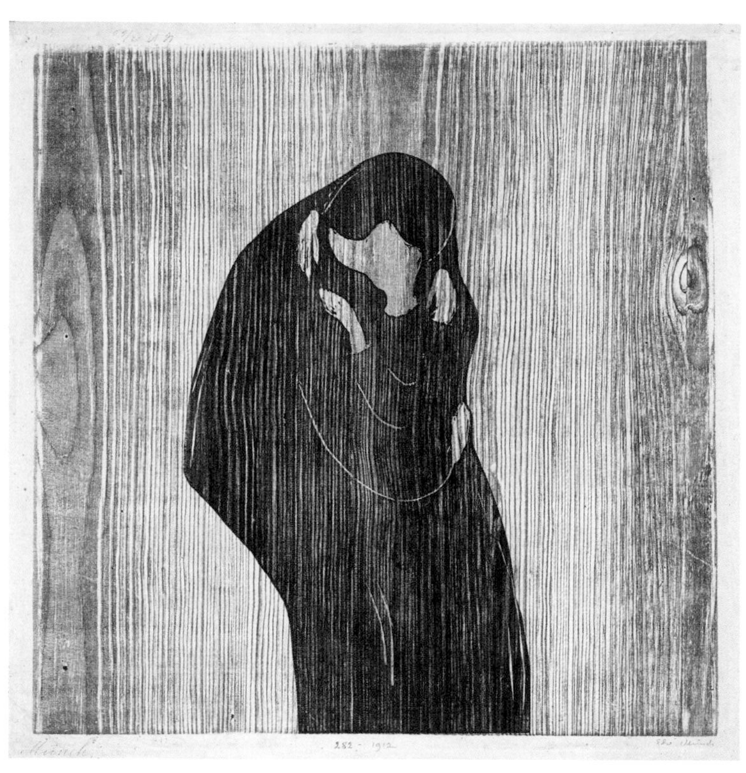

Cat. no. 53 *The Kiss* IV, 1902
Color woodcut on paper, 46.7 x 46.7 cm
Albertina, Vienna

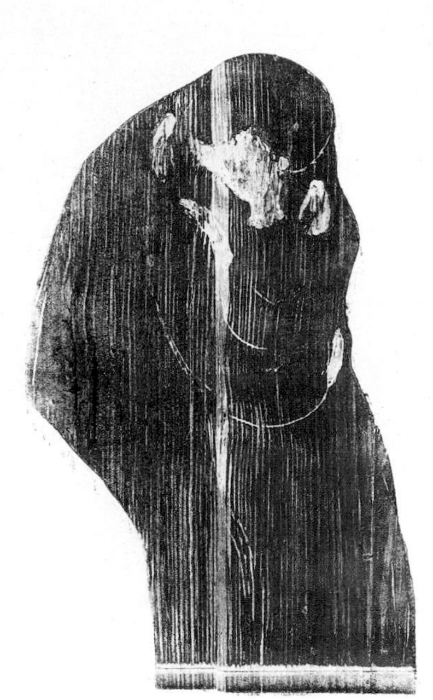

Cat. no. 54 *The Kiss* IV, 1902
Color woodcut on paper, 40.7 x 26 cm
Munch-museet, Oslo

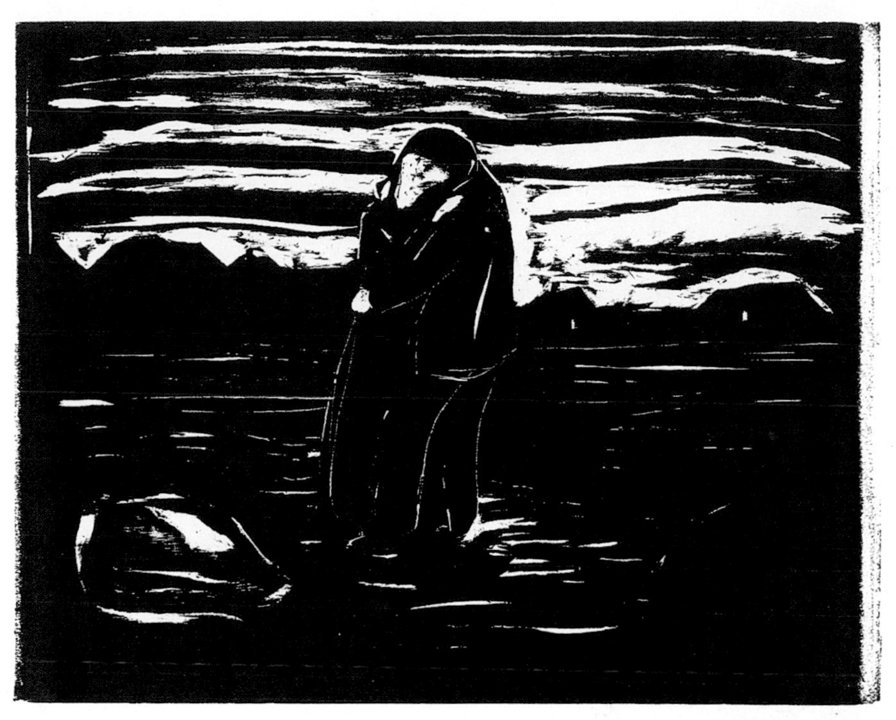

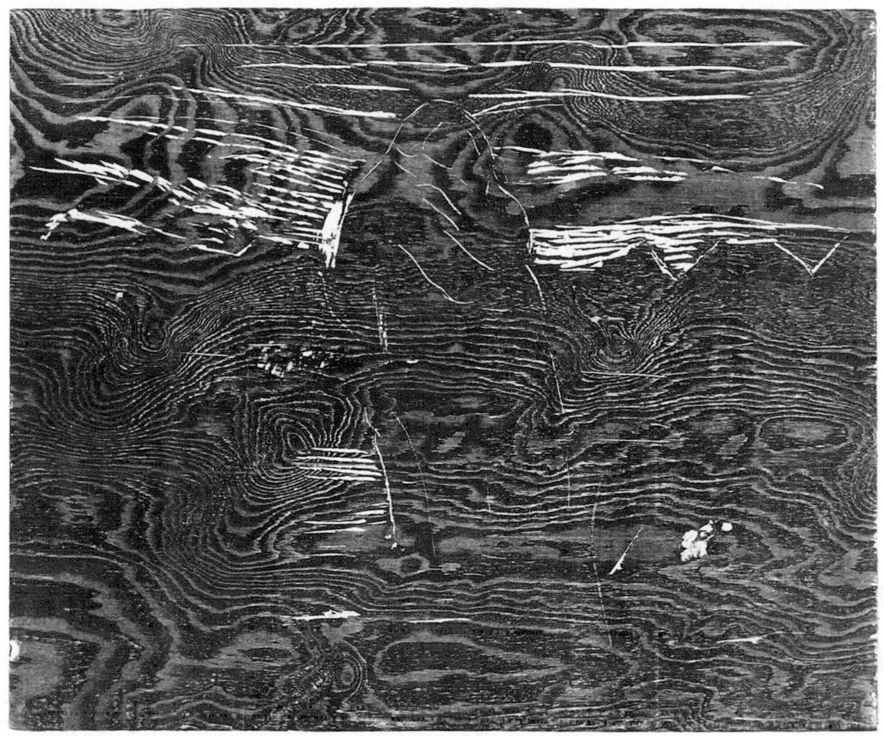

Cat. no. 55 *Kiss in the Field*, 1905
Woodcut on paper, 21 x 26.1 cm
Munch-museet, Oslo

Cat. no. 56 *Kiss in the Field*, 1943
Woodcut on paper, 40.4 x 49 cm
Munch-museet, Oslo

Towards the Forest

Pressed tightly together in a close embrace, a couple walks towards a forest that resembles an impenetrable wall. The figures are seen from the rear, moving away from the viewer, and appear fused into a single form. The man in dark clothing is outlined with fine lines, while the seemingly naked body of the woman is rendered in patches gouged from the printing block. However, a contour line beneath her feet describes the hem of a transparent robe—a garment whose transparency vacillates between exposure and potential concealment. The viewer gazes through the outer covering as if in a roentgenogram. The body is exposed to the voyeur's gaze; male desire is literally made transparent, as in *The Hands* (cat. nos. 24–26). Munch also establishes a relationship of color polarity between the genders through the contrast of light and dark in the bodies. The complete blending of the sexes achieved in most of the *Kiss* pictures no longer seems possible after the turn of the century. The embrace connects two opposing poles, but does not unite them. By affixing framelike strips of molding to the left and right sides of the wood block, Munch intensifies the voyeuristic character of the situation, as they serve as a window through which to observe the couple.

As is true of many of Munch's most important graphic works, it is difficult to date the many prints relating to this subject, as the artist often printed new variations from the same wood block at intervals of as long as several years. Munch printed varying numbers of copies and ordinarily did not number his prints. His total output, which is impossible to reconstruct today, appears to have been influenced by his interest in experimenting with a given theme and by the demands of the art market. Many of the prints represent unique experimental variations that were not repeated and are difficult to classify in the traditional sense. Later revisions of wood blocks and correlations of certain color combinations help to identify specific states and establish a sequential order.

A substantially revised variation bearing the inscription "E Munch 97" on the lower right (cat. no. 57) is identified as one of the early prints of *Towards the Forest* I.[1] In this monochrome black print, Munch achieves a new pictorial structure by applying opaque watercolor after printing. The couple walks across a meadow towards a red line marking the bank of a lake. Both motifs remain visible by virtue of the transparency of the paint. The title variation *The Lake* also confirms this duality of motif. Munch heightens the polar opposition between the genders by emphasizing the contrast between them through the dark color of the man. The striking, unorthodox interplay of graphic and painterly elements forges a link between painting and graphic art beyond the traditional boundaries separating the two media.

However, the consolidation of two background motifs does not constitute a complete re-evaluation of the subject, since the prominent horizontal grain pattern and the application of strips of color on most of the prints result in a comparable stratification of the scene. Yet it is evident that this effect was achieved using a range of very different means. While pictorial structure is achieved in the reworked print by overpainting the woodcut, it is determined in most of the other prints by the pattern of the grain in the printing block. The vertical lines of the trees and the couple are opposed by the horizontal pattern of the grain, which almost causes the motif to disappear. As a result, the prints Munch varied

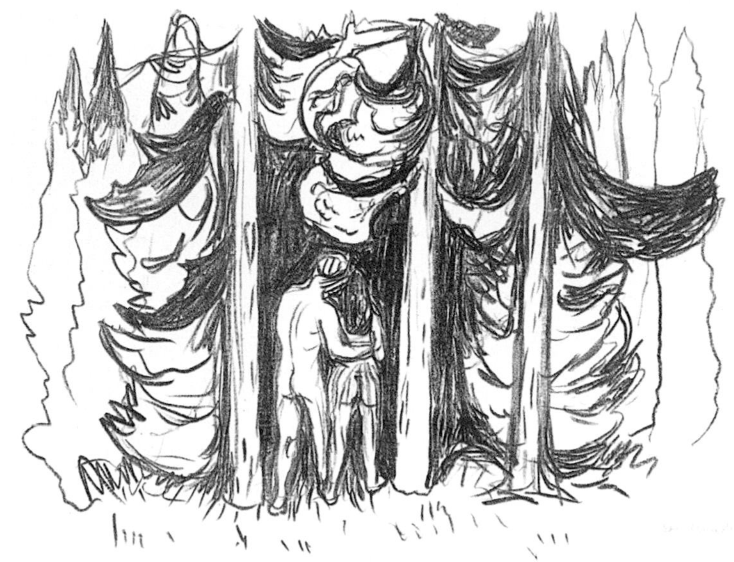

1 *The Forest*, 1908–09,
from the portfolio *Alpha und Omega*,
33 x 42 cm, Albertina, Vienna

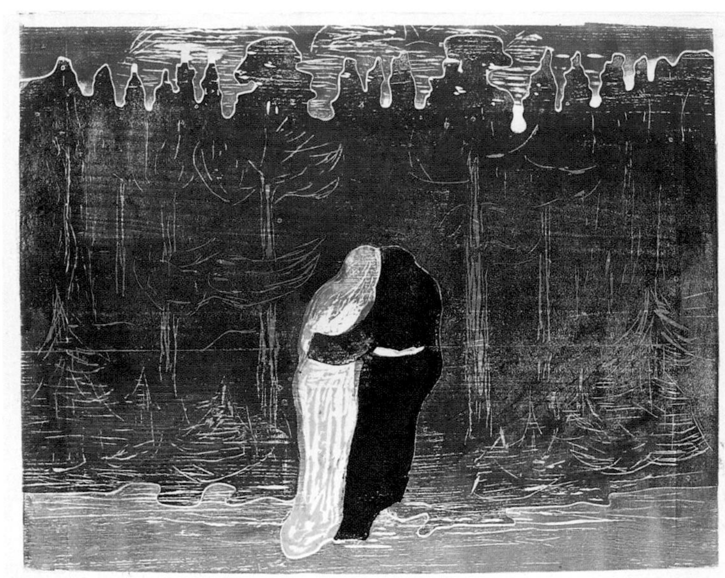

using different color combinations assume a strong atmospheric character. He printed the multicolored prints with two plates, cutting one of them into several sections in order to increase the number of possible combinations. The spectrum of associations evoked by these color experiments ranges from emotional states and moods at different times of day to seasonal atmospheres. Thus, for example, a yellow, green, and grayish-purple print produced in the 1910s (cat. no. 58) may be interpreted as a dawn scene with early-morning mist, while in another multicolored variation (cat. no. 59)—whose experimental character is evidenced by the visible roller marks in the paint—the couple appears to disappear into the fog, through which a delicate shimmer of morning light shines. The blue, green, yellow, and reds in this variation (cat. no. 60) suggest an evening scene, whereas the dark colors of another version (cat. no. 61), herald the coming of night.

In 1915, Munch reworked the printing blocks and created the second version of *Towards the Forest* II (fig. 2). He sawed the color block—now the main printing block into six parts, added details to the forest and hints of clouds in the sky. The woman in this version wears a dress which, depending upon the thickness and color of the paint, covers the nudity of the first version with a veil ranging from transparent to opaque.

Munch did variations of the couple in several drawings and in two lithographs for *Alpha and Omega* (fig. 1), a satirical love poem containing autobiographical elements. He also portrayed the now nude couple in a manner more reminiscent of Adam and Eve. No corresponding painted versions have been identified to date,[2] and thus *Towards the Forest* represents one of the few subjects associated with the *Frieze of Life* for which Munch relied entirely on graphic techniques in all variations. DB

1 Cf. Gerd Woll, *Edvard Munch. The Complete Graphic Works*, London 2001, p. 129.

2 A no longer identifiable painting entitled *Forest* is shown in the catalog for the solo exhibition at the Diorama Center in Kristiania in 1897. This title appears again the following year in a list compiled by Wolfframm at the Galerie Arno Wolfframm in Dresden. Two paintings bearing the title *Forest* are shown in the catalog for the solo exhibition at the Kunstsalon Wolfframm in 1900. Jan Kneher suggests six possible forest paintings for consideration as the latter two works, all of which are dated no earlier than 1899. Yet since Munch did not paint any straight forest landscapes prior to that time, the title *Forest* used as early as 1897 surely refers to a depiction of human figures in a forest setting rather than a forest landscape. One of the works in question may have been a painted version of *Towards the Forest* that has not survived. Cf. Jan Kneher, *Edvard Munch in seinen Ausstellungen zwischen* 1892 *und* 1912, Worms 1994, pp. 110, 125, 131 and 419, note 11.

2 *Towards the Forest* II, 1915,
color woodcut on paper, 49 x 56.5 cm,
Munch-museet, Oslo

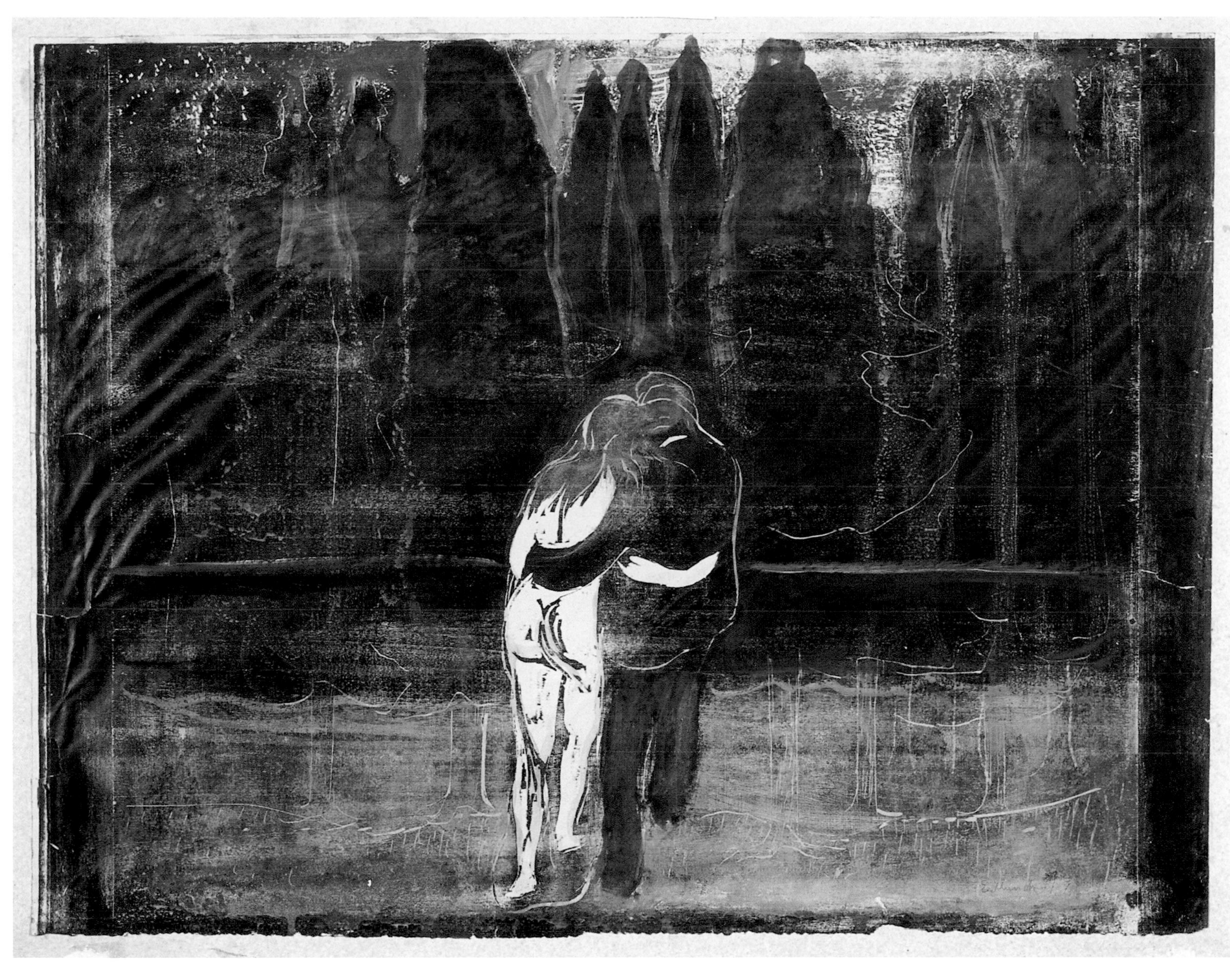

Cat. no. 57 *Towards the Forest* I, 1897
Hand-colored woodcut on paper, 49.4 x 64.7 cm
Munch-museet, Oslo

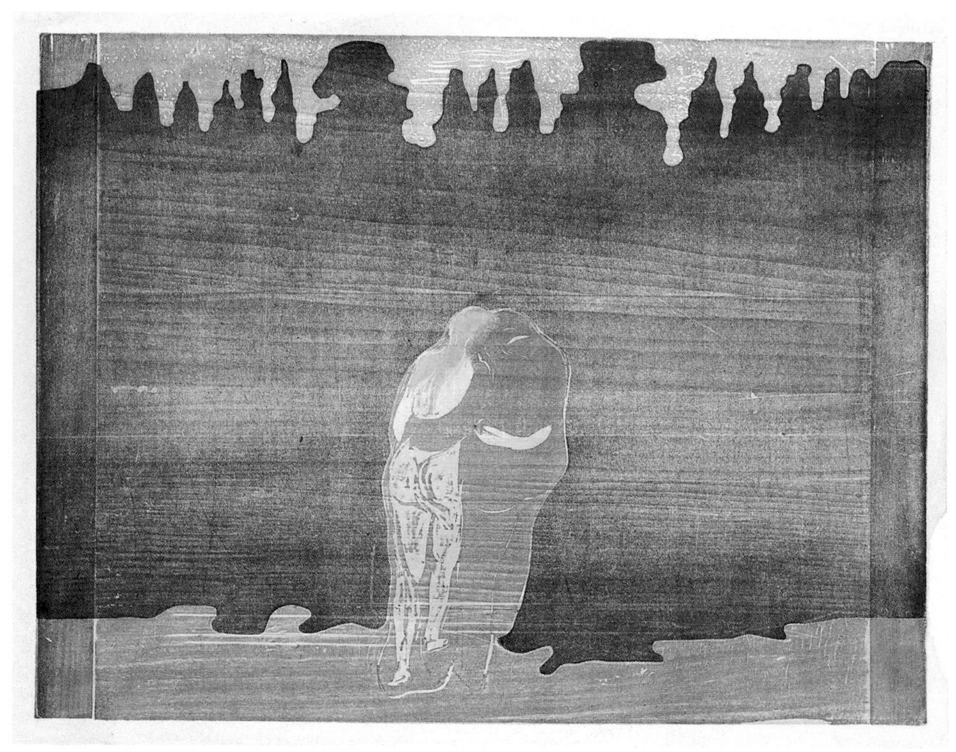

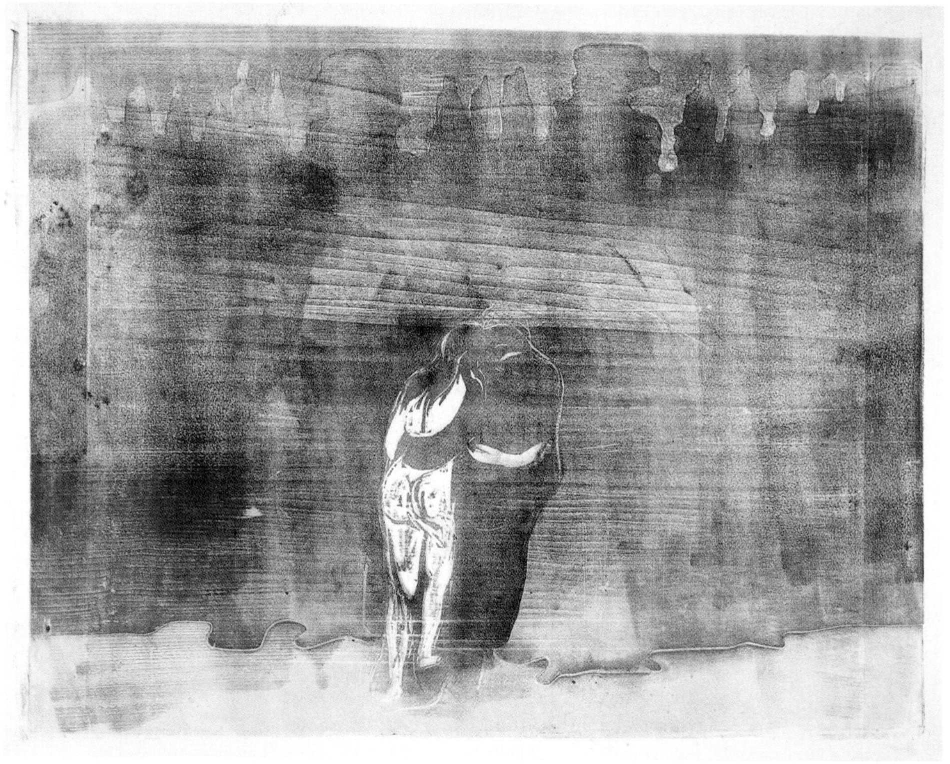

Cat. no. 58 *Towards the Forest* I, 1897
Color woodcut on paper, 50 x 64.5 cm
Munch-museet, Oslo

Cat. no. 59 *Towards the Forest* I, 1897
Color woodcut on paper, 51.7 x 65 cm
Munch-museet, Oslo

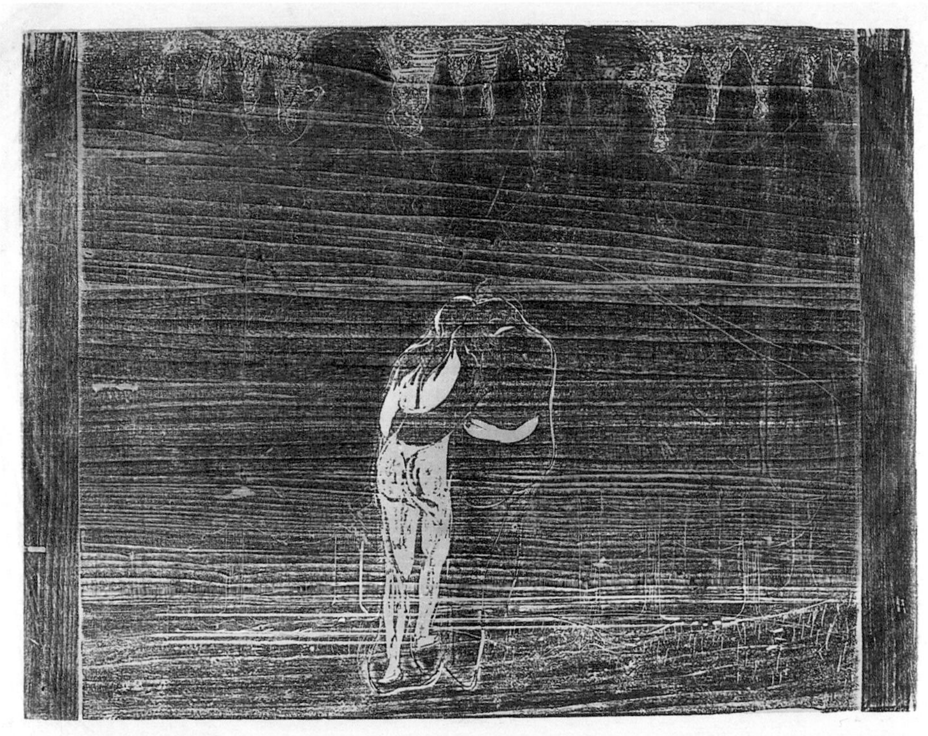

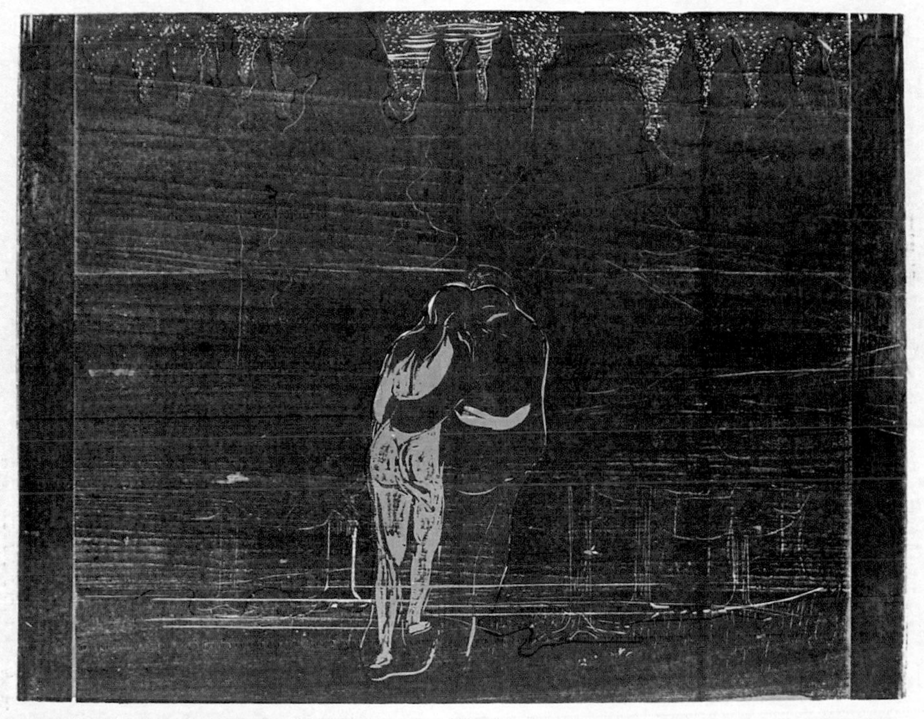

Cat. no. 60 *Towards the Forest* I, 1897
Color woodcut on paper, 49.7 x 64.5 cm
Munch-museet, Oslo

Cat. no. 61 *Towards the Forest* II, 1915
Color woodcut on paper, 50 x 64.5 cm
Munch-museet, Oslo

Vampire

The title appears to identify the subject clearly: a woman with long, red hair bending over a man, sucking the vital power from her victim's body. Like a vampire, she draws strength from the opposite sex and destroys it at the same time. We find this interpretation in a description written by Przybyszewski in 1894:

A broken man, and the face of a biting vampire on his neck... There is something terribly calm and passionless in this picture; an immeasurable, fatal quality of resignation. The man there rolls and rolls into abysmal depths, without will, powerless, and he is happy to be able to roll on with as little will as a stone. Yet he cannot rid himself of the vampire, cannot rid himself of the pain, and the woman will always sit there, biting forever with a thousand adders' tongues, with a thousand poison fangs.[1]

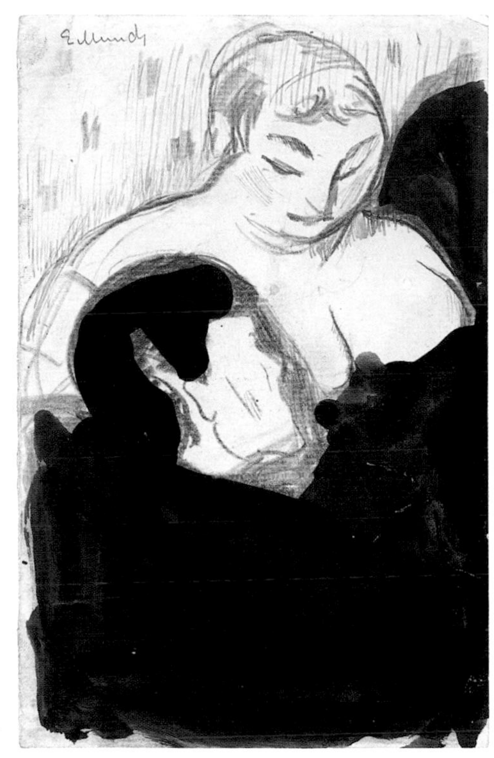

Cat. no. 62 *Young Man and Prostitute*, 1893–96
Drawing on paper, 17.7 x 11.4 cm, Munch-museet, Oslo

The views of the intellectual circle of literati in the Zum Schwarzen Ferkel group are clearly reflected in this description: the futility of love, the destructive power of sex, and the deadly threat posed to man by woman. Munch apparently adopted the word "vampire" from Przybyszewski and first employed it in Stockholm in 1894. At his *Unter den Linden* 19 presentation the year before in Berlin, he had exhibited a version—now at the Göteborg Art Museum (cat. no. 65)—that clashed with this unambiguous interpretation under the title *Love and Pain*. Munch's autobiographical notes also document his ambivalent thoughts on the subject: "It is a warning. ... This painting says that love goes hand in hand with death."[2] The vampire's deadly kiss is also a profession of love or a gesture of consolation, and the shadow behind the couple can be interpreted as a sign of doom or unity in love. Thus the literary title *Vampire* represents a narrow interpretation that conforms to Munch's intellectual environment, but it also echoes his own interests. Forty years later, he distanced himself from this ambiguity, stating soberly that "it is actually only a woman kissing a man on the neck."[3]

Arne Eggum associates the subject matter with the small drawing entitled *Young Man and Prostitute* (cat. no. 62)[4] Although the drawing exhibits a similar composition and shadow pattern, the crucial element is missing—the kiss or bite, which Munch describes definitively as such only once, namely in a 1913 etching depicting an erotic scene (cat. no. 63), in which a man appears to bite a woman in the breast in passion. Munch makes no attempt to portray this actual physical form of vampirism explicitly in *Vampire*, but instead allows the motif to vacillate between love and pain, kiss and death.

Munch completed four painted versions within a very short time between 1893 and 1894, each of which is based on the same compositional scheme. The man's head is framed by the naked arm of the woman bending over him, while her red hair falls over his head and back, which merges with the shadow. Much as in the drawing *Vampire* dated to 1895 (cat. no. 64), the shadow to the right of the couple is cast against the wall of an undefined space in three of these versions. In the fourth version (cat. no. 66), the now clearly outlined shadow envelops the pair and joins them together. Munch obviously transposed this image onto the two prints which present the scene as a mirror image. In the first version worked with lithograph chalk (cat. no. 67), he added the window and curtain, a highly stylized motif reminiscent of the etching entitled *The Kiss* (cat. no. 45), and a suggestion of spatial perspective rendered with a few lines. The larger second version exhibits the same lack of depth as the painting and focuses exclusively on the couple. In this work, Munch used both chalk and lithograph ink, placing additional accents with scratches. According to Schiefler (Sch. 34), the first multicolored prints were made in 1902. From this large group of variations, Gerd Woll has filtered out ten different combinations of two color stones, four wood blocks—each cut into several sections with a fretsaw—and a cardboard template.[5] Munch supplemented the lithograph with color plates which he did not process using the traditional woodcutting technique in which lines and areas are cut out but instead as color templates made by cutting the wood block into forms. In one case, he added different hair colored in red to an earlier black lithograph print (cat. no. 68). Other prints were made by overprinting with the same wood block with up to four different colors, using another color stone in some cases for the red hair. A comparison with two later multicolored prints shows that these variations cover a spectrum ranging from clear delineation of the shadow (cat. no. 69) to a marked development of contrast and complete blending of the shadow with the background (cat. no. 70).

Munch completed further painted versions prior to the exhibition of his *Frieze of Life* at Blomqvist's gallery in 1918. While one version conforms closely in color and motif to the earlier ones, he shifted the action in the vertical format painting *Vampire on the Beach* to a setting in a wooded fjord landscape resembling that of *Kiss on the Beach* (cat. no. 48). He used the vertical format again in the mid-1920s for *Vampire in the Forest*, but depicted his nude protagonists against the background of thick shrubbery in that work. The hand and face of the man are reddened, as if in the blush of lovemaking, and the scene suspended between the poles of pain and love, bite and kiss, is rendered in harmony with the colors of nature. DB

1 Stanislaw Przybyszewski (ed.), *Das Werk des Edvard Munch. Vier Beiträge von Stanislaw Przybyszewski, Dr. Franz Servaes, Willy Pastor, Julius Meier-Graefe*, Berlin 1894, pp. 19f.
2 Munch-museet, Oslo, MM T 2732.
3 Letter from Munch to Jens Thiis written in the early 1930s. Quoted and translated from Ragna Stang, *Edvard Munch. Der Mensch und der Künstler*, Königstein 1979, p. 108.
4 Arne Eggum, "Vampire," in Arne Eggum, *Edvard Munch. The Frieze of Life from Painting to Graphic Art*, Oslo 2000, pp. 181ff.
5 Gerd Woll, *Edvard Munch. The Complete Graphic Works*, London 2001, pp. 73f.

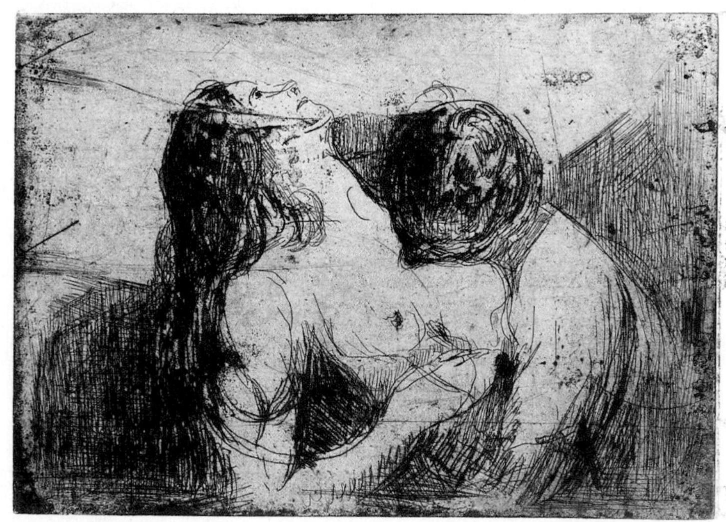

Cat. no. 63 *The Bite*, 1913
Etching on paper, 19.7 x 27.6 cm
Munch-museet, Oslo

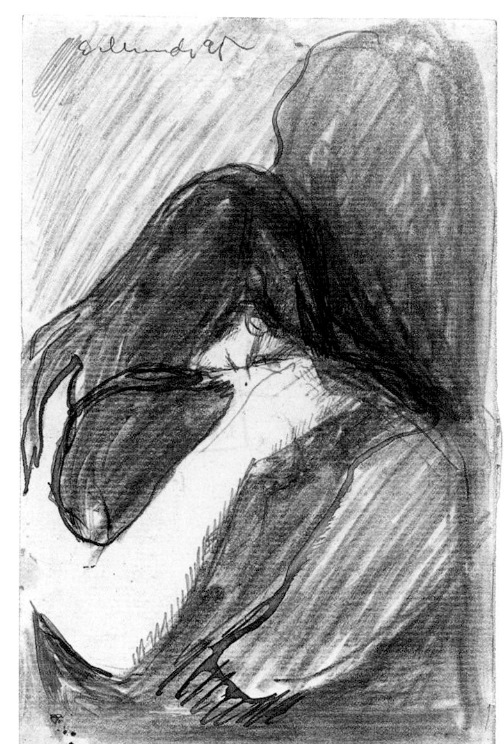

Cat. no. 64 *Vampire*, 1895
Drawing on paper, 17.8 x 11.4 cm
Munch-museet, Oslo

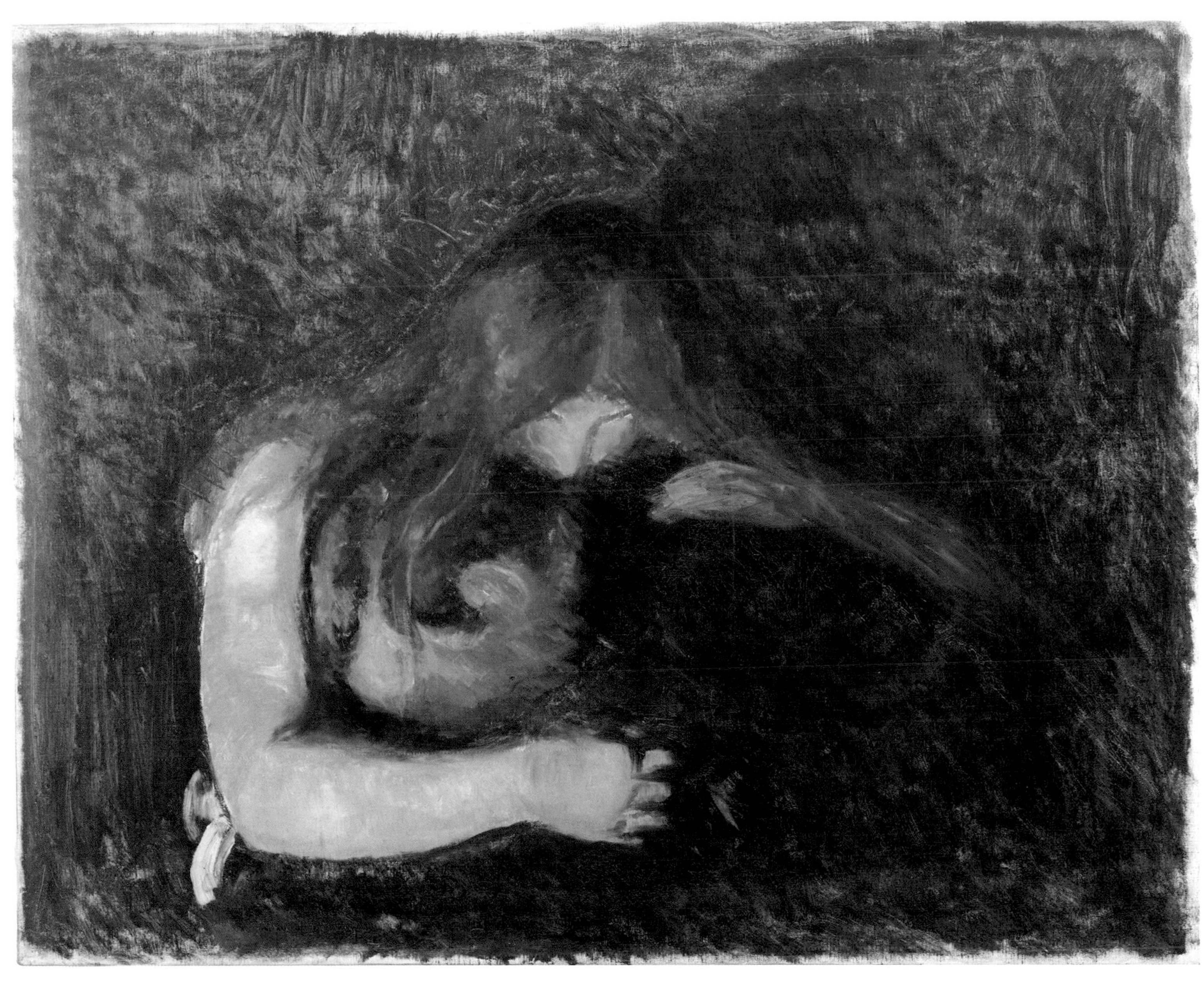

Cat. no. 65 *Vampire*, 1893
Oil on canvas, 80.5 x 100.5 cm
Göteborgs Konstmuseum, Göteborg

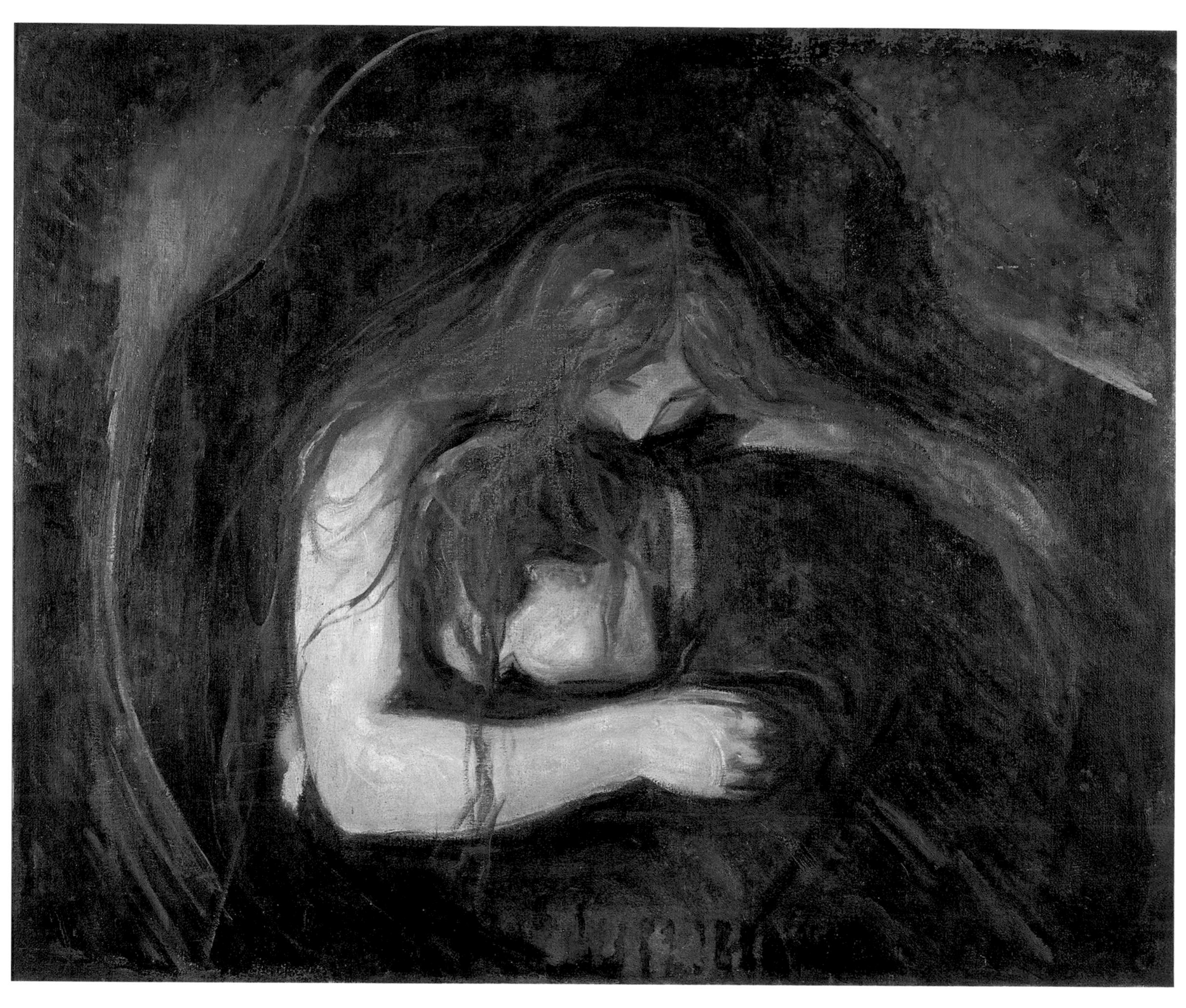

Cat. no. 66 *Vampire*, 1893–94
Oil on canvas, 91 x 109 cm
Munch-museet, Oslo

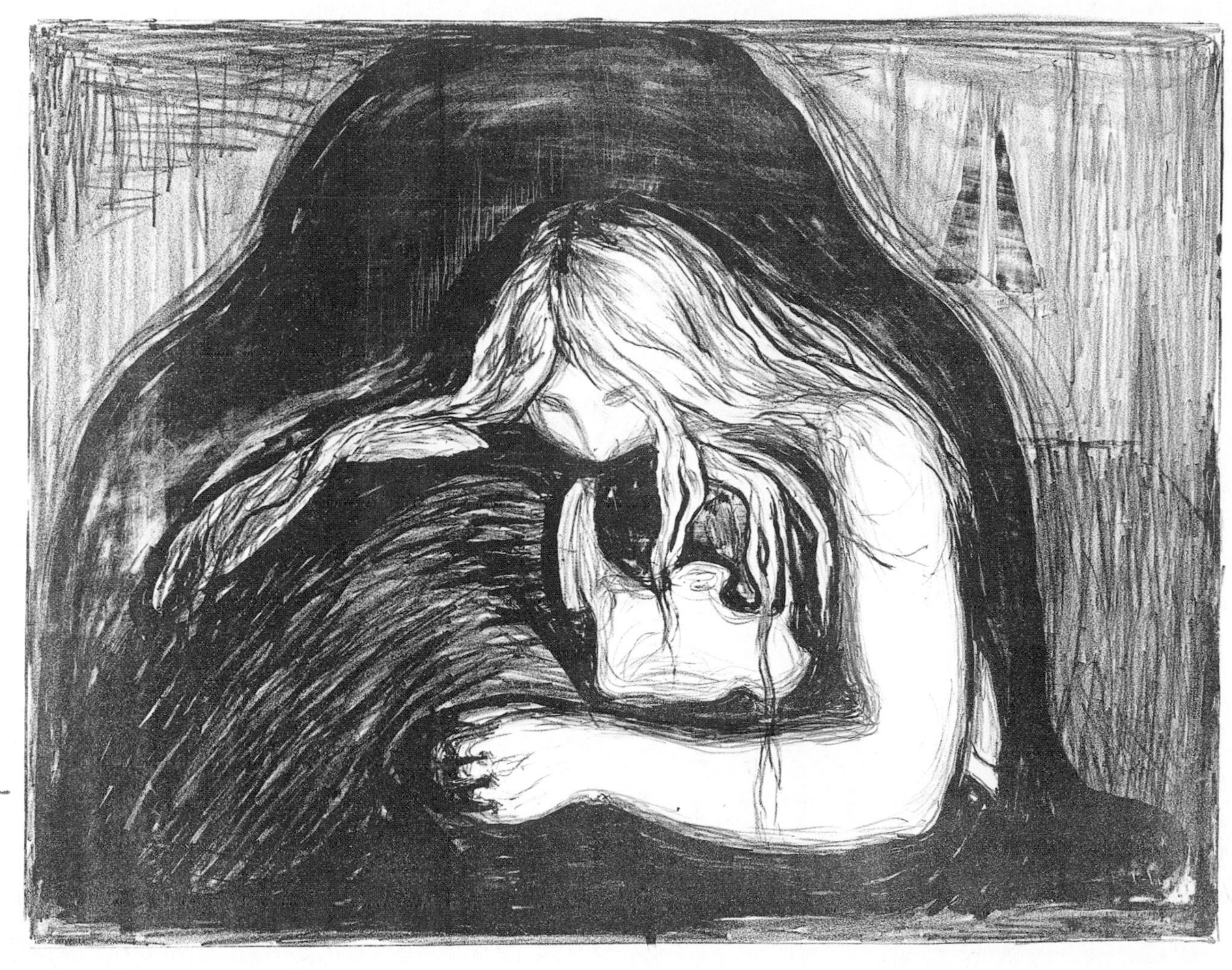

Cat. no. 67 *Vampire* I, 1895
Lithograph on paper, 38.2 x 54.5 cm
Munch-museet, Oslo

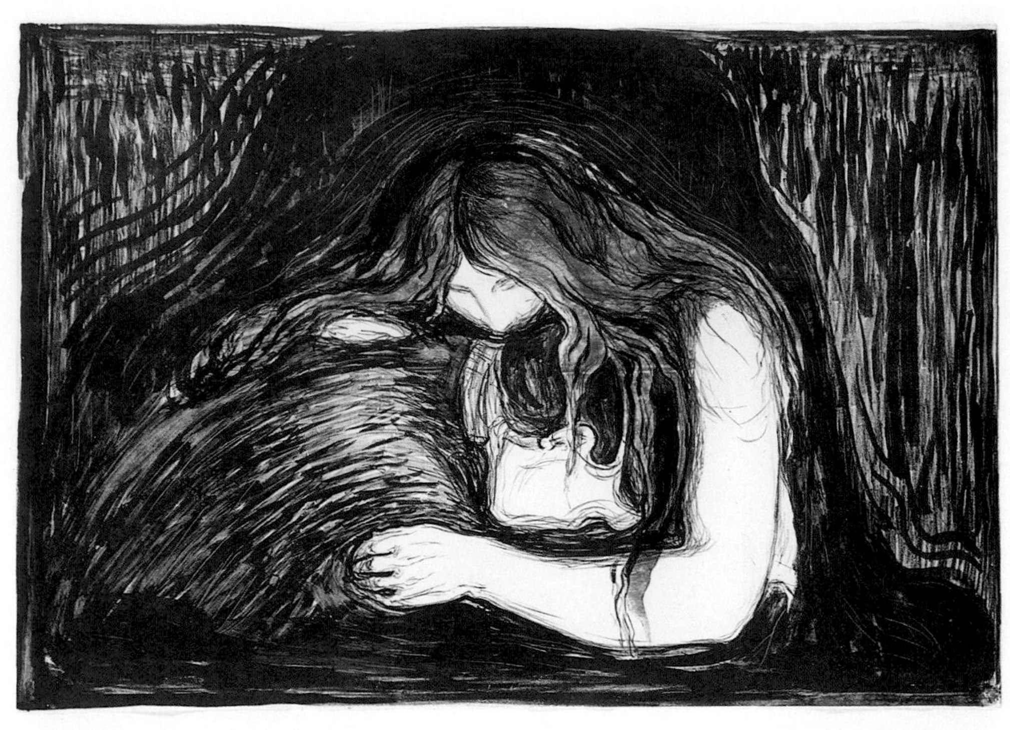

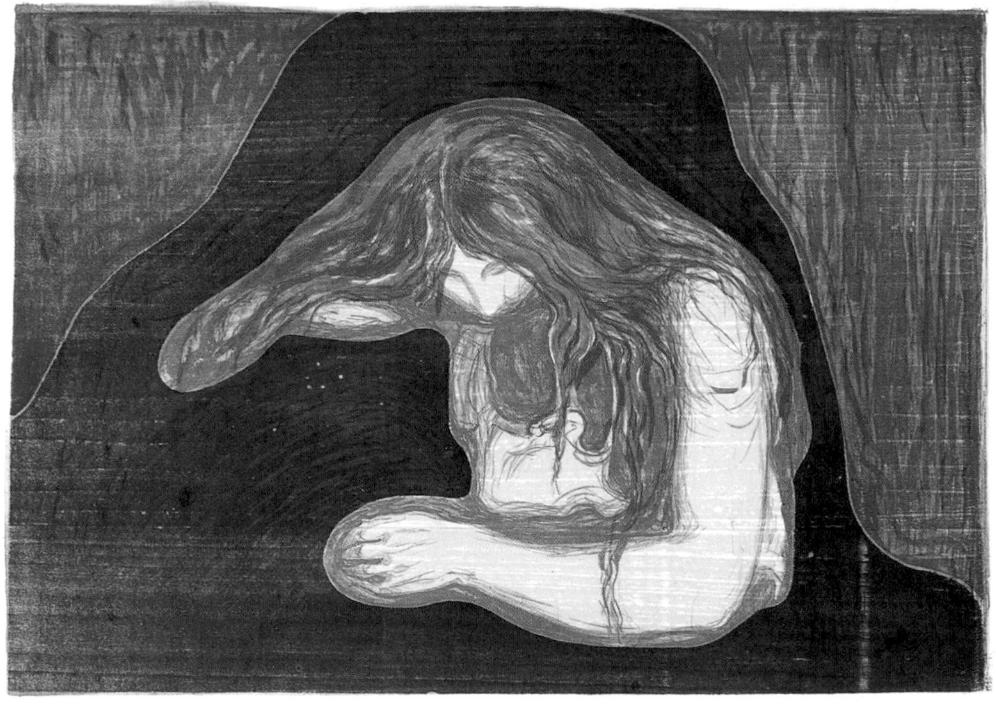

Cat. no. 68 *Vampire* II, 1895
Lithograph and woodcut on paper, 38.7 x 55.5 cm
Munch-museet, Oslo

Cat. no. 69 *Vampire* II, 1895/1902
Color lithograph and woodcut on paper, 38.7 x 55.2 cm
Munch-museet, Oslo

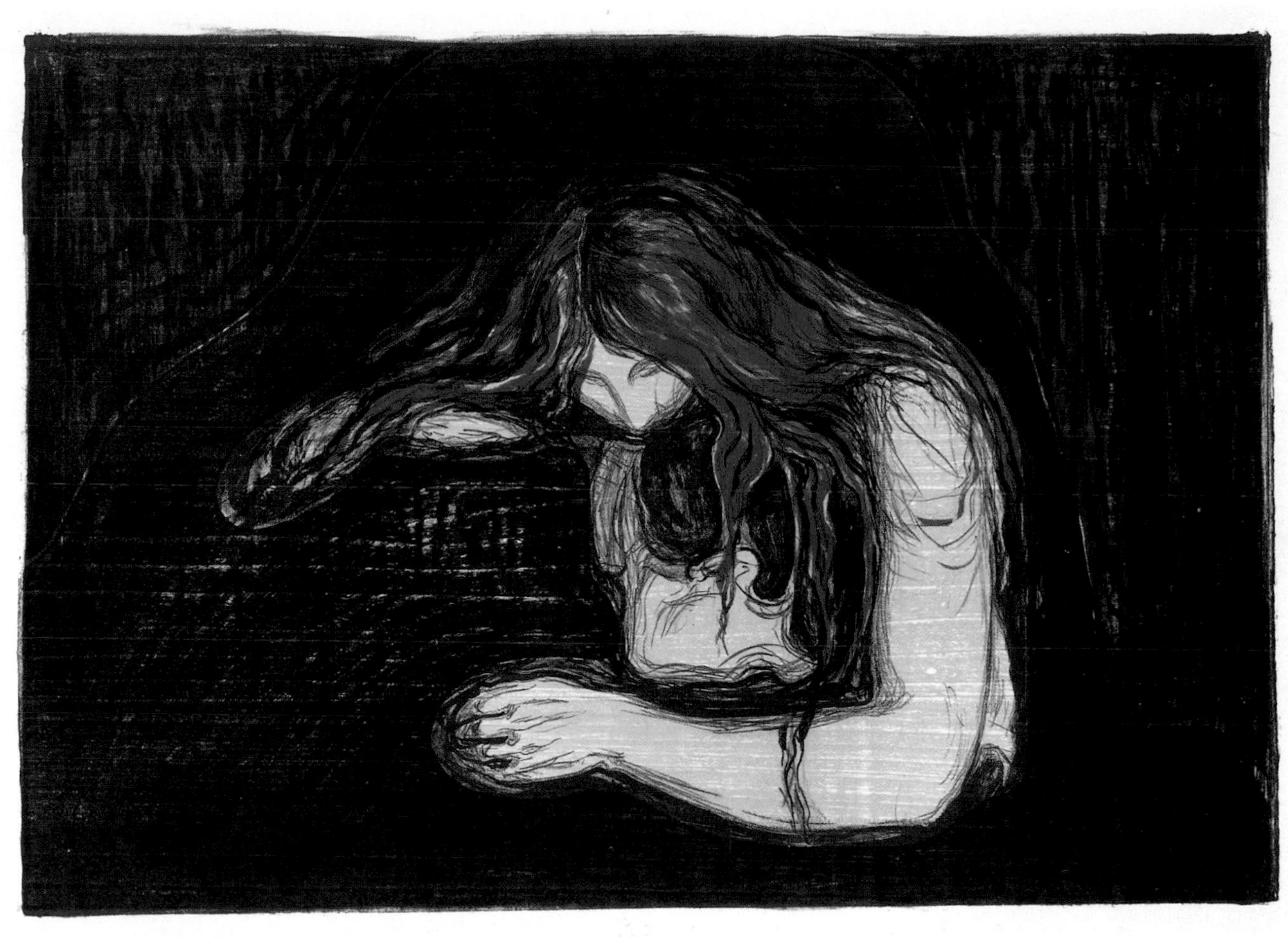

Cat. no. 70 *Vampire* II, 1895/1902
Color lithograph and woodcut on paper, 38.6 x 55.1 cm
Munch-museet, Oslo

Jealousy

"A mystical gaze of the jealous lover—in these two penetrating eyes [is] concentrated into myriad mirror images as if in a crystal—the gaze is probing, interested, full of hate and love—an essence, of it which they all share,"[1] Munch wrote with colored pencils on a page of *The Tree of Knowledge of Good and Evil*. The written words are interspersed with sketchily drawn faces whose eyes reflect different facets of jealousy, as suggested in the text.

In numerous variations involving changing protagonists and executed as lithographs, woodcuts, etchings, watercolors, drawings, and paintings, Munch remained concerned for much of his life with this theme in the field of conflict between love and hate. A study done during the winter of 1891–92 alludes to the experience of his past relationship with Milly Thaulow, whom he suspected of meeting with another lover. In this work, he associates his own grim, profiled image with the Adam-and-Eve motif of clothed primal parents, depicting the woman pointing to a nearby tree or reaching for the forbidden apple. During the preceding summer in Åsgårdstrand, he had experienced the lovers' triangle involving his friend Jappe Nilssen and Oda and Christian Krohg, which inspired the first version of *Melancholy*, a work he also originally entitled *Jealousy*. Despite the two differing titles, jealousy evolves into passive resignation the depiction of the slumped figure of the unlucky loser Nilssen.

Munch's relationship with Stanislaw Przybyszewski and Dagny Juel in Berlin presumably gave rise to his first explicit treatment of a lovers' triangle in the medium of painting in *Jealousy* of 1895 (fig. 1, p. 69). The partially obscured figure in the foreground, whose physiognomy bears a close resemblance to Przybyszewski's, faces the viewer, while the figures of Munch and Juel in the middle ground on the left-hand portion of the picture could be understood to represent Adam and Eve standing at the Tree of Knowledge. The blood-red "flower of pain" in front of the reddish-orange wall along the lower left-hand edge of the painting may be read as a reference to the pain suffered by Przybyszewski, who masochistically gave Dagny the right to choose her sexual partners freely even after their wedding and attempted to cope with these experiences in his writing. Yet an interpretation of the painting as a portrait of specific persons runs counter to the intent behind Munch's customary use of friends and acquaintances as actors in his *Frieze of Life* images. Here, they serve as models for a symbolic representation of jealousy.

This is also documented by his handling of the theme in two monochrome lithographic versions of 1896, in which he altered both the physiognomy and the frame of view. In both lithographs, the motif of the painting is presented as a mirror image. The section of wall is missing, and Eve no longer appears to reach for the apple. While the frame of view in *Jealousy* II (cat. no. 72) corresponds for the most part to that of the painting, the artist comes closer to the motif in *Jealousy* I (cat. no. 73), focusing more strongly on the figures, who are also closer together. Munch applied opaque and transparent watercolors to some of the monochrome prints. In a hand-colored version of *Jealousy* I (cat. no. 74), he accentuated the pupils of the foreground figure with luminous red, thereby creating a color connection to the background scene. Both figuratively and literally, the jealous lover with his penetrating red eyes is an expression of anger and despair; in another version, he actually appears green with jealousy. Applying deliberate color accents, Munch transposed specific feelings to the existing matrix of the lithographic print, using color as a means of expressing the prevailing mood. In a variation of *Jealousy* II (cat. no. 71), he experimented with the composition, eliminating the patch of meadow and the "flower of pain" on the right and fragmenting the male figure at the right-hand edge of the print. The woman, with the voluminous, open red dress with billowing sleeves is now positioned between the foreground figure and the other man, who is now dressed elegantly as well, in tailcoat and a top hat. Her red nipples emphasize her erotic aura and the sexual aspect. Although beleaguered by the two men, she dominates the action in a role which shifts back and forth between that of lover and prostitute.

During a stay at the seaside resort of Warnemünde in the summer of 1907, Munch once again took up the theme of jealousy in a series of joyless motifs devoted to the subject of love grouped under the title *The Green Room*. These works were inspired by his unhappy relationship with Tulla Larson and their last, dramatic dispute, during which a gunshot was fired and the artist lost a portion of his left middle finger. In *Jealousy* I (cat. no. 77), the scene is set in a windowless room with green, patterned wallpaper, a setting that also appears in *Desire*, *The Murderess* (fig. 9, p. 74), and *Hate*. Arne Eggum associates the room with a brothel, "although Munch paints the traditional red bordello interior in green."[2] The figures in this work are spatially connected, as if on a theater stage, and the dramatic tension of the scene is much more intense than in the versions done in the 1890s. This situation appears hopeless, the dramatic outcome predetermined: The male figure in the foreground cannot escape the scene, as his way out of the picture is blocked by an empty round table towards the front and to the rear by the kissing couple in the doorway of the narrow room, which is reminiscent of a wide-angle view. His yellowish-green face is framed by unruly reddish-orange hair—highlighted by the complementary blue of his shoulders which blends into the dark floor—further emphasizing his hot-blooded temperament.

In contrast to this image dominated by anger and aggression, the pale jealous lover in *Jealousy* II[3] appears strikingly phlegmatic. The situation seems less hopeless here, as the jealous lover is positioned only in front of the table, and the sense of claustrophobic closeness is lessened by the horizontal format. The image of the two lovers in the doorway, now spatially detached by the absence of the edge of the floor and transposed into the planar surface in the manner of a visual depiction of a backdrop, can be interpreted as a projection of the thoughts of the foreground figure.

This reflective character is intensified in *Surprise* (cat. no. 78). The dissolving pictorial structure can be seen as a visual manifestation of the cognitive world of the man in the right foreground, who, lost in thought, appears to direct his gaze inward. In the background is a woman shown in three different positions resembling photographic multiple exposures, like the three women in *The Woman (Sphinx)* (cat. no. 27), and in the process of dissolution, while the face of a man which intersects the left edge of the picture completes the lovers' triangle. The round, green forms presumably represent the wallpaper pattern but may also be seen as apples and thus as a reference to the Fall of Adam and Eve.

In *Jealousy* III (cat. no. 79), Munch juxtaposes innocence and sin in the figure of the woman dressed in immaculate white who offers herself and her body with her hands clasped behind her hair, her vividly blushing face alternating between shame, anger, and excitement. Despite their proximity, the figures seem isolated from one another and unable to communicate. The two men, their jealousy suggested in shades ranging from yellow to green, are separated as rivals by the woman's body, which also functions as the binding link of their desire.

Munch continued to work on variations on the theme of jealousy well into the 1930s, using a wide range of figures and settings. In two lithographs done in 1930, he expanded the theme by adding the aspect of age. In the hand-colored version of *Jealousy* III (cat. no. 75), for example, an evidently aging Adam—Munch himself with suit and hat—faces Eve, dressed in a short red dress, beneath an apple tree. In *Jealousy* IV (cat. no. 76), the older man appears as a foreground figure in contrast to the young couple seen kissing in the background. Here we find an expression of the jealousy of age towards youth, and Munch wrote the following words on one of the prints: "Jealousy (a dog's gaze)"[4]—a gaze that suggests longing, resignation, and humiliation. DB

1 Translated from a literal German translation of the original: *The Tree of Knowledge*, text page, c. 1913, 65.3 x 47.5 cm, Munch-museet, Oslo, T 2547-A43.

2 Quoted and translated from Arne Eggum, "Das grüne Zimmer," in *Munch und Warnemünde* 1907–1908, exh. cat., Munch-museet, Rostock Kunsthalle, and Ateneum, Helsinki, Oslo 1999, p. 51.

3 *Jealousy* II, 1907, oil on canvas, 57.5 x 84.6 cm, Munch-museet, Oslo, MM M 614.

4 Gerd Woll, *Edvard Munch. The Complete Graphic Works*, London 2001, p. 418.

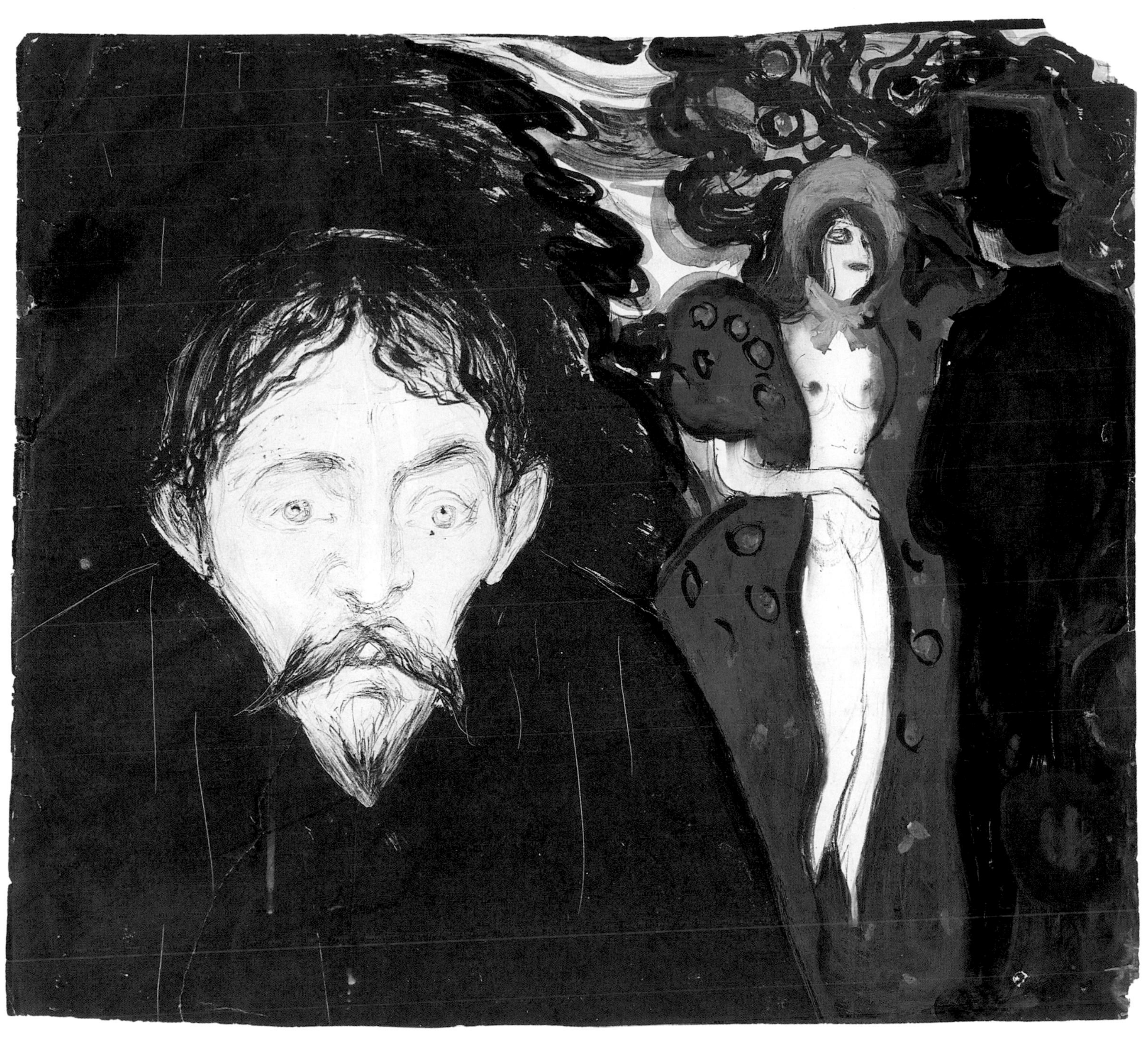

Cat. no. 71 *Jealousy* II, 1896
Hand-colored lithograph on paper, 45.4 x 51.3 cm
Munch-museet, Oslo

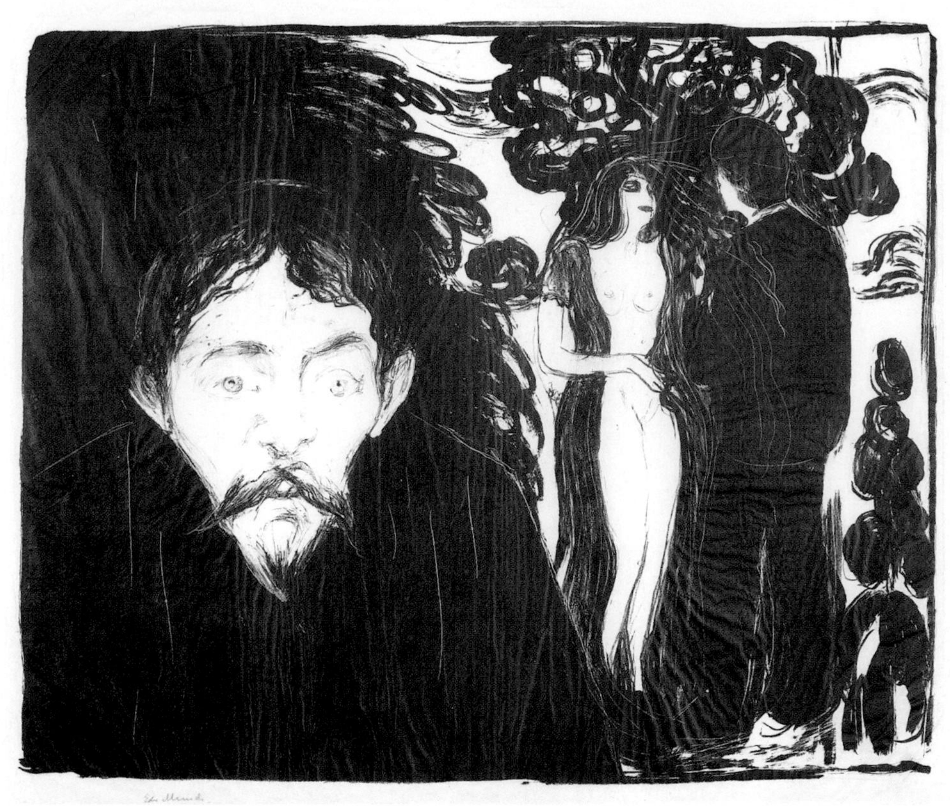

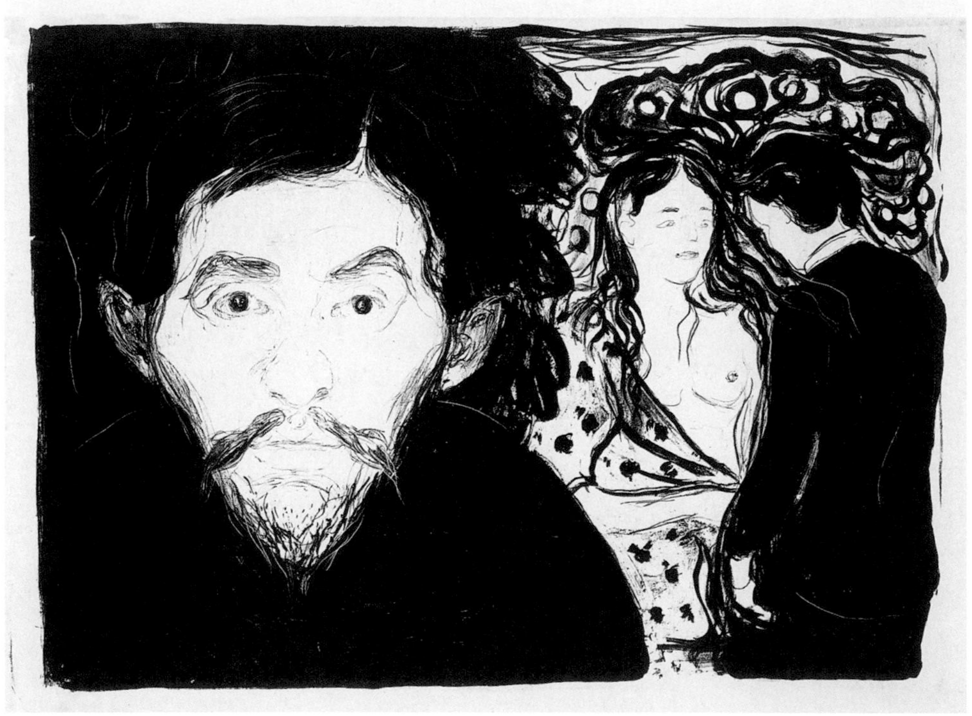

Cat. no. 72 *Jealousy* II, 1896
Lithograph on paper, 46.3 x 56.5 cm
Albertina, Vienna

Cat. no. 73 *Jealousy* I, 1896
Lithograph on paper, 33 x 45 cm
Munch-museet, Oslo

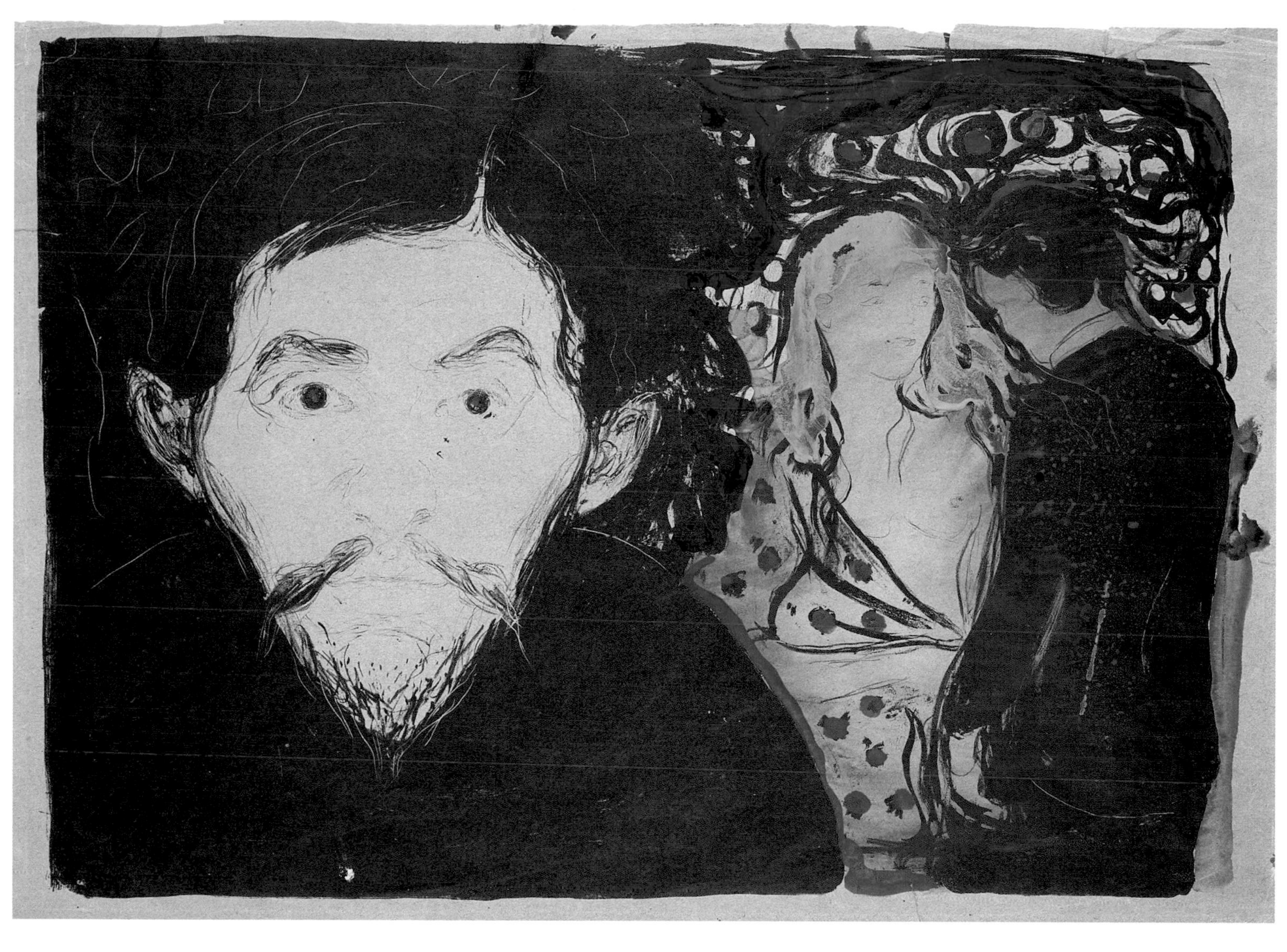

Cat. no. 74 *Jealousy* I, 1896
Hand-colored lithograph on paper, 33 x 46 cm
Munch-museet, Oslo

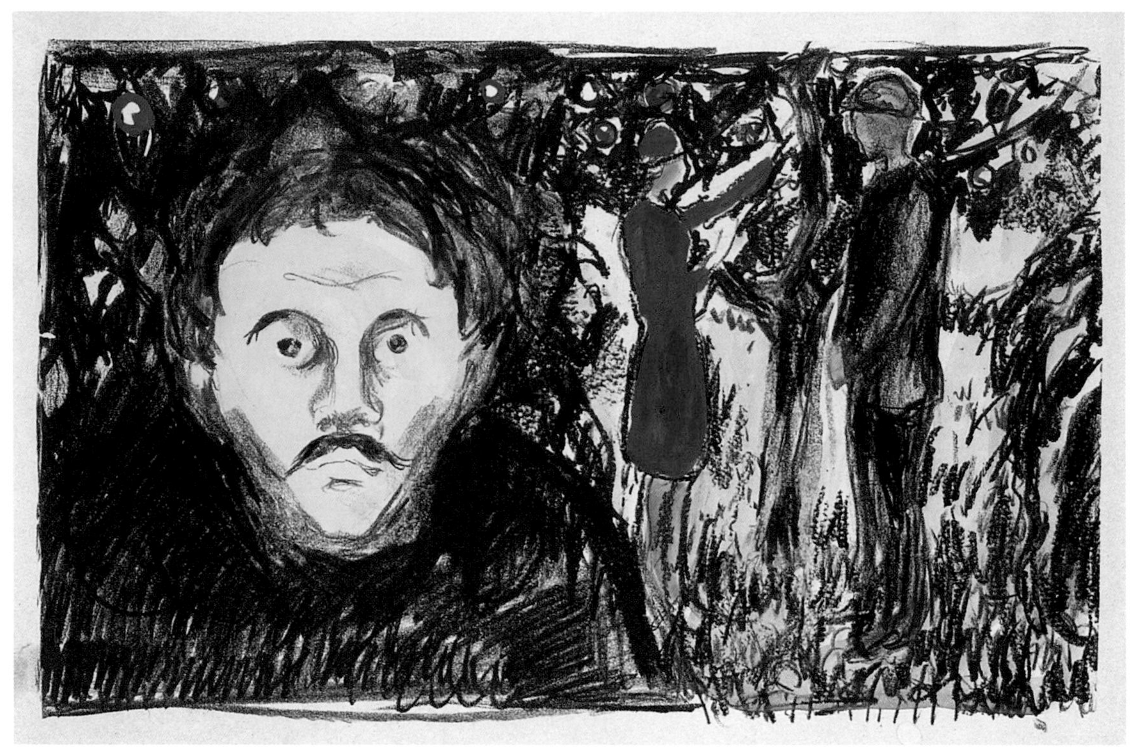

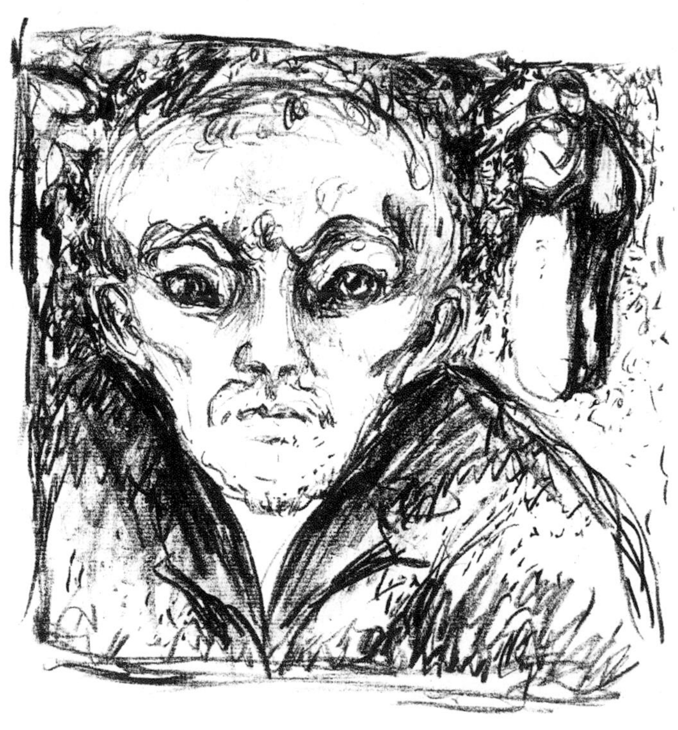

Cat. no. 75 *Jealousy* III, 1930
Hand-colored lithograph on paper, 26.5 x 41.8 cm
Munch-museet, Oslo

Cat. no. 76 *Jealousy* IV, 1930
Lithograph on paper, 23.3 x 25.5 cm
Munch-museet, Oslo

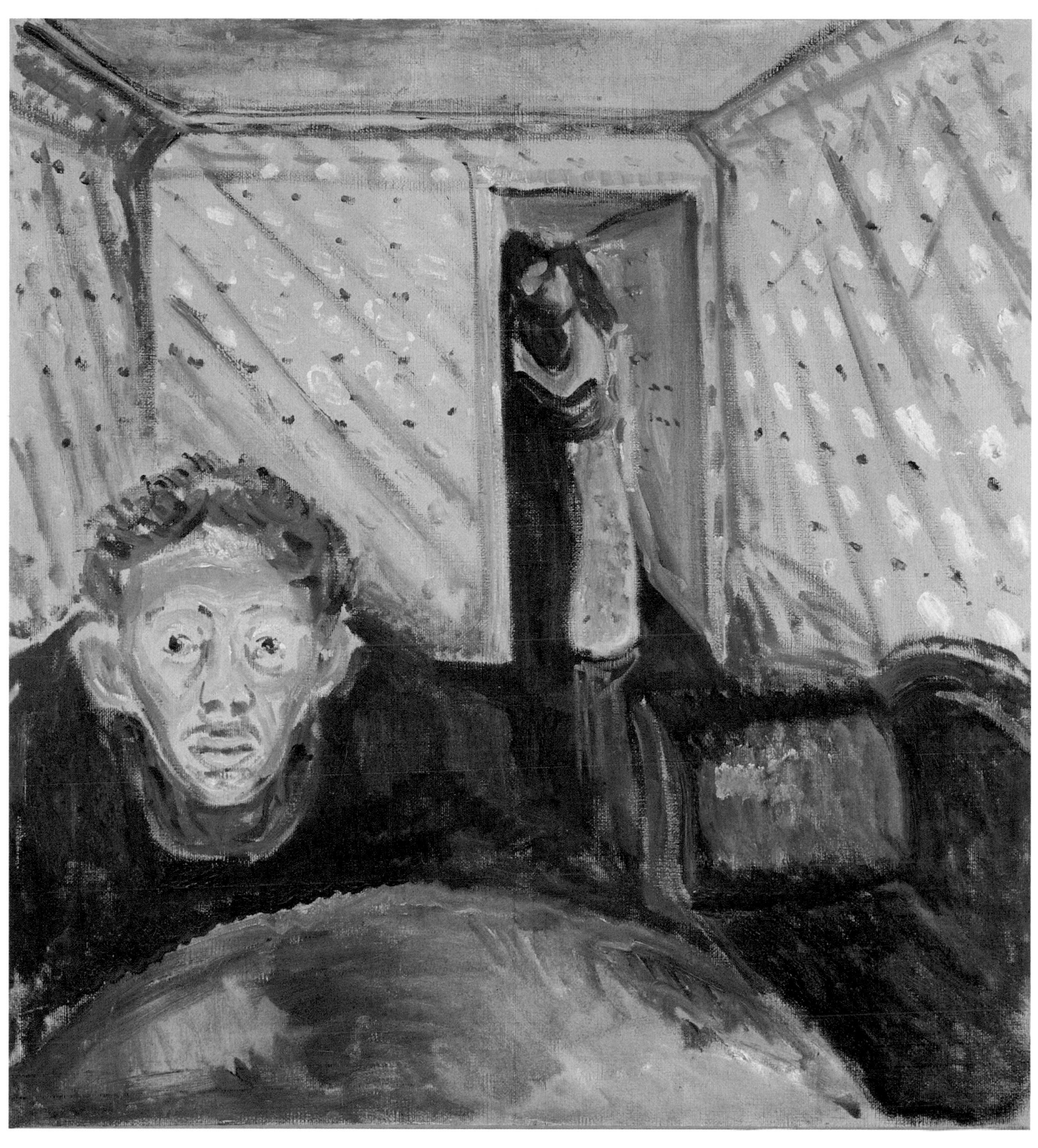

Cat. no. 77 *Jealousy* I, 1907
Oil on canvas, 89 x 82.5 cm
Munch-museet, Oslo

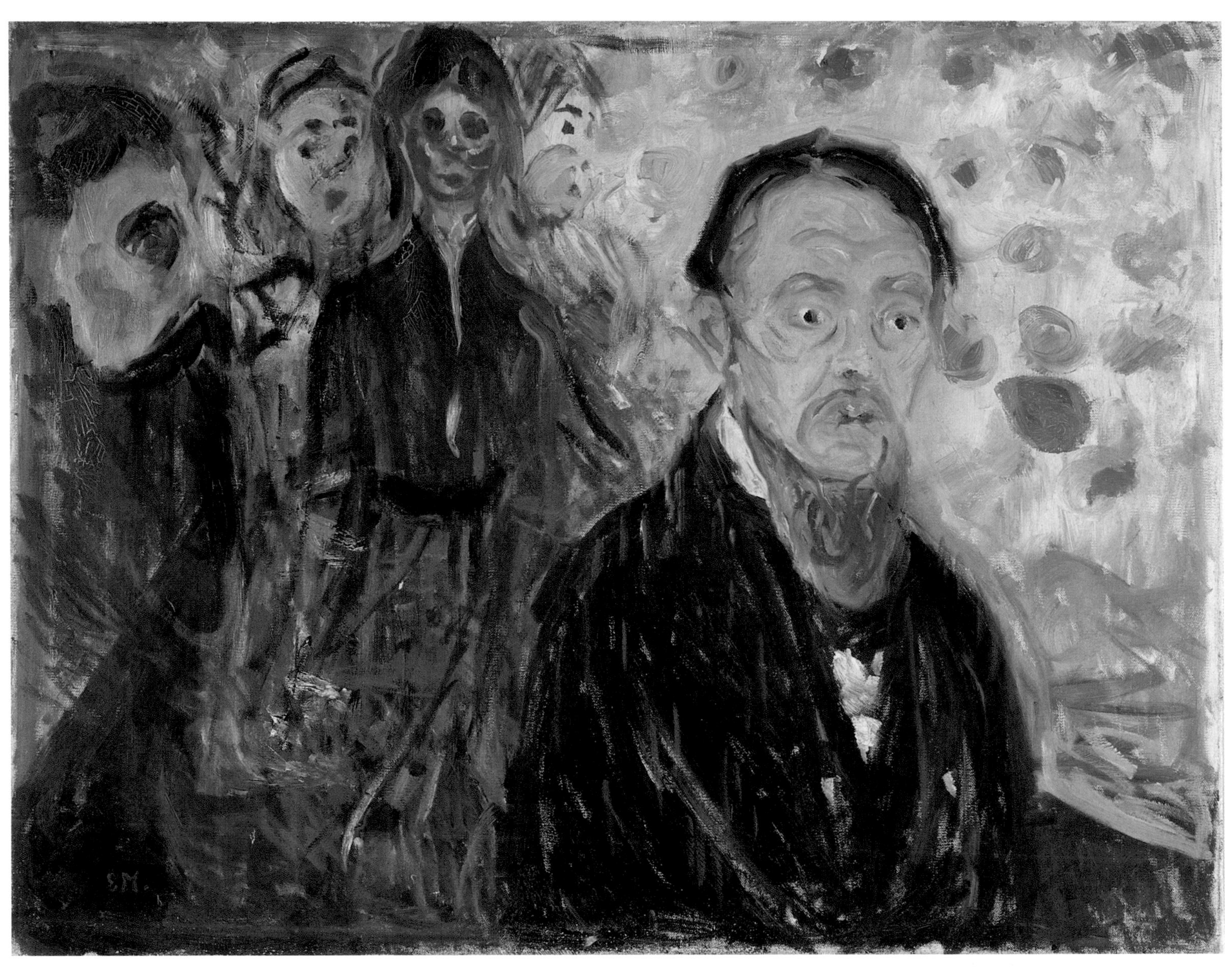

Cat. no. 78 *Surprise*, 1907
Oil on canvas, 85 x 110.5 cm
Munch-museet, Oslo

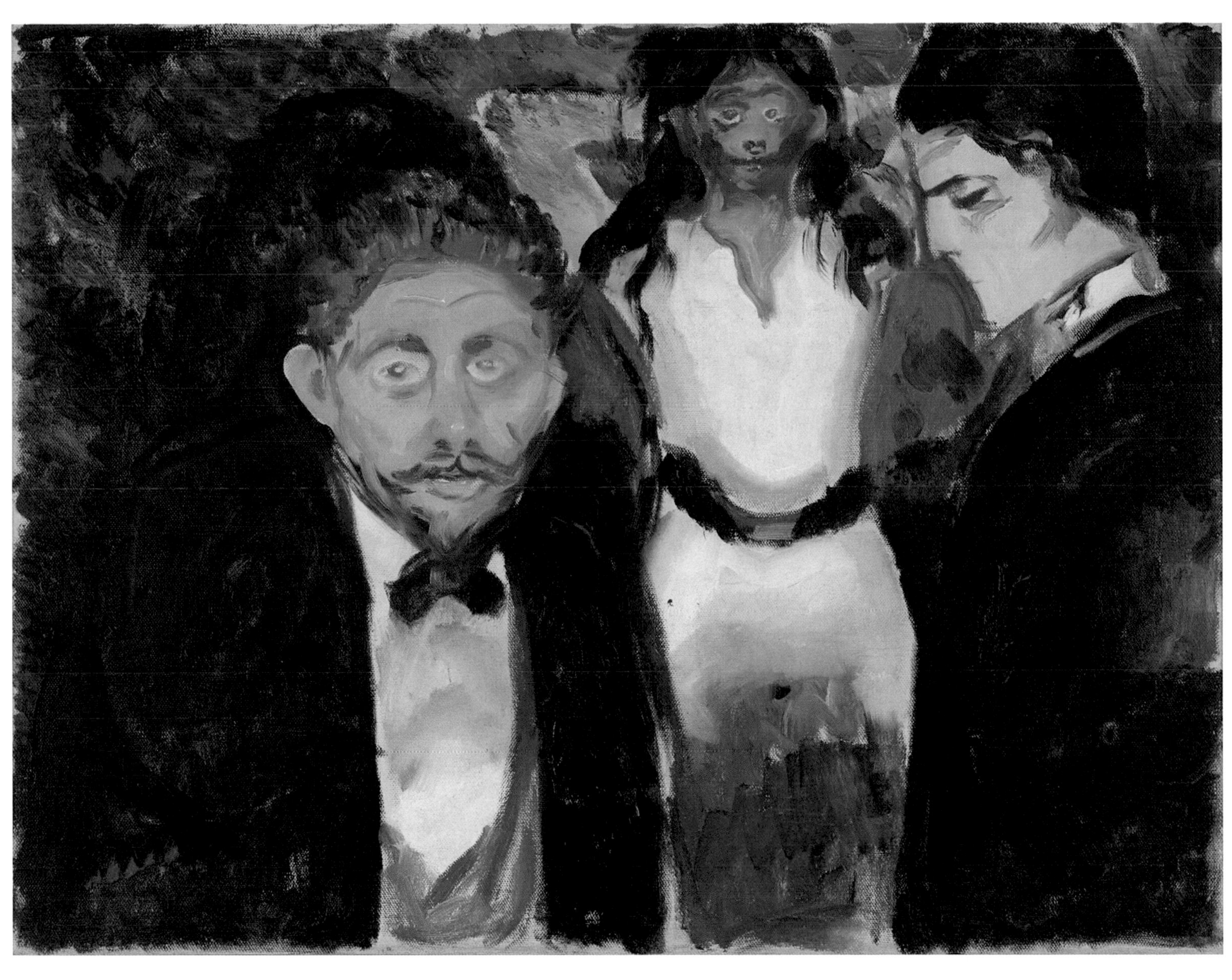

Cat. no. 79 *Jealousy* III, 1907
Oil on canvas, 75.5 x 98 cm
Munch-museet, Oslo

Melancholy

When Munch first presented the painting *Evening* (cat. no. 80) at the Autumn Exhibition in Kristiania in 1888, a critic for the *Aftenposten* wrote, "Technically speaking, E. Munch's *Evening*, no. 108, ranks even lower: a girl with a large, purple face under a yellow straw hat sitting on a blue lawn in front of a white house. The whole thing is so indescribably bad in every respect that it is almost comical. ..."[1] At first glance, this devastating review appears to have been written by a "color-blind" critic, as Jens Thiis expressed it, yet through the filter of his conservative view of art, he actually pointed out what made the painting modern—the monumentality of its foreground figure, its vivid coloration, and its color symbolism. This is the first work in which Munch set a figure cut off by the edge of the painting—his sister—against the characteristic coastal landscape of the Kristiania Fjord. Lost in thought, Laura gazes into the distance. The blue of her blouse and the sky are delicately interwoven with the green of the lawn and the white of the house. It describes the twilight of dusk and evokes a sense of the figure's loneliness and despondence.

The following year, Munch also exhibited *Inger on the Beach* under the title *Evening*, a painting for which his younger sister Inger posed as his model, sitting on a rock and staring straight ahead. Munch focused the horizonless composition on the figure, an almost patternlike form whose solitude and bowed posture mirrors her state of mind. While the interplay of figure and landscape motifs in these two *Evening* paintings evokes a mood of melancholy, Munch condensed that melancholy into despondence, sadness, and depression in *Night in St. Cloud*, a scene set in his room in St. Cloud (cat. no. 81). Although the Danish poet Emanuel Goldstein sat as model for the slumped figure at the window, this picture appears rather to reflect Munch's own emotional state after the death of his father. The shadow of the window frame describes a double cross on the floor of the empty room, and the man in the top hat seems about to dissolve into the darkness of the night. Emptiness, dissolution, darkness, and the shape of the cross allude to death, mourning, and loneliness; the interior is a mirror of the soul, the window an interface between the inner world and external reality. The shadow cast by the window frame becomes an unmistakable symbol of suffering in the mirror-image etching entitled *Night in St. Cloud* (*Moonlight*) of 1895 (cat. no. 82). Working in front of the same window he painted in *The Kiss* (cat. no. 43) in Nice in 1892, Munch realized *Girl at the Window* (cat. no. 84), a work whose diffuse blue light, round table, and window are reminiscent of *Night in St. Cloud*. The solitary girl stands out against the interior in her bluish-white nightdress and almost blends into the light falling through the window, from which she hides behind a curtain. In this painting, the curtain is a boundary between inside and outside, between melancholy and the pulsating life of the city.

The previous summer, Munch had captured the mood of resignation born of the agony of jealousy in his friend Jappe Nilssen in a painting characterized by emphatic simplification and stylization of line, form, and color (fig. 1). He exhibited the painting at the Autumn Salon under the title *Evening*, the same one he had given his pictures of Laura and Inger on the beach. Its color symbolism and striking lines inspired Christian Krohg to celebrate this painting as the first symbolist work created by a Norwegian painter: "He is the first and only [Norwegian artist] who pursues idealism, who dares to make nature, the model, etc., obedient to mood and changes mood in order to achieve more."[2] The source of this melancholy is expressed in the title variations *Jealousy* and *The Yellow Boat*. The latter alludes to the lovers' triangle involving the protagonist and the couple on the dock. In later versions of *Melancholy* (cat. nos. 85, 86), Munch adds a third figure on the dock, which now completes the triangle and prompts an interpretation of the background scene as a projection of the thoughts of the foreground figure. In the version from the Nasjonalgalleriet (cat. no. 85), which was presumably painted in Nice, the foreground figure has turned away from the beach scene.

The woodcut entitled *Melancholy* I of 1896 (cat. nos. 87, 88) recalls the painted version of 1891, which Munch adapted as a mirror-image with a lower horizon line. In many prints, Munch experimented with the motif and a series of different color combinations using one or two wood blocks, each of which he sawed in two at

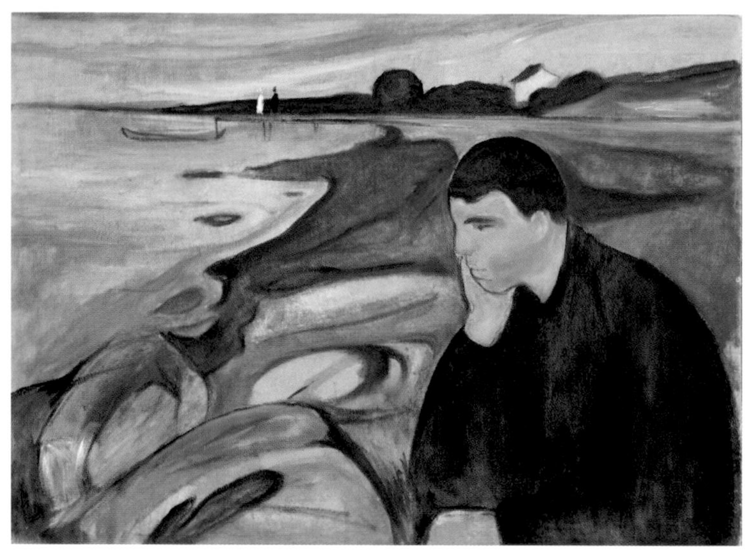

some point. The dock with the two figures and the boat are recognizable in the background of the early monochrome variations, but both motifs gradually disappear beneath successive layers of paint and as a result of the line along which the plates were cut, which leaves most of the prints concentrated on the foreground figure and its relationship to the landscape. Some of these variations are printed with sparing applications of paint and reveal the vertical grain pattern of the color plate in opposition to the horizontal grain lines and motif on the main printing plate. The overlapping layers of paint produced prints with a transparent, surface-oriented character, in which the body of the foreground figure blends into the shoreline in most cases (cat. no. 87), but is encircled by the sea in several others (cat. no. 88). Munch completed the woodcut version entitled *Melancholy* III (cat. no. 89) in 1902, possibly assuming that the plates for the first version had been lost during shipment from Norway to Berlin. This variation is a mirror-image rendition of the first woodcut version, and thus corresponds to the painted version.

Munch did another variation of the theme in the black, red, and green woodcut entitled *Melancholy* II (cat. no. 90), which shows a woman sitting on the beach. Munch cut the plate into three parts, one of which comprises her red dress, while the section for the shore contains the hollowed areas for the arm, neck, and chin and a few fine lines suggesting the hair that covers the face. In contrast to the image of Nilssen, the woman's face is obscured and thus anonymous; she is also sharply separated from her surroundings by the red color of her dress, which signals activity. She is totally immersed in herself and cut off from the outside world. Her body expresses her despair. A similar posture is found in the *Female Nude on the Beach* (cat. no. 91), a slightly larger painting executed in openly spaced brushstrokes. The nude woman is turned slightly away from the viewer and more completely integrated into the composition, as she is not cut off by the edge of the picture.

In *Melancholy* (*Laura*) (cat. no. 92), Munch intensifies the expression of passivity,

> I had the melancholy woman sit at the window, at the bright red table—she had to look large and massive and monumental in her dark, mute, boundless sadness—the melancholy woman I had seen in the asylum was sitting just that way—she didn't recognize her sister, who spoke lovingly to her—she understood nothing—her large black eyes were dull—unmoved, she stared blankly straight ahead.[3]

Here, melancholy is not depicted as a temporary state of mind or mood of sadness but instead as a state of severe psychogenic depression. Munch depicts his sister Laura, who was described as melancholy even as a child, sitting in the corner between the window and the reflected sunlight in a setting of vague spatial relationships. She is lost in thought. The tabletop is turned up and aligned with the pictorial plane. The pattern of the tablecloth calls to mind the brain sections published in journals of the day to demonstrate neurological illnesses. Munch had quite probably seen such images during his years in Berlin and presumably used this indexing gesture as a means of visualizing Laura's psychological disorder. DB

1 H-k in *Aftenposten*, quoted and translated from Jens Thiis, *Edvard Munch og Hans Samtid*, Oslo 1933, p. 148.
2 Christian Krohg, quoted and translated from ibid., p. 184.
3 Quoted and translated from Arne Eggum, *Edvard Munch. Malerei—Skizzen und Studien*, Oslo 1984, p. 164.

1 *Melancholy*, 1891,
oil on canvas, 72 x 98 cm,
private collection

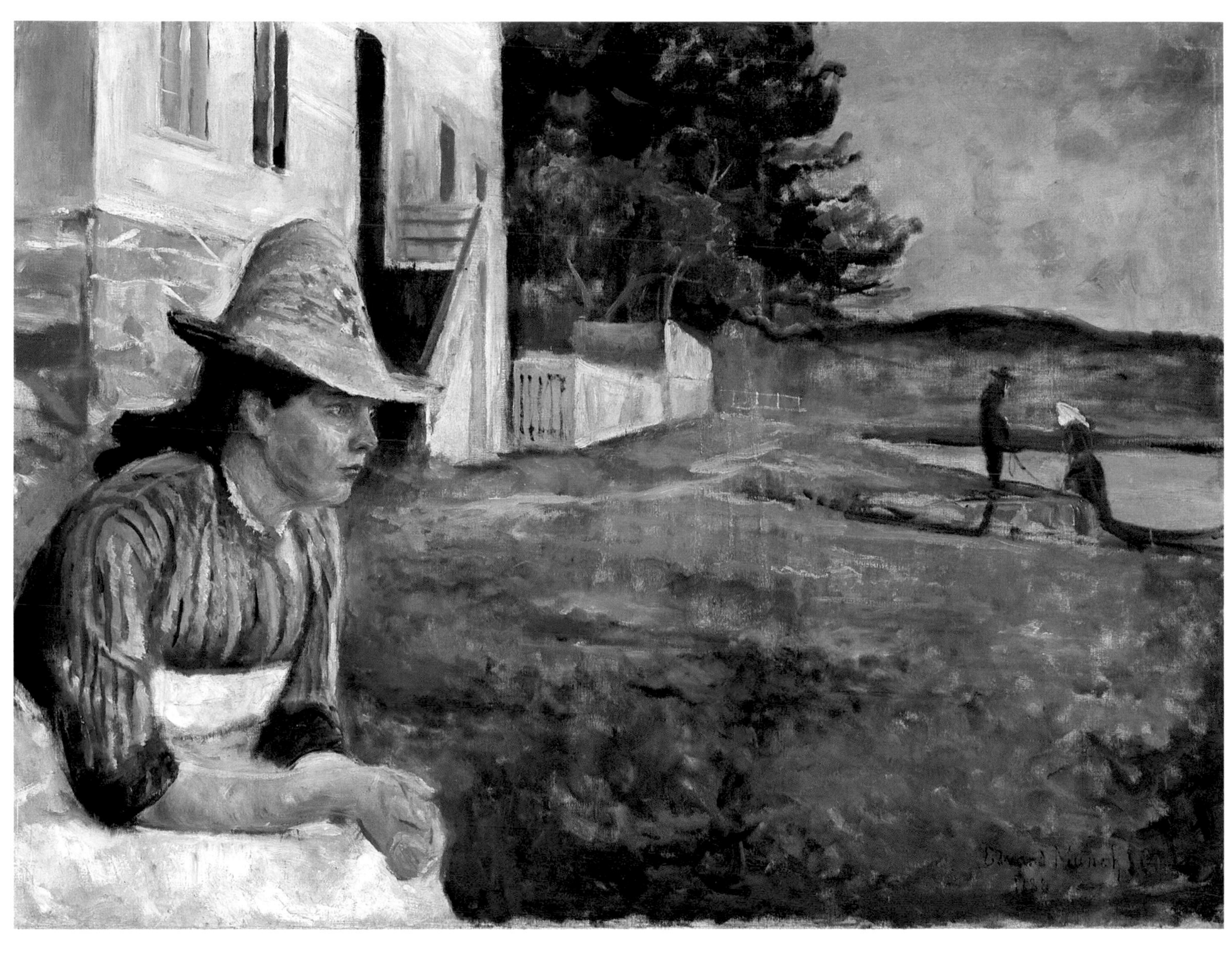

Cat. no. 80 *Evening*, 1888
Oil on canvas, 75 x 100 cm
Museo Thyssen-Bornemisza, Madrid

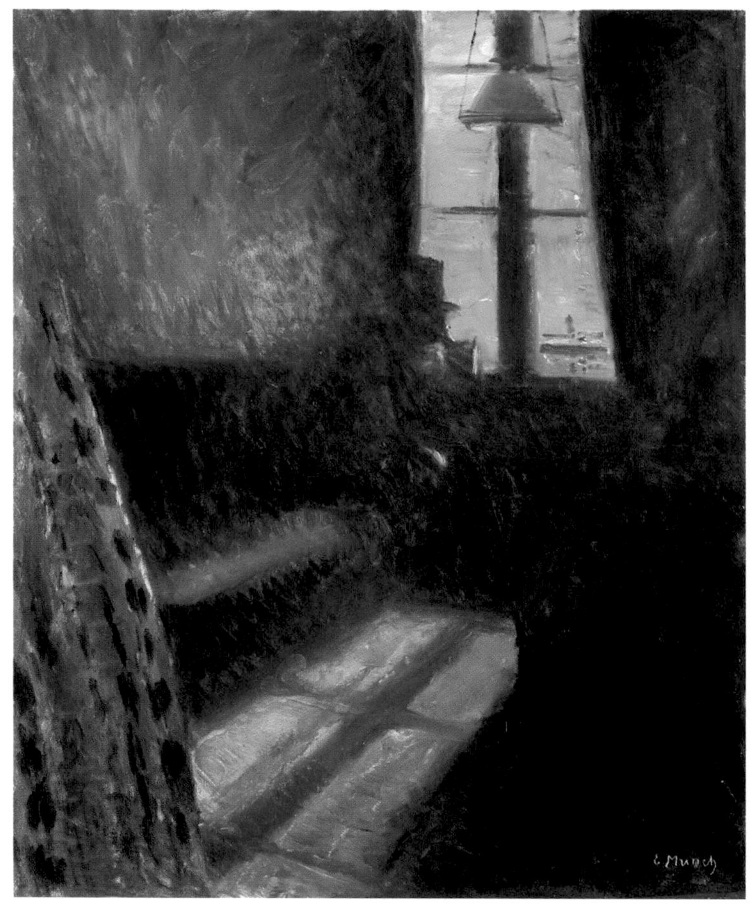

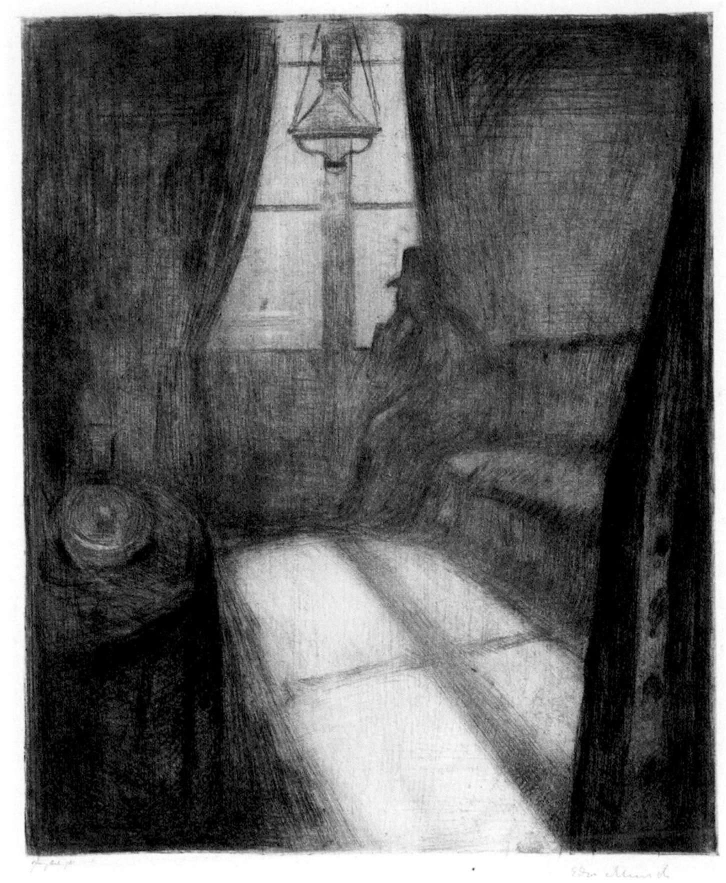

Cat. no. 81 *Night at St. Cloud*, 1890
Oil on canvas, 64.5 x 54 cm
Nasjonalgalleriet, Oslo

Cat. no. 82 *Night at St. Cloud (Moonlight)*, 1895
Etching on paper, 31 x 25.5 cm
Albertina, Vienna

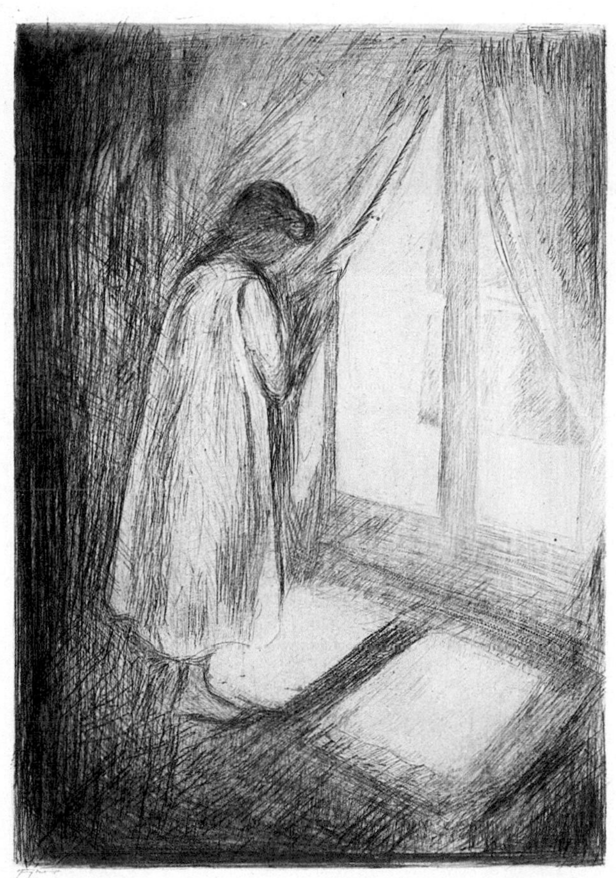

Cat. no. 83 *Girl at the Window,* 1894
Etching on paper, 20.7 x 14.5 cm
Munch-museet, Oslo

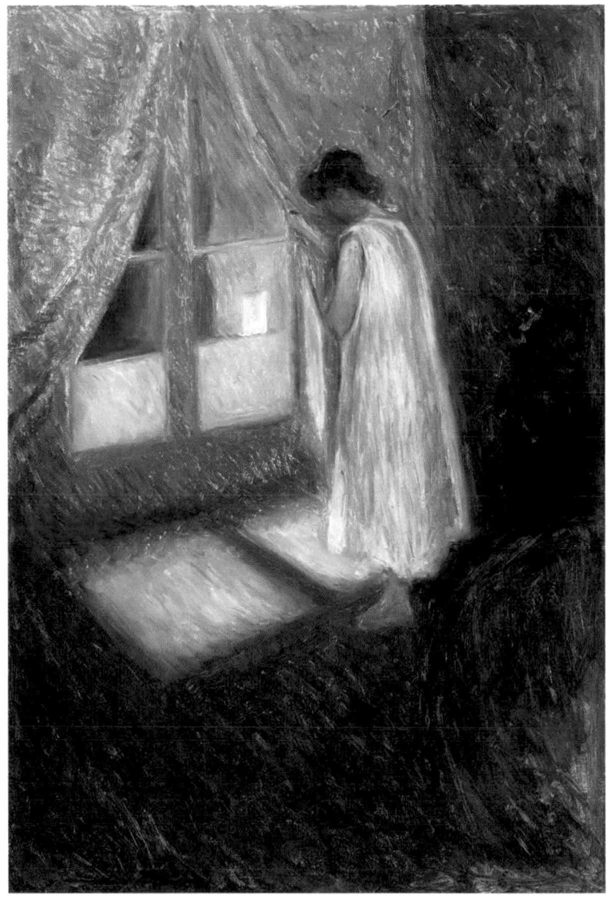

Cat. no. 84 *Girl at the Window,* 1892
Oil on canvas, 96.5 x 65.4 cm
Art Institute of Chicago, Searle Family Trust and Goldabelle McComb Finn endowments; Charles H. and Mary F. S. Worcester Collection

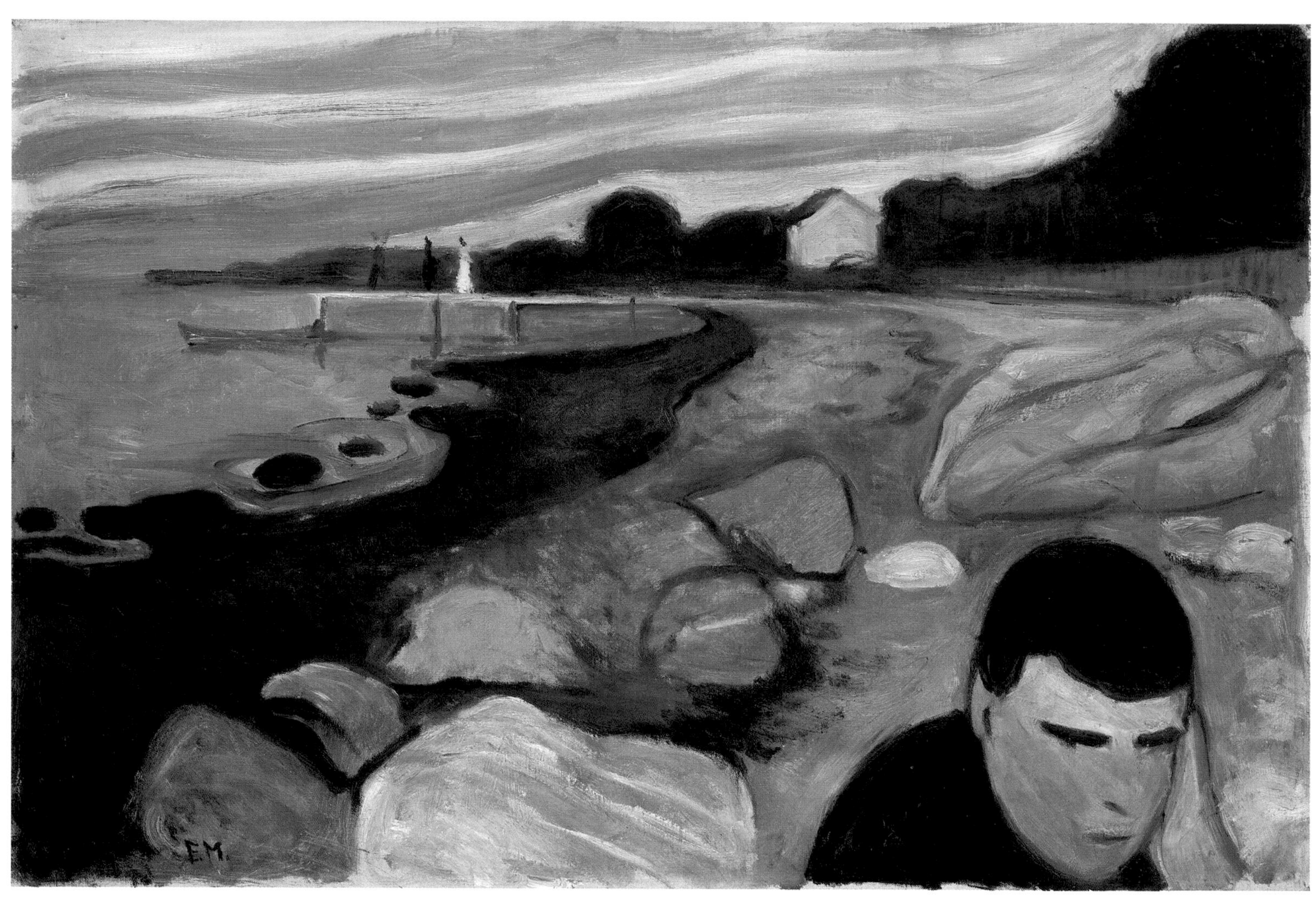

Cat. no. 85 *Melancholy*, 1892
Oil on canvas, 64 x 96 cm
Nasjonalgalleriet, Oslo

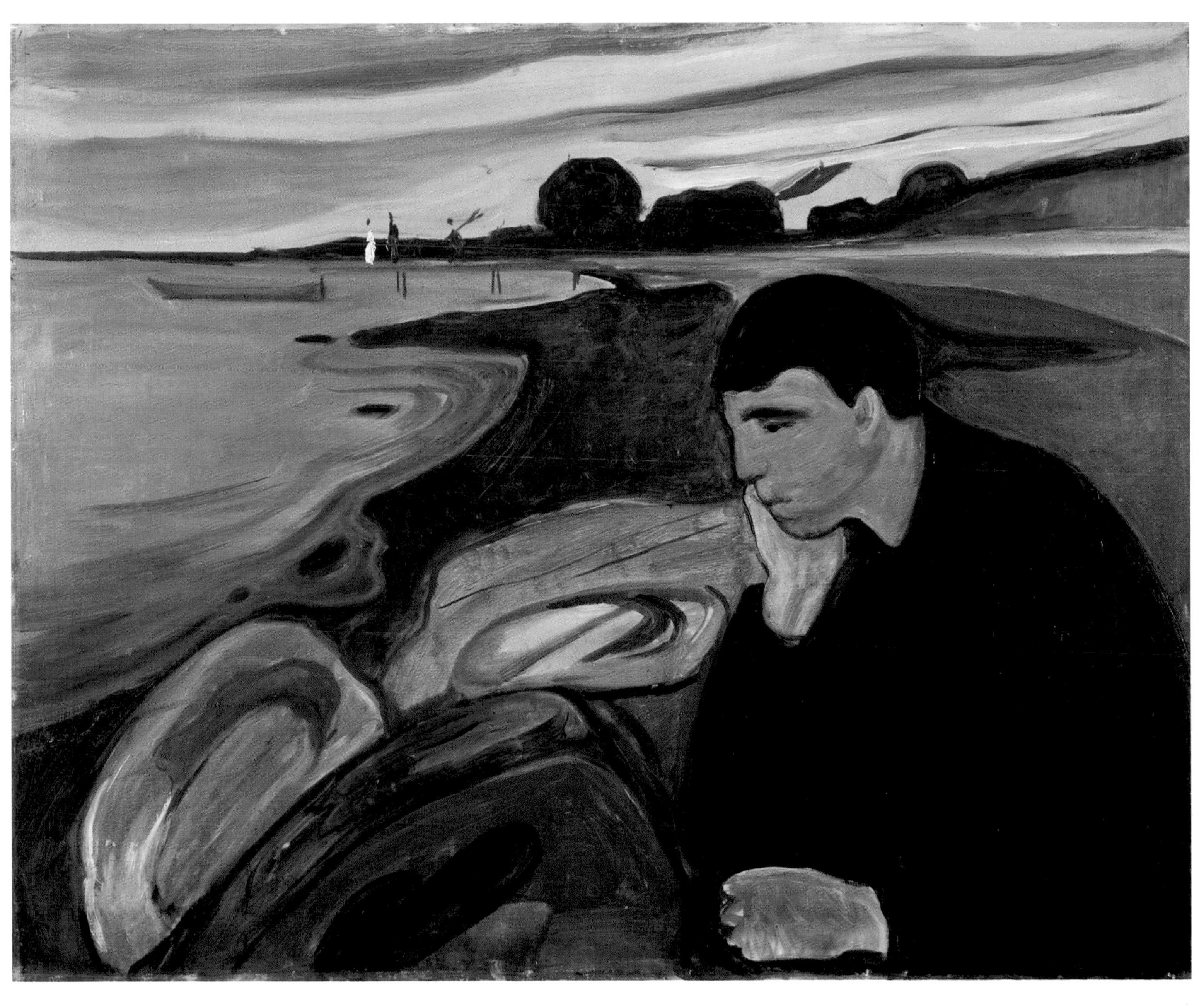

Cat. no. 86 *Melancholy*, 1894–95
Oil on canvas, 70 x 95.8 cm
Rasmus Meyers Samlinger, Bergen Kunstmuseum

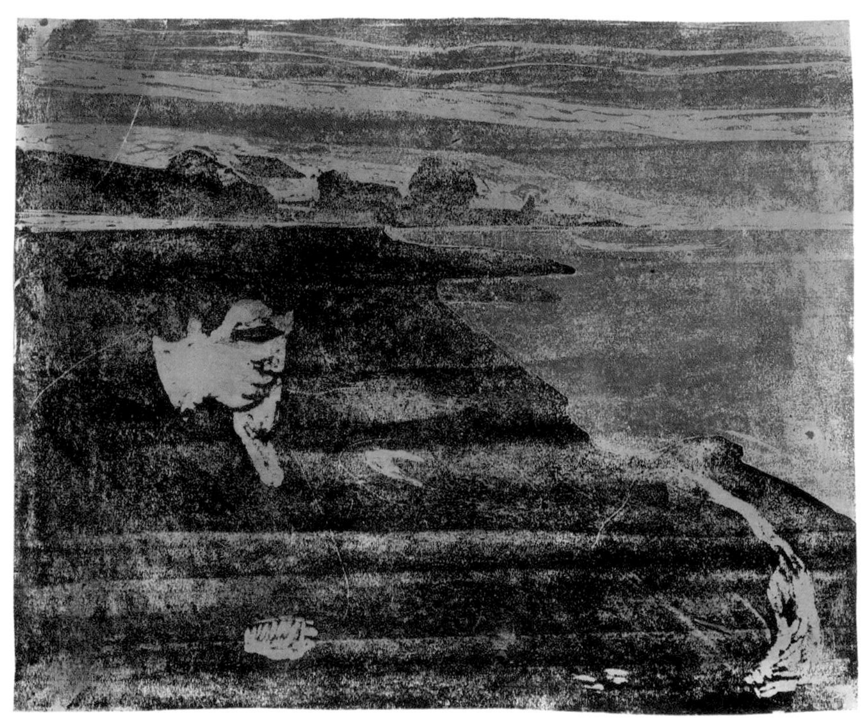

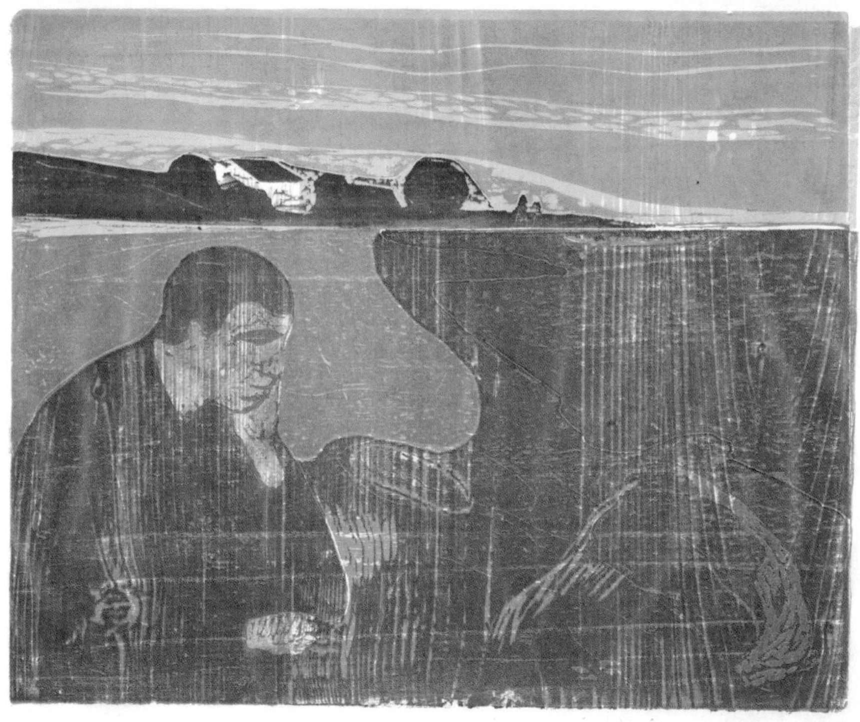

Cat. no. 87 *Melancholy* I, 1896
Color woodcut on paper, 36.8 x 44.5 cm
Private collection, Canada, courtesy of W. Wittrock, Berlin

Cat. no. 88 *Melancholy* I, 1896
Color woodcut on paper, 37.6 x 45.5 cm
Museum of Fine Arts, Boston, William Francis Warden Fund

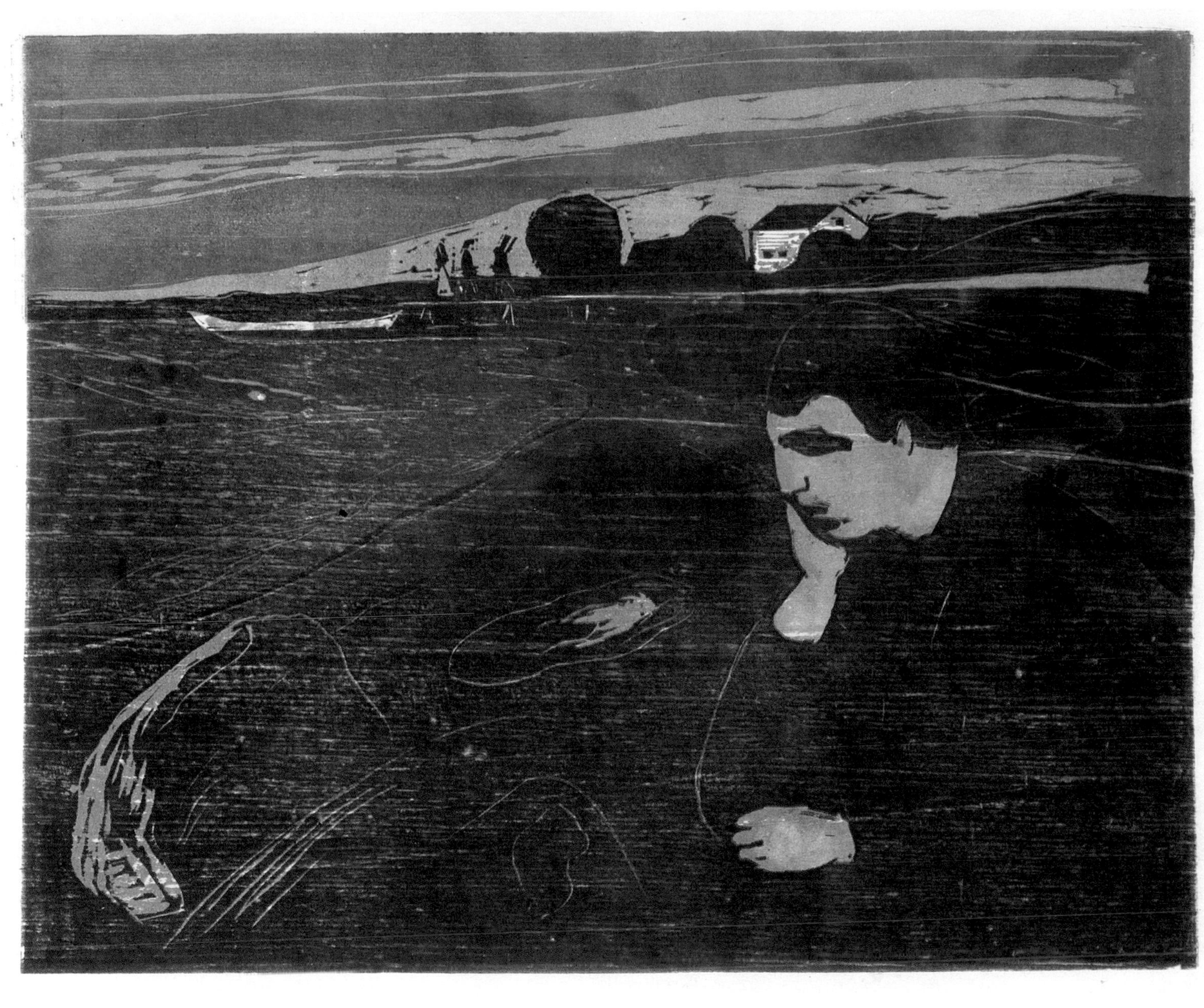

Cat. no. 89 *Melancholy* III, 1902
Color woodcut on paper, 37.6 x 47.1 cm
Epstein Family Collection

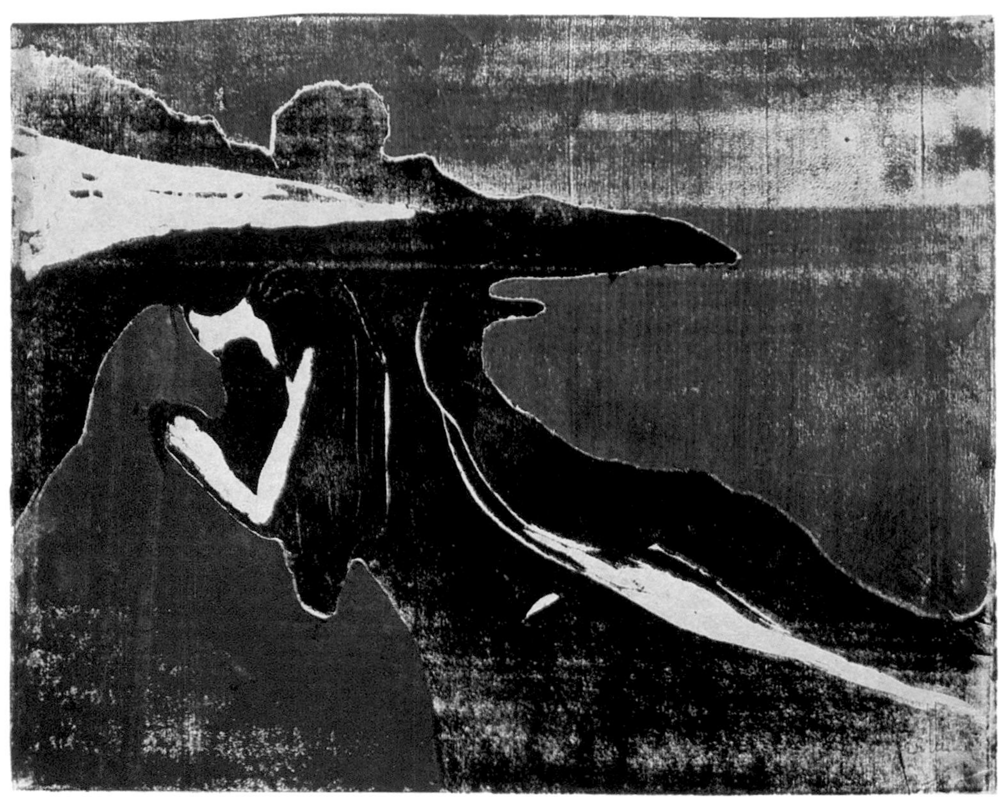

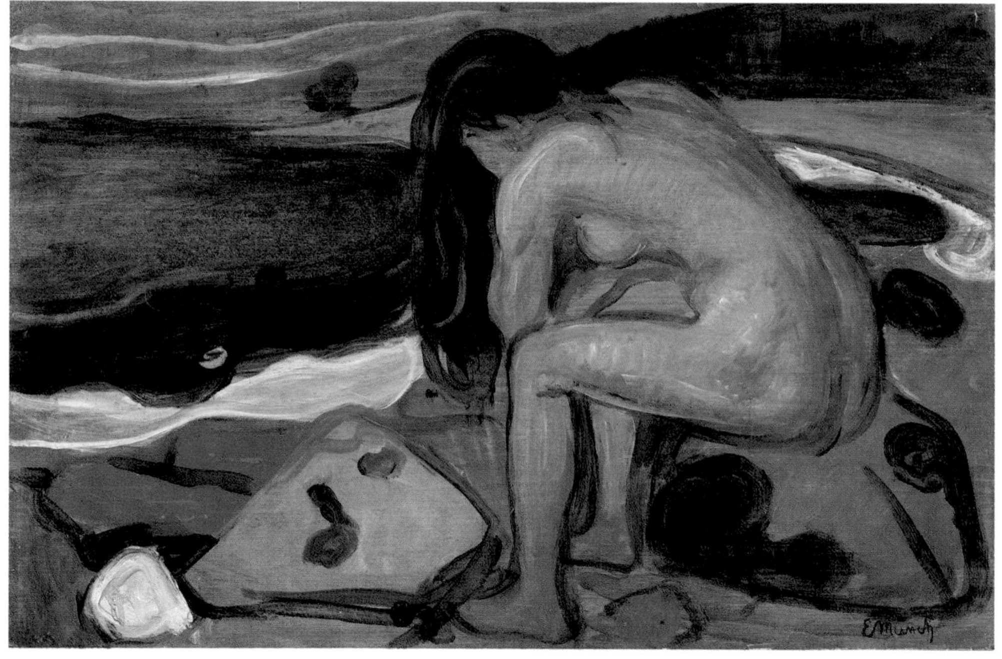

Cat. no. 90 *Melancholy* II, 1898
Color woodcut on paper, 33 x 42.2 cm
Epstein Family Collection

Cat. no. 91 *Female Nude on the Beach*, c. 1898
Oil on wood, 39.5 x 59.5 cm
Private collection

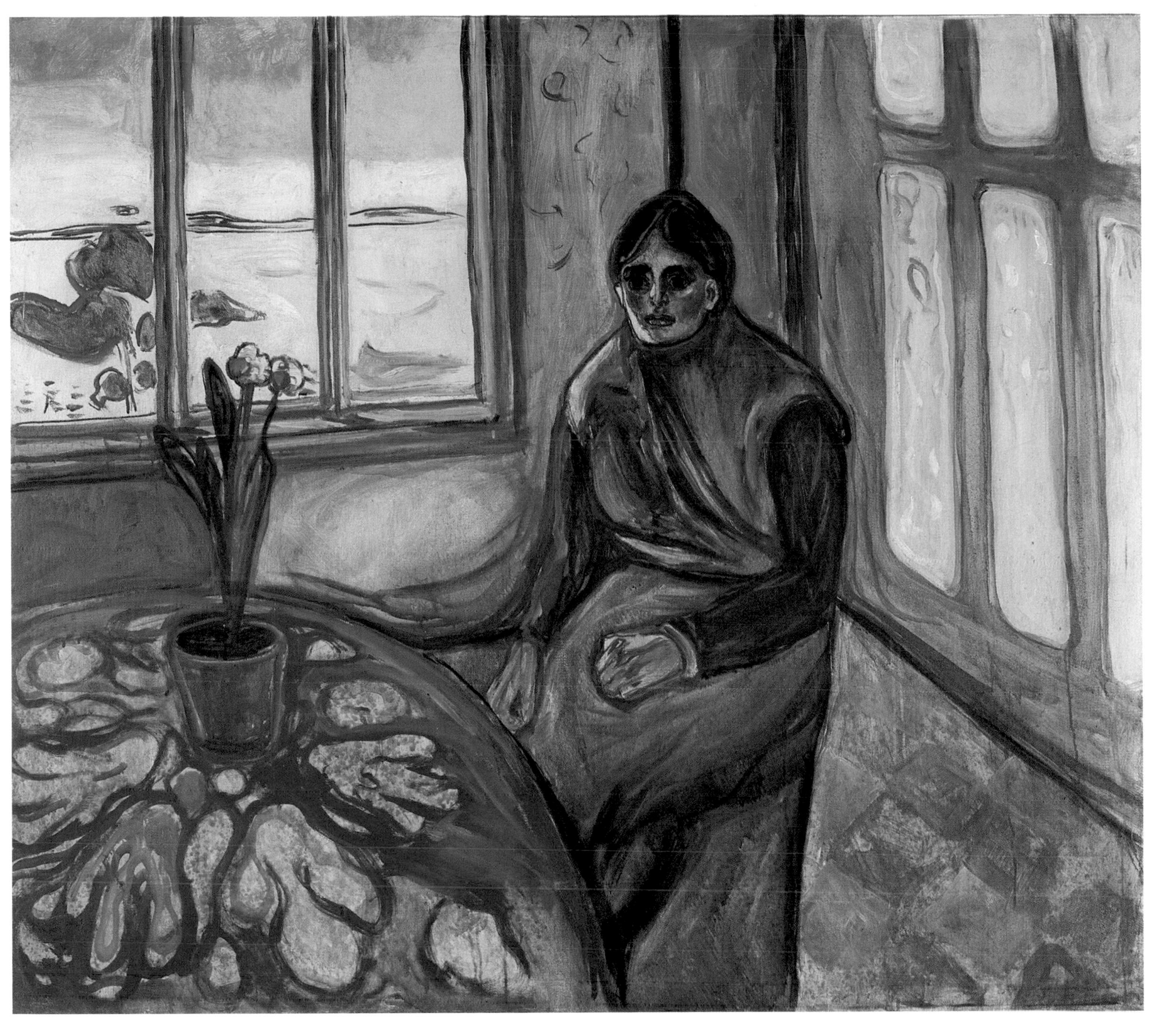

Cat. no. 92 *Melancholy (Laura)*, 1899 (1900)
Oil on canvas, 110 x 126 cm
Munch-museet, Oslo

The Lonely Ones

It is magnificent to look out over a limitless desert of water in the endless solitude of the seashore under a cloudy sky. ... And thus I became the Capuchin monk, the picture became the dune, but that to which I was to gaze out upon with longing, the sea, was missing entirely. Nothing can be sadder or more discomforting than this position in the world: the only spark of life in the vast realm of death, the solitary midpoint in a solitary circle.

In these words, Heinrich von Kleist recorded his "Sentiments in Response to [Caspar David] Friedrich's Seascape" *Monk at the Sea*.[1] He describes the rear-facing figure as a means of projection for the viewer, who through its eyes becomes a witness to a stunning, overwhelming spectacle of nature. He is not merely confronted with a pictorial scene but invited to take part in contemplation. This characteristic figure is strikingly different from Munch's foreground figures, which often move threateningly towards the viewer.

In the print entitled *Young Woman on the Beach* of 1896 (cat. no. 93–97), Munch concentrates the action of the scene on the figure of a woman with long hair dressed in white, who faces away from the viewer. She is turned towards the sea, and thus cannot communicate with the viewer. Unlike Friedrich's figure, she is not embedded in an overwhelming natural spectacle but positioned instead within a small section of a barren strip of beach. Munch achieved soft transitions using a combination of polished aquatint and drypoint etching techniques. The plate was presumably colored individually for each of the eleven surviving prints with small dollies soaked in various different colors. Gerd Woll distinguishes seven states, noting differences that may be the result of subsequent processing of the plate as well as coloring variations.[2] She identifies different lengths of the woman's hair as well as variations in the rocks and the configuration of the beach. Different color schemes reflect different times of the day. The version designated as state I, colored sparingly in shades of grayish-purple and yellow (cat. no. 97), exhibits a particularly sensitive handling of light. The reflection of the setting sun is visible in the delicate yellow on the contours of the figure and the rocks. In state II (cat. no. 95), however, the contrast between the—in some places darker—blues, the yellow, and the light pink identifies the moon as the source of light. The radiant white garment in a variation classified as state VII (cat. no. 93), in which some of the contours are reinforced in pencil, becomes a source of light itself. In contrast to Friedrich's rear-facing figures, however, it does not offer a vantage point for observation of a natural spectacle but is the symbolic medium of a mood and a projection surface that reflects the natural spectacle itself.

The first draft versions of the motif for *Young Woman on the Beach* date to 1891–92, about the same time Munch completed the first version of *Two Human Beings*, a painting that was lost in a shipwreck in 1901. The surviving photograph shows that Munch translated the motif almost literally as a mirror image into an etching (fig. 1). The light-colored female figure is now complemented by a dark male figure presented as a silhouette viewed from the rear. The man stands next to the woman with his legs spread apart, his hands in his pockets, and his head turned slightly towards her. Munch renders the two genders in dark-light contrast as opposing poles; their rigid postures, underscored by the calmness of the sea, indicate speechless silence between man and woman. Their figures are projection surfaces for Munch's personal experiences and for the viewer as well. Although the man and woman are close

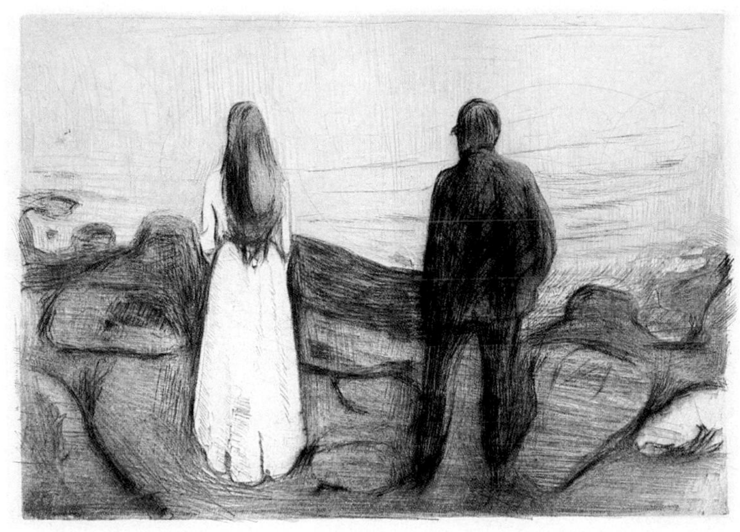

1 *The Lonely Ones (Two Human Beings)*, 1894, drypoint on copperplate on paper, 15 x 21.2 cm, Munch-museet, Oslo

to one another, the distance between them appears impossible to overcome. The two remain alone with no view of a horizon in the distance.

For the most part, the color woodcut entitled *The Lonely Ones* of 1899 (cat. nos. 98–103) conforms to the painting, although it is more highly stylized. Nearly all of the prints were presumably made with a wood block previously cut into three sections. The man's silhouette is connected to the strip of coastline, while the woman and the sea stand apart as distinct second and third forms. The sky and the sea share the same color; the horizon is marked by a fine horizontal line. Woll assumes that Munch did not print the multicolored prints until 1917.[3] The color combination and the vivid coloration support this argumentation. In the many different color combinations, some of which were hand-colored, Munch experimented with a wide range of different relationships between the protagonists. Most of these variations are characterized by the difference between the man and the woman, as the male figure blends with the color of the seashore as a part of the beach plate, while the woman stands out against the background in up to three colors. In other variations, the man's legs actually seem to disappear into the reddish-brown (cat. no. 102) or dark blue (cat. no. 98) of the beach, and his silhouette almost becomes a separate tongue of land that splits off from the beach line. In another hand-colored variation (cat. no. 99), Munch replaced this blending effect with a dark outline drawing of the man, thus adding a threatening aspect to the polar relationship. In a somewhat earlier version (cat. no. 101), he added a red band of color resembling a huge pool of blood below the two figures and colored the water purple. Munch expanded the motif in some prints (cat. no. 103) by adding a sun or moon and the phallus-shaped reflection on the water's surface, using paper templates, placing these elements between the two figures and thus incorporating the natural spectacle into the scene as in Friedrich's paintings. The division of the woman into a yellow and a blue half is internal and is not affected by ambient light.

Munch also used the templates for the moon and the sun in several later prints of the color woodcut *Two Women on the Shore* (cat. no. 109), the first variations of which were done at about the same time as those of *The Lonely Ones*. The standing female silhouette resembles the figure in *The Lonely Ones*, but is turned nearly ninety degrees towards the viewer, while her face and hair merge into an impersonal form and thus retain the character of a figure viewed from the rear. She shares the same form in the wood block cut into three sections with the seated old woman, whose skull-like face is turned towards the viewer. This figure is printed in black and represents the opposite pole to the figure dressed in white and framed in orange, thus emphasizing the oppositions of youth and age, virgin and widow, life and death. Munch continued to produce color variations of this print into the 1920s. Some of these were overprinted with a linoleum plate (cat. nos. 106, 107), while others were hand-colored (cat. no. 105).

Unlike many of his other graphic works, the woodcut entitled *Two Women on the Shore* cannot be associated directly with any of Munch's surviving paintings. However, similarities in the persons in the group call to mind the image of his aunt Karen Bjølstad, shown seated and dressed in black, and of his sister Inger, dressed in white, in the painting *Mother and Daughter* (fig. 5, p. 58), which the artist may have selected as a starting point. During the 1930s, Munch did two painted versions, of which one (cat. no. 110) relates in virtually every detail to the woodcut and the later prints (cat. nos. 108, 109) made from it, to include the division of the landscape into two distinct areas of color—an example of Munch's use of elements of his graphic works in paintings.

The moon or the sun and its reflection also appear in another variation of the theme of the Lonely Ones, namely in the woodcut entitled *Moonlight on the Beach* of 1912 (Sch. 387, Woll 419). The solitary female figure seen from the rear is turned even more markedly away from the viewer and appears to invite the observer to join her in contemplating the "magnificent, endless solitude of the seashore" against the moonlit background. DB

1 Heinrich von Kleist, "Empfindungen vor Friedrichs Seelandschaft," in *Berliner Abendblätter*, 12th issue, Oct. 13, 1810, reprint Wiesbaden 1980, pp. 47–48.

2 Gerd Woll, *Edvard Munch. The Complete Graphic Works*, London 2001, pp. 79–81.

3 *Ibid.*, pp. 163–164.

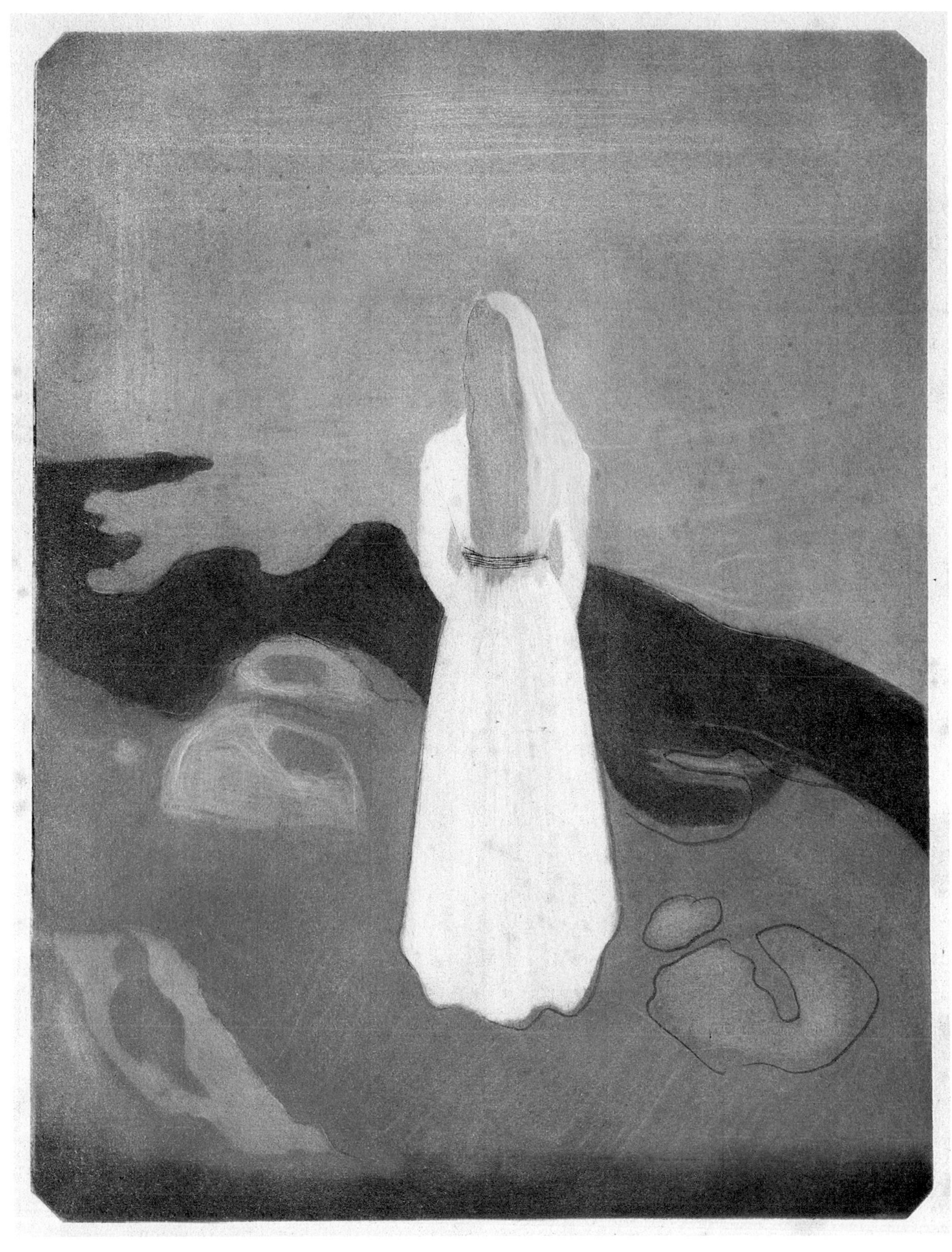

Cat. no. 93 *Young Woman on the Beach*, 1896
Aquatint and etching on paper, 28.2 x 21.3 cm
Epstein Family Collection

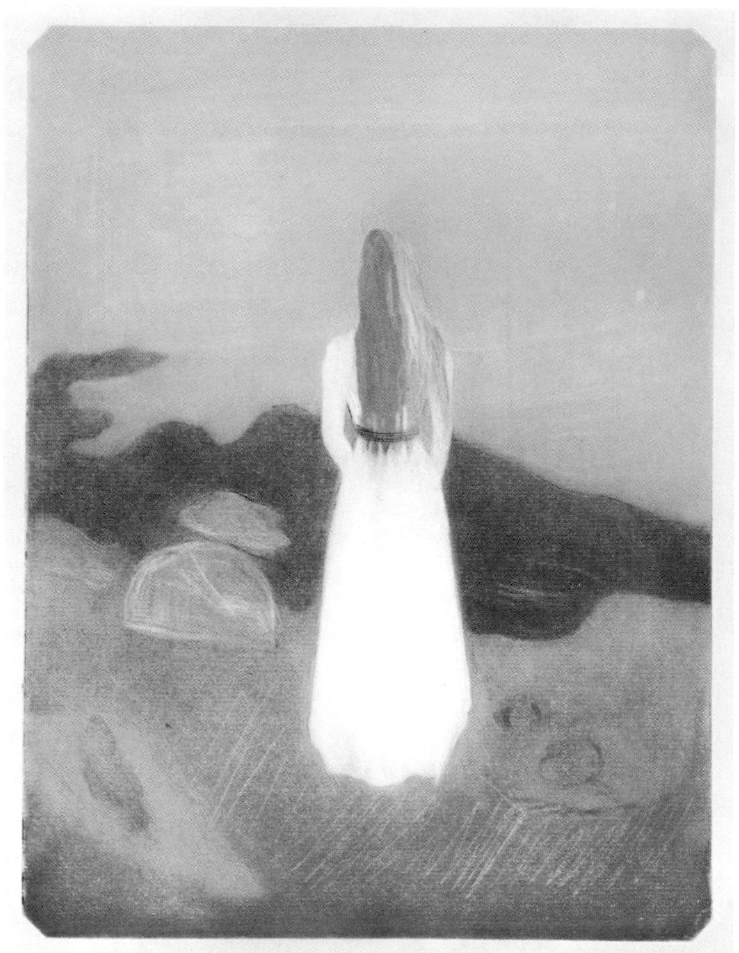

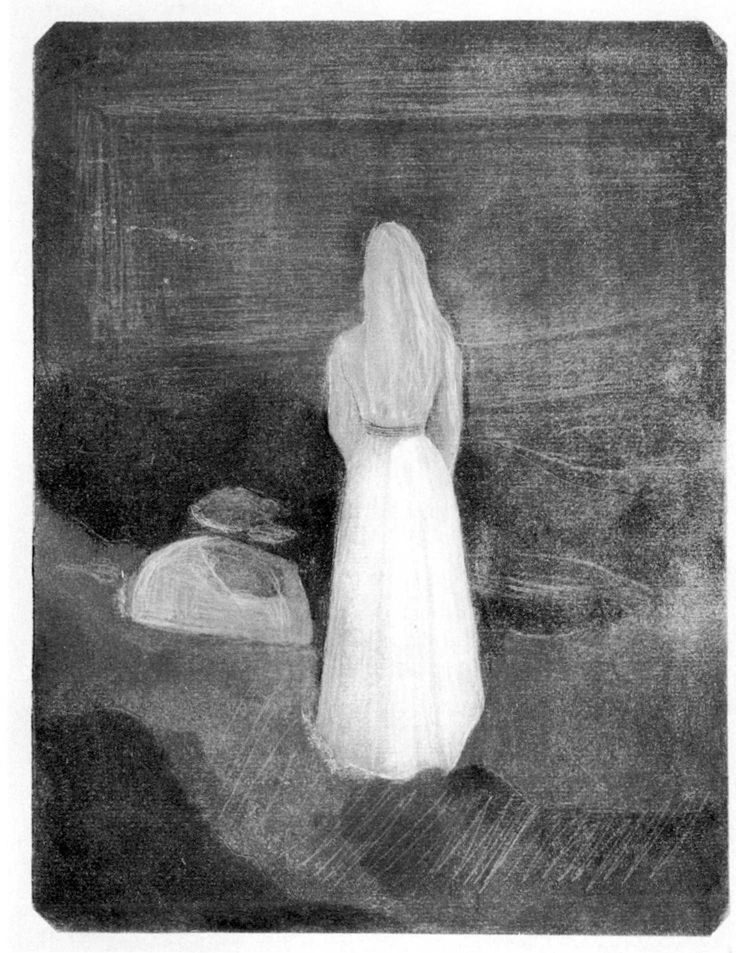

Cat. no. 94 *Young Woman on the Beach*, 1896
Aquatint and etching on paper, 28.8 x 21.9 cm
Collection of Catherine Woodard & Nelson Blitz, Jr.

Cat. no. 95 *Young Woman on the Beach*, 1896
Aquatint and etching on paper, 28.8 x 21.9 cm
Collection E.W.K., Bern

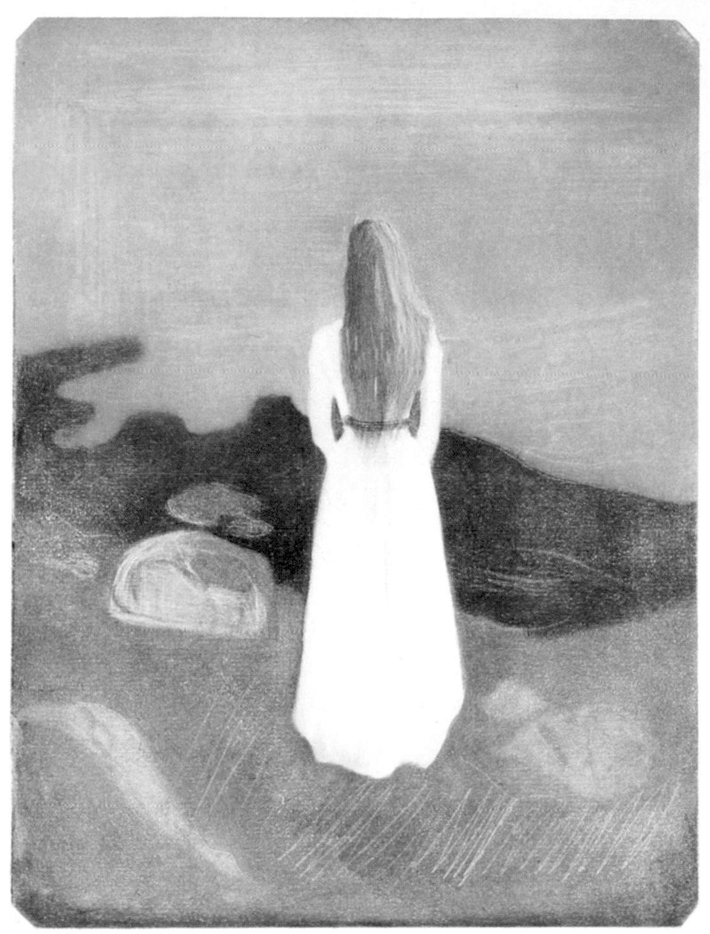

Cat. no. 96 *Young Woman on the Beach*, 1896
Aquatint and etching on paper, 28.5 x 21.6 cm
Munch-museet, Oslo

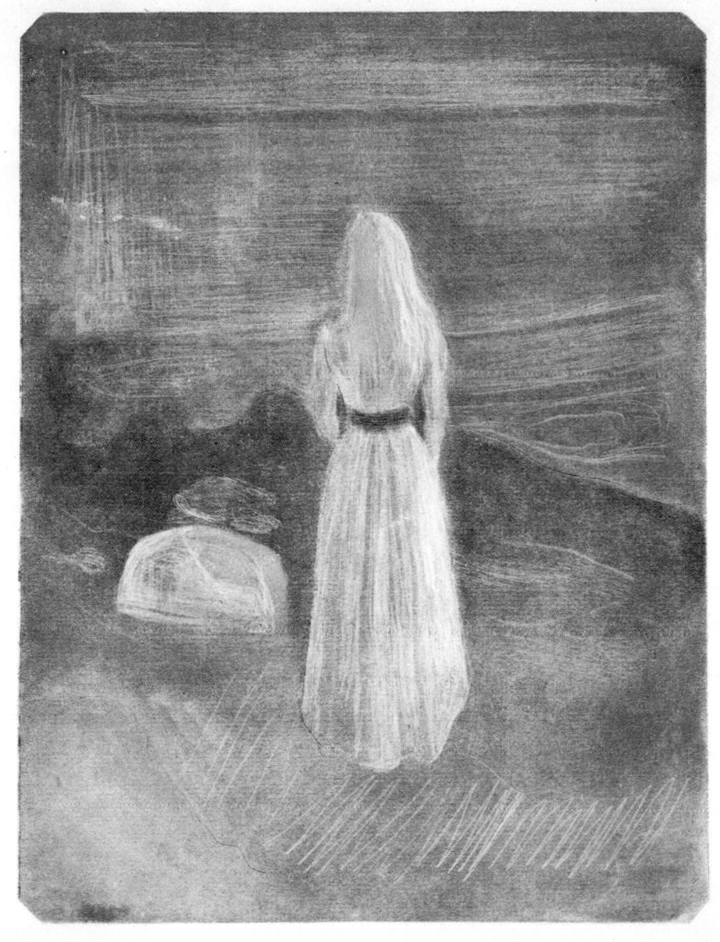

Cat. no. 97 *Young Woman on the Beach*, 1896
Aquatint and etching on paper, 28.7 x 21.6 cm
Art Institute of Chicago, Clarence Buckingham Collection

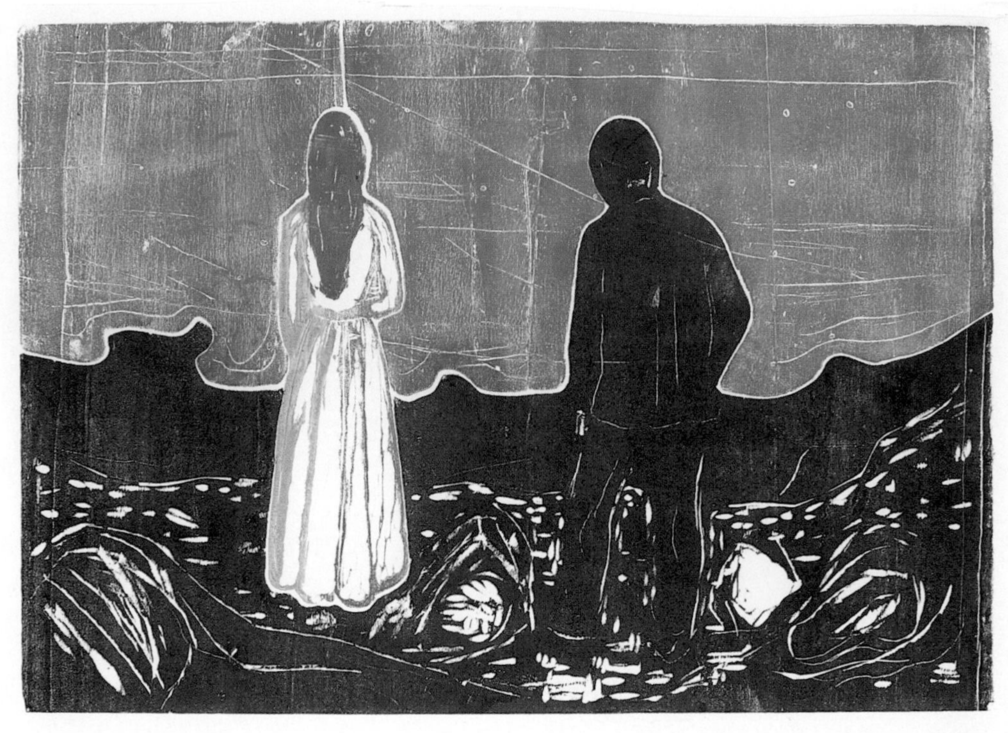

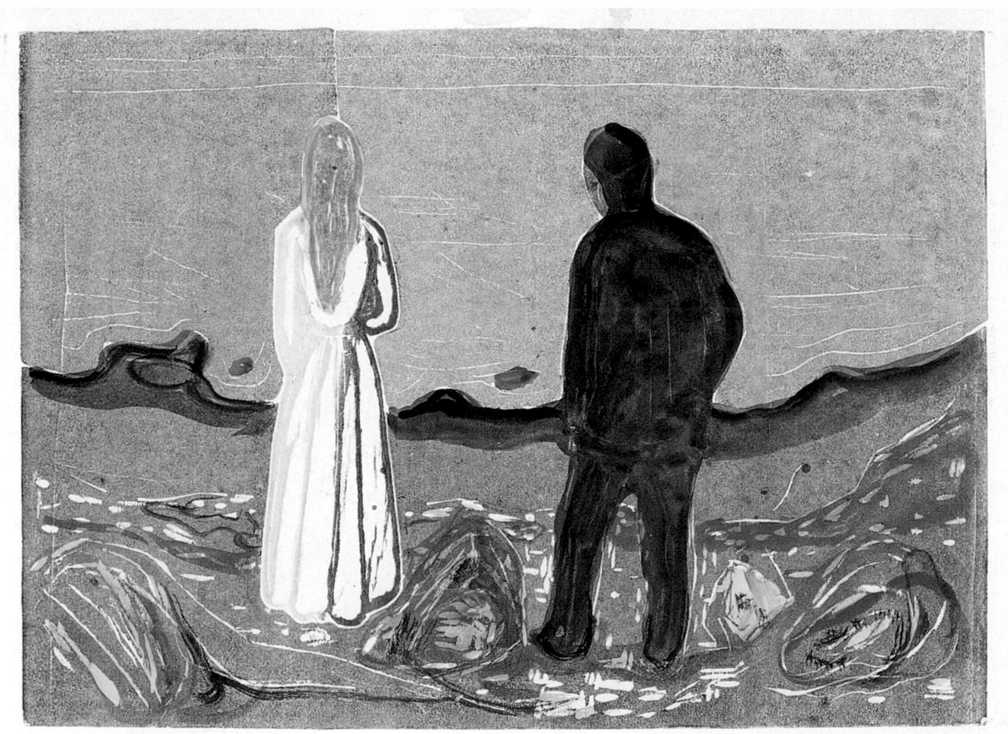

Cat. no. 98 *The Lonely Ones (Two Human Beings)*, 1899
Color woodcut on paper, 39.5 x 55.5 cm
Munch-museet, Oslo

Cat. no. 99 *The Lonely Ones (Two Human Beings)*, 1899
Hand-colored color woodcut on paper, 39.5 x 55 cm
Munch-museet, Oslo

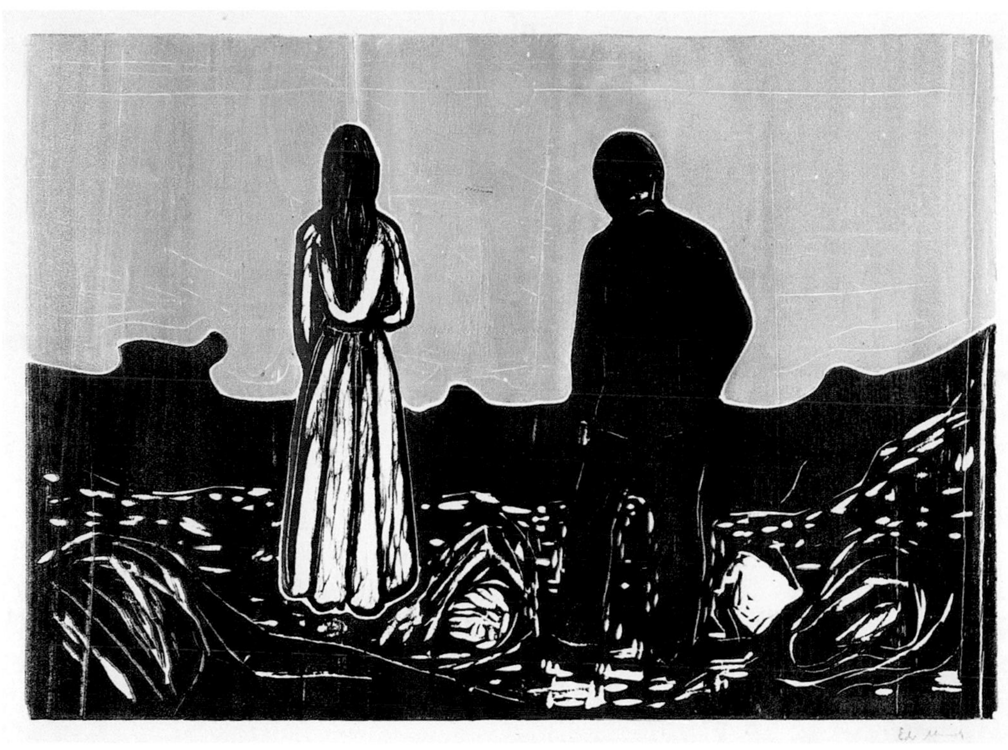

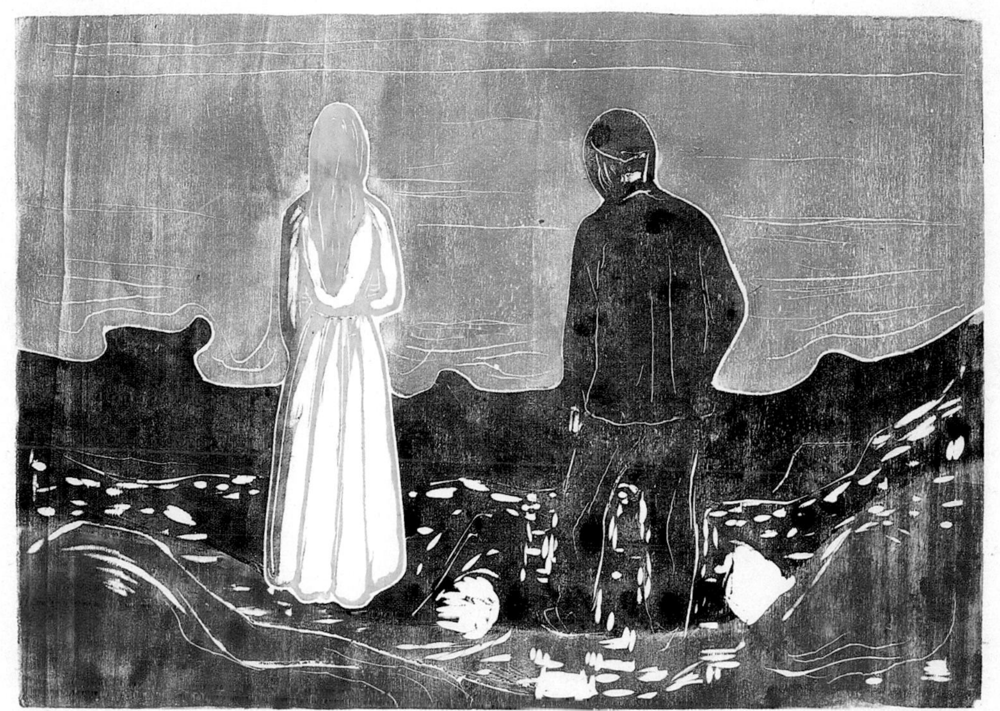

Cat. no. 100 *The Lonely Ones (Two Human Beings)*, 1899
Color woodcut on paper, 39.4 x 55.7 cm
Munch-museet, Oslo

Cat. no. 101 *The Lonely Ones (Two Human Beings)*, 1899
Color woodcut on paper, 39.5 x 55.8 cm
Munch-museet, Oslo

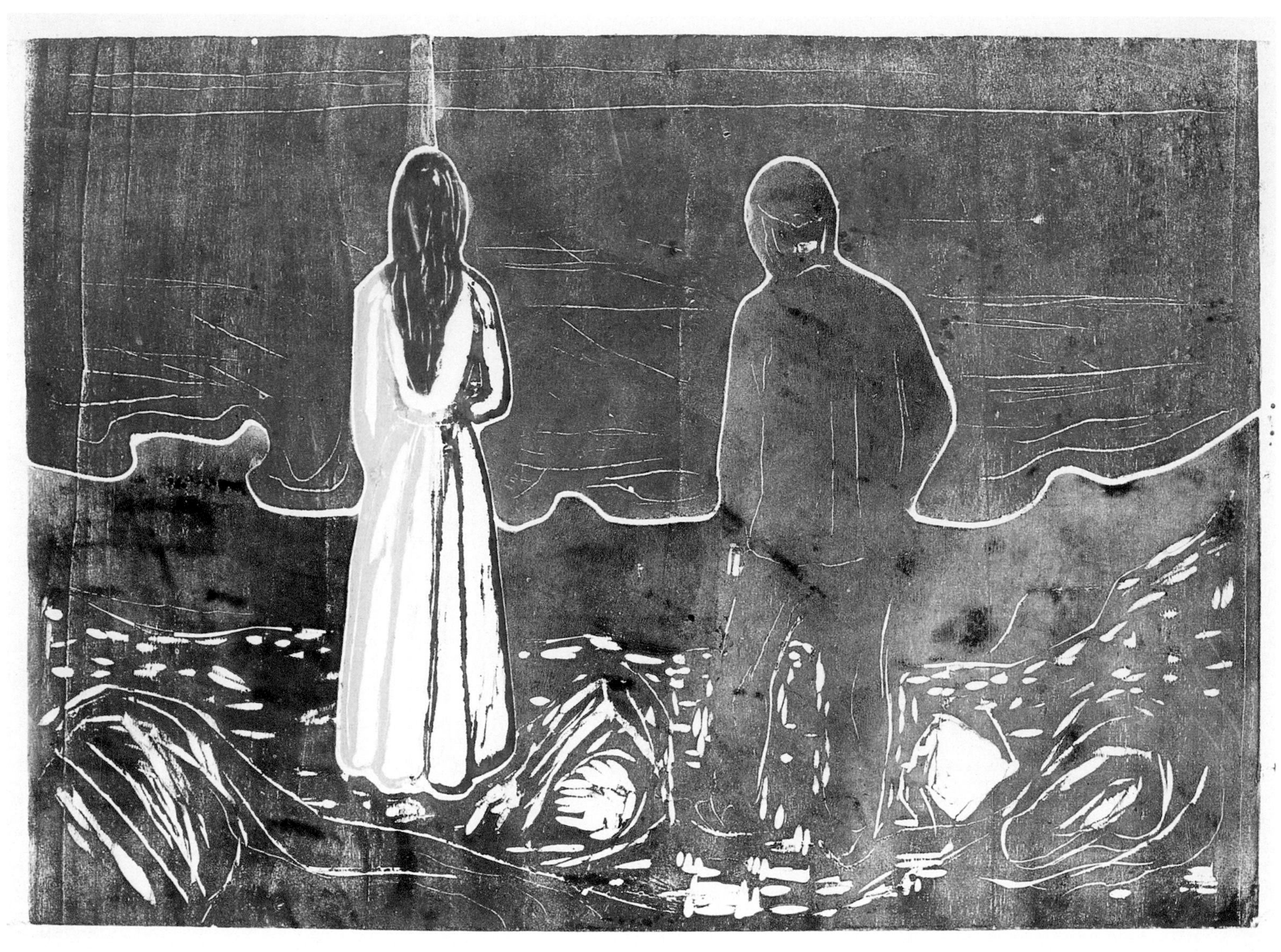

Cat. no. 102 *The Lonely Ones (Two Human Beings)*, 1899
Color woodcut on paper, 39.5 x 55 cm
Munch-museet, Oslo

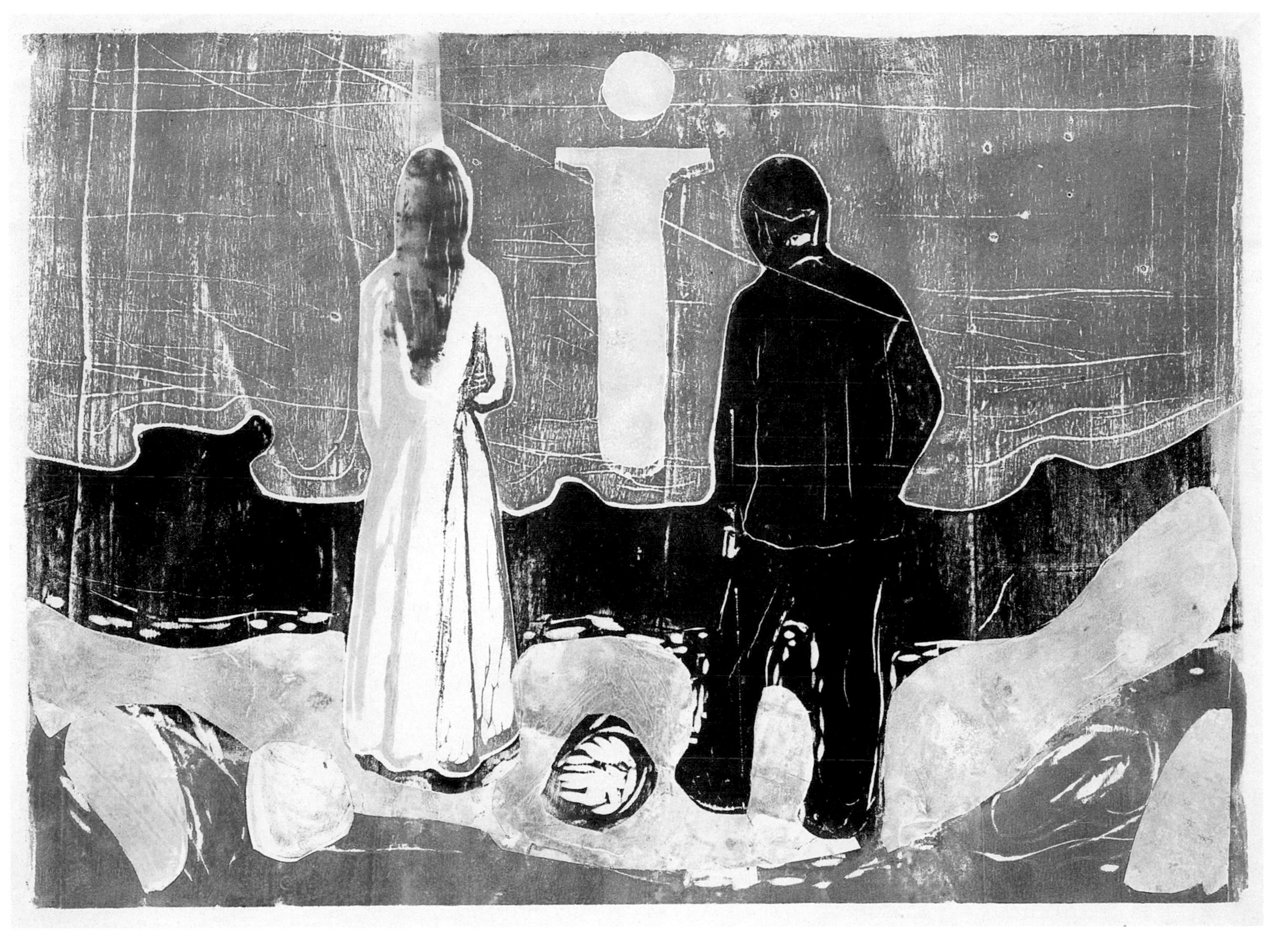

Cat. no. 103 *The Lonely Ones (Two Human Beings)*, 1899
Color woodcut and paper stencils on paper, 39.4 x 55.2 cm
Munch-museet, Oslo

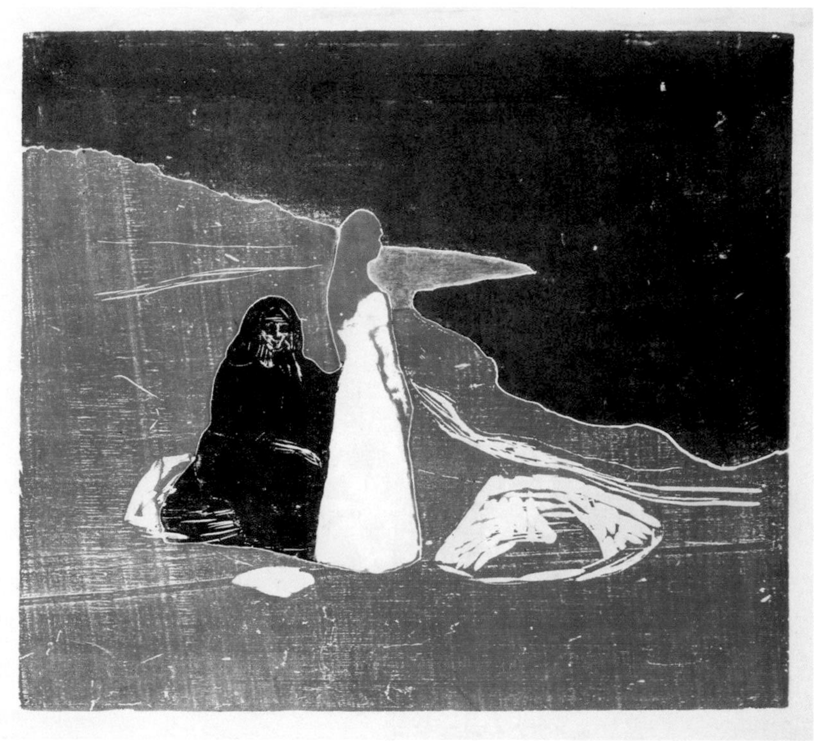

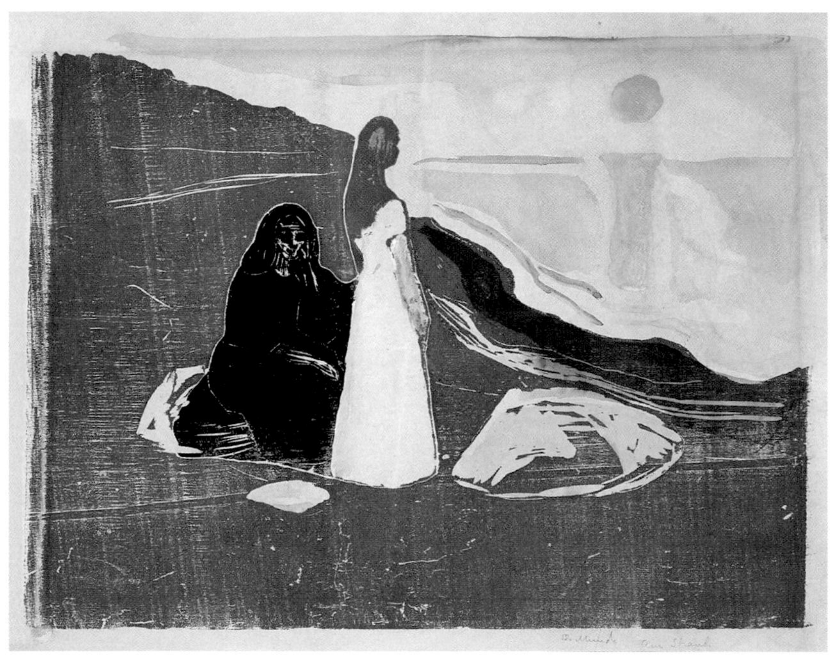

Cat. no. 104 *Two Women on the Shore*, 1898
Color woodcut on paper, 45.4 x 51.2 cm
National Gallery of Art, Washington, Print Purchase Fund
(Rosenwald Collection) and Ailsa Mellon Bruce Fund

Cat. no. 105 *Two Women on the Shore*, 1898
Hand-colored color woodcut on paper, 46.5 x 58.6 cm
National Gallery of Art, Washington, Print Purchase Fund
(Rosenwald Collection) and Ailsa Mellon Bruce Fund

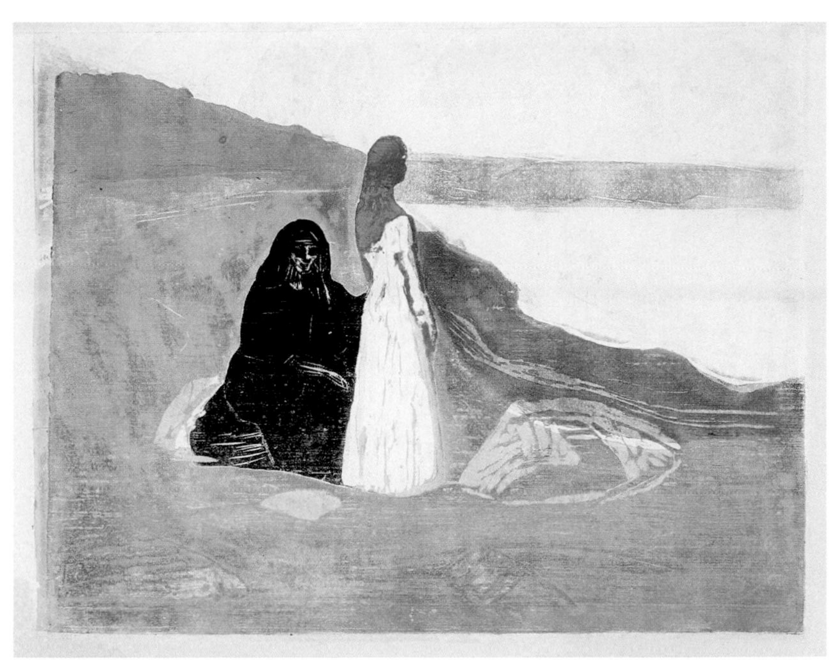

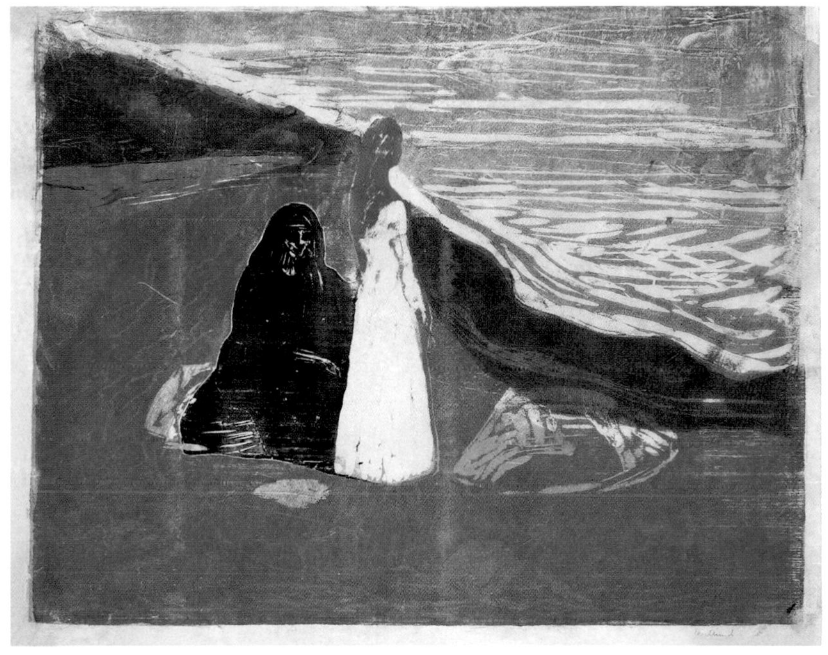

Cat. no. 106 *Two Women on the Shore*, 1900–10
Color woodcut and linoleum plate on paper, 47.4 x 59 cm
National Gallery of Art, Washington, Print Purchase Fund (Rosenwald Collection) and Ailsa Mellon Bruce Fund

Cat. no. 107 *Two Women on the Shore*, 1910s
Color woodcut and linoleum plate on paper, 43 x 55.4 cm
National Gallery of Art, Washington, Print Purchase Fund (Rosenwald Collection) and Ailsa Mellon Bruce Fund

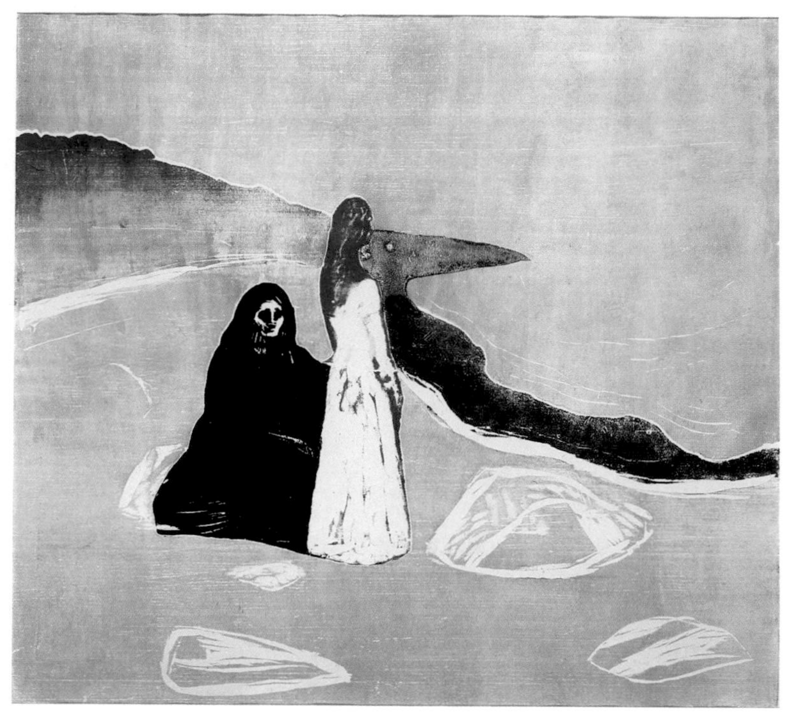

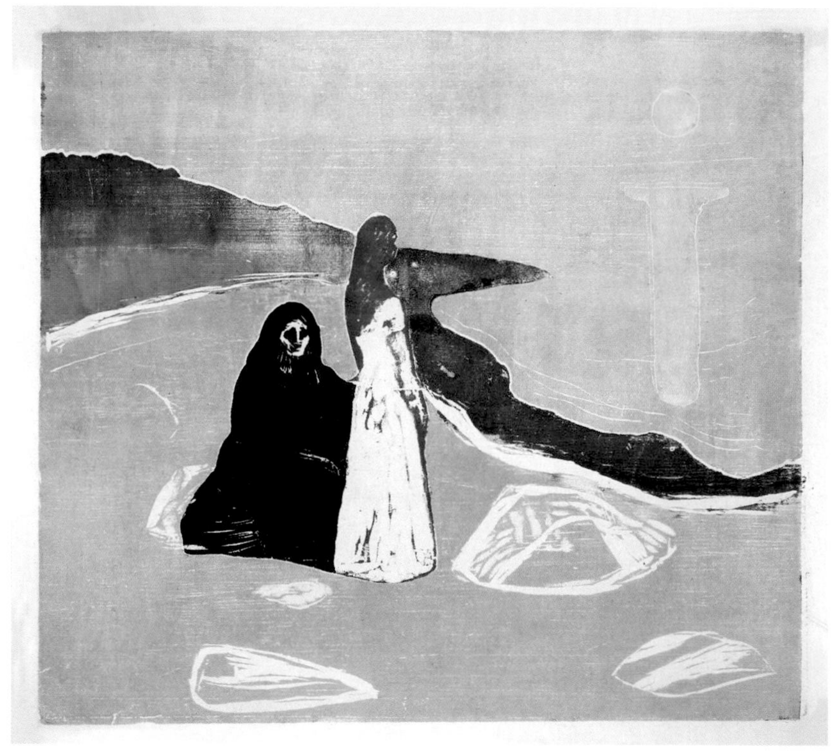

Cat. no. 108 *Two Women on the Shore*, 1920s
Color woodcut on paper, 46.2 x 51 cm
National Gallery of Art, Washington, Print Purchase Fund (Rosenwald Collection) and Ailsa Mellon Bruce Fund

Cat. no. 109 *Two Women on the Shore*, 1920s
Color woodcut and paper stencils on paper, 54 x 59.6 cm
National Gallery of Art, Washington, Print Purchase Fund (Rosenwald Collection) and Ailsa Mellon Bruce Fund

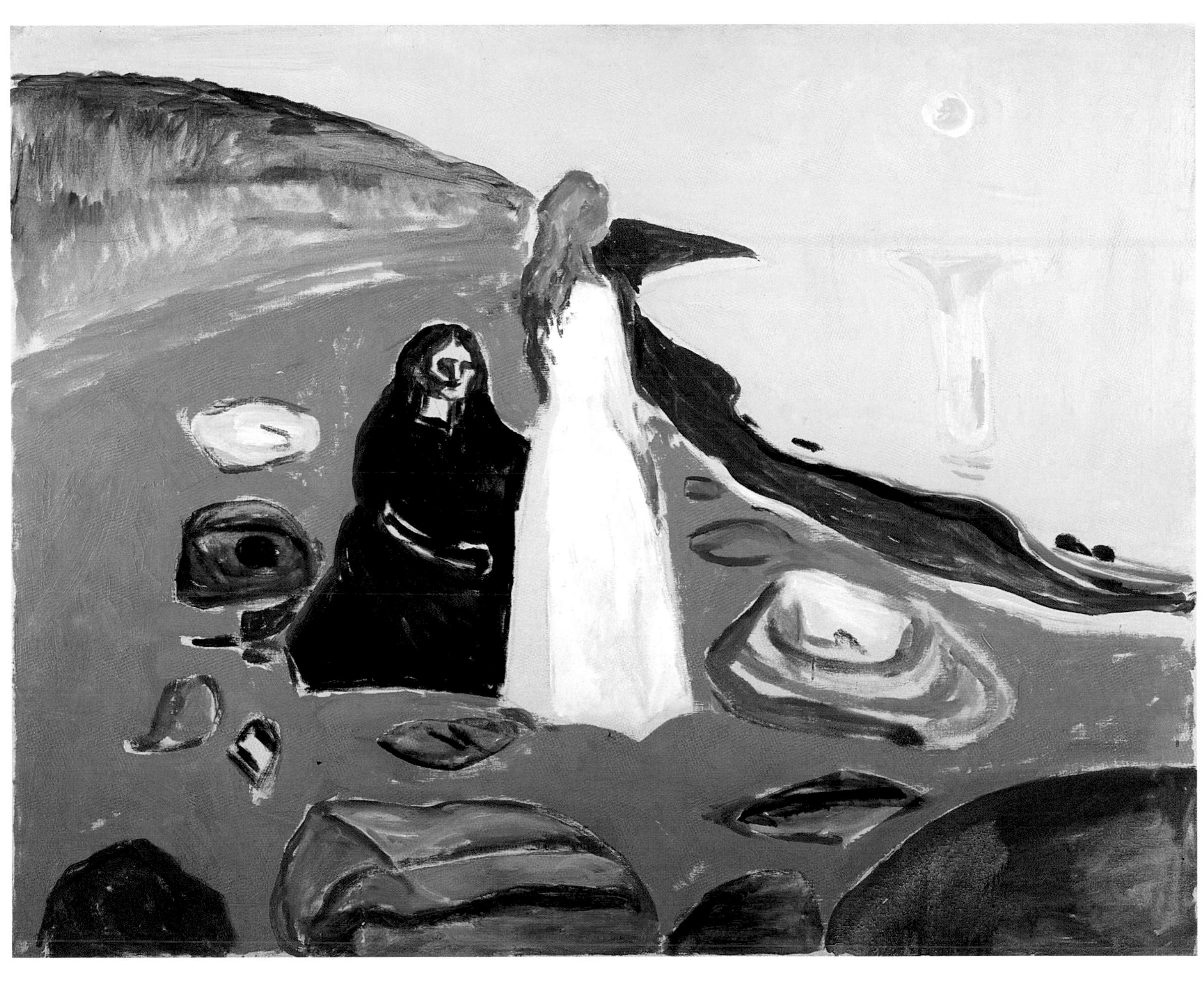

Cat. no. 110 *Two Women on the Shore*, 1935
Oil on canvas, 93 x 118 cm, Munch-museet, Oslo

Angst

According to Munch, *Despair* was the first version of *The Scream* (cat. no. 118) and, like *Evening on Karl Johans Gate* (cat. no. 114), was completed a year before it. In this painting, Munch developed a pictorial configuration that would play a central role in his work for the next several years: a single main figure – or group – cut off by the edge of the picture in the foreground and two interacting figures in the background who emphasize the isolation of the protagonist, with the landscape serving as a mirror of psychological states. *Melancholy* (cat. no. 86) and the pictures on the *Avenue* theme (cat. nos. 156–158) also represent variations.

The dominant motif in *Evening on Karl Johans Gate* of 1892 (cat. no. 114) is the massive crowd of people presented in a frontal view in the foreground. The viewer gazes directly into the masklike faces and wide-open eyes of the people in the crowd. A single male figure is seen moving away alone in the middle of the street, on the verge of disappearing from view. In *Angst* of 1894 (cat. no. 116), this figure is missing entirely. The autonomous, finely detailed vertical-format drawing of 1889 (cat. no. 111) presents yet another variation and demonstrates—as do the corresponding sketches—that Munch shortened the perspective in stages, lowering the observer's point of view from its original distant, elevated position in successive steps to the point where he ultimately stands immediately in front of the crowd. Whereas the figure with the hat seen from the rear creates distance between the viewer and the crowd in the drawing, Munch now confronts the viewer with the advancing group at close quarters. Munch was quite familiar with the world of images in James Ensor's paintings, and Eggum regards this picture as his answer to *Christ's Arrival in Brussels*. The bordering fringe of masks in his later lithograph is also attributed to the Belgian artist's influence.[1] The only known surviving print of this version (cat. no. 113) was recolored by the artist. The yellow of the faces underscores the surreal character of the scene against the cold-blue background of the sky.

By virtue of its pictorial structure, *Angst* of 1894 (cat. no. 116) is regarded as a synthesis of the scenes depicted in *The Scream* (cat. no. 118) or *Despair* and *Evening on Karl Johans Gate* (cat. no. 114). The setting alludes to the first two paintings, the crowd in the foreground to the third, although the groups of figures are composed differently. A number of interpretations have been offered with respect to the identity of the figures. The bearded man, who is visible only in this work, is said to resemble Munch's friend Stanislaw Przybyszewski. The woman—possibly "Mrs. Heiberg," Munch's first love—is depicted wearing a hat, in which some authors have recognized the form of a halo. The man in the top hat appears in all three versions. In the drawing, he walks arm-in-arm with "Mrs. Heiberg" and is thus identified as "Mr. Heiberg." Ambroise Vollard included the 1896 lithograph version of *Angst* (fig. 1) in his *Album des Peintres graveurs* that same year—a great honor for Munch. The lithograph and the woodcut differ with respect to the position and composition of the group of figures. The man with the top-hat is surrounded by three women in both, but the woodcut evokes an impression of greater concentration, achieved by positioning the foreground figures closer to the viewer and incorporating the

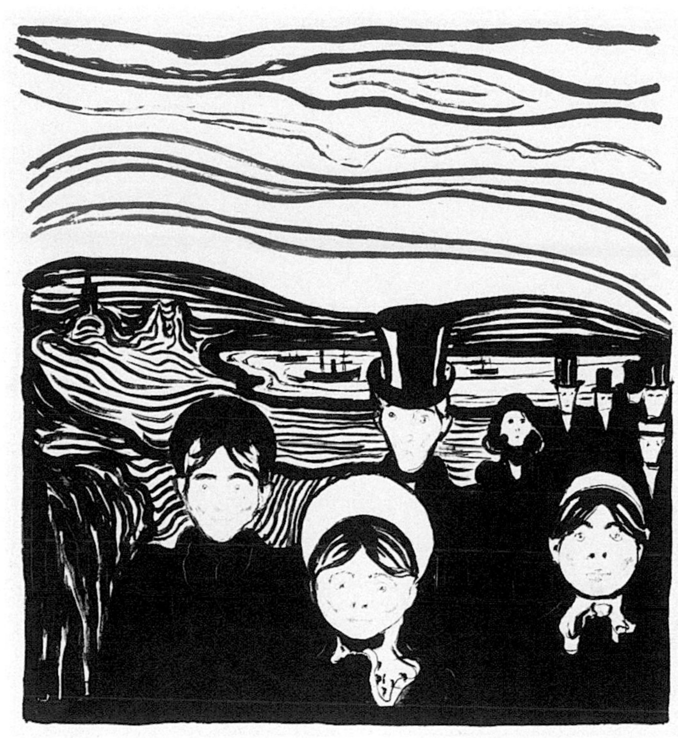

1 *Angst*, 1896,
lithograph on paper, 42 x 38.5 cm,
Albertina, Vienna

unique features of the woodcut and the wood grain, which imbues the scene with energy and dynamism, while the figures appear more deeply lost in themselves. With respect to the woodcuts, Munch wrote later that he saw "all people behind their masks—smiling—calm faces—pale corpses hurrying without pause along a winding path that ends in death."[2]

While working on these pictures, Munch writes that he saw his lost love "Mrs. Heiberg" in every woman who passed him back then:

There she comes. He felt something like an electrical shock inside—... The one in the light sheepskin coat had to be Mrs. Heiberg—wrong again—how they all looked just like her. And then she finally came. Pale and intersected by the horizon, in a black dress closed at her throat. . . . She smiled softly and passed by. I wanted to stop, but something of that old spite kept me from doing so—and then she was gone. Everything became empty, and he felt so alone.[3]

In his essay "On One of Munch's Pictorial Devices," Werner Hofmann describes *The Scream* and *Despair* as "the dramatic-dynamic epitome of the principle of frontality. In general, Munch prefers the frozen attitude, coupled with an eccentric positioning of accents with respect to pictorial space." Hofmann also contends that Munch could identify best with such figures.

The fragmented human being, who is later pressed into a frontal presentation, is derived in Munch's oeuvre from an Impressionist pictorial structure. ... While a certain eccentric mobility prevails in the works of Degas, ... Munch's people lose their mobility; they are frozen in place and fused together into amorphous masses that resist the blunt impact of the surrounding space. All of this results in a distortion of proportions that is capable of building to an impression of bottomless depth and uncertainty. The ground slides away beneath the people's feet. It is as if they were being driven passively towards us. On their frozen facial features lies the shadow of a deed or the knowledge of it (*The Murderer* [cat. no. 157], *Red Virginia Creeper* [cat. no. 155], *The Murderer on the Lane* [cat. no. 158], *Puberty* [cat. no. 161]). They no longer belong to the world the painter has given them as a background ... This helplessness and this state of abandonment as mere creatures, the expansive elaboration of which has often prompted essayistic interpretations of Munch to new verbal creations, leads to a gray area of the human condition—where the human being is nothing more than a defenseless puppet.

Hofmann also suggests that Munch's preferred spiritual-emotional mood, that of abandonment, has its roots in the nineteenth century. It leads to Daumier, who found in the visual device of frontality "a metaphor for the meaninglessness and emptiness of anonymous existence."[4]

The expression of paranoia and claustrophobia may be a direct reflection of Munch's personality, yet these themes also reflect a mood of the times that is expressed with oppressive and fascinating power in the writings of Schopenhauer, Nietzsche, and Kierkegaard and in the works of Dostoevsky, Ibsen, and Strindberg. The *Angst* paintings occupy a key position in Munch's *Frieze of Life*, and they accompanied him throughout his life, as the late photographs taken in his studio indicate (figs. 6, 7, p. 17). AH

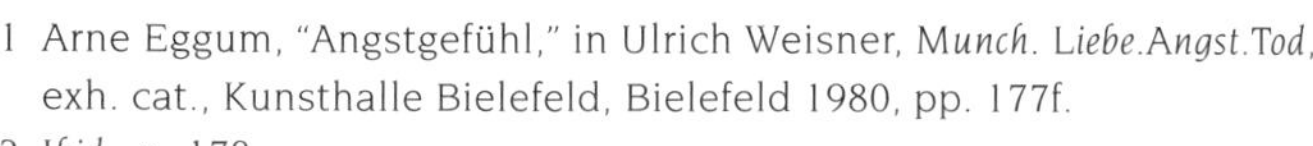

1 Arne Eggum, "Angstgefühl," in Ulrich Weisner, *Munch. Liebe.Angst.Tod*, exh. cat., Kunsthalle Bielefeld, Bielefeld 1980, pp. 177f.

2 *Ibid.*, p. 178.

3 Gerd Woll, "Angst findet man bei ihm überall," in Weisner (see note 1), pp. 317f.

4 Werner Hofmann, "Zu einem Bildmittel Munchs," in Werner Hofmann, *Bruchlinien. Aufsätze zur Kunst des 19. Jahrhunderts*, Munich 1979, pp. 125f.

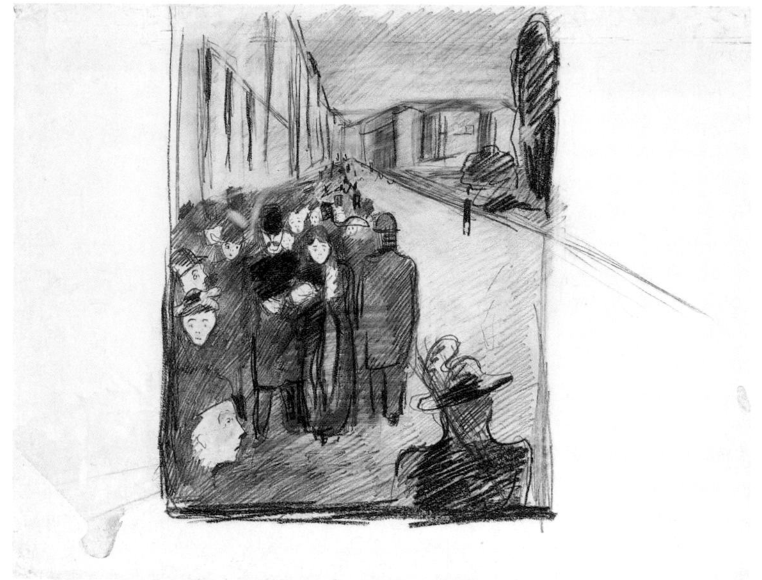

Cat. no. 111 *Evening on Karl Johans Gate*, 1889
Drawing on paper, 37 x 47 cm, Munch-museet, Oslo

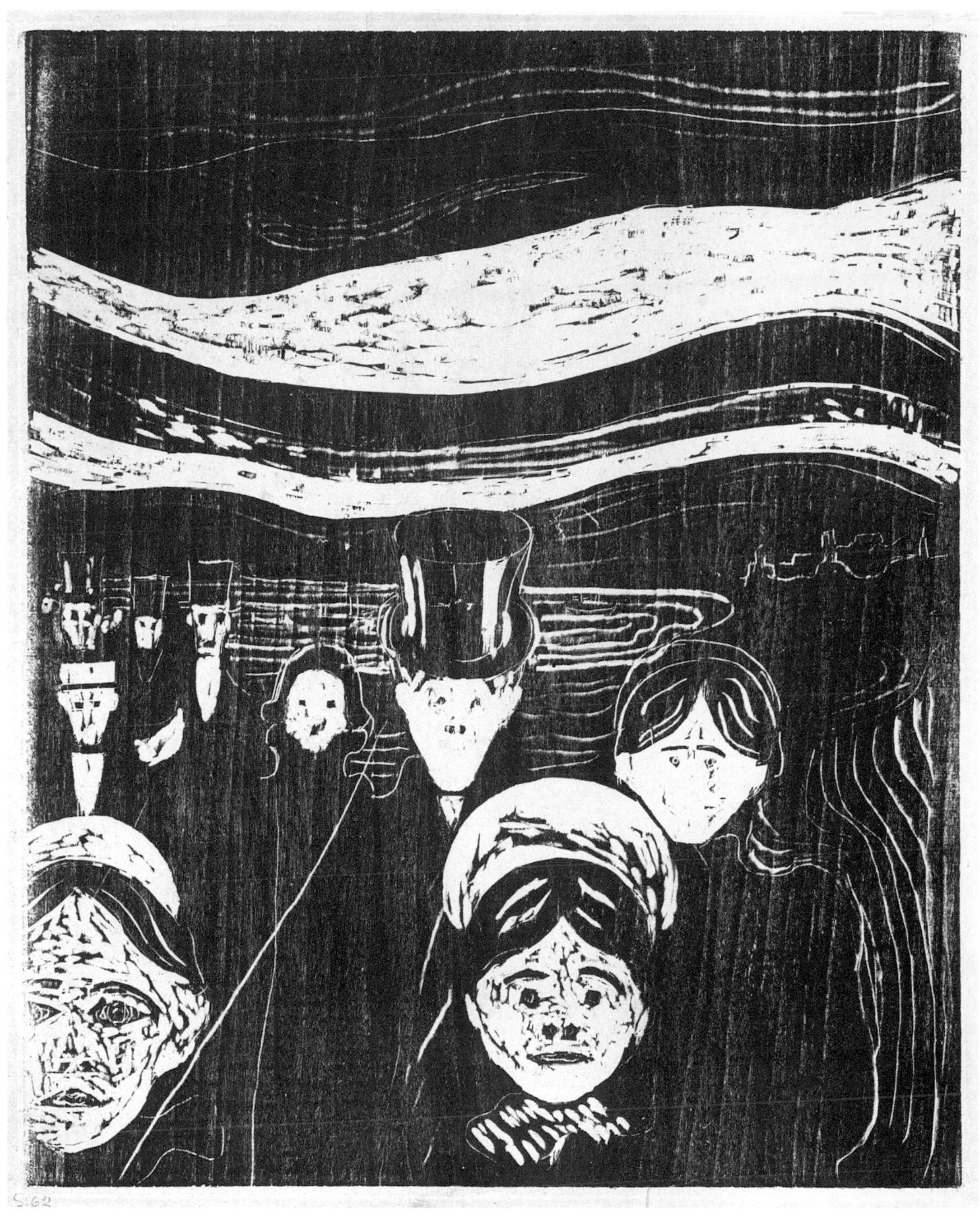

Cat. no. 112 *Angst*, 1896
Woodcut on paper, 45.9 x 37.5 cm
Munch-museet, Oslo

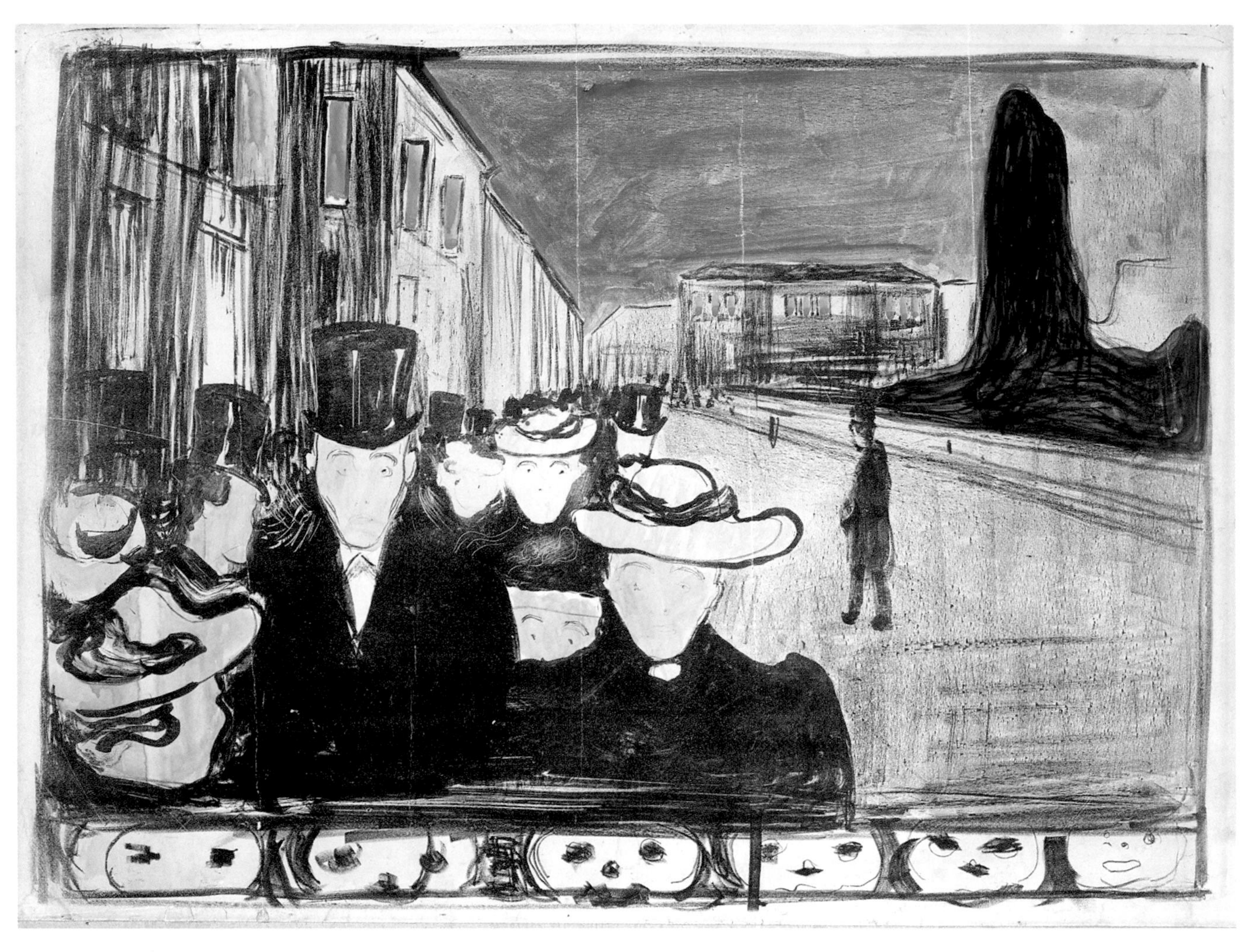

Cat. no. 113 *Evening on Karl Johans Gate*, 1896–97
Hand-colored lithograph on paper, 42.5 x 60.2 cm
Collection of Catherine Woodard & Nelson Blitz, Jr.

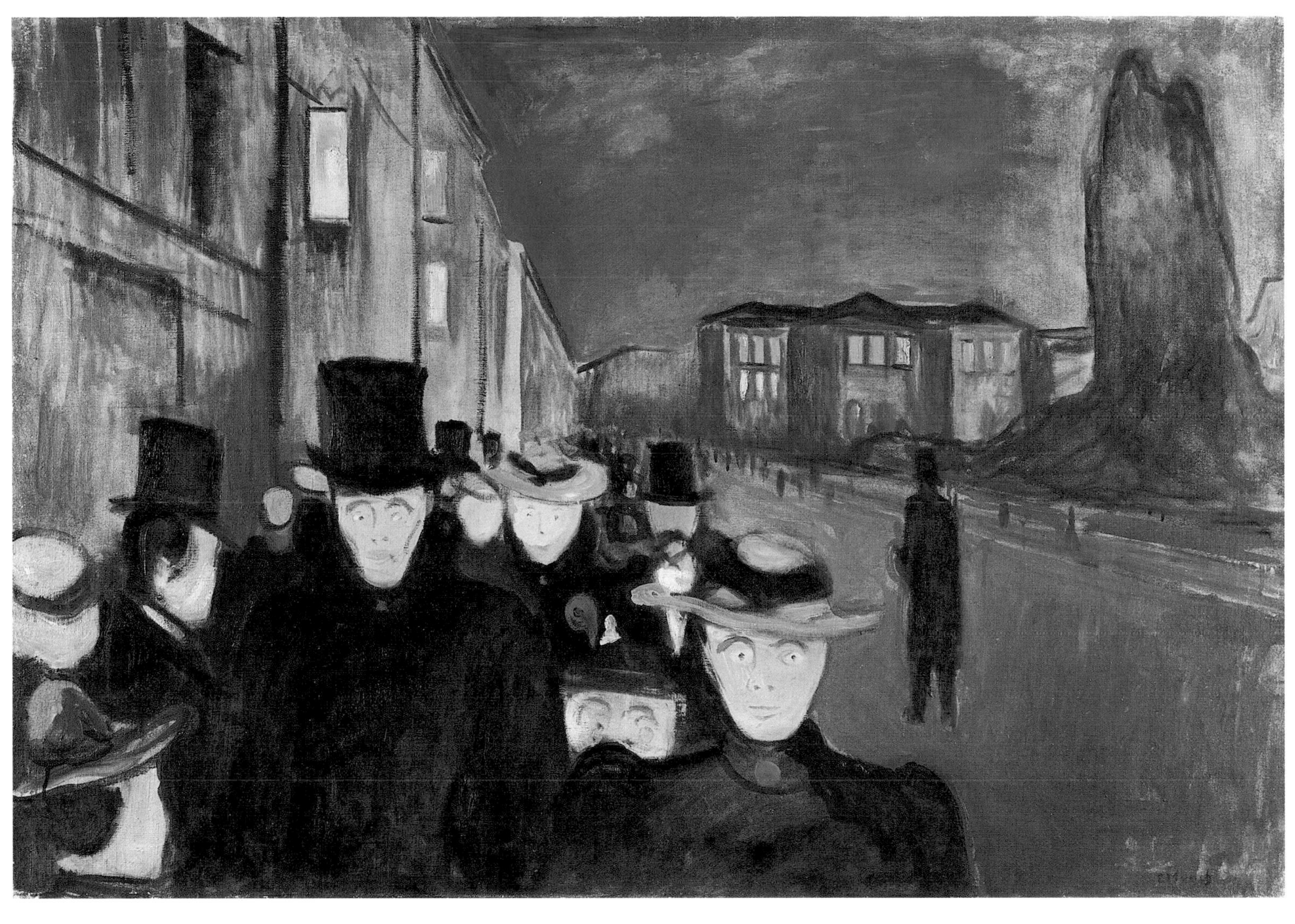

Cat. no. 114 *Evening on Karl Johans Gate*, 1892
Oil on canvas, 84.5 x 121 cm
Rasmus Meyers Samlinger, Bergen Kunstmuseum

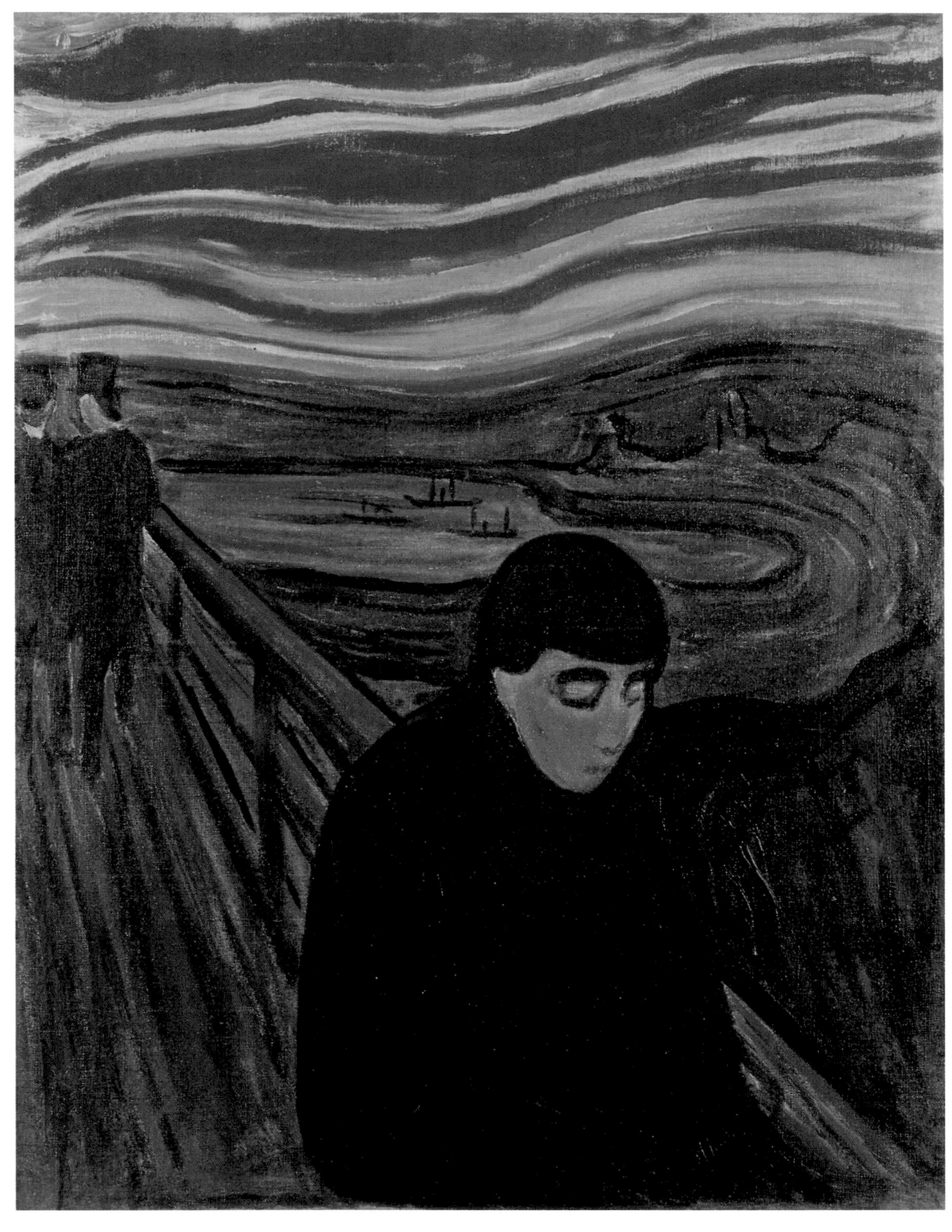

Cat. no. 115 *Despair*, 1893–94
Oil on canvas, 92 x 72.5 cm
Munch-museet, Oslo

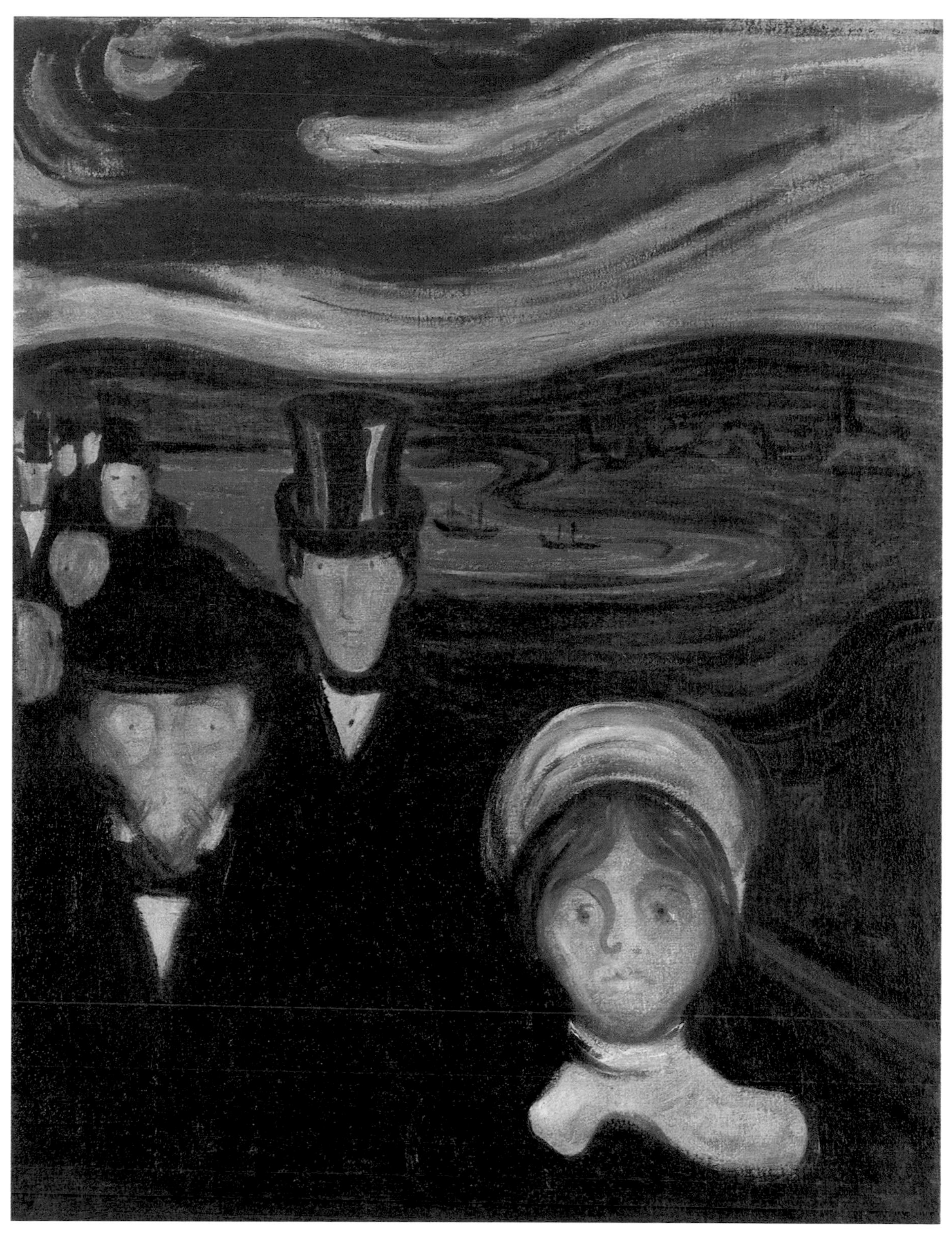

Cat. no. 116 *Angst*, 1894
Oil on canvas, 94 x 74 cm
Munch-museet, Oslo

The Scream

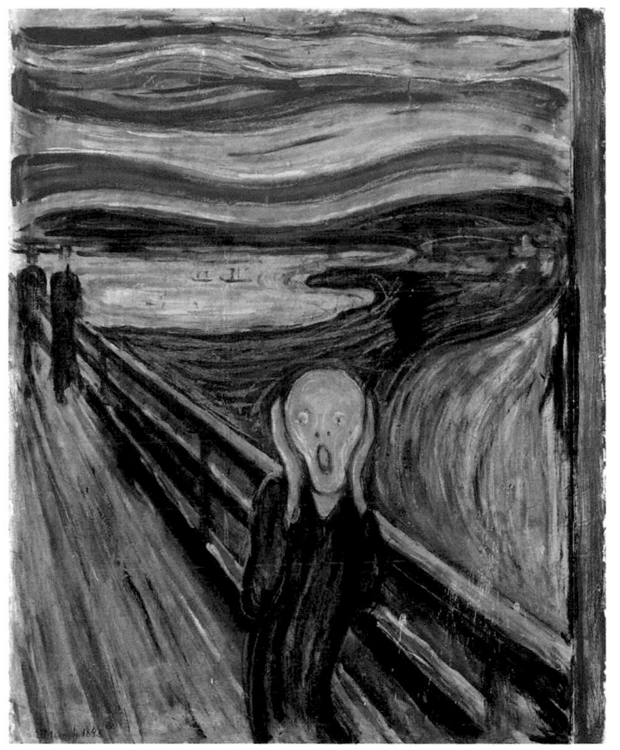

1 *The Scream*, 1893, tempera and grease crayon on cardboard, 91 x 73.5 cm, Nasjonalgalleriet Oslo

Munch's *The Scream* and his *Madonna* are among the world's best-known paintings of the modern history of art. In addition to the two famous paintings now in the collections of the Nasjonal-galleriet (fig. 1) and the Munch-museet (cat. no. 118) in Oslo, Munch also dealt with this subject in a large number of graphic variations and experimental sketches.

Munch's great visual accomplishment is the translation of angst into a universally valid metaphor. The bodiless figure with the masklike face is the concrete expression of an existential emotion. The powerful impact of this twentieth-century icon is achieved in formal terms through the juxtaposition of softly curving, vividly color-accentuated, flowing of lines in the background and the dynamic straight lines of the railing and the road, which thrust into the pictorial space from an extreme vanishing point. While the rhythmic undulating lines call to mind the surface-oriented, ornamental designs of Art Nouveau, the diagonal injects a space-exploding dynamic that puts all spheres of reality to question. The schematic figure as a vision of angst and its mute, inward scream have given rise to numerous interpretations—art-historical, psychological, and sociological—as have the open, eruptive, yet at the same time fragile painting style and the tenuous spatial structure that emphasize the ephemeral quality of this painting.

Munch drew inspiration from his own experience, but he was also well acquainted with developments in art in his time and quite capable of making use of the stimulating ideas of his contemporaries (such as Gauguin, Monet, Denis, Toulouse-Lautrec, Bonnard, Degas, and Van Gogh) in his own experimental work. "Van Gogh," wrote Munch, "was like an explosion; he burned out after five years; he became insane because he painted in the sun without a hat. ... he took advantage of the fever the sun gave him and of the fluid consistency his paints got from the sunshine. I have tried it myself, but I no longer dare to now."[1] Though Van Gogh's visual language was by no means the sole source of inspiration for Munch's composition *The Scream*, the two artists did indeed share a deep appreciation of nature and the capacity to interpret it emotionally and dynamically in their painting, in which the expressive vitality of line and the symbolic power of color play a crucial role.

The lithograph version of *The Scream* (cat. no. 117) was first printed in the important French journal *Revue blanche* in 1895, and was then on its way to becoming an "emblem of an epoch."[2] Unlike many of Munch's other subjects, the print version of *The Scream* is not a reversed presentation of the painting. Munch inscribed the following words in German on the lithograph stone: "Geschrei. Ich fühlte das große Geschrei durch die Natur" [Scream. I felt the great scream through nature]. Arne Eggum suggests that he wrote in German here because he had come to feel at home in Berlin in 1895. In some versions, the text is abbreviated to read simply "Geschrei." AH

1 Quoted and translated from Arne Eggum, "Die Bedeutung von Munchs zwei Aufenthalten in Frankreich 1891 und 1892," in Sabine Schulze (ed.), *Munch in Frankreich*, Frankfurt 1985, p. 140.

2 Cf. Hilde Zaloscer, *Der Schrei. Signum einer Epoche*, Vienna 1985.

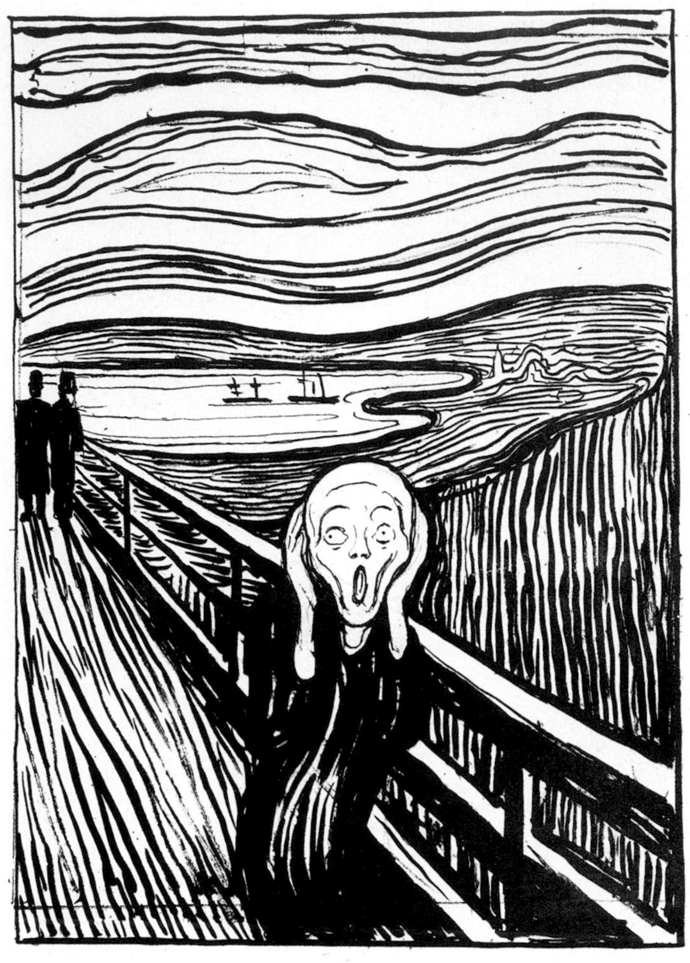

Cat. no. 117 *The Scream*, 1895
Lithograph on paper, 35.2 x 25.1 cm
Munch-museet, Oslo

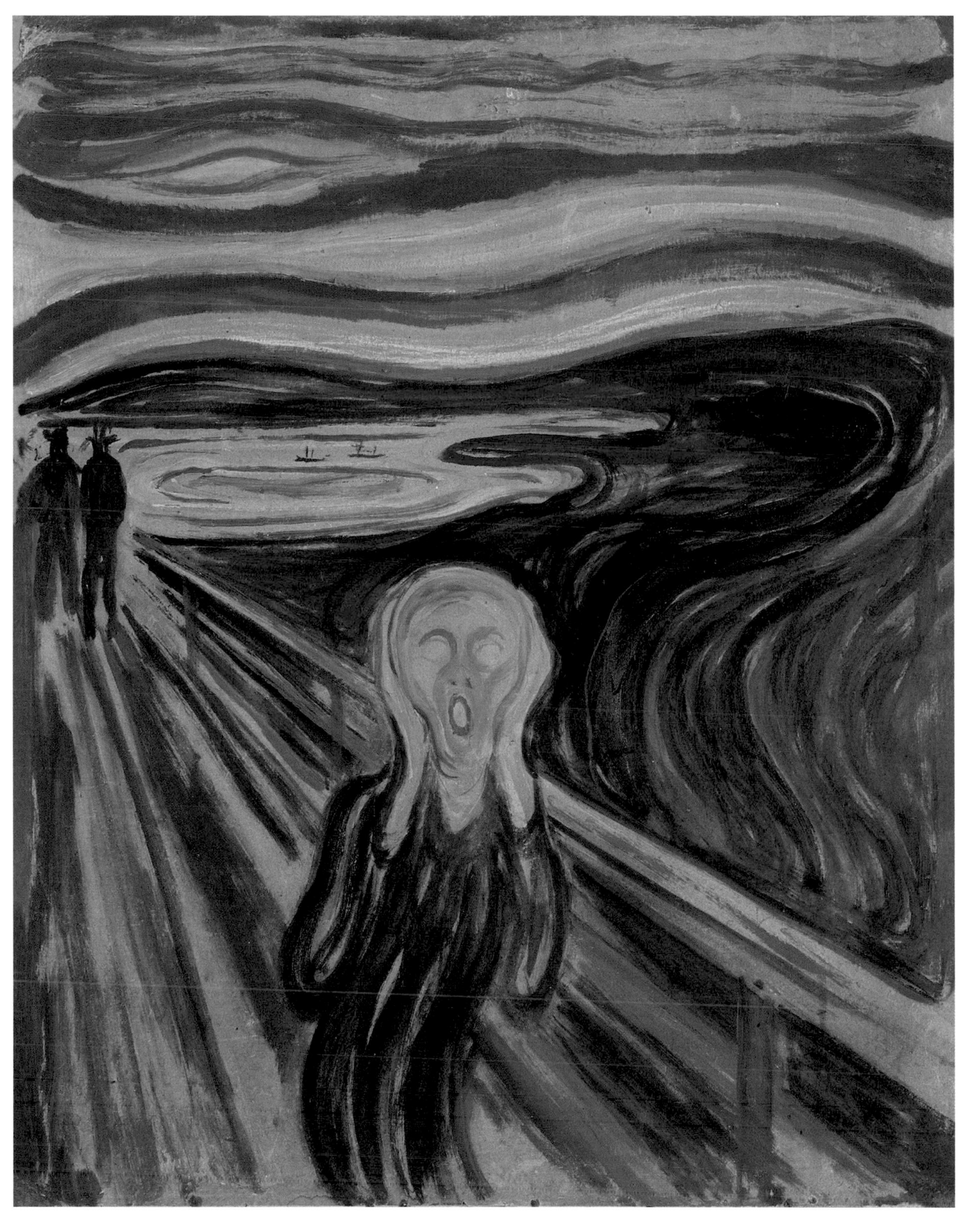

Cat. no. 118 *The Scream*, 1893
Oil, tempera and chalk on cardboard, 84 x 67 cm
Munch-museet, Oslo

The Sick Child

Munch's first presentation of *The Sick Child* (fig. 1) under the title *Study* at the *Autumn Exhibition* in Kristiania in October 1886 triggered a storm of outrage. *Study* was described as "roughly executed"[1] and as a "half-finished draft,"[2] its fragmentary aspect dismissed as the product of cursoriness. Munch later wrote that "No painting has ever caused such an uproar in Norway.—When I entered the hall in which it was hung on the opening day, there was a dense crowd of people standing in front of the painting—one heard outcries and laughter."[3]

Munch appears to have created this impression of incompleteness and sketchiness deliberately, as his choice of themes and the lengthy creative process evidenced by multiple layers of paint and numerous changes suggest. Munch recalls "[repainting] this picture frequently over the course of a year—scratching it out—letting the paint run—and trying again and again to achieve the first impression—the translucent, pale skin on the canvas, the trembling mouth, the trembling hands."[4] In the theme of the sick child, the young artist took up what was not only an autobiographical subject but also an explicit contemporary motif in the photography and painting of the 1880s and 1890s. By giving it the title *Study*, Munch established the fragmentary aspect as a programmatic principle.

In this nearly square painting, a young girl with red hair sits upright against an oversized whitish pillow (fig. 1). Her head is turned towards the bowing figure of a woman but touches the pillow only lightly. The emphatic vertical orientation conflicts with the idea of sickness and death, and the girl appears much more active than the woman. In keeping with the dry, impasto technique Munch employed in the mid-1880s, the paint contains very little binding material and calls attention to Munch's focus on the body of color and its relieflike structure. The time-consuming painting process is characterized by alternating phases of scraping off and applying layers of paint as described by Jæger: "But the mood was lost during the painting process, and so Munch vigorously painted over the whole canvas and restored the atmosphere. [He] wanted to paint it again but destroyed it time after time."[5] Munch usually tore off the nearly dry paint in horizontal strips with a palette knife or the stem of a brush. Traces of the production process remain visible and palpable in the final version of the painting.

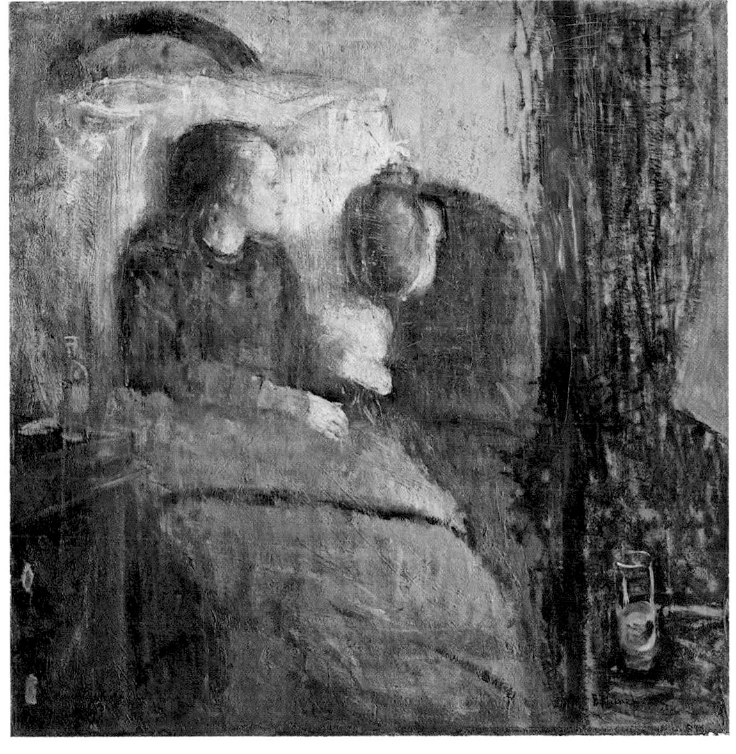

1 *The Sick Child* (*Study*), 1885–86, oil on canvas, 120 x 118.5 cm, Nasjonalgalleriet, Oslo

Munch consistently applied his scratching technique in the five subsequent versions of *The Sick Child*. The second painted version of *The Sick Child* (cat. no. 122) was done in 1896 as a commissioned piece for Olaf Schou, who wanted a "copy" for his own collection. After receiving the painting, Schou wrote, "I think you were happy with the copy. It is just like the original, although not so well done. But please do not do anything more to it. I am satisfied with it as it is."[6] Munch presumably painted the picture in Paris[7] and exhibited it along with nine other paintings at his first showing at the Salon des Artistes Indépendents. Contrary to Schou's remark, the second version differs markedly from the first. Munch used thin paints, as he did through most of the 1890s, and intensified the coloration, since he no longer modeled the paint in numerous

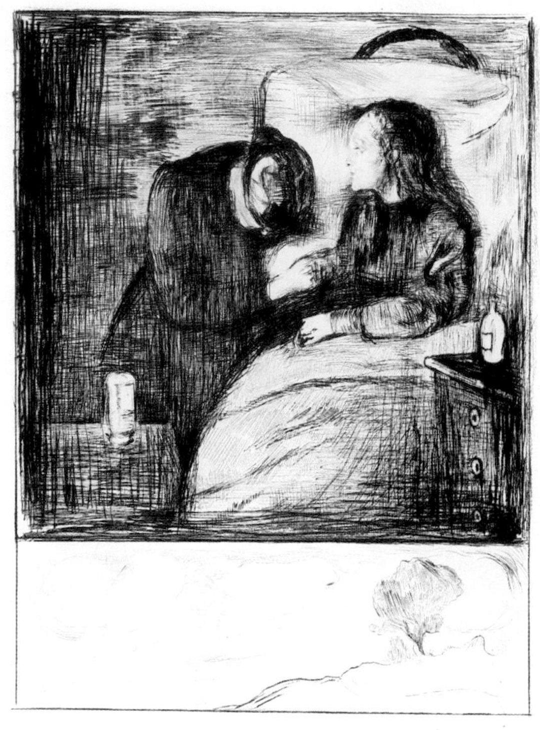

layers. The scratches no longer displace bodies of color but are fine incisions that expose the canvas—they correspond primarily to the horizontal orientation of the first version. They resemble severely scratched glass or photographs. Munch applied these scratches to the thin layer of paint in the manner of graphic hatching. The transparency that exposes the canvas forms a bond between the image-bearing surface and the motif. He does not destroy the image but instead combines elements of painting and graphic art, an approach to which he may have been inspired by his work on the etching entitled *The Sick Child* I of 1894 (cat. no. 119, 120). While Munch largely followed the model of the painting in this first graphic variation, he concentrated in the etching of 1896 (cat. no. 121)—also a mirror-image presentation—on the girl's head and shoulders. He retained this frame of view in the color lithographs *The Sick Child* I and II, which were done the same year. The rendering of the face corresponds to the physiognomy of the second painted version, although Munch left out the woman's head, as he had in the etching. As Paul Herrmann recollected, Munch's selection of colors was by no means the result of careful planning.[8] Though he did choose the colors, he left the matter of how they would be combined to the printer, thus introducing the element of chance into this series of experiments. Of the six identifiable stones, as many as five were used for a single print. The many possible combinations of stones and colors produce a broad spectrum of nuances, some of which Munch also worked over by hand-coloring. The variation and combination of cold and warm colors appear to reflect both the physical and the emotional states of the sick young girl. The red gradations that dominate in some variations (cat. nos. 125, 127) suggest hotness and fever, enabling the viewer almost to feel these conditions, while the interaction with blue (cat. no. 126) makes one think of shivering. The color effects were achieved in some cases by coloring the hair separately in red using a stone worked with lithograph ink (cat. nos. 125, 130), whereby brushstrokes and paint evoke associations with blood.

Most of the hand-colorings are transparent. They accentuate hair, a garment, or a background, or add motifs that are not present on the printing plate. In a print now held in the Epstein Family Collection (cat. no. 124), the pillow is emphasized with broad, white brushstrokes. Its contours and the garment are highlighted in

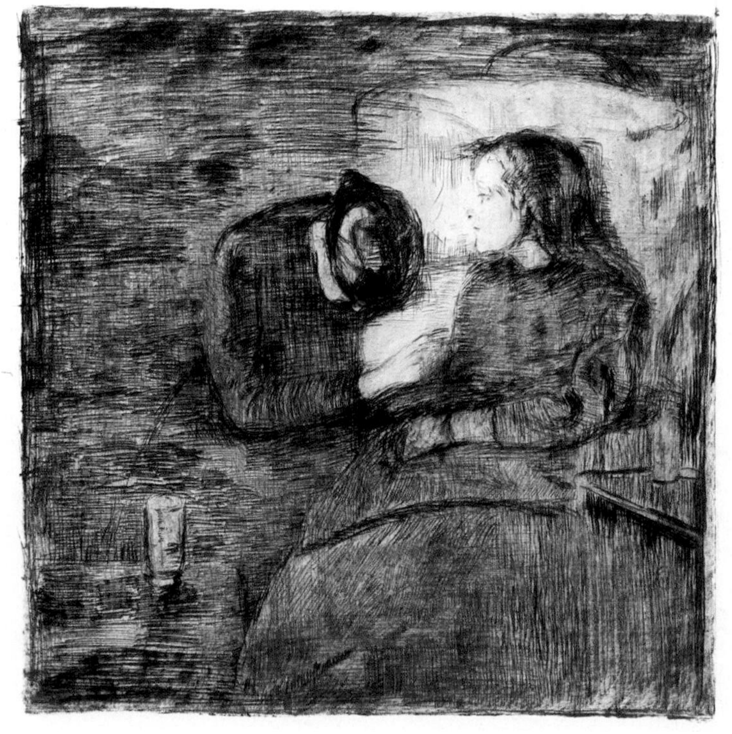

Cat. no. 119 *The Sick Child* I, 1894
Etching on paper, 36.5 x 27 cm
Albertina, Vienna

Cat. no. 120 *The Sick Child* I, 1894
Etching on paper, 27.5 x 27 cm
Munch-museet, Oslo

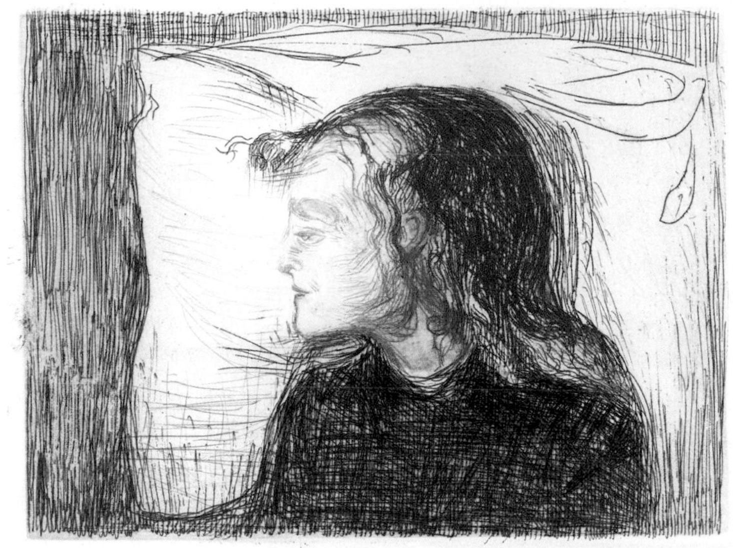

black, enhancing the vividness of the printed colors. Munch made changes in the motif in two hand-colored versions (cat. nos. 129, 130) and added a bowed woman's head in the lower right-hand corner as a transparent element reminiscent of a memory image. The aspect of transience may be interpreted as a reference to the passage from life to death.

For the entirely black lithograph print entitled *The Sick Child* II (cat. no. 128), Munch probably reworked a stone used in the first version. One notices that the artist transferred the finely incised lines characteristic of the first two painted versions onto the stone with a needle and concentrated them in the area of the head and pillow. With a degree of intensity comparable to that of the first painting, Munch appears to have tried to eradicate the girl's face, whereby the deletion of the face is facilitated by the weak contrast between her profile and the pillow. In the print shown here, Munch reduced the size of the format by cutting the sheet both along the top and bottom, as in the other versions, and along the right-hand edge, thus focusing more closely on the face and the pillow. Yet the most substantial reduction is found in the square pastel version of *The Sick Child* (cat. no. 131), which shows only the girl's head. While the dissolution of the face in the print may be interpreted as a symbolic reference to death, the pastel unites features more reminiscent of a portrait, as the white in the background strengthens the contrast with the profile, and Munch dispensed here with the concentration of focus on the area of the hair and the garment. The square may refer to the format of the paintings.

Munch painted the third version as a commissioned work for the Swedish collector Ernest Thiel in Warnemünde in 1907. This painting already reflects the impact of the marked changes in Munch's style and is characterized by vivid coloration and the direct application of paint. From the artist's correspondence with Thiel, we learn that he had taken up the theme again in earnest: "*The Sick Child* is a painting that requires a great deal of time, because it has so many fine nuances."[9] In this case, the client's reaction was euphoric: "*The Sick Child* is like a revelation. My Munch wall will be the most splendid in all of Europe."[10] Munch was presumably at work on the fourth version (fig. 2) in Warnemünde about this time, a work that was purchased by the Gemäldegalerie Dresden in 1928 after difficult negotiations with its director Hans Posse. The National Socialists declared the painting degenerate and confiscated it in 1937, after which it was purchased by a private collector from the Norwegian art dealer Harald Holst Halvorsen and later acquired by the Tate Gallery. Munch's brushwork combines extended vertical strokes in the right-hand section of the painting and a re-

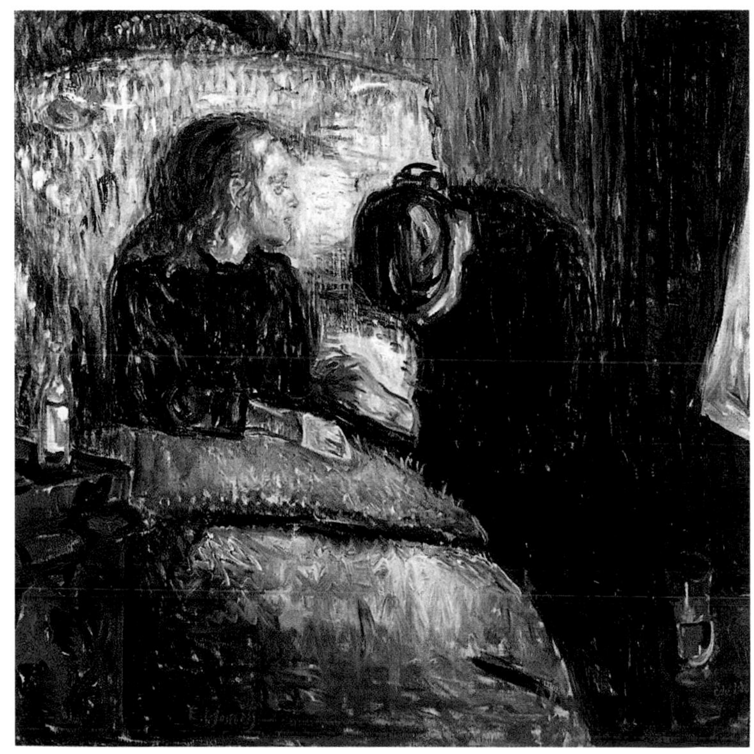

Cat. no. 121 *The Sick Child*, 1896
Color etching on paper, 12.8 x 16.8 cm
Munch-museet, Oslo

2 *The Sick Child*, 1907,
oil on canvas, 118.5 x 121 cm,
Tate, London

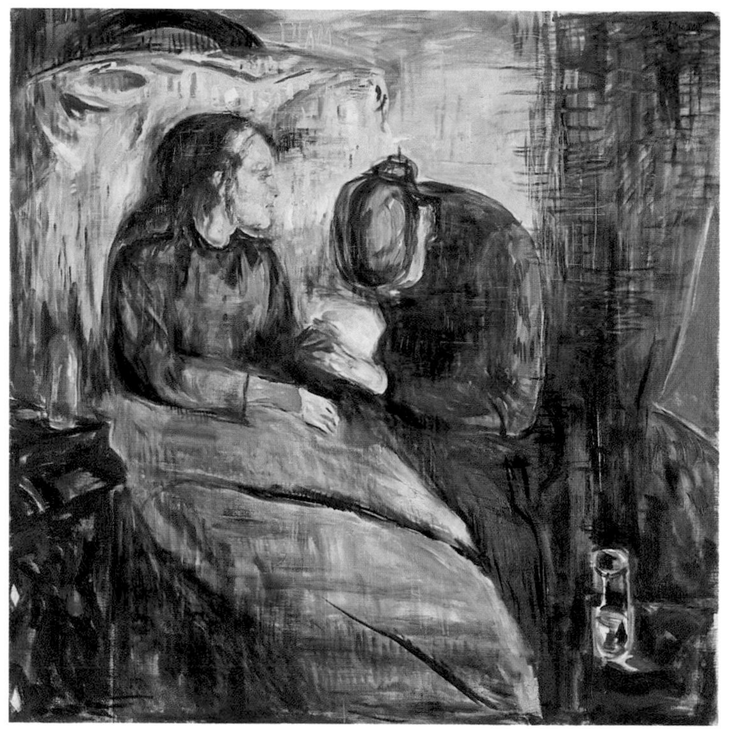

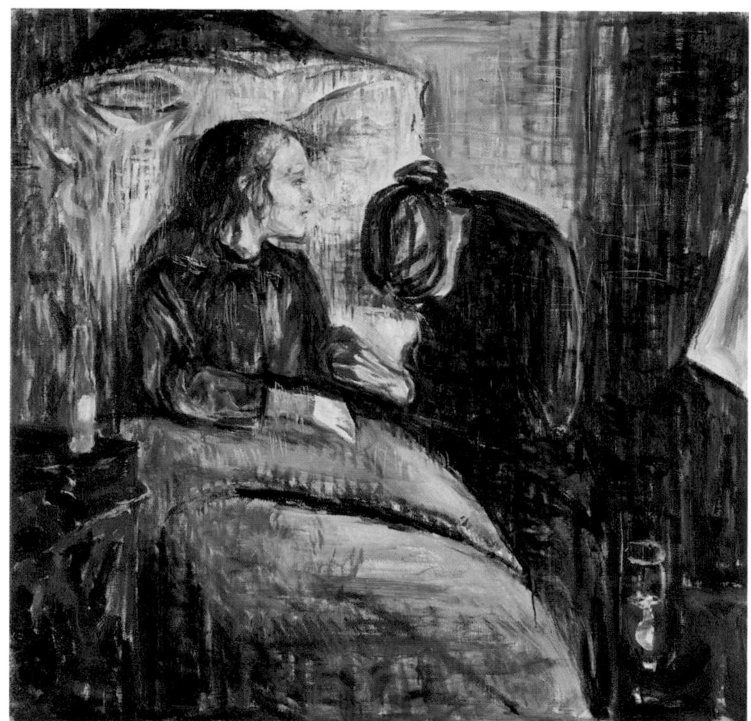

markably restless area on the side in which the girl's figure appears. Her face seems to vibrate intensely against the animated background area of the pillow, an effect evoked in part by scratches, and is considerably more active and lively than the bowing figure of the woman.

The two undated last versions done during the 1920s were still in Munch's possession at the time of his death. Eggum dates the fifth version to 1921–22 (fig. 3),[11] while the sixth and last version was completed during the latter half of the 1920s (fig. 4) and may have been done while negotiations with the Dresden Gemäldegalerie were in progress. Both of these paintings exhibit scratch marks. Characteristic of the painting style in the last version is the interplay of broad and narrow, hatchlike brushstrokes, and areas of transparent and impasto paint. The scratch marks in the agitated painted surface appear in the same area in which they were concentrated in the first version and serve as a recollected reference to Munch's early experimentation with the material characteristics of the medium of painting, the autonomy of color as a tool of pictorial expression. The glaring shades of red and orange heighten the sense of suffering and the potential for association with blood. They also allude to Munch's experience of the death of his sister Sophie, who succumbed to pulmonary tuberculosis in 1877. DB

1 Andreas Aubert, in *Morgenbladet*, Nov. 9, 1886, n. p.
2 *Ibid.*, quoted and translated from Uwe M. Schneede, *Edvard Munch. Das kranke Kind. Arbeit an der Erinnerung*, Frankfurt am Main, 1984), p. 9.
3 Edvard Munch, *Livsfrisens tilblivelse*, Oslo, n. d. [1928?], p. 10
4 *Ibid.*, p. 9. Munch also refers in other notes to the time-consuming process of developing the pictorial theme and his lengthy periods of work on the painting. Cf. Manuscript T T 2771, Munch-museet, Oslo.
5 Hans Jæger, "Utstillingen," in *Dagen*, Oct. 20, 1886, n. p.
6 Quoted from, "The Theme of Death," in *Edvard Munch. Symbols and Images*, exh. cat., National Gallery of Art, Washington 1978, p. 152.
7 Jens Thiis, *Edvard Munch og Hans Samtid*, Oslo 1933, p. 132.
8 Cf. Paul Herrmann in Erich Büttner, "Der leibhaftige Munch," in Jens Thiis, *Edvard Munch*, Berlin 1934, p. 92.
9 Letter from Warnemünde dated Sept. 21, 1907. Quoted and translated from *Munch und Warnemünde* 1907–1908, exh. cat., Munch-museet, Oslo, Rostock Kunsthalle, Ateneum, Helsinki, Oslo 1999, p. 136.
10 Undated letter, quoted and translated from *ibid.*, p. 128.
11 Eggum 1978 (see note 6), p. 153.

3 *The Sick Child*, 1921–22,
oil on canvas, 117 x 116 cm,
Munch-museet, Oslo

4 *The Sick Child*, 1925–27,
oil on canvas, 117.5 x 120.5 cm,
Munch-museet, Oslo

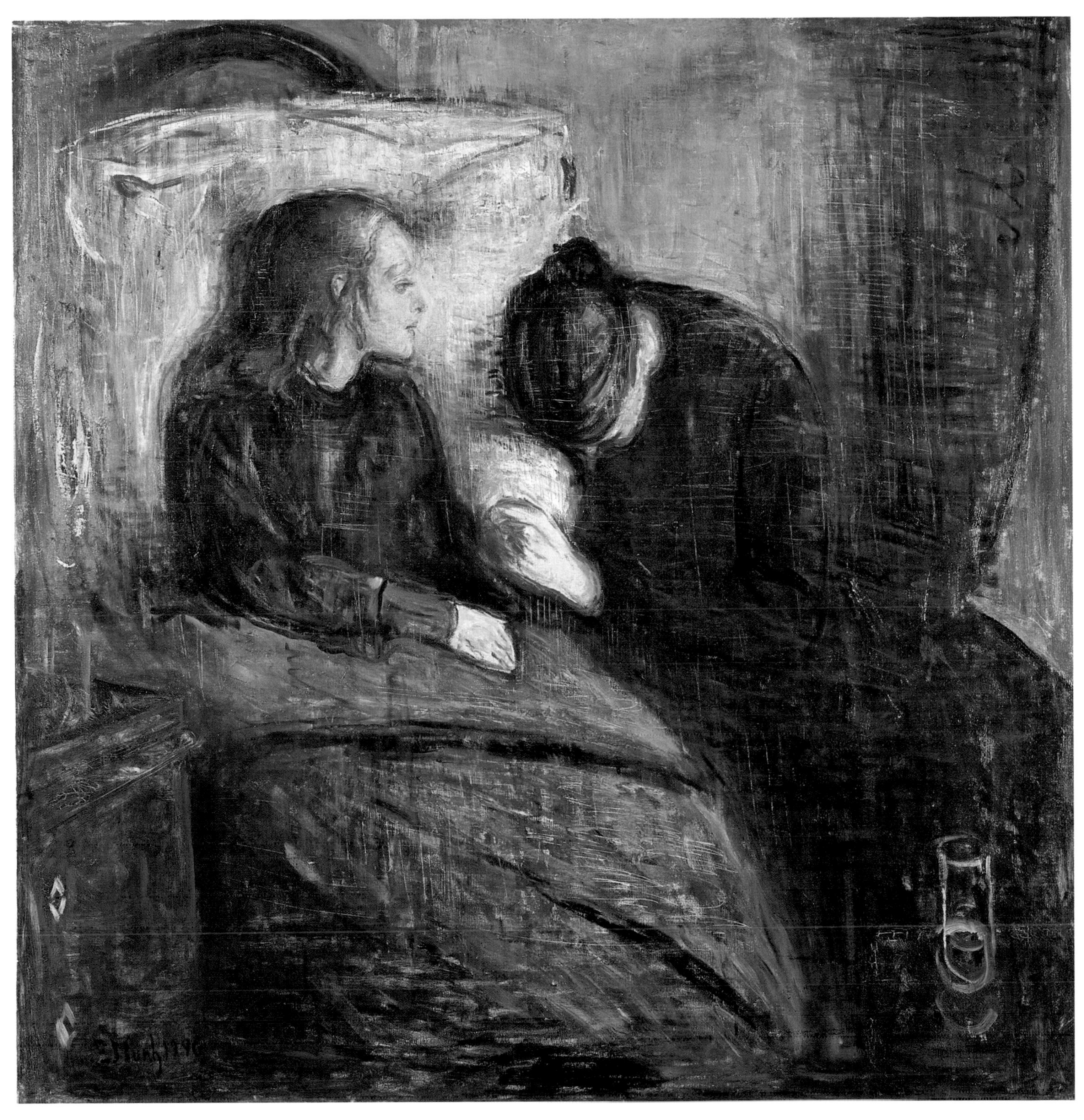

Cat. no. 122 *The Sick Child*, 1896
Oil on canvas, 121.5 x 118.5 cm
Göteborgs Konstmuseum, Göteborg

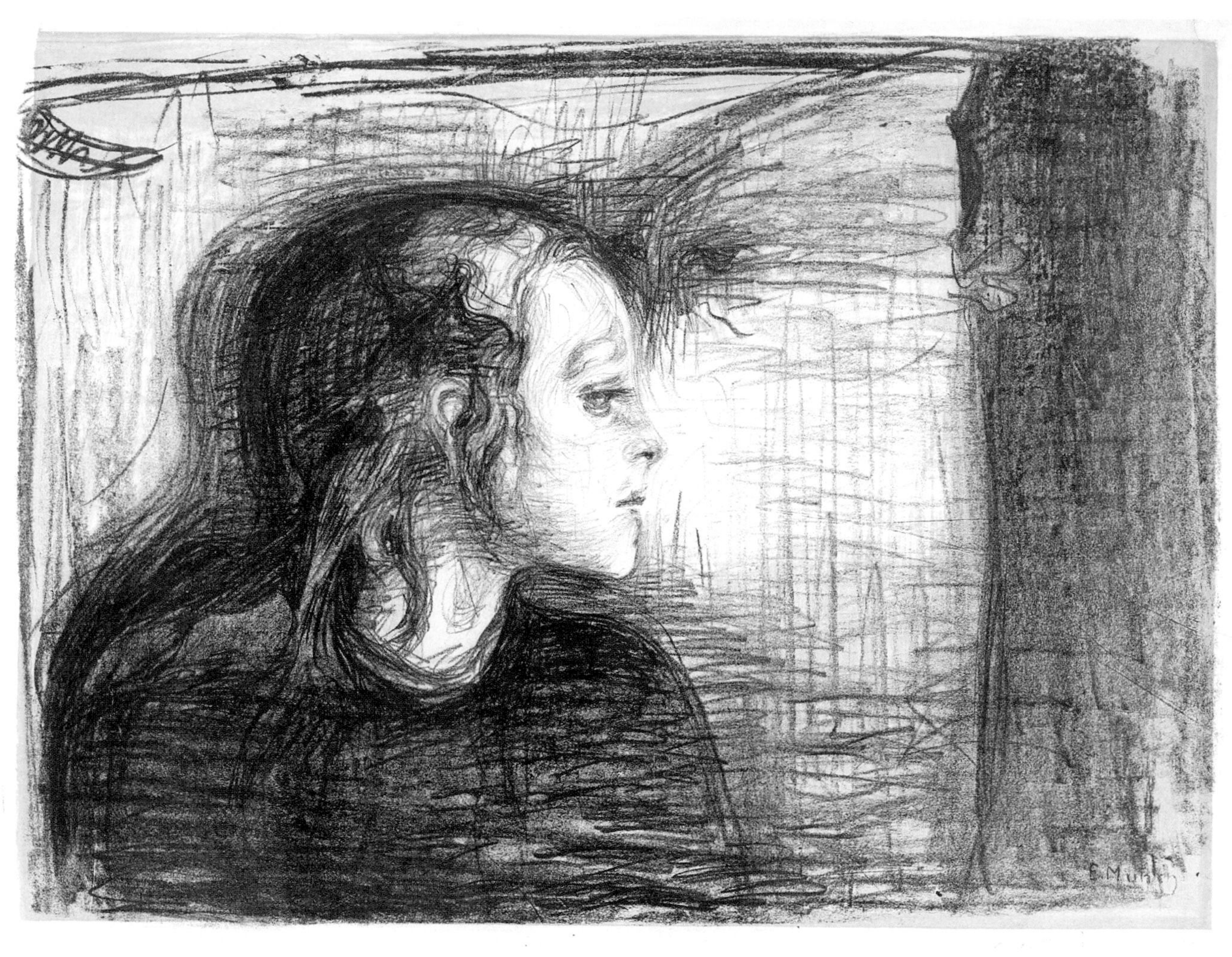

Cat. no. 123 *The Sick Child* I, 1896
Color lithograph on paper, 47.7 x 62.5 cm
Albertina, Vienna

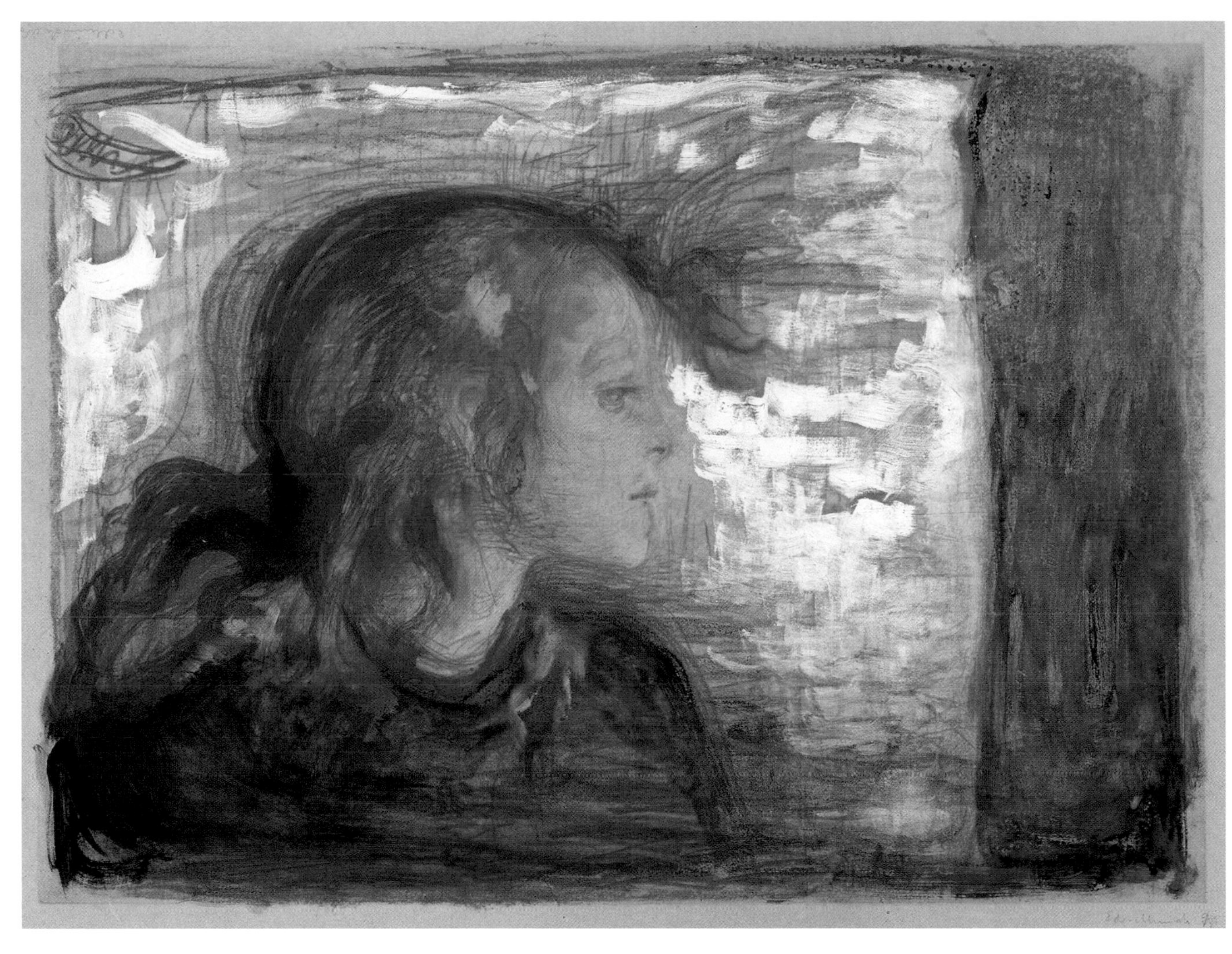

Cat. no. 124 *The Sick Child* I, 1896
Hand-colored color lithograph on paper, 42 x 56 cm
Epstein Family Collection

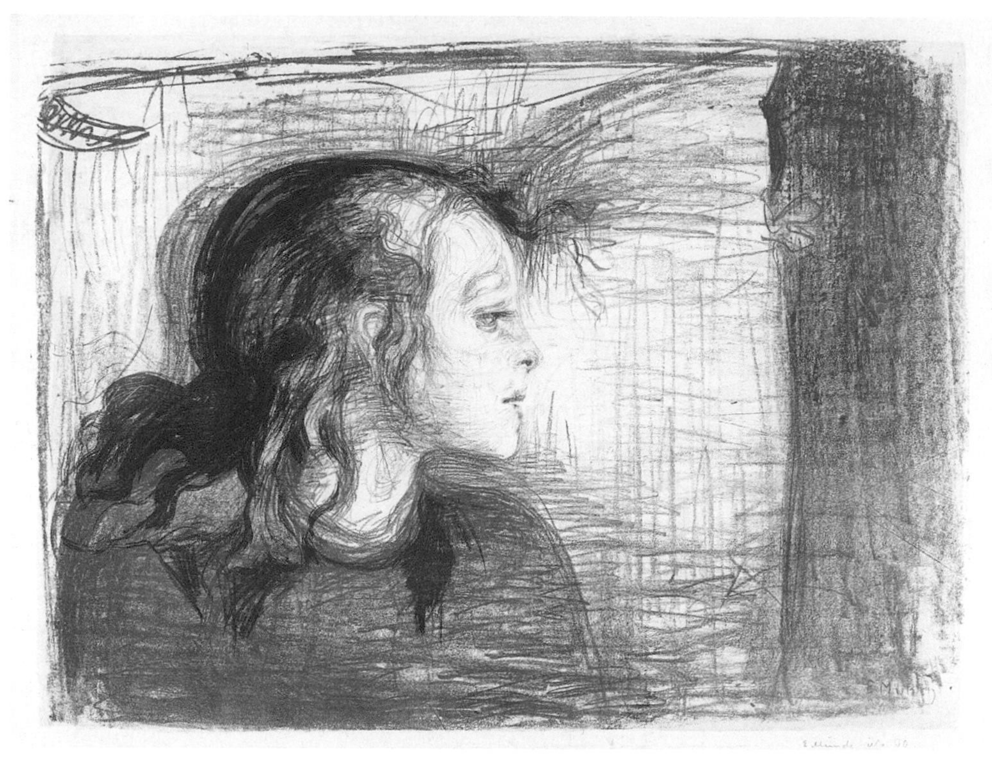

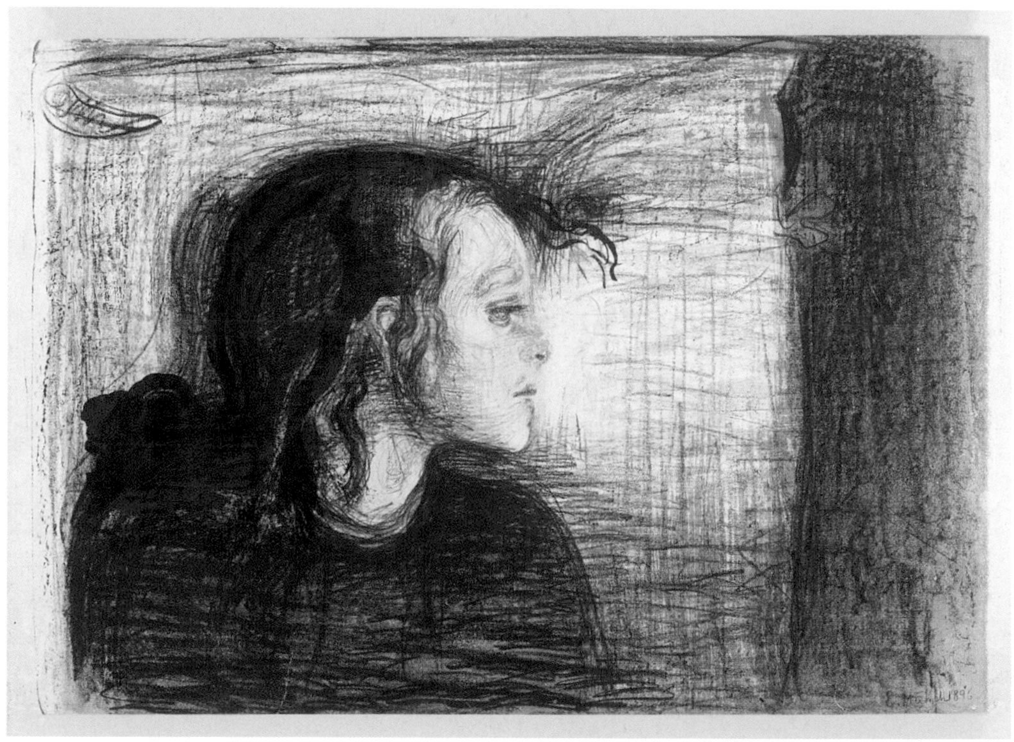

Cat. no. 125 *The Sick Child* I, 1896
Color lithograph on paper, 42 x 56.7 cm
Munch-museet, Oslo

Cat. no. 126 *The Sick Child* I, 1896
Color lithograph on paper, 41.4 x 58.8 cm
Munch-museet, Oslo

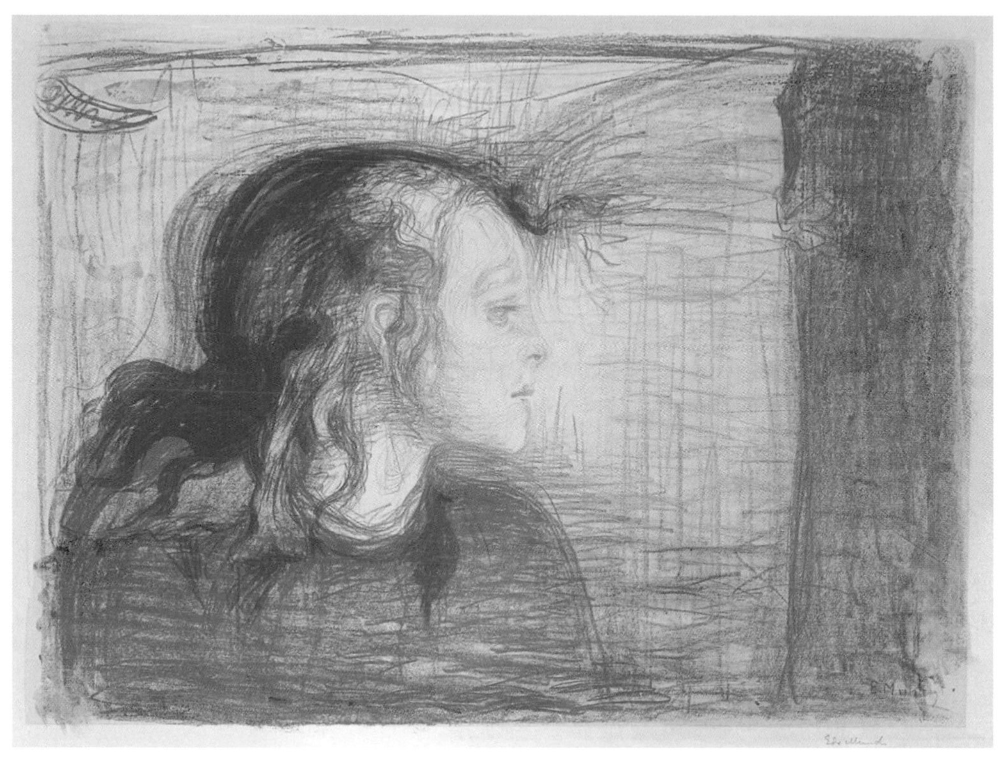

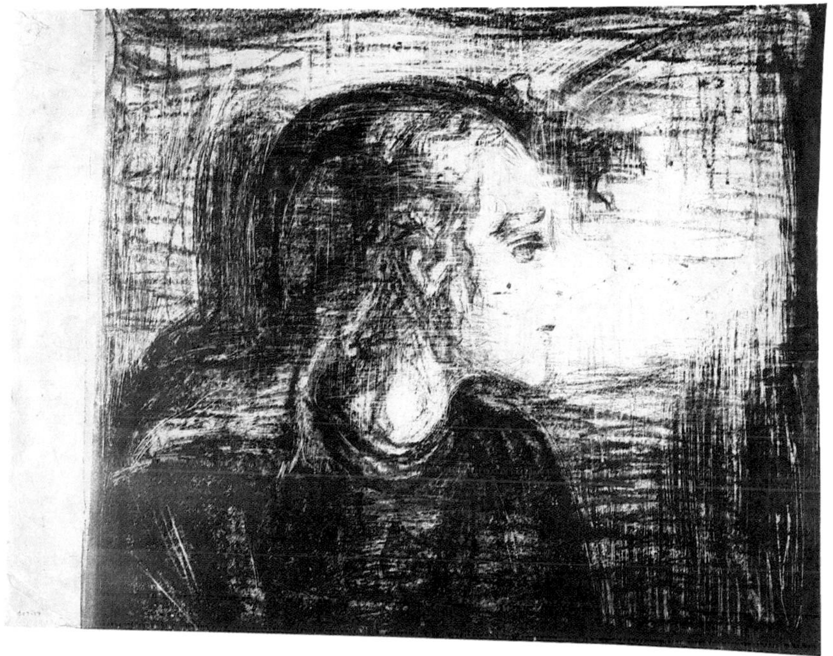

Cat. no. 127 *The Sick Child* I, 1896
Hand-colored color lithograph on paper, 42 x 60 cm
Collection of Catherine Woodard & Nelson Blitz, Jr.

Cat. no. 128 *The Sick Child* II, 1896
Lithograph on paper, 41 x 52 cm
Munch-museet, Oslo

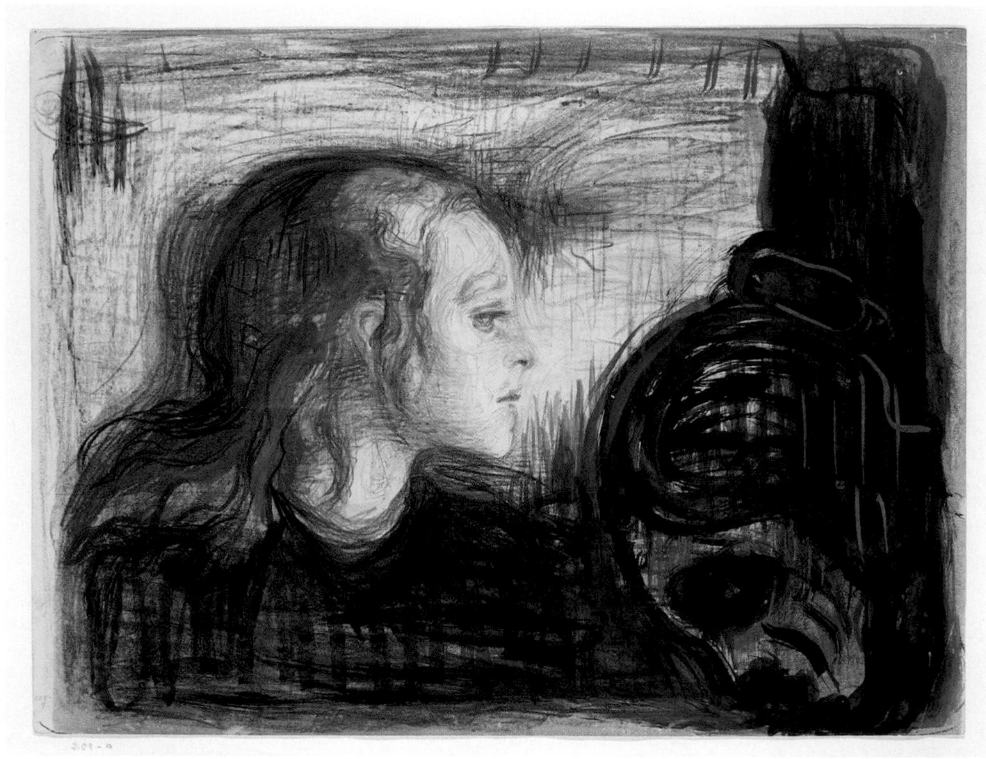

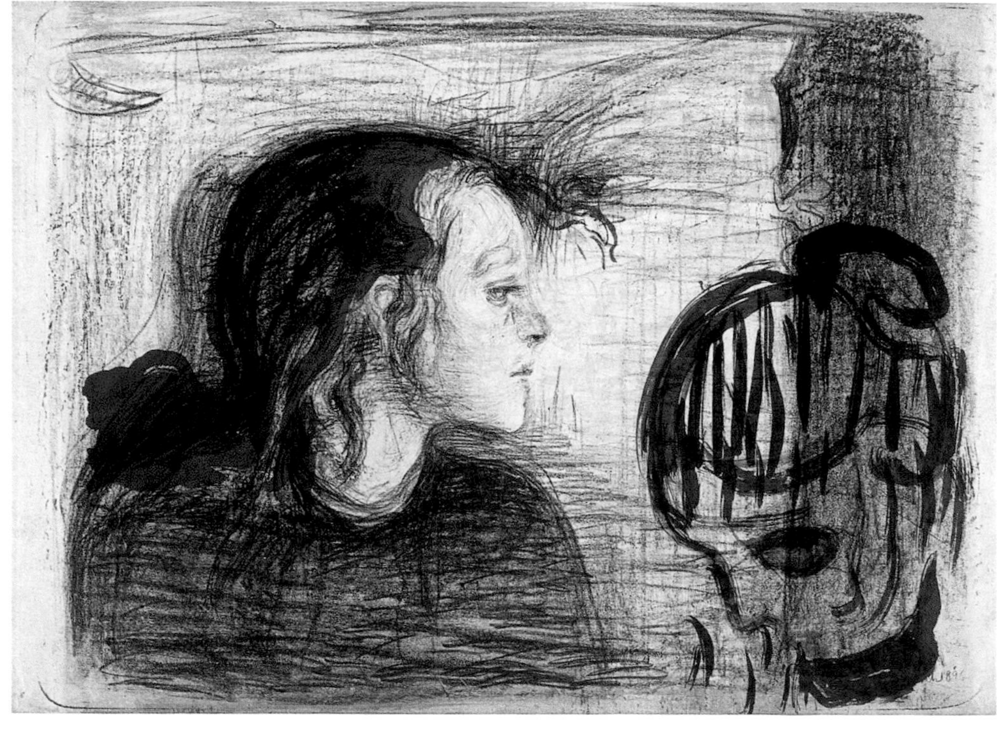

Cat. no. 129 *The Sick Child* I, 1896
Hand-colored color lithograph on paper, 43.2 x 57.3 cm
Munch-museet, Oslo

Cat. no. 130 *The Sick Child* I, 1896
Hand-colored color lithograph on paper, 41.3 x 57.2 cm
Munch-museet, Oslo

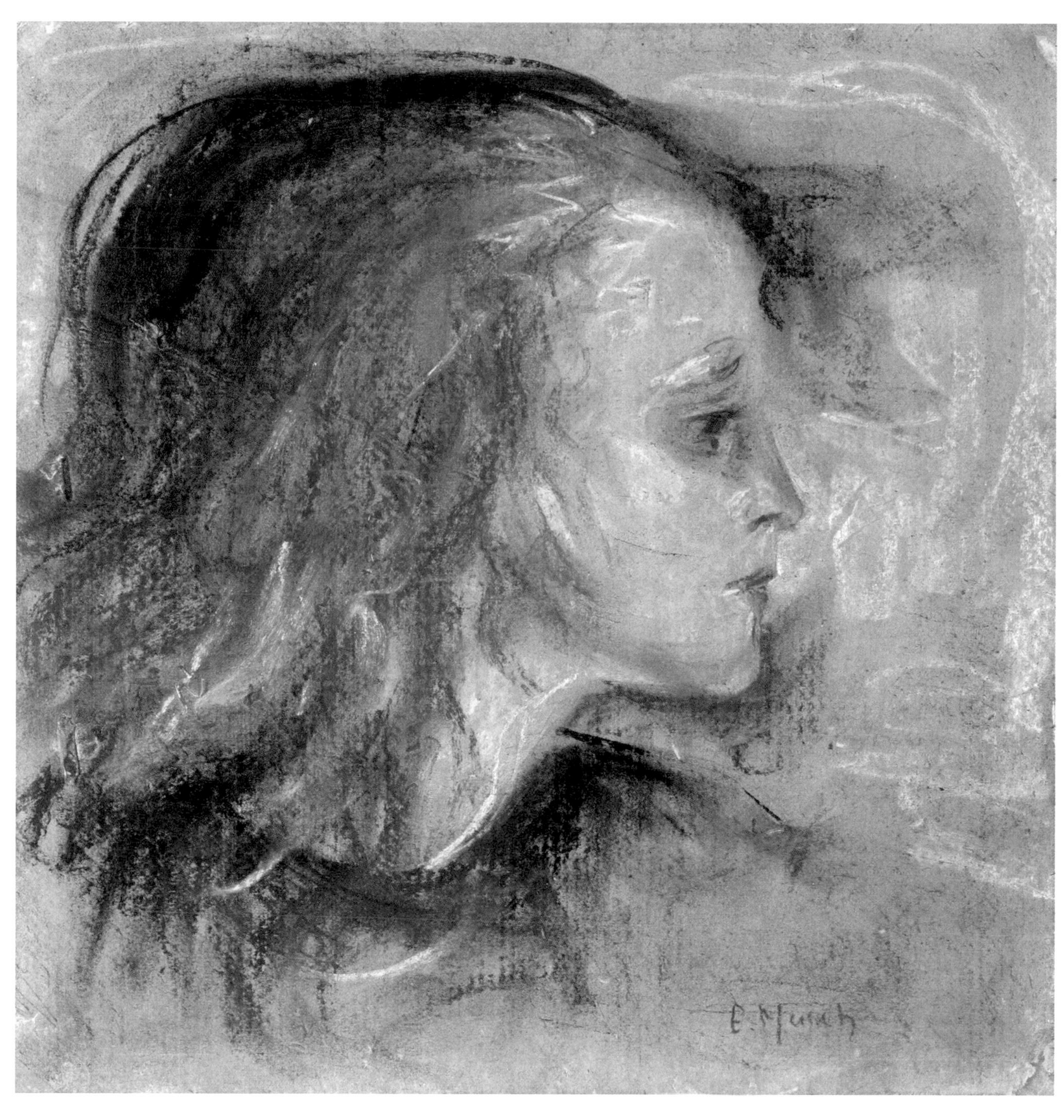

Cat. no. 131 *The Sick Child*, 1890s
Pastel on paper, 42.4 x 40.9 cm
Hamburger Kunsthalle, Kupferstichkabinett

By the Deathbed

Images of death and illness were familiar devotional motifs during the latter half of the 19th century. The adaptation of such Christian themes as suffering and death to the private context of the family as the pillar of middle-class society offered a means of identification. The visual image became a popular representative of personal experience and grief.

Edvard Munch was confronted with illness, death, and mourning even as a very young child. His mother died of tuberculosis at the age of thirty, following the birth of this sister Inger. At age thirteen, he contracted the life-threatening disease himself, which he later described in vivid, moving language: "... another attack of coughing—a new handkerchief—blood coloring nearly the whole cloth—Jesus help me, I'm dying—I mustn't die now."[1] He survived, only to witness his sister Sophie's battle with death the following year: "It was evening—Maja [Sophie] lay in bed, red and hot, her eyes shone and searched the room nervously—she was fantasizing—Dear sweet Karlemann [Edvard], take this from me, it hurts so much—won't you—she looked at him with pleading eyes—yes, you will—Do you see that head over there—it is Death."[2]

In light of these profoundly traumatic experiences, such subjects as *The Sick Child*, *By the Sickbed*, *By the Deathbed*, *Death in the Sickroom*, *Mourning Visit*, *Fever*, *Death and the Child*, and *Dead Mother and the Child* would seem to represent a kind of "working on memory."[3] The first of these "memory images," *The Sick Child (Study)* of 1885–86 (fig. 1, p. 249) depicts eleven-year-old Betzy Nielsen and Munch's aunt Karen Bjølstad, both of whom stood as models. Munch's painting does not present a memory image, however, but rather his model Betzy with her "pale head and vivid red hair on the white pillow" as she actually looked when he painted her. The subject was popular and contemporary. Munch's experimental rendering was initially rejected by the public, but it represented a milestone in his development as an artist as an early example of his unorthodox approach to material and technique: "In the sick child I broke new paths for myself—it was a breakthrough in my art."[4]

In the 1890s, Munch and his family appeared as protagonists in scenes of illness and death, all of which alluded to the dramatic events of his own childhood and youth. *Death in the Sickroom* and *At the Deathbed* deal with the death of his sister Sophie, although, in contrast to *The Sick Child*, she partially disappears from the viewer's field of vision and thus becomes anonymous. In *Death in the Sickroom* (cat. nos. 139–141), she is shown sitting on a chair in the background with her back to the viewer. Attention is concentrated on the people gathered around her and on their despair, grief, and resignation. The figures of Munch and his two sisters Laura and Inger form a compact block in the foreground. Laura sits in her own characteristic manner, her head—red in the painting of the Nasjonalgalleriet—bowed, in front of Inger, who confronts the viewer with severely reddened eyes and a pale, masklike face. Munch himself, his facial features dissolved, is turned towards the scene in the background, which comprises a group of three figures: the praying father, the chair, and his aunt Karen, shown leaning forward. In two drawings (cat. nos. 139, 140) and in a painted version now in the collection of the Nasjonalgalleriet, these figures are joined by the sheet with the bed and the foreground figures, but they are isolated in the lithograph (cat. no. 141). The visual absence of the dying or already deceased girl shifts the focus of the scene to the relatives alone. Their helplessness is particularly evident in the figure of Munch's brother Andreas in the left background, who has turned away from the scene and faces a wall or a closed door. In a charcoal drawing (cat. no. 140), he stands opposite his own shadow, a motif Munch also used in the lithograph entitled *The Insane Woman* (Woll 317), also known as *Melancholy*.

The impression that one is looking at a theater scene is evoked by the large room resembling a stage, which conflicts with the confining closeness of the actual living situation. It is also heightened by the figure of Inger, who faces the audience like a narrator and opens the field of view. The actors are not depicted at their actual ages at the time of Sophie's death but at the time Munch executed these works. The impression is that the family is acting out the scene, in which the father, who died in 1889, is depicted with highly stylized features and shifted to the background. Munch transferred his recollection into the present, adapting it in the manner of a play with a new script but with the same actors who performed in the original drama. The moment of deathly silence appears equally frozen. When he exhibited the painting for the first time at *Unter den Linden* 19 in Berlin, he entitled it *A Death*, de-emphasizing its autobiographical character and presenting it as a universally applicable statement about the loss suffered by surviving relatives.

In the painting *By the Deathbed* of 1895 (cat. no. 132), also known as *Fever* and *Struggle with Death*, Munch confronts the mourners with the anonymous figures of the dying or dead. He dispenses with theatrical references and focuses in the scene set in a barren, indefinable corner of a room on the reclining figure, whose hands rest folded on the blanket. The woman in the foreground is identifiable as his long-since deceased mother. She turns away from the scene but grips the bedpost to hold herself steady. Facing the viewer, Inger closes off the space created by the radically shortened perspective view of the bed. The absence of mouths signifies her total speechlessness and that of her siblings Laura and Andreas. The devoutly religious father prays and is connected to the reclining figure by a diagonal. His hands appear to tremble—as suggested by a second contour line on the right. This effect of motion blurring appears in all of the corresponding drawings and the lithograph of 1896 (cat. no. 134), in which the reclining figure's hands are clenched tightly as she still struggles with death. The ghostlike masks on the wall in the print and the drawings (cat. no. 133) presumably represent the fever-induced hallucinations Munch described in his account of his sister's death: "Do you see that head over there—it is Death." The figure of Death appears as a skeleton on the right in the pastel of 1893 (cat. no. 135) and forms a diagonal with the father and the deathbed. The levels of time are intermingled in these pictures. First of all, the passage from life to death is described in its several stages. Secondly, the actors are not depicted at their actual ages at the time the event occurred in 1877. Thirdly, the mother could not have been present, since she had died in 1868. By gathering the deceased and living members of his family together, Munch created—in an autobiographical sense—a devotional family portrait. In the lithograph of 1896 (cat. no, 134), the action is introduced by his mother. She is turned facing the viewer, with both hands resting on the bedpost. Of those depicted, only his sister Inger, the only sibling who outlived Edvard, and Laura were alive at that time. His brother had died previously at the young age of thirty. Laura, who died in 1926, had been moved to a hospital where she lay, unable to communicate, in a state of acute depression. Yet Munch goes far beyond the defining boundaries of a devotional scene and breaks away from the popular ideas of the 19th century. He depicts the moment of death, virtually forcing the viewer to become involved and making him experience personally the despair, the grief, and the struggle against death.

In the gouache entitled *Fever* (cat. no. 137), Munch portrays himself, surrounded by his father, his mother, and Andreas, as the sick person praying for recovery. This scene looks almost like an illustration of his own written words: "Jesus help me, I am dying—I mustn't die now." In a charcoal drawing (cat. no. 136), he is shown surrounded by large, demoniacal shadows. His sister Sophie has thrown herself across the bed in despair, while his father has already turned away and begun to pray. The scene is characterized by dynamic motion, and the trembling hands appear here once again. Years later, Munch painted the watercolor entitled *The Sick Man Rising* (cat. no. 138), signifying renewed activity and the prospect of recovery in the image of the figure rising from the chair.

DB

1 Munch-museet manuscript T 2771.

2 Quoted and translated from Arne Eggum, "Das Todesthema bei Edvard Munch," in Ulrich Weisner (ed.), *Munch. Liebe. Angst. Tod*, exh. cat., Kunsthalle Bielefeld, Bielefeld 1980, p. 364.

3 Cf. Uwe M. Schneede, *Edvard Munch. Das kranke Kind. Arbeit an der Erinnerung*, Frankfurt am Main 1984.

4 Edvard Munch, *Livsfrisens tilblivelse*, Oslo n. d. [1928?], pp. 9 and 10.

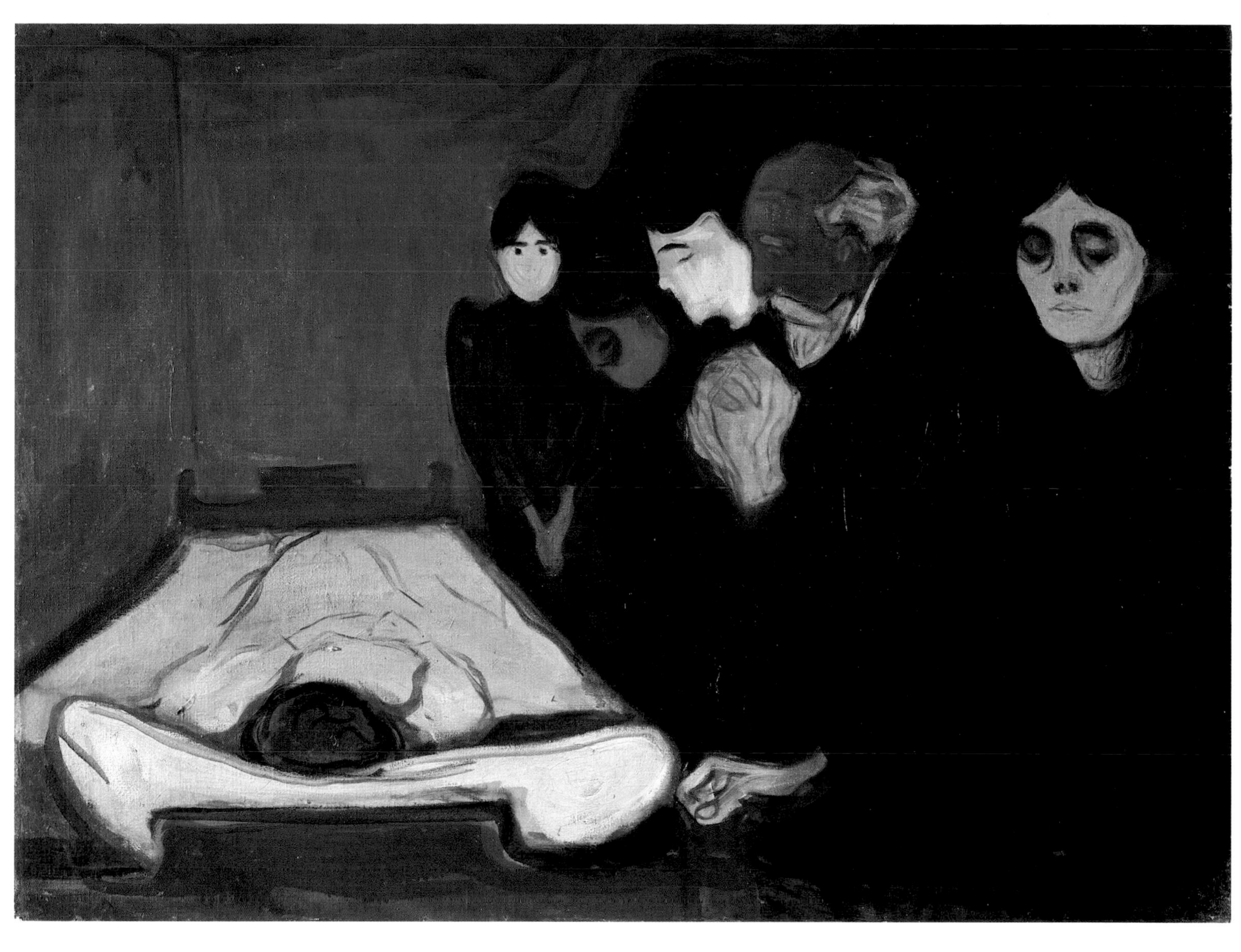

Cat. no. 132 *By the Deathbed*, 1895
Oil on canvas, 90 x 120.5 cm
Rasmus Meyers Samlinger, Bergen Kunstmuseum

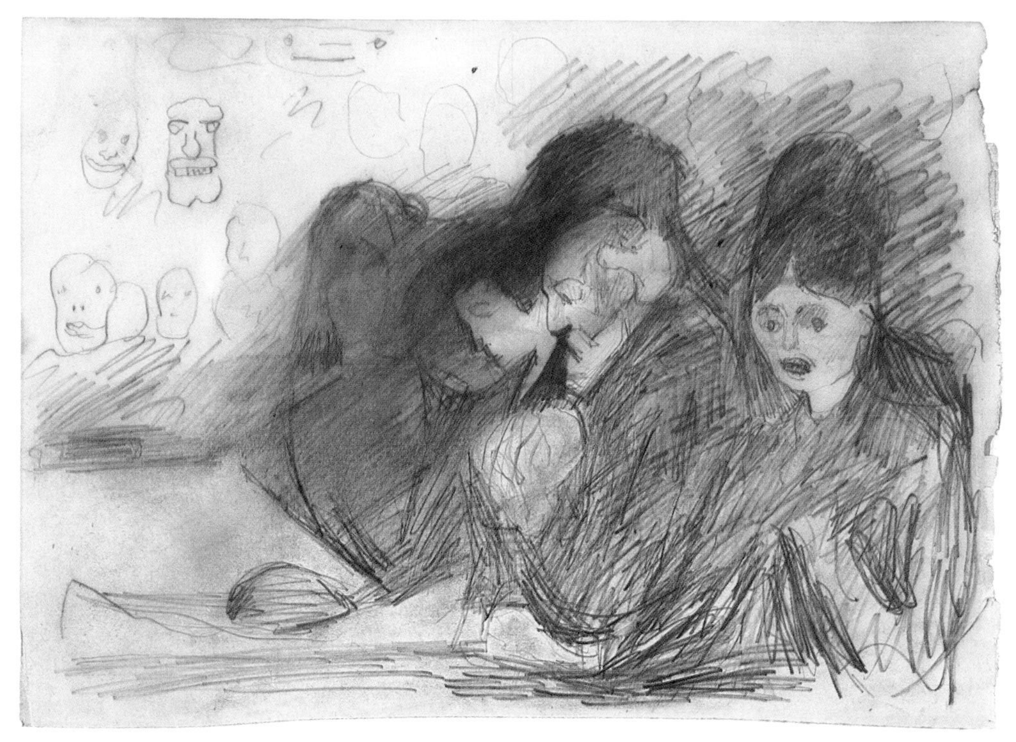

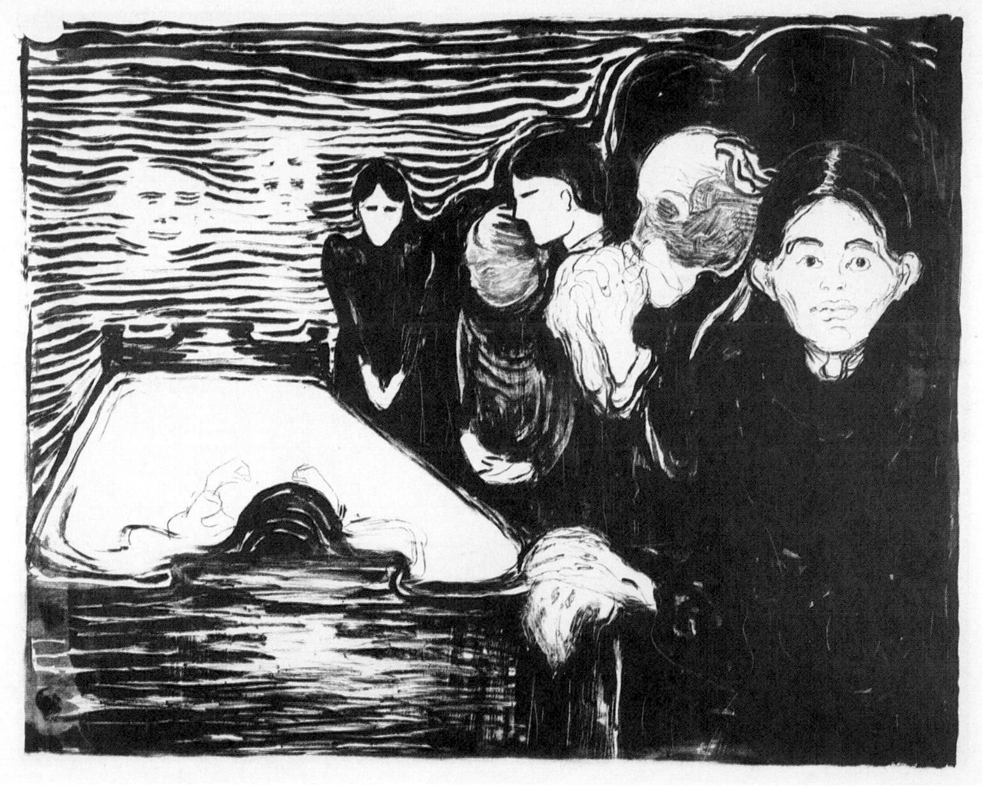

Cat. no. 133 *By the Deathbed* (*Fever*), 1893
Drawing on paper, 23 x 31.7 cm
Munch-museet, Oslo

Cat. no. 134 *By the Deathbed*, 1896
Lithograph on paper, 39.5 x 50 cm
Albertina, Vienna

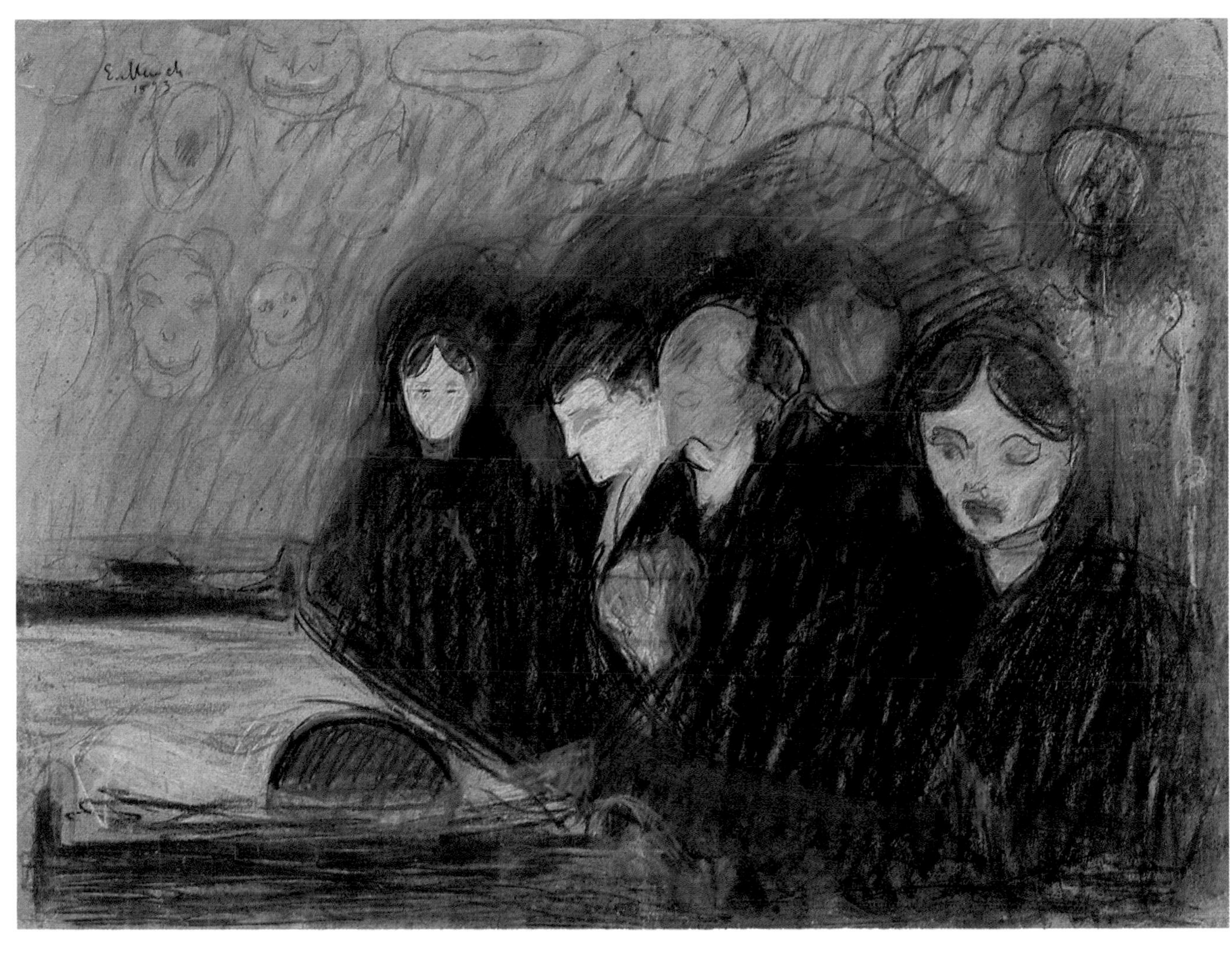

Cat. no. 135 *By the Deathbed* (*Fever*), 1893
Pastel and pencil on cardboard, 59 x 78.5 cm
Munch-museet, Oslo

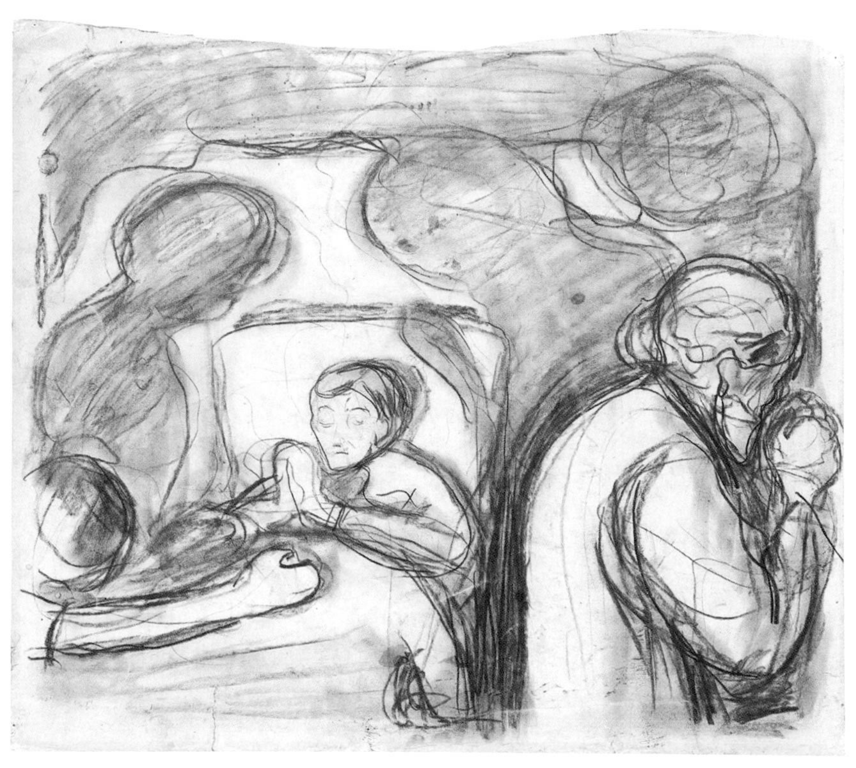

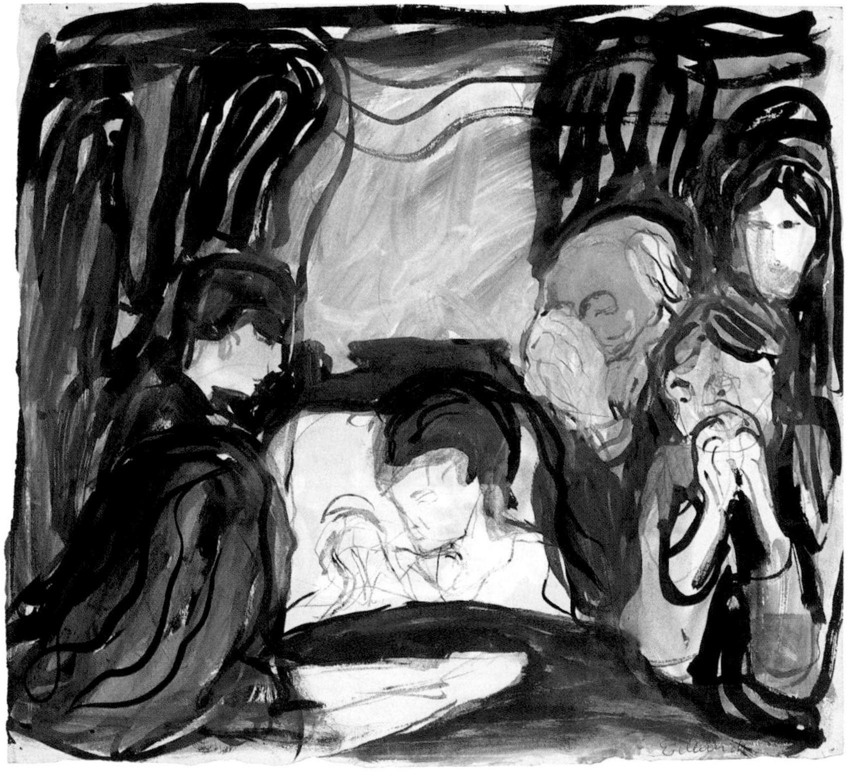

Cat. no. 136 *Fever*, c. 1894
Drawing on paper, 42.5 x 48.3 cm
Munch-museet, Oslo

Cat. no. 137 *Fever*, 1894
Drawing and gouache on paper, 31.6 x 34.7 cm
Munch-museet, Oslo

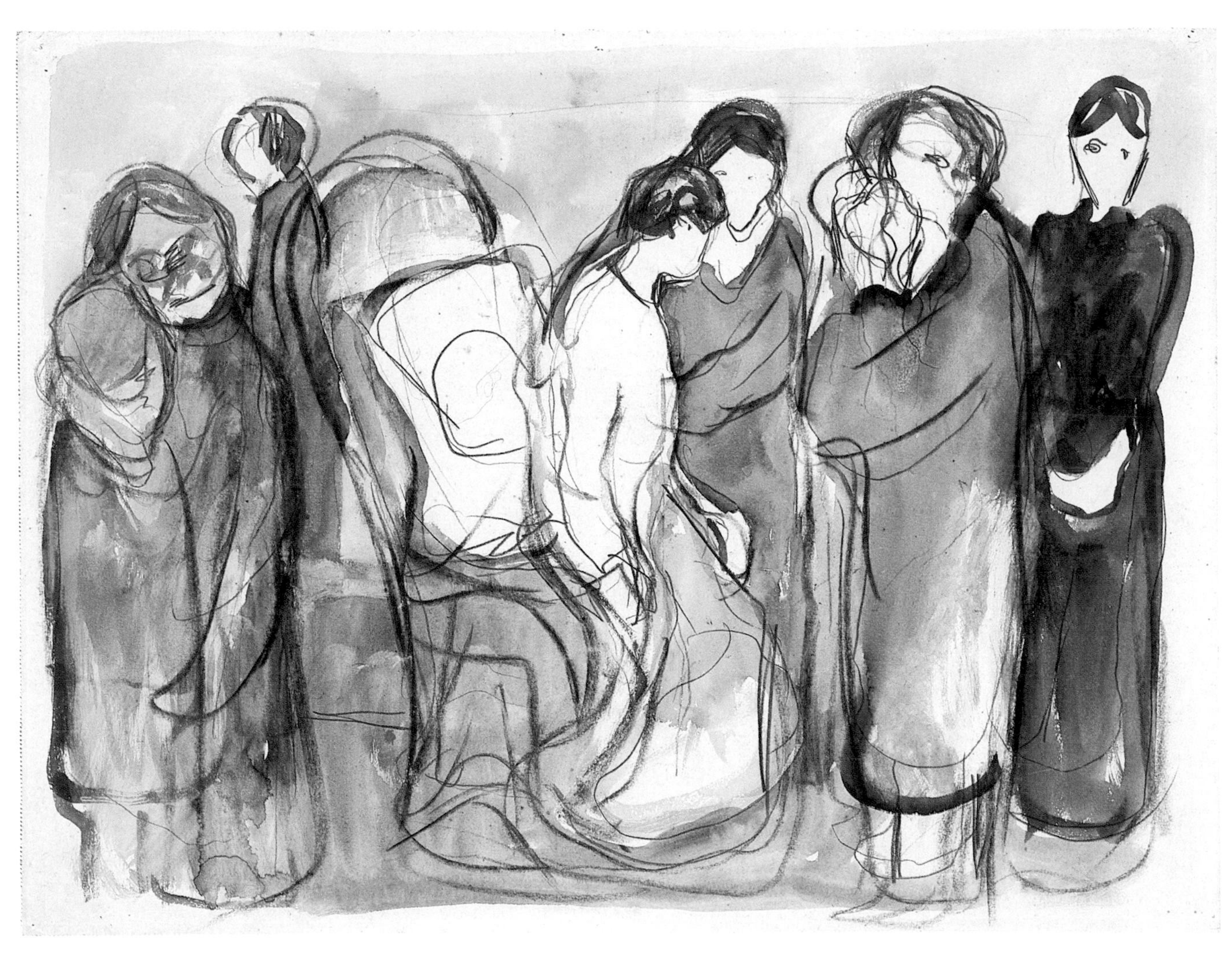

Cat. no. 138 *The Sick Man Rising*, 1907–08
Drawing and watercolor on paper, 37 x 49.4 cm
Munch-museet, Oslo

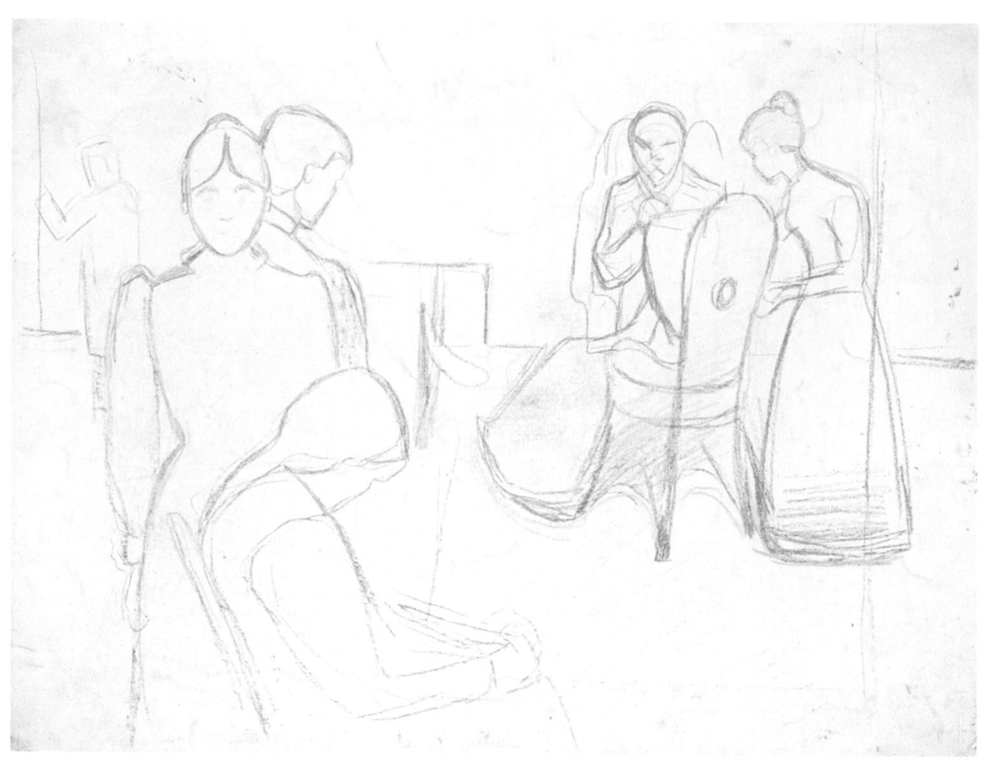

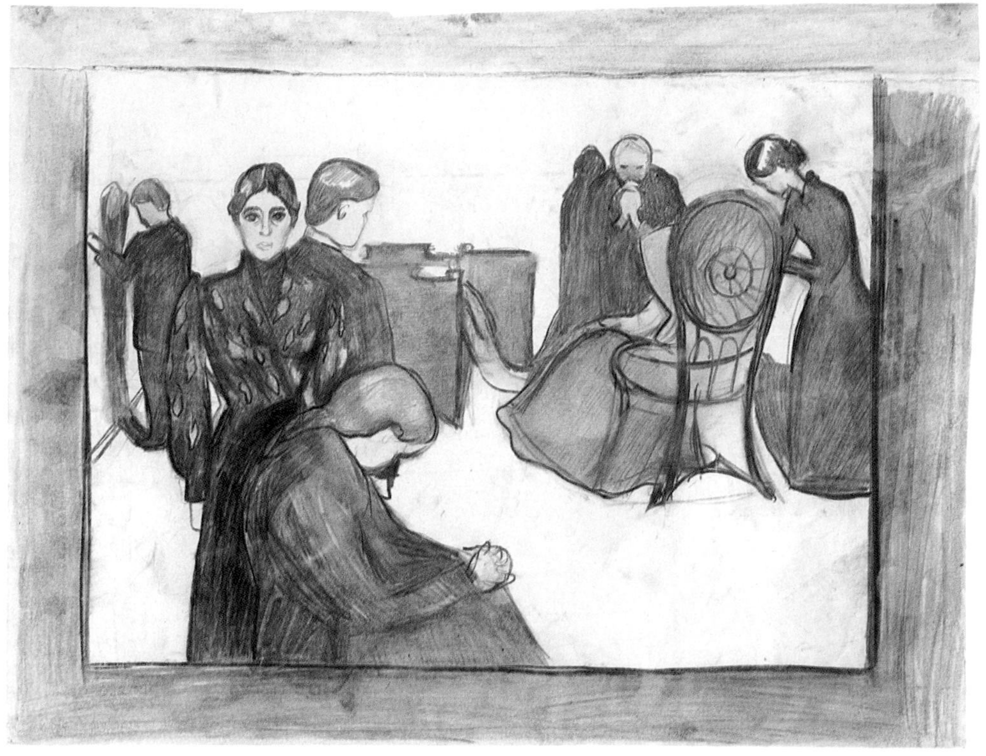

Cat. no. 139 *Death in the Sickroom*, 1894–96
Drawing on paper, 37 x 48.5 cm, Munch-museet, Oslo

Cat. no. 140 *Death in the Sickroom*, 1893
Drawing on paper, 35 x 46 cm, Munch-museet, Oslo

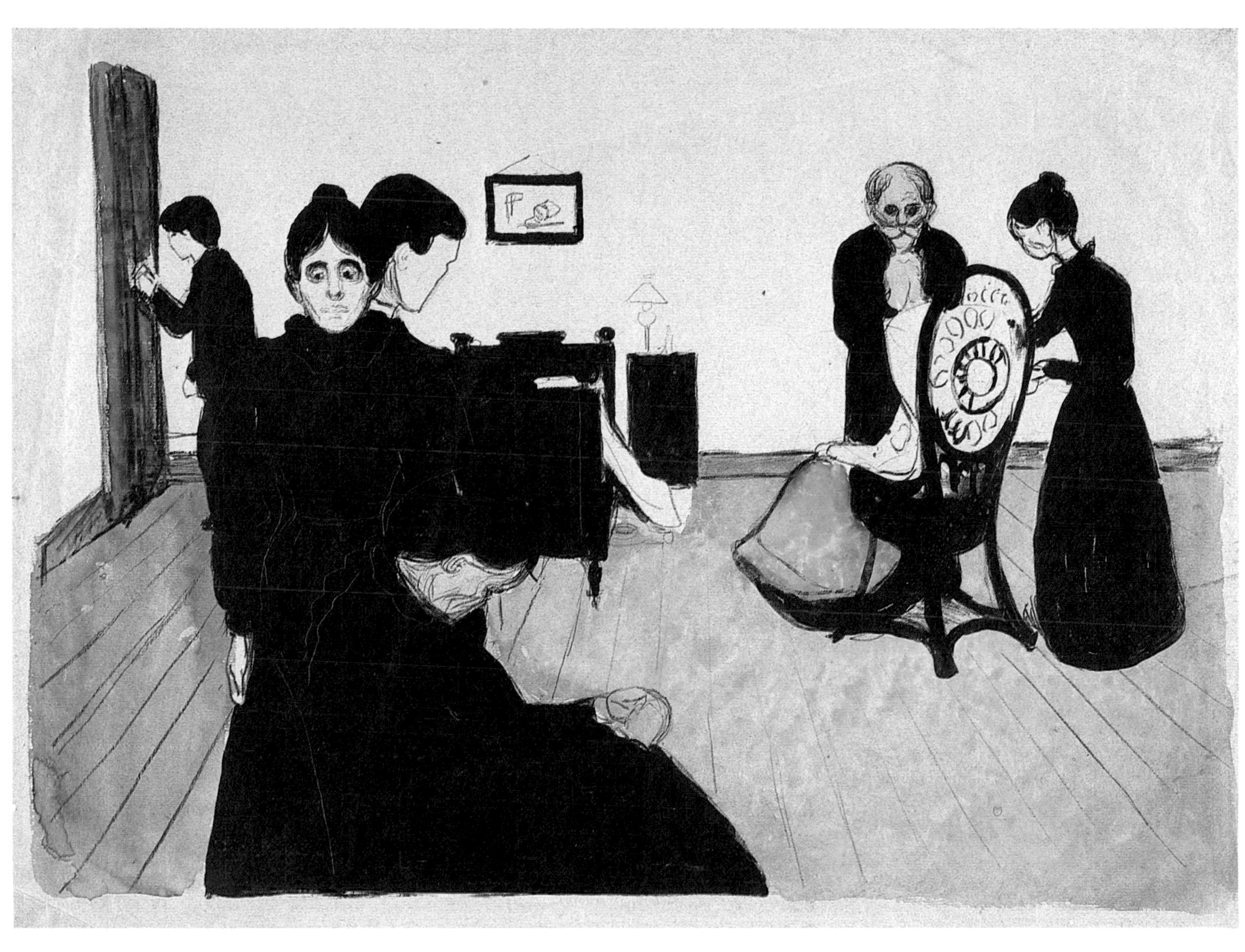

Cat. no. 141 *Death in the Sickroom*, 1896
Hand-colored lithograph on paper, 30.3 x 55.8 cm
Munch-museet, Oslo

Landscape

Munch began drawing and painting scenes in Kristiania and environs as a youth. Inspired by traditional Norwegian landscape paintings, he strove for clarity and precision in true-to-life depiction and probably used such aids as a camera obscura and a camera lucida. His decision to become a painter came in 1880, and his first small oil paintings reflect the influence of the Norwegian landscape painter Frits Thaulow, who, along with Christian Krohg, played a significant role in contemporary cultural life in Norway. Under the influence of the Kristiania bohemians, however, Munch abandoned open-air painting and focused on the human being as the central theme of his painting. His unconventional use of paint in landscapes is an expression of changes in his ideas about art:

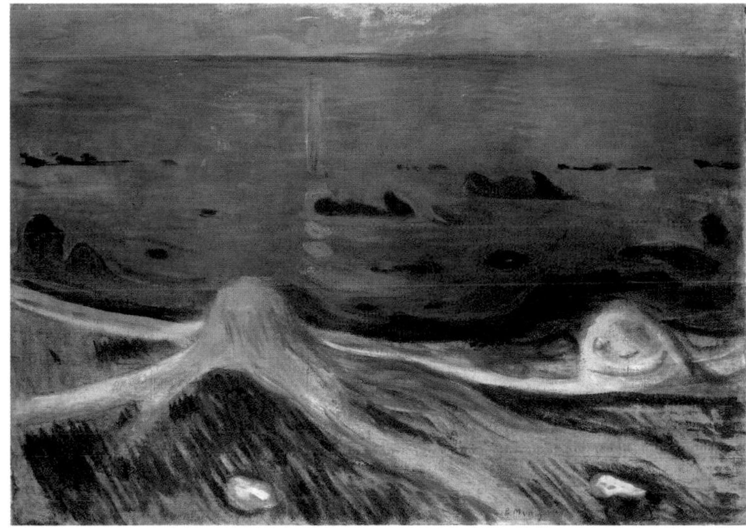

1 *Mystical Shore*, 1892, oil on canvas, 100 x 140 cm, private collection

It was the era of realism and impressionism.—It so happened that I would find myself in either a morbidly agitated state of mind or a cheerful mood when I discovered a landscape I wanted to paint.—I got out my easel, stood it up, and painted the picture from nature.—It would turn out to be a good painting—but not what I had wanted to paint. I couldn't paint it the way I saw it in my disturbed or joyful mood.—That happened often.—So in one such case I began to scratch away what I had painted—I searched my memory for the first image—the first impression—and tried to recover it.[1]

The landscape became a field for the projection of human feelings and states of mind. In paintings such as *Evening* (cat. no. 80), Munch began to establish relationships between figure and landscape, seeking to express such emotional states as loneliness and melancholy in the interplay of human and natural motifs. During his stays in France between 1889 and 1892, he experimented in views of the Seine, scenes featuring Mediterranean light, and the southern landscape around Nice with impressionist and post-impressionist painting techniques, breaking away from naturalism forever. At the Autumn Salon of 1891, Christian Krohg praised the first painted version of *Melancholy*, exhibited under the title of *Evening*, as the first symbolist work produced by a Norwegian painter. Munch strove to achieve maximum intensity of expression through the simplification of line, form, and color. The background scene of the beach is interpretable as a mental projection of the foreground figure; the choice of color is of symbolic significance.

In the summer of 1892, Munch produced his first symbolist landscapes in Åsgårdstrand, among them *Moonlight on the Shore* and *Mystical Shore* (fig. 1), which were described by a critic for the *Aftenposten* in his review of Munch's solo exhibition hosted by the jeweler Tostrup in Kristiania on September 14, 1892. In his discussion of *Moonlight on the Shore* (cat. no. 142), the critic called attention in particular to the strange reflections of the moon: "They are moons that are reflected four times on the Earth, so that they appear as a chain of gold coins above the remarkable rock formations discovered by the keen-eyed impressionist." The landscape is rendered with an open, dynamic application of paint; the stones have a very organic appearance. Against the solitary background of a beach devoid of human figures, the unused red boat is the only sign of possible human presence. The orange moon is repeated in the manner of image artifacts on the retina or the effect of backlight in photography, as if Munch had incorporated a physiological or optical phenomenon into his painting. The unusual light effect imbues the painting with an unreal, mystical atmosphere quite in keeping with Munch's ideas: "The mystical will always be present—will emerge—the more one discovers, the more things there will be that cannot be explained."[2] This sense of mysticism is uniquely heightened by the many-armed creature, the amorphous rocks, and the white, troll-like anthropomorphic figure in *Mystical Shore*. The *Aftenposten* critic soberly described the animals as "large octopuses with long arms lying lengthwise with their faces in the sand." However, this metamorphosis of nature, this humanization of the natural elements, also calls to mind the world of Nordic legends. When Munch transposed the motif into a woodcut in 1899 (cat. no. 143), he eliminated the symbolic props of mystical spirits of the sea. He translated *Mystical Shore* into a seascape with a phallus-shaped light reflection and a tree stump with roots resembling the arms of an octopus. In the painting *Summer Night on the Shore* (cat. no. 144), in which he turned his attention once again to the strip of coast near Åsgårdstrand in 1902, he emphasized the amorphous. Employing an impasto technique in some places as well as vivid coloration, he transformed the rocks into organic forms that contrast with the calm surface of the sea, which is rendered in transparent colors. The unity of the light reflection as a phallic symbol is disturbed, the moon or sun isolated from its reflection as an expression of loneliness. In the constant interplay of symbolic, rarely mystical forms, and natural structures, Munch compresses elements of the landscape, dissolves them or isolates them, creating symbolic constellations as a means of expressing specific moods.

As early as 1894, Munch established a link between his symbolist landscapes and his later *Frieze of Life* when he included *Mystical Shore* in his *Studies for a Mood Series: "Love"*. At the first comprehensive presentation of the *Frieze of Life* in Berlin in 1902, he replaced *Mystical Shore* with a version of *Starry Night* (cat. no. 38). This work is closely related to the theme of *Attraction* and alludes in both surviving versions completed during the 1890s to a human presence in the form of a ghostlike woman's head and a shadow. In contrast to the other landscapes Munch used as settings for the figures in the *Frieze of Life*, he eliminated all suggestions of human presence in *Beach near Åsgårdstrand* (cat. no. 29). The gap between the long, sweeping, dark-purple lines that define the shore and the few tree-trunks on the right creates a kind of stage as a field of projection for the viewer's thoughts.

Near the turn of the century, Munch painted a number of landscapes in Ljan, Norway, which, by virtue of their nearly monochrome coloration and the animated quality of trees and shadows, signify a high point in the development of symbolism. This is particularly true of *Starry Night* of 1901 (cat. no. 152), a view of a snow-covered forest clearing in which pictorial space is defined by three converging tree shadows. The amorphous shapes of the rocks in the foreground and the silhouettes of the trees in the background evoke an atmosphere of mystery reminiscent of a dream landscape. Munch focused once again specifically on the theme of the winter landscape in Kragerø after returning to Norway in the aftermath of his nervous breakdown in 1909. The panoramic views of the rocky, barren fjord landscape and its offshore islands (cat. no. 148) differ markedly from the seascapes done around the turn of the century. The contrast between the vast fields of snow and the rocks and strips of meadow is heightened by nuances of color, while the dynamic forms and the distant horizon celebrate the experience of nature. Munch also presented winter landscapes in a number of prints, showing forests, gardens (cat. no. 145), houses (cat. no. 147), and coastal scenes. In some woodcuts (cat. no. 146), one notes the first signs of a radical dissolution of pictorial structure.

In Ekely, where Munch explored the immediate surroundings of his estate in landscapes, garden scenes, and interiors, he once again took up the theme of the winter *Starry Night* (cat. no. 151). The shadow indicates the presence of the painter himself, while the light of the stars and the city lights of Kristiania combine to create a complex light atmosphere. The dark area in the foreground of a woodcut of 1930 (cat. no. 150) can also be read as a shadow that contrasts with the city in the background as a sign of Munch's ambivalent longing for solitude, itself an expression of loneliness. DB

1 Edvard Munch, *Livsfrisens tilblivelse*, Oslo n. d. [1928?], p. 8.

2 Quoted and translated from Ragna Stang, *Edvard Munch. Der Mensch und der Künstler*, Königstein 1979, p. 79.

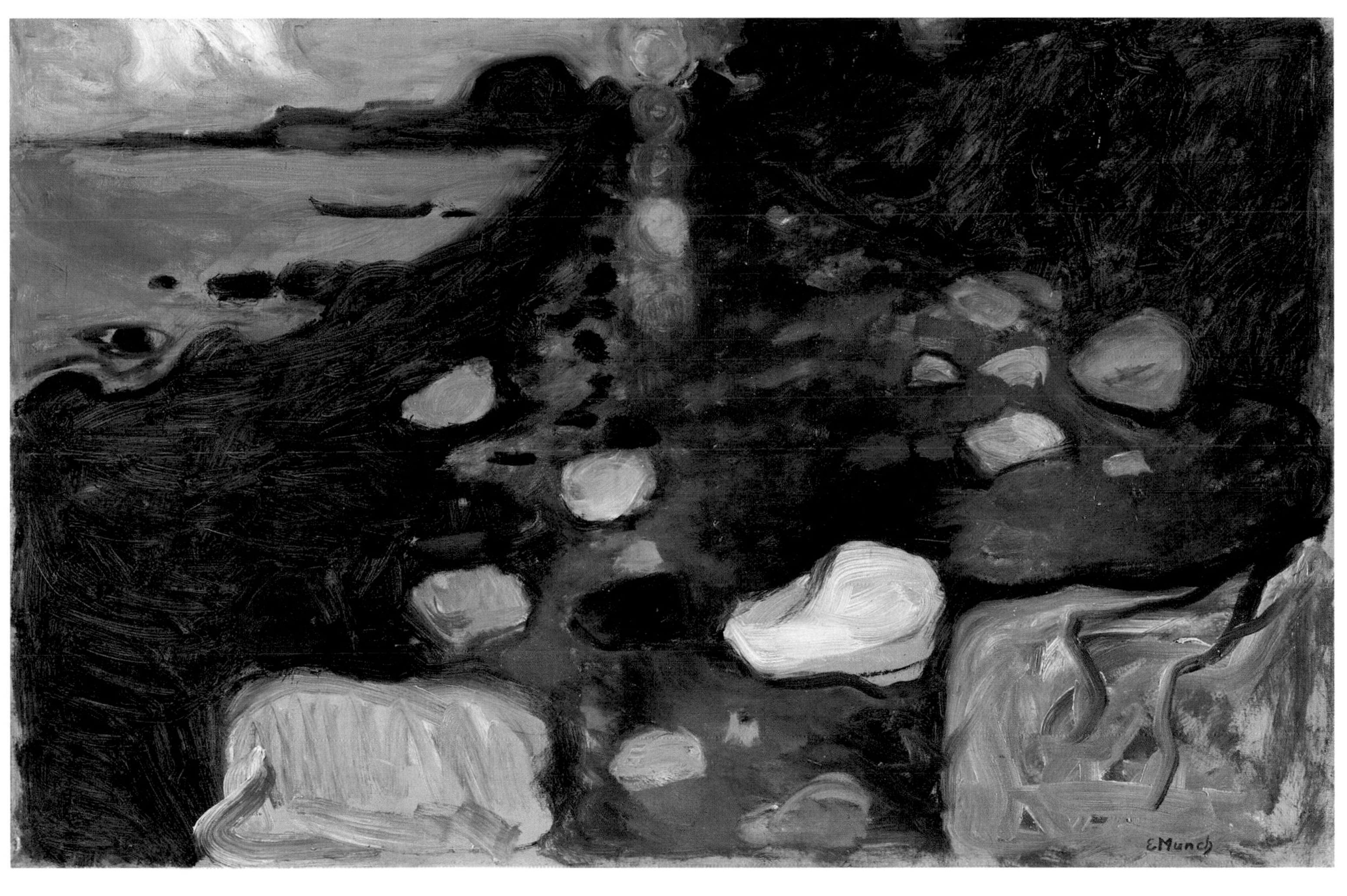

Cat. no. 142 *Moonlight on the Shore*, 1892
Oil on canvas, 62.5 x 96 cm
Rasmus Meyers Samlinger, Bergen Kunstmuseum

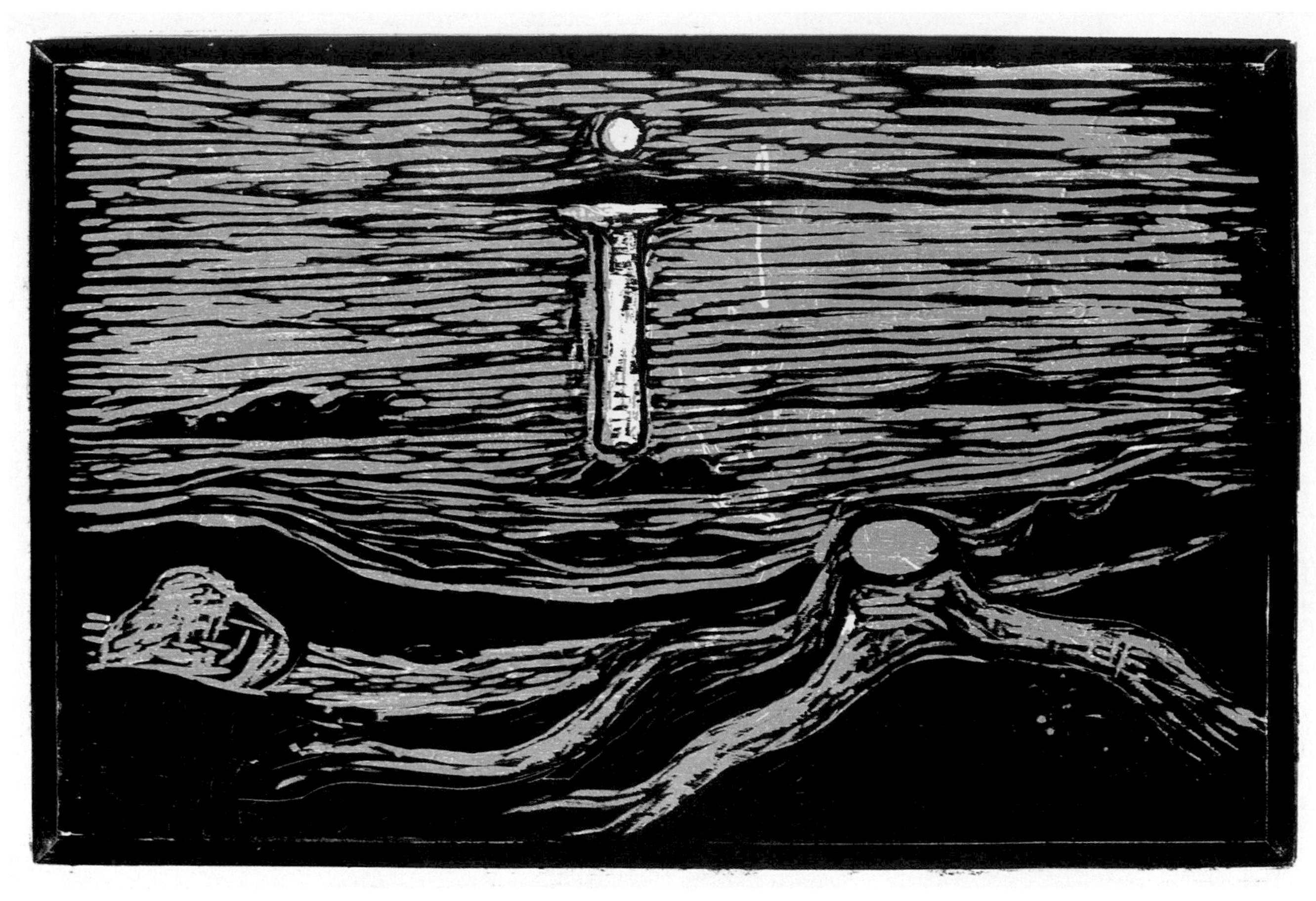

Cat. no. 143 *Mystical Shore*, 1899
Color woodcut on paper, 37 x 57.2 cm
Munch-museet, Oslo

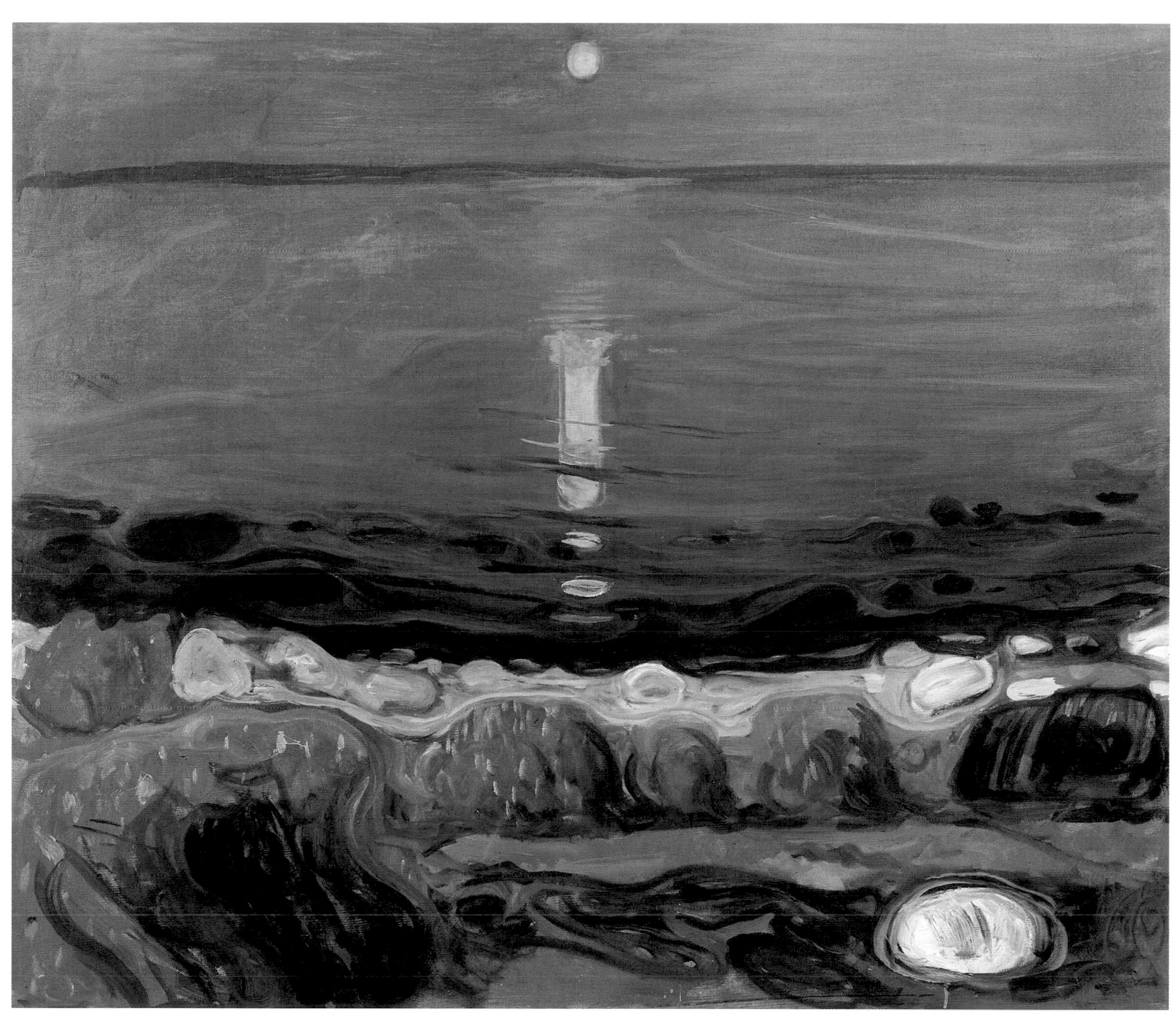

Cat. no. 144 *Summer Night on the Shore*, 1902
Oil on canvas, 103 x 120 cm
Österreichische Galerie Belvedere, Vienna

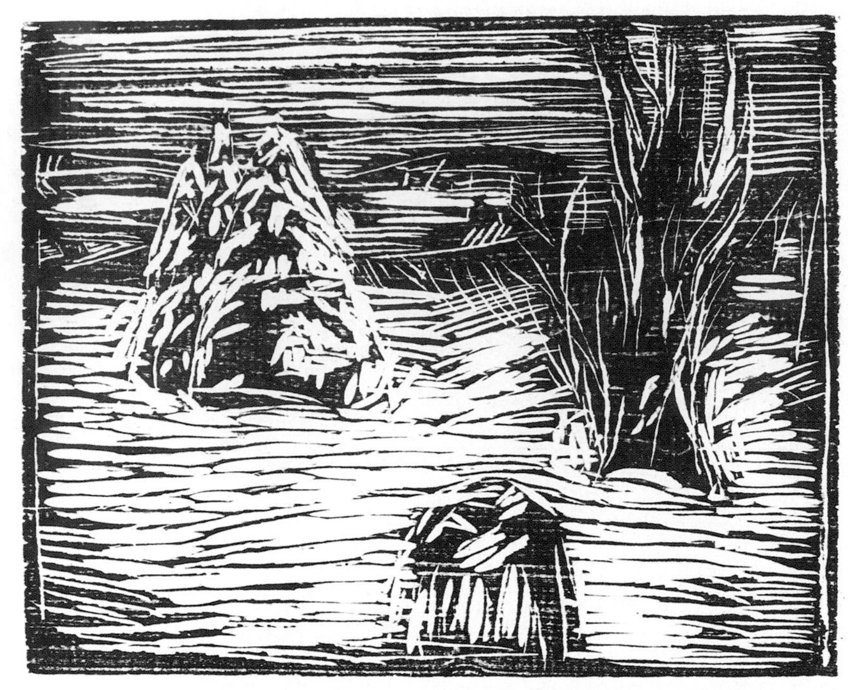

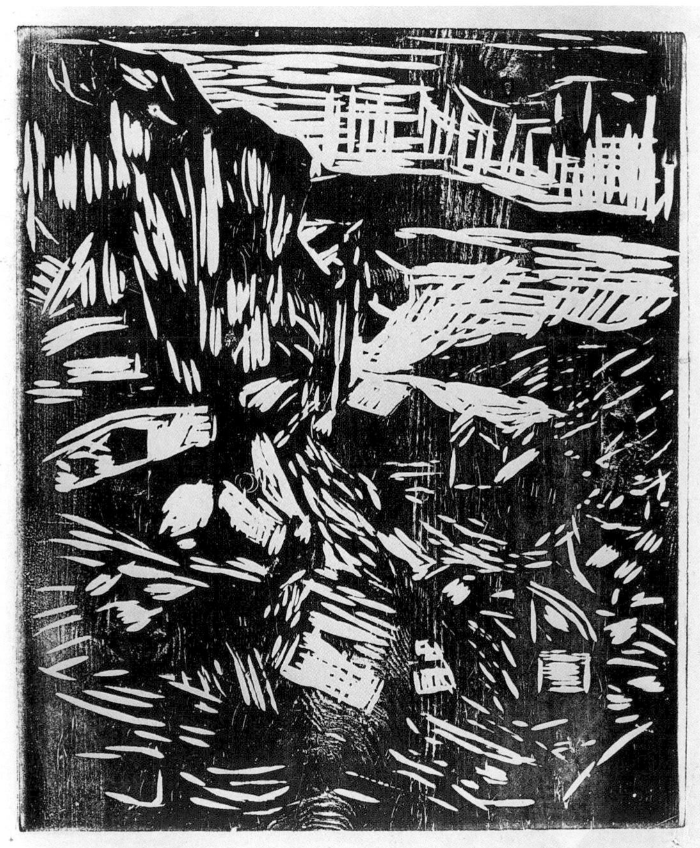

Cat. no. 145 *Garden in Snow* I, 1913
Woodcut on paper, 34.6 x 43 cm
Munch-museet, Oslo

Cat. no. 146 *Kragerø in Winter*, 1914
Woodcut on paper, 49.8 x 49 cm
Munch-museet, Oslo

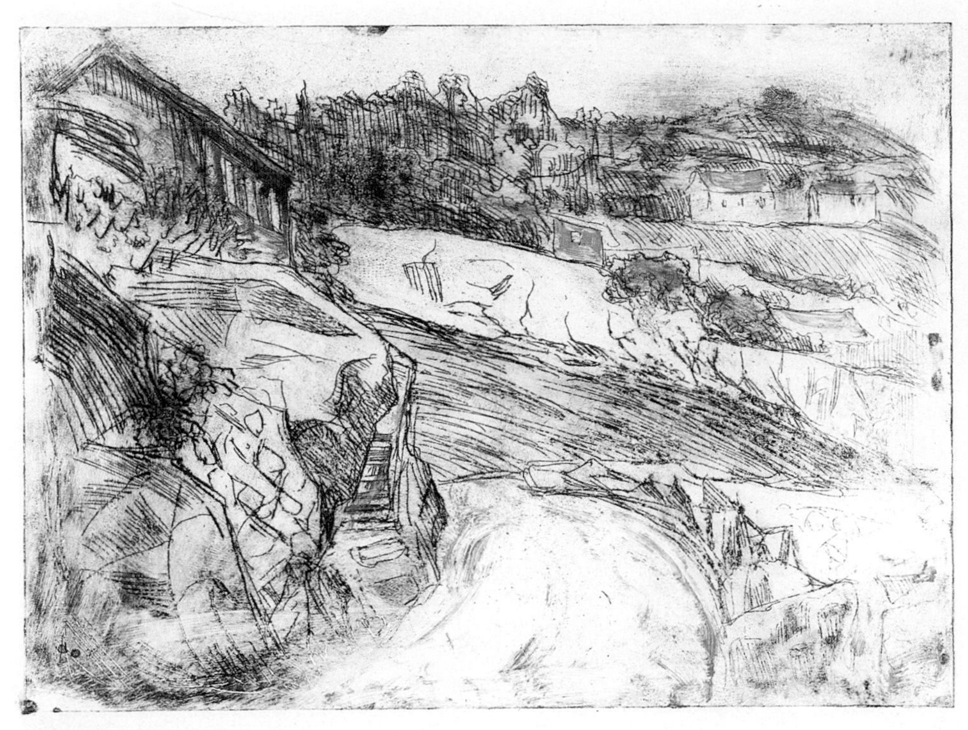

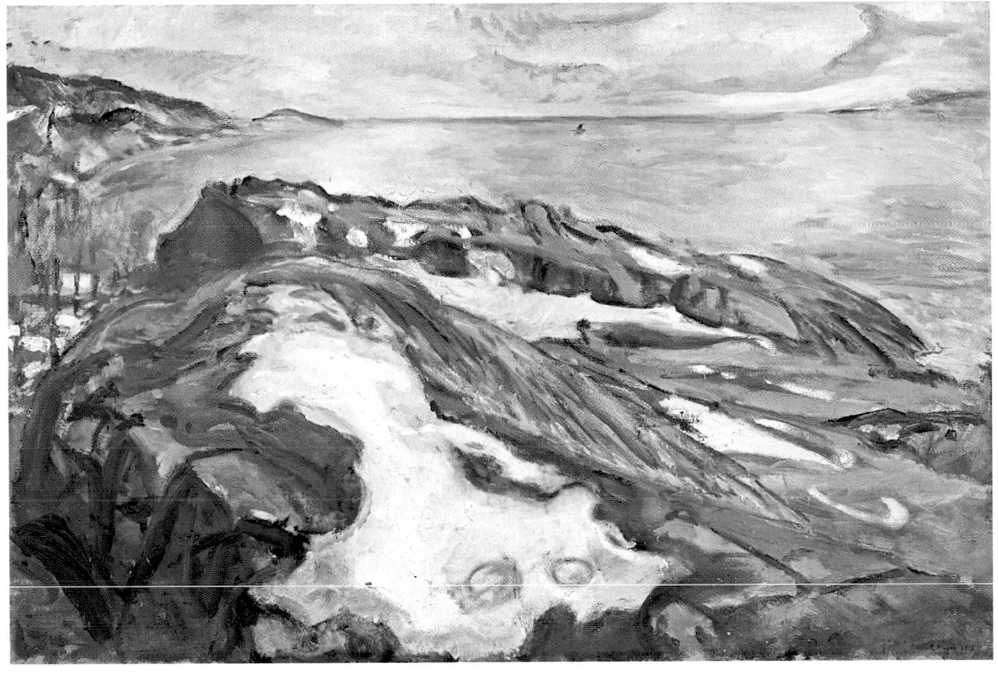

Cat. no. 147 *Houses in Kragerø*, 1915
Etching on paper, 43.9 x 59.6 cm
Munch-museet, Oslo

Cat. no. 148 *Winter Landscape*, 1915
Oil on canvas, 100 x 150 cm
Stiftung R. and H. Batliner

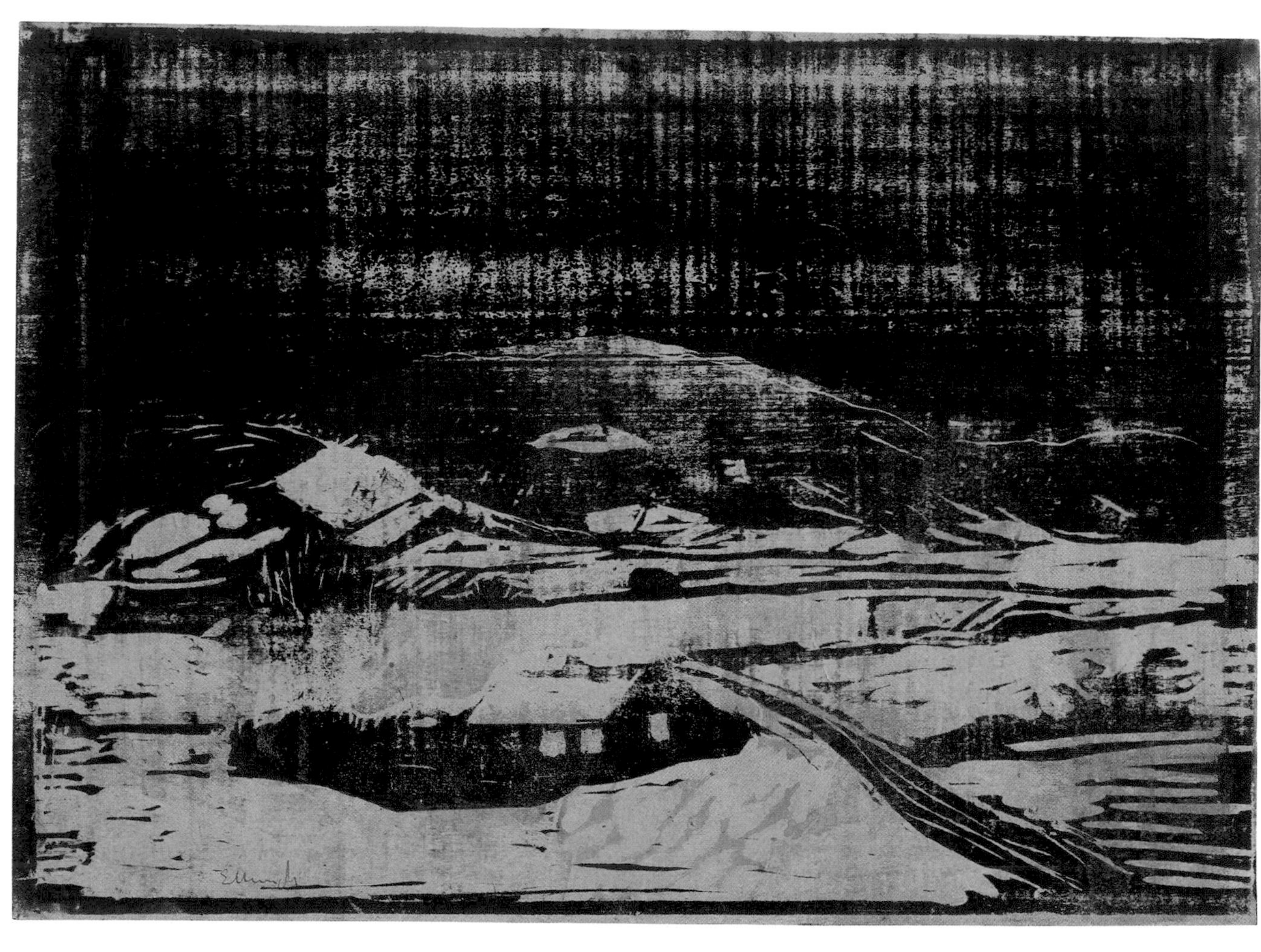

Cat. no. 149 *The Great Snow Landscape*, 1898
Color woodcut on paper, 32.9 x 45.8 cm
Museum of Fine Arts, Boston, Sophie M. Fiedman Fund

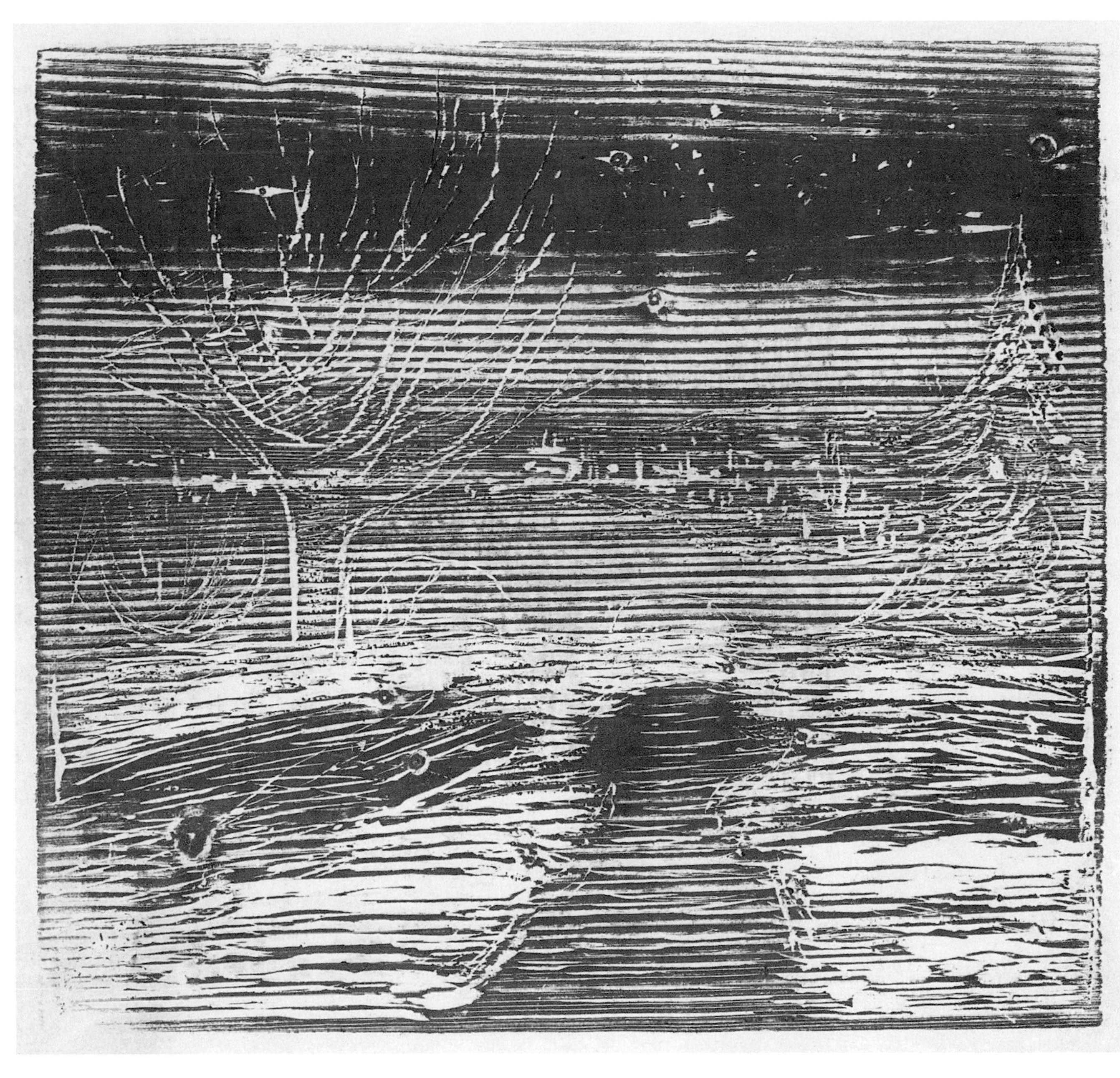

Cat. no. 150 *Starry Night*, 1930
Woodcut on paper, 37 x 40 cm
Munch-museet, Oslo

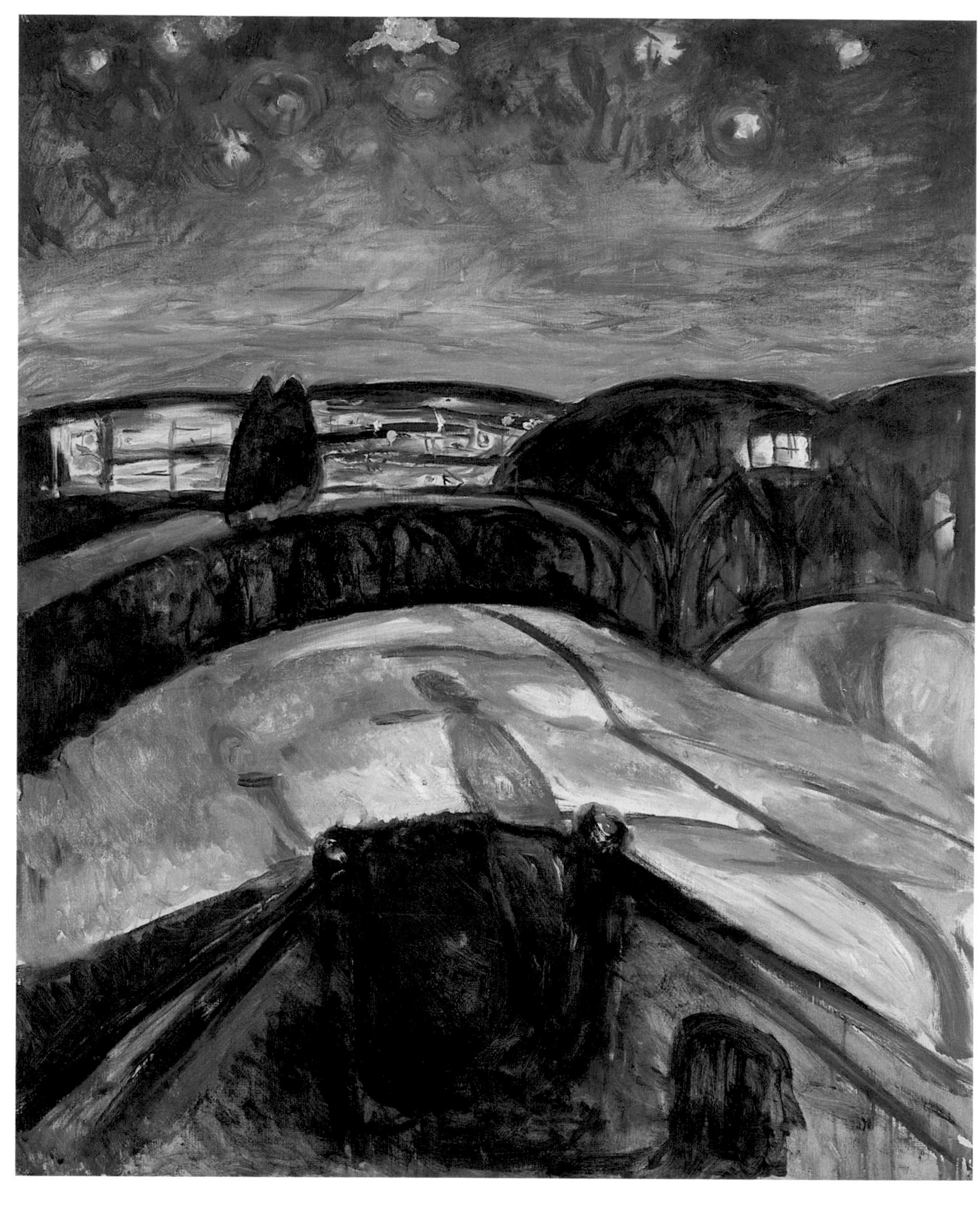

Cat. no. 151 *Starry Night* II, 1922–24
Oil on canvas, 120.5 x 100 cm
Munch-museet, Oslo

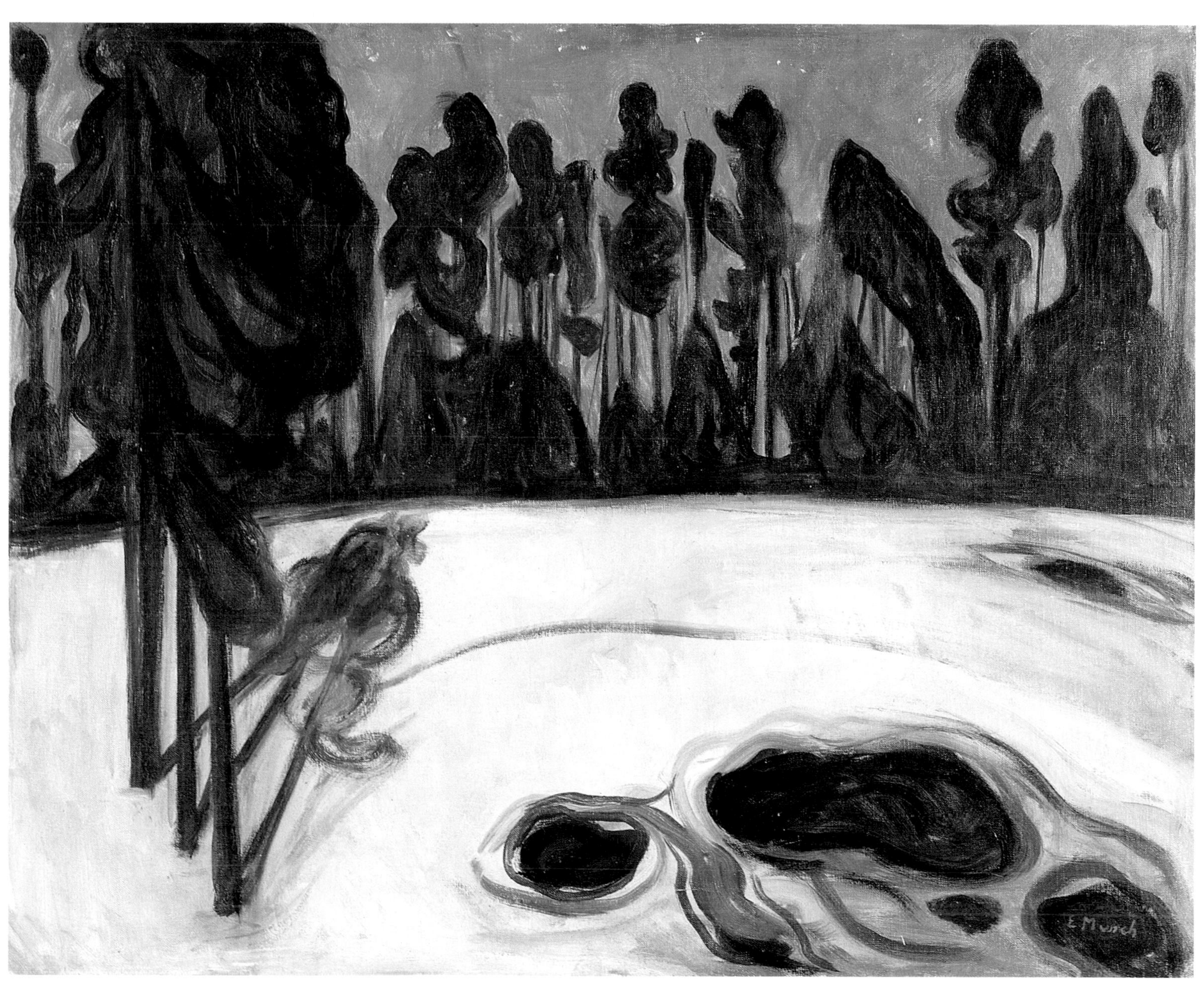

Cat. no. 152 *Starry Night*, 1901
Oil on canvas, 59 x 73 cm
Museum Folkwang, Essen

The Avenue

At the *5th Berlin Secession Exhibition* in 1902, Munch grouped *The Scream* (cat. no. 118), *Evening on Karl Johans Gate* (cat. no. 114), *Angst* (cat. no. 116), *Golgatha* (fig. 6, p. 60), and *Red Virginia Creeper* (cat. no. 155) together under the heading of *Existential Anxiety*. All five of these paintings feature a foreground figure or figures facing the viewer. In *Red Virginia Creeper*, exhibited under the title *Autumn* at the time, the figure is cut off at chest level by the lower edge of the painting. The man in the foreground with the grayish face and wide-open eyes resembles the image of Stanislaw Przybyszewski in *Jealousy* I (cat. no. 74). His eyes echo the vivid red of the building in the background, which is covered by red Virginia creeper. As in the hand-colored version of *Jealousy* I, red is used to express anger, despair, and—here in particular—fear. A path behind the foreground figure draws the viewer's gaze to the house positioned in the center of the scene. The amorphous mass of its covering of Virginia creeper appears to develop an organic life of its own. Only the leafless tree in front of the white fence cuts through the house, forming a prominent dividing line. The tree-trunk, which splits apart towards the top, may be read as a reference to an intimate relationship between two people and the stump as the jealous, excluded third person in the lovers' triangle. Evidently, Munch let thinly diluted paint run down the canvas in the area of the path, then turned the square painting ninety degrees counter-clockwise before resuming his work. These horizontal lines of paint extending from the face and the vertical ones which run downward in the lower right-hand corner clearly heighten the dramatic tension of the scene. These dramatic effects, combined with the structure of the composition, relate this painting to *The Murderer* (cat. no. 157) and *The Murderer on the Lane* (cat. no. 158), although the foreground figures in those works appear as transparent overlays on the road. The movement of the three-quarter figure striding towards the viewer in *The Murderer* of 1910 (cat. no. 157) is indicated by the leading, transparent right leg and the figure's overall fleeting quality. The lane is bordered on each side by contrasting light and dark rock formations which suggest the human duality of positive and negative, good and evil. Unlike the portrait-style facial features of the foreground figure in *Red Virginia Creeper*, the green face of the "murderer" is anonymous, a mask without mouth or nose. Yet the scene is puzzlingly ambiguous, as it is impossible to tell whether the crime has already been committed or the perpetrator is only just approaching his victim. His hands are tense, as if prepared for aggression, and the advancing figure appears to confront, indeed to threaten the viewer. His path is apparently laid out, as retreat is blocked by the background. The dramatic tension of the scene is further intensified by the purple and reddish traces of running paint and the red line bordering the lane. The transparency of the figure positions the scene between the past and the future; it is an expression of both physical and psychological movement.

In *The Murderer on the Lane* (cat. no. 158), the body of the murder victim lies like a transparent, blueish-purple shadow on the roadway. The deed has been done, and the sketchily drawn head of the murderer is on the verge of disappearing from the picture. This quality of transience may be read as a sign of real flight or as a recollection of the crime that has already been committed. The threat of direct confrontation with the viewer is apparently diminished. In contrast to the rock formations, the lane, with its rows of widely

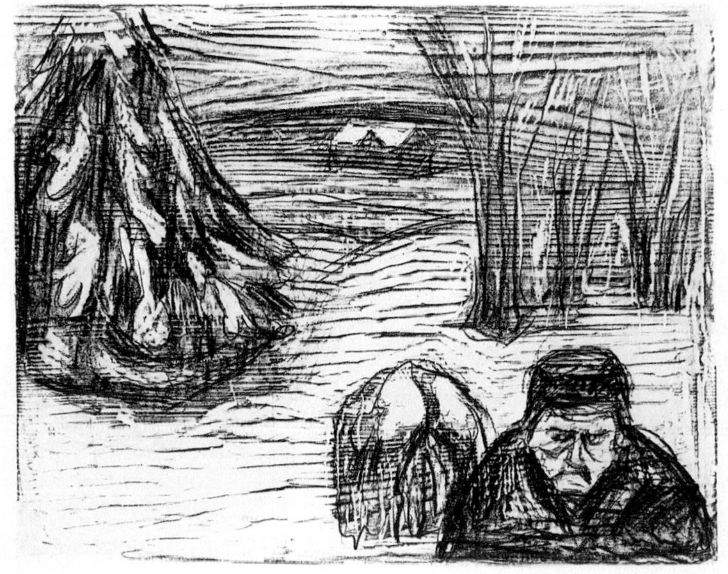

Cat. no. 153 *In the Garden*, after 1909
Woodcut and drawing on paper, 50.7 x 63.4 cm
Munch-museet, Oslo

spaced trees, marks out a permeable boundary but also creates an impression of depth in an almost cinematic perspective.

A road vanishing into the depth also dominates Munch's earlier Paris street scene *Rue de Rivoli* (1891). Rendered with just a few brushstrokes, the sketchy images of pedestrians and coaches appear to be drawn into the depth of the scene. Their fleeting quality calls to mind the effect of motion blurring achieved with extended exposure times and evokes a sense of the speed and acceleration of urban life. The viewer observes the hectic activity from a safe bird's-eye perspective.

In contrast, the crowds of people in *Evening on Karl Johans Gate* of 1892 (cat. no. 114) collide head-on with the viewer, staring him directly in the face with wide-open eyes. The vanishing stretch of Kristiania's only representative boulevard is highlighted by the lines of the roofs and curbstones; the advancing crowd remains a confusing mass in this claustrophobic situation. The theme of the threatening acceleration of urban life expressed in *Rue de Rivoli* gives way here to that of the palpable, fundamental existential anxiety of civilized man, which reaches a peak of expressive intensity in *The Scream* (cat. no. 118).

But what is the symbolic significance of the lane or road in Munch's art? In the drawing *Death Raking Leaves* of 1891–92 (fig. 1), he associates it with death in two different motifs: a skeleton dressed in scarf, blouse, and skirt raking leaves and a dark female figure riding towards the distant end of the lane. In *Snow Drift in the Avenue* (cat. no. 156), the more pronounced sense of depth, the amorphous shapes of the trees, and the two faceless, anonymous foreground figures intensify the mood of impending danger. In contrast to *The Murderer on the Lane*, the street as depicted here and in the drawing is a long, straight road which runs unobstructed into the background and is lined on both sides by uniform, dense rows of tall trees, which blend together in the background to form a wall-like boundary. The two foreground figures marked out by the snowflakes as parts of the scene are about to disappear from the picture as they move away from the pull of the depth. The painting entitled *Avenue with Children* (fig. 3) was completed about the same time. Here, the green area to the right of the road is folded open like a wall, heightening the funnel effect. The road is also open towards the background, unlike that in *Snow Drift in the Avenue*, there is a visible avenue of escape, and the colors are lighter. In yet another variation, Munch positions three men on a road in the drawing and lithograph entitled *Workers on the Lane* (fig. 2). The transparent tree-trunks expose the background to view.

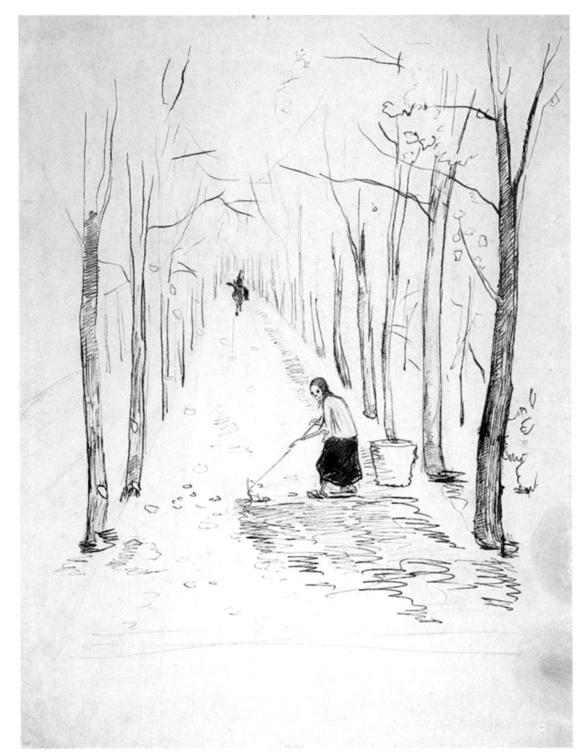

1 *Death Raking Leaves*, 1891–92,
drawing on paper, 38.3 x 29.1 cm,
Munch-museet, Oslo

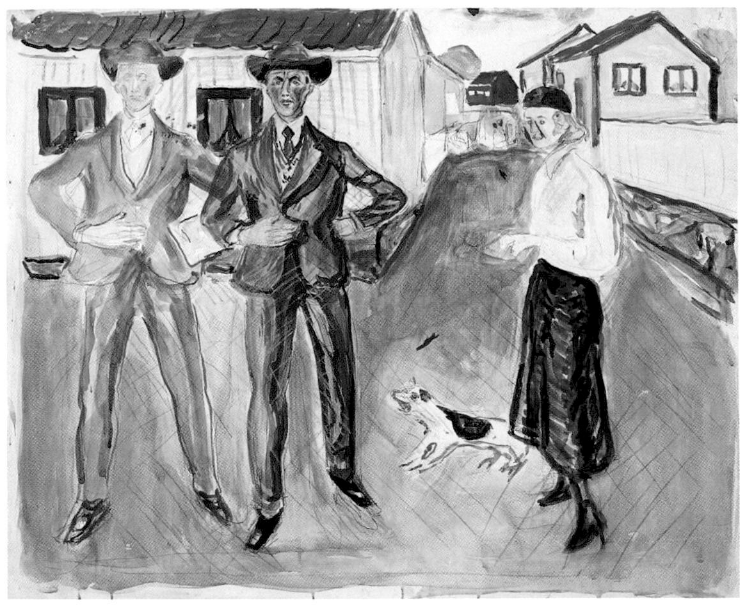

Cat. no. 154 *The Split of Faust*, 1932–42?
Drawing, watercolor and gouache on paper, 70 x 86 cm
Munch-museet, Oslo

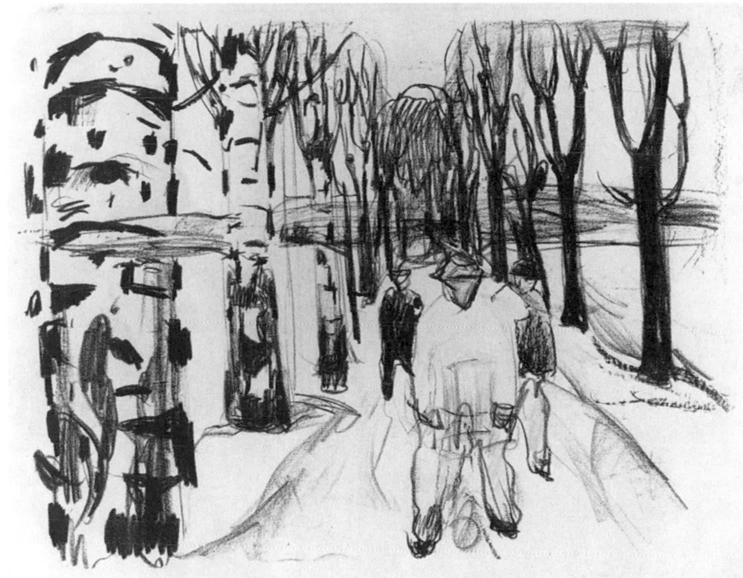

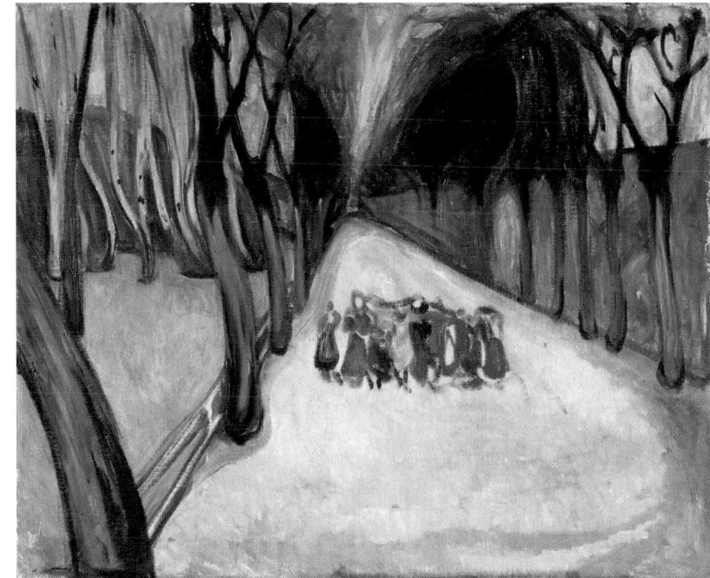

Despite the apparent diversity of Munch's iconographic associations with the avenue, it is always related to a dangerous situation or used to evoke a threatening atmosphere.

Vanishing stretches of road appear as an element of composition in many of Munch's works after the turn of the century—as a landing bridge in *Girls on the Pier* (cat. no. 163) and *Country Road* (fig. 11, p. 20), for example. In two paintings he did during his stay in Warnemünde in 1908, he used the image of two workers to symbolize the dialectic of the human soul as expressed in *The Murderer*. In *Bricklayer and Mechanic* (cat. no. 159), two male figures—one dressed in dark, the other in light clothing—face the viewer but are not intersected by the edge of the picture. In an allusion to Faust, whom Munch depicted as the epitome of the split personality in a large, washed drawing done during the 1930s (cat. no. 154), the theme of this work is the conflict of the powers of light and darkness. Yet while the division in Faust's soul is manifested in a duplication of his self, the figures in *Bricklayer and Mechanic* are two distinctly different people. The darkly dressed man with the beard hides his hands in his pants pockets, while the man in light-colored clothing expresses aggression. Thus Eggum's association of light and dark with good and evil[1] does not seem to fit the facts entirely. Munch's own inner division is actually evident in the double signature on the painting. The one appears on the upper left in pencil, the other on the lower left, entered in blue paint. Thus the artist created an opposing pair in terms of both material and color. After his release from the mental hospital in Copenhagen, Munch wrote that

The influence of alcohol caused a division of the senses or the soul to the extreme—creating the two states that pulled in opposite directions like two birds bound together and threatened to dissolve or break the chain apart—in these two states of mind a violent split emerged, more and more like a massive internal division—a severe inner conflict—a terrible struggle inside the cage of the soul.[2]

In *The Drowned Boy* (cat. no. 160), which was first exhibited as a picture of workers under the title *Mechanic and Peasant*, the dark and light-colored figures are seen from the rear. Visible in the foreground are a horse's head facing the viewer on the left and what is assumed to be a dog on the right, both transparent. The background scene, which is also completely transparent down to the substrate of the painting, shows a man in dark clothing and a dead boy. The transparency of these figures is reminiscent of Munch's photographic experiments with double-exposure, a technique used to merge two events together. As in *The Murderer on the Lane*, this effect can be interpreted as a trace of the past, like a memory

2 *Workers on the Lane*, 1919–20,
lithograph on paper, 46 x 59.5 cm,
Munch-museet, Oslo

3 *Avenue with Children*, 1906,
oil on canvas, 75.5 x 90.5 cm,
Munch-Museet, Oslo

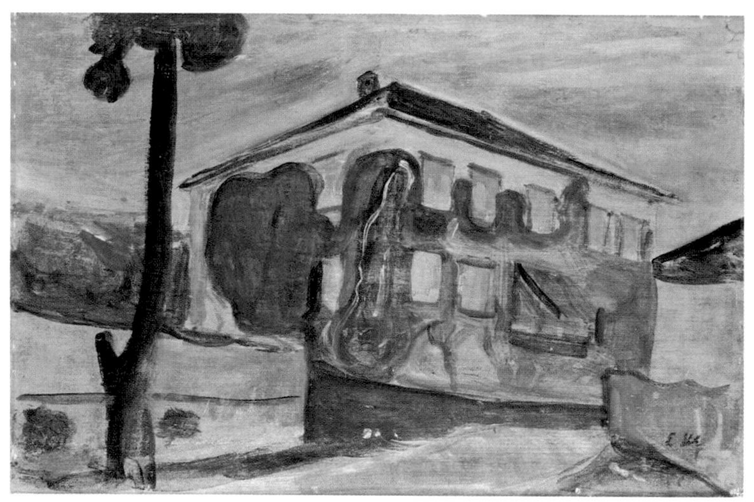

image, or as a sign of physical movement in the depicted scene. The multiple, looping outlines of the light-colored figure call to mind the kind of photographic motion blurring that appears in the street scene in *Rue de Rivoli* of 1891. Many of Munch's works dealing with workers involve the use of the road motif as a means of depicting motion. Employing the painter's device of transparency, Munch succeeds in splitting the visual image into two synchronous realities located between past and present, between bygone and future events, between life and death. DB

1 Arne Eggum, "Munch und Warnemünde," in *Munch und Warnemünde 1907–1908*, exh. cat., Munch Museet, Oslo, Rostock Kunsthalle, Ateneum, Helsinki, Oslo 1999, p. 43.

2 Manuscript, Munch-museet T 2789.

4 *Red Virginia Creeper*, c. 1900,
oil on wood, 32.5 x 48 cm, Nasjonalgalleriet, Oslo

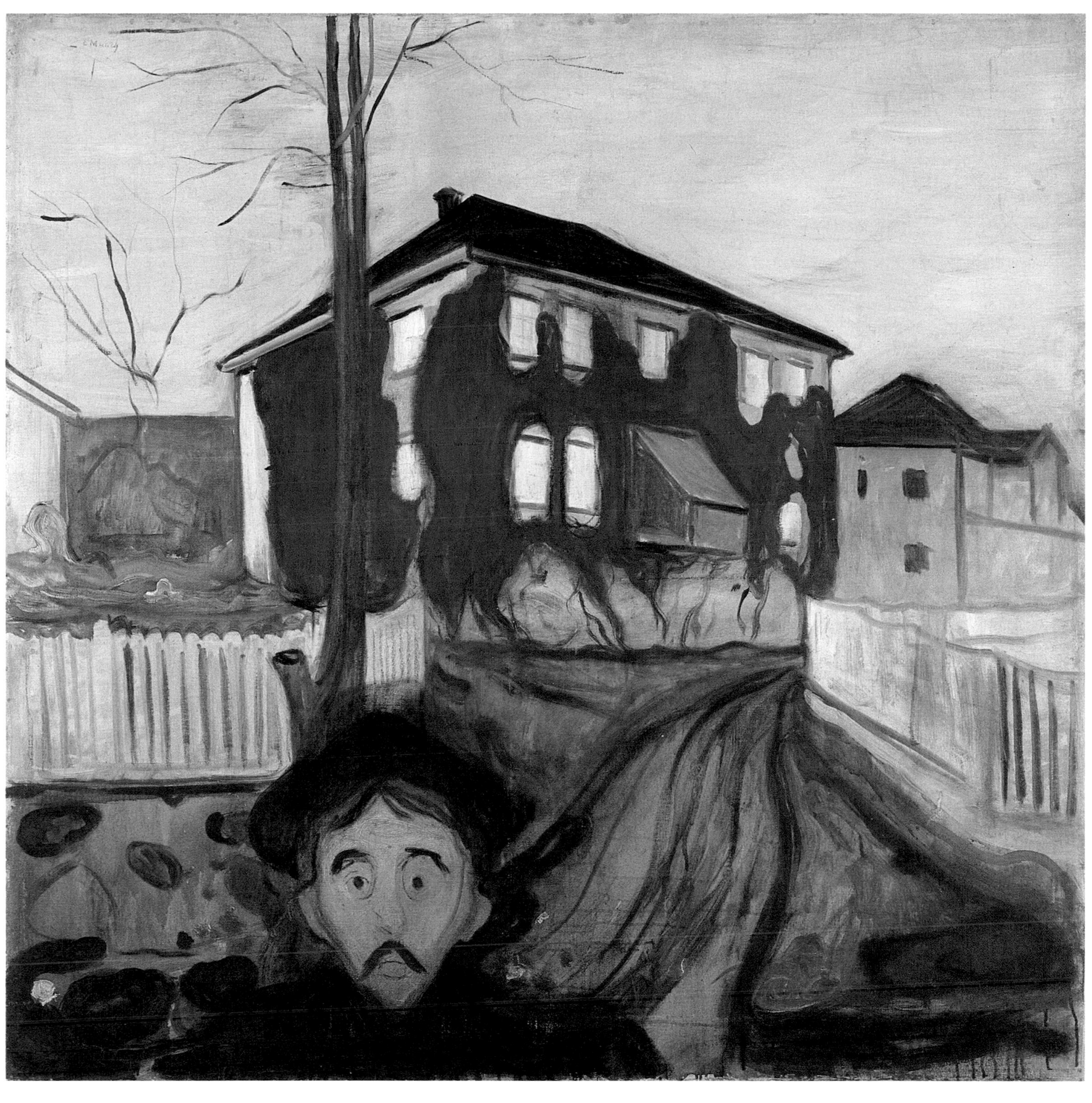

Cat. no. 155 *Red Virginia Creeper*, 1898–1900 (1899)
Oil on canvas, 119.5 x 121 cm, Munch-museet, Oslo

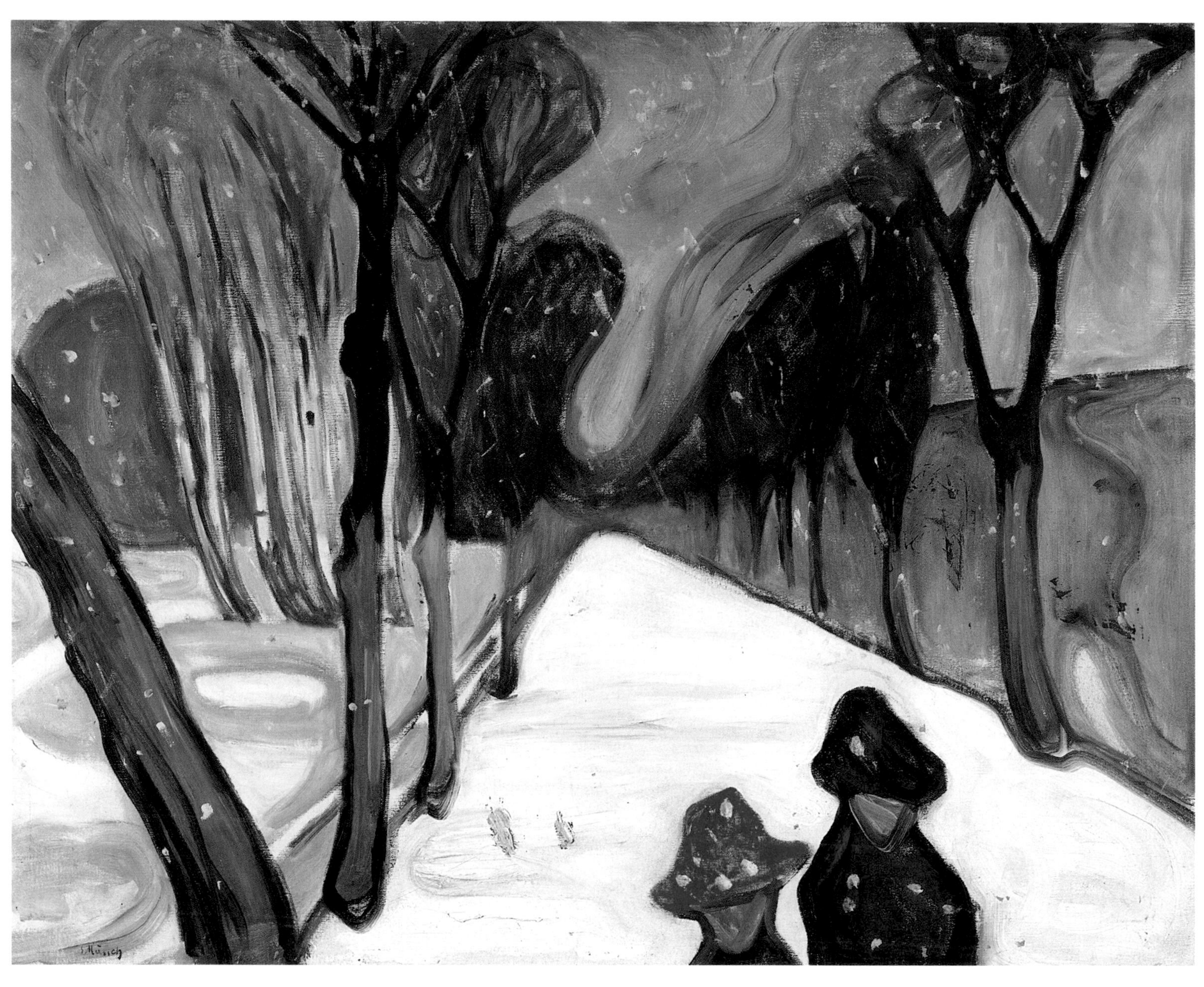

Cat. no. 156 *Snow Drift in the Avenue*, 1906
Oil on canvas, 80 x 100 cm, Munch-museet, Oslo

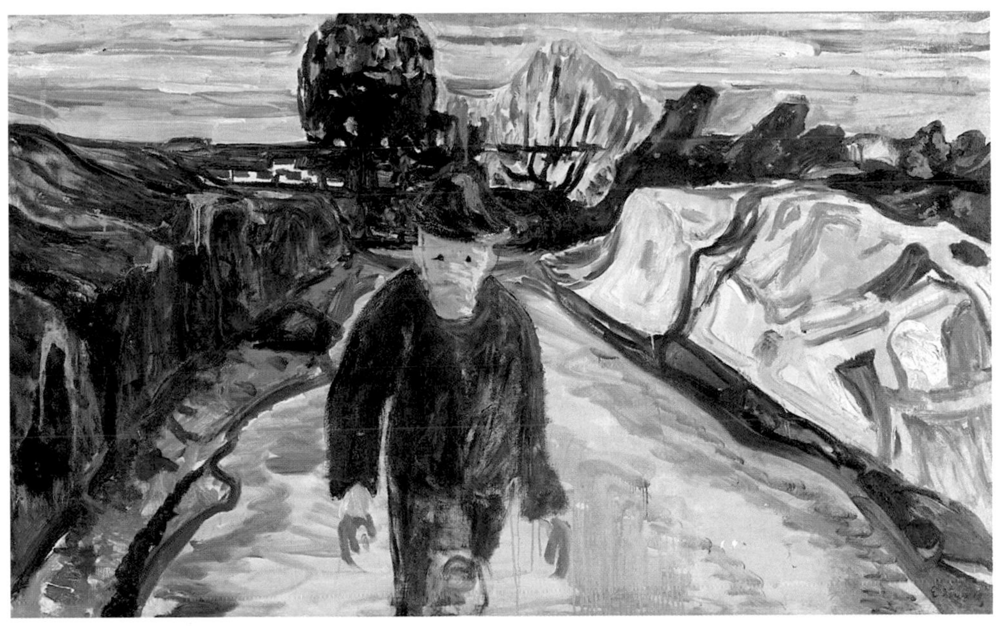

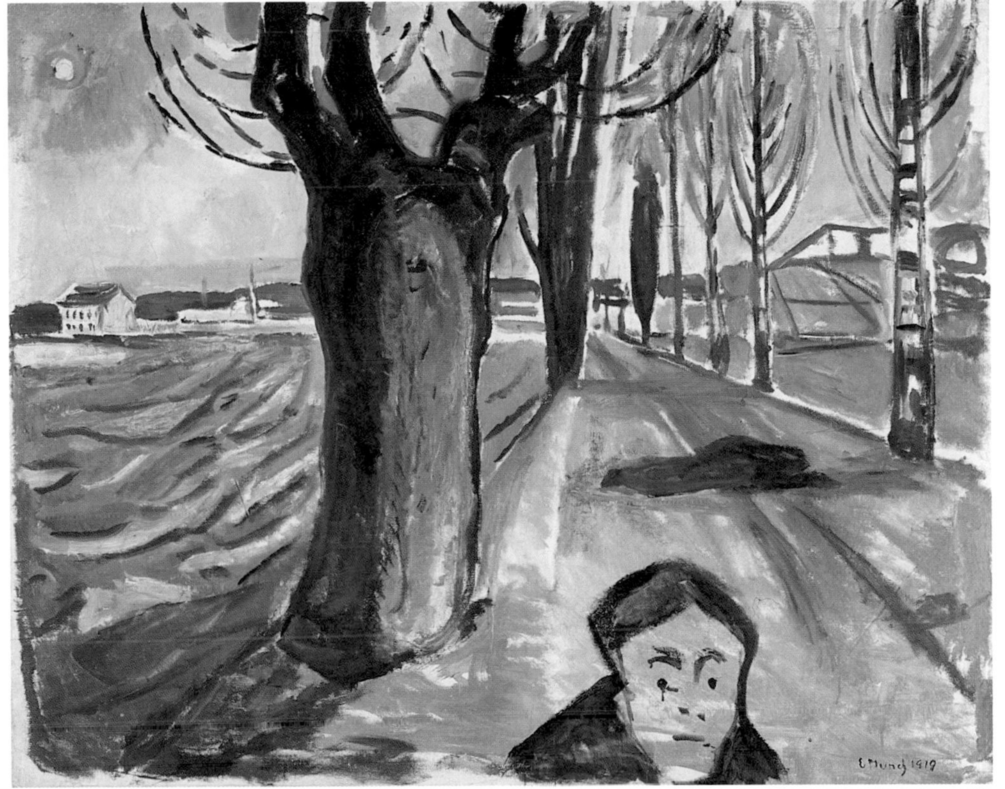

Cat. no. 157 *The Murderer*, 1910
Oil on canvas, 94 x 154 cm, Munch-museet, Oslo

Cat. no. 158 *The Murderer on the Lane*, 1919
Oil on canvas, 110 x 138 cm, Munch-museet, Oslo

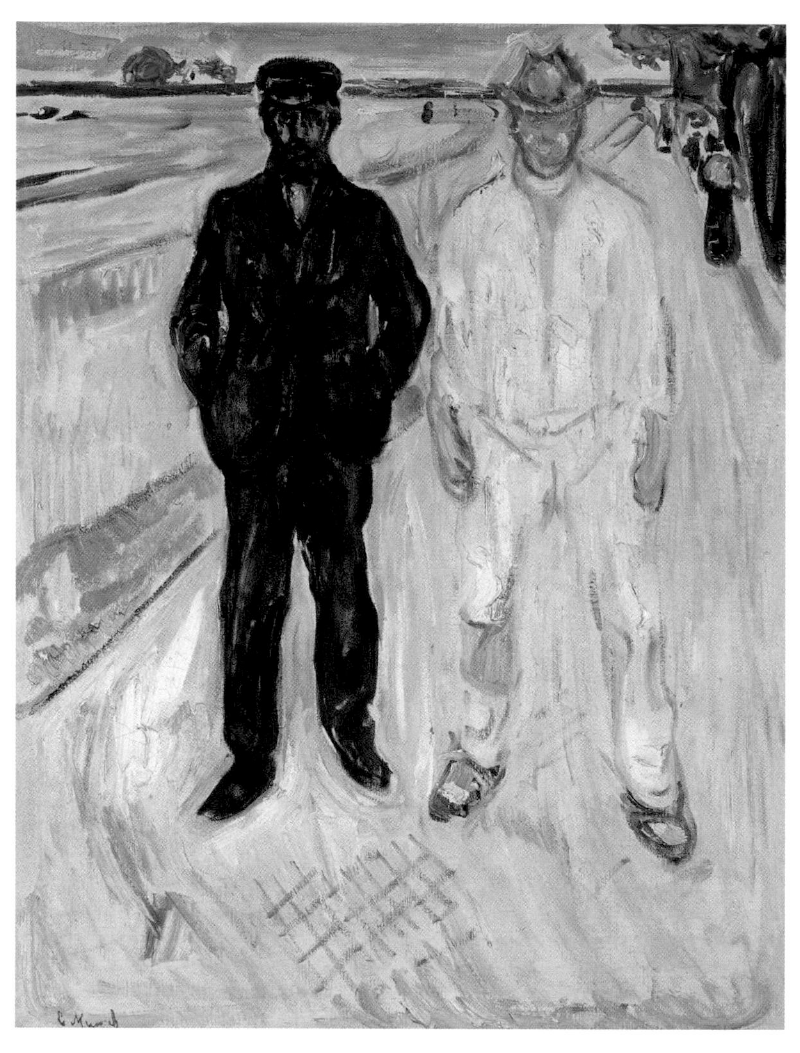

Cat. no. 159 *Bricklayer and Mechanic*, 1908
Oil on canvas, 90 x 69.5 cm, Munch-museet, Oslo

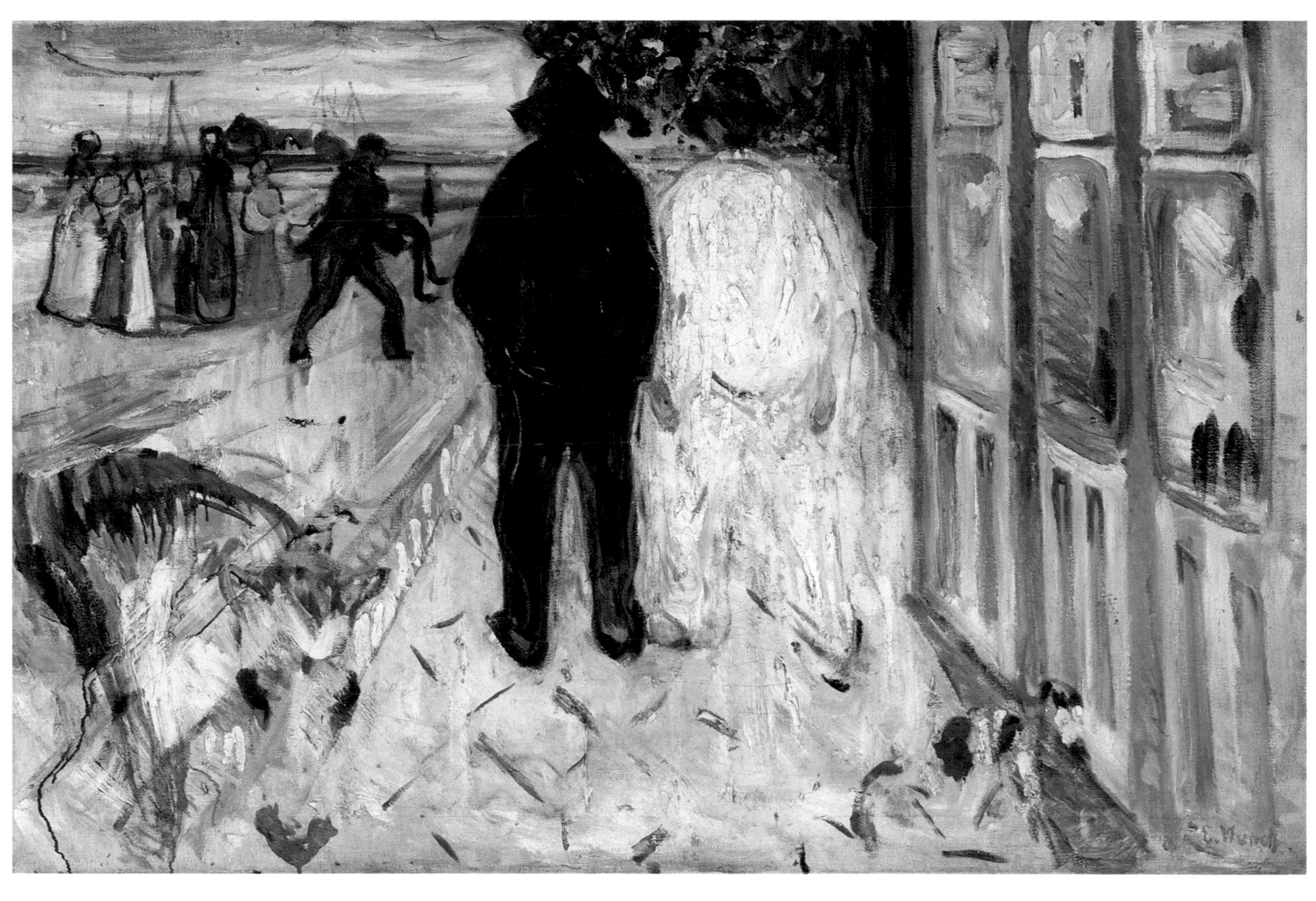

Cat. no. 160 *The Drowned Boy*, 1908
Oil on canvas, 85.5 x 130.5 cm, Munch-museet, Oslo

Girls on the Pier

Girls on the Pier provides a striking illustration of the interrelationships between different creative phases and different techniques in Munch's art. Twelve works identifiable today as paintings by Munch are devoted to this popular subject. As a surviving photograph (fig. 4, S. 340) shows, Munch chose an authentic spatial setting as his point of departure. The photo is a view of the harbor of a small fishing village near Oslo, a place where city-dwellers often went to enjoy the fresh summer air.

The first version was executed in Åsgårdstrand (cat. no. 163) in 1901. Contemporary critics praised the work enthusiastically as perhaps the most mature and accomplished painting produced by the painter Edvard Munch. The painting was also received with great enthusiasm in Berlin, where Munch showed it to fellow artists in 1902. He reports that Max Liebermann considered it his best painting. Walter Leistikow wanted to purchase the picture, but it had already been promised to the collector Olaf Schou. Schou later bequeathed it to the Nasjonalgalleriet in Oslo, where it remains today. Many people were also impressed by the fact that Ivan M. Morozow, a respected Russian collector of contemporary art, purchased a smaller version the following year. That work now hangs in the Pushkin Museum in Moscow.

The individual versions vary with respect to the composition of figure groups and the rendering of individual figures, who differ not only in age but in terms of the directions they face and colors used to depict them. Some of these figures have detailed, portrait-style features, although most are generalized. Some elements appear as props in paintings dealing with other themes and thematic complexes and thus establish interesting cross-references. The painting *Country Road* in Basel (fig. 11, p. 20), for example, combines elements from *Girls on the Pier* with motifs from the *Avenue*. Thus the mood and message of each painting is different, as is its relationship to the viewer. The angle from which the viewer sees the landing dock is also different in each variation and produces corresponding shifts in the dynamics of the composition.

The images of the girls gazing over the railing on the pier is dominated by light coloration and a clearly structured composition (cat. no. 163). The choice of color symbols for the girls recalls those used in paintings from the 1890s. White, red, and green call to mind *The Woman* (*Sphinx*), for example.[1] In the version from Cologne (fig. 9, p. 19), the thematic, compositional, and color effects are altered by the addition of a fourth figure—dressed in blue—and the fact that the girl in the white dress is turned faceless towards the viewer. These two works share a coloration that radiates in self-reliant tones reminiscent of fauvist works and exhibits certain affinities with the painting entitled *Three Parasols* (1906) by the French artist Raoul Dufy. A later variation by Munch (cat. no. 169) also shows the continuing dominance of color. Yet one does note differences in the application and consistency of the paint—consequences of changes that took place in the course of Munch's development as an artist. The colors in his later works are considerably brighter and more transparent and often appear as areas of transparent glaze.

Munch focused on the house in the background, rendering it in multiple variations as an autonomous composition. This reflects his interest in the use of landscape motifs and color accents to achieve a range of different atmospheric effects, a process in which he employed. color qualities, cold and warm shades, in diverse, contrasting constellations. In *Åsgårdstrand* (cat. no. 165), the

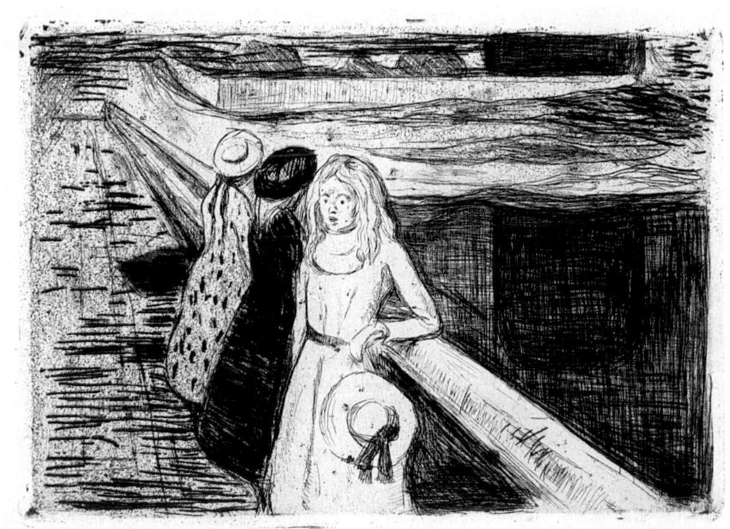

Cat. no. 161 *Girls on the Pier*, 1903
Etching on paper, 18 x 25.5 cm
Munch-museet, Oslo

horizontal axis through the middle of the painting divides reality and reflection broken by rocks and indefinable areas of shadow along the waterline. The schematic silhouette of the tree recalls comparable elements in *Starry Night* (cat. no. 38) and the graphic versions of *Attraction* (cat. no. 35). The interconnecting motif elements underscore the proximity of the motif to the highly symbolic images of the 1890s. The other version (cat. no. 164) relies more heavily on the shortened perspective, resulting in a more dynamic composition.

The question of whether these works show the sun or the moon—a long northern summer day or a nocturnal scene—has been a recurring focus of discussion with respect to all of the different interpretations in the picture. In any event, the dark-light contrasts accentuate both the color effects and the light atmosphere, while reflections and shadow expand the levels of reality in the composition.

Munch produced numerous variations of this theme using all of the standard print-making techniques—as etchings in 1903 (cat. no. 161) and 1905 (cat. no. 162), as woodcuts, some of which were printed in color, around 1918, and as lithographs beginning in 1912 (cat. no. 167, 168). In 1918, he achieved particularly striking atmospheric and color-mood variations in combination prints made with a wood block and two zinc lithograph plates (cat. no. 166). All of the prints are mirror-image presentations of the motif, as compared to the paintings, and the different formats alter the frame of view in each one.

Structurally speaking, all versions of *Girls* or *Women on the Pier* exhibit a diagonal that runs steeply across the pictorial plane and generates a strong sense of depth. This is a less dramatic variation of the fundamental idea underlying especially the *Angst* pictures, which achieves its greatest potency as a means of expressing a mood of oppression in *The Scream*.

Werner Hofmann regards this pictorial structure as a tool that enables the artist to link different levels of reality, as Gauguin did in *Jacob Wrestling with the Angel* (1888).[2] This approach to organization of the pictorial surface is found in many works around the turn of the century. Munch used the diagonal compositional structure in his first "French" paintings, although primarily as a means of visualizing spatial depth. Depending upon its position and length, the diagonal line later became a major factor and a vehicle for thematic (and atmospheric) expression in the respective subjects. Munch employed the device again in 1906 in his *Friedrich Nietzsche* (fig. 4, p. 86), arranging the composition as a mirror-image of *The Scream* (cat. no. 118), as he had also done in *Girls on the Pier*. In this portrait of the philosopher, the different levels of reality of *Angst* and *The Scream* are recalled in the turbulent sky as a mirror of internal emotional states. Although *Girls on the Pier* depicts a real and lyrical situation, it has given rise to numerous interpretations—some of them psychoanalytical—whose advocates see the levels of reality as reversed and recognized male or female forms corresponding to Munch's symbolist imagery in the reflections of the water. AH

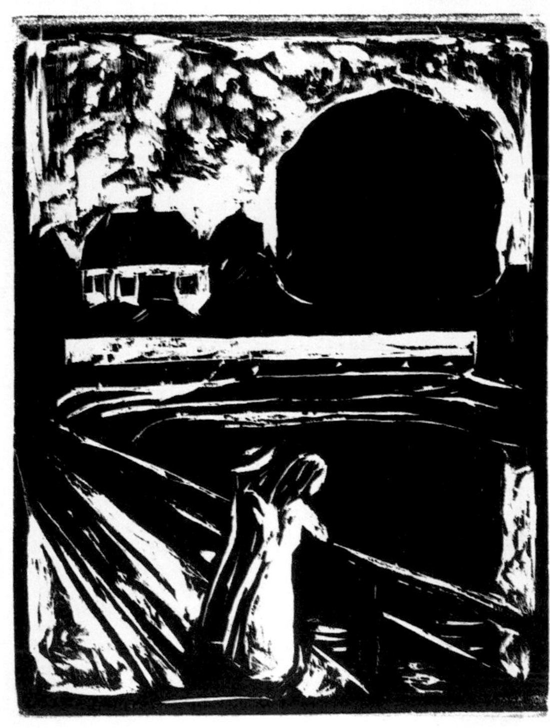

Cat. no. 162 *Girls on the Pier*, 1905
Woodcut on paper, 26.8 x 20.4 cm
Munch-museet, Oslo

1 See also the essay by Frank Høifødt in this catalog, pp. 53–65.

2 Werner Hofmann, *Von der Nachahmung zur Wirklichkeit. Die schöpferische Befreiung der Kunst* 1890–1917, Cologne 1970, pp. 21ff.

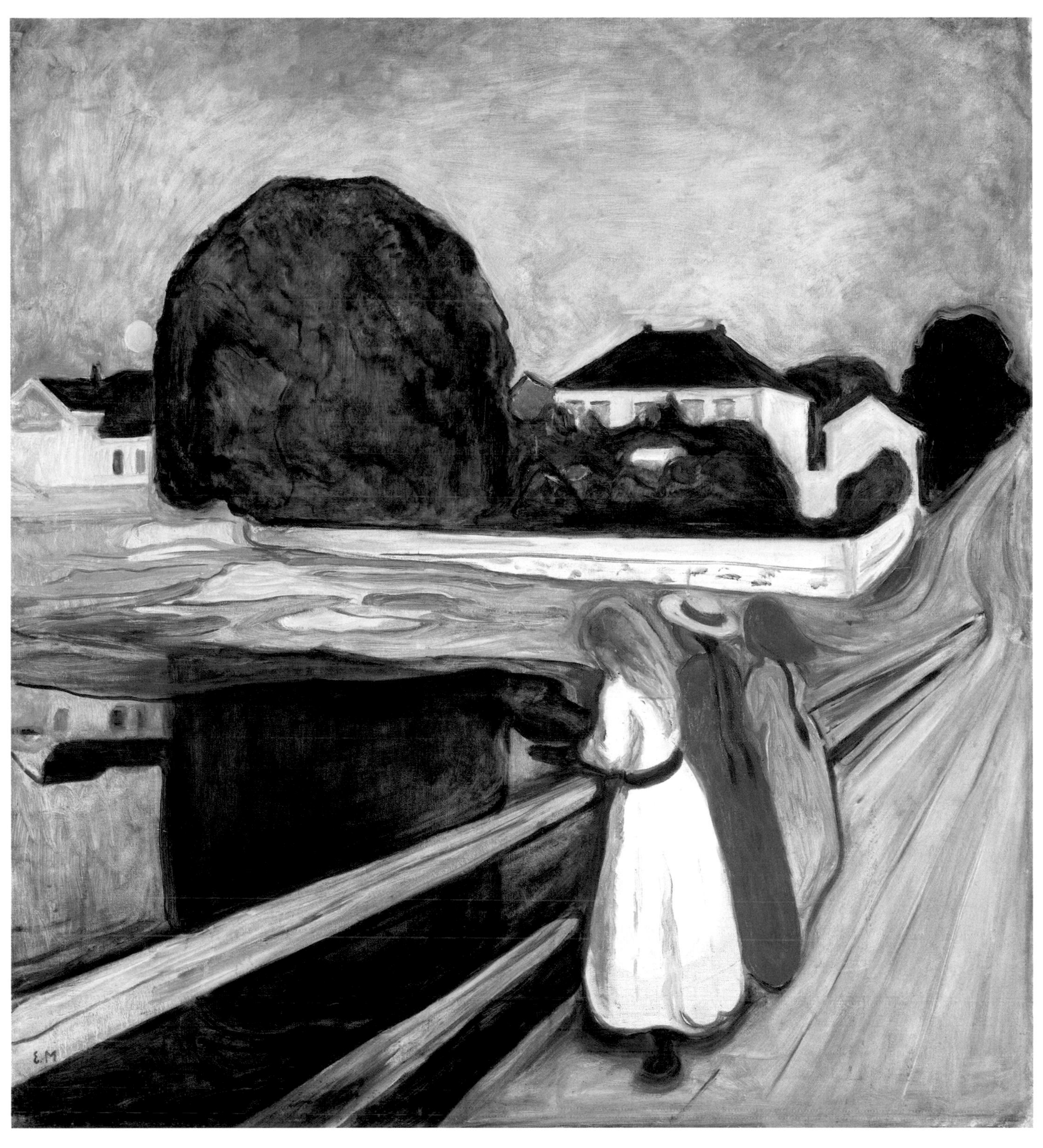

Cat. no. 163 *Girls on the Pier*, c. 1901
Oil on canvas, 136 x 125 cm
Nasjonalgalleriet, Oslo

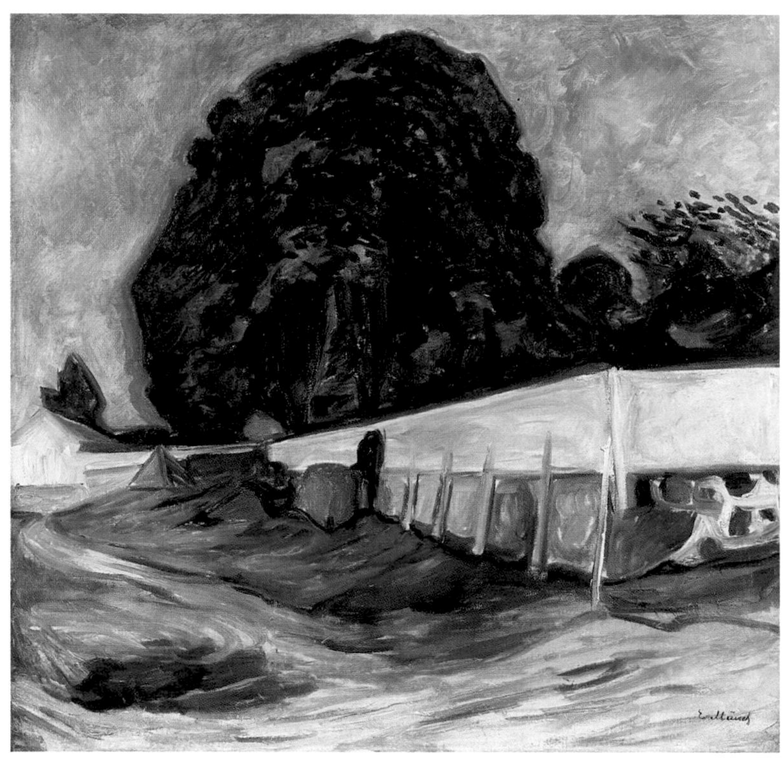

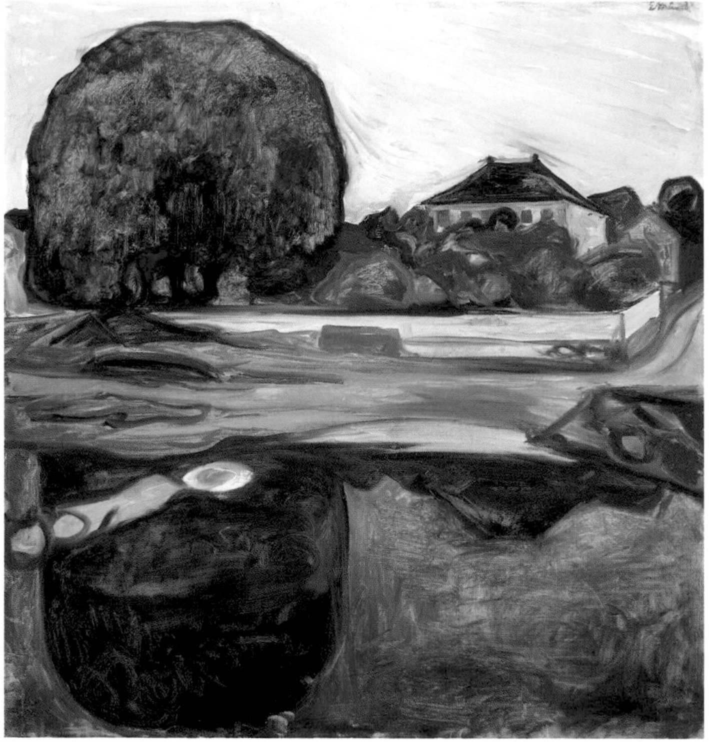

Cat. no. 164 *Summer Night in Åsgårdstrand*, 1904
Oil on canvas, 99 x 103.5 cm
Musée d'Orsay, Paris

Cat. no. 165 *Åsgårdstrand*, 1902
Oil on canvas, 100 x 95 cm
Private collection

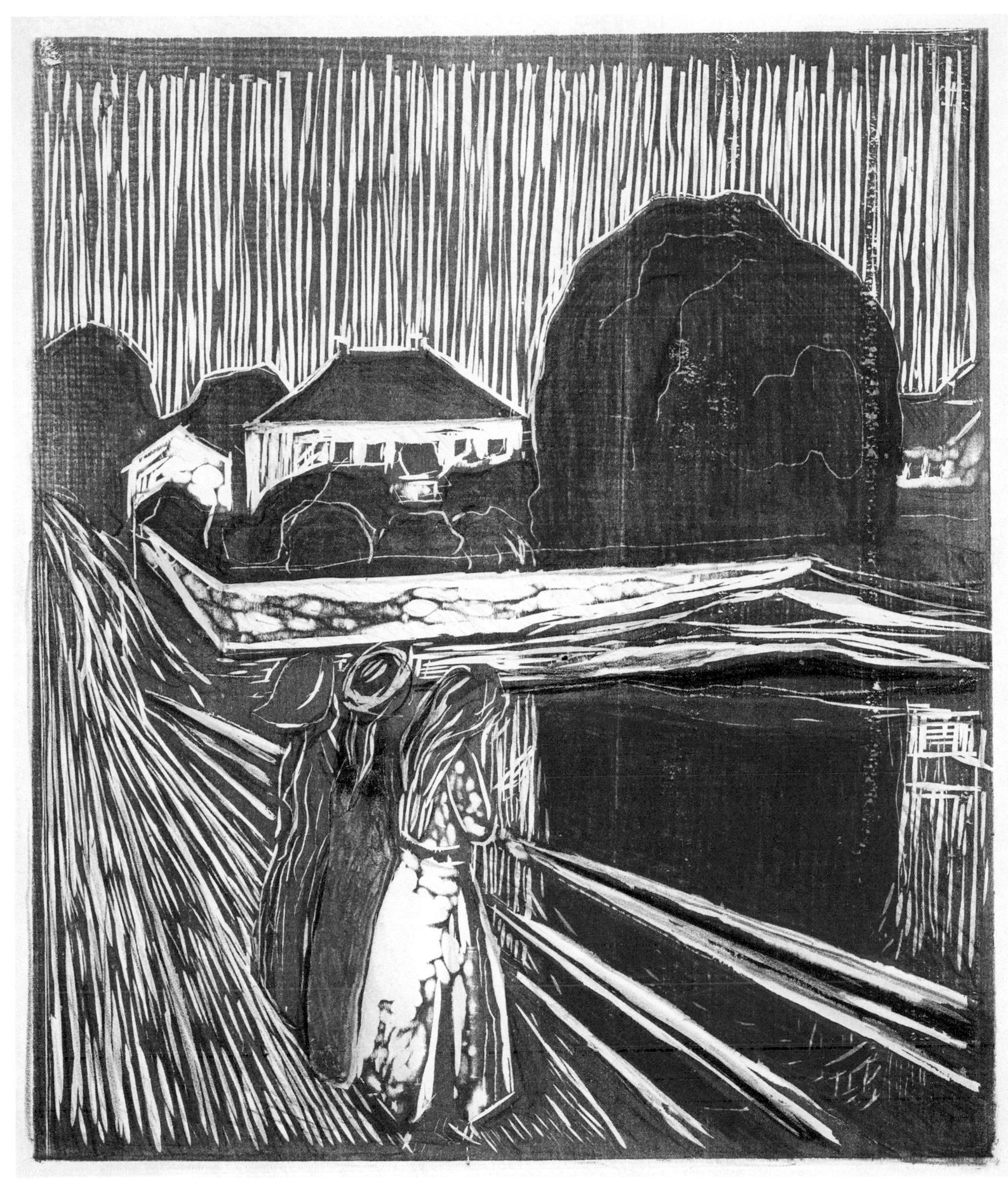

Cat. no. 166 *Girls on the Pier*, 1918
Woodcut and color lithograph on paper, 49.8 x 42.7 cm
Albertina, Vienna

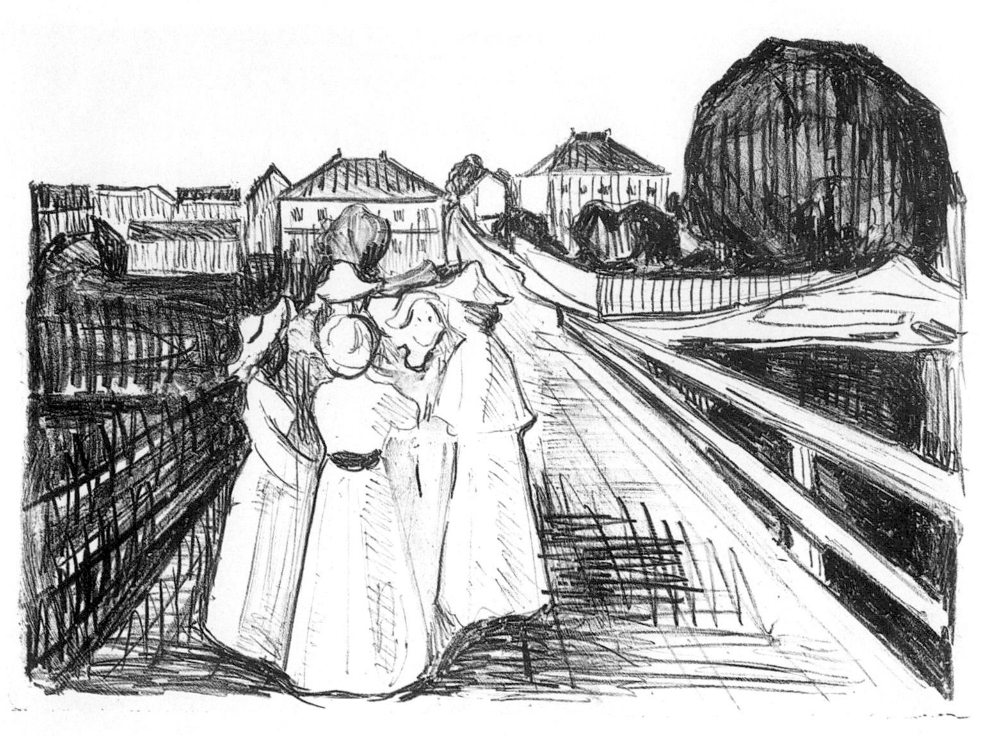

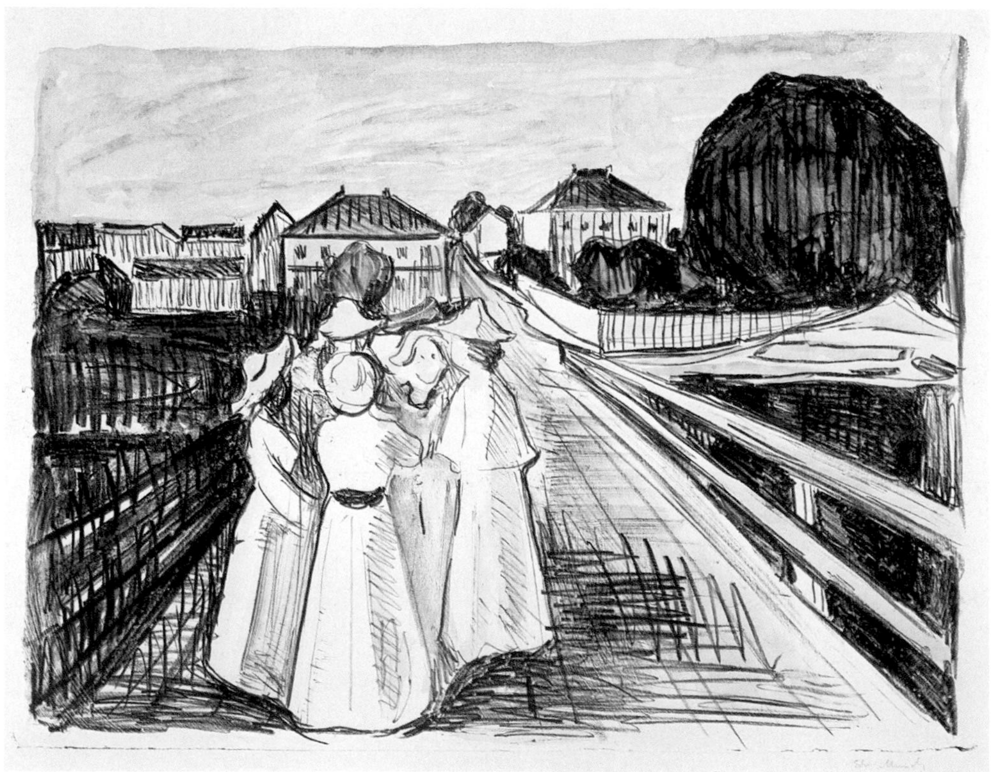

Cat. no. 167 *Girls on the Pier*, 1912–13
Lithograph on paper, 37.6 x 52.8 cm
Munch-museet, Oslo

Cat. no. 168 *Girls on the Pier*, 1912–13
Hand-colored lithograph on paper, 38 x 53 cm
Epstein Family Collection

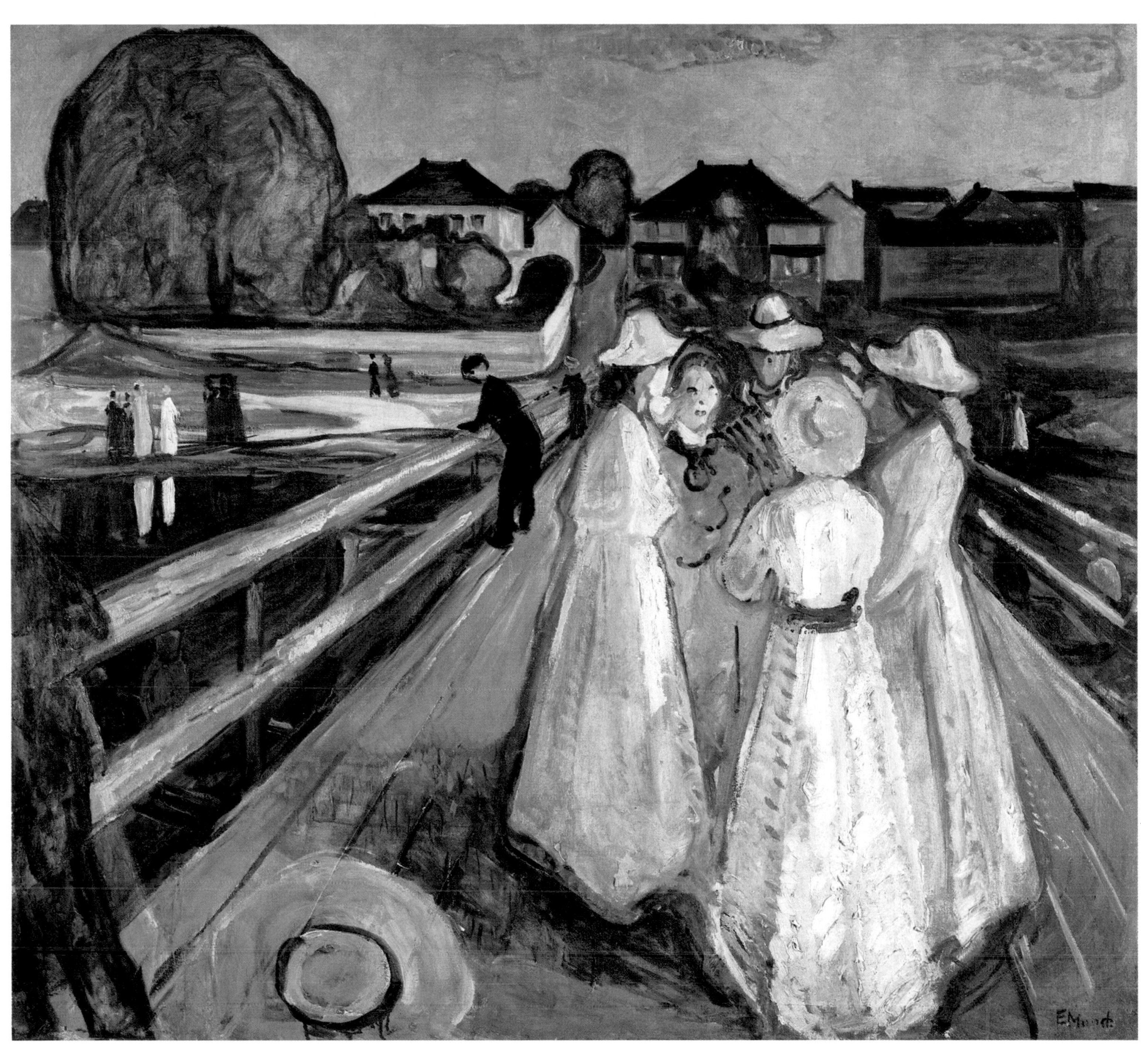

Cat. no. 169 *Girls on the Pier*, 1904–25
Oil on canvas, 143 x 158.5 cm, Munch-museet, Oslo

Nude

"The Woman is a beautiful creature, by the way; I think [I] shall paint only the woman from now on,"[1] wrote Edvard Munch to a friend in a mood of enthusiasm in 1885. Influenced by the Kristiania bohemian community, he announced an impending break with the conservative taboo associated with the painting of nude female models. In the interest of morality, male students studying the human body at art schools in the 19th century were permitted to work only with male models, and that restriction also applied to Julius Middelthun's course in the nude, which Munch attended in 1881. But the anti-bourgeois bohemians of Kristiania advocated free love. Munch's notes and sketches show that he did a number of female nudes during the latter half of the 1880s, among them the first versions of *Puberty* and *The Day After.* Eggum assumes that the artist painted over some of these nudes in deference to his deeply religious father, who did not tolerate the presence of such images in his house. According to Munch's notes, his father even destroyed several such works.[2]

Munch resumed his studies of nudes, now using female models, at Léon Bonnat's studio during his stay in Paris in October 1889 (fig. 1). His falling out with Bonnat the following year coincided with his final break with naturalism, which Munch describes in the *Manifest of St. Cloud*: "We should paint no more interiors, no more people reading or women knitting. We should paint living people who breathe and feel, suffer and love."[3] In the course of his study of impressionism and post-impressionism during the following years, Munch painted several bathing and toilet scenes, including *After the Bath* and *Woman at her Toilet*.

After moving to Berlin, Munch created a number of highly symbolic images of women which go beyond the depiction of personal moments and nudes *per se*. These works deal with such themes as love, pain, and death and take up the threads of similar paintings done in Kristiania in the mid-1880s. Working on themes for the *Frieze of Life*, he produced works with multiple levels of meaning, such as *Puberty* (cat. no. 16), *The Hands* (cat. no. 26), *Madonna* (cat. no. 19), and *The Woman* (*Sphinx*) (cat. no. 27), for which Stanislaw Przybyszewski offered a psychological interpretation as early as 1894:

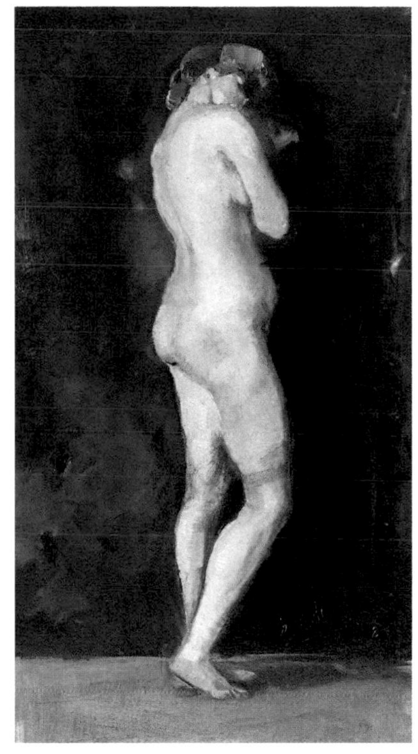

Edvard Munch is the first artist who sought to portray the most delicate and subtle emotional processes as they unfold spontaneously, completely independent of any action of the brain, at the level of pure individual consciousness. His pictures are truly painted specimens of the soul at the moment in which all reason is silent.[4]

Przybyszewski's interpretation is a measure of the extent to which Munch had already distanced himself from naturalism and impressionism and adopted symbolist views.

After returning to Paris in 1896 and presumably inspired by such French artists as Edgar Degas and Henri de Toulouse-Lautrec, Munch produced a number of aquatint, acid, and drypoint etchings, drawings, and paintings of female nudes. Although some of his subjects, like the woman in the colored drawing *Seated Nude* (cat. no. 170), bear a certain resemblance to those of the French painters, Munch made no use of their ideas in paintings such as *Parisian Model* (cat. no. 171). The model in this work is depicted in

1 *Standing Nude*, 1889?,
oil on canvas, 59 x 32 cm,
Munch-museet, Oslo

profile, seated against a background of vivid red fields of color, holding a whitish garment in front of her body. The moment of movement appears to be frozen still. Rendered in broad brushstrokes that imbue it with dynamic energy, the woman's hair and the prominent, partially looping contours of her body signify agitation as an expression of inner tension against the complementary contrasting green shadow of her back and the red of the background. A particularly striking feature is the position of her legs, which is difficult to reconstruct in physical terms, although the oval form behind her buttocks can be seen as the sole of a foot. Her face is separated from her body by a red line, and her eye is a dark cavern. Thus the nude vacillates against the aggressive red background between relaxation and tension, movement and rigid stasis, external and internal expression, physical and mental existence.

Munch devoted much of his attention during his years in Paris in 1896 and 1897 to graphic works, however. The paintings that followed are characterized by an increasingly decorative use of color, line, and surface and a striving for monumentality. One picture of a female nude, a three-quarter figure shown in profile (cat. no. 172), is indicative of these stylistic tendencies, although the title *Nude Study* associates the work with *Metabolism*, one of the central paintings in the *Frieze of Life*. Like that of the woman in *Metabolism* (fig. 1, p. 53), the face in this painting is schematic; the eyes are cavernous, and the vertical brushstrokes on the right appear to correspond to the forest. In the nude study, however, Munch altered the position of the arms, which are crossed rather than extended and cover the breasts in an apparent gesture of modesty.

The nude did not assume importance as an autonomous genre in Munch's work until 1902, after his return to Berlin. In *The Beast* (cat. no. 173), a painting shown at the *Sonderbund-Ausstellung* in Cologne under the title *Nude Female Half-Figure*, the model's gaze is fixed on the viewer. The forward-leaning attitude of her ample upper body and the frame of view shorten the distance between subject and viewer. Munch's painting technique is unorthodox, his treatment of the agitated background is almost aggressive. A phallus-shaped red form that penetrates the scene from the right at the level of the woman's hair heightens the erotic mood.

In Warnemünde, Munch used the figure of the female nude to express such emotional extremes as desire, jealousy, hate, and even murder, as the last resort, in the *Green Room* series in 1907. The square painting entitled *Weeping Nude* (cat. no. 175) is adapted from a photograph of the model Rosa Meissner taken in a hotel room in Warnemünde. The full-figure nude is shown standing in front of a bed, her head bowed, in a sparsely furnished room with checkered wallpaper. Her head is intersected by both the ceiling line and the upper edge of the painting, which generates a sense of cramped space and an oppressive atmosphere. Reminiscent of motion blurring in photography, the diffuse appearance of the red face and hair suggests sadness and despair. Munch did several painted versions of *Weeping Nude*, varying in particular the figure's relationship to its surroundings but consistently retaining the diffuse character of the head and hair. Munch transposed this form of dematerialization into a lithograph in 1930 (cat. no. 174) and a sculpture, which he had cast in bronze in 1932 (fig. 2).[5]

Only after his return to Norway in 1909 could Munch easily afford to hire models. From that point on, he focused considerable attention on the nude in addition to his work in landscape and portrait painting. He first sought models for the draft designs submitted for the competition for the decoration of the main auditorium

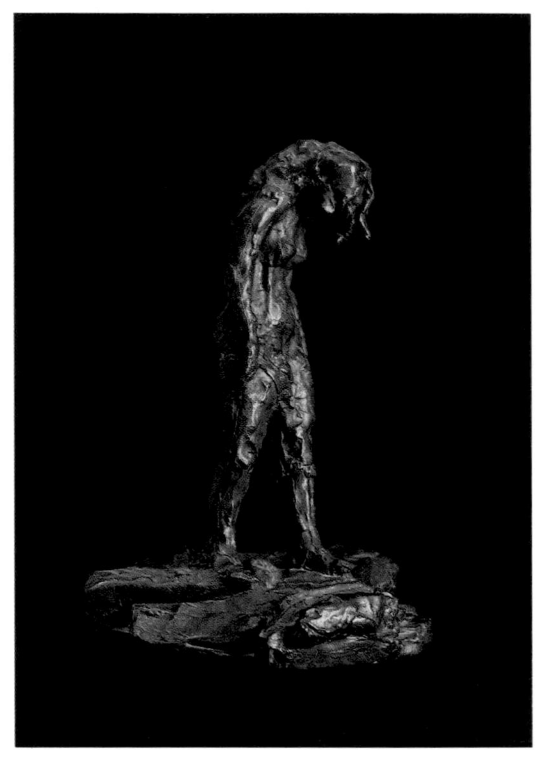

2 *Weeping Nude*, 1932,
bronze, 38.5 x 30 x 26 cm,
Munch-museet, Oslo

of the university in Kristiania. As the project neared its end, Munch turned once again to the theme of the nude after 1912. In 1913, he painted another variation of *Weeping Nude* (cat. no. 176), placing greater emphasis on the figure's physical character. The woman sits on a red bedspread with one leg bent and the other extended. Her posture recalls that of the figure in *Vampire* (cat. no. 65), although she covers her face with her hands. The dominant red heightens the emotional intensity of the scene, the sense of despair. Munch continued to explore the emotional potential of varying positions of the model in different color settings until the early 1920s. One of the works completed during this period is the gouache *In the Dressing Gown* (cat. no. 177), which exhibits similarities to *Weeping Nude* of 1907—the dot pattern of the wallpaper and the bowed head—although the impression of weeping is evoked less by dissolution than by the attitude of the woman's head and the fact that her face is covered by her hair.

Munch also worked with pairs of nudes—a man and a woman or two women—and became interested in the relationship between artist and model. After the First World War, he did a number of light-hearted watercolors that bear little resemblance to his "specimens of the soul," but instead feature female nudes in different positions. In these works, he combined energetic colored-chalk lines with transparent watercolors (cat. no. 178), used a wet-in-wet technique (cat. no. 181), let paint run across the paper, and experimented with different types of paper (cat. no. 180).

Munch pursued his work on the theme of the female nude as long as he lived. Though women played an increasingly minor role in his personal life as he retreated more into isolation at his Ekely estate, he continued to hire models. His relationships with them were always characterized by mutual trust and close personal bonds, for it was "the individual, the personal qualities of the model" that interested Munch and which he wanted to express.[6] DB

1 Munch to Olav Herman Paulsen, letter of April 3, 1885, Munch-museet, Oslo.
2 *Edvard Munch og hans modeller* 1912–1943, Arne Eggum (ed.), exh. cat., Munch-museet, Oslo 1988, p. 9. That Munch would do paintings only to paint over them again seems rather puzzling.
3 Edvard Munch, *Livsfrisens tilblivelse*, Oslo n. d. [1928?], p. 1.
4 Stanislaw Przybyszewski (ed.), *Das Werk des Edvard Munch. Vier Beiträge von Stanislaw Przybyszewski, Dr. Franz Servaes, Willy Pastor, Julius Meier-Graefe*, Berlin 1894, p. 16.
5 Eggum presumes that Munch made a clay model in Warnemünde and cast it in plaster in 1914. Cf. Arne Eggum, "Munch und Warnemünde," in *Munch und Warnemünde* 1907–1908, exh. cat., Munch-museet, Oslo, Rostock Kunsthalle, Ateneum, Helsinki, Oslo 1999, p. 33.
6 Birgit Prestøe, "Modellen," in *Norsk dameblad*, 1/3, 1954, p. 6

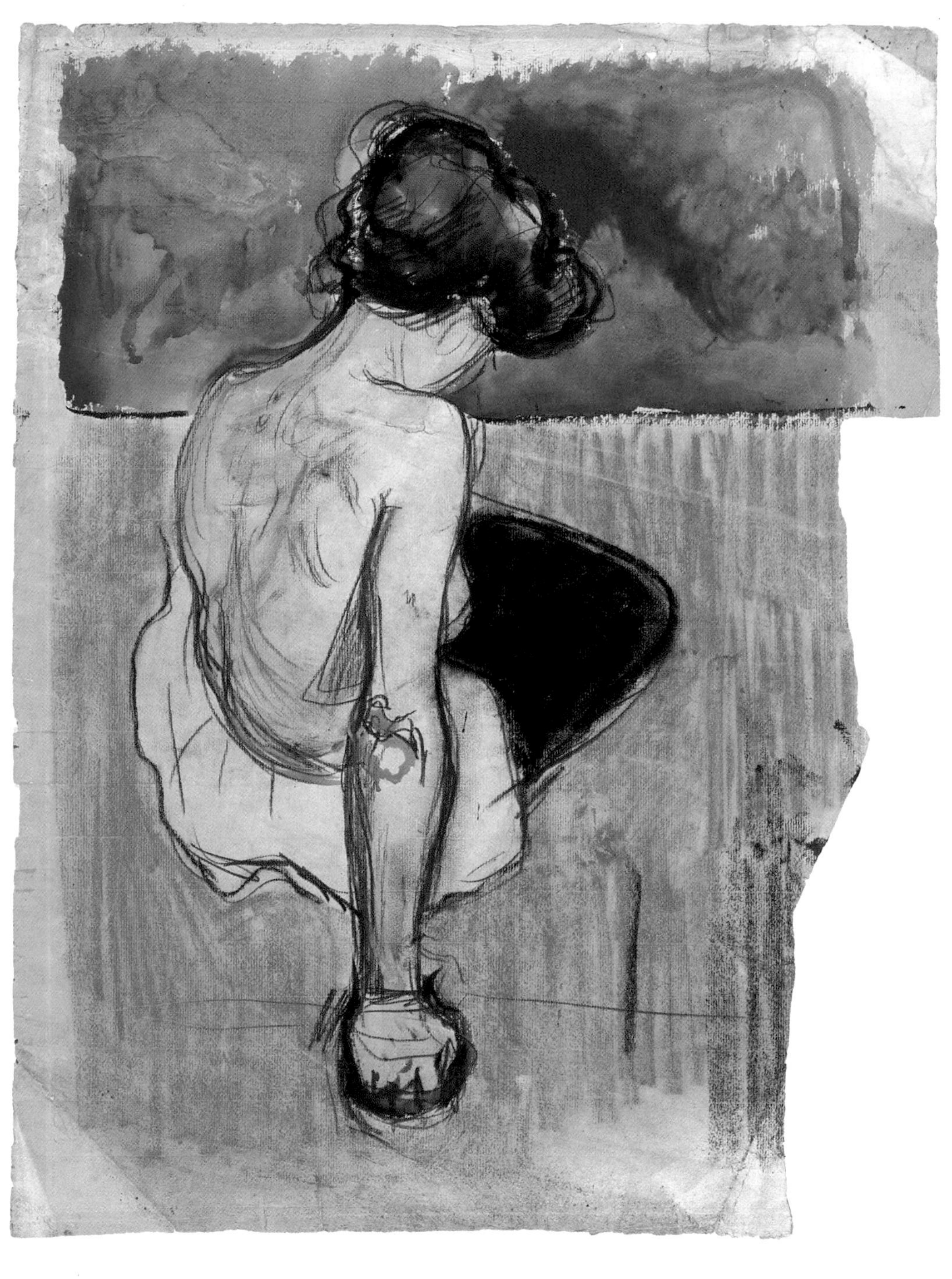

Cat. no. 170 *Seated Nude*, 1896
Drawing and watercolor on paper, 62 x 47.7 cm
Munch-museet, Oslo

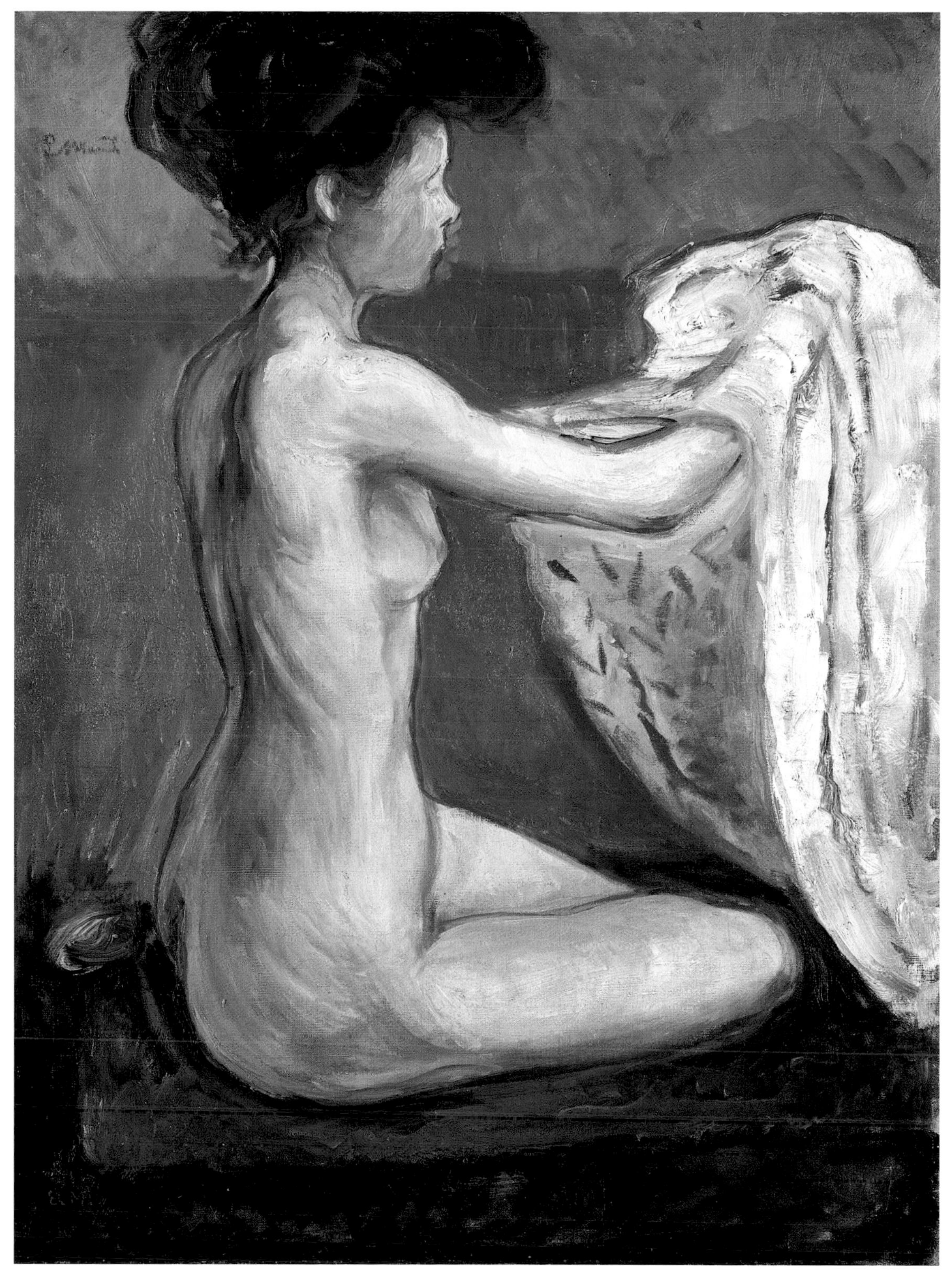

Cat. no. 171 *Parisian Model*, 1896
Oil on canvas, 80 x 60 cm
Nasjonalgalleriet, Oslo

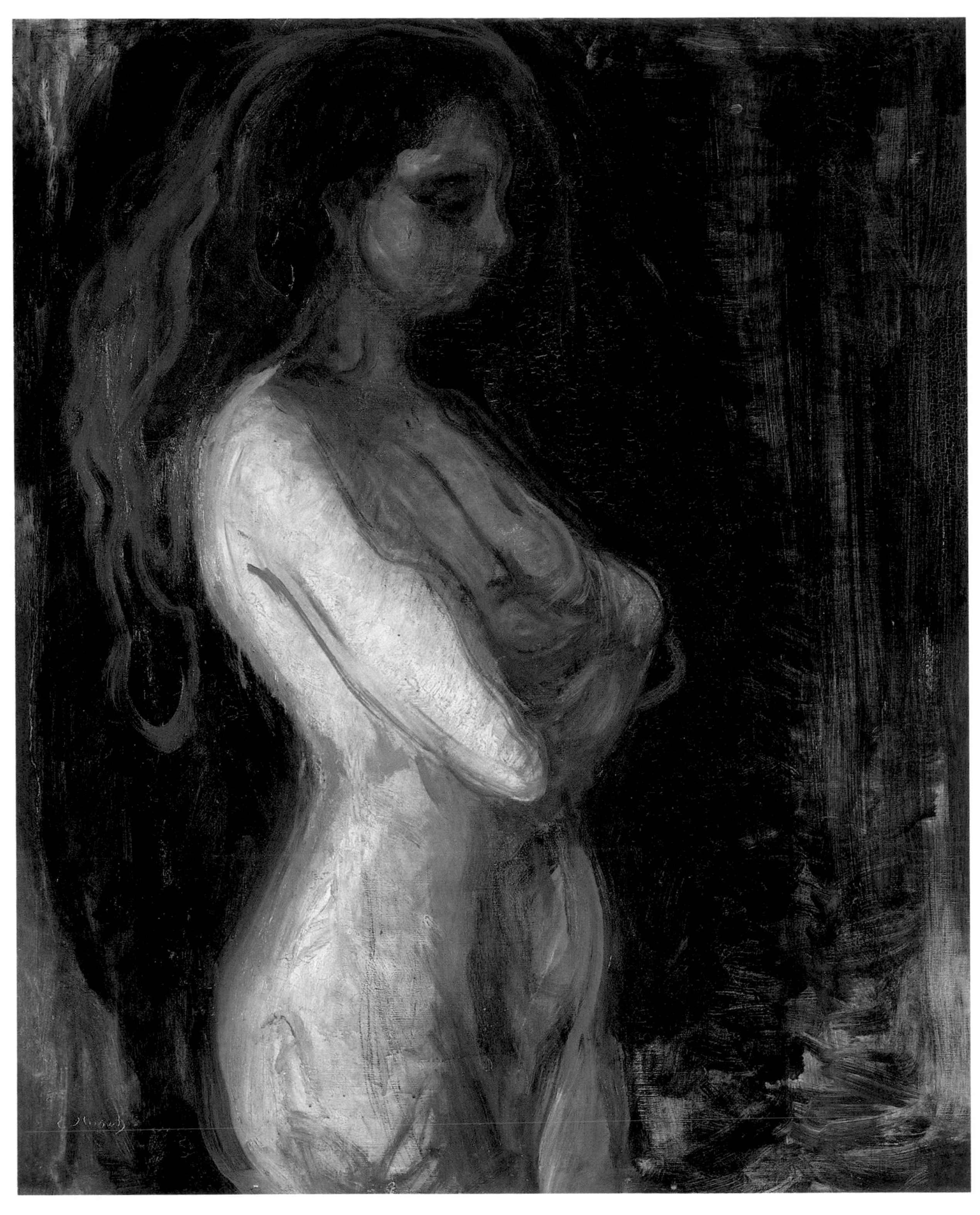

Cat. no. 172 *Nude Study*, c. 1900 (c. 1898)
Oil on canvas, 93 x 76 cm
Rasmus Meyers Samlinger, Bergen Kunstmuseum

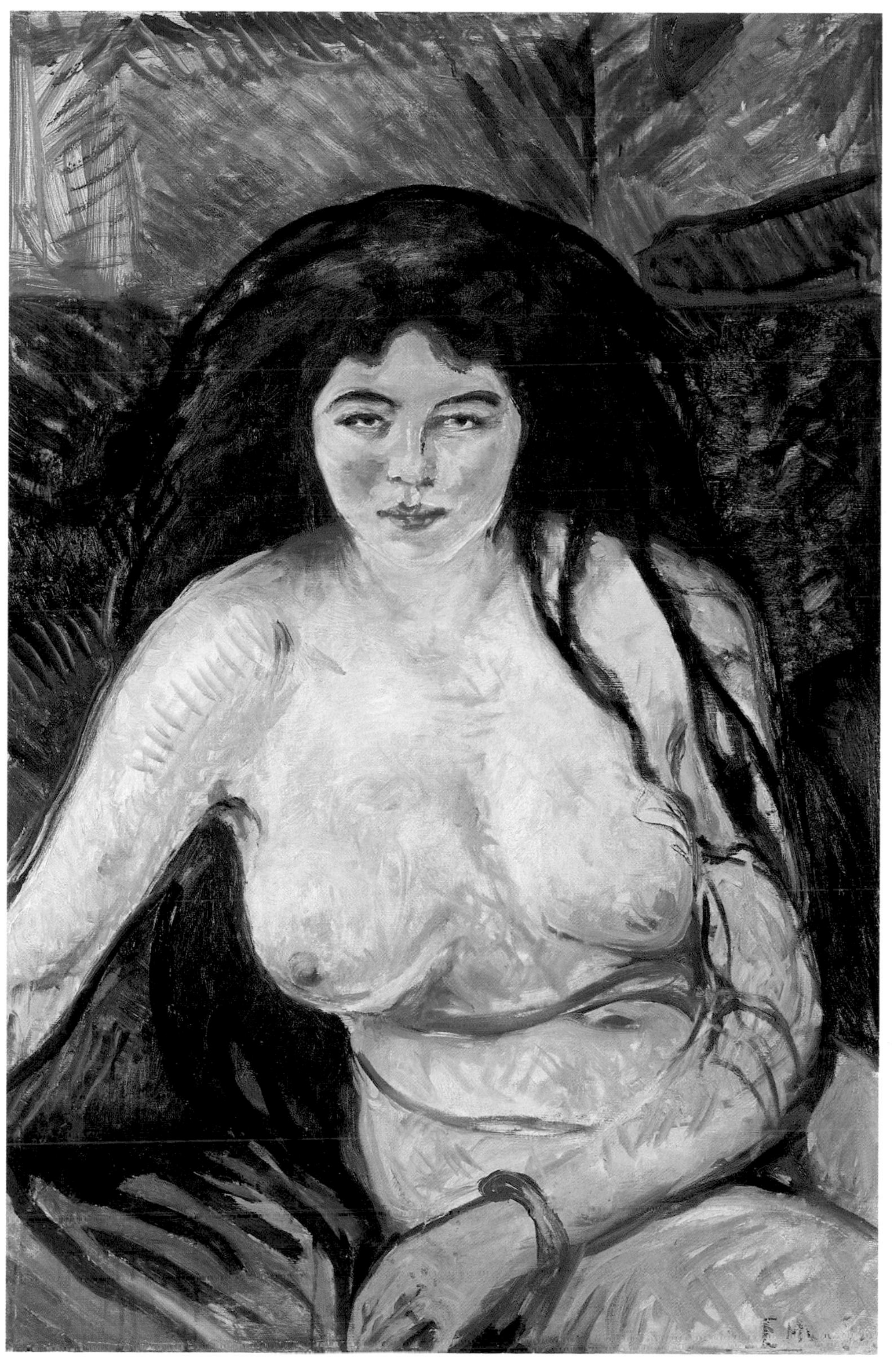

Cat. no. 173 *The Beast*, 1901
Oil on canvas, 94.5 x 63.5 cm
Sprengel Museum Hannover

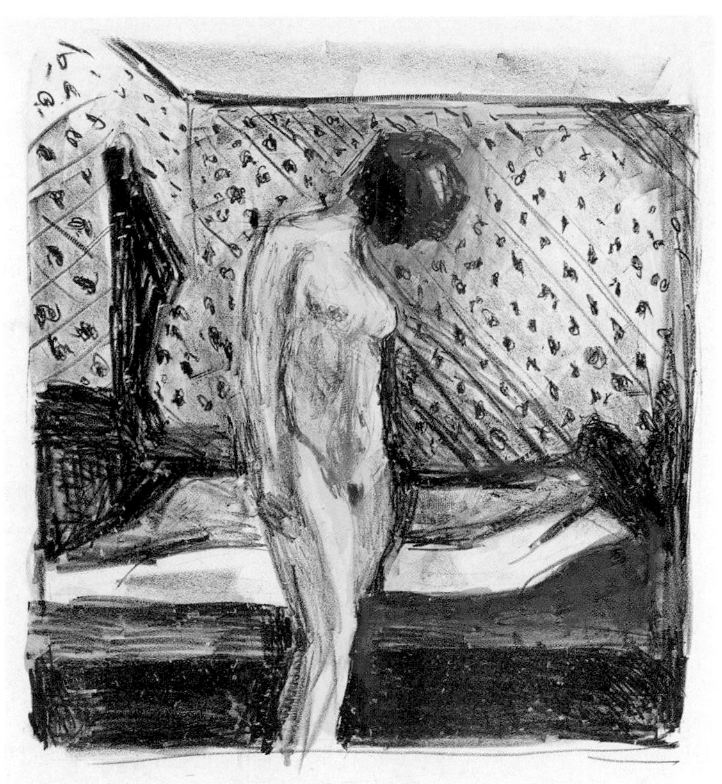

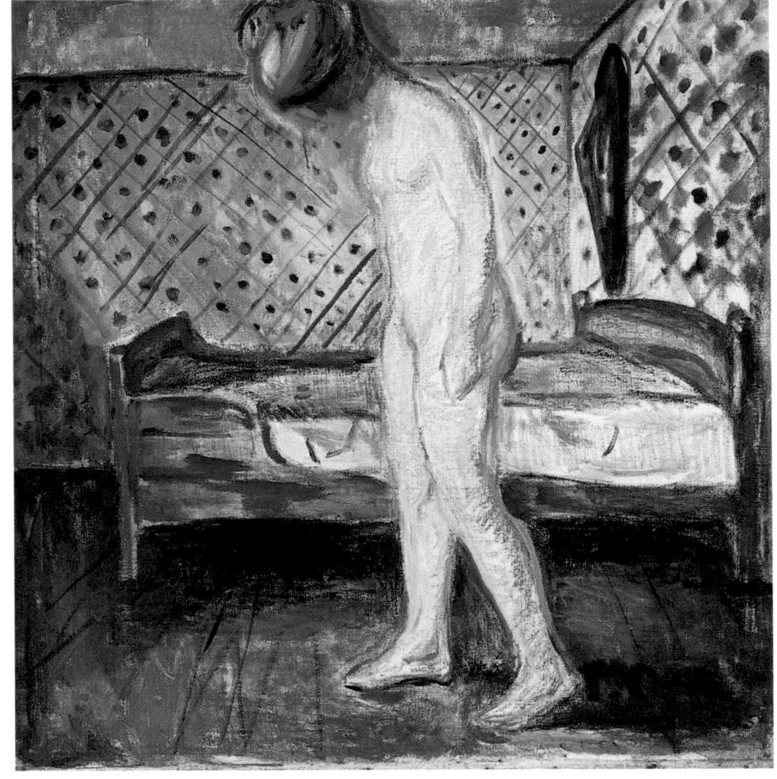

Cat. no. 174 *Weeping Young Woman by the Bed*, 1930
Hand-colored lithograph on paper, 38.3 x 36.5 cm
Epstein Family Collection

Cat. no. 175 *Weeping Nude*, 1907
Oil on canvas, 121 x 119 cm
Munch-museet, Oslo

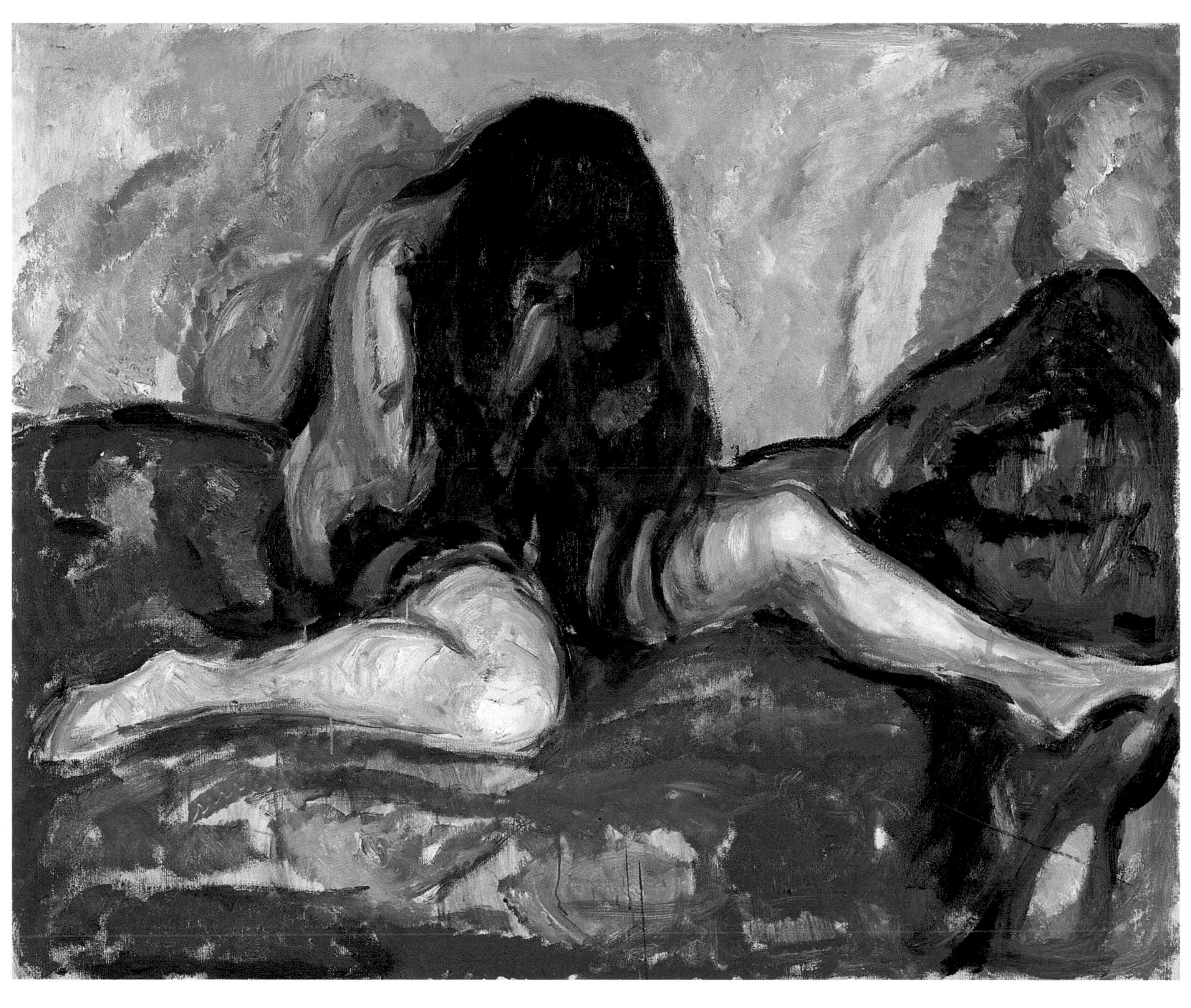

Cat. no. 176 *Weeping Nude*, 1913
Oil on canvas, 110.5 x 135 cm
Munch-museet, Oslo

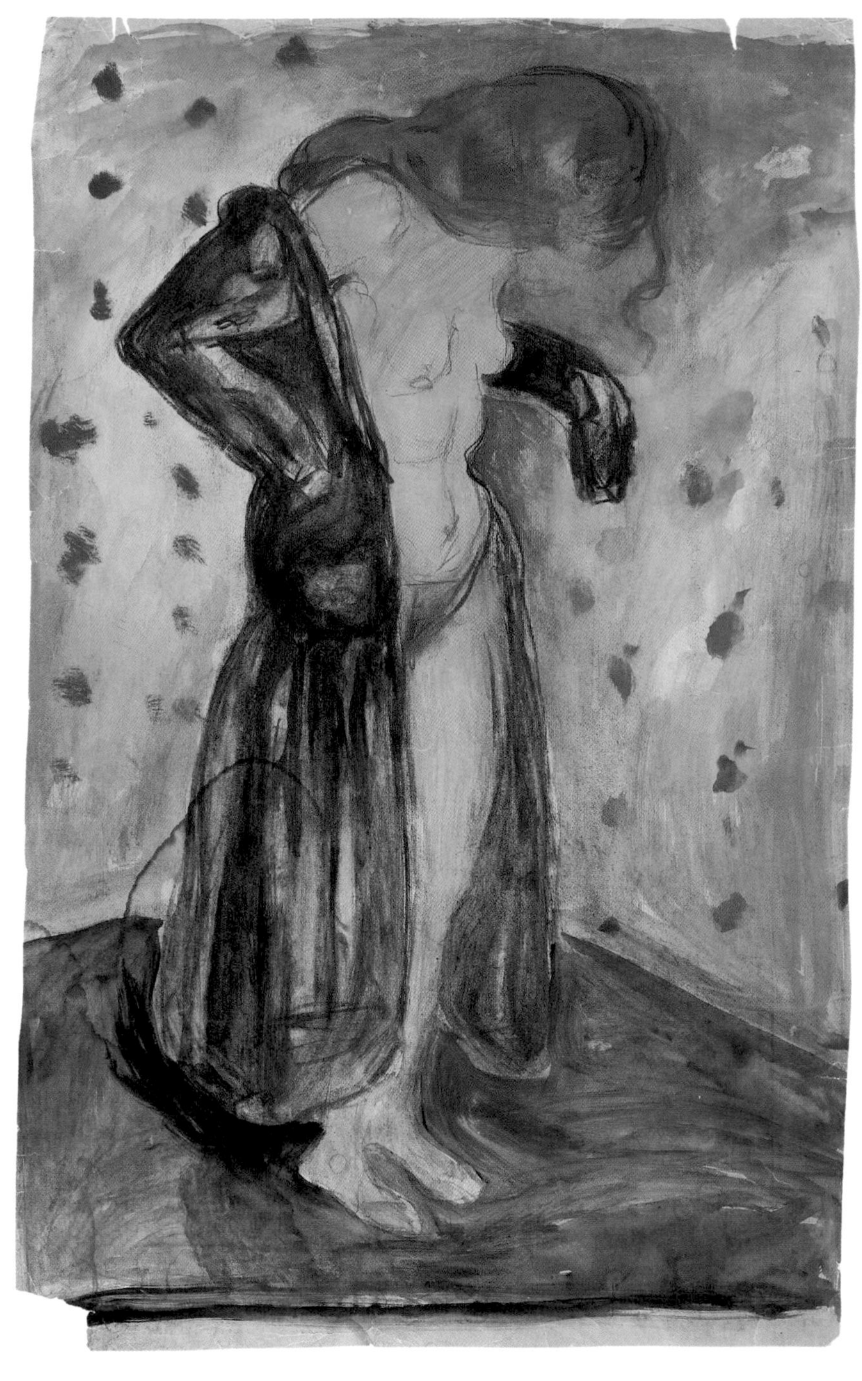

Cat. no. 177 *In the Dressing Gown*, 1919–21
Drawing and watercolor on paper, 98.1 x 60.8 cm
Munch-museet, Oslo

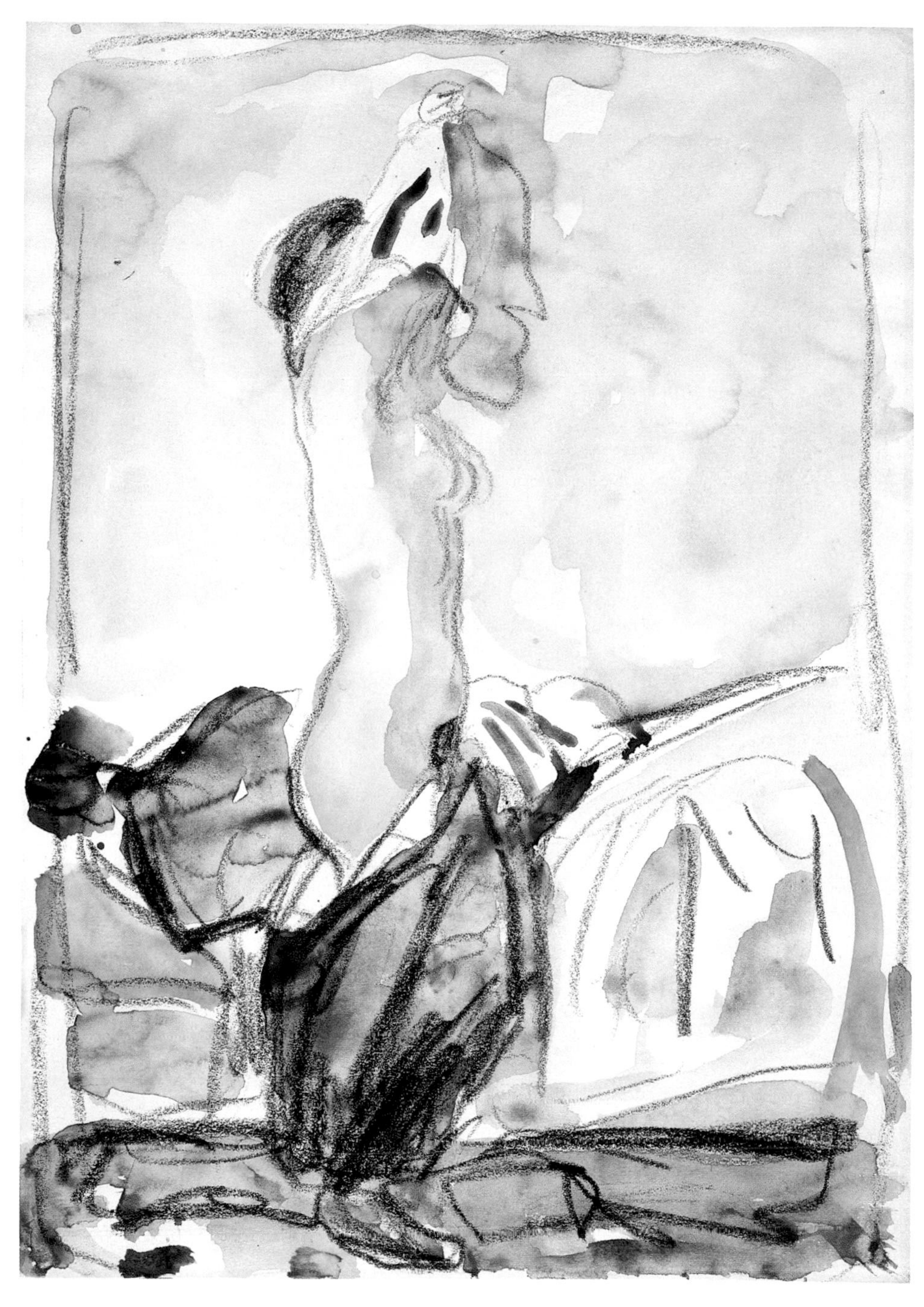

Cat. no. 178 *Nude Undressing*, c. 1920
Drawing and watercolor on paper, 35.3 x 25.7 cm
Munch-museet, Oslo

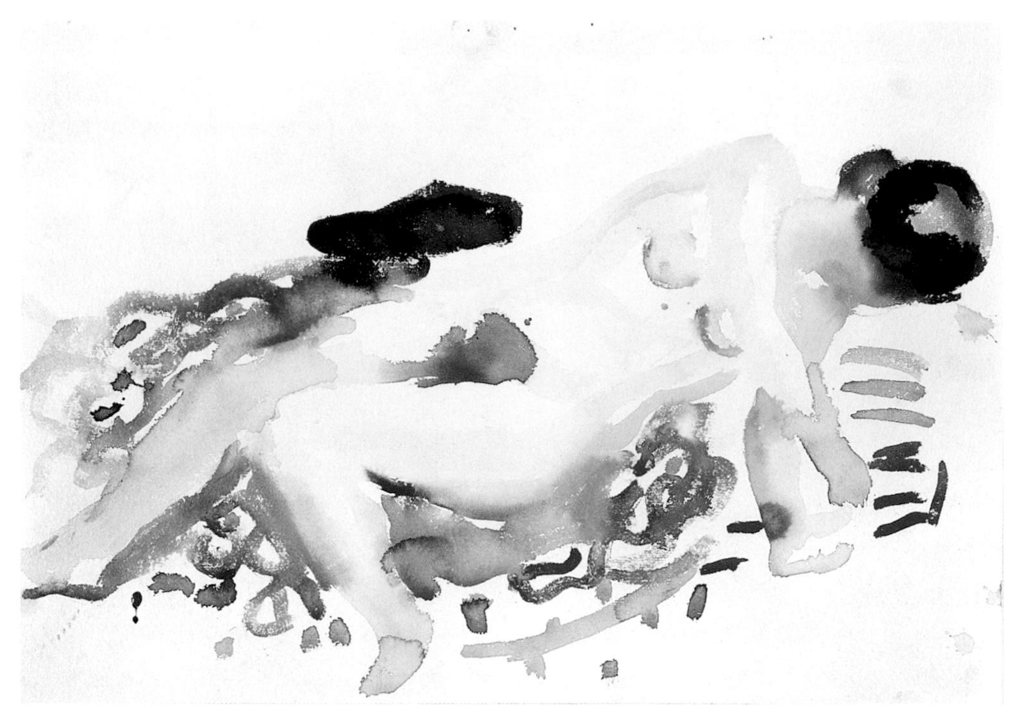

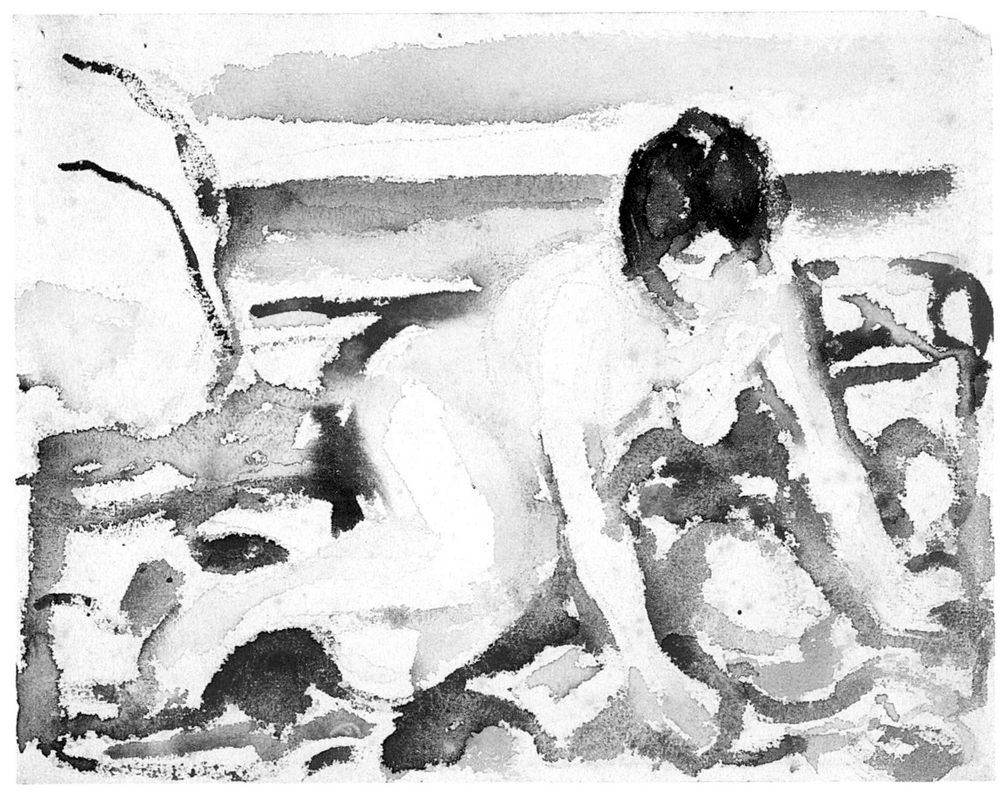

Cat. no. 179 *Reclining Nude on Patterned Carpet*, 1919–21
Watercolor on paper, 35.4 x 50.9 cm
Munch-museet, Oslo

Cat. no. 180 *Nude Bending forward on Patterned Carpet*, 1919–21
Watercolor on paper, 22.4 x 29.2 cm
Munch-museet, Oslo

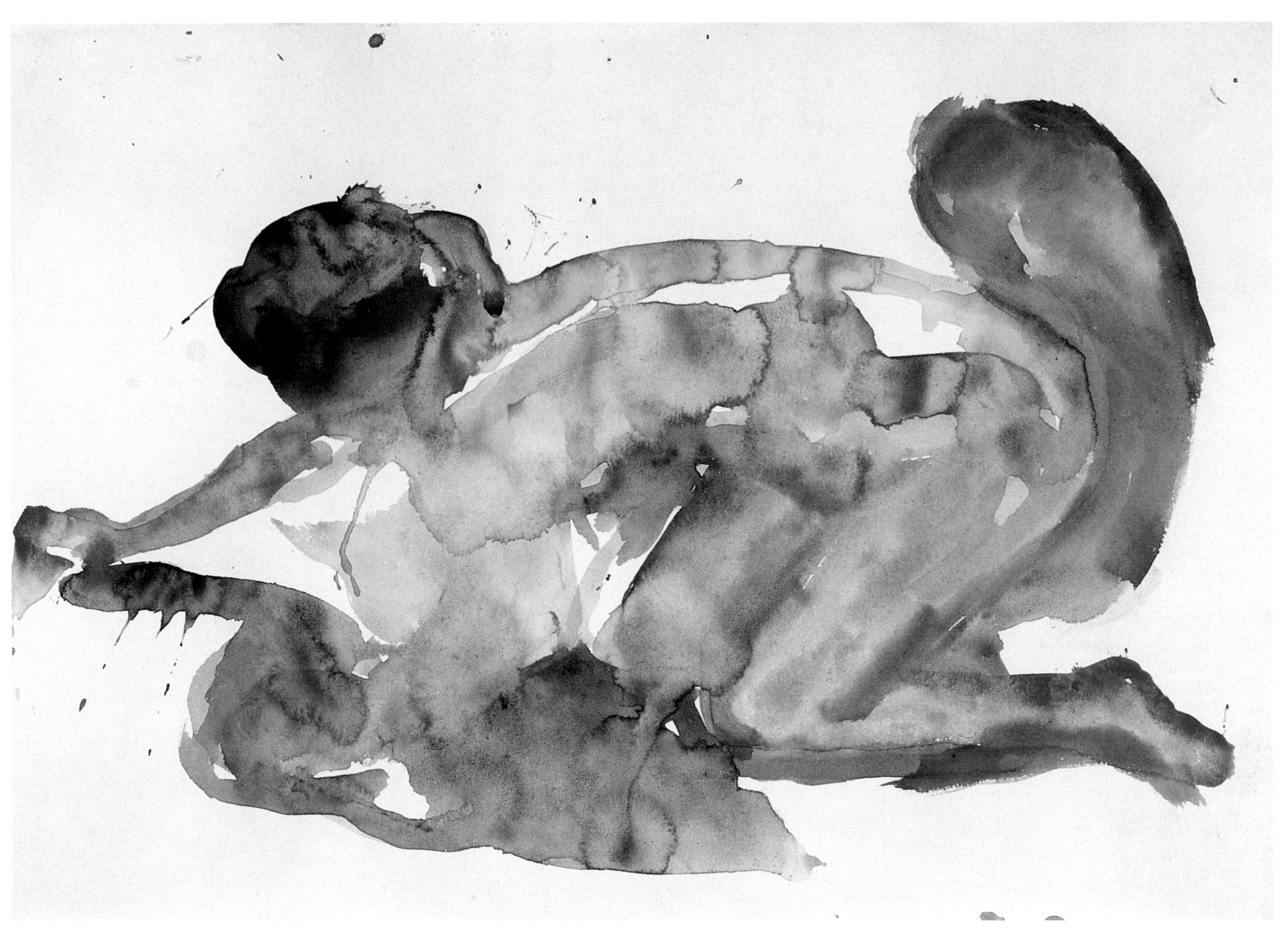

Cat. no. 181 *Kneeling Nude*, 1919–21
Watercolor on paper, 25.3 x 35.5 cm
Munch-museet, Oslo

Portrait

Portraits play an important role in Munch's oeuvre. The earliest are portraits of his family, friends, and acquaintances, many of them artists, done in Norway. By the mid-1890s, he had completed numerous portraits of members of the bohemian circle Zum Schwarzen Ferkel in Berlin, including August Strindberg (cat. no. 190), Stanislaw Przybyszewski (cat. nos. 186–189), Dagny Juel, and Julius Meier-Graefe. With its modulated monochrome coloration, the *Portrait of Dagny Juel Przybyszewska* (cat. no. 185) calls to mind his earlier Impressionist-style portraits of women, such as that of *Olga Buhre* of 1890 (cat. no. 184). In both of these paintings, the nebulous figures emerge from the background. While the shadow in the Buhre picture generates a certain sense of depth, Juel is enveloped in a spaceless, timeless blueish-purple aura.

Munch often painted two or more variations of his portraits, some of them in different techniques and formats and in certain cases only years later. He painted two extremely experimental portraits of Juel's husband Przybyszewski. The painting showing the skeleton arm (cat. no. 186) is one of the first pictures Munch exposed to the elements in a "kill-or-cure treatment." He painted the second portrait (cat. no. 187) in thin layers of paint over a charcoal drawing on grayish-brown, untreated cardboard, then sprayed the face with white and the background with red paint. That same year, he transposed Przybyszewski's facial features for the most part to the foreground figure in *Jealousy*, making him a character in his *Frieze of Life* series. He presumably made a lithograph version of the painting (cat. no. 188) the same year. He reworked the lithograph nearly two decades later and produced a hand-colored version (cat. no. 189) whose coloration comes close to that of the painting.

In the mid-1890s, Munch painted group portraits featuring members of the bohemian community, with which he was associated with in Kristiania in the 1890s. In 1895, he completed two etchings showing a group of men drinking and engaged in earnest discussion. *Kristiania Bohemians* II (cat. no. 182) corresponds for the most part to a gouache (cat. no. 195) done that same year. Oda Krohg is depicted standing at the end of a table at which all of her lovers are gathered. Accentuated in red, she is connected to the table and the basket of fruit below her lap, which symbolizes the forbidden fruit. Her first husband reaches for his glass with a trembling hand in the left foreground. The others at the table are Gunnar Heiberg, Hans Jæger, Jappe Nilssen, Christian Krohg, and Munch himself. Years later, and certainly no earlier than 1907 in Warnemünde, he painted *The First Glass* (cat. no. 197), a work which also relates to the first etching entitled *Kristiania Bohemians* I (cat. no. 196). Munch began by spraying and dripping paint over his black lithograph chalk drawing and then added contours and several details, giving the work the appearance of a large transparent watercolor. In contrast to highly individualized images such as his double portrait of *Paul Herrmann and Paul Contard* of 1897 (cat. no. 183), Munch's *The First Glass* captures the atmosphere at gatherings of the Kristiania bohemians and recalls their lengthy sessions of wine-drinking and discussion.

After the turn of the century, Munch received an increasing number of commissions from patrons, friends, and collectors, and portraiture became an important source of income for the artist. At Munch's first solo exhibition at *Den Frie Udstilling* in Copenhagen in 1904, his portraits were grouped together on a single wall as a central group of works for the first time. Although the critical

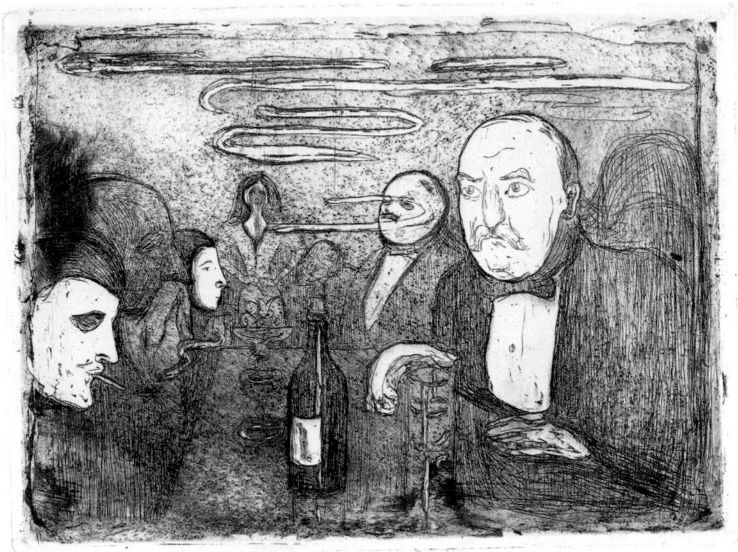

Cat. no. 182 *Kristiania Bohemians* II, 1895
Etching on paper, 28 x 37.6 cm, Munch-museet, Oslo

response was negative overall, he did earn praise for the portraits: "The most readily accessible and comprehensible works are the portraits. They are highly modern, in terms of both *'façon'* and the use of color, yet there is not a trace of obscurity in them."[1] That same year, the presentation of eighteen paintings identified as portraits at the Diorama building in Kristiania bore witness to the growing interest in Munch's portraits, which also gained a measure of recognition in the press: "The portraits are full of life and are masterfully characteristic in expression and movement."[2] Despite his otherwise critical assessment of Munch's first exhibition of portraits at Cassirer's gallery in Berlin in the winter of 1904–05, where only his portraits were shown, Hans Rosenhagen also called attention to the "fine details on the psychological side."[3]

Munch created expressive portraits in which he attempted to penetrate the surface and, in the spirit of Henrik Ibsen and other contemporary authors, to analyze the personality and the hidden human sides of his subjects: "I see all people behind their masks, smiling, calm faces, pale corpses hurrying without pause [along] a winding path that ends in death."[4] Munch's precise characterization of his subject was seldom greeted with enthusiasm by the individuals themselves. The industrialist and politician Walter Rathenau, of whom Munch did two full-figure portraits in 1907, remarked dryly with respect to his picture: "A horrid fellow, isn't he? That is what one gets when one has his portrait painted by a great artist. One looks more like oneself than one is."[5] In both versions, Rathenau assumes an extraordinarily representative pose with his legs positioned in a manner typical of Munch. The most striking difference between the two is a clearly developed, amorphous shadow on the wall (cat. no. 192) which separates from the outline of the subject's body. In the second version, Munch eliminated the threatening disassociated shadow and replaced it with a door bearing a light reflection. Gustav Schiefler, Director of the Hamburg Regional Court, gave his wife a detailed description of the process of making his portrait (cat. no. 194):

> He started with the smaller picture, the one meant for us, that is to say, for you. He drew the outline of the figure with charcoal. ... The next day, he proceeded to the head, first in the large picture, then in the smaller one. At first, he seemed to like the small one better, but then he put the small one aside, and has now nearly finished the large one. The painting starts about 10 or 10:30 in the morning. That is, I often run into M. on the stairs about then, on his way to have a glass of vermouth or something like that. Then come the endless lamentations about the woman who ruined his health. ... So he nearly completed the head first, then the background (purple oven against yellow wallpaper), and after that the figure bit by bit, going back to work on the head each time.[6]

Munch worked on the two versions, which by then had become obligatory, simultaneously, concentrating in particular on the head. Following his alcohol problems noted by Schiefler, a nervous breakdown led him that same year to the clinic of Dr. Daniel Jacobson, whose portrait he did in three painted versions and a lithograph. In the large-format version (cat. no. 191), Munch exaggerated the image of self-confidence displayed by the neurologist against a vivid yellow, orange, and red background, varying his expression within a range between superiority and arrogance.

After his recovery and return to Norway, Munch continued to work on portraits, many of them full-figure presentations (cat. no. 193) well into old age, experimenting with different media, often in multiple versions. These variations bear witness to "Munch's extraordinary ability to express the characteristic, individual traits of an individual's personality with the most sparing, striking means conceivable. Looking at some of his portraits, one has the certain feeling that he has grasped the essence of his subjects down to the very last detail. ..."[7] DB

1 Vordingborg Avis, Sept. 6, 1904, n. p.
2 b., in *Morgenbladet*, Oct. 17, 1904, n. p.
3 Hans Rosenhagen, in *KfA*, vol. 20, Jan. 19, 1905, pp. 210–211.
4 Translated into English from the author's translation of the original. *Der Baum der Erkenntnis*, after 1915, page of text in red colored pencil, 64.7 x 50 cm, Munch-museet T 2547-A41.
5 Quoted and translated from Peter Krieger, *Der Lebensfries für Max Reinhardts Kammerspiele*, Berlin 1978, p. 67.
6 Letter dated July 25, 1908. Edvard Munch/Gustav Schiefler, *Briefwechsel*, vol. 1: 1902–1914, Hamburg 1987, p. 289, no. 402.
7 Hans Rosenhagen, in *Der Tag*, Jan. 7, 1905, n. p.

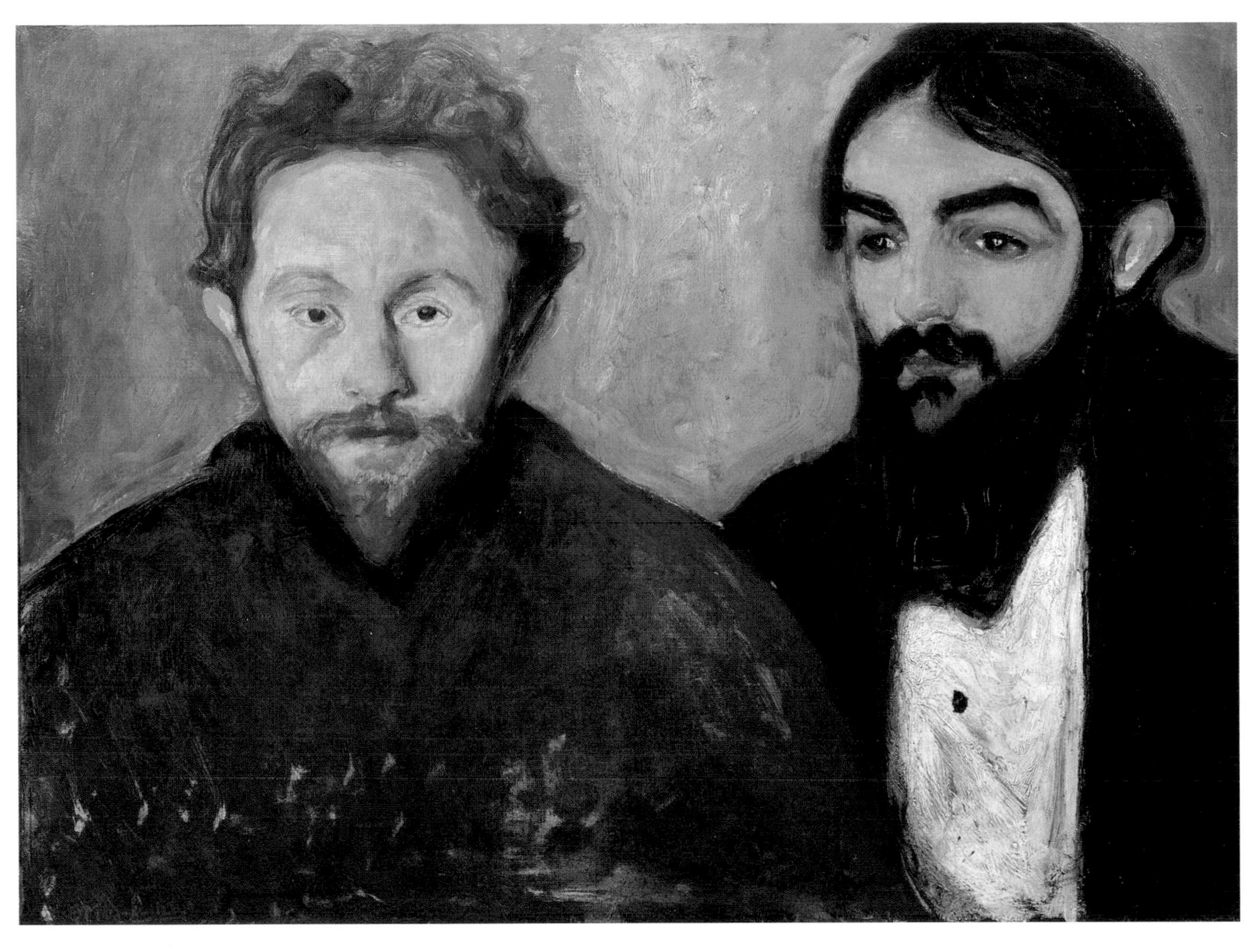

Cat. no. 183 *Paul Herrmann and Paul Contard*, 1897
Oil on canvas, 54 x 73 cm
Österreichische Galerie Belvedere, Vienna

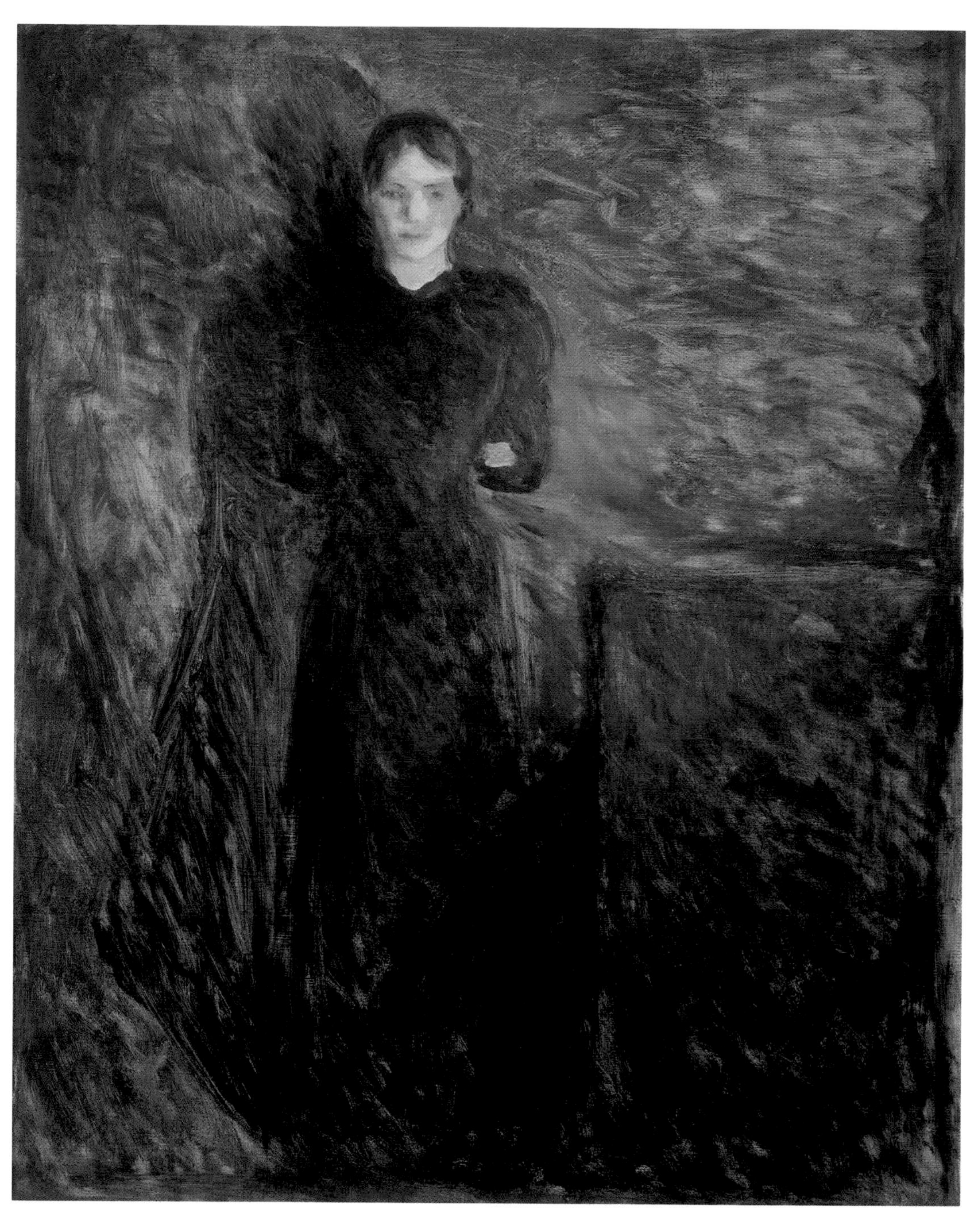

Cat. no. 184 *Olga Buhre*, 1890
Oil on canvas, 73.4 x 59.4 cm
Statens Museum for Kunst, Copenhagen

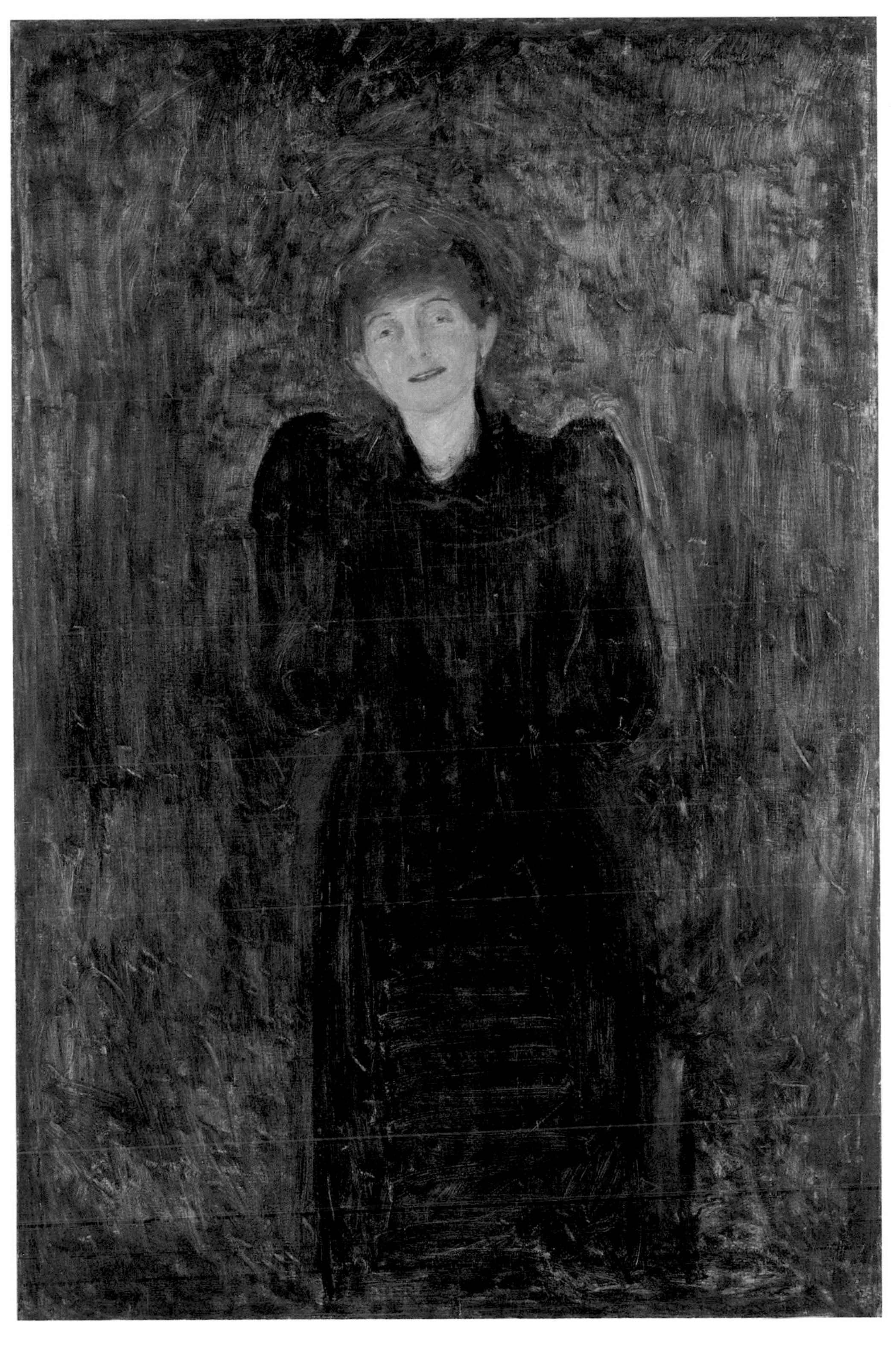

Cat. no. 185 *Dagny Juel Przybyszewska*, 1893
Oil on canvas, 148.5 x 99.5 cm
Munch-museet, Oslo

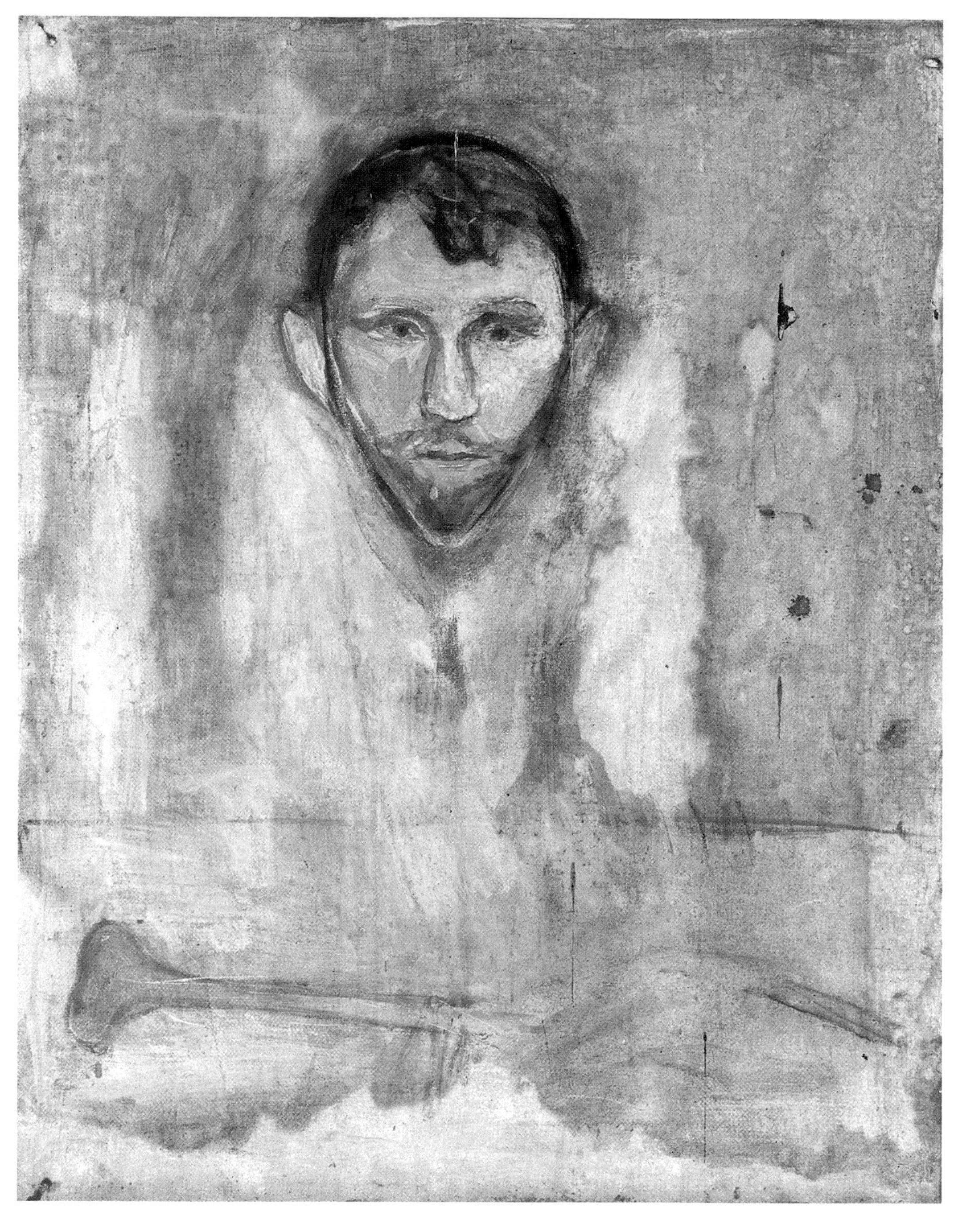

Cat. no. 186 *Stanislaw Przybyszewski (with Skeleton Arm)*, 1893–94
Tempera on canvas, 75 x 60 cm, Munch-museet, Oslo

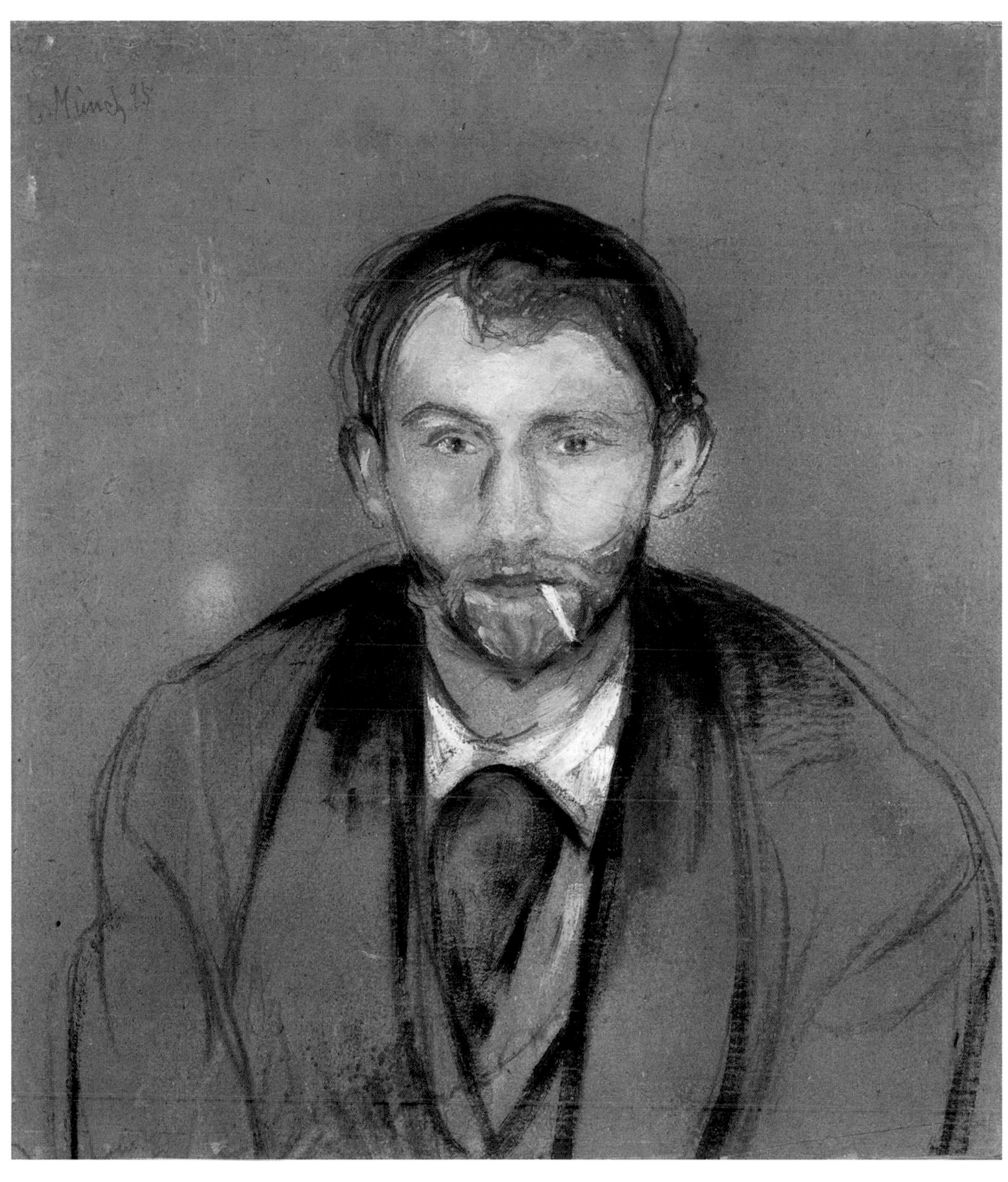

Cat. no. 187 *Stanislaw Przybyszewski*, 1895
Charcoal and oil on cardboard, 62.5 x 55.5 cm
Munch-museet, Oslo

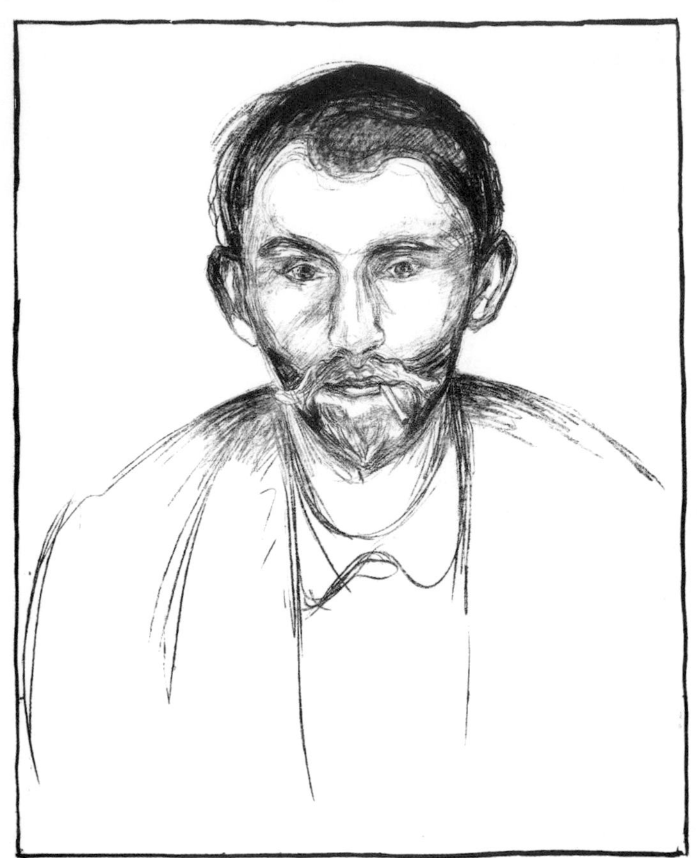

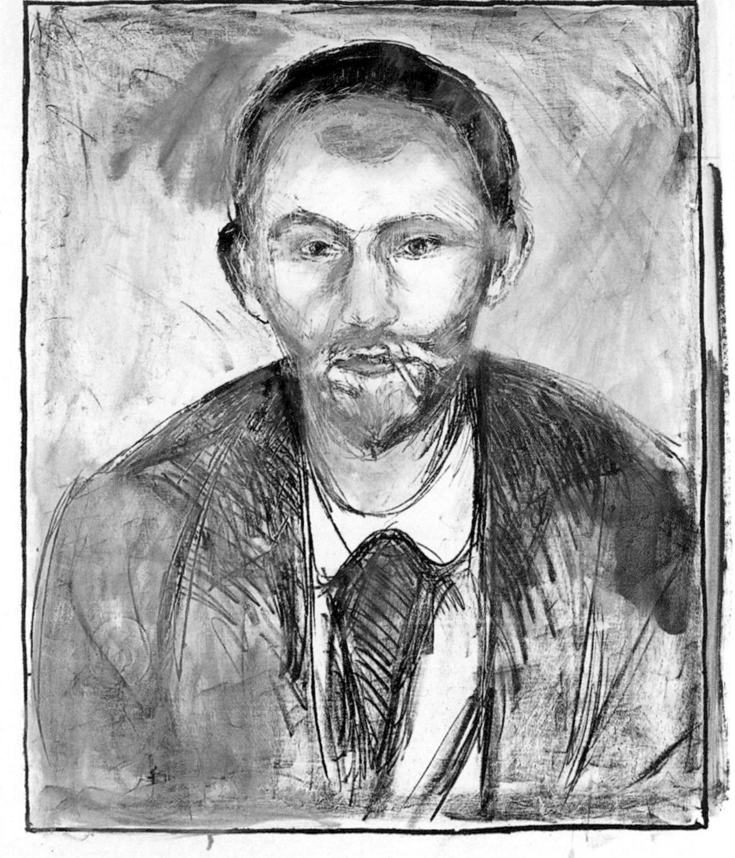

Cat. no. 188 *Stanislaw Przybyszewski*, c. 1895
Lithograph on paper, 54.6 x 44.4 cm
Albertina, Vienna

Cat. no. 189 *Stanislaw Przybyszewski*, after 1916
Hand-colored lithograph on paper, 54.5 x 45.8 cm
Munch-museet, Oslo

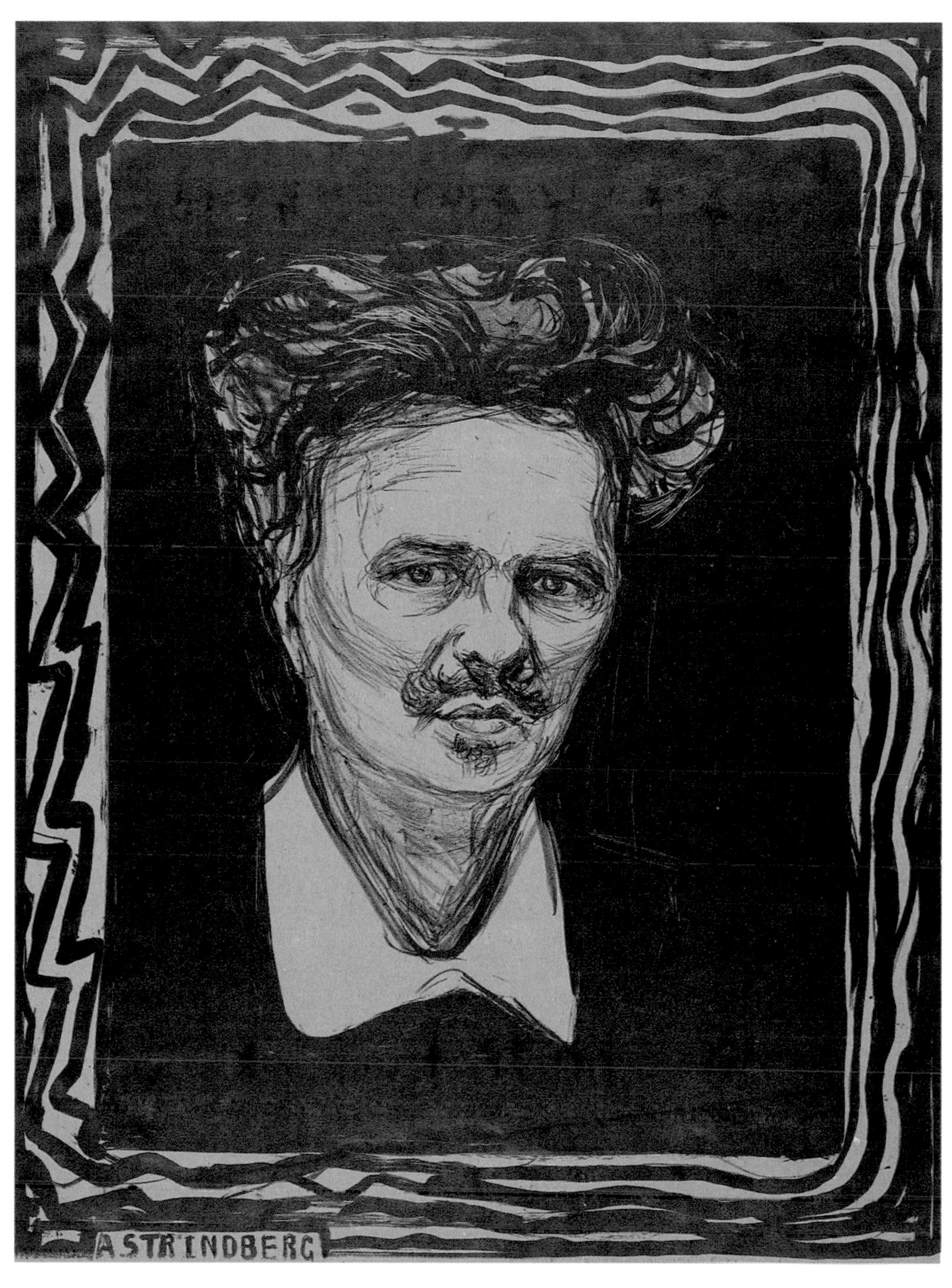

Cat. no. 190 *August Strindberg*, 1896
Lithograph on paper, 61.2 x 46.5 cm
Albertina, Vienna

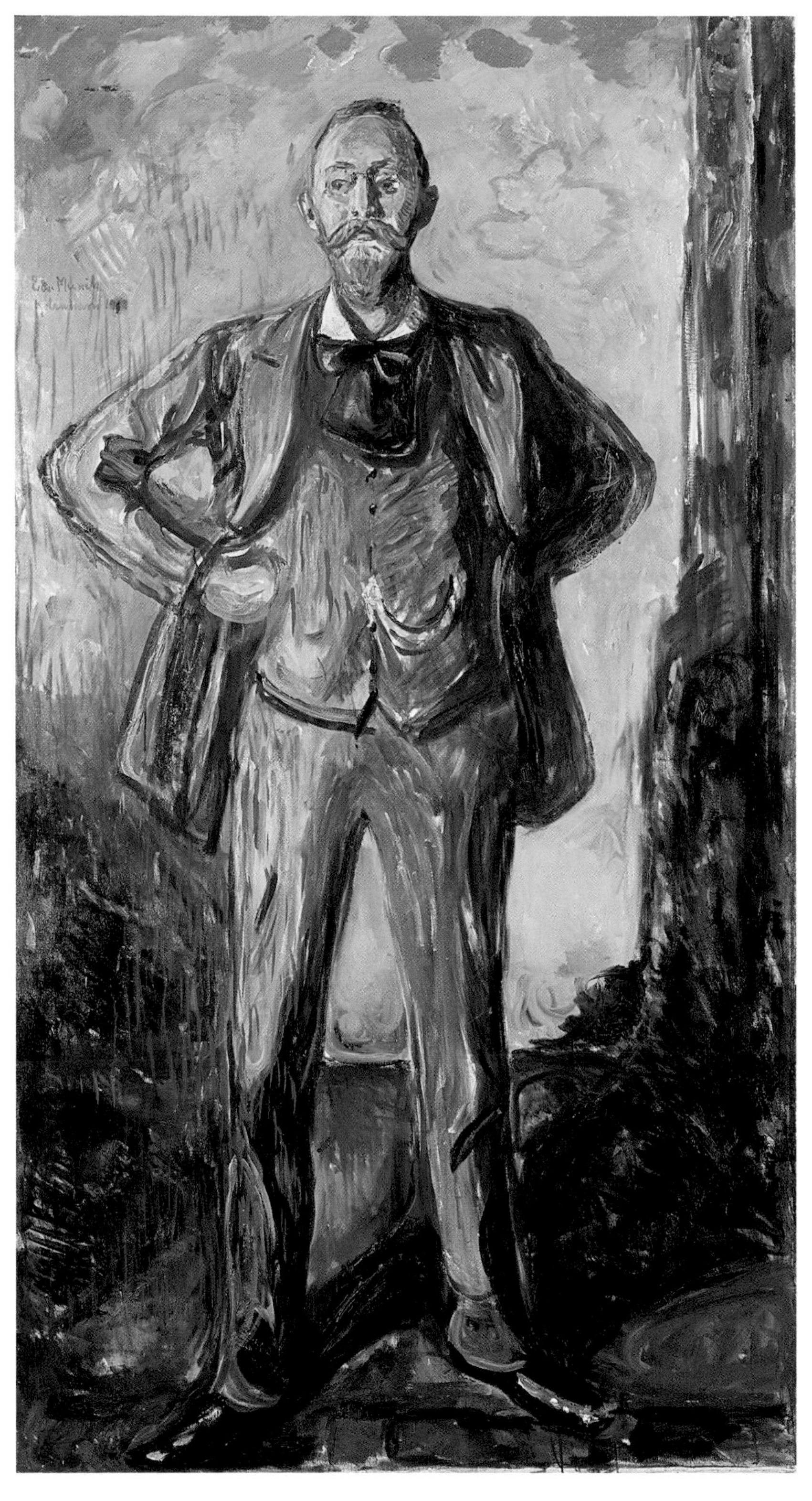

Cat. no. 191 *Professor Daniel Jacobson*, 1908–09
Oil on canvas, 203 x 111 cm, Munch-museet, Oslo

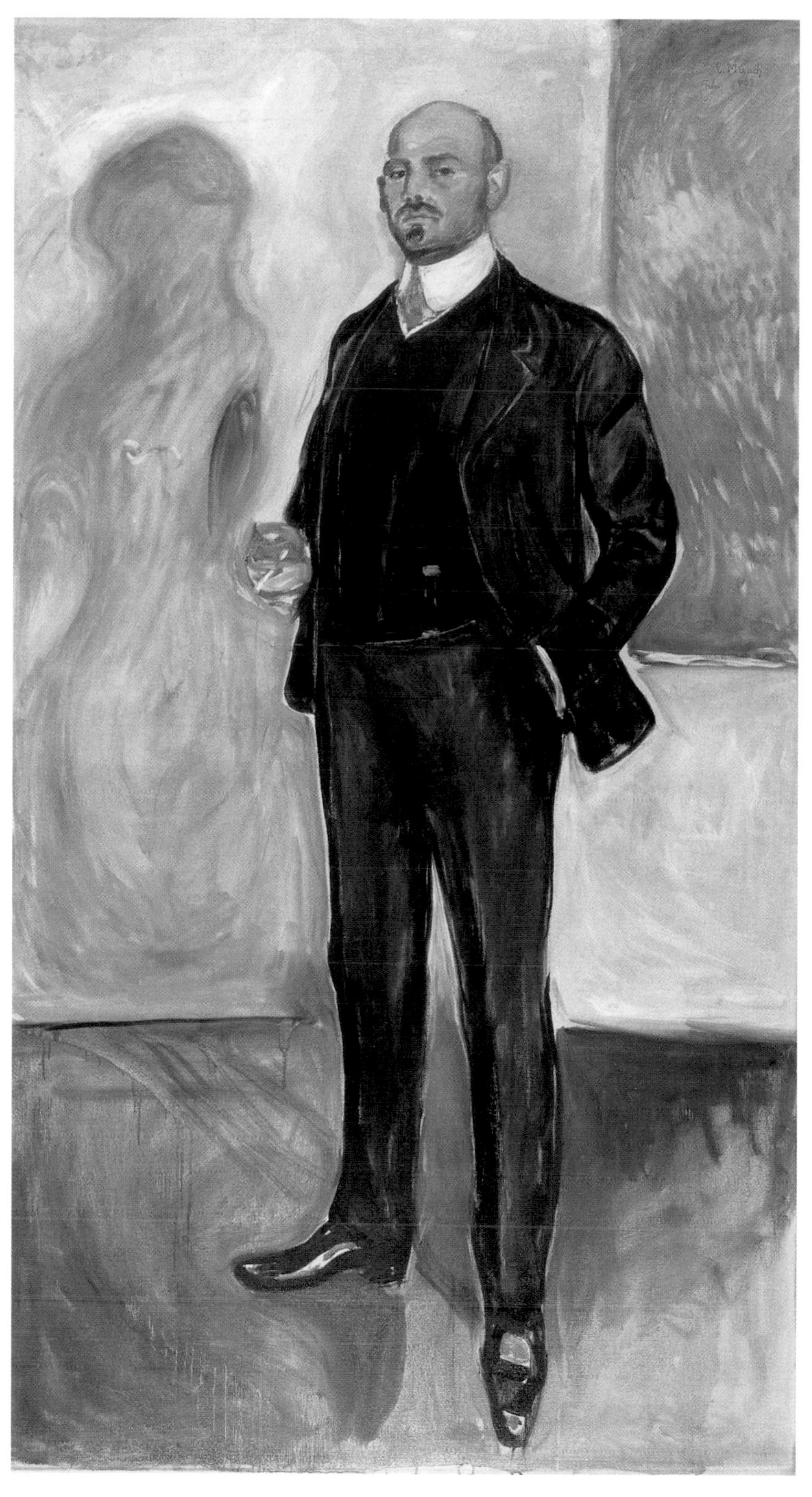

Cat. no. 192 *Walter Rathenau*, 1907
Oil on canvas, 200 x 110 cm
Stiftung Stadtmuseum Berlin. Acquired with
the support of the Ernst von Siemens-Kunstfonds

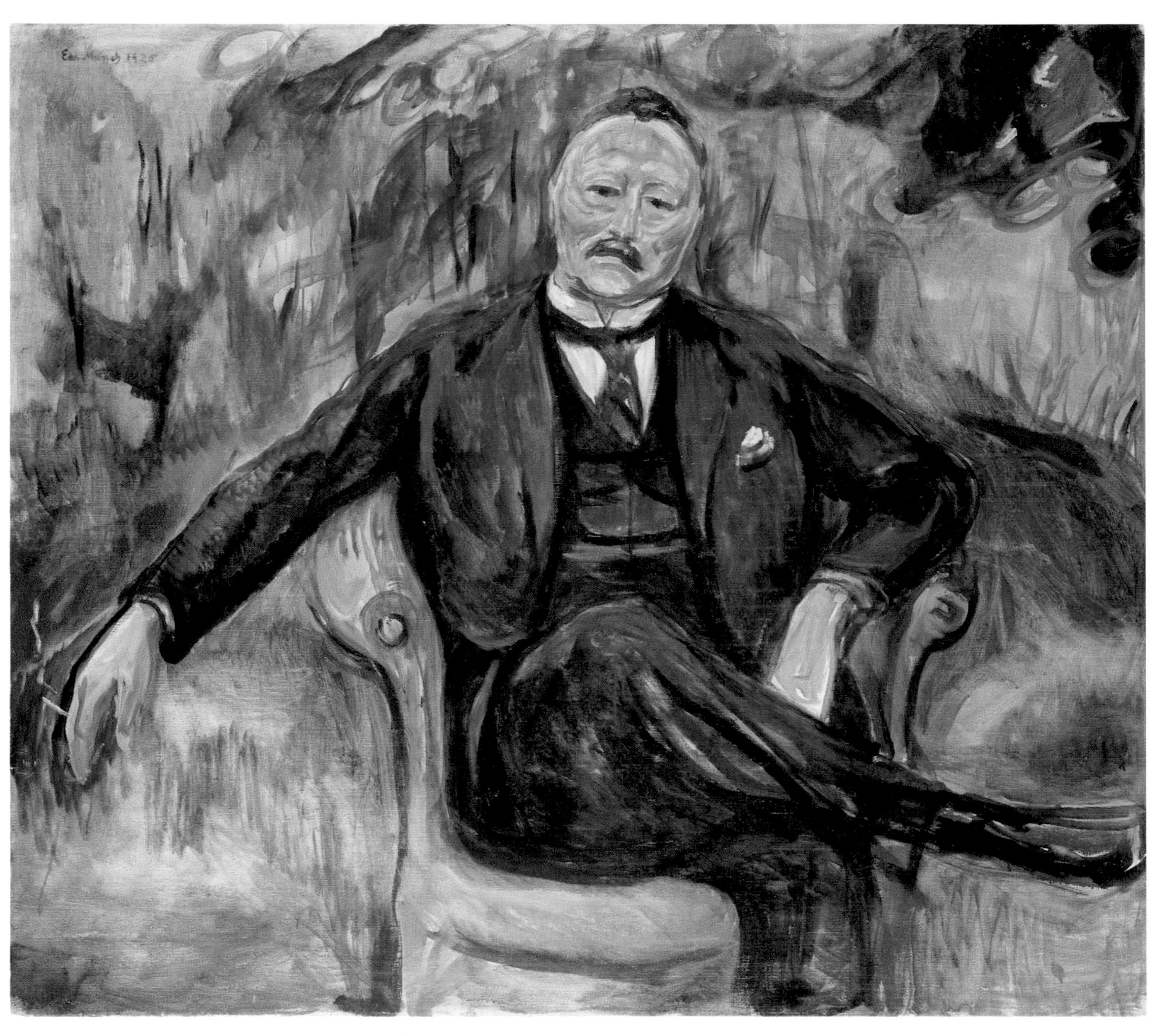

Cat. no. 193 *Heinrich Hudtwalcker*, 1925
Oil on canvas, 119.5 x 138 cm
Private collection, Switzerland

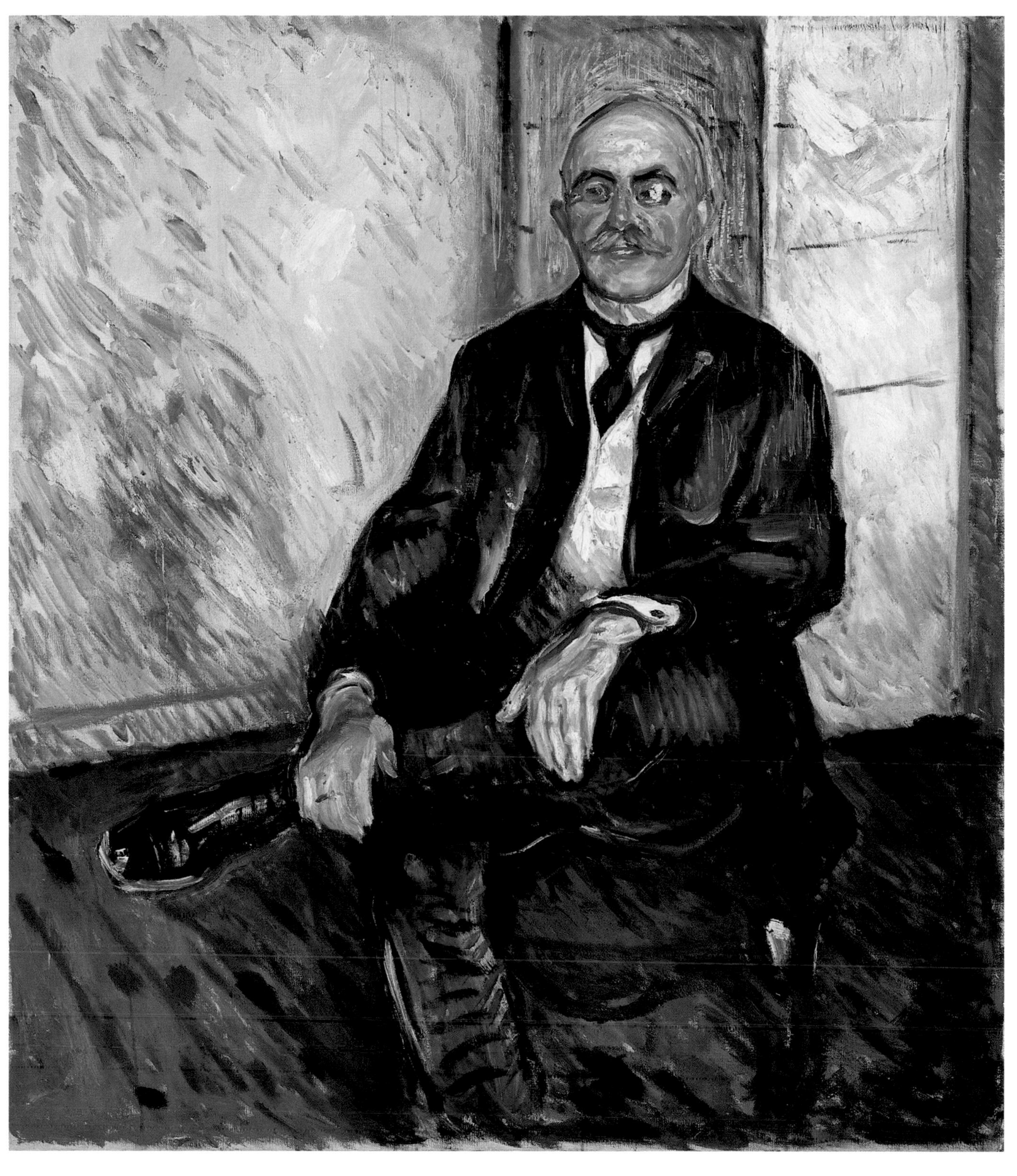

Cat. no. 194 *Gustav Schiefler*, 1908
Oil on canvas, 135 x 119.5 cm
Ateneum, Taidemuseo, Helsinki

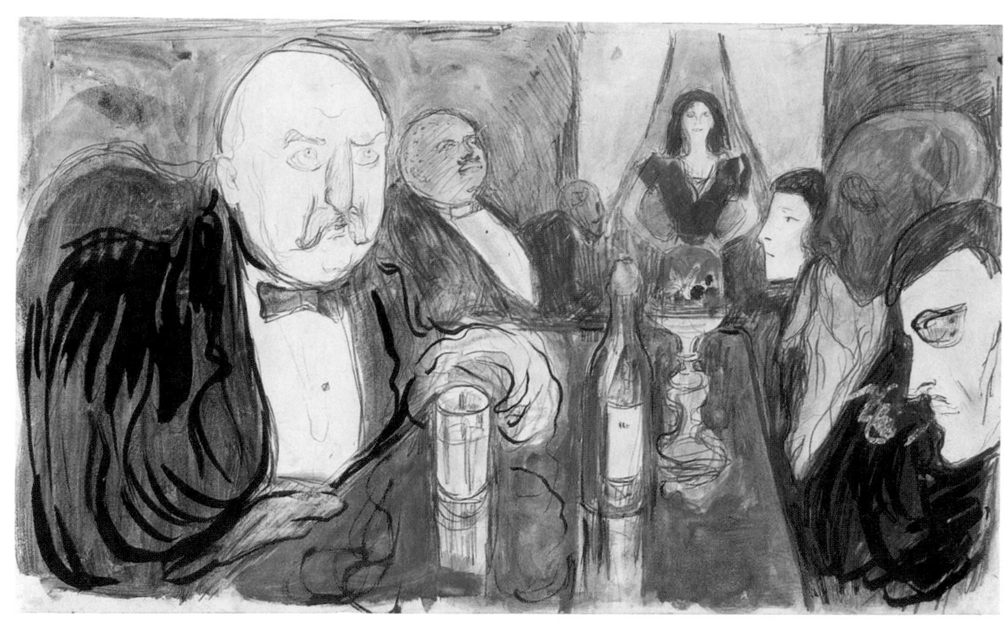

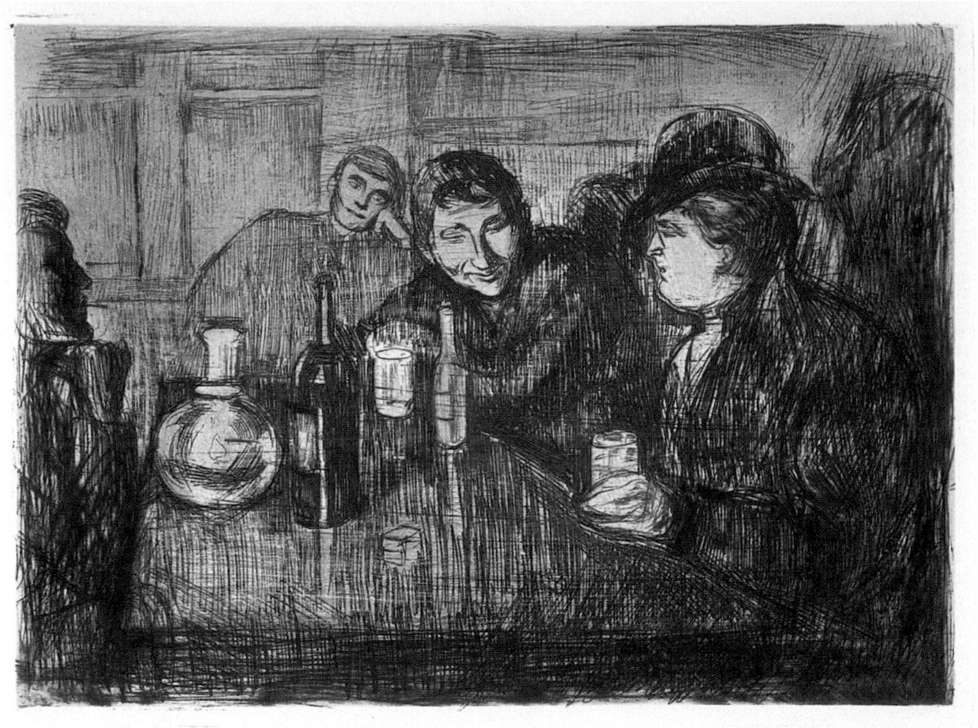

Cat. no. 195 *Kristiania Bohemians* II, 1895
Drawing, gouache and watercolor on paper, 24.8 x 41.5 cm
Munch-museet, Oslo

Cat. no. 196 *Kristiania Bohemians* I, 1895
Etching on paper, 20.9 x 28.8 cm
Munch-museet, Oslo

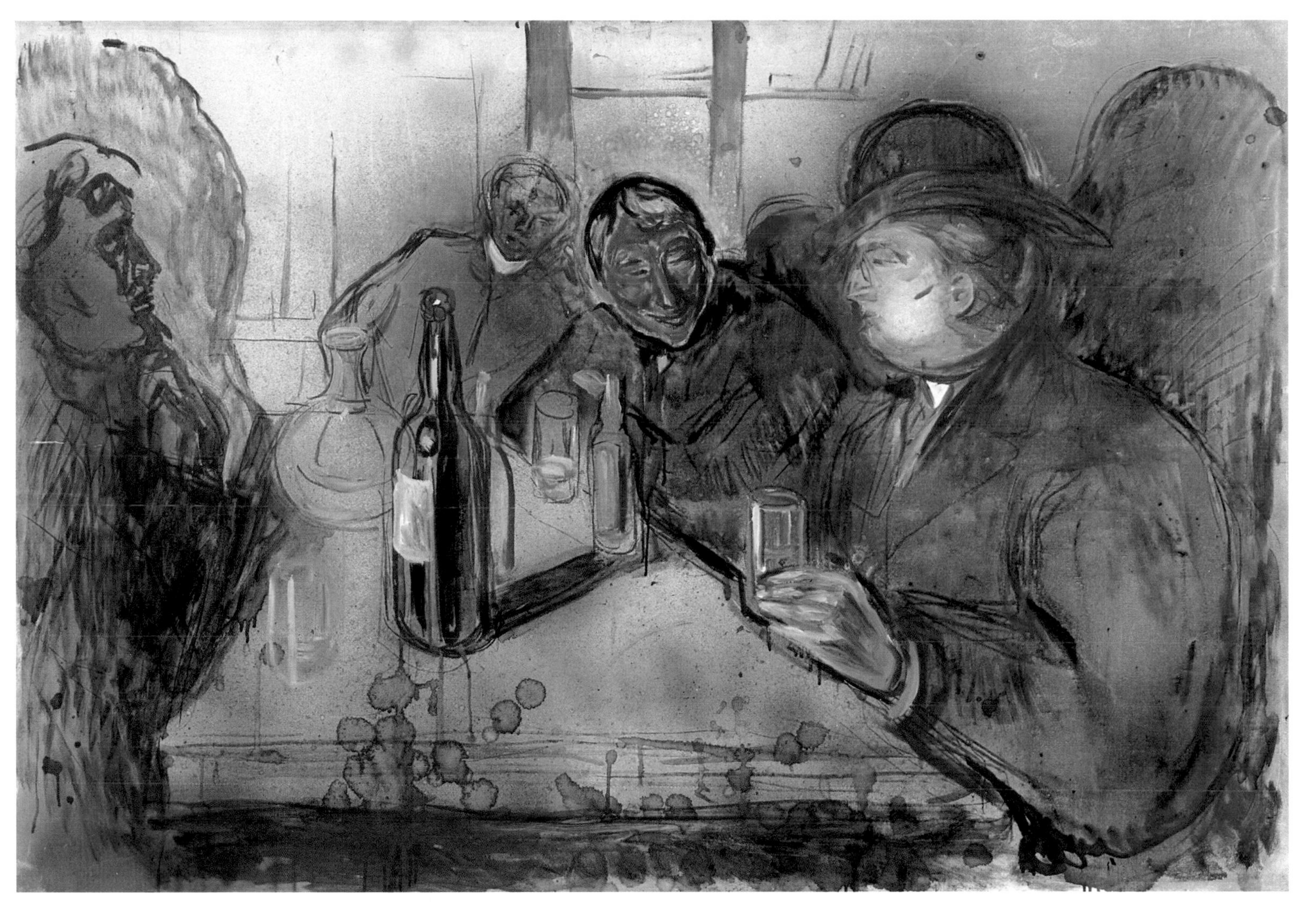

Cat. no. 197 *The First Glass*, after 1907
Oil and black crayon on canvas, 109 x 160 cm
Munch-museet, Oslo

Self-Portrait

"My way led along a chasm, a bottomless abyss. I had to leap from stone to stone. Now and then I left the path, plunging into the crowds of people in life. But I was always compelled to return to my way along the chasm. I must follow that path until I fall into the abyss. Existential fear has accompanied me as long as I can remember,"[1] Munch once wrote. Very few artists have delved as deeply and mercilessly into their own personalities as he did.

Over seventy paintings, twenty prints, and more than one hundred drawings trace his progress through life from the early 1880s to his death in 1944. There is no clear dividing line between the straight self-portraits, which are focused on his physical appearance, and his allegorical self-images. Thus the "flower of pain" or such paintings as *Golgatha* (fig. 6, p. 60) and *The Dance of Life* (fig. 4, p. 57) may be read either as allegories of art or as concealed self-portraits.[2] Conversely, a number of stylized male figures, such as those in *Death in the Sickroom* or *The Scream*, represent Munch himself and bear witness to the strands of autobiography interwoven into his oeuvre.

Munch's self-portraits consistently mirror both his reflections about himself and his artistic concerns with respect to material, technique, form, and style. In 1895, he depicted himself in the famous *Self-Portrait with Cigarette* (fig. 8, p. 102) as the "perfect image of the modern artist"[3] and created at the same time a veritable model of the symbolic self-portrait in the lithograph *Self-Portrait (with Skeleton Arm)* (cat. no. 200). In the latter, his face emerges bodiless from a field of deep black, which Munch colored in steps with lithograph ink, as an earlier state indicates. In the manner of a memorial plaque for a dead soul, the artist inscribed his name and the year in capitals along the upper edge of the picture and framed the image along the bottom with a skeletal forearm. Munch's depiction of the skeletal forearm also appears in the portrait of Stanislaw Przybyszewski (cat. no. 186) and may allude to the close ties of friendship the two shared at the time.

While these two portraits reflect Munch's self-image as a modern artist, he turned his attention near the turn of the century to allegorical themes such as *Golgatha*, in which he portrays the artist as a social outsider. It was not until after he was wounded in a shooting accident that he did a series of "straight" self-portraits during a period of severe crisis. In *Self-Portrait in Hell* (cat. no. 202), Munch exposes his vulnerability, which he had experienced in the loss of part of one finger. In a letter to Jappe Nilssen dated November 12, 1908, he wrote, "It is the wounds from Norway—that have made life a kind of hell for me." The flamelike interplay of light and shadows in the background combined with the mark suggesting a wound on his neck, which separates his reddened face from his yellow body, allude to the thin line between life and death. A photographic self-portrait taken in the summer of 1903 showing Munch with a tanned face and pale body may have provided the source for this image of the separation of the head from the body.

Munch achieved his breakthrough as an artist in Germany, yet his self-portraits bear witness to the increasingly acute crisis brought on by alcoholism and psychological problems. In the woodcut entitled *Self-Portrait in the Moonlight* (cat. no. 198), the artist is depicted as a three-quarter figure with his hands in his pockets in front of an

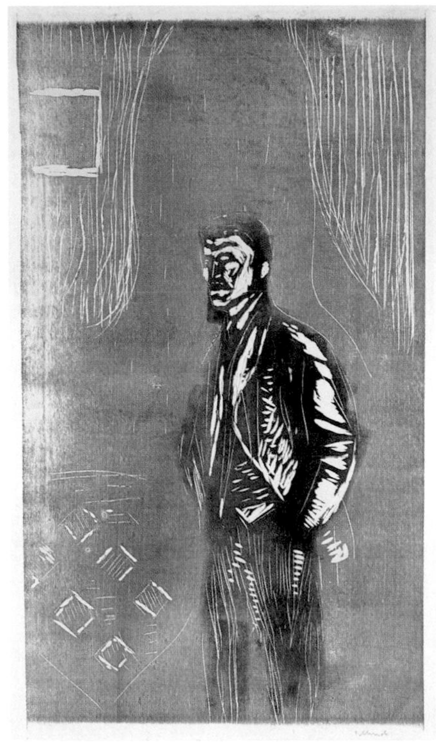

Cat. no. 198 *Self-Portrait in the Moonlight*, 1904–06
Color woodcut on paper, 73 x 41 cm
The Art Institute of Chicago, Clarence Buckingham Collection

oversized shadow. The black paint was rolled over the grayish-blue of the background and extends in places beyond the boundaries of the figure. The fire of hell is extinguished and has given way to loneliness and melancholy. In *Self-Portrait with Bottle of Wine* (cat. no. 201), Munch created a particularly striking image of his isolation and mental distress. Here, he is shown seated against a background that vanishes into the distance. His folded hands seem sapped of strength, while his head appears heated against a field of red in the background, as in *Self-Portrait in Hell*, signifying the division of the self. The glass and bottle refer to his alcoholism. Munch showed *Self-Portrait with Bottle of Wine* at all of the major exhibitions at which he appeared during the following decades and transposed it into a lithograph in 1930. Following his nervous breakdown, he wrote to Nilssen from the hospital on March 9, 1909: "There are several self-portraits, which are self-examinations in difficult years. I think the portraits I am sending, the ones showing me with the glass, are the best. They were done during the Weimar days."

Having returned to Norway following his recovery, he sought and reflected upon his newly regained psychological balance in self-portraits, turning to such themes as his relationship to the opposite sex, the seducer, or the artist as a social outsider. His bout with the Spanish influenza in 1919 led to renewed concern with mortality in a number of variations. In *Self-Portrait with Spanish Influenza*, Munch appears weak and near collapse, as in *Self-Portrait with Bottle of Wine*. Marked by his illness, he appears to be on the verge of dissolution. During a conversation with the banker and author Rolf Stenersen, Munch is said to have asked, "Doesn't it look disgusting?—What do you think?—Do you know that smell?—The smell?—Yes, can't you see that I am in the process of decomposing?"[4] Over the course of the following years, the aging artist became more and more obsessed with his loneliness and the aging process itself in his self-imposed isolation. Munch may have been prompted to do the roughly executed woodcut *Self-Portrait en face* (cat. no. 199) by a burst blood vessel in his right eye, which nearly resulted in temporary blindness. The dissolution of his face in this work reflects his intense struggle to come to grips with the fact of death in the last years of his life. In the large painting entitled *Self-Portrait between Clock and Bed* (cat. no. 205), he stands between two symbols of death, the clock and the bed. The open french doors offer a view into a room with a wall full of paintings representing his work as an artist. The separation of the shadow in *Self-Portrait* (cat. no. 204) and in the gouache *Self-Portrait at Quarter past Two in the Morning* (cat. no. 203) is an allusion to the moment of death. The transparency of the body anticipates its extinction. Speaking to his model Birgit Prestøe, he once said, "I do not want to die suddenly or in a state of unconsciousness. I want to have that last experience as well."[5] DB

1 Munch-museet, MM T 2648b. Quoted and translated from Ragna Stang, *Edvard Munch. Der Mensch und der Künstler*, Königstein 1979, p. 24.
2 In her comprehensive analysis of Munch's self-portraits, Müller-Westermann points out "that the individual self-portraits do not stand alone in the artist's oeuvre but are closely related to one another and thematically and visually interwoven with the rest of his art." Iris Müller-Westermann, *Edvard Munch. Die Selbstbildnisse*, Ph. D. dissertation, Oslo,1997, p. 202.
3 *Ibid.*, p 48.
4 Rolf Stenersen, *Edvard Munch. Nærbilde av et geni*, Oslo 1945, p. 125.
5 Birgit Prestøe, "Småtrekk om Edvard Munch," in *Kunst og Kultur*, Oslo 1946, p. 216.

Cat. no. 199 *Self-Portrait en face*, 1930
Woodcut on paper, 29 x 17.2 cm, Munch-museet, Oslo

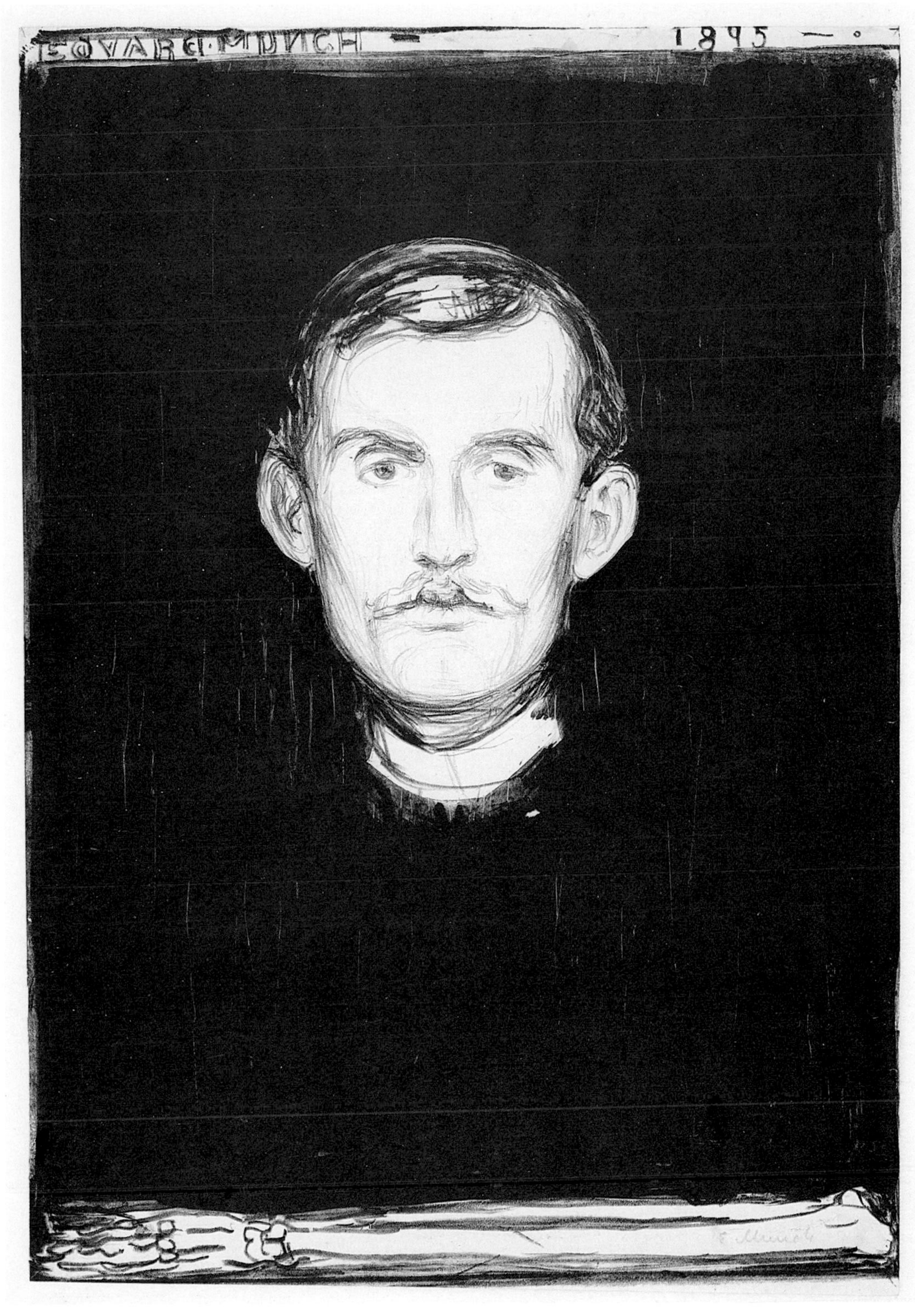

Cat. no. 200 *Self-Portrait (with Skeleton Arm)*, 1895
Lithograph on paper, 45.6 x 31.5 cm, Albertina, Vienna

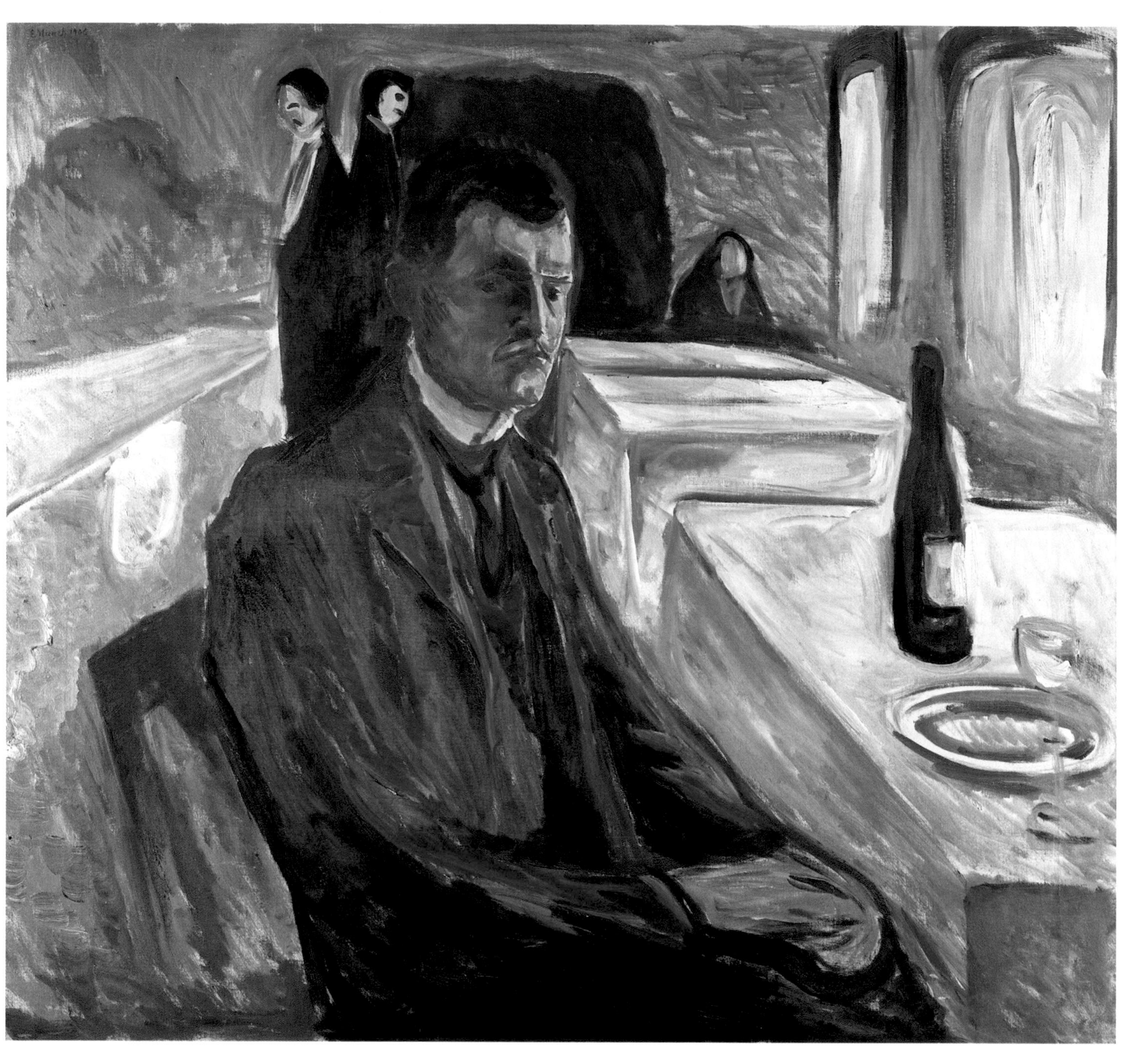

Cat. no. 201 *Self-Portrait with Bottle of Wine*, 1906
Oil on canvas, 110.5 x 120.5 cm, Munch-museet, Oslo

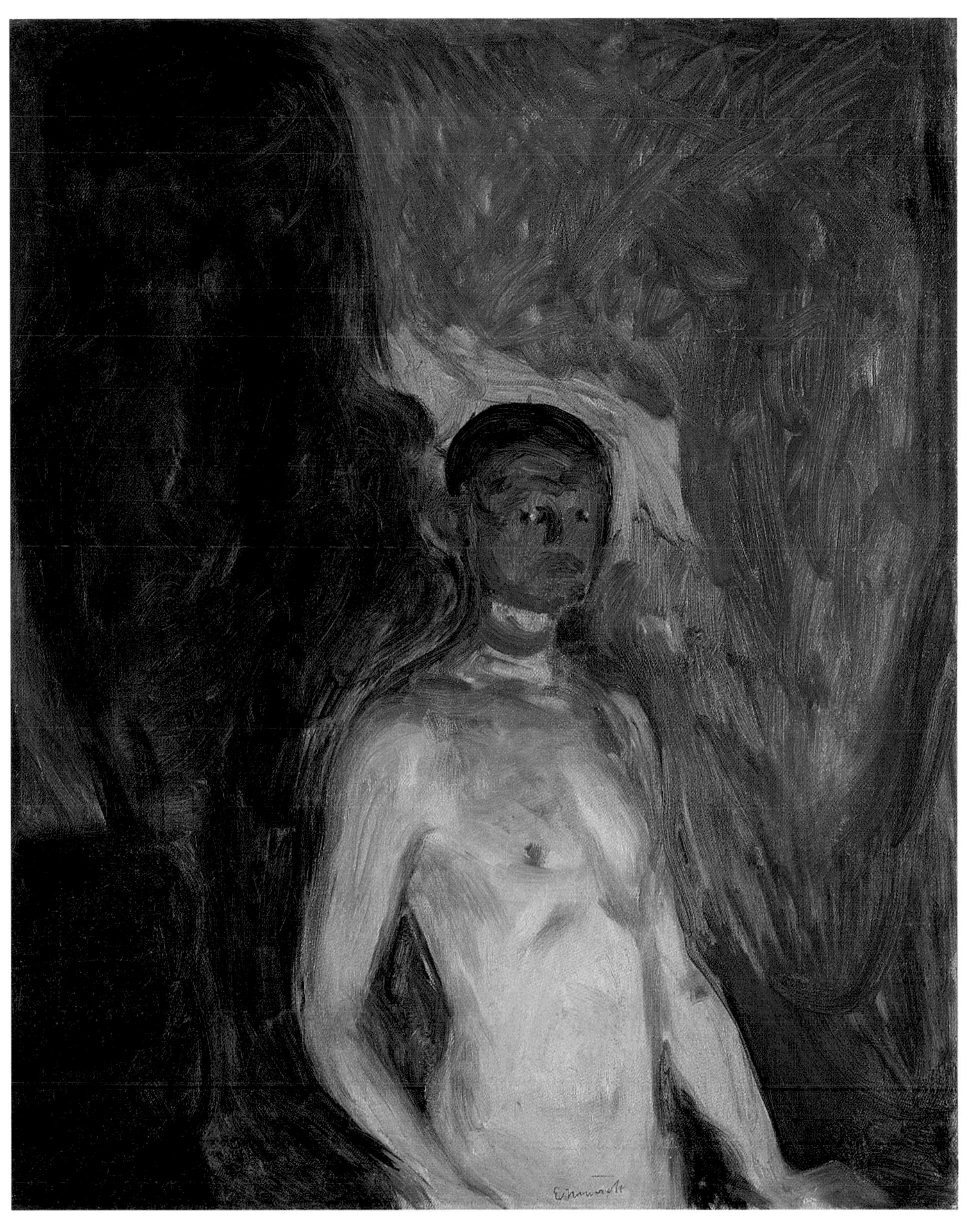

Cat. no. 202 *Self-Portrait in Hell*, 1903
Oil on canvas, 82 x 66 cm, Munch-museet, Oslo

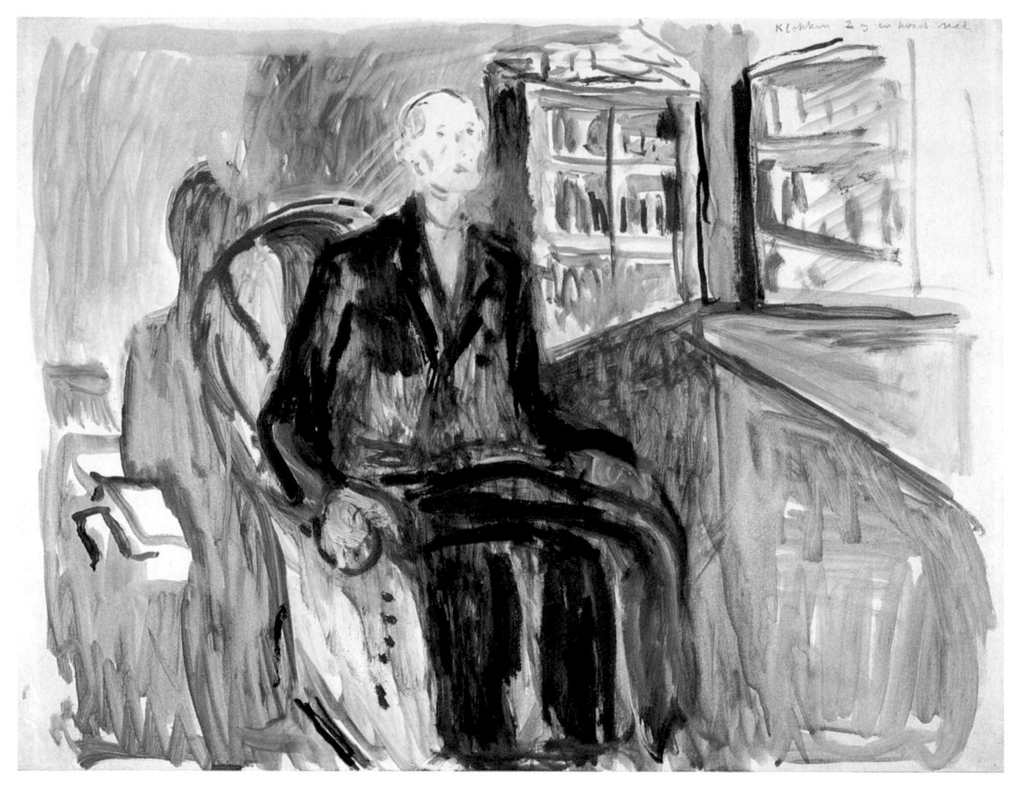

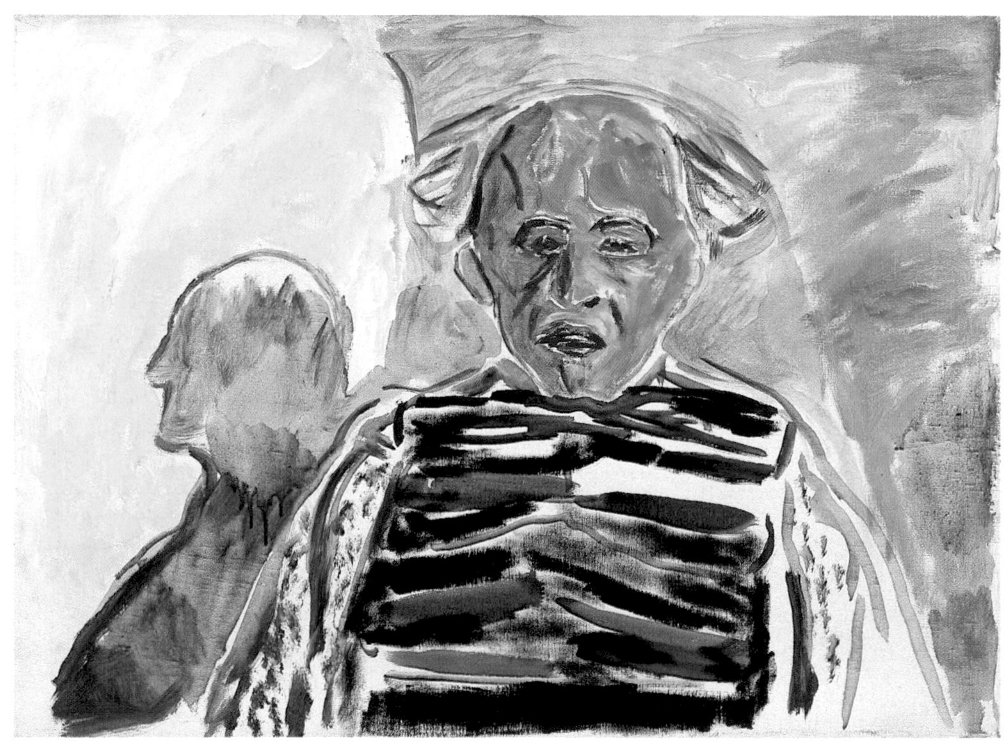

Cat. no. 203 *Self-Portrait a Quarter past Two in the Morning*, c. 1940–44 (1943)
Gouache on paper, 51.5 x 64.5 cm, Munch-museet, Oslo

Cat. no. 204 *Self-Portrait*, 1940–43 (1943)
Oil on canvas, 57.5 x 78.5 cm, Munch-museet, Oslo

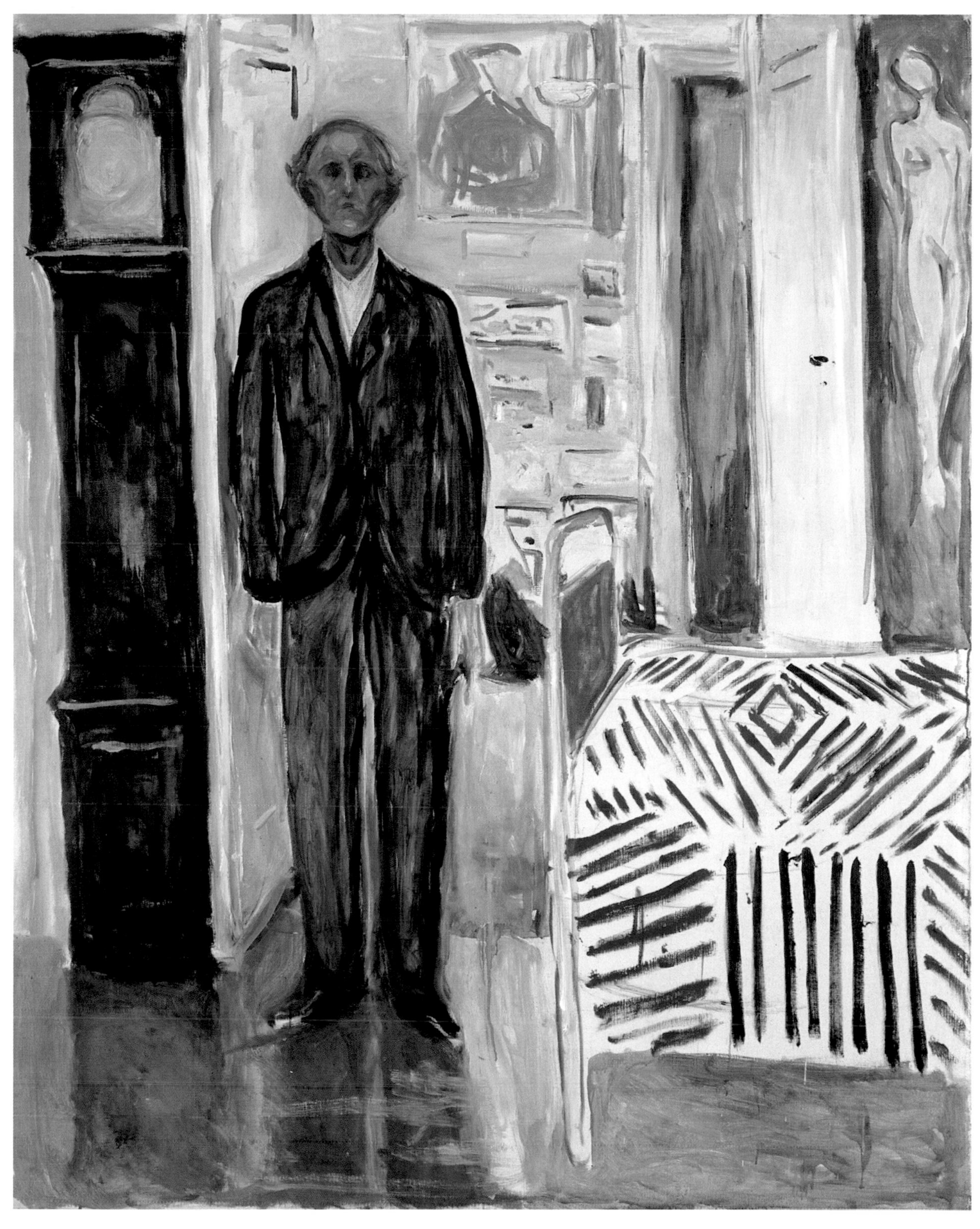

Cat. no. 205 *Self-Portrait between Clock and Bed*, c. 1940
Oil on canvas, 149.5 x 120.5 cm, Munch-museet, Oslo

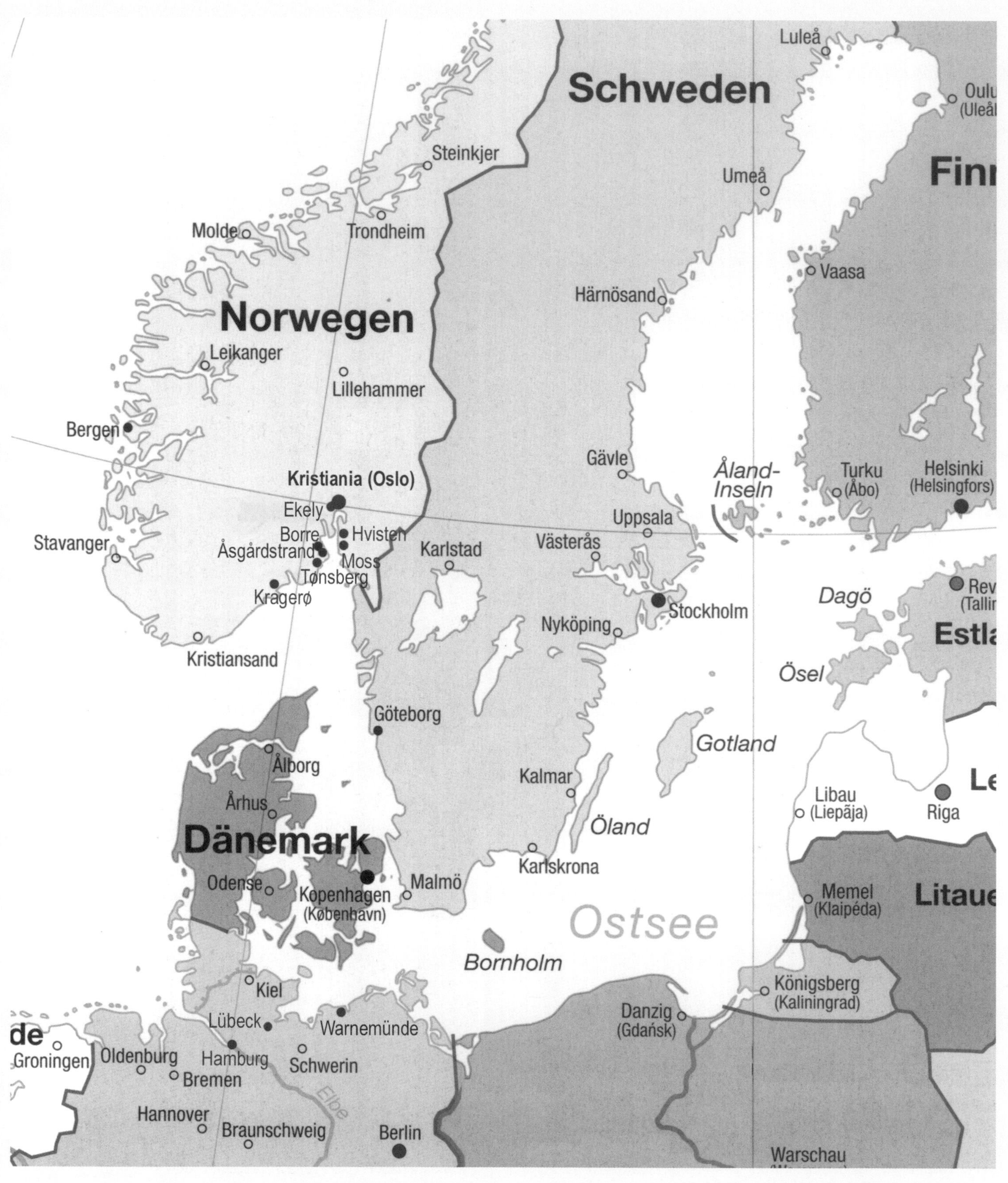

Schweden
Luleå
Oulu
(Uleå
Finn
Steinkjer
Umeå
Molde
Trondheim
Vaasa
Härnösand
Norwegen
Leikanger
Lillehammer
Bergen
Gävle
Åland-
Inseln
Turku
(Åbo)
Helsinki
(Helsingfors)
Kristiania (Oslo)
Ekely
Uppsala
Borre
Hvisten
Stavanger
Åsgårdstrand
Moss
Karlstad
Västerås
Tønsberg
Kragerø
Stockholm
Dagö
Rev
(Tallin
Nyköping
Estla
Kristiansand
Ösel
Göteborg
Gotland
Ålborg
Kalmar
Le
Århus
Libau
(Liepāja)
Riga
Öland
Dänemark
Karlskrona
Odense
Kopenhagen
(København)
Malmö
Memel
(Klaipéda)
Litaue
Ostsee
Bornholm
Kiel
Königsberg
(Kaliningrad)
Danzig
(Gdańsk)
Lübeck
Warnemünde
de
Groningen
Oldenburg
Hamburg
Schwerin
Bremen
Elbe
Hannover
Braunschweig
Berlin
Warschau

Dieter Buchhart

Childhood and Youth in Kristiania, 1863 to 1878: Illness and Death

Edvard Munch was born on December 12, 1863 at Hof Engelhaug in Løten, County of Hedmark, Norway, the second child of Dr. Christian (1817–1889) and Laura Cathrine Munch, née Bjølstad (1838–1868). His father, a surgeon in the army medical corps, came from a respected, influential Norwegian family. Munch's mother was the daughter of a wealthy farming and seafaring family. She was of delicate health and had already contracted tuberculosis before her wedding day. Edvard became particularly close to his slightly older sister Sophie (1862–1877). He also had a brother, Andreas (1865–1895), and two younger sisters, Laura (1867–1926) and Inger (1868–1952).

In the autumn of 1864, the family moved to Kristiania (spelled Christiania until 1877), now Oslo, where they changed residences a number of times during the following twenty years. Munch's mother died of tuberculosis at the age of thirty after the birth of her daughter Inger in 1868. Her sister Karen Marie Bjølstad (1839–1931), who had been helping out in the home since Edvard's birth, assumed responsibility for the family and the household. An avid painter and draftswoman herself, she promoted the artistic talents of Edvard and his sisters. Munch's drawings from his childhood and adolescent years exhibit striking clarity and precision, and they describe his immediate surroundings.

In 1877, Edvard's favorite sister Sophie died of tuberculosis at age fifteen. He would continue to deal with this painful experience throughout his life in variations on such themes as *The Sick Child*, *By the Deathbed*, and *Death in the Sickroom*. Unable to cope with these immeasurable losses, his father succumbed progressively to depression and sought refuge in a strict, puritanical religious faith which, in addition to their worsening financial situation, imposed a confining, almost claustrophobic atmosphere on the Munch family. Munch's own health suffered under these circumstances as well. He began to visit exhibitions and completed a number of

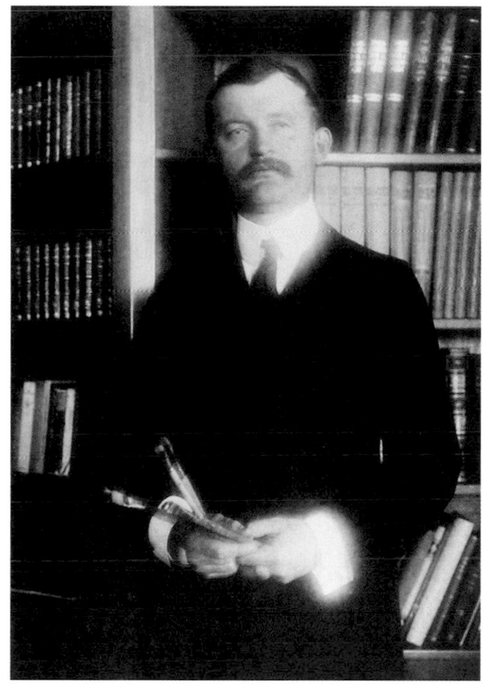

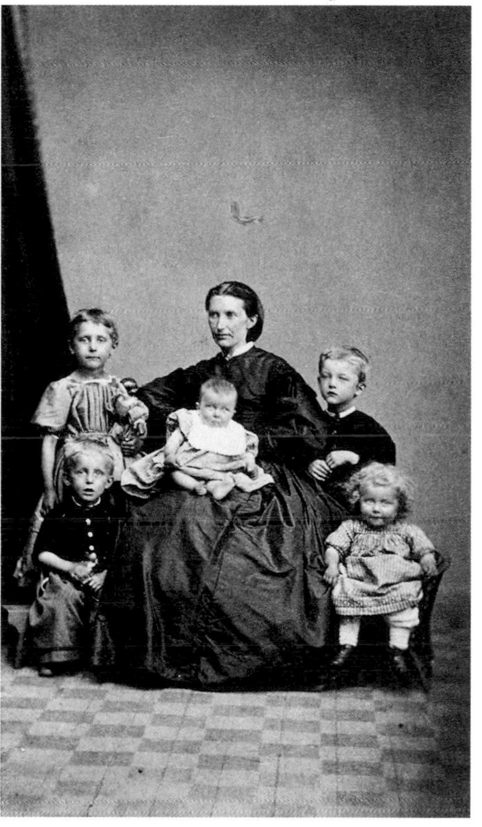

1 Edvard Munch in Herbert Esche's library, Chemnitz, 1905

2 Laura Cathrine Munch with her children; Sophie standing on the left; Andreas seated in front of her; Edvard on the right behind Laura; Inger on the lap, 1868, photo: J. Lindegaard

sketches and watercolors in which he demonstrated a sure command of the brush. On his father's advice, he enrolled as a student of engineering at the Technical University in Kristiania but attended classes only irregularly due to recurrent illness.

Early Norwegian Images, 1880 to 1889: Family Pictures, Kristiania's Bohemians, Åsgårdstrand

In November 1880, Munch decided once and for all to become a painter. He left the Technical University and enrolled at the Royal School of Drawing in Kristiania. Beginning of March in 1881, Munch attended a course in freehand drawing, followed by a class in nudes conducted by the sculptor Julius Middelthun (1820–1886) the next autumn. He devoted much of his time to still lifes, domestic scenes, and cityscapes. He sold his first works at an auction—two paintings for which he received only 26½ kroner—and repurchased a third one himself. In the fall of 1882, he rented a studio with six fellow art students at Karl Johans Gate in the center of Kristiania. The well-known and admired naturalist painter and writer Christian Krohg (1852–1925) maintained a studio in the same building and made corrections to the works of the young artists free of charge. Munch began frequenting the circles of the Norwegian naturalists and, like Krohg and Frits Thaulow (1847–1906), employed a technical drawing aid—presumably a camera obscura or a camera lucida—for his works, many of which involved highly complex perspectives.

Munch made his debut as a painter at the major industry and art exposition in Kristiania in June 1883, showing a study of a head. He also took part in the second *Autumn Salon*, a progressive alternative show rivaling the exhibition of the official local art association, at which he exhibited his painting *In the Attic Room* and two drawings. In the late summer of the following year, he attended Thaulow's "Open-Air Academy," a community of artists who painted outdoors in Modum, just outside Kristiania. With Krohg's support, he was awarded a Schäffer grant of 500 kroner, which was later extended for an additional year.

Munch attracted criticism with his painting *Morning* at the third *Autumn Salon*, which also featured three paintings by Thaulow's brother-in-law Paul Gauguin. Through Krohg, he established contact with the bohemian community in Kristiania, whose leading figures included Krogh himself and the anarchist writer Hans Jæger (1854–1910).

Aided by a grant funded by Thaulow, Munch traveled abroad for the first time in May 1885. He began his three-week journey in the company of a group of young fellow-artists with a visit to the

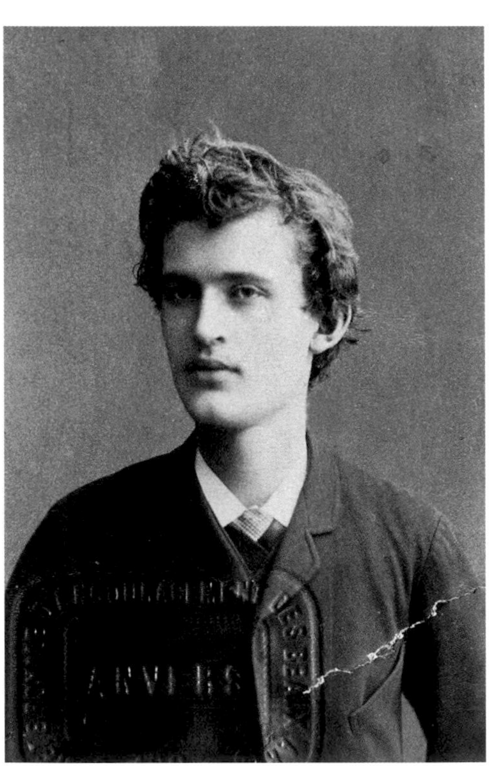

3 Edvard Munch at age twenty-two, 1885

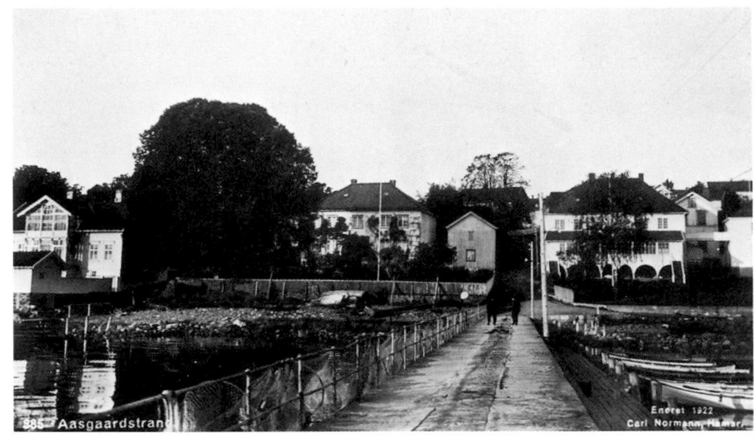

4 Landing bridge in Åsgårdstrand

World's Fair in Antwerp, where he was represented in the Norwegian section with the portrait of his sister, *Inger in Black*, and then traveled on to Paris. He studied the collections in the Louvre, where he was especially fascinated by the works of Rembrandt and Velázquez, and visited the *Salon*.

After his return to Norway in 1885, Munch spent the summer with his family in Borre, where he met Milly Thaulow, wife of the physician and medical corps captain Carl Thaulow, a brother of Frits Thaulow. His love affair with Milly, a woman three years older than he, whom he referred to in his literary notes as "Mrs. Heiberg," lasted until 1889. He exhibited again at the *Autumn Salon* in Kristiania and began work on the first versions of his major works *The Sick Child*, *The Day After*, and *Puberty*, the latter two have not survived. He would return to the themes of these paintings again and again throughout his life.

Munch's ties to the bohemian community in Kristiania grew stronger in 1886. This group included Krohg's wife-to-be Oda, her first husband Jørgen Engelhardt, the author and art critic Jappe Nilssen (1870–1931), the poet Gunnar Heiberg (1857–1929), and the painter Karl Jensen-Hjell (1861–1888), among others. Munch recalled the infamous gatherings of the Kristiania bohemians, which were often characterized by interminable discussions on political, social, and moral freedom and provocative statements by participants, years later in a number of graphic works (cat. nos. 182, 196) and paintings (cat. no. 197).

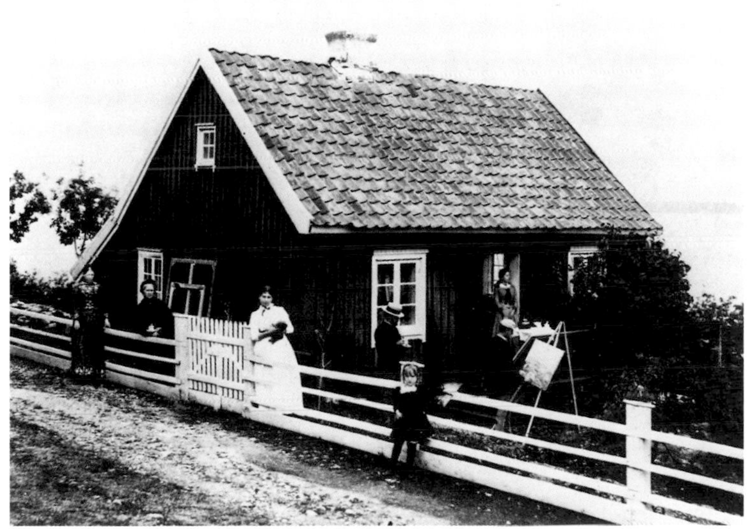

5 Edvard Munch at his easel in Åsgårdstrand; in the doorway his sister Laura; at the gate his sister Inger, 1889, photo: C.T. Thorkildsen

Munch spent the summer of 1886 painting in Hisøya near Arendal. His participation in the *Autumn Salon* in Kristiania, where he exhibited four paintings, gave rise to a scandal. His work *The Sick Child*, exhibited under the title *Study*, was attacked by the public and newspaper critics alike as unfinished "daubing." Munch wrote that "No painting has ever caused such an uproar in Norway. — When I entered the hall in which it was hung on the opening day, there was a dense crowd of people standing in front of the painting—one heard outcries and laughter." This early version of the work, which Munch first revised in the 1890s, was followed by five others, the last of which was completed during the 1920s. Munch found himself the target of criticism once again on the occasion of the *Autumn Salon* of 1887.

In the summer of 1888, Munch gained a broad overview of international modernism as a participant in a major exhibition of Nordic art, where he also met the Danish painter Johan Rohde (1856–1935). He spent much of the fall in the company of the painter Andreas Dørnberger (1864–1940) near Tønsberg and visited the small village of Åsgårdstrand, where he would spend most of his summers for the next twenty years. The painting entitled *Evening* (cat. no. 80), Munch's first attempt to come to grips with the subject of melancholy, was attacked by an irate critic of the *Autumn Salon* as "so indescribably bad in every respect." His first solo exhibition at the Student Union House in Kristiania in April 1889, featuring 109 works, including 63 paintings, brought a certain degree of reconciliation with his critics. He received a two-year grant from the government in July and exhibited a painting at the World's Fair in Paris. His painting *Inger on the Beach* was purchased by the painter Erik Werenskiold (1855–1938). Encouraged by the appeal of the Kristiania bohemians that its members "write their own life histories," he began to keep a diary, which he supplemented with illustrations.

Munch's Years in France, 1889 to 1892: Parisian Influences from Impressionism to Early Symbolism

With 1,500 kroner from his grant in his pocket, Munch departed for Paris in early October 1889. After living for several weeks at the Hotel de Champagne on 62, Rue de la Condamine, he moved into a furnished room on 37, Rue de Chartres in Neuilly in November. He attended morning lessons in Léon Bonnat's studio but was hardly an enthusiastic student. Apart from the World's Fair, there were numerous opportunities to become acquainted with the works of the contemporary avant-garde, including those of Van Gogh, Seurat, Signac, and Toulouse-Lautrec, at the *Salon des Artistes Indépendants*. Munch received news of the sudden death of his father on December 4, a day after his burial. He entered a phase of profound crisis, during which he was plagued by loneliness and melancholy.

At the end of the year, he moved to St. Cloud on the Seine near Paris. In January 1890, he moved in with the Danish poet Emanuel Goldstein (1862–1921), who explained in numerous discussions the symbolist universe to Munch, and the Norwegian officer and politician Georg Stang (1858–1907) in rooms at the Hotel Belvédère. During this period, he completed the painting *Night in St. Cloud* (cat. no. 81), a work devoted to the theme of melancholy of which he later did several versions on commission. Munch described his final break with naturalism in his often cited *St. Cloud Manifesto*: "We should paint no more interiors, no more people reading or women knitting. We should paint living people who breathe and feel, suffer and love." Under the influence of impressionism, particularly that of Monet, and of works inspired by Seurat's pointillism, he distanced himself from the realism of Bonnat and eventually broke with his mentor. He exhibited ten pictures at the *Autumn Salon* in Oslo, which also featured works by Monet, Degas, and Pissarro. Having received another government grant of 1,500 kroner, he traveled by sea to Le Havre in November, but was forced by an attack of articular rheumatism to spend two months in a hospital. In December, he was informed that five of the works he had shown at the *Autumn Salon*, among them possibly a first version of *The Voice*, had been destroyed in a fire at a depository in Oslo. The respectable sum of 750 kroner paid by the insurance company went to the Munch family, which was in dire financial straits following the death of Munch's father.

In early January 1891, Munch traveled via Paris to Nice to cure his rheumatism. In the Mediterranean light of the southern landscape he resumed his work with impressionist and post-impressionist painting techniques. He returned to Paris in late April and took rooms at 49, Rue Lafayette. He visited the *Salon des Artistes Indépendants* and viewed the many works of Van Gogh, Seurat, and Toulouse-Lautrec as well as a Gauguin exhibition. During his stay in Åsgårdstrand, he met Christian and Oda Krohg. The involvement of his friend Jappe Nilssen in a lovers' triangle with the Kroghs served as the stimulus for Munch's variations on *Melancholy* (cat. no. 85) in which Jappe is seen sitting on the beach, and for his concern with the theme of jealousy. Krohg hailed the version of *Melancholy* shown at the *Autumn Salon* as the first symbolist work by a Norwegian painter. The Nasjonalgalleriet in Kristiania demonstrated its recognition of the young artist by purchasing his painting *Night in Nice* and continued to acquire his works in the years to follow. Munch took part in his first group exhibition in Germany at the Glaspalast in Munich.

With funds from a third state grant of 1,000 kroner, Munch traveled with a friend, the painter Christian Skredsvig, via Copenhagen, Hamburg, Frankfurt, Basel, and Geneva to Nice, where the two ar-

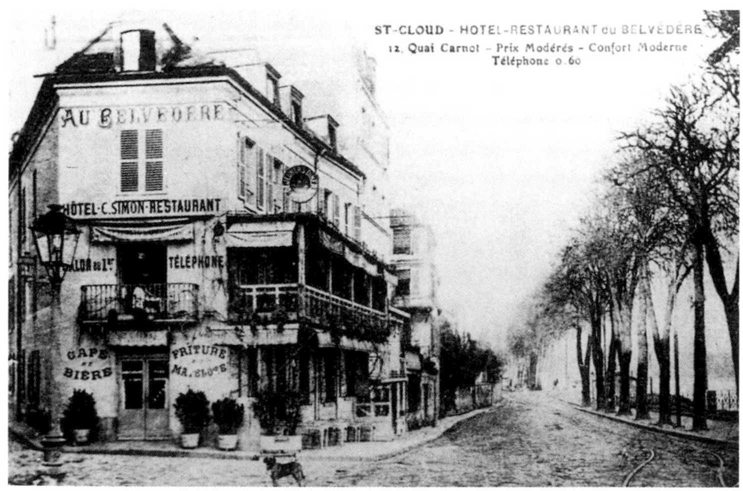

6 Hotel Belvédère, St. Cloud, postcard, early 20th century.
Munch lived in one of the rooms on the second floor.

rived in December. In Nice, Munch occupied rooms at 34, Rue de France, as he had done the year before. During the winter of 1891–92, he worked with motifs from the local casino and the theme of *The Kiss* (cat. no. 43). His literary notes and sketches contain first studies on themes for the *Frieze of Life—Vampire, Despair, The Voice, Jealousy, Moonlight*, and *The Storm*. He painted his first symbolist landscapes (cat. no. 142) in Åsgårdstrand in the summer of 1892. Munch bade farewell to the Norwegian art establishment with an exhibition of fifty paintings and eleven drawings at the Tostrupgården in Kristiania. He met the influential Danish secessionist J. F. Willumsen (1863–1958).

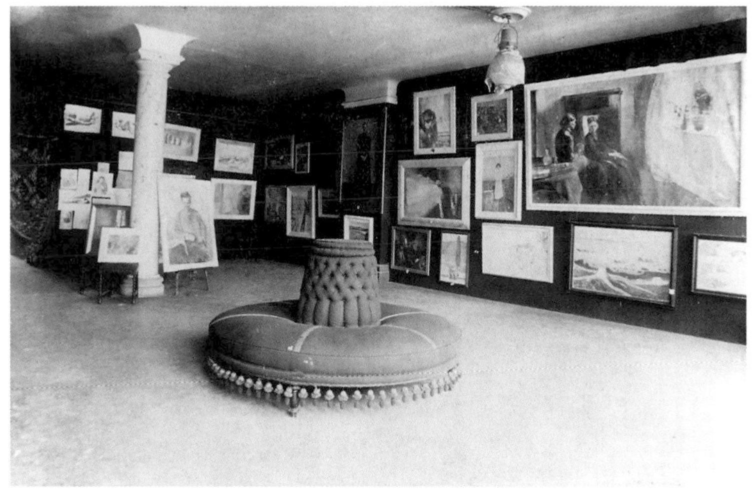

7 Munch exhibition at the Equitable-Palast, Berlin, 1892–93

Munch's Berlin Years and the Circle Zum Schwarzen Ferkel, 1892 to 1896

At the invitation of the Norwegian painter Adelsteen Normann, an extensive exhibition of Munch's art, comprising fifty-five paintings, was opened at the Verein Bildender Künstler [Visual Artists' Association] in Berlin on November 5, 1892. The paintings were criticized as incomplete and ugly, and the exhibition was closed ahead of schedule by resolution of the majority of the association's artist members. The "Munch Affair" not only contributed to the artist's fame, it also triggered the secession, led by Max Liebermann, of a group of progressive artists from the association. These artists later founded the Berlin Secession. Just few days later, the art dealer Eduard Schulte organized a Munch exhibition in Düsseldorf, which was followed by another show in Cologne. Munch moved to Berlin in December and exhibited his scandalous paintings there as well—this time under his own direction at the Equitable-Palast, charging admission for the "paid spectacle." He augmented the selection by adding the recently completed portrait of August Strindberg and then presented the exhibition in slightly modified form in Copenhagen, Breslau, Dresden, and Munich.

Munch spent the winter of 1892–93 and the three following winters in Berlin, where he frequented the literary circle at the wine tavern called Zum Schwarzen Ferkel [The Black Piglet], whose members included the writer and critic Stanislaw Przybyszewski (1968 1927) (cat. nos. 186–189), Julius Meier-Graefe (1867–1935), Richard Dehmel, Ola Hansson, Holger Drachmann, Gunnar Heiberg, Adolf Paul, and Przybyszewski's wife-to-be Dagny Juel (1867–1901) (cat. no. 185). It was probably about this time that Munch began to expose some of his pictures to the influences of the weather, subjecting them to a kind of "kill-or-cure treatment." In June, he joined Strindberg in participating in the *Freie Berliner Kunstausstellung*. In 1893, he completed variations on *The Voice, Vampire, Madonna*, and *The Scream*, which he grouped together along with a version of *The Kiss* and *Melancholy* under the title *Study for a Series: "The Love"* for presentation at a solo exhibition in Berlin. At this time he was also at work developing the principles of design for his *Frieze of Life*. Within the broader context of the Berlin exhibition, the first monograph devoted to Munch, *Das Werk von Edvard Munch* [The Art of Edvard Munch], containing articles by Stanislaw Przybyszewski, Julius Meier-Graefe, Franz Servaes and Willy Pastor, was published by S. Fischer Verlag in June 1894.

The month of October 1894 witnessed the most extensive exhibition of Munch's work to date. Arranged by Professor Helge Bäckström (1865–1932), the husband of Dagny's sister Ragnhild, the show was presented at the Art Association in Stockholm and featured seventy of Munch's paintings and drawings. Munch expanded on the *Love Series* by adding new themes and a second version each of *The Kiss, Madonna*, and *Vampire*. He developed a formal vocabulary consisting of specific pictorial elements, such as the column of moonlight and the window, which appear as painterly signals and symbols in a variety of different contexts. Upon his return to Berlin, Munch completed the first etchings and lithographs in which he rendered themes he had depicted in earlier paintings as mirror images.

In March 1895, Munch exhibited together with Axel Gallén-Kallela (1865–1931) at Ugo Barroccio's gallery in Berlin. In June, Meier-Graefe published a portfolio containing eight etchings by Munch and an extensive introduction and then began making preparations for exhibitions in Paris and Brussels. The group Zum Schwarzen Ferkel was in the process of breaking apart. Strindberg, Meier-Graefe, and the Przybyszewskis moved away, and Munch himself left Berlin. In October, he presented a number of works at the Blomqvist gallery in Kristiania, among them the first version of *Jealousy*. This exhibition, which Henrik Ibsen viewed with great interest, drew considerable attention and was also a financial success thanks to proceeds from admissions and the sale of Munch's *Self-Portrait with Cigarette* to the Nasjonalgalleriet in Kristiania. Exhibitions in Bergen and Stavanger followed. The Munch family was profoundly shaken once again by the death of Edvard's brother Andreas at the age of thirty on December 15.

Munch in Paris, Berlin, Kristiania, and Åsgårdstrand, 1896 to 1902

Munch traveled by train via Berlin to Paris on February 26, 1896 and rented a studio on 32, Rue de la Santé in Montparnasse. For the first time he took part in the *Salon des Artistes Indépendants*, presenting ten paintings, including the second version of *The Sick Child* (cat. no. 122), a work commissioned by the collector Olaf Schou. In May, Munch's special exhibition opened at Siegfried Bing's Salon de l'Art Nouveau and was reviewed by Strindberg, who had introduced Munch to the intellectual circles of Parisian society, in prose poems in *La Revue Blanche*. Munch was commissioned to illustrate the theater programs for Ibsen's *Peer Gynt* and *John Gabriel Borkman*, which were performed in Lugné-Poës's avant-garde Théâtre de l'Œuvre. Draft illustrations for *Les Fleurs du Mal* by

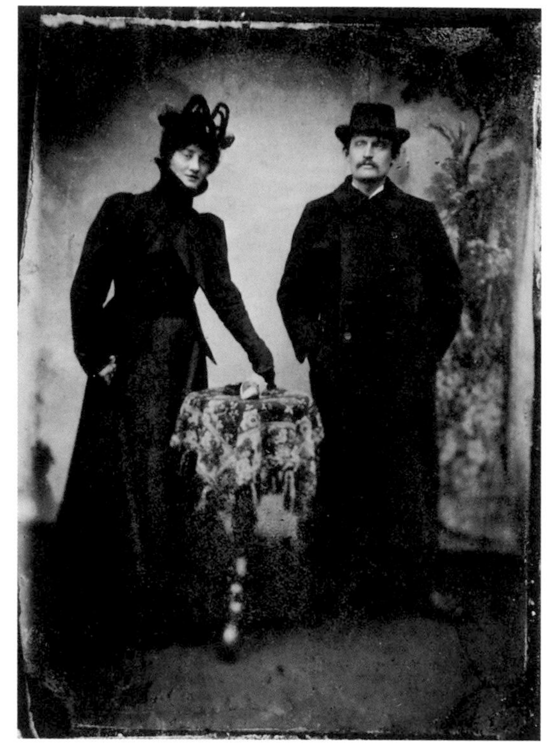

the symbolist poet Charles Baudelaire were left unpublished after the client's death. Munch did the lithograph *Angst* (fig. 1, p. 237) for Ambroise Vollard's portfolio entitled *Album des Peintres Graveurs*. His first multi-colored lithographs, including *The Sick Child* (cat. nos. 123–130), were printed at Auguste Clot's printers'. Munch was in touch with friends of Gauguin, who was already in Tahiti, and the poets Sigbjørn Obstfelder and Stéphane Mallarmé, whose famous Tuesday receptions he attended, and the English composer Frederick Delius. Munch spent the summer at the seashore in Knokke-sur-mer in Belgium. In the fall, he began working on woodcuts, among them the highly experimental variations on *Moonlight* I (cat. nos. 11–15).

Munch moved into a Hotel on 60, Rue de Seine at the turn of the year 1896/97. He exhibited ten paintings selected from the *Frieze of Life* at the *Salon des Artistes Indépendants* in 1897. Eight graphic works had been shown previously at *La Libre Esthétique* in Brussels. Munch left Paris in June and spent the summer in Åsgårdstrand, where he bought a small fisherman's house and worked on motifs of village scenes, his garden, and the neighbors' children. The

8 Tulla Larsen and Edvard Munch

largely positive response to his extensive exhibition of eighty-five paintings, sixty-five prints, and thirty-one studies at the Diorama Center in downtown Kristiania heralded his arrival as a recognized artist in Norway. In the fall, Munch took part in an exhibition of Scandinavian art in St. Petersburg.

He spent most of the following winter in Kristiania, where he shared a studio with Alfred Hauge, a close friend of Hans Jæger. His works from around the turn of the century are characterized by the highly decorative use of color, line, and surface, and such works as *Fertility* already show signs of a striving for monumentality. After exhibiting at *Den frie Udstilling* in Copenhagen, Munch traveled to Berlin in March of 1898, before proceeding on to Paris. In July, he met Tulla Larsen, the daughter of a wealthy wine merchant, in Norway. The fourth issue of *Quickborn* appeared in January 1899 and featured texts by Strindberg and pictures by Munch. In the spring, he embarked on a journey through Italy with Tulla Larsen and studied works of Renaissance art in Florence and Rome. Illness forced him to interrupt the trip. He later went on to Rome alone, as Tulla Larsen had departed for Paris early following disputes between the two. Munch returned to Åsgårdstrand via Paris in mid-May and began work on his first studies for *Girls on the Pier*. He sought help in combating his severe alcohol problems at the Kornhaug Sanatorium in Gudbrandsdalen, Norway, during the fall and winter. The crisis in his relationship with Tulla Larsen came to a head. Munch flatly opposed her wish to marry him, seeing his freedom as an artist endangered and firmly convinced that the "sickness, insanity, and death" in his family would pass on to future generations, a fear he expressed in visual terms in *The Legacy*. In March of 1900, he traveled with Tulla Larsen to Berlin, Nice, Florence, and Rome, after which he spent some time in sanatoriums in Switzerland and Como, Italy. Feeling increasingly burdened by his love affair with Tulla Larsen, Munch left her in the early summer. He showed work at solo exhibitions in Dresden and the Diorama Center in Kristiania. He completed a number of monumental, decorative paintings, including *The Dance of Life*, *Melancholy (Laura)* (cat. no. 92), and *Red Virginia Creeper* (cat. no. 155) and devoted much of the winter in Nordstrand to landscape painting.

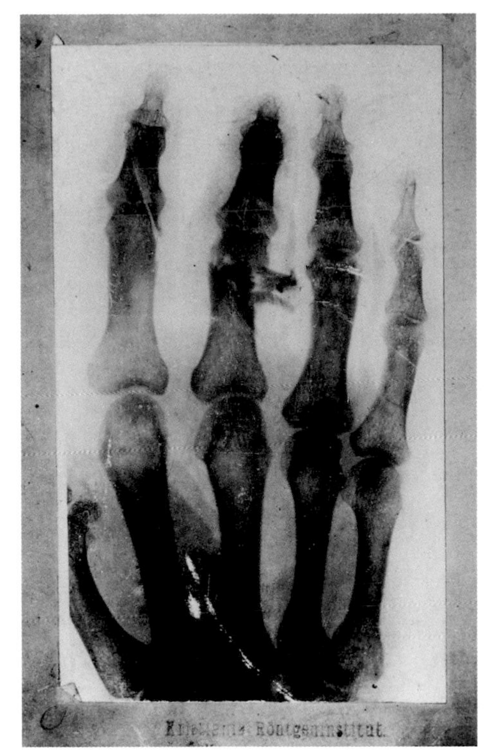

9 X-ray of Edvard Munch's left hand taken before surgery at the Rikshospitalet, showing a small bullet from a revolver in the shattered middle finger, 1902

Years of Crisis and Munch's Breakthrough in Germany, 1901 to 1908

During his summer stay in Åsgårdstrand in 1901, Munch received the sad news of the death of Dagny Przybyszewska, who had been murdered by one of her husband's students. Munch participated in the *Internationale Ausstellung* at the Glaspalast in Munich. Two of his paintings, one of which was *Angst* (cat. no. 116), were shown at the *Vienna Secession*. Although his exhibitions had been well received, Munch's financial situation remained precarious. In November, he moved to Berlin and rented a studio at 82, Lützowstrasse. In April 1902, he exhibited twenty-two paintings devoted to themes of love, fear, and death under the title *Frieze. A Series of Images of Life* at the *5th Exhibition of the Berlin Secession*. The paintings were hung high on the walls. The exhibition attracted in particular the attention of young northern European painters. Munch purchased a camera and began taking photographs, some of them highly experimental, of himself and his surroundings. He was introduced by the businessman and art aficionado Albert Kollmann (1837–1915), who devoted considerable energy to promoting recognition of Munch's art in Germany, to Dr. Max Linde (1862–1940), a Lübeck ophthalmologist and art collector, who eventually became an important client and a close friend. Munch was compelled to realize that the Norwegian press gave no coverage to his successful appearances in Germany. He completed numerous landscapes during his summer stay in Åsgårdstrand, including *Summer Night on the Shore* (cat. no. 144).

A reunion with Tulla Larsen on September 12 took a dramatic end. During a heated argument, a shot was fired, and Munch suffered a wound in his hand. The loss of a part of his left middle finger would remind him of the traumatic event for the rest of his life. In the late fall, he traveled to Lübeck to visit Max Linde, who commissioned him to make prints of his family, his house, and his garden. The product was a portfolio, known as the *Linde Portfolio*, containing 14 etchings and two lithographs. Max Linde's book *Edvard Munch und die Kunst der Zukunft* [Edvard Munch and the Art of the Future] was published at year's end. Munch spent the winter in Berlin, where he met Gustav Schiefler (1857–1935), Director of the Regional Court in Hamburg, who bought numerous prints from him over the course of the year.

Munch showed his works at thirteen different exhibitions in 1903. Following his first exhibition at the Galerie Paul Cassirer in Berlin early in the new year, he presented an extensive selection of graphic works at Cassirer's gallery in February 1903. That same month, Munch journeyed to Leipzig, where he exhibited prints and paintings at the Beyer & Sohn art dealership and hung nineteen *Frieze of Life* pictures on the wall at a height of about three meters from the floor. The eight paintings he exhibited at the *Salon des Artistes Indépendants* in Paris attracted great interest by virtue of their distinctive coloration. In Paris, Munch made the acquaintance of the violinist Eva Mudocci (cat. no. 17), a friend and model of Matisse's. The two soon developed strong bonds of friendship. Munch returned to Germany in April. In September, he exhibited his work at Blomqvist's gallery in Kristiania. Cassirer showed his works along with those of Goya in Berlin. The sale of 800 prints shown at an exhibition of graphic art organized by the Kunstfreunde [Friends of Art] in Hamburg at the turn of the year 1903–04 underscored the significance and recognition his graphic art had attained in Germany.

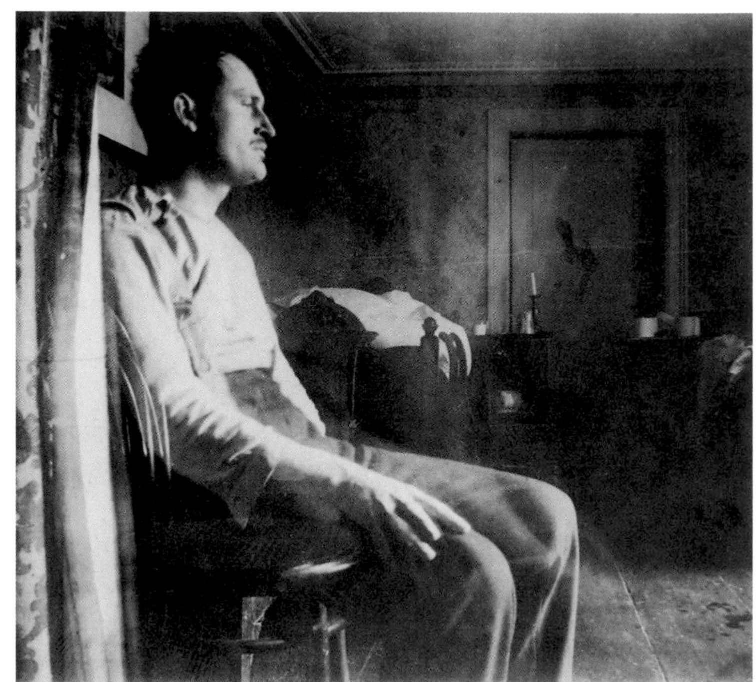

10 Edvard Munch in his room at the Kontinentet, 1906, photo: Edvard Munch, Munch-museet, Oslo

Munch signed contracts conferring exclusive rights to sell his graphic works and paintings in Germany to Bruno Cassirer in 1904 and to Commeter in Hamburg in 1905, respectively. In January 1904, the Berlin Secession honored Munch by electing him to full membership. The *19th Exhibition of the Vienna Secession* featured twenty paintings by Munch, along with works by Ferdinand Hodler, Cuno Amiet, and Axel Gallén-Kallela. He showed six paintings, including *Melancholy (Laura)* (cat. no. 92), at the *Salon des Artistes Indépendants*. Munch accepted an invitation by Harry Graf Kessler, chairman of the new museum, to come to Weimar. The offer of a studio at the Academy of Art was equivalent to the award of a professorship, but was rescinded due to Munch's excessive drinking, which produced nervousness, psychological instability, and other disorders. During the summer in Åsgårdstrand, he worked on the *Frieze* commissioned by Max Linde as a decoration in the child's room. Linde rejected his draft designs, however, as unsuitable for children. Munch's solo exhibition at *Den Frie Udstilling* in Copenhagen, for which a fistfight with the writer Andreas Haukland provided advance publicity, was followed by an extensive retrospective at the Diorama Center in Kristiania.

After an exhibition of his portraits at Cassirer's gallery in Berlin in the winter of 1904–05, which brought in numerous commissions, portraiture became an important source of income for the artist. A retrospective featuring seventy-four paintings and forty-seven graphic works, including the *Frieze of Life* presented as a grand ensemble, at the Manes Artists' Union in Prague in February 1905 was received with great enthusiasm and exerted considerable influence on many young Czech artists. Exhibitions of his graphic art were presented in Copenhagen, Paris, Stockholm, Munich, and Vienna in 1905 and 1906. Munch spent the spring in Åsgårdstrand but left Norway following a violent dispute with the painter Ludvig Karsten and did not return until 1909. Munch sought to find peace and quiet in Klampenborg near Copenhagen. In September, he painted a portrait of the Esche family in Chemnitz. In November, he entered a clinic in Bad Elgersburg, Thuringia, in the hopes of curing his severe alcohol addiction and his psychological problems. Munch spent the spring and summer of 1906 in Thuringia near the residential city of Weimar. He worked on several portrait jobs and completed the Nietzsche portrait commissioned by Ernest Thiel (1859–1947), a Stockholm banker and art collector. The portrait was painted from a photograph. His works were grouped with those of fauvist artists at an exhibition presented by the *Salon des Artistes Indépendants*. In the summer, Munch began work on set designs for Henrik Ibsen's play *Ghosts* and the decoration for the foyer of the Berliner Kammerspiele, the famous *Reinhardt Frieze* (completed in 1907), on commission of the actor and theater director Max Reinhardt (1873–1943). In Bad Kösen, he spent several periods in clinics for treatment of his alcohol addiction. In addition to his participation at the *11th Exhibition of the Berlin Secession* and the *Norwegian Exhibition* in Copenhagen, he also was presented in solo exhibitions in Magdeburg, Dresden, Chemnitz, Hamburg, Hagen, and Weimar. The artists of the Brücke group were highly impressed with his art and invited him to take part in their exhibitions in that and the two succeeding years. Munch refused to accept these invitations. He worked on set designs for Ibsen's play *Hedda Gabler* and on two full-figure portraits of the industrialist Walter Rathenau (1867–1922) (cat. no. 192).

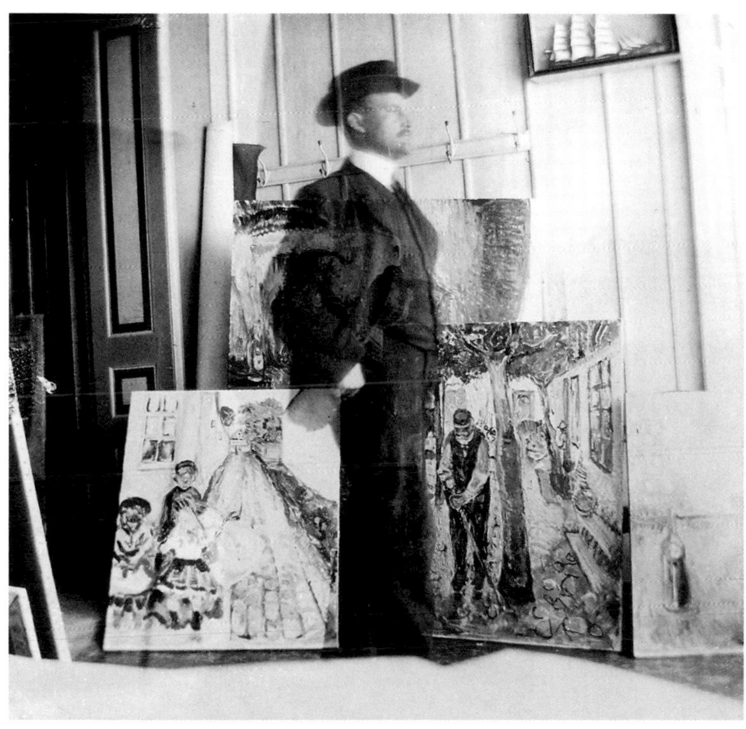

11 Edvard Munch in the hallway of 53, Am Strom, 1907, photo: Edvard Munch, Munch-museet, Oslo

Munch in Warnemünde, 1907 to 1908

In June 1907, Munch traveled to Warnemünde, a small seaside resort on the Baltic Sea, where he rented rooms at the elegant Hosmanns Hotel on 61, Am Strom, before moving somewhat later into an older fisherman's house on 53, Am Strom. His stay in Warnemünde was not devoted to rest and recovery but instead to intensive experimentation in painting and photography. In a series of joyless motifs of love entitled *The Green Room*, which includes several variations on the theme of jealousy (cat. nos. 77, 79), Munch attempted to come to grips with the experience of his failed love affair with Tulla Larsen, as he also did in the new versions of *The Death of Marat*. These works are characterized by striking coloration and the direct application of paint. The *Verzeichnis des Graphischen Werks Edvard Munchs bis* 1906 [Index of the Graphic Works of Edvard Munch until 1906], written by Gustav Schiefler, was published by Bruno Cassirer. Munch's joint exhibition with Paul Cézanne and

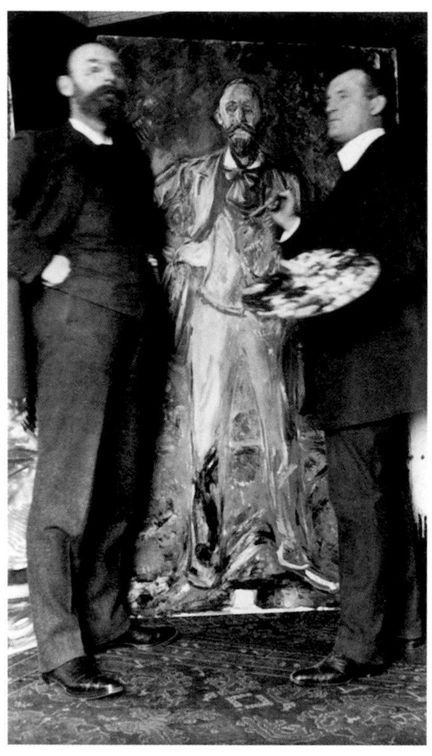

Henri Matisse was the second of his group exhibitions shown at Cassirer's gallery in Berlin that year and received favorable reviews. He met Emil Nolde, who also began to expose his pictures to weathering the following year.

Following a brief stay in Paris in February 1908, Munch returned to Warnemünde in March—before the opening of the *Salon des Artistes Indépendants*, where he offered insights into the most recent developments in his art with *The Death of Marat* and a study for the *Reinhardt Frieze*. His earliest work on the theme of modern working life included a number of such variations as *Bricklayer and Mechanic* (cat. no. 159) and *The Drowned Boy* (cat. no. 160).

Munch's Breakdown and Treatment in Copenhagen, 1908–09

Munch moved to Copenhagen in August 1908, and his mental and physical crisis came to a head about the same time. Following a period marked by alcohol abuse, hallucinations, attacks of paranoia, and early signs of paralysis in his legs, suffering a complete physical collapse Munch admitted himself to the clinic run by Dr. Daniel Jacobson (1863–1939), a Danish neurologist, on 21, Kochsvej in Copenhagen on October 3, 1908. He underwent treatment for seven months and finally left the sanatorium in stable physical and mental condition in early May 1909. In his room, which he converted into a studio, Munch produced several graphic works and paintings, including the portrait of *Daniel Jacobson* (cat. no. 191). In the spring of 1909, he wrote the prose poem entitled *Alpha and Omega*, which he illustrated with eighteen lithographs. During his stay at the clinic, a solo exhibition took place at the Art Association in Copenhagen. The show was also presented at the Ateneum in Helsinki early the following year. His presentation at the *Exhibition of Graphic Art* organized by the Berlin Secession in the winter of 1908–09 was well received and widely acclaimed. In Norway, Munch was made a Knight of the Royal Order of Saint Olav for "his achievements in art."

Long-Awaited Recognition in Munch's Homeland: Kragerø, Hvitsten, Jeløya, 1909 to 1916

After a five-year absence from Kristiania, Munch presented an large-scale retrospective at Blomqvist's gallery in March 1909, featuring some 200 prints and fifty paintings. The show was a com-

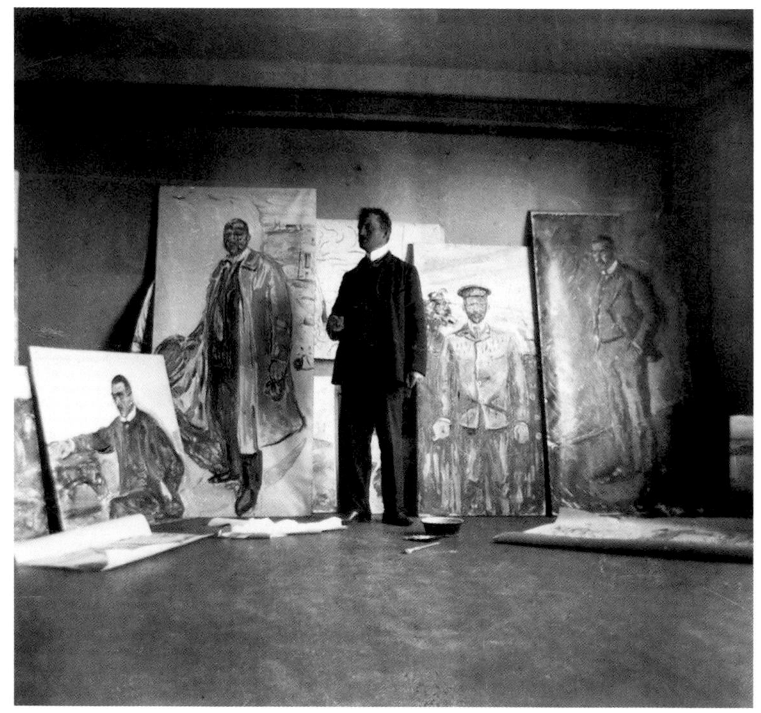

12 Munch and Dr. Jacobson at the clinic on Kochsvej, Copenhagen, 1909

13 Edvard Munch in his studio in Kragerø, 1909–10, photo: Edvard Munch, Munch-museet, Oslo

plete success and catapulted the artist to widespread recognition in his homeland. His friend Jens Thiis (1870–1942), Director of the Nasjonalgalleriet in Kristiania since 1908, purchased five major works by the artist, including *Puberty* (cat. no. 16), with special funds provided by the relevant ministry, paying only 10,000 kroner or about one-third of their market value at the time. The art patron Olaf Schou bequeathed his collection of Norwegian art to the National Gallery. Among these works were seven paintings by Munch, including the first version of *The Sick Child* and *Girls on the Pier* (cat. no. 163).

After being discharged from the sanatorium, Munch rented "Skrubben," a large wooden house in the coastal town of Kragerø, where he hoped to regain his physical and mental health. He set up a large open-air studio there and sought motifs for his art in the nearby garden, woods, and skerries and in his studio. Except for a few old friends—Ludvig Ravensberg, Jappe Nilssen, Thorvald Stang, and Christian Gierløff—he severed all social ties during this period. Solo exhibitions of his paintings and prints in Bremen, Trondheim, and Bergen and his presentations at international exhibitions in Prague, Düsseldorf, Copenhagen, Berlin, Budapest, Rome, and Vienna, where he showed four set designs for Ibsen's *Ghosts* at the *International Kunstschau*, confirmed Munch's position as an established artist. In the summer, he began work on proposals for the competition for decorative artwork at the main auditorium of the University of Kristiania. Hans Jæger died in 1910, and Munch would later devote several variations on *The Death of the Bohemian* to the theme of his death. At the Diorama Center in Kristiania, Munch organized one of the most extensive solo exhibitions of his work shown up until that time, featuring more than eighty-nine paintings and 180 prints. Olaf Schou purchased three more important works from this group, among them the second major version of *The Scream*, which he donated to the Nasjonalgalleriet.

Munch purchased the Nedre Ramme estate in Hvisten on the Kristianiafjord, which offered him more room and better working conditions. He presented a very broad selection from his oeuvre at another exhibition at the Diorama Center, a show featuring more than 300 works in all. In September, he exhibited his draft designs for the decoration of the university auditorium in Kristiania, which received a positive evaluation by the jury but were rejected for the time being. He devoted much of his time during the fall and winter in Kragerø to landscape painting.

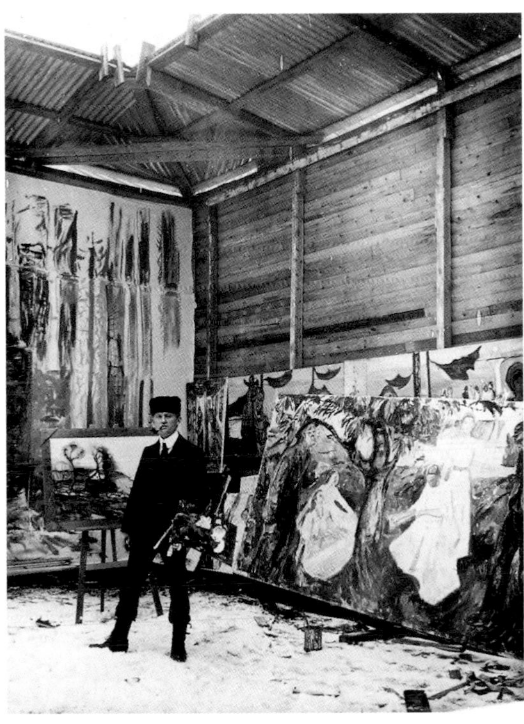

14 Open-air studio in Kragerø, c. 1913

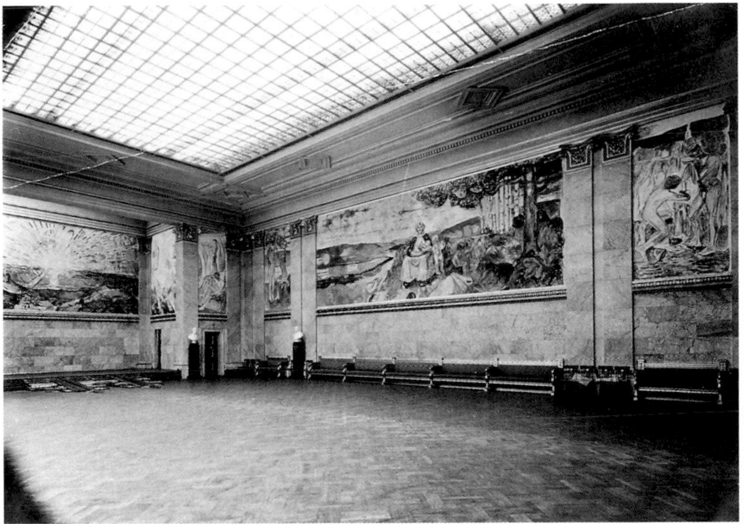

15 Decoration in the main auditorium, University of Kristiania

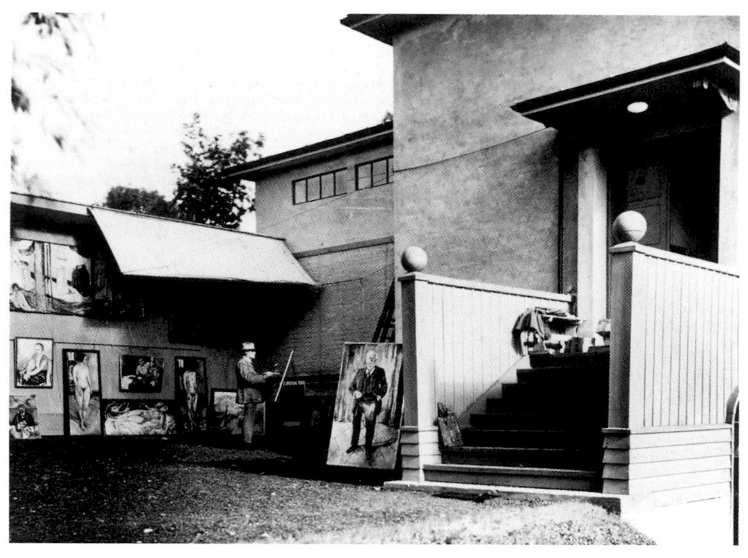

His presentation of eleven paintings, including *Self-Portrait with Bottle of Wine* (cat. no. 201) and *Melancholy (Laura)* (cat. no. 92), thirty-one prints, and the portfolio *Alpha and Omega*, at the exhibition *Norwegian Artists* organized by the Künstlerbund Hagen in Vienna in January 1912 brought him significant acclaim. Munch's currency and the guiding role his expressive art played for the younger generation were honored by the invitation to participate in the *Sonderbund-Ausstellung* in Cologne in May 1912, where he was shown in a special hall of honor as a leading representative of modern art. He met Curt Glaser of the Berliner Königliches Kupferstichkabinett [Berlin Royal Museum of Copper Engraving], who devoted a comprehensive monograph to him in 1917.

Seeking more working and storage space, Munch rented the Grimsrød mansion on the Jeløya Peninsula near Moss for two years in 1913, although he maintained his other residences as well. He presented eight etchings at the *Armory Show* in New York, a touring exhibition that later traveled to Boston and Chicago, and took part in exhibitions in Dresden, Breslau, Hamburg, Stockholm, and Berlin. Moving back and forth between Kragerø, Hvisten, and Jeløya, he devoted most of his time to monumental paintings of working people.

His draft designs for the artwork at the university were accepted on May 29, 1914 (the dedication took place on September 19, 1916). In November 1915, he presented some of his artwork for the main university auditorium at the *Norwegian Exhibition* in Copenhagen. He was awarded a gold medal in recognition of his graphic art at an international exhibition in San Francisco. Munch began at this time to provide financial support for young German painters.

Ekely, 1916 to 1944

In January 1916 Munch purchased the Ekely estate near Skøyen, west of Kristiania, where he would spend most of his time for the remainder of his life. He took part in the *Norwegian Exhibition* in Stockholm and presented solo exhibitions in Göteborg and Copenhagen in 1917. In 1918, Munch exhibited his *Frieze of Life* at Blomqvist's gallery and began working on new monumental versions of the same theme. Munch contracted the Spanish influenza in 1919. He turned his attention to the subject of artist and model and focused increasingly on the nude and the medium of watercolor. He recalled a number of earlier works in a series devoted to the theme of *Starry Night* (cat. no. 151).

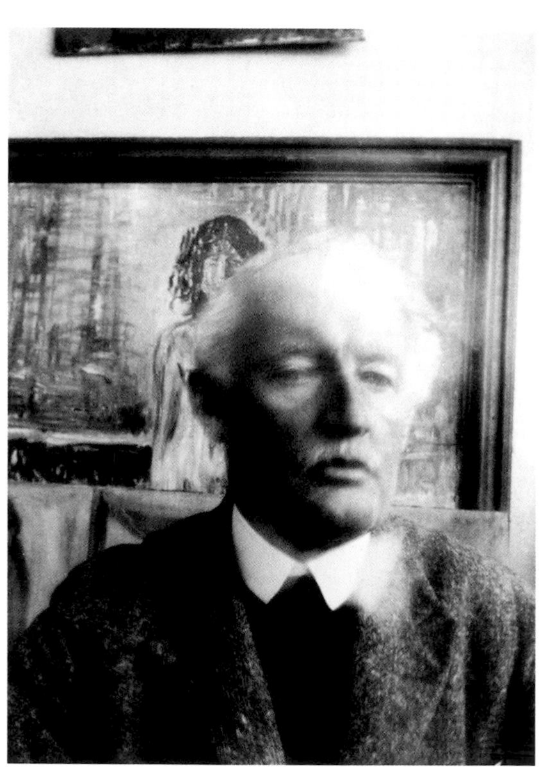

16 Edvard Munch outside his winter studio at Ekely, 1933, photo: Ragnvald Væring

17 Edvard Munch standing in front of *The Death of Marat* III, Ekely, 1930, photo: Edvard Munch, Munch-museet, Oslo

In May 1922, Munch presented his first major solo exhibition in Switzerland at the Kunsthaus Zürich, a show comprising 389 works of graphic art and seventy-three paintings which subsequently moved on to venues in Bern and Basel. He sought to provide support for German artists through the sale of more than seventy prints. During the summer, Munch painted twelve wall panels in frieze form for the workers' cafeteria at a chocolate factory in Kristiania. In May 1923, he traveled to Göteborg, where an entire room had been set aside for him as guest of honor at an exhibition devoted to the painter Willumsen. He was named a member of the German Academy and spent time in Berlin during an exhibition at the Academy building there. In 1924, he donated a number of prints for the benefit of German artists. He was named an honorary member of the Bayerische Akademie der Bildenden Künste [Bavarian Academy of Fine Arts] the following year, during which he also took part in an international exhibition at the Kunsthaus Zürich.

Munch's sister Laura, who had been suffering from depression for many years, died in 1926. After finishing numerous studies, he completed the painting entitled *Menschenberg*, which was rejected by the jury appointed to select the decoration for the university. A tireless traveler, he journeyed again the following year to Germany, Rome, Florence, and Paris. Major retrospectives were presented at the Nationalgalerie in Berlin and the Nasjonalgalleriet in Oslo in honor of the artist and his work. By this time, Munch had also gained recognition in his homeland as one of the most important representatives of modern art. Gustav Schiefler published the second part of his index of Munch's graphic works.

In 1928, Munch presented work at exhibitions in San Francisco and at the Royal Academy in London and worked on designs for wall decorations in the hall of the planned new city hall in Oslo, which were to be devoted primarily to the history of the city, the construction of the city hall, and images of working people. The commission, however, was never carried out. The next year witnessed the construction of Munch's winter studio and a comprehensive exhibition of his graphic art in Stockholm. In 1930, a ruptured blood vessel in Munch's right eye almost caused temporary

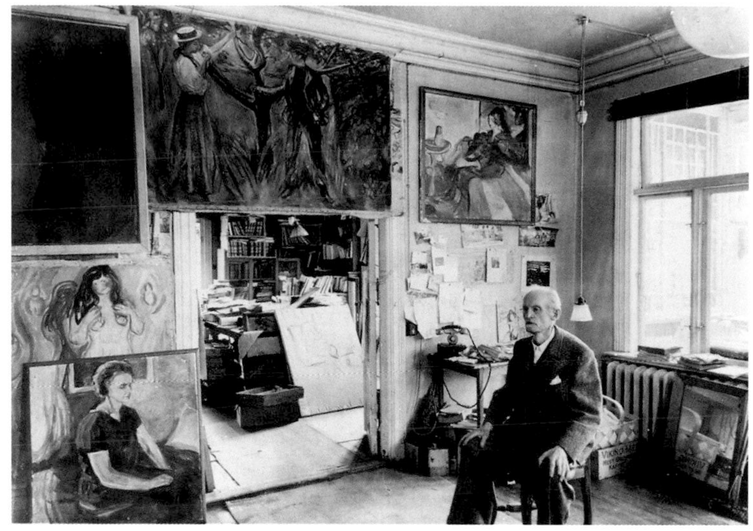

blindness. With painstaking scientific precision, Munch chronicled the progress of his illness. During this time he did a number of photographic self-portraits, all of them in close-up. In the following year, the death of his aunt Karen Bjølstad and his persistent eye disorder prompted him to focus his attention once again on the themes of age and death. He did variations on old themes and complemented them with images of the "ghost of death." Numerous exhibitions of his works were presented in Germany. In 1932, Munch was exhibited along with Paul Gauguin at the Kunsthaus Zürich and awarded the silver Goethe Medal by the German President Paul Hindenburg. Munch received many honors on the occasion of his seventieth birthday and was named Knight of the Grand Cross of the Order of Saint Olav. Pola Gauguin published the first monograph devoted to Munch in the Norwegian language.

During the mid-1930s, Munch completed several additional variations on the *Frieze of Life* themes using extremely luminous colors. In 1934, he was awarded the medal of the Legion of Merit. During these years, he lived in relative isolation—"quite like a hermit," as he expressed it himself—but continued to enjoy the support of a small circle of friends, including Christian Gierløff, Ludvig Ravensberg, the anatomist Prof. Kristian Schreiner, and the banker and writer Rolf Stenersen. Munch presented his first solo exhibition in

18 Edvard Munch in his studio at age eighty, Ekely, 1943, photo: Ragnvald Væring

London in 1936. His eye disorder forced him to discontinue work on his designs for the city hall in Oslo. He was represented at the 1937 World's Fair in Paris and at other major exhibitions in Stockholm, Amsterdam, and Bergen. That same year, eighty-two of Munch's works, most of which had been completed after the First World War, were declared "degenerate art" and confiscated from German museums and private collections. Munch provided the young German painter Ernst Wilhelm Nay with funds enabling him to spend a period of time in Norway. Munch rejected the plan proposed by Jens Thiis to establish a Munch museum in Tullinløkka in Oslo. He was plagued again the following year by his persistent eye disorder. In 1939, he rejected an invitation to participate in a major exhibition in Paris. Fourteen of his paintings and thirty-one works of graphic art were auctioned at the Galerie Harold Holst Halvorsen in Oslo, all works that had been confiscated by the National Socialists from German museums.

Munch started working on his last self-portraits (cat. nos. 203–205) in 1940. The paintings bear the imprint of his intense concern with the theme of death: "I do not want to die suddenly. I want to have this last experience as well." Munch lived in isolation in Ekely and refused all contact with the Germans, who had occupied his country in 1940, and with their Norwegian collaborators. He began growing potatoes, vegetables, and fruit on a large scale in Ekely and Hvisten. Munch's first major exhibition in the U. S. A., a presentation of his graphic art at the Brooklyn Museum in New York, opened in 1942. Numerous celebrations marked the occasion of his eightieth birthday on December 12, 1943. Munch himself printed a version of *Kiss in the Fields* (cat. no. 56) shortly afterwards. During the next few cold December days, he contracted pneumonia.

Edvard Munch died peacefully at his home in Ekely on January 23, 1944. He bequeathed his entire estate to the city of Oslo—some 1,100 paintings, 18,000 prints, 3,000 drawings and watercolors, ninety-two sketchbooks, six sculptures, 143 lithograph stones, 155 copper plates, 133 woodcut blocks, and many photographs as well as numerous as yet unpublished manuscripts, letters, newspaper clippings and his entire library. At her death in 1952, his sister Inger bequeathed fifteen additional paintings and her complete collection of correspondence with her brother to the city of Oslo. The Oslo City Parliament resolved in 1946 to build a museum for the purpose of preserving these treasures of art. The Munch-museet was officially opened in Oslo's Tøyen district on May 29, 1963, 100 years after the artist's birth.

Works in the Exhibition

The year entries in parenthese are date attribution proposed by authors of this publication.

Cat. no. 1
The Voice (Summer Night), 1893/after 1907
Oil on canvas, 90 x 119.5 cm
Munch-museet, Oslo, MM M 44

Cat. no. 2
The Voice (Summer Night), 1894
Etching and drypoint with open bite on copperplate in black on vellum, washed over and hand-colored with watercolor, 23.7 x 31.4 cm
Sch. 19, Woll 12 I
Munch-museet, Oslo, MM G 18-5

Cat. no. 3
The Voice (Summer Night), 1893
Oil on canvas, 87.9 x 108 cm
Signed lower left: E. Munch 1893
Museum of Fine Arts, Boston, Ernest Wadsworth Longfellow Fund, 59.301

Cat. no. 4
The Voice (Summer Night), 1896
Woodcut with gouges and fretsaw in black on vellum, hand-colored with watercolor and gouache, 37.8 x 56.9 cm
Sch. 83, Woll 92 II
Munch-museet, Oslo, MM G 572-3

Cat. no. 5
The Voice (Summer Night), 1896
Color woodcut with gouges and fretsaw in black, violet, brown on mould paper (Van Gelder), hand-colored with watercolor, 37.6 x 57.7 cm
Sch. 83, Woll 92 III
Munch-museet, Oslo, MM G 572-2

Cat. no. 6
The Voice (Eyes), 1893–96
Pencil and crayon on vellum, 41.5 x 50 cm
Inscribed lower center: Dine øine ere store som den halve himmel/når du står nær meg og håret dit har guldstøv/og munnen ser jeg ikke – ser blot smiler
Munch-museet, Oslo, MM T 329

Cat. no. 7
The Voice (Summer Night), 1893
Charcoal and watercolor on vellum, spray technique, 50 x 64.7 cm
Munch-museet, Oslo, MM T 2373

Cat. no. 8
Moonlight, 1893
Oil on canvas, 140.5 x 137 cm
Signed lower right: E. Munch
Nasjonalgalleriet, Oslo, NG.M.01914

Cat. no. 9
House in Moonlight, 1895
Oil on canvas, 81 x 100.5 cm
Rasmus Meyers Samlinger, Bergen Kunstmuseum, RMS.M.250

Cat. no. 10
The Storm, 1893
Oil on canvas, 91.8 x 130.8 cm
Signed lower right: E. Munch 1893
The Museum of Modern Art, New York, Gift of Mr. and Mrs. H. Irgens Larsen and acquired through the Lillie P. Bliss and Abby Aldrich Rockefeller Funds, 1974

Cat. no. 11
Moonlight I, 1896
Color woodcut with gouges in black and blue on China paper, 41.5 x 47.1 cm
Signed lower right with red color pen, then pencil: E Munch E Munch
Sch. 81, Woll 90 I
Munch-museet, Oslo, MM G 570-21

Cat. no. 12
Moonlight I, 1896
Woodcut with gouges in black on vellum, 39 x 46.8 cm
Sch. 81, Woll 90
Munch-museet, Oslo, MM G 570-1

Cat. no. 13
Moonlight I, 1896
Color woodcut with gouges and fretsaw with oilcolors on heavy cream wove, 41.2 x 47 cm
Sch. 81, Woll 90 II
Munch-museet, Oslo, MM G 570-15

Cat. no. 14
Moonlight I, 1896
Color woodcut with gouges and fretsaw with various colors on vellum, mounted on cardboard, 41.7 x 47 cm
Inscribed lower right on the cardboard: E Munch, Mondschein mit Hand gedruckt
Sch. 81, Woll 90 II
Munch-museet, Oslo, MM G 570-13

Cat. no. 15
Moonlight I, 1896
Color woodcut with gouges and fretsaw in black-blue, grass-green, blue-green, ochre, gray on paper, 41 x 46.7 cm, sheet: 47 x 54.7 cm
Signed lower right: E. Munch
Sch. 81, Woll 90 III
Albertina, Vienna, DG1961/422

Cat. no. 16
Puberty, 1894–95 (1894)
Oil on canvas, 151.5 x 110 cm
Signed lower right: E. Munch
Nasjonalgalleriet, Oslo, NG.M.00807

Cat. no. 17
The Brooch (Eva Mudocci), 1903
Lithograph with lithographic crayon, tusche, scraper in black on paper, 60 x 46 cm, sheet: 68.8 x 57 cm
Signed lower right: Edv Munch
Sch. 212, Woll 244 V
Albertina, Vienna, DG1924/443

Cat. no. 18
Woman with Red Hair and Green Eyes (The Sin), 1902
Color lithograph with lithographic crayon, tusche and scraper in dark yellow, dark orange and grass-green on paper, 69.7 x 40.2 cm, sheet: 81 x 57.8 cm
Signed lower right: Edv Munch
Sch. 142, Woll 198 II
Albertina, Vienna, DG1912/281

Cat. no. 19
Madonna, 1893–94
Oil on canvas, spray technique, 90 x 68.5 cm
Signed upper left: E. Munch
Munch-museet, Oslo, MM M 68

Cat. no. 20
Female Nude, 1893–94
Pencil and charcoal on cardboard, 73.8 x 59.8 cm
Munch-museet, Oslo, MM T 2430

Cat. no. 21
Madonna, 1894–95
Oil on canvas, 97 x 75 cm
Collection of Catherine Woodard & Nelson Blitz, Jr.

Cat. no. 22
Madonna, 1895/1902
Color lithograph with lithographic crayon, tusche and scraper in black, olive, blue, red on paper, 55.6 x 34.1 cm, sheet: 65 x 44.5 cm
Sch. 33, Woll 39 VII
Albertina, Vienna, DG1912/275

Cat. no. 23
Madonna, 1895/1902
Color lithograph with lithographic crayon, tusche and scraper in black, olive, blue and rusty brown on paper, 60.5 x 44.2 cm, sheet: 86.5 x 59.5 cm
Signed lower right: Edv Munch
Sch. 33, Woll 39 I
Albertina, Vienna, DG1946/47

Cat. no. 24
The Hands, 1895
Lithograph with lithographic crayon and tusche in black on paper, hand-colored with watercolor, 48.4 x 29.1 cm
Sch. 35, Woll 42
Epstein Family Collection

Cat. no. 25
The Hands, 1893–94
Charcoal, crayon and gouache on vellum, 67.2 x 45.2 cm
Munch-museet, Oslo, MM T 2442

Cat. no. 26
The Hands, 1893
Oil and color crayon on cardboard, 91 x 77 cm
Munch-museet, Oslo, MM M 646

Cat. no. 27
The Woman (Sphinx), 1893–94
Oil on canvas, 72 x 100 cm
Munch-museet, Oslo, MM M 57

Cat. no. 28
The Woman (Salome Paraphrase), 1895
Pencil on vellum, 30.5 x 46 cm
Munch-museet, Oslo, MM T 2762

Cat. no. 29
Beach near Åsgårdstrand, 1895–96
Oil on canvas, 57.5 x 83.5 cm
Signed lower right: E. Munch
Collection of Catherine Woodard & Nelson Blitz, Jr.

Cat. no. 30
Red and White, 1894 (1899)
Oil on canvas, 93.5 x 129.5 cm
Munch-museet, Oslo, MM M 460

Cat. no. 31
The Woman (Sphinx), 1899
Lithograph with lithographic crayon, tusche and scraper in black on paper, 46 x 59.6 cm, sheet: 50 x 65 cm
Signed lower right: E. Munch
Sch. 122, Woll 147 II
Albertina, Vienna, DG1921/188

Cat. no. 32
The Woman II, 1895
Aquatint and drypoint on copperplate in black on vellum, hand-colored with watercolor and gouache, 28.7 x 33.5 cm
Signed lower right: E Munch 95
Sch. 21B III, Woll 22 V
Munch-museet, Oslo, MM G 20-1

Cat. no. 33
Eye in Eye, 1894 (1896–98)/after 1907
Oil on canvas, 136 x 110 cm
Signed lower right: E. Munch
Munch-museet, Oslo, MM M 502

Cat. no. 34
Attraction I, 1896
Lithograph with lithographic crayon, tusche and scraper in black on paper, 59.3 x 43.2 cm
Signed lower right: Edv Munch
Sch. 65, Woll 75
Albertina, Vienna, DG1924/433

Cat. no. 35
Attraction I, 1895
Etching and drypoint with open bite and drypoint and burnisher on copperplate in black on vellum, hand-colored, 32 x 23.9 cm
Sch. 17, Woll 19 II
Munch-museet, Oslo, MM G 16-2

Cat. no. 36
Attraction II, 1895
Drypoint and etching on copperplate in blue-gray, brown and yellow, 26.7 x 33.1 cm
Signed lower right: E Munch
Sch. 18, Woll 20 I
The Museum of Modern Art, New York. Given anonymously, 1942, 5.341.942

Cat. no. 37
Attraction II *(Two Heads)*, 1896
Lithograph with lithographic crayon in brown, yellow, blue on vellum, 41 x 63.5 cm
Signed lower left: Edv. Munch
Sch. 66, Woll 76 II
Munch-museet, Oslo, MM G 208-4

Cat. no. 38
Starry Night, 1895–97
Oil on canvas, 108.5 x 120.5 cm
Von der Heydt-Museum Wuppertal, G 1179

Cat. no. 39
Separation II, 1896
Lithograph with lithographic crayon on transfer paper in blue on paper, 41 x 64 cm, sheet: 49 x 66 cm
Signed lower right on the stone: E. Munch, signed lower right: E. Munch
Sch. 68, Woll 78 I
Albertina, Vienna, DG1914/252

Cat. no. 40
Separation, 1896
Oil on canvas, 96.5 x 127 cm
Munch-museet, Oslo, MM M 24

Cat. no. 41
Rouge & Noir, 1898
Color woodcut with gouges, fretsaw and chisel in black and red on heavy cream wove, 25.2 x 19 cm
Sch. 115, Woll 131 I
Munch-museet, Oslo, MM G 587-5

Cat. no. 42
Adieu (Scene in the Studio), 1889
Pencil on vellum, 27 x 20.5 cm
Inscribed lower center: Adjö
Munch-museet, Oslo, MM T 2356

Cat. no. 43
The Kiss, 1892
Oil on canvas, 73 x 92 cm
Signed lower left: E. Munch 1892
Nasjonalgalleriet, Oslo, NG.M.02812

Cat. no. 44
Death and the Maiden, 1893
Oil on canvas, 128.5 x 86 cm
Munch-museet, Oslo, MM M 49

Cat. no. 45
The Kiss, 1895
Etching and drypoint on copperplate in brown on paper, 32.7 x 26.3 cm, sheet: 58.5 x 43.7 cm
Signed lower left: Edv Munch, signed lower right: Edv. Munch
Sch. 22, Woll 23
Albertina, Vienna, DG1912/283

Cat. no. 46
The Kiss, 1897
Oil on canvas, 99 x 81 cm
Signed lower right: E. Munch 97 [?]
Munch-museet, Oslo, MM M 59

Cat. no. 47
Lovers in the Park (*Linde Frieze*), 1904
Oil on canvas, 91 x 170.5 cm
Munch-museet, Oslo, MM M 695

Cat. no. 48
Kiss on the Beach, c. 1914
Oil on canvas, 77 x 100 cm
Signed upper right: E. Munch, date illegible
Munch-museet, Oslo, MM M 41

Cat. no. 49
The Kiss I, 1897
Woodcut with gouges in black on vellum, 45.7 x 38 cm
Sch. 102B, Woll 114 I
Munch-museet, Oslo, MM G 578-3

Cat. no. 50
The Kiss II, 1897
Color woodcut with gouges in black and blue on cardboard, 58.8 x 46.1 cm
Signed lower right: Edv Munch
Sch. 102A, Woll 115 II
Munch-museet, Oslo, MM G 577-5

Cat. no. 51
The Kiss III, 1898
Color woodcut with gouges and fretsaw in black, gray on China paper, laminated on paper, 40 x 45.6 cm
Sch. 102C, Woll 124 I
Munch-museet, Oslo, MM G 579-10

Cat. no. 52
The Kiss III, 1898
Color woodcut with gouges and fretsaw in black, gray on China paper, laminated on paper, 40.6 x 46.3 cm
Sch. 102C, Woll 124 I
Epstein Family Collection

Cat. no. 53
The Kiss IV, 1902
Color woodcut with gouges and fretsaw in black and gray on gray paper, 46.7 x 46.7 cm, sheet: 50.2 x 51.3 cm
Signed lower right: Edv. Munch
Sch. 102D, Woll 204 IV
Albertina, Vienna, DG1912/282

Cat. no. 54
The Kiss IV, 1902
Color woodcut with gouges and fretsaw in light blue, dark blue and brown on vellum, 40.7 x 26 cm
Sch. 102D, Woll 204 IV I
Munch-museet, Oslo, MM G 580-3

Cat. no. 55
Kiss in the Field, 1905
Woodcut with gouges in black on vellum, 21 x 26.1 cm
Sch. 232, Woll 270
Munch-museet, Oslo, MM G 614-1

Cat. no. 56
Kiss in the Field, 1943
Woodcut with gouges in brown on vellum, 40.4 x 49 cm
Woll 746
Munch-museet, Oslo, MM G 707-1

Cat. no. 57
Towards the Forest I, 1897
Woodcut with gouges and fretsaw in black on vellum mounted on cardboard, hand-colored with Gouache and watercolor, 49.4 x 64.7 cm
Signed lower right: E Munch 97, signed lower right on cardboard: E Munch, verso: Unverkauflich
Sch. 100, Woll 112 I
Munch-museet, Oslo, MM G 575-5

Cat. no. 58
Towards the Forest I, 1897
Color woodcut with gouges and fretsaw in grayish violet, green, yellow on Japan paper, 50 x 64.5 cm
Sch. 100, Woll 112 II
Munch-museet, Oslo, MM G 575-29

Cat. no. 59
Towards the Forest I, 1897
Color woodcut with gouges and fretsaw in black, violet, light green, dark green and red on vellum, 51.7 x 65 cm
Sch. 100, Woll 112 II
Munch-museet, Oslo, MM G 575-14

Cat. no. 60
Towards the Forest I, 1897
Color woodcut with gouges and fretsaw in blue, pink, green, yellow, orange on Japan paper, 49.7 x 64.5 cm
Sch. 100, Woll 112 II
Munch-museet, Oslo, MM G 575-8

Cat. no. 61
Towards the Forest II, 1915
Color woodcut with gouges and fretsaw in black, green, ochre on vellum, 50 x 64.5 cm
Sch. 444, Woll 644 II
Munch-museet, Oslo, MM G 575-9

Cat. no. 62
Young Man and Prostitute, 1893–96
Charcoal and tusche on paper, 17.7 x 11.4 cm
Signed upper left: E Munch
Munch-museet, Oslo, MM T 380

Cat. no. 63
The Bite, 1913
Etching on copperplate in black on vellum, 19.7 x 27.6 cm
Sch. 396, Woll 472
Munch-museet, Oslo, MM G 142-2

Cat. no. 64
Vampire, 1895
Charcoal and tusche on vellum, 17.8 x 11.4 cm
Signed upper left: E Munch 95
Munch-museet, Oslo, MM T 379

Cat. no. 65
Vampire, 1893
Oil on canvas, 80.5 x 100.5 cm
Signed lower right: E. Munch 1893
Göteborgs konstmuseum, Göteborg, GKM 640

Cat. no. 66
Vampire, 1893–94
Oil on canvas, 91 x 109 cm
Munch-museet, Oslo, MM M 679

Cat. no. 67
Vampire I, 1895
Lithograph with lithographic crayon in black on vellum, 38.2 x 54.5 cm
Signed lower right: Edv Munch
Sch. 34A, Woll 40
Munch-museet, Oslo, MM G 567-27

Cat. no. 68
Vampire II, 1895
Lithograph with lithographic crayon, tusche and scraper in black and woodcut with fretsaw in red on China paper, 38.7 x 55.5 cm
Sch. 34, Woll 41 VII
Munch-museet, Oslo, MM G 567-31

Cat. no. 69
Vampire II, 1895/1902
Lithograph with lithographic crayon, tusche and scraper and woodcut with fretsaw in blue, green, ochre, brown-red and gray on vellum, 38.7 x 55.2 cm
Sch. 34, Woll 41
Munch-museet, Oslo, MM G 567-81

Cat. no. 70
Vampire II, 1895/1902
Lithograph with lithographic crayon, tusche and scraper and woodcut with fretsaw in black, ochre, dark green, dark blue and red on light cream wove, 38.6 x 55.1 cm
Sch. 34, Woll 41
Munch-museet, Oslo, MM G 567-74

Cat. no. 71
Jealousy II, 1896
Lithograph with lithographic crayon, tusche and scraper in black on vellum, hand-colored with watercolor and gouache, 45.4 x 51.3 cm
Sch. 58, Woll 69
Munch-museet, Oslo, MM G 202-11

Cat. no. 72
Jealousy II, 1896
Lithograph with lithographic crayon, tusche and scraper in black on Japan paper, 46.3 x 56.5 cm, sheet: 65.5 x 95 cm
Signed lower left: Edv. Munch
Sch. 58, Woll 69
Albertina, Vienna, DG1912/274

Cat. no. 73
Jealousy I, 1896
Lithograph with lithographic crayon, tusche and scraper in black on Japan paper, 33 x 45 cm
Sch. 57, Woll 68
Munch-museet, Oslo, MM G 201-17

Cat. no. 74
Jealousy I, 1896
Lithograph with lithographic crayon, tusche and scraper in black on vellum, hand-colored with watercolor, 33 x 46 cm
Sch. 57, Woll 68
Munch-museet, Oslo, MM G 201-2

Cat. no. 75
Jealousy III, 1930
Lithograph with lithographic crayon on transfer paper in black on vellum, hand-colored with watercolor, 26.5 x 41.8 cm
Woll 709
Munch-museet, Oslo, MM G 542-2

Cat. no. 76
Jealousy IV, 1930
Lithograph with lithographic crayon on transfer paper in black on vellum, 23.3 x 25.5 cm
Sch. 503, Woll 710
Munch-museet, Oslo, MM G 543-7

Cat. no. 77
Jealousy I, 1907
Oil on canvas, 89 x 82.5 cm
Munch-museet, Oslo, MM M 573

Cat. no. 78
Surprise, 1907
Oil on canvas, 85 x 110.5 cm
Initialed lower left: E.M.
Munch-museet, Oslo, MM M 537

Cat. no. 79
Jealousy III, 1907
Oil on canvas, 75.5 x 98 cm
Munch-museet, Oslo, MM M 447

Cat. no. 80
Evening, 1888
Oil on canvas, 75 x 100 cm
Signed lower right: Edvard Munch 1888
Museo Thyssen-Bornemisza, Madrid

Cat. no. 81
Night in St. Cloud, 1890
Oil on canvas, 64.5 x 54 cm
Signed lower right: E Munch
Nasjonalgalleriet, Oslo, NG.M.01111

Cat. no. 82
Night in St. Cloud (Moonlight), 1895
Drypoint and etching on copperplate in brown on paper, 31 x 25.5 cm, sheet: 59 x 43.9 cm
Signed lower right: Edv Munch
Sch. 13, Woll 17 III
Albertina, Vienna, DG1911/450

Cat. no. 83
The Girl at the Window, 1894
Drypoint with roulette and burnisher on copperplate in brownish black on vellum, 20.7 x 14.5 cm
Inscribed lower left: O. Felsinger Berlin gdr
Sch. 5 V, Woll 5 VI
Munch-museet, Oslo, MM G 5-20

Cat. no. 84
The Girl at the Window, 1892
Oil on canvas, 96.5 x 65.4 cm
The Art Institute of Chicago, Searle Family Trust and Goldabelle McComb Finn endowments Charles H. and Mary F.S. Worcester Collection, 2000.50

Cat. no. 85
Melancholy, 1892
Oil on canvas, 64 x 96 cm
Initialed lower left: E.M.
Nasjonalgalleriet, Oslo, NG.M.02813

Cat. no. 86
Melancholy, 1894–95
Oil on canvas, 70 x 95.8 cm
Rasmus Meyers Samlinger, Bergen Kunstmuseum, RMS.M.245

Cat. no. 87
Melancholy I, 1896
Color woodcut with gouges, chisel and fretsaw in black, gray with brown tone plate, 36.8 x 44.5 cm
Sch. 82, Woll 91
Private collection Canada, Courtesy W. Wittrock, Berlin

Cat. no. 88
Melancholy I, 1896
Color woodcut with gouges, chisel and fretsaw in green, blue, yellow-green and orange on paper, 37.6 x 45.5 cm, sheet: 45.4 x 57.8 cm
Sch. 82, Woll 91 IV
Museum of Fine Arts, Boston, William Francis Warden Fund, 57.356

Cat. no. 89
Melancholy III, 1902
Color woodcut with gouges and fretsaw in black, orange, green and blue on paper, 37.6 x 47.1 cm
r.u: Edv. Munch
Sch. 144, Woll 203 III
Epstein Family Collection

Cat. no. 90
Melancholy II, 1898
Color woodcut with gouges and fretsaw in black, green and red on paper, 33 x 42.2 cm
Signed lower right in print area: Edv Munch
Sch. 116, Woll 132
Epstein Family Collection

Cat. no. 91
Female Nude on the Beach, c. 1898
Oil on Wood, 39.5 x 59.5 cm
Private collection

Cat. no. 92
Melancholy (Laura), 1899 (1900)
Oil on canvas, 110 x 126 cm
Signed lower right: E Munch 189..
Munch-museet, Oslo, MM M 12

not illustrated
Two Women on the Shore, 1898
Color woodcut with gouges, fretsaw and chisel in black, green, dark gray-blue, brown on Japan paper, reworked with crayon, 54.5 x 51.6 cm
Sch. 117, Woll 133 II
Munch-museet, Oslo, MM G 589-9

Cat. no. 93
Young Woman on the Beach, 1896
Burnished aquatint and drypoint on zinc plate in blue, brown, yellow, orange on paper, reworked with pencil, 28.2 x 21.3 cm
Inscribed lower right. E Munch 97 No 5
Sch. 42, Woll 49 VII
Epstein Family Collection

Cat. no. 94
Young Woman on the Beach, 1896
Burnished aquatint and drypoint on zinc plate in blue, black, yellow, ochre on paper, ca. 28.8 x 21.9 cm
Signed lower right: E Munch, inscribed lower right: 3te Druck
Sch. 42, Woll 49 V
Collection of Catherine Woodard & Nelson Blitz, Jr.

Cat. no. 95
Young Woman on the Beach, 1896
Burnished aquatint and drypoint on zinc plate in blue, yellow, light pink on handmade paper (Arches), 28.8 x 21.9 cm
Signed lower right: Edv Munch
Sch. 42, Woll 49 II
Collcetion E.W.K., Bern

Cat. no. 96
Young Woman on the Beach, 1896
Burnished aquatint and drypoint on zinc plate in blue, black, yellow, ochre on handmade paper (Arches), 28.5 x 21.6 cm
Signed lower right: Edvard Munch, inscribed lower right: 2te Druck
Sch. 42, Woll 49 IV
Munch-museet, Oslo, MM G 816-1

Cat. no. 97
Young Woman on the Beach, 1896
Burnished aquatint and drypoint on zinc plate in grayish violet, yellow on handmade paper, 28.7 x 21.6 cm, sheet: 44 x 31 cm
Signed lower right: Edv. Munch
Sch. 42, Woll 49 I
The Art Institute of Chicago, Clarence Buckingham Collection, 1.969.252

Cat. no. 98
The Lonely Ones (Two Human Beings), 1899
Color woodcut with gouges and fretsaw in dark blue, light blue, ochre, red on vellum, 39.5 x 55.5 cm
Sch. 133, Woll 157 III
Munch-museet, Oslo, MM G 601-1

Cat. no. 99
The Lonely Ones (Two Human Beings), 1899
Hand-colored color woodcut with gouges and fretsaw in violet, light blue, dark blue, yellow, red on vellum, hand-colored with watercolor, 39.5 x 55 cm
Sch. 133, Woll 157 III
Munch-museet, Oslo, MM G 601-9

Cat. no. 100
The Lonely Ones (Two Human Beings), 1899
Color woodcut with gouges and fretsaw in black, light blue on vellum, 39.4 x 55.7 cm
Signed lower right: Edv. Munch
Sch. 133, Woll 157 III
Munch-museet, Oslo, MM G 601-46

Cat. no. 101
The Lonely Ones (Two Human Beings), 1899
Color woodcut with gouges and fretsaw in black, violet, yellow, red on Japan paper, 39.5 x 55.8 cm
Sch. 133, Woll 157 II
Munch-museet, Oslo, MM G 601-42

Cat. no. 102
The Lonely Ones (Two Human Beings), 1899
Color woodcut with gouges, fretsaw, in violet, green-blue, yellow, red and blue on paper, 39.5 x 55 cm
Sch. 133, Woll 157 III
Munch-museet, Oslo, MM G 601-12

Cat. no. 103
The Lonely Ones (Two Human Beings), 1899
Color woodcut with gouges and fretsaw and paper stencils in black, green, green-blue, red, light ocher, pink on vellum, 39.4 x 55.2 cm
Signed lower right: Edv Munch
Sch. 133, Woll 157 VII
Munch-museet, Oslo, MM G 601-30

Cat. no. 104
Two Women on the Shore, 1898
Color woodcut with gouges, fretsaw and chisel in black, green, orange and blue on paper, 45.4 x 51.2 cm
Sch. 117, Woll 133 II
National Gallery of Art, Washington, Print Purchase Fund (Rosenwald Collection) and Ailsa Mellon Bruce Fund, 1991.31.1

Cat. no. 105
Two Women on the Shore, 1898
Color woodcut with gouges, fretsaw and chisel in black, green, orange and yellow on paper, hand-colored with watercolor, 46.5 x 58.6 cm
Signed lower right: Edv Munch
Sch. 117, Woll 133 II
National Gallery of Art, Washington, Print Purchase Fund (Rosenwald Collection) and Ailsa Mellon Bruce Fund, 1978.15.1

Cat. no. 106
Two Women on the Shore, 1900–10
Color woodcut with gouges, fretsaw and chisel and color linoleum plate in black, gray, yellow, orange on paper, 47.4 x 59 cm
Sch. 117, Woll 133 III
National Gallery of Art, Washington, Print Purchase Fund (Rosenwald Collection) and Ailsa Mellon Bruce Fund, 1978.15.2

Cat. no. 107
Two Women on the Shore, 1910s
Color woodcut with gouges, fretsaw and chisel and color linoleum plate in black, violet, light blue, yellow, orange on paper, 43 x 55.4 cm
Signed lower right: Edv Munch
Sch. 117, Woll 133 III
National Gallery of Art, Washington, Print Purchase Fund (Rosenwald Collection) and Ailsa Mellon Bruce Fund, 1978.15.3

Cat. no. 108
Two Women on the Shore, 1920s
Color woodcut with gouges, fretsaw and chisel in black, light green, dark green, light blue, light orange, dark orange on paper, 46.2 x 51 cm
Sch. 117, Woll 133 IV
National Gallery of Art, Washington, Print Purchase Fund (Rosenwald Collection) and Ailsa Mellon Bruce Fund, 1978.15.4

Cat. no. 109
Two Women on the Shore, 1920s
Color woodcut with gouges, fretsaw and chisel and paper stencils in black, blue, light green, dark green, light blue, yellow, light orange, dark orange on paper, 54 x 59.6 cm
Sch. 117, Woll 133 IV
National Gallery of Art, Washington, Print Purchase Fund (Rosenwald Collection) and Ailsa Mellon Bruce Fund, 1978.15.5

Cat. no. 110
Two Women on the Shore, 1935
Oil on canvas, 93 x 118 cm
Munch-museet, Oslo, MM M 866

Cat. no. 111
Evening on Karl Johans Gate, 1889
Pencil and black crayon on vellum, 37 x 47 cm
Munch-museet, Oslo, MM T 2390,

Cat. no. 112
Angst, 1896
Woodcut with gouges and chisel in red
on China paper, 45.9 x 37.5 cm
Sch. 62, Woll 93
Munch-museet, Oslo, MM G 568-1,

Cat. no. 113
Evening on Karl Johans Gate, 1896–97
Lithograph with lithographic crayon and tusche in black on gray-white China paper, hand-colored with watercolor, 42.5 x 60.2 cm
Woll 87
Collection of Catherine Woodard & Nelson Blitz, Jr.

Cat. no. 114
Evening on Karl Johans Gate, 1892
Oil on canvas, 84.5 x 121 cm
Signed lower right: E. Munch
Rasmus Meyers Samlinger, Bergen Kunstmuseum, RMS.M.245

Cat. no. 115
Despair, 1893–94
Oil on canvas, 92 x 72.5 cm
Munch-museet, Oslo, MM M 513

Cat. no. 116
Angst, 1894
Oil on canvas, 94 x 74 cm
Munch-museet, Oslo, MM M 515

Cat. no. 117
The Scream, 1895
Lithograph with lithographic crayon and tusche in black on vellum, 35.2 x 25.1 cm
Inscribed lower center printed: Geschrei, printed lower right: Ich fühlte das grosse Geschrei durch die Natur
Sch. 32, Woll 38
Munch-museet, Oslo, MM G 193-2

Cat. no. 118
The Scream, 1893
Oil, tempera and crayon on cardboard, 84 x 67 cm
Munch-museet, Oslo, MM M 514

Cat. no. 119
The Sick Child I, 1894
Drypoint and etching on copperplate in black on paper, 36.5 x 27 cm, sheet: 57 x 38.8 cm
Signed lower right: Edv Munch 95
Sch. 7, Woll 7 VI
Albertina, Vienna, DG1917/514

Cat. no. 120
The Sick Child I, 1894
Drypoint with roulette and burnisher on copperplate in black on vellum, 27.5 x 27 cm
Sch. 7, Woll 7 II
Munch-museet, Oslo, MM G 7-12

Cat. no. 121
The Sick Child, 1896
Etching and drypoint on copperplate in greenish black, yellow, red-brown, green on mould paper (Arches), 12.8 x 16.8 cm
Sch. 60, Woll 59
Munch-museet, Oslo, MM G 43-6

Cat. no. 122
The Sick Child, 1896
Oil on canvas, 121.5 x 118.5 cm
Göteborgs konstmuseum, Göteborg, GKM 975

Cat. no. 123
The Sick Child I, 1896
Color lithograph with lithographic crayon, tusche and scraper in black, light blue, yellow on paper, 47.7 x 62.5 cm
Signed lower right: E Munch
Sch. 59, Woll 72 IX
Albertina, Vienna, DGNF7446

Cat. no. 124
The Sick Child I, 1896
Color lithograph with lithographic crayon, tusche and scraper in red, yellow on paper, hand-colored with oil and watercolor and wax resistant color, 42 x 56 cm
Sch. 59, Woll 72 X
Epstein Family Collection

Cat. no. 125
The Sick Child I, 1896
Color lithograph with lithographic crayon, tusche and scraper in red, yellow on China paper, 42 x 56.7 cm
Signed lower right on the stone: E Munch, signed lower right: E Munch No 30
Sch. 59, Woll 72 X
Munch-museet, Oslo, MM G 203-2

Cat. no. 126
The Sick Child I, 1896
Color lithograph with lithographic crayon, tusche and scraper in red, blue, yellow on vellum, 41.4 x 58.8 cm
Signed lower right on the stone: E Munch 1896
Sch. 59, Woll 72 V
Munch-museet, Oslo, MM G 203-22

Cat. no. 127
The Sick Child I, 1896
Color lithograph with lithographic crayon, tusche and scraper in red shades on paper, hand-colored, 42 x 60 cm
Sch. 59, Woll 72
Collection of Catherine Woodard & Nelson Blitz, Jr.

Cat. no. 128
The Sick Child II, 1896
Lithograph with lithographic crayon and scraper in black on China paper, 41 x 52 cm
Woll 73
Munch-museet, Oslo, MM G 203-13

Cat. no. 129
The Sick Child I, 1896
Color lithograph with lithographic crayon, tusche and scraper in red, blue, yellow on vellum, hand-colored, 43.2 x 57.3 cm
Sch. 59, Woll 72 III
Munch-museet, Oslo, MM G 203-5

Cat. no. 130
The Sick Child I, 1896
Color lithograph with lithographic crayon, tusche and scraper in black, red, blue, yellow on vellum, hand-colored, 41.3 x 57.2 cm
Signed lower right on the stone: E Munch 1896
Sch. 59, Woll 72 V
Munch-museet, Oslo, MM G 203-4

Cat. no. 131
The Sick Child, 1890s
Pencil and pastel crayon on brownish paper, 42.4 x 40.9 cm
Signed lower right: E. Munch
Hamburger Kunsthalle, Kupferstichkabinett, 1999/44

Cat. no. 132
By the Deathbed, 1895
Oil on canvas, 90 x 120.5 cm
Signed lower left: E. Munch
Rasmus Meyers Samlinger, Bergen Kunstmuseum, RMS.M.251

Cat. no. 133
By the Deathbed (Fever), 1893
Pencil on vellum, 23 x 31.7 cm
Munch-museet, Oslo, MM T 2366

Cat. no. 134
By the Deathbed, 1896
Lithograph with lithographic crayon, tusche and scraper in black on paper, 39.5 x 50 cm, sheet: 50 x 63.7 cm
Sch. 72, Woll 64 IV
Albertina, Vienna, DG1914/253

Cat. no. 135
By the Deathbed (Fever), 1893
Pastel and pencil on cardboard, 59 x 78.5 cm
Signed upper left: E. Munch, 1893
Munch-museet, Oslo, MM M 121

Cat. no. 136
Fever, c. 1894
Pencil on vellum, 42.5 x 48.3 cm
Munch-museet, Oslo, MM T 2381R

Cat. no. 137
Fever, 1894
Pencil and gouache on vellum, 31.6 x 34.7 cm
Signed lower right: E Munch
Munch-museet, Oslo, MM T 2470

Cat. no. 138
The Sick Man Rising, 1907–08
Charcoal, pencil and watercolor on vellum, 37 x 49.4 cm
Munch-museet, Oslo, MM T 2467

Cat. no. 139
Death in the Sickroom, 1894–96
Pencil and crayon on vellum, 37 x 48.5 cm
Munch-museet, Oslo, MM T 297R

Cat. no. 140
Death in the Sickroom, 1893
Charcoal on vellum, 35 x 46 cm
Munch-museet, Oslo, MM T 2380

Cat. no. 141
Death in the Sickroom, 1896
Lithograph with lithographic crayon and tusche in black on bluish gray handmade paper (MBM), hand-colored, 30.3 x 55.8 cm
Sch. 73, Woll 65
Munch-museet, Oslo, MM G 215-7

Cat. no. 142
Moonlight on the Shore, 1892
Oil on canvas, 62.5 x 96 cm
Signed lower right: E Munch
Rasmus Meyers Samlinger, Bergen Kunstmuseum, RMS.M.248

Cat. no. 143
Mystical Shore, 1899
Color woodcut with gouges in black and blue on vellum, 37 x 57.2 cm
Sch. 125, Woll 117 III
Munch-museet, Oslo, MM G 593-5

Cat. no. 144
Summer Night on the Shore, 1902
Oil on canvas, 103 x 120 cm
Signed lower left: E Munch
Österreichische Galerie Belvedere Wien, 3772

Cat. no. 145
Garden in Snow I, 1913
Woodcut with gouges in black on vellum, 34.6 x 43 cm
Signed lower right: Edv Munch
Sch. 418, Woll 467
Munch-museet, Oslo, MM G 636-4

Cat. no. 146
Kragerø in Winter, 1914
Woodcut with gouges in black on vellum, 49.8 x 49 cm
Woll 492
Munch-museet, Oslo, MM G 688-1

Cat. no. 147
Houses in Kragerø, 1915
Etching on zinc plate on vellum, monotype with oilcolor, 43.9 x 59.6 cm
Woll 503
Munch-museet, Oslo, MM G 174-4

Cat. no. 148
Winter Landscape, 1915
Oil on canvas, 100 x 150 cm
Signed lower right: E Munch 1915
Stiftung R. und H. Batliner

Cat. no. 149
The Great Snow Landscape, 1898
Color woodcut with gouges and fretsaw in black, gray, light blue, yellow-green on paper, 32.9 x 45.8 cm
Signed lower left: E Munch
Sch. 118, Woll 134 III
Museum of Fine Arts, Boston, Sophie M. Fiedman Fund, 631.367

Cat. no. 150
Starry Night, 1930
Woodcut with gouges in red-brown on vellum, 37 x 40 cm
Woll 717
Munch-museet, Oslo, MM G 677-1

Cat. no. 151
Starry Night II, 1922–24
Oil on canvas, 120.5 x 100 cm
Munch-museet, Oslo, MM M 32

Cat. no. 152
Starry Night, 1901
Oil on canvas, 59 x 73 cm
Signed lower right: E Munch
Museum Folkwang, Essen

Cat. no. 153
In the Garden, after 1909
Woodcut (Woll 467) and drawing, black crayon on paper, 50.7 x 63.4 cm
Munch-museet, Oslo, MM T 2097

Cat. no. 154
The Split of Faust, 1932–42?
Pencil, charcoal, crayon, watercolor and gouache on vellum, 70 x 86 cm
Munch-museet, Oslo, MM T 2125

Cat. no. 155
Red Virginia Creeper, 1898–1900 (1899)
Oil on canvas, 119.5 x 121 cm
Signed upper left: E. Munch
Munch-museet, Oslo, MM M 503

Cat. no. 156
Snow Drift in the Avenue, 1906
Oil on canvas, 80 x 100 cm
Signed lower left: E. Munch
Munch-museet, Oslo, MM M 288

Cat. no. 157
The Murderer, 1910
Oil on canvas, 94 x 154 cm
Signed lower right: E. Munch
Munch-museet, Oslo, MM M 793

Cat. no. 158
The Murderer on the Lane, 1919
Oil on canvas, 110 x 138 cm
Signed lower right: E. Munch 1919
Munch-museet, Oslo, MM M 268

Cat. no. 159
Bricklayer and Mechanic, 1908
Oil on canvas, 90 x 69.5 cm
Signed upper left and lower left: E. Munch
Munch-museet, Oslo, MM M 574

Cat. no. 160
The Drowned Boy, 1908
Oil on canvas, 85.5 x 130.5 cm
Signed lower right: E. Munch
Munch-museet, Oslo, MM M 559

Cat. no. 161
Girls on the Pier, 1903
Etching on copperplate in black on vellum, 18 x 25.5 cm
Sch. 200 III, Woll 232 II
Munch-museet, Oslo, MM G 95-10

Cat. no. 162
Girls on the Pier, 1905
Woodcut with gouges and chisel in black on vellum, 26.8 x 20.4 cm
Sch. 233, Woll 271
Munch-museet, Oslo, MM G 615-1

Cat. no. 163
Girls on the Pier, c. 1901
Oil on canvas, 136 x 125 cm
Initialed lower left: E.M.
Nasjonalgalleriet, Oslo, NG.M.00844

Cat. no. 164
Summer Night in Åsgårdstrand, 1904
Oil on canvas, 99 x 103.5 cm
Signed lower right: E Munch
Musée d'Orsay, Paris, RF 1986-58

Cat. no. 165
Åsgårdstrand, 1902
Oil on canvas, 100 x 95 cm
Signed upper right: E Munch
Private collection

Cat. no. 166
Girls on the Pier, 1918
Woodcut with gouges in blue and lithograph with lithographic crayon transferred on zinc plates in yellow, orange and green on paper, 49.8 x 42.7 cm, sheet: 63 x 52.9 cm
Signed lower right: Edv. Munch
Sch. 488, Woll 628 III
Albertina, Vienna, DG1921/180

Cat. no. 167
Girls on the Pier, 1912–13
Lithograph with lithographic crayon in blue on paper, 37.6 x 52.8 cm
Sch. 380, Woll 416
Munch-museet, Oslo, MM G 360-2

Cat. no. 168
Girls on the Pier, 1912–13
Lithograph with lithographic crayon in black on paper, hand-colored with watercolor, 38 x 53 cm
Signed lower right: Edv Munch
Sch. 380, Woll 416
Epstein Family Collection

Cat. no. 169
Girls on the Pier, 1904–25
Oil on canvas, 143 x 158.5 cm
Signed lower right: E. Munch
Munch-museet, Oslo, MM M 795

Cat. no. 170
Seated Nude, 1896
Charcoal, pencil, pastel and watercolor on Mould paper (CF), 62 x 47.7 cm
Munch-museet, Oslo, MM T 2459

Cat. no. 171
Parisian Model, 1896
Oil on canvas, 80 x 60 cm
Initialed lower left: E.M., signed upper left: E. Munch
Nasjonalgalleriet, Oslo, NG.M.02816

Cat. no. 172
Nude Study, c. 1900 (c. 1898)
Oil on canvas, 93 x 76 cm
Signed lower left: E Munch
Rasmus Meyers Samlinger, Bergen Kunstmuseum, RMS.M.256

Cat. no. 173
The Beast, 1901
Oil on canvas, 94.5 x 63.5 cm
Signed lower right: E Munch
Sprengel Museum Hannover, KA 18/1965

Cat. no. 174
Weeping Young Woman by the Bed, 1930
Lithograph with lithographic crayon in black on paper, hand-colored with watercolor, 38.3 x 36.5 cm
Signed lower right: Edv Munch
Woll 713
Epstein Family Collection

Cat. no. 175
Weeping Nude, 1907
Oil on canvas, 121 x 119 cm
Munch-museet, Oslo, MM M 689

Cat. no. 176
Weeping Nude, 1913
Oil on canvas, 110.5 x 135 cm
Munch-museet, Oslo, MM M 540

Cat. no. 177
In the Dressing Gown, 1919–21
Charcoal, watercolor and gouache on heavy cream wove, 98.1 x 60.8 cm
Munch-museet, Oslo, MM T 813

Cat. no. 178
Nude Undressing, c. 1920
Crayon and watercolor on vellum, 35.3 x 25.7 cm
Munch-museet, Oslo, MM T 2464

Cat. no. 179
Reclining Nude on Patterned Carpet, 1919–21
Watercolor on handmade paper, 35.4 x 50.9 cm
Munch-museet, Oslo, MM T 1077

Cat. no. 180
Nude Bending forward on Patterned Carpet, 1919–21
Watercolor on handmade paper, 22.4 x 29.2 cm
Munch-museet, Oslo, MM T 1118

Cat. no. 181
Kneeling Nude, 1919–21
Watercolor on vellum, 25.3 x 35.5 cm
Munch-museet, Oslo, MM T 870

Cat. no. 182
Kristiania Bohemians II, 1895
Drypoint with roulette and burnisher on copperplate in black on vellum, 28 x 37.6 cm
Sch. 11, Woll 16 III
Munch-museet, Oslo, MM G 10-5

Cat. no. 183
Paul Herrmann and Paul Contard, 1897
Oil on canvas, 54 x 73 cm
Signed lower left: E. Munch 97
Österreichische Galerie Belvedere Wien, 3838

Cat. no. 184
Olga Buhre, 1890
Oil on canvas, 73.4 x 59.4 cm
Statens Museum for Kunst, Copenhagen, KMS 2096

Cat. no. 185
Dagny Juel Przybyszewska, 1893
Oil on canvas, 148.5 x 99.5 cm
Munch-museet, Oslo, MM M 212

Cat. no. 186
Stanislaw Przybyszewski (with Skeleton Arm), 1893–94
Tempera on canvas, 75 x 60 cm
Munch-museet, Oslo, MM M 618

Cat. no. 187
Stanislaw Przybyszewski, 1895
Charcoal and oil on cardboard, spray technique, 62.5 x 55.5 cm
Signed upper left: E. Munch 95
Munch-museet, Oslo, MM M 134

Cat. no. 188
Stanislaw Przybyszewski, c. 1895
Lithograph with lithographic crayon, tusche and scraper in black on vellum, 54.6 x 44.4 cm, sheet: 59.5 x 48.7 cm
Signed lower right: Edv Munch
Sch. 105, Woll 45 I
Albertina, Vienna, DG1914/255

Cat. no. 189
Stanislaw Przybyszewski, after 1916
Lithograph with lithographic crayon, tusche and scraper in black on vellum, hand-colored with gouache and watercolor, 54.5 x 45.8 cm
Signed lower right: E Munch
Sch. 105, Woll 45 III
Munch-museet, Oslo, MM G 231-9

Cat. no. 190
August Strindberg, 1896
Lithograph with lithographic crayon, tusche and scraper in black on olive colored paper, 61.2 x 46.5 cm, sheet: 64.7 x 49.5 cm
Signed lower right: E. Munch
Sch. 77, Woll 66 II
Albertina, Vienna, DGNF5000

Cat. no. 191
Professor Daniel Jacobson, 1908–09
Oil on canvas, 203 x 111 cm
Inscribed upper left: Edv. Munch København 1909
Munch-museet, Oslo, MM M 359-a

Cat. no. 192
Walter Rathenau, 1907
Oil on canvas, 200 x 110 cm
Inscribed upper right: E. Munch Febr 1907
Stiftung Stadtmuseum Berlin, acquired with the support of the Ernst von Siemens-Kunstfonds, VII 93/53 x

Cat. no. 193
Heinrich Hudtwalcker, 1925
Oil on canvas, 119.5 x 138 cm
Signed upper left: Edv. Munch 1925
Private collection, Switzerland

Cat. no. 194
Gustav Schiefler, 1908
Oil on canvas, 135 x 119.5 cm
Ateneum, Taidemuseo, Helsinki, A II 856

Cat. no. 195
Kristiania Bohemians II, 1895
Pencil, tusche, gouache and watercolor on vellum, 24.8 x 41.5 cm
Munch-museet, Oslo, MM T 2383

Cat. no. 196
Kristiania Bohemians I, 1895
Etching and drypoint on copperplate in black on vellum, 20.9 x 28.8 cm
Signed lower right: E Munch
Sch. 10, Woll 15 II
Munch-museet, Oslo, MM G 9-36

Cat. no. 197
The First Glass, after 1907
Oil and black crayon on canvas, spray technique, 109 x 160 cm
Munch-museet, Oslo, MM M 15

Cat. no. 198
Self-Portrait in Moonlight, 1904–06
Color woodcut, printed in black and gray-blue, 73 x 41 cm
Signed lower right: E Munch
The Art Institute of Chicago, Clarence Buckingham Collection, 1.963.290

Cat. no. 199
Self-Portrait en face, 1930
Woodcut with gouges in greenish black on vellum, 29 x 17.2 cm
Woll 724
Munch-museet, Oslo, MM G 700-1

Cat. no. 200
Self-Portrait (with Skeleton Arm), 1895
Lithograph with lithographic crayon, tusche and scraper in black on paper, 45.6 x 31.5 cm
Signed lower right in printing area: E Munch
Sch. 31, Woll 37 III
Albertina, Vienna, DG1910/454

Cat. no. 201
Self-Portrait with Bottle of Wine, 1906
Oil on canvas, 110.5 x 120.5 cm
Signed upper left: E. Munch 1906
Munch-museet, Oslo, MM M 543

Cat. no. 202
Self-Portrait in Hell, 1903
Oil on canvas, 82 x 66 cm
Signed lower center: E. Munch
Munch-museet, Oslo, MM M 591

Cat. no. 203
Self-Portrait a Quarter past Two in the Morning, 1940–44 (1943)
Gouache on vellum, 51.5 x 64.5 cm
Inscribed upper right with blue crayon: Klokken 2 og en kvart nat
Munch-museet, Oslo, MM T 2433

Cat. no. 204
Self-Portrait, 1940–43 (1943)
Oil on canvas, 57.5 x 78.5 cm
Munch-museet, Oslo, MM M 611

Cat. no. 205
Self-Portrait between Clock and Bed, c. 1940
Oil on canvas, 149.5 x 120.5 cm
Munch-museet, Oslo, MM M 23

Bibliography

Dieter Buchhart and Lasse Jacobsen

General

Bielefeld 1980
Weisner, Ulrich (ed.). *Munch. Liebe. Angst. Tod.* Exh. cat. Kunsthalle Bielefeld. Bielefeld 1980.

Eggum 1989
Eggum, Arne. *Munch and Photography*. New Haven/London 1989.

Eggum 2000
Eggum, Arne. *Edvard Munch. The Frieze of Life from Painting to Graphic Art*. Oslo 2000.

Essen/Zurich 1987
Magnaguagno, Guido (ed.). *Edvard Munch*. Exh. cat. Museum Folkwang Essen, Kunsthaus Zürich. Bern 1987.

London 1992
Edvard Munch. The Frieze of Life. Exh. cat. National Gallery, London 1992.

Munich/Hamburg/Berlin 1994
Munch und Deutschland. Exh. cat. Kunsthalle der Hypo-Kulturstiftung, Munich, Hamburger Kunsthalle, Nationalgalerie—Staatliche Museen zu Berlin. Stuttgart 1994.

Oslo 2002
Edvard Munchs Livsfrise. En rekonstruksjon av utstillingen hos Blomqvist 1918. Exh. cat. Munch-museet, Oslo. Oslo 2002.

Oslo/Rostock/Helsinki 1999
Munch und Warnemünde 1907–1908. Exh. cat. Munch-museet, Oslo, Kunsthalle Rostock, Ateneum, Helsinki. Oslo 1999.

Paris/Oslo/Frankfurt 1992
Munch in Frankreich. Exh. cat. Musée d'Orsay, Paris, Munch-museet, Oslo, Schirn Kunsthalle Frankfurt. Stuttgart 1992.

Schütz 1985
Schütz, Barbara. *Farbe und Licht bei Edvard Munch*. Ph.D. Saarbrücken 1985.

Toronto 1996
Prelinger, Elizabeth and **Parke-Taylor, Michael** (ed.). *Edvard Munch. The Symbolist Prints of Edvard Munch. The Vivian and David Campbell Collection*. Exh. cat. Art Gallery of Ontario, Toronto. New Haven 1996.

Washington 1978
Edvard Munch. Symbols & Images. Exh. cat. National Gallery of Art, Washington 1978.

The Themes (Selection)

The Voice

Bruteig, Magne. "Images on the Way. Three Drawings by Edvard Munch." In Gether, Christian and Reenberg, Holger. *Echoes of the Scream*. Exh. cat. Arken Museum of Modern Art, Munch-museet, Oslo. Ishøj 2001, pp. 124–137.
Eggum, Arne. "Sommernacht." In Bielefeld 1980, pp. 57–64.
Eggum, Arne and **Biørnstad, Sissel**. "The Voice." In London 1992, pp. 58–60.
Eggum, Arne. "The Voice/Summer Night." In Eggum 2000, pp. 26–39.
Gup, Audrey Rosa. *Munch's The Voice. An Image of Woman*. *Thesis*, Brown University, Providence 1984.
Heller, Reinhold. *Edvard Munchs Life Frieze. Its Beginnings and Origins*, Ph.D. Indiana University 1969, pp. 155–163.
Mørstad, Erik. "Kjærlighetens forvandlinger." In Oslo 2002, pp. 84–87.
Prelinger, Elizabeth. "The Voice (Summer Night)." In Toronto 1996, pp. 84–86.

Moonlight

Eggum, Arne. "Mondschein." In Bielefeld 1980, pp. 121–128.
Eggum, Arne. "Moonlight." In Eggum 2000, pp. 40–47.
Hansen, Dorothee. "Bilder der Empfindung. Munch und die deutsche Malerei im späten 19. Jahrhundert." In Munich/Hamburg/Berlin 1994, pp. 142–153.
Kurosaki, Akira. "Moonshine. A Study of the Paper Used for Edvard Munch's Color Woodcut." In *Journal of Kyoto Seika University*, 4, 1993, pp. 103–128.
Prelinger, Elizabeth. "Moonlight." In Toronto 1996, pp. 155–158.
Skedsmo, Tone and **Lerberg, Ellen J.** "Moonlight." In London 1992, pp. 56–57.
Woll, Gerd. "Der Grafiker." In Paris/Oslo/Frankfurt 1992, pp. 268, 273 and 276.

Puberty

Eggum, Arne. "Puberty." In Eggum 2000, pp. 236–239.
Friedel, Helmut. *Der Kampf der Geschlechter. Der neue Mythos in der Kunst* 1850–1930. Exh. cat. Städtische Galerie im Lenbachhaus, Munich. Cologne 1995, pp. 116–117.
Klüsener, Erika. "Das erwachende Bewusstsein. Zur Ikonographie der Malerei des 19. Jahrhunderts." In *Münster*, no. 3, 1975, pp. 145–153.
Prelinger, Elizabeth. "Puberty." In Toronto 1996, pp. 195–197.
Rapetti, Rodolphe. "Munch im Kontext des Symbolismus. Französische Einflüsse." In Paris/Oslo/Frankfurt 1992, pp. 162–164.
Sherman, Ida L. "Edvard Munchs 'Pubertet' og Felicien Rops." In *Kunst og Kultur*, vol. 59, 1976, no. 4, pp. 243–258.
Skedsmo, Tone and **Lerberg, Ellen J.** "Puberty." In London 1992, pp. 105.
Svenæus, Gösta. *Idé och innehåll i Edvard Munchs konst*, Oslo 1953, pp. 17–20.
Svenæus, Gösta. *Edvard Munch. Das Universum der Melancholie*, Lund 1968, pp. 55–58.

Madonna

Eggum, Arne. "Madonna." In Bielefeld 1980, pp. 29–45.
Eggum, Arne. "Madonna." In Eggum 2000, pp. 184–203.
Gerner, Cornelia. *Die "Madonna" in Edvard Munchs Werk. Frauenbilder und Frauenbild im ausgehenden 19. Jahrhundert*. Ph.D. Morsbach 1993.
Hodin, Josef Paul. "Munch als Vorläufer des Surrealismus. Ein Madonna Motiv im Werke Munchs und Dalis." In *Phantastische Kunst*, special no. of *Das Kunstwerk*, 1955, pp. 51–54.
Høifødt, Frank. "Kvinnen – kjærlighet og død – dommedag." In Oslo 2002, pp. 96–100.
Müller-Westermann, Iris. "Im männlichen Gehirn. Das Verhältnis der Geschlechter im 'Lebensfries'." In Munich/Hamburg/Berlin 1994, pp. 36–37.
Prelinger, Elizabeth. "Catalogue of the Exhibition." In Toronto 1996, pp. 99–105, 139–141, 188–192 and 206–209.
Schloesser, Stephen. "From Spiritual Naturalism to Psychical Naturalism. Catholic Decadence, Lutheran Munch, Madone Mystérique." In Howe, Jeffery. *Edvard Munch. Psyche, Symbol and Expression*. Exh. cat. Charles S. and Isabella V. McMullen

Museum of Art, Boston College. Boston 2001, pp. 75–110.
Skedsmo, Tone and **Lerberg, Ellen J.** "Madonna." In London 1992, pp. 72–75.
Thurmann-Moe, Jan. "Sprühtechnik." In idem. *Munchs "Roßkur". Experimente mit Technik und Material.* Exh. cat. Hamburger Kunsthalle, Hamburg 1994, pp. 18–21.

The Woman (Sphinx)

Eggum, Arne. "Das Weib." In Bielefeld 1980, pp. 47–55.
Eggum, Arne. "The Woman/Sphinx." In Eggum 2000, pp. 96–111.
Friedel, Helmut. *Der Kampf der Geschlechter. Der neue Mythos in der Kunst* 1850–1930. Exh. cat. Städtische Galerie im Lenbachhaus, Munich. Cologne 1995, p. 251.
Graen, Monika. *Das Dreifrauenthema bei Edvard Munch.* Ph.D. Frankfurt am Main 1985.
Heller, Reinhold. *The Riddle of Edvard Munch's Sphinx.* Papers of the X. AICA-Kongress, Munch-museet, Oslo 1969.
Høifødt, Frank. *Kvinnen, kunsten, korset. Edvard Munch anno* 1900. Ph.D. Oslo 1995.
Høifødt, Frank. "Kvinnen – kjærlighet og død – dommedag." In Oslo 2002, pp. 96–100.
Hübener, Kristin. *Edvard Munch und Henrik Ibsen. Bild- und texthermeneutische Studien zu Munchs "Die Frau in drei Stadien" und Ibsens "Wenn wir Toten erwachen" vor dem Hintergrund der Künstler – Leben – Problematik um* 1900. Thesis. Frankfurt am Main 1994.
Junillon, Ingrid. "Dialogue ou influence. 'Quand nous nous réveillerons d'entre les morts', ekphrasis de 'Sphinx'?." In idem. *Le théatre d'Henrik Ibsen dans l'œuvre d'Edvard Munch . scénographie, "illustration" et variations graphiques.* Ph.D. Lyon 2001, pp. 392–402.
Lande, Marit. "Red and White." In London 1992, pp. 64–65.
Prelinger, Elizabeth. "Woman (Woman in Three Stages)." In Toronto 1996, pp. 86–89.
Wilson, Mary G. "Edvard Munch's Woman in Three Stages. A Source of Inspiration for Henrik Ibsen's When We Dead Awaken." In *The Centennial Review,* vol. 24, no. 4, 1980, pp. 492–500.

Attraction

Eggum, Arne. "Anziehung." In Bielefeld 1980, pp. 77–86.
Eggum, Arne. "Attraction." In Eggum 2000, pp. 74–85.
Hofer, Gunter. "Edvard Munch 'Anziehung' und 'Loslösung'." In Bielefeld 1980, pp. 307–314.
Høifødt, Frank. "Kvinnen – kjærlighet og død – dommedag." In Oslo 2002, pp. 101–106.
Lande, Marit. "Starry Night." In London 1992, pp. 54–55.
Lippincott, Louise. *Starry Night.* Malibu 1988.
Maurer, Simon. "Sternennacht, 1893/97." In Essen /Zurich 1987, cat. no. 52.
Müller-Westermann, Iris. "Eye in Eye." In London 1992, pp. 62–63.
Müller-Westermann, Iris. "Im männlichen Gehirn. Das Verhältnis der Geschlechter im 'Lebensfries'." In Munich/Hamburg/Berlin 1994, pp. 30–31.
Prelinger, Elizabeth. "Attraction." In Toronto 1996, pp. 130–133.
Schlemm, Jürgen von. "Sternennacht." In *Edvard Munch. Sommernacht am Oslofjord, um* 1900, Kunsthalle Mannheim. Mannheim 1988, pp. 128–131.
Schütz, Barbara. "Auge in Auge, 1893." In Schütz 1985, pp. 35–41.

Separation

Eggum, Arne. "Loslösung." In Bielefeld 1980, pp. 87–99.
Eggum, Arne. "Separation." In Eggum 2000, pp. 86–95.
Friedel, Helmut. *Der Kampf der Geschlechter. Der neue Mythos in der Kunst* 1850–1930. Exh. cat. Städtische Galerie im Lenbachhaus, Munich, Cologne 1995, pp. 120–121 and 261.
Hofer, Gunter. "Edvard Munch 'Anziehung' und 'Loslösung'." In Bielefeld 1980, pp. 307–314.
Høifødt, Frank. "Separation." In London 1992, pp. 84–85.
Mørstad, Erik. "Kjærlighetens forvandlinger." In Oslo 2002, pp. 88–90.
Müller-Westermann, Iris. "Im männlichen Gehirn. Das Verhaltnis der Geschlechter im 'Lebensfries'." In Munich/Hamburg/Berlin 1994, pp. 35–36.
Prelinger, Elizabeth. "Seperation I und II." In Toronto 1996, pp. 134–138.
Schultze, Jürgen. "Loslösung, 1894." In Essen/ Zurich 1987, cat. no. 45.

The Kiss

Berman, Patricia G. *Edvard Munch. Mirror Reflections.* Exh. cat. The Norton Gallery of Art, West Palm Beach, Florida 1986, pp. 34–39.
Bisanz, Hans. "Zur Bildidee 'Der Kuss'." In *Klimt und die Frauen.* Exh. cat. Österreichische Galerie Belvedere, Vienna. Cologne 2000, pp. 226–234.
Eggum, Arne. "Der Kuss." In Bielefeld 1980, pp. 17–28.
Eggum, Arne. "Kiss." In Eggum 2000, pp. 156–171.
Hansen, Dorothee. "Der Linde-Fries 1904." In Munich/Hamburg/Berlin 1994, pp. 194–199.
Nergaard, Trygve. "Tema med Variasjoner – Kyss – Piken og døden – Vampyr – Trøst." In Oslo 2002, pp. 114–123.
Prelinger, Elizabeth. "The Kiss." In Toronto 1996, pp. 90–92 and 161–166.
Tomek, Ines. *Der Kuss als Bildmotiv bei Edvard Munch.* Thesis. Berlin 1996.
Winter, Gundolf. "Sinnbildlichkeit als Bildsinn. Zum Gestaltungskonzept des frühen Munchs." In Bielefeld 1980, pp. 419–432.
Woll, Gerd. "The Kiss." In London 1992, pp. 66–67.

Towards the Forest

Eggum, Arne. "Zum Walde." In Bielefeld 1980, pp. 149–156.
Eggum, Arne and **Biørnstad, Sissel** (ed.). *Edvard Munch. Alpha and Omega,* Munch-museet Oslo, Oslo 1981.
Eggum, Arne. "Torwards the Forest." In Eggum 2000, pp. 146–155.
Wivel, Mikael. "Mod skoven. Edvard Munch." In idem. *Fremkaldelser,* Copenhagen 1999, pp. 143–147.

Vampire

Buvik, Per. "Kunst, ideologi og historie. omkring et maleri av Munch. 'Vampyr'." In *Med og utan rammer,* Oslo 1984, pp. 55–66.
Eggum, Arne. "Vampir." In Bielefeld 1980, pp. 65–76.
Eggum, Arne. "Vampire." In Eggum 2000, pp. 172–183.
Hansen, Merethe. *Ulike tolkninger av Edvard Munchs maleri Vampyr.* Thesis. Bergen 2001.
Müller-Westermann, Iris. "Im männlichen Gehirn. Das Verhältnis der Geschlechter im 'Lebensfries'." In Munich/Hamburg/Berlin 1994, pp. 32–34.
Nergaard, Trygve. "Kunsten som det evige kvinnelige – en vampyrgåte." In *Kunst og Kultur,* vol. 57, 1974, pp. 251–262.
Nergaard, Trygve. "Tema med Variasjoner – Kyss – Piken og døden – Vampyr – Trøst." In Oslo 2002, pp. 114–123.
Prelinger, Elizabeth. "Vampire" and "The Fat Whore." In Toronto 1996, pp. 105–111 and 179–181.
Schneede, Uwe M. "Vampir von Edvard Munch." In *Kunst und Antiquitäten,* no. 11, 1990, pp. 46–47.
Schneede, Uwe M. "Munchs 'Lebensfries', zentrales Projekt der Moderne." In Munich/Hamburg/ Berlin 1994, pp. 24–25

Schütz, Barbara. "Vampir, 1893." In Essen/Zurich 1987, cat. no. 34.
Woll, Gerd. "Vampire." In London 1992, pp. 66–67.

Jealousy

Boe, Roy A. "'Jealousy'. An Important Painting by Edvard Munch." In *The Minneapolis Institute of Arts Bulletin*, vol. 45, no. 1, 1956.
Eggum, Arne. "Eifersucht." In Bielefeld 1980, pp. 101–114.
Eggum, Arne and **Biørnstad, Sissel**. "The Green Room." In London 1992, pp. 122–130.
Eggum, Arne. "Munch und Warnemünde." In Oslo/Rostock/Helsinki 1999, pp. 31–33.
Eggum, Arne. "Das grüne Zimmer." In Oslo/Rostock/Helsinki 1999, pp. 51–64.
Eggum, Arne. "Jealousy." In Eggum 2000, pp. 126–135.
Hofmann, Werner. "Zu einem Bildmittel Edvard Munchs." In *Alte und neue Kunst. Wiener Kunstwissenschaftliche Blätter, Bruchlinien. Aufsätze zur Kunst des 19. Jahrhunderts*, vol. 3, no. 1, 1954, pp. 20–40.
Prelinger, Elizabeth. "Jealousy II." In Toronto 1996, pp. 116–118.
Ydstie, Ingebjørg. "Jealousy." In London 1992, pp. 79–81.

Melancholy

Berg, Knut. "Om dateringen av et Munch-maleri." In *Kunst og Kultur*, vol. 76, 1993, no. 4, pp. 213–222.
Eggum, Arne. "Melancholie." In Bielefeld 1980, pp. 129–136.
Eggum, Arne. "Melancholy." In Eggum 2000, pp. 112–125.
Howe, Jeffery. "Nocturnes. The Music of Melancholy, and the Mysteries of Love and Death." In idem. *Edvard Munch. Psyche, Symbol and Expression*. Exh. cat. Charles S. and Isabella V. McMullen Museum of Art, Boston College, Boston 2001, pp. 48–74.
März, Roland. *Edvard Munch. Melancholie aus dem Reinhardt-Fries* 1906/07, Berlin 1998.
Nergaard, Trygve. "Despair." In Washington 1978, pp. 112–141.
Plahter, Leif Einar. "Atelierleder Leif Einar Plahters rapport." In *Kunst og Kultur*, vol. 76, 1993, pp. 222–223.
Prelinger, Elizabeth. "Melancholy. Girl on Shore" and "Melancholy (Evening)." In Toronto 1996, pp. 167–169 and 192–195.
Skedsmo, Tone and **Magnaguagno, Guido**. "Melancholie, 1891." In Essen/Zurich 1987, cat. no. 25.
Ydstie, Ingebjørg. "Melancholy." In London 1992, pp. 86–87.

The Lonely Ones

Eggum, Arne. "Die Einsamen." In Bielefeld 1980, pp. 137–148.
Eggum, Arne. "Two Human Beings/The Lonely Ones." In Eggum 2000, pp. 48–63.
Prelinger, Elizabeth. "Two Women on the Shore", "Two People (The Lonely Ones)" and "Moonlight by the Sea." In Toronto 1996, pp. 170–173, 182–188 and 214–216.
Woll, Gerd. "Two People" and "Young Girl on the Shore." In London 1992, pp. 88.

Angst

Askeland, Jan. "Angstmotivet i Edvard Munchs kunst." In *Kunsten idag*, vol. 78, no. 4, 1966, pp. 5–57.
Bjerke, Øivind Storm. "Skrik – Angst – Døden og barnet – Dødskamp – Morderen og de badende børn." In Oslo 2002, pp. 127–129.
Eggum, Arne. "Angstgefühl." In Bielefeld 1980, pp. 174–186.
Eggum, Arne. "Evening on Karl Johan Street" and "Angst." In Eggum 2000, pp. 208–219.
Halbreich, Uriel. "The Characteristics of Tension-provoking Composition and Lines in Munch's Paintings." In *Confinia Psychiatricia*, vol. 23, no. 3, 1980, pp. 188–192.
Høifødt, Frank, **Ydstie, Ingebjørg** et al. "Anxiety." In London 1992, pp. 92–101.
Nergaard, Trygve. "Despair." In Washington 1978, pp. 112–141.
Prelinger, Elizabeth. "Anxiety." In Toronto 1996, pp. 127–129.
Winter, Gundolf. "Sinnbildlichkeit als Bildsinn. Zum Gestaltungskonzept des frühen Munchs." In Bielefeld 1980, pp. 410–418.
Woll, Gerd. "Angst findet man bei ihm überall." In Bielefeld 1980, pp. 315–334.

The Scream

Askeland, Jan. "Angstmotivet i Edvard Munchs kunst." In *Kunsten idag*, vol. 78, no. 4, 1966, pp. 5–57.
Bjerke, Øivind Storm. "Skrik – Angst – Døden og barnet – Dødskamp – Morderen og de badende børn." In Oslo 2002, pp. 124–127.
Crockett, Campbell. "Psychoanalysis in Art Criticism." In *The Journal of Aesthetics and Art Criticism*, vol. 17, no. 1, 1958, pp. 34–44.
Eggum, Arne. "Geschrei." In Bielefeld 1980, pp. 187–194.
Eggum, Arne. "Scream." In Eggum 2000, pp. 220–235.
Flaatten, Hans-Martin Frydenberg. "Skrik som ikon og dikt." In Oslo 2002, pp. 67–77.
Gether, Christian and **Reenberg, Holger**. *Echoes of the Scream*. Exh. cat. Arken Museum of Modern Art, Munch-museet, Oslo. Ishøj 2001.
Heller, Reinhold. *Edvard Munch. The Scream*, London 1973.
Kristoffersen, Sigrid Fløttum. "Jobs skrik? Et bidrag til tolkningen av Edvard Munchs maleri." In *Kunst og Kultur*, vol. 83, no. 1, 2000, pp. 50–61.
Lind, Ebba. "På sporet av et 'Skrik'." In *Kunst og Kultur*, vol. 80, no. 2, 1997, pp. 98–105.
Lund, Hans. "Edvard Munchs Skrik som kulturell ikon." In *Agora*, no. 2–3, 2001, pp. 20–41.
Prelinger, Elizabeth. "When the Halted Traveler Hears the Scream in Nature. Preliminary Thougths on the Transformation of Some Romantic Motifs." In *Shop Talk. Studies in Honor of Seymour Slive*, Harvard University Art Museums. Cambridge, Mass., 1995, pp. 198–203.
Prelinger, Elizabeth. "The Scream." In Toronto 1996, pp. 96–99.
Prelinger, Elizabeth. "Music to our Ears? Munch's Scream and Romantic Music Theory." In *The Arts Entwined. Music and Painting in the Nineteenth Century*, New York/London 2000, pp. 209–225.
Rugi, Goriano. "Anatomia del grido." In *Psiche. rivista di cultura psicoanalitica*, vol. 4, no. 1, 1996, pp. 82–100.
Skedsmo, Tone and **Lerberg, Ellen J.** "The Scream." In London 1992, pp. 96–98.

The Sick Child

Eggum, Arne. "The Theme of Death." In Washington 1978, pp. 142–183.
Eggum, Arne. "Das kranke Kind." In Bielefeld 1980, pp. 195–206.
Eggum, Arne. "Das Todesthema bei Edvard Munch." In Bielefeld 1980. 335–375.
Eggum, Arne. "The Sick Child." In Eggum 2000, pp. 242–257.
Hellerstedt, Kahren. *An Examination of Edvard Munch's Sick Child*. Thesis. Pittsburgh 1971.
Magnaguagno, Guido. "Munch als Maler." In Magnaguagno, Guido (ed.). *Edvard Munch*, Essen/Zurich 1987, pp. 63–67.
Plahter, Leif Einar. "Det syke barn – spekulasjoner og fakta om maleriets opprinnelige utseende." In *Kunst og Kultur*, vol. 75, 1992, no. 2, pp. 85–99.
Plahter, Leif Einar. "Beneath the Surface of Edvard Munch. Technical Examinations of Four Paintings by Edvard Munch." In Nordisk Konservatorforbund, Den norske seksjon (IIC Nordic Group)

(ed.). *Conservare necesse est. Festskrift til Leif Einar Plahter på hans 70-årsdag*. Oslo 1999, pp. 111–127.
Prelinger, Elizabeth. "The Sick Child", "The Sick Child II" and "Head of Sick Child." In Toronto 1996, pp. 68 and 119–126.
Schneede, Uwe M. *Edvard Munch. Das kranke Kind. Arbeit an der Erinnerung*. Frankfurt am Main 1984.
Schneede, Uwe M. *Im Blickfeld. Edvard Munch. Das Kranke Kind*. Exh. cat. Hamburger Kunsthalle. Hamburg 2002.
Schütz, Barbara. "Das kranke Kind, 1885/86." In Schütz 1985, pp. 12–22.
Skedsmo, Tone. "Tautrekking om det syke barn." In *Kunst og Kultur*, vol. 68, no. 3, 1985, pp. 184–195.

By the Deathbed

Bjerke, Øivind Storm. "Skrik – Angst – Døden og barnet – Dødskamp – Morderen og de badende børn." In Oslo 2002, pp. 130–134.
Eggum, Arne. "'Am Totenbett' und 'Tod im Krankenzimmer'." In Bielefeld 1980, pp. 207–235.
Eggum, Arne. "Das Todesthema bei Edvard Munch." In Bielefeld 1980, pp. 335–375.
Eggum, Arne. "At the Deathbed/Fever" and "Death in the Sickroom'." In Eggum 2000, pp. 258–275.
Forssman, Erik. "Tanz und Tod im Werk Edvard Munchs." In *Tanz und Tod in der Kunst und Literatur. Schriften zur Literaturwissenschaft*, vol. 8. Berlin 1993, pp. 299–315.
Gercken, Günther. "Todesangst und Todesvisionen im Werk von Edvard Munch." In *Todesbilder in der zeitgenössischen Kunst mit einem Rückblick auf Hodler und Munch*. Exh. cat. Kunstverein in Hamburg, Städtische Galerie im Lenbachhaus, Munich. Hamburg 1983, pp. 9–15.
Héran, Emmanuelle u.a. *Le Dernier Portrait*. Exh. cat. Musée d'Orsay, Paris 2002.
Høifødt, Frank, Ydstie, Ingebjørg u.a. "Death." In London 1992, pp. 108–115.
Klein, Janine. Edvard Munch. 'Der Tod im Krankenzimmer'. Thesis, 1994.
Nergaard, Trygve. "Das Todesmotiv bei Munch." In *Munch-Symposium in der Kunsthalle Bremen*. Bremen 1970, pp. 2–18.
Plante, Anne Marie. *Edvard Munch's By the Deathbed and Nineteenth-Century Spiritualism*. (USA) 1986.
Prelinger, Elizabeth. "Death in the Sickroom." In Toronto 1996, pp. 142–144.

Landscape

Anderson, Katherine E. *The Landscapes of Edvard Munch. A Medium of Communication and the Continuation of a Tradition*. Thesis. Michigan 1985.
Berg, Knut. "The Landscape Motif in Munch's Art." In *Edvard Munch*. Exh. cat. National Museum of Modern Art, Tokyo. Tokyo 1981, pp. 246–251.
Bøe, Alf and **Høifødt, Frank**. "The Winter Paintings of Edvard Munch." In *Winterland. Norwegian Visions of Winter. Winter Themes through Two Centuries of Norwegian Art*. Exh. cat. The Fernbank Museum of Natural History, Atlanta 1993, pp. 41–48 and 123–145.
Czymmek, Götz (ed.). *Landschaft als Kosmos der Seele. Malerei des nordischen Symbolismus bis Munch 1880–1910*. Exh. cat. Wallraf-Richartz-Museum, Cologne. Heidelberg 1998.
Dreier, Franziska. *Landschaft als Spiegel der Seele. Edvard Munch. Sternennacht*. Thesis. Göttingen 2000.
Edvard Munch. Sommernacht am Oslofjord, um 1900. Exh. cat. Kunsthalle Mannheim. Mannheim 1988.
Lange, Marit. *Da Dahl a Munch. romanticismo, realismo e simbolismo nella pittura di paesaggio norvegese*. Exh. cat. Palazzo dei Diamanti, Ferrara 2001.
Lippincott, Louise. *Edvard Munch. Starry Night*. Malibu 1988.
Moen, Arve. *Edvard Munch. Tier und Landschaft*., Munich 1958.
Norwegische Landschaftsmalerei. von Dahl bis Munch. Exh. cat. Kunsthalle Bremen. Bremen 1977.
Wieldpolski, Beate. "Zur Stimmungslandschaft um 1900." In *Mitteilungen der Gesellschaft für vergleichende Kunstforschung in Wien*, vol. 46, 1994, pp. 6–12.

Avenue

Eggum, Arne. "James Ensor and Edvard Munch. Mask and Reality." In *James Ensor. Edvard Munch, Emil Nolde*. Exh. cat. Norman Mackenzie Art Gallery University of Regina, Saskatchewan 1980, p. 29.
Eggum, Arne. "Roter Wilder Wein, 1898/1900." In Essen/Zurich 1987, cat. no. 50.
Høifødt, Frank. "Rød villvin." In *Vi ser på kunst*, no. 4, 1989, pp. 26–27.
Høifødt, Frank. "Red Virginia Creeper." In London 1992, pp. 102–103.
Høifødt, Frank. *Kvinnen, kunsten, korset. Edvard Munch anno* 1900. Ph.D. Oslo 1995, pp. 134–141.
Maurer, Simon. "Der Mörder, 1910." In Essen/Zurich 1987, cat. no. 86.
Mørstad, Erik. "Kjærlighetens forvandlinger." In Oslo 2002, pp. 90–93.
Schütz, Barbara. "Roter Wilder Wein, 1898." In Schütz 1985, pp. 46–51.
Schütz, Barbara. "Allee im Schneegestöber, 1906." In Essen/Zurich 1987, cat. no. 70.
Winter, Gundolf. "Sinnbildlichkeit als Bildsinn. Zum Gestaltungskonzept des frühen Munchs." In Bielefeld 1980, pp. 407–418.

Girls on the Pier

Eggum, Arne. "Mädchen auf der Landungsbrücke." In Bielefeld 1980, pp. 167–174.
"Erwerbungen für die Gemälde-Galerie und die Sammlung neuerer Plastik im Jahre 1961." In *Jahrbuch der Hamburger Kunstsammlungen*, vol. 7, 1962, pp. 111–134.
Høifødt, Frank. *Kvinnen, kunsten, korset. Edvard Munch anno* 1900. Ph.D. Oslo 1995, pp. 205–211.
Magnaguagno, Guido. "Munch als Maler." In Essen/Zurich 1987, pp. 67–71.
Prelinger, Elizabeth. "On the Jetty" and "Girls on the Jetty." In Toronto 1996, pp. 212 and 217–219.
Revold, Reidar. "Omkring en motivgruppe hos Edvard Munch." In *Oslo Kommunes Kunstsamlinger, Årbok* II, 1952–1959, pp. 38–51.

Nude

Bimer, Barbara Susan Travitz. *Edvard Munch's Fatal Women. a Critical Approach*, Ph.D. Texas 1997.
Eggum, Arne (ed.). *Edvard Munch og hans modeller 1912–1943*. Exh. cat. Munch-museet, Oslo 1988.
Grotmol, Kirsti. "Edvard Munch. the Artist from the Model's Point of View." In *Scandinavian Review*, no. 3, 1991, pp. 57–62.
Heller, Reinhold. "'Ich glaube ich male nur noch Frauen'. Die Aktdarstellung im Werk von Edvard Munch." In Mössinger, Ingrid, Ritter, Beate and Drechsel, Kerstin (ed.). *Edvard Munch in Chemnitz*. Exh. cat. Kunstsammlungen Chemnitz. Cologne 1999, pp. 285–292.
Moen, Arve. *Edvard Munch. Woman and Eros*. Oslo 1957.
Munch and Women. Image and Myth. Exh. cat. San Diego Museum of Art, Portland Museum of Art, Portland, Yale University Art Gallery, New Haven. Alexandria, Virginia 1997.
Munch og kvinnen. Exh. cat. Bergen Kunstmuseum. Bergen 2001.
Prestøe, Birgit. "Småtrekk om Edvard Munch." In *Edvard Munch. Mennesket og kunstneren*. Oslo 1946, pp. 133–144.
Schmidt, Johann-Karl and **Zeller, Ursula** (ed.). *Edvard Munch und seine Modelle*. Exh. cat. Galerie der Stadt Stuttgart. Stuttgart 1993.
Stubbe, Wolf. "Den sørgende pike var ikke sørgmodig. Edvard Munch og hans modell." In *Kunst og Kultur*, vol. 55, 1972, pp. 105–108.

Portrait

Affentranger-Kirchrath, Angelika. "Die Frage nach dem Menschen. Porträtmalerei um 1900 am Beispiel Ferdinand Hodlers und Edvard Munchs." In *Zeitschrift für Schweizerische Archäologie und Kunstgeschichte*, vol. 51, 1994, pp. 295–308.
Bisanz, Hans. *Edvard Munch und seine Bedeutung für den mitteleuropäischen Expressionismus*. Ph. D. Vienna 1959.
Bisanz, Hans. "Edvard Munch og portrettkunsten i Wien etter 1900/Edvard Munch und die Wiener Porträtmalerei nach 1900." In *Oslo Kommunes Kunstsamlinger, Årbok*, 1963, pp. 68–101 and 136–144.
Brünniche, Eigil H. "Edvard Munch og to danske læger." In *København. Statens Museum for Kunst. Kunstmuseets årsskrift*, 1992, pp. 40–43.
Cortenova, Giorgio and **Eggum, Arne**. *Edvard Munch. l'io e gli altri*. Exh. cat. Palazzo Forti, Verona. Milano 2001.
Eggum, Arne. "Portrait Painting and Photography 1896–1908." In Eggum 1989, pp. 65–92.
Eggum, Arne. *Edvard Munch. Portretter*. Exh. cat. Munch-museet, Oslo. Oslo 1994.
Heller, Reinhold. *The Portrait Art of Edvard Munch*. Thesis. Indiana 1965.
Magnaguagno, Guido. "Munch als Maler." In Essen/Zurich 1987, pp. 71–75.
Magnaguagno, Guido. "Edvard Munch. Heinrich Hudtwalcker." In *El Greco bis Mondrian. Bilder aus einer Schweizer Privatsammlung*. Exh. cat. Aargauer Kunsthaus, Aarau, Von der Heydt-Museum, Wuppertal, Staatliche Kunstsammlungen Dresden. Cologne 1996, pp. 188–191.
Prelinger, Elizabeth. "Portrait of August Strindberg." In Toronto 1996, pp. 145–148.
Schultze, Jürgen. "Portrait Dagny Juell Przybyszewska, 1893", "Portrait Stanislaw Przybyszewski, 1893/95", "Portrait Walther Rathenau, 1907" and "Portrait Gustav Schiefler, 1908." In Essen/Zurich 1987, cat. nos. 32, 33, 72 and 73.
Timm, Ingo. "Edvard Munch. Das Walther-Rathenau-Bildnis. Bemerkungen zur Maltechnik des Berliner Porträts." In *Restauro. Zeitschrift für Kunsttechniken, Restaurierung und Museumsfragen*, no. 4, 1996, pp. 248–252.

Self-Portrait

Arnold, Matthias. "Gemalte Biographie. Die Selbstbildnisse Edvard Munchs." In *Kunst und Antiquitäten*, no. 4, 1986, pp. 70–79.
Berman, Patricia G. "Edvard Munch's Self-Portrait with Cigarette. Smoking and the Bohemian Persona." In *Art Bulletin*, no. 4, 1993, pp. 626–646.
Chéroux, Clément. "Edvard Munch. Visage de la Mélancolie. Autoportraits Photographiques." In *La Recherche photographique*, no. 14, 1993, pp. 14–17.
Cortenova, Giorgio and **Eggum, Arne**. *Edvard Munch. l'io e gli altri*. Exh. cat. Palazzo Forti, Verona. Milano 2001.
Edvard Munch. Selvportretter. Exh. cat. Munch-museet, Oslo 1963.
Eggum, Arne. "Munch's Self-Portraits." In Washington 1978, pp. 11–33.
Eggum, Arne. "Selbstbildnisse und Selbstdarstellungen." In Bielefeld 1980, pp. 243–268.
Eggum, Arne. "Munch's Experiments as an Amateur Photographer, 1902–1910 and 1926–1932." In Eggum 1989, pp. 93–148 and 161–190.
Göpel, Erhard. *Edvard Munch. Selbstbildnisse und Dokumente*. Munich 1955.
Krieger, Peter. "Selbstbildnisse." In *Edvard Munch. Der Lebensfries für Max Reinhardts Kammerspiele*. Exh. cat. Nationalgalerie, Berlin 1978, pp. 86–95.
Langaard, Johan H. *Edvard Munchs selvportretter*, Oslo 1947.
Müller-Westermann, Iris. "Mit Kopf und Hand. Zu Munchs Selbstverständnis als Künstler." In Munich/Hamburg/Berlin 1994, pp. 39–45.
Müller-Westermann, Iris. "The Head in the Hand – and the Hand in his Blood." In Paszkiewicz, Piotr (ed.). *Totenmesse. Modernism in the Culture of Northern and Central Europe*. Warschau 1996, pp. 79–87.
Müller-Westermann, Iris. *Edvard Munch. Die Selbstbildnisse*, Ph.D. Oslo 1997.
Prelinger, Elizabeth. "Self-Portrait with Skeleton Arm" and "Self-Portrait with Wine Bottle." In Toronto 1996, pp. 95–96 and 221–223.
Schneede, Uwe M. (ed.). *Edvard Munch. Höhepunkte des malerischen Werks im 20. Jahrhundert*. Exh. cat. Kunstverein in Hamburg. Hamburg 1984.
Självporträtt. Exh. cat. Göteborgs Konstmuseum, Göteborg. Göteborg 1998.

Catalogues raisonnés

Schiefler, Gustav. *Verzeichnis des graphischen Werks Edvard Munchs bis* 1906. Berlin 1907.
Schiefler, Gustav. *Edvard Munch. Das graphische Werk* 1906–1926. Berlin 1928.
Woll, Gerd. *Edvard Munch. The Complete Graphic Works*. London 2001.

Biographies (Selection)

Arnold, Matthias. *Edvard Munch*. Reinbek 1986.
Bjørnstad, Ketil. *Edvard Munch. Die Geschichte seines Lebens*. Frankfurt am Main 1995.
Eggum, Arne. *Edvard Munch. Painting, Sketches and Studies*. Oslo 1984.
Gauguin, Pola. *Edvard Munch*. Oslo 1933.
Heller, Reinhold. *Edvard Munch. His Life and Work*. London 1984.
Lande, Marit. *På sporet av Edvard Munch – mannen bak mytene*. Oslo 1996.
Stang, Nic. *Edvard Munch*. Oslo 1972.
Stang, Ragna. *Edvard Munch. The Man and the Artist*. London 1979.
Stenersen, Rolf E. *Edvard Munch – Close-Up of a Genius*. Oslo 1994.
Thiis, Jens. *Edvard Munch og hans samtid*. Oslo 1933.
Thiis, Jens. *Edvard Munch*. Berlin 1934.
Tøjner, Poul Erik. *Munch in his Own Words*. Munich 2001.

Photo Credits

© Munch-museet, Oslo, photo Andersen/de Jong: cat. nos. 1, 2, 4–7, 11–14, 19, 20, 25–28, 30, 32, 33, 35, 37, 40–42, 44, 46–51, 54–64, 66–71, 73–79, 83, 92, 96, 98–103, 110–112, 115–118, 120, 121, 125, 126, 128–130, 133, 135–141, 143, 145–147, 150, 151, 153–162, 167, 169, 170, 175–182, 185–187, 189, 191, 195–197, 199, 201–205; fig. 5 (p. 16), fig. 9, 10 (p. 19), fig. 13 (p. 21), fig. 5 (p. 27), fig. 8 (p. 31), fig. 9 (p. 32), fig. 10 (p. 33), fig. 13 (p. 37), fig. 2, 3 (p. 45), fig. 4 (p. 46), fig. 5, 6 (p. 47), fig. 7 (p. 49), fig. 8 (p. 50), fig. 1 (p. 53), fig. 6 (p. 60), fig. 7 (p. 61), figs. 3, 4 (p. 71), figs. 5, 6 (p. 72), figs. 7, 8 (p. 73), fig. 9 (p. 74), figs. 10, 11 (p. 75), fig. 12 (p. 76), fig. 13 (p. 77), fig. 14 (p. 78), figs. 15, 16 (p. 79), figs. 17, 18 (p. 80), fig. 1 (p. 83), fig. 4 (p. 86), fig. 5 (p. 87), figs. 6, 7 (p. 88), fig. 10 (p. 90), fig. 10 (p. 103), fig. 16 (p. 107), fig. 1 (p. 133), fig. 2 (p. 134), fig. 1 (p. 137), fig. 2 (p. 158), fig. 5 (p. 159), fig. 6 (p. 160), fig. 3 (p. 172), fig. 1 (p. 188), fig. 1 (p. 223), figs. 3, 4 (p. 252), fig. 1 (p. 284), figs. 2, 3 (p. 285), fig. 1 (p. 301), fig. 2 (p. 302)
Archive of Munch-museet: fig. 4 (p. 15), figs. 6, 7 (p. 17), fig. 8 (p. 18), fig. 12 (p. 20), fig. 2 (p. 24), fig. 3 (p. 25), fig. 7 (p. 30), fig. 11 (p. 35), fig. 12 (p. 36), fig. 2 (p. 56), fig. 8 (p. 62), fig. 1 (p. 114), fig. 2 (p. 138), fig. 3 (p. 158), fig. 4 (p. 159), fig. 1 (p. 171), fig. 2 (p. 172), fig. 4 (p. 173), figs. 1–18 (pp. 339–351)
© Nasjonalgalleriet, Oslo, photo J. Lathion: cat. nos. 8, 16, 43, 81, 85, 163, 171; fig. 1 (p. 23), fig. 4 (p. 57), fig. 5 (p. 58), fig. 5 (p. 100), fig. 8 (p. 102), fig. 1 (p. 157), fig. 1 (p. 245), fig. 1 (p. 249), fig. 4 (p. 286)
Albertina, Vienna, photo Peter Ertl: cat. nos. 15, 17, 18, 22, 23, 31, 34, 39, 45, 53, 72, 82, 119, 123, 134, 166, 188, 190, 200; fig. 3 (p. 14), figs. 1, 2 (p. 92), fig. 3 (p. 93), figs. 4, 5 (p. 94), figs. 6, 7 (p. 95), fig. 1 (p. 187), fig. 1 (p. 237)
Öffentliche Kunstsammlung Basel: fig. 11 (p. 20)
© Rasmus Meyers Samlinger, Bergen Kunstmuseum: cat. nos. 9, 86, 114, 132, 142, 172; fig. 1 (p. 69), fig. 2 (p. 70),
© Stadtmuseum Berlin, Berlin, photo Christel Lehmann: cat. no. 192
© Museum of Fine Arts, Boston: cat. nos. 3, 88, 149
© Courtesy Museum of Fine Arts, Boston: fig. 9 (p. 63)
© The Art Institute of Chicago: cat. nos. 84, 97, photo Greg Williams: cat. no. 198
© Museum Folkwang, Essen: cat. no. 152
Göteborgs Konstmuseum: cat. nos. 65, 122
Hamburger Kunsthalle, Kupferstichkabinett, photo Elke Walford: cat. no. 131
© Sprengel Museum Hannover: cat. no. 173
© Finnish National Gallery, Helsinki, Central Art Archives, photo Jukka Romu: cat. no. 194
© Statens Museum for Kunst, Copenhagen, photo Hans Petersen: cat. no. 184
© Landesgalerie Linz: fig. 3 (p. 99)
© Tate, London: fig. 2 (p. 251)
© Museo Thyssen-Bornemisza, Madrid: cat. no. 80
Bayrische Gemäldesammlungen, Schack-Galerie, Munich: fig. 2 (p. 84)
© Glyptothek, Munich: fig. 2 (p. 13)
© The Museum of Modern Art, New York: fig. 9 (p. 89), fig. 11 (p. 104), cat. nos. 10, 36
Narodnic Galcric, Praguc: fig. 3 (p. 57)
Kungliga Bibliotheket Stockholm, photo Jan O. Almerén: fig. 4 (p. 26)
© Board of Trustees, National Gallery of Art, Washington: cat. nos. 104–109
Österreichische Galerie Belvedere, Vienna: cat. nos. 144, 183; fig. 2 (p. 98), fig. 4 (p. 100), fig. 13 (p. 105)
© Leopold-Museum – Privatstiftung, Vienna: fig. 7 (p. 102)
© Prof. Dr. Rudolf Leopold, Vienna: fig. 9 (p. 103)
Von der Heydt-Museum, Wuppertal: cat. no. 38
© Kunsthaus Zürich. All rights reserved: fig. 3 (p. 85)
© Photo RMN, Paris: fig. 6 (p. 29);
Jean Schormans: cat. no. 164, fig. 8 (p. 89)
Stiftung R. und H. Batliner: cat. no. 148
Sammlung E. W. K., Bern: cat. no. 95
Courtesy Galleri Faurschou: cat. no. 91, fig. 1 (p. 271)
© José Mugrabi Collection: fig. 1 (p. 13)
© Collection of Lawrence and Ronald Schönberg and Nuria Schönberg Nono: fig. 6 (p. 102)
Courtesy W. Wittrock, Berlin: cat. no. 87
Collection of Catherine Woodard & Nelson Blitz, Jr.: cat. nos. 21, 29, 94, 113, 127
Photo Bara-King: cat. no. 174
Photo Dean Beasom: cat. no. 24
Photo Philip Charles: cat. nos. 89, 90, 93, 124, 168
Photo Tim Druckerey: cat. no. 52
Photo R. Lorenzson: cat. no. 165; fig. 1 (p. 212)
Photo Lutz & Co., Berlin: fig. 12 (p. 20)
Photo Atelier Marschalk: fig. 4 (p. 343)
© Photo Franz Schachinger: fig. 1 (p. 97)
© Photo Lothar Schnepf: fig. 17 (p. 107)

This catalog is published
on occasion of the exhibition
Edvard Munch—Theme and Variation
at the Albertina, Vienna,
March 15 to June 22, 2003

Editors
Klaus Albrecht Schröder
Antonia Hoerschelmann

Editing
Antonia Hoerschelmann
Dieter Buchhart

Translations
From the Norwegian: Elinor Ruth Waaler
From the German: John Southard

Graphic design
Gabriele Sabolewski

Typesetting
Weyhing digital, Ostfildern-Ruit

Reproductions
C+S Repro, Filderstadt

Paper and font
LuxoSamtoffset, Novarese

Printed by
Dr. Cantz'sche Druckerei, Ostfildern-Ruit

Published by
Hatje Cantz Publishers
Senefelderstrasse 12
73760 Ostfildern-Ruit
Germany
phone +49 711 44 05 0
fax +49 711 44 05 220
www.hatjecantz.de

ISBN 3-7757-1270-4 (English edition)
ISBN 3-7757-1250-X (German edition)

Front cover
Edvard Munch, *Girls on the Pier*, c. 1901
(detail of cat. no. 163)

Back cover
Edvard Munch, *Girls on the Pier*, 1918
(detail of cat. no. 166)

Frontispiece
Edvard Munch, *Self-Portrait (with Skeleton Arm)*, 1895
(cat. no. 200)

Exhibition

Idea
Klaus Albrecht Schröder

Concept
Klaus Albrecht Schröder
Antonia Hoerschelmann

Curator
Antonia Hoerschelmann

Assistant
Dieter Buchhart

Exhibition organization
Margarete Heck

Assistant
Cornelia Zöchling

Conservators
Albertina, Vienna: Karine Bovagnet, Ulrike Ertl, Monica Festetics, Rudolf Leberwurst, Momar Sall, Hannah Singer, Elisabeth Thobois.
Munch-museet, Oslo: Magdalena Ufnalewska Godzimirska, Kirsten Korff, Biliana Topalova-Casadiego, Mette Havrevold, Mattias Malmberg, Pablo Gracia.

410th exhibition of the Albertina